BIG STORY

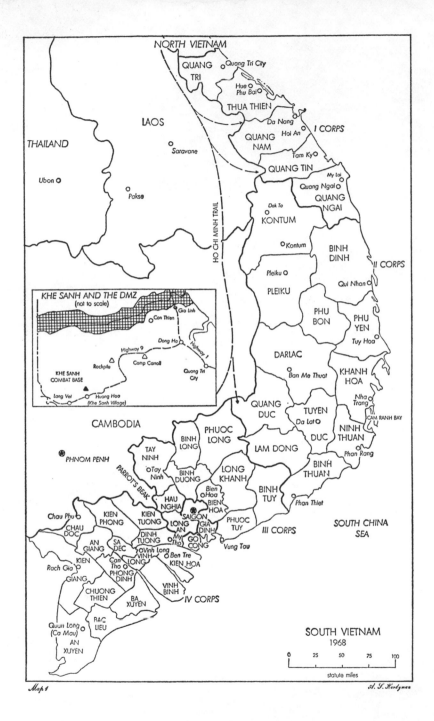

NORTH VIETNAM

QUANG TRI

Quang Tri City

Hue
Phu Bai

THUA THIEN

LAOS

Da Nang
Hoi An

I CORPS

THAILAND

Saravane

QUANG NAM

Tam Ky

QUANG TIN

My Lai

Ubon

Pakse

Dak To

KONTUM

Kontum

Quang Ngai

QUANG NGAI

II CORPS

BINH DINH

Pleiku

Qui Nhon

PLEIKU

PHU BON

PHU YEN

Tuy Hoa

DARLAC

KHANH HOA

Ban Me Thuot

Nha Trang

CAM RANH BAY

KHE SANH AND THE DMZ
(not to scale)

Gio Linh
Con Thien

Dong Ha

Highway 9

Rockpile

Camp Carroll

Highway 1

Quang Tri City

KHE SANH COMBAT BASE

Lang Vei

Huong Hoa
(Khe Sanh Village)

QUANG DUC

TUYEN DUC

Da Lat

NINH THUAN

CAMBODIA

PHUOC LONG

Phan Rang

BINH LONG

LAM DONG

BINH THUAN

PHNOM PENH

TAY NINH

Tay Ninh

BINH DUONG

LONG KHANH

PARROT'S BEAK

Bien Hoa

BIEN HOA

BINH TUY

Phan Thiet

HAU NGHIA

SAIGON

Chau Phu

KIEN PHONG

KIEN TUONG

LONG AN

GIA DINH

PHUOC TUY

III CORPS

SOUTH CHINA SEA

CHAU DOC

DINH TUONG

My Tho

GO CONG

AN GIANG

SA DEC

Vinh Long

Ben Tre

Vung Tau

KIEN GIANG

Rach Gia

Can Tho

VINH LONG

KIEN HOA

PHONG DINH

CHUONG THIEN

VINH BINH

IV CORPS

BA XUYEN

Quan Long
(Ca Mau)

BAC LIEU

AN XUYEN

SOUTH VIETNAM
1968

0   25   50   75   100

statute miles

Map 1

A. S. Hardyman

Big Story

*How the American Press and Television
Reported and Interpreted the Crisis of Tet 1968
in Vietnam and Washington*

ABRIDGED EDITION

PETER BRAESTRUP

YALE UNIVERSITY PRESS   NEW HAVEN AND LONDON

Library of Congress Cataloging in Publication Data

Braestrup, Peter.
  Big Story.
    Includes bibliographical references and index.
    1. Tet Offensive, 1968.   2. Vietnamese Conflict,
1961-1975—Journalists.   3. Press—United States.
4. Television broadcasting of news—United States.
I. Title.
DS557.8.T4B7   1983   959.704'342   82-11041
ISBN 0-300-02953-5
ISBN 0-300-02807-5 (pbk.)

10   9   8   7   6   5   4   3   2

This book is dedicated to the memory of
those foreign journalists who died in
Indo-China in 1961–75, with the hope that
their colleagues still listed as missing
will someday return.

Those who died were:

Vietnam

MICHAEL Y. BIRCH
JOHN L. CANTWELL, *Time-Life*
SAM CASTAN, *Look*
DICKEY CHAPELLE, Free Lance
CHARLES CHELLAPAH
CHARLES EGGLESTON, UPI
ROBERT J. ELLISON, Free Lance
IGNACIO EZCURRA
BERNARD B. FALL, Free Lance
RONALD D. GALLAGHER, Free
  Lance
BERNARD KOLENBERG, AP
RONALD B. LARAMY, Reuters
HIROMICHI MINE, UPI
HUYNH THANH MY, AP
OLIVER NOONAN, AP
BRUCE PIGOTT, Reuters
JERRY ROSE, Free Lance
TATSUO SAKAI, *Nihon Keizai
  Shimbun*

PAUL SAVANUCK, *Stars and
  Stripes*
PHILIPPA SCHUYLER, *Manchester
  Union Leader*
FRANCOIS SULLY, *Newsweek*
PIETER RONALD VAN THIRL,
  Free Lance

Laos

LARRY BURROWS, *Life*
HENRI HUET, AP
KENT POTTER, UPI
KEISABURO SHIMAMOTO, *News-
  week*

Cambodia

FRANK FROSCH, UPI
GERALD MILLER, CBS
KOICHI SAWADA, UPI
GEORGE SYVERTSEN, CBS

Those still listed as missing are:

Cambodia

CLAUDE ARPIN, *Newsweek*
DIETER BELLENDORF, NBC
GILLES CARON, Gamma Agency of Paris
ROGER COLNE, NBC
SEAN FLYNN, *Time*
GEORG GENSLUCKNER, Free Lance
WELLES HANGEN, NBC
GUY HANNOTEAUX, *L'Express*
ALAN HIRONS, UPI
TAIZO ICHINOSE, Free Lance
TOMOHARU ISHII, CBS
AKIRA KUSAKA, Fuji Television
RICHARD A. MARTIN, Free Lance

WILLY METTLER, Free Lance
TERRY REYNOLDS, UPI
KOJIRO SAKAI, CBS
DANA STONE, CBS
TOSHIIHI SUZUKI, Nippon Dempa News
YUJIRO TAKAGI, Fuji Television
TAKESHI YANAGISAWA, Nippon Dempa News
YOSHIHIKO YURINO, Nippon Dempa News
YOSHIHIKO WAKU, NBC

Vietnam

ALEXANDER SHIMKIN, *Newsweek*

Contents

Introduction

This book is one newsman's effort to examine and explain the performance of America's major press and television organizations under conditions of unusual stress, complexity, and uncertainty. Such conditions prevailed in Vietnam and Washington during the February–March 1968 Tet crisis, whose domestic political impact in Washington helped to topple a President, Lyndon Johnson, and led to later changes in the conduct of the Vietnam war.

The Tet drama began with the January 30–31, 1968, surprise attacks by the North Vietnamese and their southern allies, the National Liberation Front (Vietcong), involving perhaps 84,000 men in the first waves, against most of South Vietnam's major cities and towns. Sappers hit the U.S. Embassy in Saigon. North Vietnamese regulars pressed the siege of the Marine outpost at Khe Sanh and for three weeks occupied most of the former imperial city of Hue. Not since major U.S. forces first entered Vietnam in 1965 had Hanoi undertaken so ambitious a military effort— aimed largely at South Vietnamese installations amid calls for a popular uprising against the Thieu regime and its American allies.

An astute American eyewitness, Don Oberdorfer, spelled out the principal elements of the ensuing setback suffered by the North Vietnamese and Vietcong—in Vietnam, if not in Washington:

" . . . It is clear that the attack forces—and particularly the indigenous Vietcong, who did most of the fighting and dying—suffered a grievous military setback. Tens of thousands of the most dedicated and experienced fighters emerged from the jungles and forests of the countryside only to meet a deadly rain of fire and steel within the cities. The Vietcong lost the best of a generation of resistance fighters, and after Tet increasing numbers of North Vietnamese had to be sent south to fill the ranks. The war became increasingly a conventional battle and less an insurgency. Because the people of the cities did not rise up against the foreigners and puppets at Tet—indeed, they gave little support to the attack force—the communist claim to a moral and political authority in South Vietnam suffered a serious blow."*

Soon after the events, the authoritative *Strategic Survey—1969*, published by the Institute for Strategic Studies, London, declared: "The main 'success' for the United States was the revelation of the extent to which North Vietnam and the Vietcong had suffered during 1968. The enormous losses incurred by North Vietnamese units during their major offensives of February and May 1968 destroyed the elite of North Vietnam's army. That army showed little sign of complete recovery during 1969.

"The Vietcong also experienced increasingly serious recruiting difficulties during 1969. They had been forced in 1968 to abandon much of their rural power base, in the form of territory under their control, in order to launch the assault upon the cities. That assault having failed, they found in retreat that their rural base, once neglected, had begun to crumble."

Other post-mortems, of varying colorations, have echoed the same themes. For example, the journalist Frances Fitzgerald, in her best-selling, often passionate indictment of U.S. involvement in Vietnam, *Fire in the Lake* (New York: Atlantic–Little, Brown, 1972), observed that "the curious aspect of the American public [and press] reaction to the Tet offensive was that it reflected neither the judgment of the American officials nor the true change in the military situation in South Vietnam." The South Vietnamese Army, she noted, "was not routed; the GVN did not fall; and as a year would show, the Tet offensive had weakened the Front and forced [*sic*] the GVN to recruit the troops necessary to support American operations and occupy much greater areas of the countryside." It should be added that, to Fitzgerald, the communist military setback at Tet was irrelevant in the face of the "real question"—whether U.S. intervention served any good purpose. She felt, emphatically, that it did not; and that the future, in any case, belonged to the communists, whose "narrow flame of revolution" would

---

*Don Oberdorfer, *Tet!* (New York: Doubleday & Co., 1971), pp. 329–30. According to Oberdorfer, Communist dead during the period January 29–March 31, 1968, by official allied count, totalled 58,373; 3,895 U.S. servicemen died, as did 214 South Koreans, Australians, New Zealanders and Thais. So did 4,954 South Vietnamese servicemen and 14,300 South Vietnamese civilians. (All U.S. estimates of enemy dead, civilian losses, and enemy manpower were necessarily based at least partly on guesswork.)

"cleanse" Vietnam of the "corruption and disorder of the American war."

The observations of Oberdorfer, Fitzgerald, and other writers* differ markedly from most of the media's 1968 "message." That message, most simply put, was: DISASTER IN VIETNAM! The generalized effect of the news media's contemporary output in February–March 1968 was a distortion of reality—through sins of omission and commission—on a scale that helped shape Tet's political repercussions in Washington and the Administration's response.

Why the distortion? I find simple "ideological" explanations of media flaws gravely insufficient, particularly as applied to the Tet coverage. In my view, the distortions at Tet resulted from the impact of a rare combination of circumstances on the various habits, incentives, economic constraints, and managerial and manpower limitations peculiar to each of the major U.S. news organizations. Tet sharply illuminated these limitations, which, to varying degrees, affect news coverage to this day.

One possible underlying explanation of the unusual media malfunction during the Tet period needs more emphasis here. This involves the public performance of President Johnson.

Particularly during a foreign policy crisis, the Chief Executive plays a special role with respect to the practical needs of the press and television. American news managers (like other Americans) look to him to define the new situation, at least initially, and to provide a coherent response to it. Congress and the public can wait for a week or two, if necessary. But the editors and TV producers cannot. Faced with the competitive task of providing instant reportage and prompt explanation, they are ill-equipped psychologically to tolerate lingering uncertainty or ambiguity. They need a clear story line, an agenda, a framework, a plausible answer to that recurrent journalistic question: "What next?"

If the man in the White House, however beleaguered, does not soon satisfy this need, newsmen look elsewhere and his troubles are magnified. Vague reassurances and exhortations are not enough. In word and deed, the President must be seen to seize the initiative. If he does not do so, his domestic foes will edge onto the stage and win increasing media attention for *their* definitions of the crisis and *their* solutions; the President's

---

*For example, Herbert Schandler, *The Unmaking of a President* (Princeton, 1977); Leslie H. Gelb with Richard K. Betts, *The Irony of Vietnam* (Washington: Brookings, 1979); Harry G. Summers, Jr., *On Strategy: The Vietnam War in Context* (Presidio Press, 1982).

subordinates and political allies will be shaken or silent; contending bureaucratic factions within his Administration will attempt to exploit uncertainty and influence policy through news "leaks"; the hesitant will side with his critics. Lacking a clear White House action-reaction scenario for the story, many news managers, especially TV newsmen, will hastily design their own, yielding to a penchant for drama, controversy, and "worst case" speculation. The difficulties abroad will loom ever larger.

Neither the President nor his prior policy need be "popular" to supply the press with a reassuring scenario. Popularity helps, as it helped John F. Kennedy during the Berlin Wall crisis of 1961 and the Cuban missile crisis of 1962—and Lyndon Johnson during his riposte to the North Vietnamese in the Gulf of Tonkin in 1964 and his intervention in the Dominican Republic in 1965. But Richard Nixon got along without it after Hanoi launched its powerful, tank-led 1972 "Easter offensive" against South Vietnam. He provided the news media (and political Washington) with what they needed most. There was not only clear prior warning by the Administration, but also a decisive White House reaction to the enemy thrust—renewed bombing of the North, the mining of Haiphong harbor, a renewed but conditional peace offer. Despite the fevers of election year, despite the antiwar candidacy of George McGovern, despite the enemy's initial battlefield successes, the newsmen, in Washington and Vietnam, were not overwhelmed by the story in 1972, as they were in early 1968. No Washington crisis occurred.

Before and during Tet, as will be seen in the chapters that follow, Lyndon Johnson, willy-nilly, helped to create conditions that led to an unusual failure in U.S. crisis journalism. Six months prior to the Tet attacks, he orchestrated a "progress" campaign; to shore up public support, he and his subordinates presented an optimistic view of the Administration's limited war of attrition in Vietnam. Shortly before the Tet attacks he received ample warning from Saigon that Hanoi was planning a major battlefield effort of some sort; he did not warn the American people, but rather stressed his quest for "peace." When the Tet attacks came, he confined his initial reaction to a hastily called, untelevised news conference several days later. He left the detailed explanations to subordinates. Amid the clamor of an election year, he took no major retaliatory actions (e.g., more bombing, or mining); instead, he hunkered down, besieged, apparently trying to buy time. Finally, on March 31, he addressed the nation, announcing a new bombing pause, a new peace offer, and his withdrawal from the 1968 presidential race. For two months he had left a vacuum—which others hastened to fill. Simply to describe the alarums and distortions of the TV and the press in February–March 1968 as "deliberate" or "ideological" ignores both prior Administration performance and the President's own failure to respond decisively to the sudden turn of events in Vietnam. Possibly owing to the deep contradictions in his own "guns and butter" war policy, Johnson did not give the news media (or the public) a coherent scenario. In that sense, the President's political crisis in Washington after Tet was a self-inflicted wound.

Did the reporting after Tet, particularly TV's portrayal, suddenly turn the American people against the war? This has long been the claim of both critics and champions of television news. This claim is highly speculative, it seems to me. No one has yet produced empirical evidence linking the content of news coverage to changes in public opinion; such links are simply assumed to exist. In any event, the polls did not show any drastic shifts in mass attitudes toward the war during February–March 1968, even as Lyndon Johnson's popularity ratings sank to new lows (and recovered a bit after his March 31 speech).

However, as Oberdorfer observes in *Tet!*, the crisis apparently provided an opportunity for many "opinion-leaders"—politicians, pundits, educators—long uneasy about LBJ's war policy to come out against it. Their public statements often echoed media themes. And I do suggest that, at Tet, the news coverage from Vietnam demonstrably affected the perceptions and early reactions of political Washington, of the President's allies and his foes, and, thanks in part to the White House "vacuum," seemed to aggravate the growing disarray.

My explanations are not all-encompassing. As the Washington *Post*'s Saigon bureau chief, I was an active, if less than omniscient, participant in the Vietnam coverage I describe. My accounts of the journalistic atmosphere in Washington and New York during February–March 1968 are necessarily based on the recollections of others, long after the event.

Nor does this book—a study of an "extreme case" of crisis journalism—serve as a complete history of the Tet period (other sources are cited). As with the Indo-China war as a whole, despite some refreshingly dispassionate new scholarship, much research remains to be done, especially on the decisions, plans, and expectations of Hanoi's leaders, on the South Vietnamese experience, and on the changing hopes, fears, and intentions of Lyndon Johnson and his domestic foes. Still more research needs to be done on the performance of the U.S.

news media during the entire Vietnam period: on the ebb and flow of news managers' attention, particularly before 1965 and after the U.S. withdrawal in 1973 made Vietnam no longer a "hometown story"; on the shabby, even shameful media treatment given the Vietnam veteran, commonly depicted on TV as either victim or psychopath, through the 1970s; and on the slowness of news managers to recognize the significance of the exodus of the "boat people" after 1975 from a Communist Vietnam.

Of late, one sees certain signs of journalistic self-consciousness. Old media clichés about Vietnam, some dating back to Tet '68, die hard. But public discussion of media performance has greatly increased since the mid-1970s. In early 1982, as conflict spread in Central America, *Time* and the *Times* and *Post* reported, not uncritically, on television's enduring thirst for emotive "bang-bang" stories—news as entertainment, gunfire and corpses—in El Salvador. The *Wall Street Journal*'s editorial page took reporters elsewhere to task for romanticizing Latin guerrillas, and a debate over coverage of the Mideast perked along in magazines and journalism reviews. Arguments still persisted over the press's role in Indo-China.* But on the whole, I see no reason to change the conclusions in *Big Story*.

This book is divided into "subject chapters" covering various major aspects of the Tet offensive and its aftermath in Vietnam and the United States. This approach has advantages for the analyst in terms of selection, clarity, and cohesion. It does not reflect, indeed it distorts, the way that reporters, editors, and TV producers must deal day by day with heterogeneous bits and pieces of available information. This special journalistic process would be better reflected in a chronology of TV and press performance over the two-month Tet period. But such a chronology—my original approach—quickly proved unwieldy and kaleidoscopic.

For lack of space, I did not explicitly single out several subsidiary strands in the media coverage. I decided against a special chapter, for example, on press discussions of U.S. military strategy, a subject that recurs throughout but whose treatment by itself seemed both too technical and too confused by badly articulated official statements and lazy press commentary. (At Tet, as during other periods of the war, the crucial military advantage to Hanoi of "sanctuaries" in Laos and Cam-

---

*See Robert Elegant's "How to Lose a War," *Encounter*, August 1981, and "An Exchange," involving Mr. Elegant and this writer, in *Encounter*, April 1982.

bodia was seldom cited in Congress or on TV; Lyndon Johnson's policy was "no wider war," and somehow, this policy turned Vietnam into an island in media analyses of the allies' military problem.) Nor did I write extensively about the history, tradition, and internal ethos of the parent news organizations and their Washington news bureaus; these factors are only noted in passing. Nor, for space reasons, did I undertake extensive analyses of TV and press coverage in Indo-China long prior to (or after) Tet or of the erosion of the virtually unanimous editorial (and Congressional) consensus behind the Johnson Administration's initial troop commitment in 1965.

My own experience in and out of Vietnam no doubt shaped my perceptions of Tet and of press performance. Like most of my colleagues in Vietnam, I was more interested in *how* the war was going than in the more general questions, so fiercely debated at home, of whether the United States should have committed itself to Vietnam or whether Administration war policy made sense. The war and the policy were a "given," and so treated by most American newsmen in 1965–68 in Saigon. As a Marine veteran of Korea, I was perhaps less shocked by war's waste and destruction than were my colleagues witnessing these for the first time; I was probably also more interested in such military matters as logistics, "foxhole strength," enemy tactics, and allied deployments than they were. My career as a "word man," rather than a TV reporter, made me, no doubt, less tolerant than others of television techniques and commentary. Indeed, Professor Lawrence Lichty, a distinguished analyst of TV and contributor to this study who was not in Vietnam at Tet, found certain individual network news reports considerably less alarmist and simplistic than I did. Lastly, I shared many of my colleagues' misperceptions at Tet, as will be seen.

This inquiry was broadly conceived and funded in 1970 by Freedom House (20 West 40th Street, New York, New York 10018), a non-profit, non-partisan organization. Its chairman was Margaret Chase Smith, then United States Senator from Maine. Freedom House's trustees and its director, Leonard Sussman, a former newsman, scrupulously refrained from seeking to impose their views on my work. The research and conclusions were mine alone. As indicated by many of the reviews of earlier editions of this book, these conclusions disappoint extreme partisans, would-be reformers, and those of my colleagues who argue, as some still do, that because the Johnson Administration was "wrong," the press and TV were "right."

This edition of *Big Story* is abridged and updated for the student and the general reader, and the notes, which are an important complement to the text, begin on page 530. No less important are the additions and corrections that follow the notes. With this caveat, scholars and researchers are directed to the original two-volume edition (published in 1977 by Westview Press, Boulder, Colorado), which is illustrated with 110 photos of newsmen and other actors in the Tet drama and which contains some 700 pages of documentation. It includes a roster of accredited Vietnam correspondents; story and picture lists; transcripts of news conferences, briefings, and key TV programs; and certain special studies, including a revealing analysis of published news photographs and a detailed chapter by Burns W. Roper on public opinion polls before, during, and after Tet.

Mr. and Mrs. Carl B. Braestrup provided support and encouragement throughout the project. My employer, the Washington *Post*, granted several short leaves of absence and sent me back to Vietnam in 1972. My wife and children bravely shared the burden.

Finally, I am grateful to the Woodrow Wilson International Center for Scholars at the Smithsonian for a fellowship which enabled me to complete the book and to Yale University Press and the Institute for Educational Affairs for making this new edition possible.

Peter Braestrup

Washington, D.C.
March 1982

A BRIEF CHRONOLOGY OF THE TET PERIOD

1968

JANUARY

Sun	Mon	Tues	Wed	Thurs	Fri	Sat
	1	2	3	4	5	6
7	8	9	10	11	12	13
14	15	16	17	18	19	20
21	22	23	24	25	26	27
28	29	30	31			

FEBRUARY

Sun	Mon	Tues	Wed	Thurs	Fri	Sat
				1	2	3
4	5	6	7	8	9	10
11	12	13	14	15	16	17
18	19	20	21	22	23	24
25	26	27	28	29		

MARCH

Sun	Mon	Tues	Wed	Thurs	Fri	Sat
					1	2
3	4	5	6	7	8	9
10	11	12	13	14	15	16
17	18	19	20	21	22	23
24	25	26	27	28	29	30
31						

1967

Nov. 21: In Washington, General Westmoreland predicts U.S. troop withdrawals can start in two years.
Dec. 18: In Detroit, General Wheeler warns of possible enemy offensive.
Dec. 20: Westmoreland privately tells Washington of communists' decision to try countrywide win-the-war effort.
Dec. 21: President Johnson confides to Australian officials he expects "kamikaze" attacks in Vietnam. Later, he publicly discusses Vietnam, does not mention "kamikaze" attacks.

1968

Jan. 20: Siege of Khe Sanh begins.
Jan. 22: Westmoreland tells NBC he expects major enemy effort around Tet (Lunar New Year) holidays.
Jan. 23: North Koreans seize U.S. intelligence ship *Pueblo*.
Jan. 29: Tet holiday cease-fire begins. Saigon's troops on 50 percent holiday leave. Curfew lifted.
Jan. 30: (Saigon time)—Communists launch surprise attacks in II Corps, hit Da Nang and Hoi An in I Corps.
Jan. 31: (Saigon time)—Attacks throughout South Vietnam, including Hue, Ben Tre, Saigon's Tan Son Nhut Air Base, the U.S. Embassy, and the Presidential Palace.
Feb. 1: Westmoreland predicts more enemy initiatives.
Feb. 2: Johnson says Tet offensive was a military failure, but predicts more hard fighting.
Feb. 5: Hanoi's *Nhan Dan* claims impending victory.
Feb. 7: Communists take Lang Vei outpost near Khe Sanh, hang on in Hue and Saigon outskirts, but have withdrawn from other urban areas.
Feb. 8: Senator Robert Kennedy assails Johnson's policy.
Feb. 13: Pentagon sending 10,500 more men to Vietnam.

Feb. 18:   Communist gunners shell 45 cities and bases, but only four ground attacks are launched.
Feb. 24:   Hue city cleared of enemy forces.
Feb. 25:   In AP interview, Westmoreland is optimistic, but says he may need additional U.S. forces in future.
Feb. 27:   In special report, CBS's Walter Cronkite says negotiation is only way out of the war.
Feb. 28:   After trip to Saigon, Wheeler presents complex 206,000-troop request; Johnson orders task force under incoming Secretary of Defense Clark Clifford to study it. Administration and Congress divided on war.
Mar. 1:   Last major communist push at Khe Sanh repelled.
Mar. 6:   In "backgrounder," Westmoreland sees Hue as more likely enemy target now than Khe Sanh; says allies are going on the offensive.
Mar. 8:   Wheeler cables Westmoreland "cheerless counsel" that chances of getting troop increase are all but dead.
Mar. 10:   New York *Times* reports that Westmoreland has asked for 206,000 more men, "to regain the initiative." NBC's Frank McGee says U.S. is losing the war.
Mar. 11:   *Newsweek* features "Agony of Khe Sanh," calls for peace.
Mar. 12:   Senator Eugene McCarthy wins 42 percent of vote in New Hampshire Democratic primary.
Mid-month: Under heavy bombing, communists cut back forces around Khe Sanh, as UPI reports.
Mar. 16:   Robert Kennedy announces candidacy.
Mar. 21:   Thieu announces 135,000-man Army increase.
Mar. 22:   Johnson announces that Westmoreland will become Army Chief of Staff (in mid-1968).
Mar. 30:   Gallup poll reports all-time low in public approval of Johnson's performance as President.
Mar. 31:   Johnson gives first nationwide TV speech since Tet; he announces partial bombing pause, willingness to negotiate with Hanoi, and his decision not to run for re-election.

1

The Press Corps in Vietnam

In June 1962, Peter Arnett, a tough little 27-year-old Associated Press correspondent from New Zealand, who had worked in Thailand and Laos and been expelled from Indonesia, showed up in Saigon as a legman for Malcolm Browne, the somewhat austere one-time chemist who was then AP's only permanent reporter in Vietnam. A year out of the Baltimore bureau, Browne was "beating a two-finger tattoo on his old Remington the day I arrived," Arnett recalled, "trying to complete the daily 700 words of copy we used to send then to Tokyo by Morsecast—a far cry from the batteries of teleprinters that would eventually grace a much expanded AP bureau."

On the wall of Browne's cubbyhole hung a "withered hand," Arnett added, brought back by "our Vietnamese photographer who had been to an ambush scene. Browne had hitched it to the wall to remind visitors that there was a war beyond the casually luxurious life of the foreign community in Saigon in the early Sixties."

Indeed, Arnett noted, until 1968, the war rarely showed its ugly face in downtown Saigon. In 1962, reporters could sit on the terrace of the Hotel Continentale Palace ("Graham Greene's hotel," where he reportedly wrote *The Quiet American*), ogle the graceful girls strolling down Tu Do street (the Rue Catinat in the French time) in their *ao dais,* and "talk politics into the warm evening hours." Then, as later, it was exotic. Both Arnett and Browne were to meet and marry Vietnamese girls of good family.

The other newsmen in Saigon in the 1962–63 period included Peter Kalischer of CBS (who was to return at Tet); Charles Mohr of *Time;* Beverly Deepe, a free-lancer who took over from Francois Sully as *Newsweek*'s Saigon correspondent when the latter was expelled by Diem in late 1962 (she later joined the *Christian Science Monitor* and Sully returned to Saigon); and Neil Sheehan of UPI, who came in April 1962. Browne himself had taken up residence in Saigon in November 1961. In addition, fresh from the Congo, David Halberstam was to succeed Homer Bigart of the New York *Times*, who departed in mid-1962.

These journalists' experiences grew increasingly turbulent in 1962–63. For a decade, their views helped shape the attitudes of newly arriving U.S. newsmen toward U.S. officialdom, successive Saigon regimes, the South Vietnamese fighting man, and the enemy.

The Beginnings of Abrasion

Only a small band of American newsmen was on hand in Saigon as the Kennedy Administration fitfully increased its commitment of military advisors (to 6,000 in May 1962, to 16,000 by the end of 1963), of helicopters, and of high-level attention to President Ngo Dinh Diem's regime. The Kennedy policy was, in essence, to prevent South Vietnam from "going communist," albeit short of all-out U.S. intervention. This policy, however vague, was widely endorsed by U.S. editorial writers. But the shortcomings of Diem's "counterinsurgency" effort against the Hanoi-backed Vietcong guerrillas in the countryside contrasted with official expressions of optimism. These shortcomings were recounted to newsmen by frustrated U.S. Army field advisors and helicopter pilots, then as later prime sources of information. The resultant "negative" reporting upset official Washington, anxious not to frighten the public or alarm Congress.

In May 1962, press-government tensions were already apparent. Homer Bigart (with a half-dozen wars in his by-line file) duly reported Robert S. McNamara's conclusions after the Defense Secretary's first flying trip to Vietnam. No more U.S. advisors would be needed, McNamara told newsmen at Tan Son Nhut airport—U.S. aid had reached a peak and would level off. Bigart wrote: "After forty-eight hours in South Vietnam, Mr. McNamara said, he was 'tremendously encouraged' by developments. He said the Vietnamese people had more security."

Then Bigart noted his own impressions: "The Kennedy Administration is still rigidly following its sink or swim with Diem line . . . the Administration believes the American correspondents here are giving a distorted picture . . . of American involvement in the shooting war. The Administration feels the reporters are magnifying incidents where American servicemen find themselves in combat situations, and are writing too much about American casualties."

The Saigon newsmen, Bigart reported, "petitioned Mr. McNamara to ease the United States information policy [in Saigon]. They [the newsmen] are convinced that information on American casualties is being withheld or at least subjected to unnecessary delays. They complained that South Vietnamese officers had intervened successfully to prevent the correspondents from riding on United States helicopters engaged in transporting combat units to the battlefields."

It was not an easy time for Bigart, Browne, Arnett, and the others. Caught in the middle was John Mecklin, the U.S. Mission information chief, himself a former *Time* war correspondent, who wrote: "A man from Mars admitted to official [U.S.] inner circles in both Vietnam and Washington could have been excused if he got the impression that the newsmen, as well as the Vietcong, were the enemy." In his memoir, *Mission in Torment,* Mecklin added: "No responsible U.S. official in Saigon ever told a newsman a really big falsehood, instead there were endless little ones."

Within the various, often rival U.S. bureaucracies in Saigon, there was strong pressure to report only "progress" up the chain of command, to minimize failure on the part of the Army of the Republic of Vietnam (ARVN), to eschew "pessimism" in favor of "can do" positive thinking. U.S. Ambassador Frederick G. Nolting and Gen. Paul D. Harkins, the U.S. military commander, were at the same time both instigators and victims of this conformity. Strongly committed to Diem, seeing no stable alternative, they could not countenance "negative" facts, whether reported by frustrated subordinates in the field or published in the newspapers back home. It was "sink or swim with Ngo Dinh Diem."

From Browne, Arnett got a mimeographed guide for newcomers to the AP bureau, which included a warning that the Diem regime looked no more kindly on frank reporting than the U.S. government: "You can expect very little help from most official sources, and news comes the hard way. Correspondents in Vietnam are regarded by the Saigon government as 'scabby sheep' and treated accordingly." Diemist harassment of foreign reporters was to grow in 1963 as the Buddhist demonstrations and self-immolations began. Madame Nhu, Diem's sister-in-law, was to denounce Halberstam and other newsmen by name, and Diem's police, on occasion, cracked newsmen's heads.

Hostility between the newsmen and the many official U.S. organizations (including the military) which made up the U.S. Mission in Saigon also grew apace. The Battle of Ap Bac, southwest of Saigon, in January 1963 was a breaking point. The South Vietnamese 7th Division put three battalions into an effort to encircle the elusive 514th Vietcong Battalion in a long-sought set-piece battle. Air strikes and artillery were used. The attack was a debacle: The ARVN commanders failed to press their ground attacks or close off the foe's escape route, and in the confusion shelled their own troops—nearly killing the senior U.S. advisor, as well as Neil Sheehan and Reuters' Nick Turner. At the ARVN command post, Halberstam and Arnett confronted General Harkins. " 'We've got them in a trap [Harkins said], and we're going to spring it in half an hour.' We looked at him, completely bewildered," Halberstam wrote later.

General Harkins described the operation as a "victory, not a defeat." And Adm. Harry Felt, Honolulu-based commander of U.S. forces in the Pacific, told Sheehan: "You ought to talk to some of the people who've got the facts." Sheehan, Halberstam, and Arnett had, of course, talked to the prime American sources of battlefield facts— Lt. Col. John Paul Vann and his fellow advisors in the Delta, whose own reports on ARVN performance were regarded by Harkins as excessively "pessimistic."

The credibility gap widened rapidly thereafter. Halberstam and his colleagues privately supported the U.S. commitment to South Vietnam—if not the U.S. Mission's "sink or swim" endorsement of the Diem regime. Indeed, Halberstam was to write in 1964: "I believe that Vietnam is a legitimate part of that [U.S.] global commitment . . . perhaps one of only five or six nations in the world that is truly vital to U.S. interests. If it *is* this important it may be worth a larger commitment on our part but if so we should be told the truth, not spoon-fed clichés as in the past."[1] But the newsmen were described by the U.S. Mission—and by the Diemists—as handmaidens of the foe. They were criticized by their visiting elders, including Joseph Alsop and Marguerite Higgins. And *Time,* in a celebrated exercise, attacked the Saigon press corps in September 1963 for distorted reporting, "helping to compound the very confusion that [the press] should be untangling for its readers at home." (*Time*'s Charles Mohr resigned in protest to join the New York *Times;* his partner, Merton Perry, also quit, and eventually joined *Newsweek.*)

The ouster of Diem in November 1963 by the ARVN generals (with U.S. approval) and the subsequent added revelations of his regime's ineptitude and paranoia served both to justify the reporting of Halberstam, Sheehan, Browne, and their colleagues, and to underscore the "credibility gap." Halberstam and Browne shared a 1964 Pulitzer Prize for international reporting; Sheehan, in Halberstam's view, was denied his rightful share of the glory only because his wire service, UPI, had insisted that he take a vacation just prior to the anti-Diem coup.

The impression was later widespread—among both critics and admirers—that Browne, Halberstam, and Sheehan had combined forces in the face of U.S. Mission hostility, eschewing the usual journalistic rivalries. As Arnett later emphasized (in a 1974 interview), this was not what happened. After his arrival in August 1962, Halberstam shared a Saigon house with his friend from Congo days, AP photographer Horst Faas, who was to log more "field time" in combat than any other newsman in Vietnam. Halberstam also used the AP office; *Times* men overseas liked to establish informal alliances with wireservice bureaus, mostly to profit from the latter's broader coverage of "spot" news.

But Halberstam, a gregarious, ambitious young Harvard graduate, and Browne, a loner, indifferent to U.S. Embassy social snubs, did not hit it off. At one point, Halberstam openly criticized Browne's dispatches in the AP office. It ended with Halberstam divorcing AP and moving to the cubbyhole office of Neil Sheehan, an intense young reporter just in from Tokyo. Although Faas and Arnett remained Halberstam's friends, the AP bureau often found itself competing with a hard-working rival combine—Halberstam, Sheehan, and Nick Turner. If Browne generally shared Halberstam's critical views of the Diem regime and U.S. Mission policy, Arnett recalled, he came to his conclusions independently.

After the replacement, in mid-1963, of Nolting as U.S. Ambassador by Henry Cabot Lodge (the GOP 1960 vice-presidential candidate), and the subsequent ouster of Diem later that year, tension eased. Indeed, Lodge had used "leaks" to the press as part of his campaign to change U.S. policy toward Diem. Never again was government-press hostility in Saigon so fierce. But a "credibility gap" had been established, and remained. Under Lyndon Johnson, on many issues besides Vietnam, the "gap" was later to grow wider in Washington.

In May 1964, six months after Diem's ouster, Hanson Baldwin, the *Times*'s hawkish military editor, scored Secretary McNamara and President Johnson for "alternate optimism and pessimism," and attacked the Administration's "misleading and sometimes distorted picture" of conditions in South Vietnam where "the Vietcong have extended their control over large sections . . . since the overthrow of the Diem government." Baldwin noted the Joint Chiefs' desire to fish-or-cut-bait on Vietnam. He cited the Administration's on-again, off-again internal discussions of stronger war measures.

In 1965, having left Vietnam after 18 months, Halberstam published his *Making of a Quagmire,* and Browne published his *New Face of War,* garnished by an introduction by Ambassador Lodge. Later there appeared the collected long pieces on Vietnam of Robert Shaplen, the *New Yorker*'s roving Hong Kong-based correspondent. These books—together with John Mecklin's Vietnam memoir, Graham Greene's brilliant, pessimistic Saigon novel, *The Quiet American,* and Bernard Fall's analysis of the French and American Indo-China wars, *The Two Vietnams*—became part of the inner landscape of many reporters who went to Vietnam in the 1960s. The authors variously recounted the hopes, self-deceptions, and miscalculations of Western policy in Indo-China; the tenacity of the Vietnamese communists; and the failings of the Diem regime. These writers, of course, were outsiders, visitors. They did not speak Vietnamese. By and large, they focused on the *Western* experience in Indo-China, a focus that was to be shared by the newsmen who followed them.

1964–65: A Neglected War

Not many American newsmen joined Halberstam, Browne, Sheehan, Faas, Arnett, and the others after the climactic events of 1963. Vietnam, in terms of permanent assignment of U.S. correspondents, remained a backwater even after the fall of Diem and the commitment of 23,000 U.S. advisors. In mid-1964 there were only 20-odd American and other foreign correspondents in Saigon. Most of them were pinned down in the capital by political turmoil—a series of Army-led coups that lasted until mid-1965, with "instability" succeeding "dictatorship" as the prime U.S. complaint about Saigon. To Jim Lucas of the Scripps-Howard newspapers, an ex-Marine and journalistic veteran of the Korean War, this preoccupation with Saigon politics seemed excessive. "In the six months I lived in the Delta [1964]," Lucas wrote later, "I was the only correspondent regularly assigned to working and living with combat troops . . . this is the only war of recent memory which has not been covered to saturation." But as Saigon governments rose and fell, the "war" spread in 1964 from the easy-to-reach Delta to the remote center and north of South Vietnam. Even AP lacked enough manpower for sustained field coverage. As is often the case, the media were light on the take-off, heavy after the landing.

Yet, ironically, at home throughout 1964, Vietnam loomed largely, if irregularly, as an election-year "story." Widely publicized were attacks on U.S. destroyers in the Gulf of Tonkin, U.S. reprisal bombing of North Vietnam's ports, and a subsequent Congressional resolution backing Presidential action in Southeast Asia. Senator Barry Goldwater, the hawkish GOP contender, was depicted by Democrats as trigger-happy, eager to escalate in Vietnam. President Johnson played down the idea that American troops would be imminently involved in combat. On September 28, in Manchester, New Hampshire, in the course of the campaign, he said, "I have not thought that we were ready for American boys to do the fighting for Asian boys . . . we are not going north and drop bombs at this stage of the game, and we are not going south and run out and leave it for the communists to take over."

Meanwhile, a year after Diem's ouster, the New York *Times*'s Peter Grose was reporting from Saigon that the war had reached a "stage more desperate for South Vietnam than ever," with deterioration having set in prior to the Diem coup. The erosion was accelerated by the political turnover and resultant instability in the army and administration. AP's Horst Faas, John Wheeler (up from Kuala Lumpur), Browne, and Arnett had been gradually stepping up field coverage of ARVN's plight, especially on major engagements.

But such warnings, and even increasing U.S. involvement, did not bring "saturation" coverage. Then as now, cable charges and other costs made foreign coverage expensive and—it was widely felt—not worth it in terms of selling papers. Moreover, service abroad was not part of the professional experience of most American news executives

—those who allocated budgets—or of many of the harried telegraph editors forced to choose among wire-service offerings from abroad, Washington, and nearby states. American newspapers are primarily locally oriented businesses, and resources are allocated accordingly. The more affluent or ambitious news organizations maintained Washington staff bureaus. But all but a handful of newspapers and broadcast organizations left foreign news coverage to the tightly budgeted AP, UPI, or Reuters—or to the New York *Times,* Los Angeles *Times,* or Washington *Post* news services. Then as now, in terms of space allotments, news from abroad steadily ranked well below the comics and sports, and below local, state, and Washington news.[2]

The net effect was visible in Vietnam. With the commitment of U.S. ground forces in March 1965, the press corps there did indeed at last begin to grow. But among those major U.S. newspapers which did not staff Vietnam even after that commitment were the 31 Gannett papers (circ. 1,470,000), the 22 Newhouse papers (3,055,000), the Chicago *Tribune* (805,000), the rival Chicago *Sun-Times* (545,000), the St. Louis *Post-Dispatch* (345,000), and the six Knight papers (1,466,000). Asked why his chain did not staff Vietnam, a Knight executive told this writer in the winter of 1970–71 that, as far as he knew, the subject never came up. (In Knight's defense, however, it must be added, the organization sent some of its best Washington reporters to Vietnam for 60-day tours, notably including Don Oberdorfer and Robert Boyd.)

Nor was much attention paid within the trade to the quality of Vietnam reporting or the "operational" and "intellectual" problems of coverage. The quarterly *Bulletins* of the American Society of Newspaper Editors (ASNE) in 1965–68 reflected executives' concern over proper reporting of elections and domestic issues such as civil rights and ghetto disturbances, but published no comment on Vietnam coverage. The annual Associated Press Managing Editors (APME) convention summary in 1967 barely mentioned Vietnam, despite AP's relatively strong manpower commitment there. The quarterly *Columbia Journalism Review* published no major examination of Vietnam coverage prior to Tet. The *Nieman Reports* held off until 1969. *Editor and Publisher* only on occasion printed interviews with returning Vietnam reporters. Trade periodicals such as *Broadcasting* and the Overseas Press Club's annuals focused largely on "freedom of information" issues and the "credibility gap."

The Press Corps at Tet

Only with the commitment of U.S. ground troops in 1965 did the number of accredited American reporters and photographers in Vietnam begin to grow by leaps and bounds. It was then that the New York *Times*, for example, with six men in Paris (and a total of 42 men overseas), permanently beefed up its one-man Saigon bureau to a three-man post. *Newsweek* and *Time* followed suit, and other newspapers began to staff the place on a regular basis. The Washington *Post*'s first full-time correspondent, John Maffre, arrived in 1964; not until 1968 did the *Post* add a second staffer. For a long time after 1965, as it seemed to many newsmen in Saigon, managements back home thought of Vietnam as a "temporary" expense, an "extra" post, despite its growing contributions to page one. Such accessories as cars, office space, and files were slow in coming. By all accounts, only Richard Clurman, chief of foreign correspondents for *Time-Life*, arranged communications and working space in Saigon that were adequate from the start.

The U.S. troop commitment grew, from 75,000 in mid-1965 to almost 500,000 in late 1967. So did the U.S. press and TV contingent in Saigon: 131 in December 1965, 175 in December 1966, 207 at the end of 1967. By January 1968, the collective strength—all nationalities—of accredited media representatives in Saigon was sizable, involving a combined multimillion-dollar annual outlay (mostly by the TV networks for logistics) and a local payroll covering perhaps 100 messengers, secretaries, and translators. The press corps provided prime customers for the Aterbea, the Guillaume Tell, and other French-owned restaurants and hotels: the modernistic Caravelle (where CBS and ABC were headquartered), the high-ceilinged Continentale Palace, with its terrace bar overlooking Lam Son Square, and the riverfront Majestic (favored by columnist Joseph Alsop, when he was not staying at the U.S. ambassador's residence). Vietnamese drivers, parked in front of the Caravelle, drove correspondents around Saigon for $25 a day, in aging Pontiacs and Ramblers.

All told, as of January 19, 1968, two weeks before Tet, there were 464 men and women accredited under the local rules to both the South Vietnamese government and to the Office of Information of the United States Military Assistance Command, Vietnam (MACV).

Americans made up a minority of the total, with 179. There were 114 Vietnamese and 171 other "non-U.S. citizens."[3]

This large number of accredited "media representatives," often cited by outsiders as evidence of an information "glut," gave a misleading impression. The 179 Americans included a dozen freelancers, as well as representatives of the *National Catholic Welfare News,* the *Baptist Mission Press,* the *Dartmouth* (College) *Daily News,* the *Twin Cities Courier,* and *Christianity Today.* Another half-dozen were wives of newsmen.[4] Moreover, the total list of 464 included journalists in Vietnam on brief visits, part-time "stringers" (journalists who worked on a fee or contract basis for several organizations), secretaries, managers, and interpreters. Television sound men and cameramen, as well as still photographers, were also necessarily accredited, although their "fact-finding" or "reporting" functions may have been minimal. Furthermore, departure from Vietnam did not mean loss of accreditation prior to the MACV card's expiration date, thus swelling the official list of correspondents.

Thus, the "fact-finding" manpower available in Saigon during the Tet offensive was far less impressive than the official figures indicated. In terms of resident representatives of "major media"—those news publications, news agencies, and TV networks with national U.S. audiences—there were perhaps 60 newsmen in all.[5] The breakdown was as follows:

Wire services: AP (servicing 1,262 U.S. newspapers, 3,221 radio or TV subscribers) had eight reporters and deskmen in Vietnam; UPI (1,200 newspapers, 3,200 broadcast clients), eight; Reuters (45 U.S. client newspapers), four; and Agence France Presse (AFP) (one U.S. subscriber—the New York *Times*), three.

Radio-television networks: NBC (est. 15,000,000 listeners to evening news) had six reporters; CBS (est. 15,100,000 listeners), six; and ABC (est. 4,600,000), four.[6]

Newspapers: The New York *Times* (circ. 895,000 with 320 news service clients) had four American reporters; and the Washington *Post* (circ. 480,000) and the Los Angeles *Times* (circ. 950,000), with 308 U.S. clients for their joint news service, had two reporters each.

News magazines: Time (U.S. circ. 3,700,000) had six reporters; *Newsweek* (circ. 2,090,000), two staff men plus two American stringers; and *U.S. News and World Report* (circ. 1,580,000), one reporter.

A number of other organizations were also represented in Saigon. The Minneapolis papers, the Scripps-Howard chain, the Chicago *Daily News*, the *Wall Street Journal*, the New York *Daily News*, the Baltimore *Sun*, the Washington *Star*, the Detroit *News*, the *Christian Science Monitor*, and *Newsday* each maintained one reporter largely based in Saigon at this time. (The *New Yorker*'s roving Robert Shaplen was based in Hong Kong.)

But even this reduced roster was misleading as an indicator of the "breadth" of war "information" reaching the individual U.S. reader-viewer. The focus, in fact, was quite narrow. Why? First, of course, these 60 fact-seekers did not work "collectively" in any systematic sense. They were not employees of a central fact-finding agency. They informally exchanged gossip, impressions, rumors. But like their colleagues in Washington and other news centers, they did not "divide up the story," disperse to cover all its aspects, and then later pool information. Each bureau, in the U.S. tradition, operated in competition with its counterparts—AP versus UPI, CBS versus NBC, *Time* versus *Newsweek,* and, to a far lesser degree, the *Times* versus the *Post.*

Secondly, for competitive reasons, much of each bureau's scarce manpower in Vietnam was typically devoted to "matching" coverage, for the most part, of the *same* subject matter. Before Tet, for example, the common focus was on the battles of Con Thien and Dak To, and the 1967 Vietnam elections. This was particularly true of the wire services and networks. The pattern—in terms of page one and evening TV news subject matter—was heavily duplicative, not complementary, for each bureau strove not to be "left behind" by its competitor. The chronic rebuke of media management to subordinates is: "Why didn't *we* have that story?"

Thirdly, in Vietnam, despite all the editorial writers' talk at home of the war's complexities and "political" dimensions, the media focus was on the American presence. No American reporter spoke Vietnamese in early 1968; prior language training was regarded as a costly frill by media managers, if it was considered at all. (The New York *Times* routinely assigned Moscow-bound correspondents to appropriate language courses, but not its Vietnam men). Moreover, even after the State Department opened its hospitable Vietnam Training Center in Arlington, Virginia, for U.S. military and civilian pacification advisors, in mid-1967, few, if any, Saigon-bound newsmen were permitted by their managements to spend a guest fortnight there learning something of Vietnam's history and geography, and the nuts-and-bolts of the U.S. effort in that country.

Another blank spot in the experience of most newly arrived American newsmen in Vietnam was the military—at least the U.S. military apparatus and "language" of the 1960s. Few, for example, understood the differences between, say, a mortar and a howitzer, brigades and divisions, logistics and tactics, or between overall U.S. personnel strength in Vietnam (approaching 500,000 in January 1968) and the relatively small number of men actually firing weapons at the enemy (perhaps 100,000, including helicopter and fighter-bomber crews, artillerymen, tank crews, Navy riverboat teams, and the so-called "grunts," or infantrymen). As one result, many newsmen were ill-equipped to understand, let alone question, official or unofficial explanations of military deployments, problems, and progress. They had to learn, in highly unsystematic, patchwork fashion, while on the job. And, as Tet was to show, this was insufficient.

In Vietnam, the "learning curve" was flattened by the short tour of most American newsmen. A year to 18 months was the standard stay for newspaper and news magazine reporters, in deference to the demands of family life. AP men tended to stay 18 months or more. AFP representatives stayed for three years. In early 1968, in the *major* "print media," old hands were present: Charles Mohr of the New York *Times* had been in Vietnam in 1963; Merton D. Perry of *Newsweek,* since 1963; Peter Arnett of AP, since 1962. But they were there by choice and, except for Arnett, started out working in Vietnam for other publications. The majority of the reporters had no such lengthy exposure; for the ambitious there were few incentives to stay more than one year. Twelve to 18 months in Vietnam was a good merit badge for young reporters out of the city room. It was a boon for young unknowns in TV news. But a long-term performance in Vietnam gave one reporter no particular career advantage over another who, under fewer hardships, covered politics at home or ran a bureau in Western Europe.

In 1966–68, the television networks were perhaps the least "serious" in this respect. Their bureau chiefs were assigned to Vietnam for one year; the reporters came and went on tours varying from one to six months. A few, including Murray Fromson (Bangkok) and Bernard Kalb (Hong Kong) of CBS, had been in Southeast Asia for several years. Of the 18-odd network correspondents in Saigon when Tet hit, only half had been accredited four months earlier. As a CBS network reporter put it, "There was no premium on experience or expertise in our business. The networks see no harm in running a standup piece on the war's progress by a guy who has just come in the country two days earlier." The Tet coverage was to make this plain.

In brief, for all these reasons, the net unduplicated informational output of the Saigon press corps in 1968—far bigger and better-equipped than its counterpart of the Browne-Sheehan-Halberstam era—was a good deal smaller than the sizable flow of film and words would indicate.

Press and Bureaucracy

Even as the U.S. military buildup grew into sizable proportions by January 1968, so did the American bureaucracy in Saigon. It spawned its own mini-ministry of information, the Joint United States Public Affairs Office (JUSPAO), headed by Barry Zorthian. A Yale-educated career United States Information Service (USIS) official of Armenian descent, who had been in Vietnam since 1964, Zorthian was a swarthy, soft spoken former Marine, who projected an air of reasonableness, world-weariness, and great energy. His military-civilian press organization was headquartered in a six-story concrete building at the corner of Le Loi and Nguyen Hue streets, close by Saigon's old City Hall, and next-door to the U.S. Army officers' billet at the Rex Hotel, which featured a rooftop restaurant and steaks from the United States.

In addition to panelled offices for Zorthian and his top aides, the JUSPAO building contained a post office for U.S. correspondents (who could use the U.S. military postal system), a 200-seat auditorium—scene of the official daily military news briefings—and a first-floor warren of small offices for military and civilian advisors to various U.S. forces and the ARVN.

JUSPAO's roster included 119 American civilians, and 128 U.S. military and 370 Vietnamese employees. Much of its work was acting as a surrogate for the Government of South Vietnam (GVN), running "psychological" and propaganda efforts directed at the Vietnamese population. But JUSPAO also provided an abundance of services to newsmen. The "special projects" office quickly arranged reservations on the daily Air Force C-130 transport flights upcountry and did the paperwork required for MACV accreditation, PX and commissary cards. JUSPAO held periodic screenings of the network TV

news shows—kinescopes made by a Pentagon contractor—so that the
TV newsmen could see, often with chagrin, what got on the screen
back home. It provided copies of the USIS "Vietnam Roundup"—a
compilation of news clippings on Vietnam—and made available, on a
less systematic basis, U.S. Embassy translations of both enemy documents and the Saigon press. In short, by late 1967, JUSPAO was an
extremely helpful, even luxurious, logistics center for newsmen. But
aside from Zorthian himself, few JUSPAO officials had been in Vietnam longer than 18 months. Like the rest of the American bureaucracy there, JUSPAO had no "memory."

Permanent correspondents gave Zorthian a silver tray as a gift
when he left Vietnam in July 1968. He had been accused, on occasion, of shrewdly tailoring his explanations of U.S. (and South Vietnamese) policy to the listener's bias, of riffling through reports osten-
tatiously tagged "SECRET" to give a roomful of newsmen the
flattering sense that they were "in" on affairs of state, even as he
disclosed only trivia. But he was widely regarded as well-informed,
and he was a valuable source of instant history and background information in a U.S. diplomatic-military community whose average
tour of duty was a very short one. In 1966–68, when there was constant pressure from the White House to "present the bright side" of
Vietnam, Zorthian resisted the "all's well" syndrome. His view of the
press was publicly benign, with a good deal of private skepticism. He
would argue, "Anyone who comes to Vietnam with a particular point
of view can find stories to justify it."

But he was careful—far more careful than officials in the United
States or some of the top officials in Saigon—not to mislead reporters.
He volunteered favorable news, not the unfavorable. But his advice if
pressed was: "Don't take my word for it. Get out of town and look
for yourself." In an October 14, 1968, speech to the Industrial College of the Armed Forces, Zorthian looked back at Vietnam:

> In the world of 1968 you don't make propaganda, at least not in the
> old-fashioned way. You must communicate through the hard realities of
> your actions.
>
> The trained communicator is less a publicity man than a "substance"
> man. He has a professional appreciation for political realities. He has a
> feel for the people of a country, for what and how they think; he can
> sense how they are likely to react to a given policy or action. The profes-
> sional communicator also knows how to use the media to best advantage.

He knows their limitations and their capabilities and how to circumvent the one and exploit the other. . . .

Too often, in Vietnam, we found ourselves trying to catch up with stories about which half the world had already made up its mind. The classic case was the use of tear gas, a perfectly legitimate and humane weapon, widely used, as you know, in riot control. Yet, we were coy and secretive about it when it was first used in the field [in 1965]. Two correspondents who happened to be on the scene rushed out with a story, based on incomplete information, under a headline proclaiming that American troops in Vietnam had used gas. . . . If we had taken the initiative and put out a full and frank account of the facts, I am convinced we could have avoided most of the damage that was done.

At "Pentagon East," the two-story MACV headquarters completed in 1967 at the sprawling Tan Son Nhut military and civilian airfield on Saigon's outskirts, was the inter-service MACV Office of Information (MACOI). It consisted of some 49 officers and men headed by Brig. Gen. Winant K. Sidle, an Army artilleryman and a veteran information officer from the Pentagon. Eighteen of Sidle's people dealt with the civilian press. His staff prepared daily communiqués (9 a.m. and 4:30 p.m.) from operational reports received at the MACV combined operations center and then journeyed downtown in late afternoon to conduct the military portion of the daily briefings ("Five O'Clock Follies") in the JUSPAO building auditorium. They also compiled monthly chronologies of U.S. military actions, whose optimism could be disregarded. (Their 1967 year-end summary was entitled "Year of Progress," and read like a corporation's annual report.)

Sidle suffered from two major handicaps: (1) he worked in a military bureaucracy that regarded the press as a necessary evil; and (2) unlike Zorthian, he was not free to travel extensively in the countryside, and had to depend largely on information available at MACV for his own background. Most of his subordinate officers were even worse off. Assigned to MACOI for their entire one-year tour in Vietnam, they had little field experience or historical perspective to add to the bare bones of the communiqués.

For information on military "fundamentals," such as shifts in allied or enemy units, or the tactical rationale for the long-term efforts of Gen. William C. Westmoreland (who replaced General Harkins as commander in 1964), Saigon newsmen had to go via Sidle to busy MACV staff officers. In times of fast-moving action, as at Tet, this was difficult. There was no "war room" for U.S. newsmen—even those from the major media—with maps and charts showing the overall military situation. In the field, such information was usually available to newsmen who bothered to seek it out, but in Saigon details were skimpy.

For his part, besides working a 16-hour day, General Westmoreland, a crisp 52-year-old West Pointer, was under severe Administration pressure to present the war in its most favorable light. The White House called him almost daily to urge better "image-making." At LBJ's request, Westmoreland journeyed to Washington in April and November 1967 to assure Congress and the nation that the war was looking better, that "progress" was being made, and that American sacrifices were beginning to pay off.

Between mid-1964 and mid-1967, Westmoreland had his difficulties with what he thought of as "cynical elements" of the press, although no personal animus existed. AP picked on him for playing tennis; he stopped playing. (He had contemplated censorship, but was persuaded that it was impractical.) He was not prone, as a troop leader, to airing his vast problems in public, least of all to civilian newsmen. Beginning before the late Diem era in 1962–63, the U.S. Mission in Saigon had been pressed to stress the positive side of the conflict, not its costs, difficulties, and imponderables; Westmoreland obeyed the orders of his civilian bosses. Nor did he attempt to use the press as a vehicle for expressing his dissenting views on how to fight the war. As a result, during his occasional background briefings, with his blackbound briefing books and charts, Westmoreland sounded to many newsmen like an Administration spokesman, a "true believer" in McNamara statistics. Even as he stressed the enemy's burdens, not his own, the "credibility gap" deepened. Thus, when the Tet offensive came, there was only headshaking among newsmen as Westmoreland claimed a military setback for the foe. (Months later the Westmoreland judgment became widely accepted, but without retroactive credit to the General.)

Indeed, by late 1967, Saigon newsmen felt that Westmoreland and the military spokesmen at MACV, under pressure from Washington, were gilding the lily, presenting the war of attrition in black and white terms (U.S. progress, enemy decline) instead of in the grays that the realities demanded. There was a built-in suspicion of U.S. claims, created by the generalized over-optimism expressed by high U.S. officials since 1962, from McNamara on down. To some, including the Washington *Post*'s Ward Just, the net result was cynicism, a feeling that "there are no facts" about the war; among others grew a sour determination to counter official blandness with exposure of the mishaps and horrors of the war—which had a ready market at home.

Moreover, on a more prosaic level, both MACV and the press were bedeviled by the problem of describing an unconventional war in conventional news terms—a problem never solved. Most of the war news published or broadcast at home had its source in the so-called "Five O'Clock Follies," or daily press briefings.

When my wife visited me in Saigon in October 1966, I took her to one of these sessions, an event which she promptly labeled a "happening." On the JUSPAO auditorium stage was a display of maps affixed with cardboard bombs to show the location of raids on North Vietnam ("Air North") and cutouts of aircraft to indicate where U.S. planes were downed. An Army major supplied "updates" on the day's communiqué ("In item 7 of your release, it should read 'seven U.S. KIA and 32 enemy KIA'"), as 100 American, British, German, Vietnamese, Japanese, and French newsmen shuffled paper and scribbled notes, and a small crowd of Public Information Officers (PIOs) stood in the back and listened.

Three or four newsmen asked questions: "How far was that strike from the Chinese border?" "What was the name of that battalion commander?" The amount of extra information available was limited; few briefing officers had ever been outside Saigon, and the communiqués were necessarily made up of fragmentary reports sent in from the field. There were repeated squabbles about "body counts" and the lack of available detail, especially on allied mishaps, such as bombing friendly troops or "friendly" villages.

A fair-sized sandwich of paper was issued by the military at each "Follies": an overall MACV account of major U.S. Army, Air Force, Navy, and Marine actions of the preceding day in the four corps areas, Air North, and Air South; a U.S. Army-Vietnam (USARV) handout on actions by U.S. Army divisions (statements from division information officers, not tactical reports); and mimeographed bulletins by the 7th Air Force and the U.S. Navy amplifying their accomplishments. On occasion, the Republic of Korea and Australian forces would also add their bit.

Of necessity, given the seemingly episodic nature of the war, these communiqués resembled a collection of accident reports, or police-blotter excerpts; an unrelated jumble of "contacts," with score-keeping of enemy and friendly casualties and of enemy and U.S. bombardments. In effect, the daily catalogue of these fragmentary "scores" and "contacts" substituted for the daily gauge of progress used in more conventional wars—the movement and location of the front lines. It was quite obvious to newsmen in Saigon that the "Follies" war wrap-ups did not convey the realities of the conflict or even the tactical rationale that produced the battles. Moreover, many small-scale tactical setbacks to the U.S. forces were either minimized or glossed over, and enemy losses exaggerated, as reports came up the chain of command. And, these built-in distortions were supplemented by those of the media. Inevitably, a dramatic event—for example, the loss of an aircraft—regardless of its significance, was stressed by the press in a war where, by and large, the loss or gain of terrain features meant little. This tendency was to crop up repeatedly during the 1968 Tet offensive, especially as Hanoi's pressure on the cities waned.

But the communiqués were tailored to the "spot news" demands of all the media (except the weekly news magazines). The goat had to be fed; the communiqués were the best daily fodder available. No news agency had the money or manpower to duplicate the military reporting system.

The January 1968 U.S. Mission telephone directory was some 180 pages thick. A mini-Washington had been created in Saigon, with more than 2,000 American civilians ranging from railroad experts, textbook specialists, and propagandists, to analysts of captured documents. Besides those in the employ of the military and JUSPAO, hundreds of Americans also worked for contractors—Raymond-Morrison-Knutsen, Philco, and Pacific Architects and Engineers.

There were three sizable official American civilian groups with whom newsmen could deal:

1. The U.S. Embassy was housed in a new chancery on Thong Nhat Street. It included the political section, with a specialist on Hanoi and the CIA station chief. The latter was "special assistant" to Ambassador Ellsworth Bunker. Bunker, rarely given to meetings with newsmen, headed the Mission Council, which consisted of heads of all U.S. activities in Vietnam, including the CIA and military. The embassy political section drew on its own dozen political reporters in the field, a valuable if not omniscient secondary source of information, as well as its Vietnamese-speaking officers watching parliament and the Thieu cabinet in Saigon.

2. The U.S. Agency for International Development (USAID), headed by Donald G. MacDonald, which provided the U.S. civilian advisors to the GVN's ministries (Communications, Agriculture, Interior, Labor, Education, etc.), tried to monitor the AID program and published translations of GVN documents. It also served as the embassy's economic analysis section, keeping an eye on Vietnamese prices, wages, and other economic indicators. USAID was a prime source of bread-and-butter news about the GVN.

3. Civil Operations and Revolutionary Development (CORDS), with 3,900 men, was the civil-military subsidiary of MACV under Ambassador Robert Komer, headquartered at Pentagon East. Unlike USAID, CORDS worked outside Saigon, and it provided newsmen with grass-roots observers of varying, but generally impressive, perspicacity throughout rural Vietnam. Reorganized in mid-1967, the CORDS advisory effort paralleled the South Vietnamese administrative hierarchy in the country's four military regions (or "corps areas"), 44 provinces (the equivalents of states), and 242 districts (the equivalents of counties). Its men supplied "advice," aid, and logistics to the government in the hinterland, including the militia units. Its personnel included old Asia hands, young Vietnamese-speaking State Department officers, middle-aged USAID specialists, Filipino technicians, CIA men, and, especially at province and district level, some of the more impressive young lieutenant colonels, majors, and captains from the U.S. Army, as well as a handful of Australians. The bush pilots of Air America provided regularly scheduled light plane service for CORDS to remote districts and province capitals— with room for newsmen.

Komer's conglomerate included most of the American old hands in Vietnam. John Paul Vann, a prime source for newsmen in 1962–63, who had quit his beloved Army in disgust over high-level rejection of his "pessimistic" reporting and joined AID, was top CORDS man in the III Corps area around Saigon. Maj. Jean Sauvageot, the Army's most fluent speaker in Vietnamese, was at the Revolutionary Development Center at Vung Tau. Komer's best operatives, he felt, were the military and young Foreign Service men; often the problem with senior State officials in CORDS was that their prior diplomatic careers did not include high-pressure *management* experience.

No such panoply of sources, official or unofficial, was available to American newsmen in Saigon from the GVN. It took a lot more time, risk, and effort to get the Vietnamese story from the Vietnamese. The government-run Vietnam Press twice daily published mimeographed news bulletins, AP style; ARVN communiqués in English were available; the English-language Saigon *Post, Vietnam Guardian,* and Saigon *Daily News* did little reporting of their own.

Like their counterparts in most of the world's armies, the South Vietnamese were uneasy with the American tradition of military public relations and access by newsmen to both troops and senior officers. The daily Republic of Vietnam Armed Forces (RVNAF) war briefing, then conducted on the second floor of the shabby National Press Center on Tu Do Street, was ill-attended by Americans. ARVN spokesmen had far more limited access to operational information than did MACOI briefers. Cautious and noncommittal—and polite in the face of occasional heckling from U.S. newsmen—they seldom went beyond the day's communiqué, itself a highly laundered version of reality. (The *weekly* ARVN summary, however, was a useful guide to trends.) Their superiors would not have had it otherwise. Gen. Cao Van Vien, chief of the Vietnamese Joint General Staff, was "not in" to newsmen. In 1967 a letter from the RVNAF press office in Saigon was required for a visit to an ARVN unit (not until early 1968 did Westmoreland get Saigon's approval to set up a division-level PIO "advisory" effort for ARVN, although corps-level American PIOs already existed). Above all, there was a language barrier, especially between Western newsmen and ARVN enlisted men or junior officers, whose English or French was rudimentary at best.

Consequently, it was easier to listen to the American advisors, and most newsmen's information about the South Vietnamese came from such Americans, themselves short of experience and local knowledge, and unfamiliar with the Vietnamese language.

The "Story"

The Vietnam War even prior to Tet demanded a great deal of the serious newsman. Yet, in terms of physical mobility (helicopters, C-130 transports), he was far better off than his counterparts had been in World War II and the Korean conflict. Furthermore, while in Vietnam official ignorance and evasion were present, there was no formal censorship; rarely did President Thieu expel an offending U.S. newsman. Communications inside Vietnam—by military telephone— were difficult and time-consuming, but not impossible. From Saigon, depending on the affluence of his employer, the newsman could employ one of several Telex channels to his home office. (By 1972, he could telephone directly to the United States.) TV film was shipped from Saigon by Air Force transport or commercial airliner as a matter of routine.

Nevertheless, for all media, even prior to Tet, Vietnam coverage required a lot of stamina, a lot of man-hours per story. For example, to reach a U.S. Marine unit in the field south of the Demilitarized Zone (the DMZ—created by the 1954 Geneva Accords as a buffer area between North and South Vietnam), a Saigon reporter rose before dawn and took a regularly scheduled early morning C-130 flight to Da Nang. Then he usually had to stay overnight at the press center there, catch a dawn plane to the 3rd Marine Division base at Dong Ha, and hope to get out to the unit via a supply helicopter. Getting back to Dong Ha depended on the vagaries of war: it might be by means of a returning supply helicopter or one carrying out wounded. From Dong Ha, the reporter took whatever means he could find back to Da Nang, and dictated his story from there to Saigon by telephone. Getting one story could take 72 hours or more. During the Tet offensive, aircraft delays stretched available productive reporting manhours even thinner. And sheer exhaustion dulled perceptions.

In intellectual terms, understanding the war in Vietnam demanded a great deal more than had prior U.S. overseas conflicts. In military terms alone, it was a complicated, shifting war, without a front line to signal progress. It was a war of "trends" which Administration officials, seeking to dispel the ambiguities, described statistically in such terms as "kill-ratios," North Vietnamese infiltration rates, weapons seized and lost, hamlets "pacified" to varying degrees, or population under government control.

The ambiguities were magnified in discussions at home in America, as every returning Vietnam correspondent was soon to discover. Was Vietnam a "political war," and, if so, what did this mean? The "counterinsurgency" cult, which blossomed under the Kennedy Administration, quoted Mao Tse-tung and Che Guevara, or cited British experience in Malaya to explain Vietnam. Secretary of State Dean Rusk sometimes seemed to regard Vietnam as a second Korea, an extension of cold-war containment policy, with Communist China the ultimate foe being contained. Senate doves and many academic critics saw U.S. involvement in Vietnam not as an effort to ward off a communist takeover directed from the outside, but as shameful intervention in a remote civil war—on the side of corrupt reaction, against the revolution led by Ho Chi Minh. A "political" solution was widely discussed, if vaguely defined, at Washington dinner parties in 1966–67.

Such views, however fashionable in New York and Washington, gained little currency in Saigon. For newsmen on the spot, much of the recurrent discussion of solutions in Washington seemed irrelevant to the war's realities. First of all, South Vietnam was at war, hard as this was to perceive in Saigon or the more peaceful portions of the countryside. It was a limited war for America, in the sense that U.S. policy barred both full mobilization at home and, abroad, invasion or blockade of the enemy's homeland or (until 1970–71) of his vital sanctuaries in neighboring Laos and Cambodia. As in Korea, U.S. survival was not at stake. However, it was an unlimited war for the Vietnamese, whose opposing leaders saw the struggle as a long fight to the finish for control of the South. Perceiving this, few newsmen in Saigon—or their Vietnamese stringers—saw much likelihood of a negotiated compromise, a coalition government, a painless cease-fire.

In another, geographic sense, the war was unlimited. It pervaded most of rural South Vietnam, leaving few families untouched. At the same time, the war was localized and fitful. In 1966–67, its intensity varied greatly from, say, the once-Demilitarized Zone to the Delta. Along the DMZ, tactics were semi-conventional—the North Vietnamese used artillery (1967) and regular troops; south of Da Nang, guerrillas and, above all, booby traps exacted a constant toll. Still farther south, in the Central Highlands, the North Vietnamese made forays with several regiments at a time. In the southernmost Delta, it was an ARVN-Vietcong guerrilla struggle.

The U.S. forces, the ARVN, and the foe suffered from varying weaknesses and enjoyed contrasting assets. The civilian population was caught in the middle. In 1965–67, tactics evolved as a result of the increase both in enemy firepower (e.g., rocket, artillery, and mortar bombardments) and in allied troop strength (more "clear and hold" efforts added to "search and destroy" operations). The growing air war against the North had its counterpart in the far heavier but less publicized bombing in the South. There were also the scattered nightly rounds of Vietcong kidnapings, terrorism, and hit-and-run mortar attacks in the rural areas. It was, all in all, a changing pattern that lent itself to "vignette" journalism, but to few generalizations. Individual battles, while often revealing the two sides' relative assets, seldom proved decisive in terms of overall military progress. It was a war of attrition, with the outcome, ultimately, dependent on each side's relative willingness and ability to stay the course. In 1967, these factors were matters of intense speculation among newsmen. Hanoi, despite perennial U.S. predictions of "monsoon offensives," had yet to commit sizable (multi-division) forces in sustained, concerted attacks. Shaken by past coups and current politics, the American-equipped South Vietnamese army and militia in 1966–67, by joint allied decision, played a relatively passive territorial role (although suffering the lion's share of allied casualties) while the U.S. battalions took over the inconclusive "big war." Prior to Tet, neither side had been put to a severe test—militarily or politically.

In 1967 the top priority on reporting in the field was given to coverage of "our boys," and this coverage of U.S. forces was abetted by the sizable Army PIO structure. Even the U.S. 25th Infantry Division west of Saigon, not engaged in dramatic action, had a fairly large number of visitors during the year. Most of the newsmen, TV crews excepted, did not venture beyond the Cu Chi Base Camp. The division PIO reported the following "visits" tally for 1967, albeit with some garbled name-tags:

Press: 178, representing AP (23), UPI (6), NEA (1), Reuters (1), Copley News Service (1), INS (1), NANA (1), Hearst (1), New York *Times* (8), Baltimore *Sun* (3), Los Angeles *Times* (1), Chicago *Defender* (1), Rochester *Times Union* (2), Tacoma *Dispatch* (1), Detroit *News* (2), San Francisco *Chronicle* (1), New York *Daily News* (1), Honolulu *Star Bulletin* (1), Honolulu *Advertiser* (2), Newark *News* (2), Harrisburg *Patriot* (2), Philadelphia *Bulletin* (3), Chicago *Tribune* (1), Fort Worth *Star Telegram* (1), Arkansas *Press* (1), *La Croix* (1), Paris *Stuttgarter* (1), *Gaumont* (3), *AIU Saigon* (1), Municher *Zeitung* (1), Jyllands *Posten* (1), *Aftenposten* (1), Essen *Zeitung* (1), Zurich *Blick* (1), Ryuku *Shimbum* (2), *Tretride* (1), London *Daily News* (1), London *Times* (1), *Time* (11), *Newsweek* (7), *Reader's Digest* (1), *National Review* (1), *Esquire* (1), *Cosmopolitan* (1), *National Health Magazine* (1), National Catholic News Service (1), *NA Mag* (1), *Virginia Magazine* (1), *Contact* (2), *Stars and Stripes* (19), *Overseas Weekly* (13), Globe Photo Inc. (3), AFP (1), *Top Blade* (1), free-lance (17), *Empire News* (8).

Television: 73, representing ABC (24), CBS (22), NBC (14),

KORL-Honolulu (1), WIRI-TV (1), WFTV-ABC (1), KHVH-TV
(1), WTAR-TV (1), WLBW-TV Miami (1), Mutual Broadcasting
Co. (1), WMT-TV (1), KMTV-Omaha (1), WEMS-TV (1), WBC
(1), NHK-Japan (1).

U.S. forces in action, however, were not covered firsthand by
many journalists, despite ease of access to the battlefield. Relatively
few (perhaps 40 of those correspondents accredited) saw any combat
(i.e., at battalion level or below) prior to Tet. And for those who did,
technology, even as it eased access, limited exposure. The helicopter
was a special boon to wire services and television, with their competitive preoccupation with in-and-out journalism. One could reach the
battle or its environs and leave it—with luck—in three to six hours.
Reporters and photographers were plunged alongside uniformed
strangers in a remote, often dangerous locale for a brief time, and
then whisked away, often with "good film" but without any notion of
either why the fight started or its "before" and "after." There was little incentive to stay on; television could not film at night, and the
wire services wanted chiefly "spot" copy or features.

In the newspapers, if not on TV, the novelty of American troops in
combat had worn off by 1968; combat features were relegated to the
back pages. "Hero stories" were off the menu. Thus, in late 1967, it
was rare for newsmen to spend the night with a U.S. company or battalion in the field, or to live with a division, as journalists did in
World War II, long enough to see the struggle as the troops or their
leaders saw it. To many newsmen, the outcome of a skirmish or even
of a major action seemed irrelevant amid the shock of seeing Americans die or Vietnamese peasants huddled beside their ruined huts. To
many, the difference between braving a dozen noisy rounds of enemy
mortar fire and seeing a 200-round barrage accompanied by a
300-man assault was imperceptible: it was all equally important, impressive, and terrifying, especially on television.

However, when single prolonged battles occurred along the South
Vietnamese borders, involving allied capture or possible loss of Vietnamese hills, these actions drew maximum press attention. They had
conventional drama: ground to be taken or held. They fitted formula
hard-news journalism, and could be described in wire-service bulletins in World War II clichés—"Hard-charging U.S. Marines swept up
Hill 881 today." Such battles were the Marines' bloody May 1967
regiment-sized hill fights west of Khe Sanh, the September 1967 artillery "siege" of the Marine battalion outpost just below the DMZ at

Con Thien (a *Time* cover story), and the Army's costly November 1967 battle at Dak To in the Central Highlands.[7]

In a sense, the coverage of Con Thien foreshadowed the coverage of the Khe Sanh siege four months later during Tet. There was fierce sporadic ground fighting by Marines in the neighborhood, but not by the Con Thien garrison; yet the attention of the press centered on the garrison's plight, under artillery fire from across the DMZ, and facing the threat of enemy assault across the barbed wire.

Con Thien, a battalion-sized forward outpost built of sandbags and timber on a low-lying hill, was an unpleasant place. But it was accessible to newsmen by road and helicopter. It had good "visual impact" on film, and it was easily explainable—a frontier bastion under siege. To those who had not undergone (or read about) far heavier bombardments in Korea or World War II, the amount of "incoming" (enemy mortar, rocket, and artillery shells), unprecedented in Vietnam, seemed awesome.[8] Fewer than 100 Marines, by Marine count, died at Con Thien under this bombardment during September. Many more Marines died in unpublicized battles in the scrub outside the outpost and in other operations, notably in the Que Son Valley that fall. But Con Thien, with its life-and-death drama, was spotlighted. For some media analysts, Con Thien briefly gained value as a "symbol" of the war's cost to America, or of faulty "static" U.S. tactics.

Few such dramas involved the ARVN. Unlike the South Korean forces in 1950–53, the South Vietnamese forces were not under U.S. (United Nations) command, although they were as dependent on U.S. material support and firepower as the South Koreans had been, and more dependent on U.S. advisors. In this war of no front lines, the South Vietnamese military performance was one key to what Westmoreland, in effect, defined as military "victory" under the Johnson policy well before Tet: the gradual takeover of the war and the countryside by the South Vietnamese against a foe weakened by U.S. mobile forces and firepower. Thus, ARVN health was a crucial ever-changing component of the Vietnam story.

Unlike their predecessors in 1962–64, newsmen skimped on firsthand reporting of ARVN and Regional and Popular Forces militia. Aside from the difficulties mentioned earlier, there were two reasons. First, the U.S. presence by 1967 was overwhelmingly visible and U.S. forces were easily accessible. Second, U.S. newsmen and officials were highly ethnocentric (just as they were during the

Korean War). The accepted thinking in 1966–67 was that the American troops were doing the important fighting, with the South Vietnamese (by design) relegated to territorial defense. It was seldom noted that the annual total of South Vietnamese battle dead exceeded the annual U.S. total by a substantial margin every year of the war.[9]

In 1967, the lack of *firsthand* coverage of ARVN in all media was striking. The New York *Times,* the Washington *Post,* and the Los Angeles *Times* show no more than six firsthand stories of ARVN in combat for the three months preceding Tet. The evening network news shows did no better. There were major articles written about the ARVN, and commentary on TV, but these analyses appeared to have been developed from conversations with frustrated U.S. medium- and high-echelon advisors. This trend continued well into 1968.[10]

Still another aspect of the Vietnam "story" was the performance of the central government in Saigon. It was the end product of the 1963 ouster of Diem, the 1964–65 series of military coups, and an election of sorts in 1967. President Nguyen Van Thieu, himself a general, and Catholic convert, headed a nominally centralized French-style administration, which was not structurally dissimilar from the army-dominated regimes found in many other former European colonies in Africa or Asia. Despite intermittent crackdowns, a divided but vociferous noncommunist civilian opposition was allowed to exist, possibly to appease U.S. opinion, and, in the 1967 elections, Thieu's 10 competing foes were permitted to garner 65 percent of the votes counted. The inner "military" politics of the government, its administrative performance *as measured by Vietnamese,* and its relations with its rich, impatient American ally, were difficult to get at, and seldom reported. But these matters were of prime importance to Americans, if only because the GVN was the hinge of the whole U.S. commitment.

As noted, the Thieu government had no equivalent of the American public-relations apparatus in Saigon, and no inclination to open itself up to the queries of foreign newsmen. During the 1967 election campaign, however, Premier (and Air Vice Marshal) Nguyen Cao Ky was fond of hosting foreign newsmen at breakfast at Independence Palace (at the instigation of Nguyen Ngoc Linh, director of Vietnam Press, who had studied in the United States, rung doorbells during Adlai Stevenson's Presidential campaign in 1956, and worked as a copy boy for the New York *Times*). Foreign newsmen were allowed to accompany Ky in his four-engined DC-6 or, courtesy of

MACV, to follow him on "nonpolitical" junkets in the field. Similarly, MACV provided transport to newsmen to cover the tour of the 10 civilian candidates in 1967.

Ky enjoyed a certain popularity among resident U.S. newsmen. Whatever his qualities as a statesman, and his predilection for purple scarves and black flying suits, the Premier (later Vice President) usually said something interesting or outrageous. Thieu, a cautious man, seldom exposed himself to the give-and-take of the news conference; he spoke on TV and addressed the National Assembly, but, until late 1968, did not lay himself open to the press.

Prior to Tet, there was much talk in home news offices of the importance of Vietnamese politics and "reporting what the Vietnamese think," notably during the 1967 elections. Such firsthand reporting, however, was beyond the capability of most U.S. journalists—foreigners in an Asian nation and an Asian war. In practice, most of them depended heavily on the U.S. Embassy's political section and other limited American sources. In addition, they relied on a very few Vietnamese politicians and Vietnamese stringers.

Typically, the stringers met over Coca-Cola at Givral's snack bar or the Café Pagode on Tu Do Street at 6 p.m., traded rumors and gossip, and later bore their story—an informally syndicated, composite version—back to rival U.S. reporters. Each Vietnamese newsman had his own fears and hopes, his own viewpoint (Buddhist or militant Buddhist, pro-Thieu and anti-Ky or vice-versa, moderate or hawk Catholic) and his own personal friends and enemies in Saigon politics. Few had any contacts outside the capital. Few liked traveling in the hinterland. Several were draft dodgers, others supplied dubious information on a fee basis to the Japanese and other foreign embassies in Saigon. Fewer still had professional training. (I had the good fortune, while serving with the New York *Times* and the Washington *Post,* to work with Nguyen Ngoc Rao and Vu Thuy Hoang, two professionals.)

Election periods aside, Vietnamese officials and their political foes were occasionally helpful to U.S. newsmen, over tea or drinks, for background information, especially if one spoke fluent French. But on a breaking story, they rarely were sure of their facts, and if they were, seldom thought it prudent to communicate their knowledge to foreigners. When crisis appeared to loom, the American was often left with only a series of rumors and his own fallible instincts.

Another difficult part of the total scene was the "pacification" program, a culmination of trial-and-error stretching back to the early 1960s. It was the U.S.-South Vietnamese response, often shrouded in the Great Society rhetoric of social uplift ("winning hearts and minds"), to the Vietcong effort to "control" the rural population. The typical newspaper or news magazine story about pacification resulted from a visit to a provincial capital, an overnight stay and "talk-fest" (concerning local corruption, the province chief's complicity, the quality of the militia) in the U.S. advisors' compound, perhaps a brief interview with the province chief himself, and a tour of nearby areas by jeep. But rarely did American newsmen spend a night in a district town or go on operations with the Regional and Popular Forces militia.[11] At Tet, the impact of the enemy offensive on pacification was a major question; for lack of a "market," few newsmen had done enough field reporting beforehand to have an indication of what that impact might be.

There was also the effect of the war on the Vietnamese: the "trauma" of refugees, attributed to U.S. bombing or simply to the local ground fighting or Vietcong pressure; the strange (to Westerners) combination of bravery and corruption in some province chiefs; the fluctuating stoicism, ferocity, and "live and let live" attitude of both sides in a war without apparent end; and the get-rich-quick fervor and occasional xenophobia of Saigon's middle class, spurred by wartime inflation and U.S. spending.

South Vietnam, once you were there, was a lot larger than it looked to editors at home on two-column newspaper maps: 650 miles from the DMZ to Quan Long in the South, 400 miles from Saigon north again to Da Nang. The war, in all its aspects, was constantly ebbing and flowing in intensity in every one of the four corps areas, 44 provinces (few newsmen visited even half of them), and 242 districts.

In some rural areas the war, even in 1967, was virtually invisible, notably in the Delta province of An Giang, where the dominant Hoa Hao sect, through tacit agreement or popular support, suffered little from Vietcong incursions. Similarly tranquil was Hue, the old imperial capital, with its 19th-century palace-museum and its tombs and temples; the city was a center of the 1966 Buddhist agitation led by Thich Tri Quang, and no source of support for the Saigon government. Along the four-province coastal stretch south of Da Nang, historically strong Vietminh and Vietcong influence persisted despite the periodic, destructive sweep-and-clear operations of the allies. In the

Central Highlands, the Montagnard autonomy movement periodically surfaced, a protest against domination by the lowland South Vietnamese. All through the densely populated Delta, there were local political intrigue and factionalism. Indeed, as newsmen discovered anew during the 1967 election campaign, South Vietnam was locally oriented and politically diverse, with no strong national organizations outside the Vietcong, the South Vietnamese military, the Administration (dominated by the military), and, to some extent in the cities, the Vietnamese Confederation of Labor.

For the editors back home, there was, finally, another aspect of the Vietnam story: the Johnson Administration's ambiguous, "incremental" war policy, its confusing, often misleading, rhetoric,[12] and the growing domestic opposition. The debate, such as it was, was inflamed by a distrust of what the White House said, not only about Vietnam but other matters as well. It was complicated by a split within the Democratic Party and, thus, within the Administration itself over war policy. By 1968, an election year, the debate required a special—scarce—brand of journalistic perception: how to separate the demagoguery from the legitimate issues; how to defend the reader against the more polemical assertions of hawk and dove, especially those assertions, on Capitol Hill or in White House "background" sessions, about the situation in Vietnam. To repeat, the usual gauge of military progress—the shifting front lines—was missing in Vietnam in 1965–67. There were no Gallup polls of the Delta population. There was very little available independent objective information, academic expertise, or journalistic experience against which to measure the contradictory claims of Administration spokesmen and their critics in Congress and on the campus.[13]

Media Pressures

Each of the major media has its own peculiar technical limitations, editorial problems, and processing demands. All affect coverage, and all were to become more acute at Tet.

The wire services. To an extent seldom recognized by academic critics, the 24-hour wire services, AP and UPI, are basic sources of information for the U.S. public. Their 50- to 600-word dispatches, edited and rewritten in New York headquarters, then rewritten again by anonymous network news writers, became the scripts for the nonfilm reports of Walter Cronkite and other TV anchormen. The wires also kept "rip and read" radio news announcers supplied, and furnished the overwhelming bulk of the material from abroad (or, indeed, from out-of-town) printed in most newspapers. Given the news emphases of broadcasters and local newspapers, one may argue that both AP and UPI provided more coverage of Vietnam and Washington than their clients really wanted.

No less important, an AP or UPI story, coming off the news tickers before anything else, heavily influenced big-league editors and producers on the "tilt" of a given event, even if they later received contrary advice, or a contrary account from their own staffman. Indeed, there were often complaints from newsmen abroad that nothing *became* news until AP picked it up.

Under deadline pressure, the wire services, geared to serving a.m. and p.m. cycles, across four time zones in the United States, had little time to spend analyzing or evaluating stories; what checking was possible had to be done fast. Hence, in swift-moving events, first bulletins were sometimes in error. The wire services were also sometimes wrong on late-breaking Saigon stories, when even rudimentary checking was difficult. AP and UPI could not wait until the fog of war cleared and this was to be the case in the early hours of the Tet attacks on Saigon.

For both services, the gauge of success was the "play" given to one agency's story over its rival's in newspapers using both UPI and AP. In 1967, Joe McGinniss of the Philadelphia *Bulletin,* visiting Saigon, dropped in on George Esper, who was writing the AP war wrap-ups. Esper, McGinniss wrote later, was engaged in "a private war with UPI: a war in which victories were not measured by body count but by percentage. What percentage of newspapers that subscribed to both services used his story and what percentage used UPI's? Tell him he had scored 65 percent three days in a row and he might ease up enough to take an hour for dinner instead of 20 minutes. Let him hear that somehow, a week ago Tuesday, he had slipped below 50 percent, and he would stop eating altogether."[14]

What it all meant to a wire-service man in the field, in a continuing crisis, was that he had to run (or helicopter) back to a telephone to dictate his fragments as fast as he got them. A rewrite man or a fellow staffer would take the story down in the Saigon bureau, merge it with the rest of the war's developments (or send it as a separate "sidebar"), and hand it to the bureau's Telex operator, who sent it on to Tokyo, Manila, or Singapore. From there it was relayed to the home office. This pressure put the wire-service reporter at the mercy, at least initially, of unverified reports, official announcements, and rusty translations from the Vietnamese.

With any breaking story, or even with the war wrap-up, cyclic requirements and time pressures led to successive new lead paragraphs ("ledes") "topping" earlier stories, and to "subs" (substitute paragraphs) correcting or bringing up to date paragraphs sent earlier. It could be confusing to clients, as well as a strain on wire-service reporters and editors. The point was made in an AP managing editors' report:

> The AP's war roundups out of Saigon—the main story each day for both a.m.'s and p.m.'s—came in for much criticism. Editors found the stories too long, too disorganized, too jerky from many shifts in spheres of action and topics.
>
> Richard Nokes of the Portland *Oregonian,* looking at Vietnam coverage [for one month], saw the daily omnibus lead this way: "It covers too much not well enough, thus is a dull recitation of action and political highlights that, I am sure, leaves our readers in a state of apathy. Several editors say they often use the AP lead inside, or not at all, using for page one a story on some particular development."
>
> Nokes cited a story which began with attacks on Saigon, switched to Ben Tre 150 miles away, then returned to Saigon, went to the Demilitarized Zone near Khe Sanh, then on to Con Thien, and thence to several paragraphs on Navy and Air Force jets hammering North Vietnam.
>
> "What results [he said] is a two-paragraph summary of each of a half-dozen developments . . . a sort of 'meanwhile back at the ranch' treatment. There's not enough depth on any one action to satisfy either editor or reader. It's difficult to separate the very important from the not-so."
>
> Ben Bassett, AP's foreign news editor, had taken note of such criticism earlier in the year—in March—and said the problem was "partly because we are trying to package the story for papers that want 300 words as well as those that want 800 or so."[15]

On the ground in Vietnam, the two American wire services deployed the most manpower of any U.S. news organization.

The Associated Press bureau, located in the Eden Building on Le Loi Street, around the corner from JUSPAO, was the heavyweight of the Vietnam press corps in terms of experienced manpower. At Tet, its bureau chief was Robert Tuckman (in Vietnam since 1966), with Edwin C. White (who arrived in 1963) as his second in command, and these other reporters: Peter Arnett (1962), George McArthur (1965), John Wheeler (1965), John Lengel (1967), Robert D.

Ohman (1967), and George Esper (1965), plus Lewis Simons (1967), and Barry Kramer (1967). Horst Faas (1962), AP's chief photographer, was, with Arnett, a 1966 Pulitzer Prize winner.

All told, the AP strength was approximately 20 deskmen, reporters, and photographers, including Vietnamese; but since the bureau ran 24 hours a day, Tuckman, White, and Esper were tied to the office. The effective reporting strength was approximately eight men, with occasional reporting by AP photographers as well. As Arnett noted in a letter to this writer, when Tet came, there were "not enough bodies," given the wire-service pressure for a continuous relay of information, to cover it all during the first hectic weeks.

In response to client interests, the AP forte was the on-scene action feature involving U.S. troops or advisors. From 1965 to early 1968, AP tended to keep its manpower based in Saigon, or at a sub-bureau in the Marines' Da Nang press center alongside *Time-Life,* UPI, AFP, *Newsweek,* Reuters, and the major networks. In 1967 it did not assign men to "area coverage" in the Delta or Central Highlands, where action, except for the November 1967 Dak To battle, was undramatic. Its coverage of U.S. Mission activity in Saigon was as good—or bad—as anyone's, for AP reporters shared the common difficulty of sorting out South Vietnamese politics. In contrast to some, however, AP generally eschewed: (1) South Vietnamese rumors, (2) inferring more than the known facts warranted, and (3) "fortunetelling." Nor did its New York editing provoke the kind of complaints heard from UPI men about their home office.

AP efforts at overall analysis of military and political situations, or of the South Vietnamese themselves, were considerably less distinguished than its action stories, especially during Tet. New York dispatched its resident analyst, William Ryan, to do these chores during Tet, but with no better results. Saigon-written war wrap-ups—the prime daily product—varied in quality with the writer, and with the editing in New York. Although prone to all the flaws inherent in the genre, they were generally far less florid in tone and more comprehensive than those of competitors (despite the criticism by APME on form). Yet, AP's best war wrap-ups during Tet were contained in its daily "map summaries," intended as concise guides for newspaper mapmakers. But these were seldom published.

The United Press International bureau, a crowded suite of offices at 19 Ngo Duc Ke Street, as usual had to compete against AP with relatively green, lower-paid men. Its bureau chief was Eugene V.

Risher, later UPI White House correspondent, who came to Saigon in 1967 from the New York office. However, its staff included four men who had been in Vietnam since 1966: Robert Kaylor, Thomas Corpora, Daniel Southerland, and Alvin Webb. Richard Oliver, Thomas Cheatham, William Hall, and Kate Webb all arrived after mid-1967.

UPI's overall strength, including free-lance photographers accredited to it, was approximately the same as that of AP. So was its reporting strength at Tet: eight men, although photographers did some reporting as well. AP's big advantage, as Risher later noted, was sheer professional experience, which averted foul-ups and conclusion-jumping, and led to fewer errors.

Like AP, UPI aimed at colorful features and at action involving U.S. personnel. During the 1967–early 1968 period, UPI tended to move its manpower around Vietnam somewhat more often than did AP; it covered geographical areas more than AP did, as showed up in stories filed during Tet. AP mostly outshone UPI in Saigon coverage of the U.S. Mission; while UPI in 1967 ran AP a good race through the maze of Vietnamese politics.

UPI's big problem—in terms of acceptance by the major media—was credibility, dating back in Saigon to 1966. In its stress on competing with AP, UPI tended to exaggerate the facts through "color," "fresh angles," and, especially, too hasty rewriting in New York. On occasion, UPI's tight, well-organized writing style made its war wrap-ups more concise and easier to understand, despite use of traditional overheated sports-page clichés ("giant eight-engined B-52 bombers"). But, according to UPI alumni, the bureau's New York desk drastically rewrote and edited Vietnam copy, either to give it more impact, or simply to rearrange an a.m. cycle story to provide a new lead for the p.m. cycle. Distortion and errors resulted.

The television networks. Well before Tet, the character and impact of television's Vietnam coverage had been widely discussed, deplored, and defended—far more than the impact of the print media. It is important, as a number of this writer's TV colleagues emphasized, to differentiate between the various facets of that Vietnam coverage.

First, there was the defense of Vietnam policy by President Johnson and other Administration figures at home—a coverage that was essentially "radio plus pictures."

Second, there was coverage of antiwar statements by Senator J. William Fulbright, Senator Eugene McCarthy, and others, as well as dramatic film of antiwar protesters.

Third, there were spot reports, recycled out of AP and UPI bulletins by New York writers into commentary by the anchormen of the news shows, such as Cronkite of CBS, and Huntley and Brinkley of NBC, coupled with "standup" reports from the network newsmen at the White House, the State Department, or the Pentagon.

Fourth, there was the film-plus-commentary by TV reporters from Vietnam, which focused primarily on vignettes of action, or, more often, the aftermath of action.

In 1967, Elmer W. Lower, president of ABC News, discussed the processing and costs of Vietnam film:

> The daily package of war news from Vietnam averaged half a dozen film stories. If one of these is, say, a *bold new terror raid*, the correspondent knows that his producer is already sketching a four- or five-minute spot into the Jennings show lineup. The film flies to Tokyo for instant developing and editing. A satellite waits to bridge the Pacific.
>
> Other Vietnam footage, timely and perishable but *less spectacular*, flies a more routine route. In New York, producers and assignment editors huddle over the correspondent's advisory cable: 150 feet of North Vietnamese air-raid scenes, competitive because all three networks have obtained prints, en route in a sack, on a jet due at 11 a.m. in Seattle.
>
> With a 5:30 p.m. air time, competition dictates a decision: the film will be screened and edited on the West Coast and fed electronically from there. Other footage may be unloaded in San Francisco, Chicago, or Washington. Feature stories, independent of clock and competitor, reach New York for more leisurely processing.
>
> More leisurely, and less expensive, too. A report from Vietnam, fed by satellite from Tokyo to New York, bears a $4,000 price tag. The North Vietnamese air raid, fed by a cable from Seattle, costs $3,000.
>
> . . . In the days before coaxial-cable switches, before satellite feeds, a producer in New York could personally evaluate every foot of exposed film—some 600 to 1,200 feet for the average story that may run three minutes, or 180 feet. We still look at everything that reaches New York, and at least 40 percent of the stories never see air.[16]

In Saigon, the big three—NBC, CBS, and ABC—were also the big spenders. Much of their manpower and money was used up simply in logistics and in moving film and tape back to the United States. ABC, with 30 Saigon staffers (including cameramen, sound men, editors, producers, and Vietnamese helpers) spent upwards of $1 million on Vietnam coverage, crowded news of the war into about one-fifth of the time of its regular news shows, and devoted all of its weekly half-hour "Scope" show to the subject, as well as four one-hour specials yearly. NBC, with a Saigon staff of 25, spent $1 million on war and related coverage in 1966, was spending $2 million, and in the United States provided about 120 hours of regular programming and 15 hours of specials, including Presidential addresses and news conferences in 1967. CBS declined to reveal the size of its budget, but with a Saigon crew of 45 and a record of having provided some 24 hours of specials on Vietnam since September 1966 ("CBS Reports" programs among them), in addition to its regular news-show programming, its costs probably rivaled NBC's.

None of the networks had permanently based correspondents with the Vietnam longevity of a Peter Arnett or a Charles Mohr, but they had some people who had been around before. ABC's Lou Cioffi was accredited in December 1967 as in April 1965. CBS's Murray Fromson (based in Bangkok) and Bernard Kalb (in Hong Kong) had been in and out of Saigon since 1965 and before. There were also a few others with similar experience. But rarely did a network bureau chief stay longer than a year.

In the January 1968 issue of *Television,* in addition to discussing the budgets, Leonard Zeidenberg did a wrap-up of shop talk in Saigon and New York about Vietnam coverage (emphasis added):

Certainly the everyday horrors of war have never been made so easily available for viewing—crisply edited down to essentials, flashed on the home screen between the film clips of the Everett Dirksens, Stokely Carmichaels, Lyndon B. Johnsons and other staples of the television journalistic scene. . . .
But there is among the newsmen an undercurrent of dissatisfaction. Some say that massive as television's effort already is in reporting the war and its collateral aspects, its coverage should be enlarged. A check of network and station correspondents currently in Vietnam or who had been there in the past 18 months, turned up some who thought half-hour news shows should be extended to an hour, that more half-hour and hour-long documentaries should be presented, that more time should be given for "standuppers"—reporters simply standing in front of a camera and explaining and attempting to put an incident in the news into perspective.
A number also spoke of the need for more specialization by correspondents; generally network reporters spend six months to a year in Vietnam (pressmen generally stay longer), and, because of the rigors of the assignment, are often young. . . .
CBS's Mike Wallace has . . . spoken of the need for TV correspondents willing to spend the time needed "to soak up the background and understanding essential to putting the story in perspective." . . .

[But] there seems to be little interest in proposals for radical innovations in the coverage. . . .

Edward N. Fouhy, CBS bureau manager in Saigon, recalls some footage that John Laurence and a CBS crew produced on "a small but brutal fire fight" in which one American was killed. Laurence had reported: "There are a hundred platoons fighting a hundred small battles in nameless hamlets like this every day of the war; they are called fire fights and in the grand strategy of things this fire fight had little meaning for anyone but the redheaded kid who was killed here."

Such reporting—*which seems to encapsulate much of what the Vietnam war is all about*—says Fouhy, "is the best answer I can think of to those know-nothings who are so quick and so uninformed in their eagerness to criticize television's coverage of the war." . . .

In providing combat scenes, the men in the field and their editors in New York are meeting what they regard as the *demands* of their medium and of their craft. They feel they can't overlook the fact that the end product of television is pictures—and that combat makes a compelling picture. "The sensationalism in Vietnam is obviously the combat," says one reporter still there covering it. "Editors want combat footage. They will give it good play."

Nick Archer, director of basic news for ABC, concedes that "a good fire fight is going to get on over a good pacification story."

Leslie Midgely, executive producer of CBS's "Evening News with Walter Cronkite," adds, "If you get a really great piece of war film, it's irresistible."

Or, as Robert Northshield, executive producer of NBC's "Huntley-Brinkley Report," puts it: "There is no alternative (on the evening shows) to what we do. Something over 100 guys a week are getting killed there. It seems to me that by any standard, that's news."

In 1968, Kurt Volkert, CBS News cameraman, provided a clue to the stresses of TV coverage apart from the burden of carrying the 16 mm., 40-pound Auricon sound camera. His was a photographer's eye, not quite the same as a reporter's:

A cameraman feels so inadequate being able to record only a minute part of the misery, a minute part of the fighting. You have to decide what the most important action is. Is it the woman holding her crying baby? Is it the young girl cringing near her house because of the exploding grenades? Or is it the defiant-looking Vietcong with blood on his face, just after his capture?

. . . .

Before you go into the fighting, carrying the sound cameras and battery, linked to the sound man with a cable, you feel scared. The only

the battle of Dak To, NBC on November 24 mentioned the ARVN forces' role but only showed the Americans on film. According to Lichty and Hoffer, the little reporting that was done on the ARVN was neither sweeping nor particularly nasty. But the total coverage seems to confirm the complaints of Saigon TV correspondents that what got on the air was "U.S. GIs in combat." The general cumulative impression given was that it was an American war.

Nevertheless, it is important to note, the television news audiences of the three networks were not overwhelmed by a cornucopia of filmed reports from Vietnam. Most TV news reports on Vietnam consisted of a few sentences rewritten from AP and UPI dispatches and read aloud on camera by anchormen in "visual" variations of the nightly radio news of previous decades. Indeed, this was true even during Tet. According to the Lichty-Hoffer analysis, home-based TV newsmen, mostly anchormen, supplied 339 of 457 TV network weekday evening news reports on the Vietnam fighting and its ramifications during the period from January 29 to March 29, 1968. Network newsmen supplied only 118 reports *from* Vietnam.

This pattern stemmed from practical considerations. Direct transmission of film by satellite, as noted, was costly, and this method was seldom used. Delays of up to 48 hours might elapse between the filming of events in Vietnam and the film's broadcasting. Hence, Vietnam correspondents were instructed to produce film reports analogous to newspaper feature stories, which would "hold up," if necessary, for several days. To supply their nightly audiences with "the news of today," therefore, network producers had to rely on brief amalgams of UPI and AP news reports rewritten by a busy network editor and read aloud by broadcasters 12,000 miles from the battle. In quantitative terms (aside from the question of "visual impact"), the networks relied far more heavily on AP and UPI than on their own few overworked correspondents—although the wire services were seldom cited on the air as TV's primary sources of news.

During the Khe Sanh siege, which accounted for 25 percent of all TV reports in February–March 1968 (filmed and nonfilmed), no less than 80 reports of wire-service origin were made by anchormen, while only 30 came from newsmen in Vietnam. Similarly, only 18 reports concerning the combat in Hue came from Vietnam, while 44 were synthesized in New York from wire-service sources.

In short, the function of the network correspondent in Vietnam—as elsewhere abroad—differed radically from that of his colleagues in the print media. His primary job was not to produce news in the sense of "fact-finding" and interviewing. Often involving great risks, his job was to obtain and produce film vignettes usable in one-to-two-minute snippets; his own hasty commentary served only as support and explanation. Given the TV format, this film had to be presented as "typical," or a "microcosm," not as that small part of the total action or total situation which cameramen were able to record in Vietnam and which the network producer was able to fit in a tight 24-minute program. What resulted on film was more "personal" and "conclusive" than anything permitted newspapermen or wire-service reporters.

Controversy over this approach broke out soon after U.S. combat involvement in the war, when, on August 5, 1965, CBS showed its now-famous—and highly atypical—film of U.S. Marines using cigarette lighters to set ablaze thatched huts in the hamlet of Cam Ne in retaliation for Vietcong fire. In a "standupper," CBS correspondent Morley Safer concluded with a highly personal view of the significance of Cam Ne, relating it to President Johnson's war policies and to the overall U.S. effort in Vietnam:

The day's operation . . . wounded three women, killed one baby, wounded one Marine, and netted these four prisoners. Four old men who could not answer questions put to them in English. Four old men who had no idea what an I.D. card was. Today's operation is the frustration of *Vietnam in miniature*. There is *little doubt* that American firepower can win a *military victory*. But to a Vietnamese peasant whose home means a lifetime of back-breaking labor—it will take more than *Presidential promises* to convince him that we are on his side.[18]

Such microcosmic commentary—and insights into Vietnamese psychology—were to bloom repeatedly on TV during February and March 1968.

The news magazines. Essentially, the "group journalism" process of *Time* and *Newsweek* is an assembly line with reporters providing some but not all of the raw material. Early each week, each magazine bureau files a list of story suggestions to New York, with a brief for each story. After a story conference in New York, those ideas accepted, plus any others initiated in the New York office, become the basis for a series of questionnaires ("queries") by the New York writers. These are cabled back to the bureaus. The reporter in the field must usually write the story, his "file" (1,500–2,000 words and up), soon enough to get it to the writer in New York by Friday morning.

Functioning as a kind of rewrite man, the New York writer is aided by a researcher who has been compiling newspaper clippings, notably from the New York *Times*, and querying other bureaus, as well as stringers, on the same story. (*Time* and *Newsweek* routinely queried Washington concerning official reaction to developments in Vietnam.) The writer pulls together the reporter's file plus the additional material to produce a tight story ranging from 450 to 800 words. His output in turn is worked over by the foreign editor and, thus revised, revised again by higher-echelon editors.

New questions arise during this process. More queries go back to the field reporter, with answers due back by early Saturday, New York time. Moreover, if events require, the field reporter may bring his file up to date until closing night.

The following week, not surprisingly, the reporter may open the magazine to recognize 20 lines—or perhaps only five—of his work in an 80-line story for which he may have risked his life.

The news magazines' great appeal to the "middle-brow" reader was their "packaging" and processing of the week's news in such a fashion as to make it clear, colorful, and concise. Thus, the tendency of the writer and his editors, in the face of space limitations, was to avoid ambiguities and complexities, to fashion a clear story-line with a beginning, middle, and snappy close. Facts and "color" were selected which supported the thesis in hand: "Algeria is (or may be) going communist"; "The South Vietnamese Army is improving (or unimprovable)"; or "The *Pueblo*'s loss means a new crisis in Asia." With similar constraints (although of time rather than space), TV correspondents and producers tended to use the same technique.

A major problem for the New York magazine editors was the lag of two to five days before their magazine appeared on newsstands or in subscribers' mailboxes. Hence the need to write a story which would "project" beyond Saturday night, and hold up in the face of new developments.

Moreover, simply reporting what happened last week was not magazine policy; the "significance" and possible consequences of the week's events had to be added, often before such were clear. Again, for different reasons, TV networks had the same compulsion, which often resulted in prophecy, veiled or otherwise.

In covering and reporting the faraway Vietnam War, in which only one side's objectives, deployments, and handicaps were known (and imperfectly at that), the thesis-analysis-prophecy approach was especially prone to error. This approach had its counterpart in newspaper and wire-service "news analyses," but constituted a relatively small, if prominent, percentage of the total output of those media. In the case of the news magazines, the "analytic" flavor, refined in New York headquarters, had become an integral part of the whole product; it was especially noticeable during Tet.

In Saigon, *Time-Life,* thanks to good planning, money, and willingness to use both, had perhaps the best layout of any of the press bureaus. The office was housed in a whitewashed villa at 7 Han Thuyen Street, near the Saigon Cathedral and next-door to Reuters' humbler offices. Most important, the *Time* staffers had their own Telex communications with New York (as did the wire services and networks), which made for easier, faster last-minute checking. They had a supporting group (too sizable in some *Time* men's eyes) of a dozen Vietnamese messengers, drivers, secretaries, and managers to spare the reporters nonjournalistic chores, which in Vietnam could consume much time and energy. And they had a good set of files, perhaps the best in Saigon. At Tet, they had just taken on a new bureau chief, William Rademaekers, from Eastern Europe. But the other Americans were "Asian experienced," if not old hands: Don Sider, Glenn Troelstrup, H.D.S. (David) Greenway, John Cantwell, and Walter Terry. Normally, *Time* kept one man in Da Nang.

In 1962–66, when *Time* policy on Vietnam was optimistic, even euphoric, a *Time* reporter in Saigon would open the magazine to find the tone and import of the published story considerably different from what he had reported. Managing Editor Otto Fuerbringer was "pro-war effort" to the end. By late 1967, however, *Time* was less euphoric, occasionally even gloomy; there were fewer complaints of "twisting" from *Time-Life* men in Saigon, even if the inherent frustrations of "group journalism" continued.

Time Editor-in-Chief Hedley Donovan (since 1964) made explicit the magazine's early optimism on the war, in an article that baffled and angered the then Saigon bureau chief, Frank McCulloch, an ex-Marine and seasoned combat reporter. The article was "Vietnam: The War Is Worth Winning" (*Life,* February 25, 1966); in it Donovan said that "there is a reasonably good chance that the present phase of the war can be successfully wound up in 1967, or even late 1966." In a later issue of *Life* (June 2, 1967), after a trip to Vietnam, Donovan wrote a less optimistic but hopeful piece entitled "Vietnam: Slow, Tough But Coming Along." Associate Editor Jason McManus told the *Wall Street Journal* in July 1967, "It's the right war in the right place at the right time." Later, however, *Time* grew more somber in tone, saying the "agony of the Vietnam equation is that for the enemy simply not to lose is, in a measure, to win; for South Vietnam and the United States, not to lose is simply not enough" (*Time*, July 14, 1967, page twenty-one). Later the "siege" of Con Thien produced further *Time* misgivings about the war's cost. But to say that, by the time of Tet, or even at Tet, *Time* had swung over to the dove side, or "given up on the war," overstates the case. During Tet, a continuous debate occurred in New York each week over the content and tone of Vietnam-related coverage. Fuerbringer still presided over the magazine; there were still sharp queries to Saigon from both the relatively optimistic foreign-news editors and the relatively pessimistic, Washington-oriented national editors; and as one Saigon *Time* staffer recalled, "you had to really back up any generalizations in your files [stories] to New York."

This in-house debate, although wearying to the correspondents answering editors' queries, was probably, in retrospect, healthy. It probably contributed to *Time*'s relatively balanced Vietnam coverage, compared to what came out of a sudden "consensus" at *Newsweek* at the time of Tet. *Newsweek* had variously blown hot, cold, and lukewarm, depending on the writers and editors involved. Foreign Editor Robert Christopher, until Tet at least, and Managing Editor Osborn Elliott tended to be tepid supporters of Johnson war policy.

Newsweek lived in relative austerity in Saigon in early 1968, using a rented French villa at 10 Duy Tan Street, and subletting part of the house to photo agencies. *Newsweek* had no direct Telex to ease communications. But for the reporters there was some consolation—the magazine was prone to print signed pieces, often highly opinionated, by its men in the field. If *Newsweek* did not, as its promotion men long claimed it did, clearly "separate fact from opinion" in its unsigned news columns, it also provided opinion under staff by-lines (a practice that *Time* later followed). *Newsweek* also had some old Vietnam hands aboard in Saigon. The widely respected Merton Perry had first come to Vietnam for UPI in 1961, and Francois Sully was a French journalistic veteran of the first Indo-China war. Sully was known for his bravery, close ties to Vietnamese military sources, and ready explanations of Hanoi's strategy. Two young $50-a-day stringers completed the thin *Newsweek* roster of Westerners.

The then bureau chief, Everett Martin, due to leave anyway, was ordered out before Tet by the Vietnamese after he urged in print that the ARVN be integrated into the U.S. forces under U.S. command.[19] It was the latest such proposal in *Newsweek,* which had begun even prior to Tet to zigzag toward a more ideological stance in New York. It was a switch of roles with *Time,* which, following the death of co-founder Henry Luce, had become less ideological, more evenhanded —a trend that was to steadily grow in the early 1970s. At Tet, Osborn Elliott later recalled, *Newsweek*'s New York editors reached a "consensus" on Vietnam that was translated into a special cover story, "The Dusty Agony of Khe Sanh" (March 18, 1968), calling for a peace negotiation.[20]

The newspapers. Among newspapers represented in Saigon, the New York *Times* was the heavyweight. In late January 1968, it was established in a crowded, $300-a-month one-room office, a former apartment on Tu Do Street across from the Hotel Continentale. R. W. Apple, Jr., the bureau chief in 1967, had moved the *Times* from the noisy quarters it shared in 1965–66 with Reuters, hired a Vietnamese secretary, and set up a long-overdue file system.

The *Times* at this point had three staff reporters, normally on a year's tour, and a stringer—a professional named Sidney White, who normally wrote the daily war wrap-up to free the staffers for other stories. However, it was not uncommon in 1967 for a staff reporter in Saigon, feeling at loose ends or desirous of getting on page one when the wrap-up looked promising, to write the wrap-up himself. The *Times,* in this sense and in others, was "duplicating" the wire services; but its reporters often went much further than the wires to flesh out communiqués with detail and background.

While the *Times* might run AP or Reuters features inside the newspaper, especially on a late-breaking story, the preference in 1966–68 was for a *Times*-written story on "spot" political, military, or other developments, especially for page one. To a considerable degree, this tied down the staff when breaking news was hot; but it also gave *Times* coverage more detail and often more length than the wire services could reasonably expect to sell to their average local newspaper client, who had neither the interests nor the audience of the *Times.* It was rare, however, that the *Times* reporters, rated among the best in Saigon, could spare enough energy and time to do the longer wrap-up pieces for the Sunday magazine, or even for the daily. Among the problems for the *Times*, as for other newspapers, was the tight news hole at home. Except in periods of major developments, such as the 1967 Vietnam elections (which got almost a full page in the paper), the *Times* men in Saigon, as elsewhere abroad, had to compete—there were 42 foreign correspondents for 18 to 22 650-word columns of foreign news—and the stories that did get into the paper were often cut severely. There was no "Vietnam specialist" on the foreign copy desk in New York;[21] news from Vietnam was handled with no more special knowledge than news from Afghanistan. Saigon reporters occasionally complained of copy editors' butchery and misemphasis, but an exchange of cables could take 36 hours and such fights were frowned upon. On home leave, some *Times* reporters had the impression that the senior editors were reluctant to concede the complexity of the Vietnam story as reported from Vietnam, and that they gave excessive attention to what seemed easier to understand—diplomacy, as well as the Vietnam debate on the campus, in New York political circles, and in Washington.

In early 1968, the *Times* senior editors, led by Executive Editor Turner Catledge (who had no overseas experience) and Managing Editor Clifton Daniel, shared no common opinion on Johnson war policy. Nor was there a conscious *Times* news "policy." However, it is safe to say, those editors who did display strong feelings were doves. John Oakes's editorial page favored a bombing halt and Administration receptivity to Hanoi's proposals for a negotiated settlement. The "bullpen" editors, who handled page one, gave unusual prominence to reports of diplomatic "peace feelers" and apparent changes in Hanoi's negotiating stance. No other major newspaper seemed to give as much space in 1966–67 to the antiwar movement, partly, perhaps, because that movement was strong among New York intellectuals and on northeastern campuses. Harrison Salisbury, an assistant managing editor, famed (and controversial) because of his December 1966 dispatches from Hanoi on the U.S. bombing, lectured widely on his Vietnam experiences without hiding his hostility toward Administration war policy. A *Times* assistant Sunday editor, Gerald Walker, was permitted to help organize and publicize an antiwar effort by intellectuals. Foreign Editor Seymour Topping (who had been chief for Southeast Asia in 1963–66) privately felt that the U.S. war effort in Vietnam was doomed, harking back to his own experience as war correspondent in French Indo-China and the

1945–49 Chinese civil war.[22] This sentiment was never expressed to Saigon correspondents by Topping, a respected professional; but it may have contributed to the receptivity of the *Times* foreign desk at Tet to the analogy with Dienbienphu, and to "peace feelers."

When Tet came, the *Times*'s Saigon bureau was in the process of change-over. Bureau Chief R. W. Apple had departed after more than two years of Vietnam duty. Charles Mohr, the Hong Kong bureau chief, and himself the New York *Times* Saigon chief in 1965–66, had arrived to ease the transition, as Gene Roberts, fresh from Atlanta, took over. Also on hand on a special assignment ("The Negro GI") was Thomas A. Johnson, an Army veteran. Bernard Weinraub, normally part of the *Times* bureau, was on duty in Korea in the wake of the *Pueblo* seizure (a good many Saigon regulars were away at Tet, either in Korea or covering Hanoi's push in Laos). There was also Tom Buckley, an Army veteran with almost a year in Vietnam.

Just prior to Tet, in mid-January 1968, Topping had accompanied A. M. Rosenthal, then assistant managing editor, on a flying visit to Saigon for sessions with U.S. officials. Rosenthal was later to recall that Lt. Gen. Frederick Weyand, U.S. commander in the (III Corps) area around Saigon, told his *Times* visitors of an ominous concentration of enemy forces closing on the capital.

Despite the *Times*'s antiwar editorial stance, there was no pressure on the Saigon bureau to conform to a "line." Whatever biases crept into individual *Times* stories were those of the reporter, not of the copy desk. When Tet broke, as we shall see, the antiwar or anti-Johnson ethos in New York appeared, by all accounts, to help shape the *choice* of Vietnam-related stories for page one, although a widely shared journalistic predilection for "disaster" stories may have shaped these choices more than anything else.

In January 1968, the Washington *Post*'s fledgling foreign service (14 overseas reporters) beefed up its Saigon staff to two, plus a Vietnamese reporter. These men set up another one-room office, just down the hall from the New York *Times*. The two American *Post* reporters were Lee Lescaze, with six months in Vietnam, and this writer, who had been traveling into Vietnam from Bangkok since May 1966 and had quit as the New York *Times*'s Bangkok correspondent (covering Thailand, Laos, and Cambodia) to take over in Saigon as senior partner for the *Post*. Like the *Times* and *Newsweek,* the *Post* had no communications of its own, but relied on Reuters.

In contrast to that of the *Times,* the *Post's* policy was to leave the daily war wrap-up to one wire service (usually AP), or to a "from news dispatches" amalgam written on the foreign desk out of Reuters, UPI, AP, and, on occasion, the Los Angeles *Times-Washington Post* foreign wire.

The *Post's* foreign editor, Philip Foisie, was an old China hand (and brother of the Los Angeles *Times* veteran war correspondent, Jack Foisie) who warned his staff against needless expense. Faced with the New York *Times's* superior resources, he called his men the "thin red line." Although it shared a joint news service with the Los Angeles *Times,* the *Post* did not combine forces with that newspaper's two-man bureau in Saigon. Both newspapers wanted their own page-one stories.[23] The Los Angeles *Times* reporters—William Tuohy, in Vietnam since 1964, and John Randolph, who won the Silver Star for heroism in Korea—tended to operate in mutually independent fashion. The *Post* editors made occasional use of their copy.

In Washington, the *Post* was split on the war. President Johnson was a close friend of J. Russell Wiggins, its highly regarded editor, who generally backed Administration war policy, albeit not without criticism. His deputy in charge of the editorial page, Philip Geyelin, formerly *Wall Street Journal* diplomatic reporter, was less optimistic about the war's outcome. The *Post* published few sharp editorials about Vietnam during the Tet crisis—in contrast to the New York *Times's* outpourings.

In any case, these high-level concerns did not affect *Post* reporters in Saigon. Although his wife had participated in peace marches, Benjamin Bradlee, the managing editor, told this reporter in December 1967, "Just tell us like it is." Foisie also stressed a nonpartisan approach. The *Post's* institutional biases, as we shall see, were "journalistic" rather than ideological, and shared with many other papers.

Largely because of its Washington location, the *Post's* primary interest was in domestic party politics, including the growing controversy within Democratic ranks over Vietnam. The *Post* did not share the preoccupation of the New York *Times* with campus protest over the war. These differences were reflected in space allotments for news.

In Saigon, the *Post* had yet to get settled in Room 16, 203 Tu Do Street, in late January 1968. It was helped by Vu Thuy Hoang, one of the best informed, most professional Vietnamese reporters (and was soon to hire the New York *Times's* able Nguyen Ngoc Rao as replacement when Hoang was recalled by ARVN to active duty). Unlike the *Times* men, the *Post* staff also had adequate transport, a rented Volkswagen for each reporter, and, as March approached, good files and an extremely able American secretary, Mrs. Joyce Bolo, wife of the AFP bureau chief.

But when Tet came, the *Post* staff still operated out of its separate living quarters. Mrs. Becky Lescaze functioned as unpaid dictationist for stories telephoned by her husband and me from the hinterland: a laborious process involving taping the dictated story, then transcribing the tape, calling the military police for escort through the curfew, and getting the story to Reuters.

After Tet broke, the *Post* was to receive reinforcements—Stanley Karnow from Hong Kong stayed in Saigon for a fortnight in February, and George Wilson, the *Post*'s Pentagon man, arrived in March. But in practical terms, the *Post* force was the smallest of any serving the major media, and heavily outmatched by the *Times*. For the Baltimore *Sun*'s John Carroll, Knight's visiting Don Oberdorfer, and the *Wall Street Journal*'s Robert Keatley and Peter R. Kann, among others, the solution was to choose one's own story and go after it. Some excellent reporting resulted.

But Tet underscored the peculiarly Vietnam-wide character of the war, and the inescapable conclusion, even before Tet made it obvious, is that the U.S. major media, rich as they were in the 1960s, devoted insufficient resources and insufficient critical attention to the conflict. With their various technical and manpower limitations, editorial predilections, and journalistic biases, the media, as the offensive began, were overwhelmed.

2
Prelude

The crisis of the Tet offensive did not erupt in a vacuum. Few crises do. Tet came at an always shaky time in U.S. journalism and politics: the start of a Presidential election year. To newsmen and politicians alike, any major turn of events unfavorable to the incumbent Administration seems to have dramatic, potentially catastrophic political effects. In this particular case, the war was already a serious issue; at the behest of antiwar Democrats, Minnesota Senator Eugene McCarthy was a declared (if underpublicized) challenger to the President, focusing on Johnson's Vietnam policy. Senator Robert F. Kennedy, a more serious threat, was being pressed by his friends to join the "dump Lyndon" contest. Important segments of the Protestant and Jewish suburban middle classes—and their draft-age progeny on the campus—were hostile to Lyndon Johnson and the war, as the media reported extensively. So also were vocal elements of the liberal clergy, the Ivy League faculties, and the civil rights movement. Congress was acquiescent but uneasy;[1] Senator Fulbright and the doves did not command a majority, but enthusiastic backers of Administration war policy were few, on Capitol Hill as elsewhere. The war was inconclusive, ambiguous. By American standards, it had already lasted a long time (almost three years of involvement by U.S. ground forces). It had cost 16,022 American lives as of December 31, 1967, and had required a commitment of almost 500,000 men and approximately $75 billion in far-off Southeast Asia.[2] The Washington mood was sour, volatile.

"Progress"

In the most immediate sense, for the media at home, Tet was a shock piled upon a surprise. It erupted while the headlines, television commentary, and Congressional oratory were focused on another Asian crisis: the aftermath of the January 23, 1968, seizure of the U.S. intelligence ship *Pueblo* off the coast of North Korea. More important, however, the Tet attacks—indeed the enemy's capacity to attack at all—seemed to materialize out of the blue after repeated Administration assurances that, as General Westmoreland put it on November 21, 1967, in Washington, "We have reached an important point when the end begins to come into view." "Where Were We? Where *Are* We?" asked the Washington *Daily News* in a front-page editorial. "What the hell is going on," Walter Cronkite of CBS exclaimed when he saw the first bulletins. "I thought we were winning the war."[3]

Indeed, on January 31, 1968, and on subsequent winter days, as the first pictures, TV film, and commentary concerning the Tet offensive poured out across the land, the Johnson Administration was to pay dearly for an earlier, highly publicized offensive of its own: the fall 1967 "progress" campaign. The campaign was an intensification of repeated Administration efforts since late 1965 to "sell" the war, efforts that had aroused repeated criticism in the media. The White House notion was, by all accounts, to drown out the critics, and the assertions of "stalemate," and shore up support for its "limited war" policy. This effort involved a mid-November flood of credible, optimistic statements following the South Vietnamese elections and the November inauguration of Thieu and Ky. Not only the President and his entourage in Washington, but also the leaders of the U.S. war effort in Vietnam, spoke out: Ambassador Bunker, Ambassador Komer, and, above all, General Westmoreland, whose "image" and credibility remained relatively intact, even among those newsmen who questioned his public view of Vietnam's realities.

Leaving the details to others, Johnson laid out the "progress" line at his November 17, 1967, press conference:

> We are making progress. We are pleased with the results we are getting. We are inflicting greater losses than we are taking. . . . The fact that the population under free control has constantly risen . . . is a very encouraging sign . . . overall we are making progress.[4]

It was not a call to blood, sweat, and tears. It was an assurance that the nation's costly investment in Vietnam was beginning to show a profit.

Ambassador Bunker had shown up at the White House earlier, on November 13 (and followed this with an appearance on NBC's "Meet the Press" on November 19), to indicate there was pacification progress. At the White House, he gave these answers:

Q.: Mr. Ambassador, you speak of the progress in extending the proportion of population under government control. What is the proportion now and how does that compare with six months ago?
Bunker: I don't know about six months or a year ago. A year ago it was about 55 percent under government control. Now the Vietnamese figure is 70 percent. Ours is a little more conservative. We say 67 percent. About 17 percent according to our figures is under VC control and the rest is in contested areas.
Q.: Are you talking about population?
Bunker: Yes.[5]

"Under government control" was a misleading phrase that would haunt the Administration at Tet. It was used by Bunker, Defense Secretary McNamara, and others as shorthand to describe the status of the populations of 12,000 hamlets rated by the monthly, computerized Hamlet Evaluation Survey in Saigon as "relatively secure." "Relatively secure" meant only that no terrorist incident, raid, or other enemy activity had occurred (as reported by the U.S. district advisor) that appeared serious enough to *contest* the local South Vietnamese government presence, such as it was. It did not mean that the hamlet's population was, as Bunker and others seemed to imply, under permanent government *control,* impervious to future Vietcong activity. In fact, individual hamlet ratings fluctuated from month to month, as some newsmen in Saigon pointed out.

Ambassador Komer was also home to discuss pacification. He talked to newsmen at the White House and then, on NBC's "Today" show, on November 22, said:

The point I was trying to make yesterday at the White House was that in pacification, as opposed to the anti-main force military effort, you're just not going to have the kind of dramatic progress, the kind of dramatic forward surge, the kind of decisive turning-point battles that you would have in more conventional military operations.
Pacification is a matter of working in 12,600 different hamlets. . . .
It's a matter of winning hearts and minds or cementing the allegiance to

the farmer. And this, by its very nature, is a fragmented process. It's the sort of thing where you don't jump 10 or 15 percent in the course of a month or even in the course of six months. And it's very hard to assess the progress.

. . . .

If you're going to build solidly, if you're going to avoid the mistakes of all previous pacification programs, which were that the military and the pacifiers of the Vietnamese government moved into the villages and then soon again moved out, I think you've got to do it slowly and gradually. Pacification essentially means you've got to get in and protect the hamlet and be willing to stay. The farmer is only going to give you his allegiance slowly, as he realizes that you're there to stay at long last and you're not going to either get kicked out by the Vietcong or leave and go on to the next village.[6]

On the November 26 "Meet the Press," Vice President Humphrey also joined in the Administration campaign: "I do think it is fair to say that there has been progress on every front in Vietnam; militarily, substantial progress, politically, very significant progress, with the Constitution and the freely elected government. Diplomatically, in terms of peace negotiation, that is the place where there has been the stalemate. There is no military stalemate. There is no pacification stalemate."

Perhaps no single speech by the Administration or by its military commanders was to become so great a target during Tet as the "Progress Report" Westmoreland delivered before the National Press Club in Washington on November 21. Westmoreland said: "I am absolutely certain that whereas in 1965 the enemy was winning, today he is certainly losing." He did not warn that heavy fighting was ahead. He cited no problems. He concluded: "We are making progress. We know you want an honorable and early transition to the fourth and last phase [when U.S. units can begin to phase down]. So do your sons and so do I. It lies within our grasp—the enemy's hopes are bankrupt. With your support we will give you a success that will impact not only on South Vietnam but on every emerging nation in the world."

After the speech, Westmoreland answered questions from the floor. First, he repeated a prediction which was to be much mocked during Tet:

. . . it is conceivable to me that, within two years or less, it will be possible for us to phase down our level of commitment and turn more of the burden of the war over to the Vietnamese armed forces, who are improving and who, I believe, will be prepared to assume this greater burden. Now, I made the point that at the outset this may be token, but hopefully progressive, and certainly we're preparing our plans to make it progressive.

In essence, this was the first Administration definition of "success" or "victory," i.e., turning the war over to the Vietnamese and allowing the United States to "phase down." The process began, on schedule, in 1969, as the start of the Nixon Vietnamization effort.

The General was polite to the Press Club time-wasters:

Q.: General, has civilian marksmanship training any value to the American soldier in Vietnam?

Westmoreland: Well, marksmanship is an important part of a soldier's training and I'm confident that if a young man has been exposed to rifle marksmanship at an early age, it will facilitate his training when he puts on a uniform. . . .

Q.: In your considered military judgment, and in light of all known intelligence, both friendly and enemy, who do you think will be the victor in the Army-Navy games?

Westmoreland: Well, it is a bit awkward for me to be parochial since I have a joint command, but I say—GO ARMY!

Then he returned to a serious theme to rule out a conventional military victory (although it was repeatedly argued by inattentive critics then and later that such a victory was contemplated by the military even under the limited Administration policy):

It's rather difficult to conceive a military, total military victory, in the classic sense. I think one would have to assume that such would [only] be the case if the enemy were to surrender. . . . You might say, in a strategic sense, we're on the defensive.

He defended the U.S. "pre-emptive" attacks on the enemy around Dak To in the Central Highlands near the Cambodian border, and, from there, went on to defend such frontier efforts in general:

Why do we fight him along the Cambodian and Laos border? Well, if we didn't fight him there we would have to fight him further inland by virtue of his movements. He would cut the roads. He would overrun hamlets and villages. We would have a major refugee problem on our hands. We would find that the provincial and district seats would be isolated and we would be able to communicate with them only by air and, shortly, we'd find ourselves in an enclave posture, which would be completely unacceptable to me because we would have surrendered the initiative.[7]

He also noted that it had taken considerable time (March 1965 to mid-1967) to build from scratch "the facilities to support ground troops in sustained combat":

. . . we have had the wherewithal to put real pressure on the enemy for a little over one year. This applies to the enemy in the South and it also applies to our air pressure campaign in the North, because the target restrictions did not permit putting pressure on the enemy along his lines of communications and his support areas during the first year of the war. But now we have the wherewithal to continue to put pressure on the enemy and to accelerate that pressure.[8]

Finally, the General responded discreetly, if defensively, to a question about the press (without mentioning that he had once thought of imposing Korean War-style censorship):

There were in Saigon a number of individuals that I would categorize as cynical. There was a group of cynics in Saigon. . . . Saigon was a city of rumor. From time to time there were stories based on isolated instances—the stories portraying the situation as a generality . . . as a general statement, the reporters covering the war in South Vietnam are doing a good job. It's a very complex task. The war differs from any we have experienced in history. It's difficult to make an appraisal of how the war is going because you cannot follow it on a battle map. We've had to resort to certain statistical data and although we've tried our best to make this statistical data accurate, I'm sure there have been cases where there have been some inaccuracies. But, I think, the inaccuracies have been on the conservative side as much as on the exaggerated side.

This speech, as intended, got major press coverage. It was the lead page-one story in the Washington *Post* the next day under the headline: "War's End in View, Says Westmoreland/General on Master Plan: South Vietnam Troops to Join DMZ Fighting." A partial text of the address was printed inside. A *Post* editorial found what Westmoreland had to say "encouraging," but "only as far as it goes."[9] The New York *Times* also put the story on page one—"Westmoreland Says Ranks of Vietcong Thin Steadily"—with text excerpts on page two.

One of the few official spokesmen to specify any problem in Vietnam was the Marine Corps commandant, Gen. Wallace M. Greene, Jr. He reflected the Joint Chiefs' worries—and those of Marine com-

manders in Vietnam—over inadequate manpower, particularly in the
northern I Corps region where the Marines were. His views, however,
attracted little attention in Washington, and none in the major media.
General Greene had spoken earlier, on September 15, to the Chicago Executives Club:

In the Marines' area of South Vietnam alone, we have 1,282,000 peo-
ple inside our security screen. We must double that number. This will
take time—and fighting men on the ground.
We have over 2,000 square miles of territory inside that same screen of
security. But we need a total of 3,000 square miles.
Again, it will take time—and fighting men on the ground to do this.
I cite those figures just to give you some idea of the problem—in the
Marines' area alone.

Most generals were bullish, at least for the record, trying to
counter what they viewed as excessively negative reporting. One of the
most bullish was Gen. Harold K. Johnson, Army Chief of Staff, in a
September 11, 1967, U.S. News and World Report interview:

If you exclude the two northernmost provinces of South Vietnam, just
south of the Demilitarized Zone, you find that the major forces of the
enemy have already been largely broken up. They will have an occasional
ability to mount an attack in a force of up to 2,500 in any single group-
ing. And there may be multiple groupings of 2,500 in poorly coordinated
attacks. But this will be periodic and somewhat spasmodic, because I do
not believe that they any longer have the capability of regular, planned
·reinforcement. [Emphasis added.]

Of all the speeches made by the Administration and top military
men in the fall of 1967, only one, by Gen. Earle G. Wheeler,
Chairman of the Joint Chiefs of Staff, held out the prospect of a
major offensive by the foe. On December 18, addressing the Detroit
Economic Club, Wheeler laid out the "steady progress" line, but also
the possibility of a major enemy assault, of hard fighting ahead:

As far as the future is concerned, however, I must point out that the
North Vietnamese are not yet at the end of their military rope. Although
North Vietnam—as well as the Vietcong—is feeling a manpower pinch,
they still have the ability to send additional troops to the south. Thus,
there is still some heavy fighting ahead—it is entirely possible that there
may be a communist thrust similar to the desperate effort of the Germans
in the Battle of the Bulge in World War II.[10]

This warning, it should be emphasized, came in sharp contrast to prior Administration statements. The Chairman of the Joint Chiefs, the country's top soldier, was sounding the alert. It was news. But the speech was not given in Washington (although the text was available there), and the warning was largely ignored by Washington newsmen, even those in the Pentagon. The wire services focused on Wheeler's brief reprimand, in the same speech, to critics of Administration war policy. So did the Washington *Post*'s Pentagon man, George C. Wilson, in his page-one story, "Wheeler Reproves War Critics," on December 19. At the very end of the *Post* story, however, Wheeler's warning was mentioned: "Wheeler said that 'there is still some heavy fighting ahead.' He said there might be a Battle of the Bulge type of desperation thrust by the enemy." On the same day, the New York *Times* buried its report of the speech, omitting the warning entirely, in a brief page-twelve story which led off with criticisms of Administration war policy by David Shoup, retired U.S. Marine Corps commandant, as given in a radio interview.

The journalistic focus in Washington and New York in December 1967 was on dissent and peace diplomacy, not the possibility of massive enemy attacks.

Signs and Warnings

On December 20, 1967, Westmoreland sent the following message to Washington:

> The enemy has already made a crucial decision concerning the conduct of the war. In late September, the enemy decided that prolongation of his past policies for conducting the war would lead to his defeat, and that he would have to make a major effort to reverse the downward trend. The enemy was forced to this grave decision by the deterioration of his position over the last six months, and a realization that the trends were running heavily against him. . . . His decision therefore was to undertake an *intensified countrywide effort*, perhaps a maximum effort, over a relatively short period. We fix the date of this key decision from a study of enemy documents and subsequent implementing actions. Shortly after the 14–16 September publication of General [Vo Nguyen] Giap's article (proclaiming a protracted war of attrition and conservation of forces), captured documents began to indicate a change of policy. His forces were exhorted to make a maximum effort on all fronts (political and military) in order to achieve victory in a short period of time. If the enemy is successful in winning a significant military victory somewhere in South Vietnam, or gaining even an apparent position of strength, he may seek

to initiate negotiations. . . . In short, I believe that the enemy has already made a crucial decision to make a maximum effort. The results of this effort will determine the next move.[11]

This warning was not made public. Nor was General Wheeler's warning in Detroit repeated by Administration officials in Washington, although the schedule of troop deployments (e.g., the 101st Airborne Division) to Vietnam was speeded up. Just before Christmas, the President made a round-the-world flight. He talked to other allied leaders in Australia, cheered on the Air Force pilots at Khorat air base in Thailand who were involved in the costly bombing effort against North Vietnam, rallied the ground troops at Cam Ranh Bay in South Vietnam, and, finally, visited Pope Paul in the Vatican. But he did not mention Wheeler's or Westmoreland's warnings in public during the trip. In his January 17 State of the Union message, the President barely mentioned Vietnam, except to discuss hopes for peace talks with North Vietnam:

Since I reported to you last January: Three elections have been held in Vietnam—in the midst of war and under the constant threat of violence. A President, a Vice President, a House and Senate, and village officials have been chosen by popular, contested ballot. The enemy has been defeated in battle after battle. The number of South Vietnamese living in areas under government protection tonight has grown by more than a million since January of last year.

These are all marks of progress. Yet: The enemy continues to pour men and material across frontiers and into battle, despite his continuous heavy losses. He continues to hope that America's will to persevere can be broken. Well—he is wrong. America will persevere. Our patience and our perseverance will match our power. Aggression will never prevail.

But our goal is peace—and peace at the earliest possible moment.

Right now we are exploring the meaning of Hanoi's recent statement. There is no mystery about the questions which must be answered before the bombing is stopped.

We believe that any talks should follow the San Antonio formula that I stated last September, which said: The bombing would stop immediately if talks would take place promptly and with reasonable hopes that they would be productive. And the other side must not take advantage of our restraint as they have in the past. This nation simply cannot accept anything less without jeopardizing the lives of our men and of our allies.

If a basis for peace talks can be established on the San Antonio foundations—and it is my hope and my prayer that they can—we would consult with our allies and with the other side to see if a complete cessation of hostilities—a really true cease-fire—could be made the first order of business. I will report at the earliest possible moment the results of these explorations to the American people.

In short, the President did not sound the alarm in public. Privately, however, he warned allied leaders in Australia on December 21, after the message from Westmoreland, that he expected "kamikaze tactics" and "a wave of suicide attacks."[12] The August–November progress campaign had shored up, temporarily at least, the Administration position in the polls, and soothed, if not extinguished, much of the agitation on Capitol Hill. In a lower key, the Administration continued the campaign. The White House staff, notably Walt Rostow, the President's articulate chief assistant for national security affairs, continued to press the U.S. Mission in Saigon for success stories, and to counter unfavorable reporting about ARVN performance and the progress of pacification with emphatic "backgrounders" for selected newsmen in his White House basement office.

This pre-election year stress on the positive did not go unnoticed by newsmen.[13] Merton Perry, the *Newsweek* correspondent in Saigon, later recalled hearing about John Paul Vann's trip to Washington during that period:

John Vann followed the Big Three (Westmoreland, Komer, Bunker) into Washington in December. As usual, his line was considerably less optimistic. But he said nobody in Washington wanted to hear it; after all they had just had the word from the horse's mouth. Anyway, Vann, after much standing around in corridors, was finally given an audience with Walt Rostow. Rostow listened somewhat impatiently for awhile, and then told Vann something like this: "Vann, I know your pitch; I read all the reports, but don't you agree that the war will be over by July?"
Vann shot back: "Oh, hell, no, Mr. Rostow; I'm a born optimist—I think we can hold out longer than that."[14]

David Halberstam, a close friend of Vann and of Perry from Diem days, published a much-noted report in the December 1967 *Harper's* magazine on his summer visit to Vietnam, quoting Perry as asking Barry Zorthian, the JUSPAO chief: "What's all this crap Komer (the chief of pacification, rank of ambassador, six photos of Lyndon Johnson on his office wall) is putting out about the war being over in six months?"[15] In essence, Halberstam went on to report, nothing much had changed since his feuds with the U.S. Mission and the time of the Diem government, and, furthermore, the war was unwinnable.

Halberstam's friends in Saigon were tolerant; Dave had fallen into an old newsman's vice, that of rewriting his past stories. Much *had* changed since the Halberstam era, the "advisory" era of U.S. intervention; it was a far different war—perhaps unwinnable, but different. Halberstam related the old second-hand Saigon horror stories (corruption, ARVN incompetence, tacit truces with the foe), and checked out his old haunts in the Delta. He did not see the bloody, semiconventional war on the DMZ, or live with U.S. troops or ARVN in the Highlands. He did not visit the refugee camps in Quang Ngai province or fly, as did the *New Yorker's* Jonathan Schell, with the forward air controllers over the ruined hamlets of Quang Tin province. But back in the United States, if not in Saigon, his vivid, anecdotal report seemed to pinpoint the war's futility, which he saw as due mainly to the utter worthlessness of America's Vietnamese allies and the superiority of the Vietcong. *Harper's* editor, Willie Morris, splashed the title on a bright blue and red cover: "Return to Vietnam."

Halberstam's was not the only negative story with which Rostow had to contend at the turn of the year. Only *U.S. News* and *Reader's Digest* were optimistic. *Life* challenged what it saw as Westmoreland's emphasis on remote hinterland operations and called for another bombing pause to test North Vietnamese willingness to talk peace. *Newsweek* saw no hope in the GVN and the ARVN. *Time* had switched from "hurray" to "where do we go from here?"[16]

Joseph Alsop appears to have been the first Washington columnist to raise the possibility of a drastic "new phase" in enemy military strategy, including the threat to Khe Sanh. Between annual trips to Vietnam, Alsop in Washington used a variation of the "Chinawatching" technique employed by U.S. newsmen in Hong Kong. He had good access to the CIA and the Pentagon and to their analysis and translations of reams of North Vietnamese and Vietcong documents captured in the field. (Tons of such documents were seized in one operation alone in early 1967.) He periodically discussed what the documents—and the CIA analysts—were saying, and then drew his own conclusions. What the documents said was often contradictory; Alsop's critics contended his conclusions were tainted by his hawkishness; and few newsmen had the time or incentive in Saigon or Washington to become Hanoi-watchers.

However, in December 1967, Alsop's taste for captured documents—once derided in print by columnist Art Buchwald—produced some prescient reporting amid the progress campaign. If nothing else, Alsop suggested that heavy, climactic fighting lay ahead, linked to a renewed Hanoi effort to negotiate a coalition government for South Vietnam:

Yet there is no real answer to the problem of the abrupt change in the enemy's line.

There is no doubt, meanwhile, that Hanoi's home army is as much involved in the new line as the Vietcong-North Vietnamese forces already in the South. Not only are three to five regiments of the North Vietnamese home army being sent southward, stripping the Northern coastal defenses, as already revealed in this space. Furthermore, instead of using the customary obscure and slow infiltration trails, they are using the swifter truck routes through Laos. The Marine strongpoint at Khe Sanh is already threatened.

Few who have watched the signs and read the new documents dare to go quite so far as one analyst who sees indications of "a last big flurry." Almost certainly, in fact, that is going much too far. But it is at last clear that anyone who speaks of "a sprint-phase of the revolution" either believes that some sort of early end is in sight, or wishes to convey the impression that it is in sight. As noted, too, a time for this end has even been given—'67–'68.[17]

On January 8, as the war picked up in intensity, Alsop wrote:

After long years of waiting, almost everyone in the narrow circle of informed persons is at last convinced that Hanoi is on the verge of a major drive for a negotiated settlement in Vietnam. Yet there is little rejoicing for two quite different reasons.

The first and simplest reason is the kind of enemy effort that must be expected in the very near future, which will be aimed to create a favorable climate for the kind of talks that Hanoi obviously wants. This can, perhaps, cost all too many American and allied lives.

For example, Khe Sanh, the most westerly of the Marines' fortified outposts on the DMZ, is now held by less than two battalions of troops. It enjoys overwhelming artillery support, but at this season it is very hard to resupply. And no less than six regiments of the North Vietnamese home army—the equivalent of two divisions—have been moving into place around this outpost held by less than two battalions.

The temporary evacuation of Khe Sanh is imaginable. General Westmoreland may perhaps order evacuation in order to throw the very slow-moving enemy off balance for a while, anchoring the western end of the Marine line on the DMZ on the more easily defensible Rock-Pile position. But there is no sign of any such plan. . . .

There have been a whole series of sapper and even ground force attacks on districts and provincial capitals in South Vietnam in recent weeks. These will no doubt continue throughout this month at a minimum. . . .[18]

Most year-end roundups, including *Newsweek*'s "How Goes the War?" (with the cover photo showing wounded U.S. soldiers at a helicopter pad), Hanson Baldwin's New York *Times* series (expressing the "cautious optimism" of the military in Vietnam, citing American home-front morale as the key to success),[19] and *Time*'s pro-and-con "ARVN: Toward Fighting Trim,"[20] did not differ radically in tone from that of Defense Secretary McNamara's farewell posture statement to the Senate Armed Services Committee, January 22, eight days before Tet. None, including McNamara, echoed General Wheeler's warning (and Alsop's) of a drastic switch in Hanoi's strategy.

McNamara told the Senate that the utility of costly bombing of North Vietnam's well-defended Hanoi-Haiphong area was debatable. In South Vietnam, he said, overall progress was highly "uneven," with serious shortfalls in pacification and government performance. There was clear superiority for U.S. troops in the "big war," but the North Vietnamese, absorbing their heavy losses, were moving new divisions south. Unhappily for the Administration's already eroded credibility, McNamara's analysis was not made public until February 1, after the Tet attacks; McNamara did not predict these attacks, but he presented a far more candid view of the war's difficulties and of the strength of the North Vietnamese Army (NVA) than anything that came out of the White House or the Pentagon prior to Tet.[21]

Merton Perry was uneasy, as he recalled later, about *Newsweek*'s year-end wrap-up: "It was waffled. Predictions were tentative . . . but the general flavor was optimistic. I did the reporting on [the Delta and the III Corps area around Saigon] for that cover story and was not happy with how it came out in the magazine." Citing the confidence of Lieutenant General Weyand (commander of II Field Force in the 11-province area around Saigon) about both shielding the population and fighting on the Cambodian border, Perry commented: "He was quoted in the magazine. I couldn't knock down what he had said with any concrete facts, but I had, based mostly on a feeling, tried to qualify his remarks to the extent that not everyone I talked with had agreed with Weyand. . . . Remember also, the Komer machine had just puked out the startling 'truth' that more than

67 percent of the population was under the control of the government."[22]

Yet, as it turned out, very few of the claims made by "optimists" or "pessimists" concerning "progress" in Vietnam had much immediate relevance to the radically changed situation that followed the January 30–31 Tet attacks. Perhaps out of shock, the Johnson Administration was to respond with caution and relative candor to the new situation; however, the press and TV, especially in commentary at home, were to hark back immediately to Johnson's autumn progress campaign and cry, in effect, "Tet proved that you were all wrong and, thus, that the critics were right."

This reaction lacked discernment. The onset of the Tet offensive, per se, did not show that the war was winnable or unwinnable, worthwhile or not, moral or immoral. By February 1968, one did not need Tet to make a judgment on these issues. Tet showed that the enemy had scored a major surprise, and its ultimate effect was initially obscure. It did not *prove* that either optimists or pessimists were right or wrong on the much-debated 1967 "facts," except on two points. First, Westmoreland was wrong in publicly underestimating (in November) the enemy. Second, the media pessimists were wrong to write off South Vietnamese ability to fight and "muddle through with U.S. help." Americans did not know enough about Vietnamese, North or South.

In a more fundamental, even ethical, sense, of course, the President was wrong both to launch the rose-colored progress campaign and to persist in it without warning the U.S. public of what he knew: that possible heavy fighting lay ahead. As for Wheeler's warning, by the time Tet broke—such is the nature of the media—it was forgotten. Journalists' memories skipped back to Westmoreland's star role in the progress campaign, to his promise that "success" was discernible on the horizon.

In Saigon, as 1967 ended, newsmen had no special insights.

New Year's Eve was a warm, cloudy night. Bernard Weinraub of the New York *Times,* a young reporter who had spent Christmas with GIs in Dak To, was one of those invited to a costume party at the villa at 47 Phan Thanh Gian Street, in the high rent district. His hosts were some of the younger members of the U.S. Mission who had rented the villa since 1964. The guests included their Mission colleagues, a few newspapermen and their wives, some of the slender

Vietnamese women who worked at USAID and CORDS, and some of the Mission bosses. The invitation was properly irreverent:

The Flower Children of Saigon Invite You
to See the Light at the End of the Tunnel

Weinraub later described the party with a kind of romantic melancholy, characteristic of many newsmen's view of Saigon:

. . . A Vietnamese rock-'n'-roll band plays "Downtown." A diplomat wears a flight suit and a hat with four stars. There are Chaplinesque tuxedoes, Indian headdresses, beads, and medallions. Japanese lanterns shimmer over the lawn, which is packed with Americans sipping champagne. The band plays "I Left My Heart in San Francisco."

Somehow the mood is forced and too giddy—as if the jazzy costumes and psychedelic lighting and the vague smell of marijuana are masking a peculiar grubbiness. Partially, perhaps, it is Vietnam—the air is oppressive, the street is filthy, flares light the sky, helicopters hum overhead, somewhere—faintly—artillery booms.

. . . The Vietnamese band plays "I Can't Get No Satisfaction." Perhaps it is the swarms of officials, young and middle-aged, from the agencies whose initials are part of the dialogue here—USAID, CORDS, JUSPAO, CIA, USIS, MACV. There is, about some of them, an intense honesty and commitment, a sensitivity to the Vietnamese that sometimes leads to exhaustion, anger. . . .

There are other young men who care and learn Vietnamese and fall in love, openly, with the country, the women.

There are others. The glibly arrogant, with smooth Ivy-League chatter that masks emotion, commitment.

For others, however, there is something more: the country and the people and the war give a sense of personal meaningfulness, relevance. Trivialities fade. . . . The problems are so enormous and complex. The war. The peasants. The army. The government. The countryside. Corruption. . . .[23]

That afternoon, this writer talked with the *Times* bureau chief, R. W. Apple, in Saigon's Café Pagode on Tu Do Street. Once a café worthy of the Midi, now it was an enclosed, air-conditioned hangout for Vietnamese youths. Apple was heading home after more than two years in Vietnam, and glad to be going. Idly, he wondered if "New York will lose interest in the story," if editors were exhausted and bored by DMZ battles, Air North, pacification, Saigon politics, and progress reports. "I'm not worried," I said. "It's an election year in the United States. Either Lyndon or Hanoi will try for a 'turn' in the war."

What kind of turn? I had no idea.

Then we talked about the red tape involved in shipping his household goods home from Saigon.

A few days later, it became apparent that the war was intensifying. Stepped-up action was reflected in wire-service files, the front pages of newspapers, and the news magazines, but to a lesser extent on TV. In the III Corps area, in particular, the enemy was beginning to exert unprecedented pressure—attacking province capitals and U.S. firebases fairly close to Saigon, and using tactics to be used later at Tet.

Commentators back home speculated as to the meaning of a new Hanoi bid for peace talks,[24] but in Saigon there was action and the talk of action.

On the Brink

On January 5, JUSPAO distributed a translation of an enemy notebook captured in November 1967, and reading in part:

> The central headquarters has ordered the entire army and people of South Vietnam to implement general offensive and general uprising in order to achieve a decisive victory . . . use very strong military attacks in coordination with uprisings of the local population to take over towns and cities. Troops should flood the lowlands. They should move toward liberating the capital city, Saigon, take power and try to rally enemy brigades . . . to our side.

Oddly enough, this report got little attention in the press. Neither the *Times* nor the *Post* used the story. One reason, of course, was that JUSPAO had issued previous translations of captured documents which had not proved to be of particular significance. Another was that the source—a notebook—was not taken too seriously by most newsmen, or, for that matter, in public by U.S. officials. "Big offensives" had been customary in Hanoi documents.

There was still some "chins-up" talk. In a Saigon press conference, after 30 months as senior U.S. military advisor in the Delta (IV Corps), Brig. Gen. William R. Desobry noted new enemy weaponry and a substantial increase in Vietcong activity. But, he said, the ARVN was doing well. "We have gained the upper hand," he declared. He suggested that a fall-off in enemy defections was due to the winter offensive launched in the Delta.[25]

On January 8, in addition to increasingly bloody contacts with U.S. units along the DMZ (Con Thien) and in the Que Son Valley, the Vietcong and NVA hit at the district town of Phu Loc, between Hue and Da Nang. Most significantly, they also hit Khiem Cuong, capital of the small border province of Hau Nghia, only 21 miles northwest of Saigon, and held it for several hours before pulling back at dawn. Khiem Cuong got page-one coverage in the New York *Times* and Washington *Post,* among others. *Newsweek* used the Khiem Cuong attack and others to write a story for the following week's issue (January 22) entitled "Winter Offensive." The magazine cited the captured notebook translation issued by JUSPAO on January 5, adding what Vietcong officers were "reportedly" telling their troops. As usual, mind-reading crept in:

> The enemy has repeated his Khiem Cuong tactics all over South Vietnam in recent weeks. After months spent gathering their strength in forest and mountain strongholds, Vietcong battalions have been slinking back through U.S. and South Vietnamese lines[26] to strike at the heavily populated areas where the South Vietnamese government has concentrated its pacification efforts.
>
> ·
>
> All told, the Vietcong have launched since January 1 no less than 42 attacks against district and provincial capitals, as well as scores of raids against smaller towns, airstrips and outposts. . . .
>
> [Hanoi's] aims seem to be twofold: first, Hanoi hopes that more aggressive tactics will inflict higher casualties on American troops, and thus make the cost of the war unbearable to the American public. Secondly, by hitting constantly at populated areas, the *enemy hopes* to destroy *whatever faith* the people have in their government and to deflate Saigon's claim that it controls the majority of the South Vietnamese population. . . .
>
> But the new enemy offensive has undone a lot of patient pacification work, and for such results, the communists may well be willing to bear heavy losses for some time to come. *Ominously,* the peasants of South Vietnam, who have an uncanny instinct for the enemy's intentions, seem to expect the offensive to continue. . . .[27]

Time ignored Khiem Cuong. January in Saigon was a period of flux—old correspondents leaving, new ones arriving. No one did much serious exploring in the hinterland. And as the month dragged on, the eyes of most newsmen seemed turned largely toward the north, where Westmoreland was moving troops.

Like *Newsweek*'s Saigon staff, the Knight newspapers' Don Oberdorfer, visiting Vietnam, caught a whiff of the new situation. In an interview with Lieutenant General Weyand, Oberdorfer discovered that Weyand felt the enemy was about to make a new move of some kind. It was vague, but Weyand's unease reflected top-level discussions, later resulting in troop redeployments closer to Saigon and other province capitals. Excerpts of Oberdorfer's story give Weyand's view of the situation:

Communist tactics in Vietnam recently have undergone "marked changes," a top U.S. general said Thursday, and may be connected with the latest peace feeler from Hanoi. . . .

Lt. Gen. Frederick C. Weyand, commander of U.S. field forces surrounding Saigon, suggested that the military moves could tie in with current communist political actions and talk of a "coalition government" for South Vietnam.

Weyand admitted this is "conjecture," but the same thoughts are being entertained by responsible American civilian officials here.

There is a growing hunch on the part of many of them that the next month or two is likely to bring critical—perhaps spectacular—moves on the part of the enemy.

The next three weeks—from now until Tet, the Vietnamese Lunar New Year—are considered particularly important. . . .

The South Vietnamese government is excited and concerned. One top Vietnamese official told an American friend that he expects Saigon to be attacked by the enemy in the next few weeks, perhaps with mortars or rockets, as part of the psychological warfare campaign.

According to Weyand, at least three to four enemy battalions are now positioned within a few miles of Saigon.[28]

The stepped-up enemy activity was noted in Washington, at least by the *Evening Star*'s Pentagon reporter, Orr Kelly, who discussed the reports of rising enemy pressure around Saigon (January 14, 1968):

While the attacks in the vicinity of Saigon have been of particular significance, they are not unrelated to what has been going on in the rest of the country.

American commanders long have felt that the enemy leaders would like to mount a three-pronged offensive: striking in from the sanctuaries along the North Vietnamese, Laotian and Cambodian borders, overrunning towns as they did at Tan Uyen and Khiem Cuong, and provoking anti-American demonstrations and violence in the cities.

If this is the enemy goal, then there has apparently been some serious slippage in plans. . . .

It may be that a coordinated offensive is yet to come.

Indeed, as Oberdorfer and Kelly indicated, the concern about III Corps was growing within the U.S. command as time for a planned Tet holiday truce approached, but few specifics leaked out.[29] Then the enemy raids against district and province towns eased.

On January 17, breaking a long public silence, and following a New York *Times* report on the U.S. buildup around Khe Sanh and the DMZ, General Westmoreland got TV network play and page-one attention in the New York *Times,* Washington *Post,* and other papers via an AP interview. It was cut down in the *Post,* whose big headline went to peace feelers: "North Vietnam Presses Talks; Johnson Insists on Reciprocity."

The AP story (as it appeared in the Washington *Evening Star* on page three) ran like this:

The communists "seem to have temporarily run out of steam," Gen. William C. Westmoreland said today as the ground war in South Vietnam slipped into another one of its periodic lulls.

Only small, scattered ground clashes were reported. But Westmoreland, the top American commander in Vietnam, said he anticipates "a resurgence of enemy initiatives just before or after Tet," the Vietnamese Lunar New Year on January 30.

"Most of the communist initiatives have political motives," Westmoreland said in an interview. "Tet is an emotional time when families and friends gather. Any display of strength would benefit the enemy both psychologically and politically. They like to develop the image of strength and try to give the people the impression they're winning."

For the first 10 days after the January 1 New Year's cease-fire, the Vietnamese took the offensive, invading and temporarily holding provincial capitals and district towns, shelling American air bases and launching attacks on U.S. ground units across the country.

Westmoreland said he expects the next major communist campaign in the northernmost I Corps area, primarily in Quang Tri and Thua Thien provinces, the two northernmost provinces just below the Demilitarized Zone.

Trying to check or blunt the anticipated communist offensive, U.S. B-52 heavy bombers blasted the buildup area in the northwest corner of the country again yesterday.

A few days later, Westmoreland pointed north again in a filmed interview (also picked up by AP) with NBC for the "Huntley-Brinkley Report" of January 22, 1968:

Huntley: So thinly are the Marines spread out near the DMZ that soon they'll be supplemented by a large unit of the Army, according to authoritative military sources.

Hours before the offensive [*sic*] began Saturday [attacks on Khe Sanh's outposts], Gen. William Westmoreland . . . told [NBC's] Howard Tuckner what enemy activity to expect:

Westmoreland: We see now developing a buildup in the northern part of this area, south of the DMZ, and in the direction of Laos. We detect this buildup from the amount of trucks that are moving down through Laos and through their observations; and from patrols that have been placed in the area in the northwest quadrant of Quang Tri province.

Tuckner: Do you look for the enemy trying to score some spectacular victory before the upcoming Tet truce?

Westmoreland: I think so. I think his plans concern a major effort to win a spectacular battlefield success along the eve of Tet, which takes place at the end of the month.

Tuckner: Why do you feel that way? Is it because of any possible peace negotiations that he might hope to strengthen his position?

Westmoreland: Possibly. It's associated with this. All of his military campaigns are associated with a political objective or a psychological objective, and if he can win a spectacular victory, he would be portrayed in the eyes of the world and the South Vietnamese people as a strong force.

On January 20–21, the first big enemy push began at Khe Sanh: The main base was heavily hit by bombardment (blowing up the ammunition dump). South of the base, the lightly defended district town (Khe Sanh village) was abandoned. This action further focused attention up north on the DMZ, as the relative lull continued in the south in III Corps. There are no indications that any reporters from the major media toured the hinterland in III Corps during this pre-Tet period—close as it was to Saigon: The journalistic traffic was all to Da Nang and the north. Others, including Oberdorfer, went to Laos, where NVA troops were menacing (seasonally) the royal capital of Luang Prabang. Then, after the January 23 seizure of the *Pueblo*, that incident, as we have seen, became the main preoccupation of both the media and the Administration. Several newsmen, including Bernard Weinraub of the New York *Times*, were ordered from Saigon to Seoul.

On January 27, spotlighting developments in the north again for

the third time since mid-January, General Westmoreland announced
in Saigon that the NVA had "mounted a sizable invasion" from the
DMZ and from Laos. More U.S. troop shifts northward were announced by MACV (unhappily for the allies, these were to be still
uncompleted in northern I Corps when Tet came). Next day the 37th
ARVN Ranger Battalion—below full strength, with only 350 men—
joined the Marines at Khe Sanh.

At the same time, it was clear that the Vietnamese were preoccupied with the Tet holiday. Firecrackers began going off in Saigon several days before the evening of January 29, when the 36-hour truce
approved by Thieu was to go into effect. The Vietcong had announced a seven-day Tet truce, from January 27 until the early
morning of February 3; past violations had been minor, and it was
widely assumed that any serious fighting—at Khe Sanh or elsewhere—
would come later. Not only the Vietnamese, but many U.S. and
French civilians and Western diplomats took advantage of the holiday, going by commercial airliner over guerrilla-infested hills to Da
Lat or Hue, or to Hong Kong and Singapore. Posted in U.S. billets
were warnings of possible "terrorist attacks," but such warnings had
come before; terrorism was now a sometime thing in Saigon if not in
the hinterland.

The official ARVN history paints this picture of the pre-Tet atmosphere:

At the approach of Tet, with the exception of Khe Sanh, a relative lull
seemed to be prevailing all over South Vietnam. In the context of this situation, leaves were readily granted the troops for the Lunar New Year
and measures were taken by the Administration to give the common people as normal a Tet as possible.

Premier Nguyen Van Loc, for example, signed an order authorizing
the people to enjoy the practice of using firecrackers in the four-day period ending February 2, as may be deemed fit by the local authorities.
The sound of firecrackers could be heard in Saigon-Cholon over 10 days
before the New Year actually began. The people had forgotten about the
dying war. They wanted to celebrate Tet with as much fervor as in the
old days.

. . . .

On the very first day of the Year of the Monkey (January 30), Radio
Saigon denounced the communists for their blatant violations of the holiday cease-fire [in the north] and announced the abrogation of the truce
order.

In the joy of Tet, nonetheless, little attention was paid to these developments. Particularly in Saigon, where members of local garrisons were ordered back to their barracks, there were many who failed to listen to the radio and did not have the slightest idea what it was all about. In small provincial and district towns the authorities were more successful in communicating their orders to the local troops. . . .

At the start of the Tet offensive only two general reserve battalions were in Saigon, the 1st and 8th Airborne Battalions. They were preparing to go . . . to help with the battle of Khe Sanh and another battle in the Highlands.[30]

It should also be noted that, despite the "alert," and a subsequent U.S. cancellation of the truce on January 30, few of the U.S. advisors or units remaining in Saigon were ready for any major action. The 716th U.S. Army Military Police Battalion, protecting more than 130 U.S. installations in the Saigon-Gia Dinh area, had just over one third of its 1,000 men on duty when the attacks came—attacks that cost the unit 27 killed and 44 wounded; and no armor had been provided them beforehand. Similarly, only about 25 of the 300 Vietnamese military police were on hand for normal duty with the MPs.[31]

This failure of the Americans in Saigon to bolster local security went unknown and unreported by the press. So also did the fact, later disclosed by U.S. officials, that ARVN was only at half-strength due to holiday leaves. During those last days before the Tet attacks, Khe Sanh and the DMZ were the "action."

Opening Attacks

The Tet fighting began far from Saigon in the early morning of Tuesday, January 30. The NVA and Vietcong launched attacks against allied bases and towns in I Corps and II Corps, prompting allied forces to call off their announced cease-fire at 11 a.m. (Vietnam time) on Tuesday, January 30. Hit by ground attacks were Da Nang (a raid against ARVN I Corps headquarters on the south edge of town) and Hoi An in I Corps; and Pleiku, Kontum, Qui Nhon, Ban Me Thuot, Nha Trang, and the Dak To area in II Corps. MACV's morning release listed the towns hit, and there were telephone calls to Saigon news bureaus from the Da Nang press center and from wire-service correspondents in II Corps. The word quickly spread: It was "serious."[32]

Robert Wildau, a young Dartmouth '65 graduate, with six months' experience as a $13-a-day AFP correspondent, described the scene at the riverside III Marine Amphibious Force (MAF) press camp, a former motel, in Da Nang:

Against the background of what looked like a real tragedy developing at Khe Sanh, Tet really began for me up in Da Nang on the morning of January 30 when the VC worked their way up behind I Corps headquarters. We had all stood out on the dock the night before, watching the tracers rip into the sky and assuming it was just the ARVN celebrating the new year, and went to bed figuring somebody had probably gotten hurt with all that lead flying around, but never imagining how much of it was for real.

We were awakened before dawn by Lt. Olsen (a Marine PIO) who seemed scarcely able to suppress some kind of mad glee when he walked into the big room at the inland end of the press camp and snapped on the light. "Okay, gentlemen," he said, his voice swelling as if to imply that the Marines had staged the whole thing to satisfy the press corps' lust for action. "Okay, gentlemen, they're in Quang Tri, Hoi An, and down the coast, and we've had rockets at Da Nang and Marble Mountain." Something like that: "Okay, gentlemen, here's the disaster you've all been hoping for."

In that atmosphere very few reporters were willing to go wandering around in the darkened city, but we walked out to the road and looked down toward I Corps, where the sky was reddening from the flames of the village [Ap Ba] burning directly behind the compound. Dana Stone [an AP photographer] hopped on his Honda and drove down there. At daybreak, of course, almost everybody went down and there was action enough for all, continuing into the afternoon in that village, and at Nam O, above the big Fleet Logistics Command base north of town. We still thought at the end of that day that we had the big story of the week because Saigon wasn't hit till the next day. Late that afternoon I tried to find out what was going on in Hoi An, where I knew there was fighting, and the only place I could get a phone line into was the command bunker down there. I believe it was [an] NCO who picked up the call very courteously and I explained that I was a reporter just wanting to know how they were doing down there, against a background of heavy excited radio traffic in the bunker. I don't remember whether they thought they were facing a reinforced battalion or a whole regiment, but as he talked, they were firing beehive shells into the enemy ranged right outside the perimeter. I thanked him and said I wouldn't hold him up any longer for details, but he apparently hadn't understood who I was because he stopped me: "Sir," he said, "can you get us some more gunships? We could sure use some gunships down here."[33]

This writer missed the Da Nang furor. He had spent a peaceful

cease-fire Monday at Khe Sanh—walking about the encircled base's
perimeter, interviewing confident Marines and cocky ARVN Rangers,
visiting Hill 861 aboard a CH-46 resupply helicopter, listening to the
laconic base commander, Col. David E. Lownds, and talking to busy
staff officers. The weather was unseasonably bright and sunny. There
was little "incoming" during the day. But that night, at 6 p.m., just as
George McArthur of AP and this writer sat down next to a Lister
bag to open up our C-rations, the Marine 105 mm. howitzers near
the aid station began firing. The truce, we learned, had been called off
by Saigon for the I Corps area. Something was up. We slept badly in
a bunker.

Next day, B-52 bombers and jets once more worked over the surrounding hills. The rockets and mortars began coming in intermittently. A half-dozen Marines were killed or wounded. The newsmen crouched in a trench. It was with relief that some of us
scrambled aboard a fast-moving C-130 for the noon ride back to the
safe rear at Da Nang.

At Da Nang, however, things had changed. Even the Air Force
ground personnel were running about in flak jackets and helmets.
"The VC hit I Corps compound," explained one fellow. "Rockets
and mortars. They're all over the place."

This proved an exaggeration. The Vietcong had staged a spectacular, if abortive, predawn raid on the I Corps ARVN headquarters.
But military traffic was still normal at Da Nang, although the base
was under curfew. I hitched a ride to the press camp and we went by
the I Corps compound on the city's edge, where the slain enemy
sappers had been neatly laid out in rows along the road for a curious
crowd to view (and to be impressed by the ARVN's military prow-
ess). Fighting was still going on in the hamlets to the south of Da
Nang, the Navy driver said. The Da Nang press camp was in an uproar. I scurried around to get the bare bones of the story, deciding to
fly back to Saigon and file both that and the Khe Sanh feature instead
of dictating them by telephone. Saigon at least, I thought, would be
peaceful; and I and my *Post* partner, Lee Lescaze, could figure out
what to do about the Central Highlands battles. They seemed more
severe, judging by fragmentary official reports available in Da Nang,
than the action in I Corps.

Saigon was indeed peaceful: No curfew had been imposed at all,
despite the alarms up north. The firecrackers were still going off,
crowds were in the streets, and the war seemed far away. I wrote and

filed my copy, talked to Lescaze, and, exhausted, went to bed at 2
a.m., ready to head north next day.

As Lescaze noted in a story filed that night, that was the direction
to which MACV spokesmen in Saigon were still pointing:

American spokesmen stressed tonight that the allies are in control of
all the towns that were attacked and that control had never been lost except in Tan Canh.

"Today's attacks were probably intended to be diversionary since they
were widespread, obviously coordinated, but did not appear to involve
sufficient commitment of forces for a sustained effort," the American military command said in a written statement.

"If so, they were probably intended to confuse and draw attention
from the major area of threat, the northern part of I Corps."

"It is also possible," the U.S. military command said in its statement,
"that the attacks were part of a larger offensive plan which, for reasons
not yet known, failed to materialize."

Lescaze also filed a long description (unfortunately cut in the January 31 *Post* because the Saigon attacks pre-empted space) accurately portraying the holiday mood even on Tuesday in Saigon:

The Vietnamese government, except for President Thieu's statement
canceling the cease-fires, remained shut and the skeleton staffs assigned to
military headquarters were not visibly reinforced.

"Come back at 4 p.m.," a Vietnamese military officer told a reporter
who woke him from a mid-morning nap to ask for information about the
war. "Yes, it's pretty important," the officer said when pressed, "come
back at 4." His colleague on duty did not wake up during the brief interview.

William Tuohy of the Los Angeles *Times* added more flavor in his
account, transmitted that night at 11 p.m., Saigon time:

On Tuesday night the Vietnamese government ordered all its troops on
full alert despite the fact that the holiday was still in full swing.

U.S. high commanders were known to be angry at what they considered the lack of vigilance on the part of Vietnamese units during Monday
night, New Year's Eve.

Traditionally, Tet, for civilians and military alike, is a time of great
relaxation from the war. At midnight in Saigon, red tracers from Vietnamese machine guns were seen arching over the Saigon River, as sky-
rockets soared and cannon crackers exploded in the streets.

During Tuesday, for instance, U.S. officials found it almost impossible
to get in touch with Vietnamese officials about the cancellation of the

cease-fire: most of the government leaders were either out of town or in-communicado as is customary during the official four-day holiday.

There were widespread reports Tuesday that the Vietcong might send terror teams into Saigon to attack U.S. or Vietnamese military instal-lations, and police were on the alert. All American servicemen were under a 7 p.m. curfew. . . .

Though American officials had no real answer for the Vietcong attack, they speculated that, in addition to being a diversionary move, it might have been part of a nationwide offensive which failed to materialize in southernmost III and IV Corps. Another possibility offered was that it was a simple show of strength. In any case, said U.S. officials, the attack "did not appear to involve sufficient commitment of forces for a sustained effort."

In his counterpart to Tuohy's story, Lescaze voiced a widespread belief among newsmen that Westmoreland's recent reinforcement of I Corps had hurt security in II Corps (Central Highlands), mostly be-cause two of the three brigades of the 1st Cavalry Division (Airmo-bile) had been moved hastily north from coastal Binh Dinh province, a favorite visiting place for newsmen and a onetime pacification show-case.[34] Lescaze wrote:

Reports of the fighting reaching Saigon were still confused late tonight, but two points seemed clear:

Security in the II Corps in the Central Highlands and coastal regions has declined sharply as more and more American troops have been shifted north to meet the enormous threat south of the Demilitarized Zone, particularly around Khe Sanh. . . .

Considerable numbers of U.S. troops have been moved north from the II Corps and the southern part of I Corps, where the Tet attacks took place, to meet the North Vietnamese force of about 40,000 men believed to be present in the northern part of the I Corps.

It has long been one of the communists' publicly stated objectives to draw American troops away from populated areas in order to give com-munist guerrillas and cadres freer access to the people and to fight the Americans in the difficult terrain near the borders.

The wire services gave the story full play. The TV networks echoed the wire services. But the enemy attacks, already the most se-vere of the war, did not get the lead back home in the January 30 newspapers; there was still an overwhelming preoccupation with the *Pueblo* incident.

After filing, both Tuohy and Lescaze went home through the unguarded streets. Before leaving Reuters at midnight (his copy did not move until two hours later, so great was the jam), Tuohy sent this cable to Bob Gibson, Los Angeles *Times* foreign editor, which indicates the general move underway among newsmen in Saigon to get to the Central Highlands:

I AM CANCELLING PLANNED TRIP TO DA NANG TOMORROW IN ORDER TO TAKE ADVANTAGE, I HOPE, OF A VIETNAMESE AIR FORCE FLIGHT TO PLEIKU FOR ON-SCENER [story] OF BIG TOWNS HIT LAST NIGHT. I HOPE TO FILE FROM SAIGON WEDNESDAY P.M., THENCE THURS-DAY TO DA NANG AND KHE SANH. RANDOLPH [John Randolph, Tuohy's partner in the Los Angeles *Times* bureau] IS DELAYING R AND R PLANS IN ORDER TO STAND BY FOR MILITARY ACTION STORIES. REGARDS.

Similarly, Lescaze closed his 1,400-word story (destined for foreign desk butchery due to subsequent events) with:

PETER WILL BE BACK IN DA NANG TOMORROW AND EYE HEADING FOR PLEIKU. EYE WOULD EXPECT FILES FROM US BOTH. ANYWAY, THEY FOUND SOMETHING BESIDES KHE SANH TO MAKE NEWS, WHATEVER LIGHT THERE IS IN THE TUNNEL.

3

First Reports Are Always Partly Wrong

As the Tet offensive broke, the first day's stories of the Saigon fighting focused on the assault, after midnight on Tuesday, January 30 (Saigon time), by a 19-man Vietcong sapper group on the U.S. Embassy—a complex of a half-dozen buildings, surrounded by an eight-foot-high wall and dominated by the new concrete chancery building. The embassy was in downtown Saigon, within half a mile of the news bureaus.

That night, only five guards were on duty. The sappers blew a hole in the wall and killed two U.S. MPs in the darkness. Then they attacked the chancery, hitting the facade with several bazooka rounds and trying to enter by the front door. Dismayed by wire-service bulletins, Washington officials urged Westmoreland to give the embassy fight top priority, almost at all costs. U.S. forces (MPs and Marine guards) arrived and an intermittent six-hour hide-and-seek battle ensued in the compound in the darkness. A helicopter coming in to evacuate the wounded was driven off by ground fire. One by one, the sappers died in the yard. After sunrise, MPs rushed the gate, ending the fight, just as a platoon of airborne troops landed by helicopter on the chancery roof to ensure the embassy's security.

Compared to the far larger attacks on Tan Son Nhut air base, as well as other actions in the Saigon area, the embassy fight was minor. But because of its "symbolism" and, above all, its accessibility to newsmen, it dominated the initial Tet coverage. Moreover, because of confusion and haste, the first reports made it seem that the foe had succeeded, not failed, in seizing his objective: the embassy chancery.

Even as the fog cleared, corrections were slow in coming. Newsmen, this reporter included, were willing, even eager, to believe the worst. It was a classic case of journalistic reaction to surprise.

It is instructive to read the account of Barry Zorthian, JUSPAO director, who was the U.S. Mission's chief spokesman during that Tuesday evening and Wednesday morning in Saigon:

Let me start with Monday, the 29th of January. George Jacobson, the U.S. Mission Coordinator who lived in the house in the embassy compound to the right rear as you faced the chancery front, had a Tet reception that evening. It was a typical Saigon reception with lots of people and considerable small talk. The atmosphere was not particularly tense. Both sides had declared a cease-fire of differing lengths for the Tet season. George's reception was capped by a handsome fireworks display—a huge firecracker cluster—on the embassy grounds. We all got home reasonably early. Servants were taking off for the holiday and everyone was looking forward to a quiet few days.

Tuesday [Tet] was technically a holiday for the Mission, but it hardly turned out that way. If you remember, II Corps exploded and reports started coming in during the day of large-scale VC attacks throughout the Corps with particularly major attacks in Nha Trang and the various provincial capitals. In Saigon, we were fairly active during the day, receiving, digesting, and disseminating the reports. There were some additional [minor] precautions taken at the embassy and Westmoreland put out a MACV alert, but certainly we had no specific warning of the attacks coming that night although there were many rumors and some pieces of intelligence. John McGowan [Zorthian's deputy] and I were home for a rare quiet and private dinner.

The noise of the Saigon attacks started in the evening, but since we always heard distant shooting in the city, the sounds did not arouse much curiosity at first. It soon became clear, however, that something unusual was going on. . . . I got in touch with the [MACV] Combat Operations Center [at Pentagon East], as I usually did on such occasions to get the latest available information. The first reports of the attacks were starting to come in but, as you might expect, they were still quite fragmentary. Actually, I think the first reports were about the [sapper] attack on the Palace, and since these came from Vietnamese sources, they were diluted even more than usual by the time they got to MACV. The one thing that seemed clear, however, was the fact that there were more than isolated hit-and-run attacks underway. It looked like the start of a wide-scale assault on Saigon itself. . . .

After midnight, I received word from COC that it had reports of shooting at the embassy. I tried to get a call through, and I was at a loss to get the type of detailed information that I felt was necessary to answer the questions which I knew I would be getting from correspondents as soon as they heard the sound of shooting and confirmed the existence of an attack.

I had PTT [Saigon civilian telephone system], Tiger [military], and ARVN phones in the house, as well as the embassy Mercury radio net for emergency use. I was unable to get through to the embassy on any of them. The duty officer and the Marines [guards] were understandably in touch with MACV and the embassy security channel and were actually seeking reinforcements at that time.

I finally thought of George Jacobson . . . and I finally got through to him on the PTT line. And there, with George leaning out his second-story window, I got an eyewitness report on everything he saw—the initial shooting in the yard, the action around the chancery proper, the movement of the VC. Finally (and here I am not certain of the time, but I believe it was about 2 or 3 a.m.) the embassy activity seemed to die down and George and I ended our marathon conversation.

Meanwhile, of course, I had been receiving phone calls from the correspondents but had not had much detail to give them. With the lull at the embassy grounds, I started a systematic call-out to the spot news list—the wires, the nets, the specials, and the news magazines. I remember I gave AP and Ron Steinman at NBC George Jacobson's house telephone number with the thought that they could get some eyewitness material. I got through finally to most of the list and gave them as much detail as I had with the obvious qualification that this was preliminary and fragmentary. I finally got to sleep about four, but as you know, the action broke out again just before dawn and we were up and at it once more.

My calls to correspondents during the night were in keeping with my practice of providing them all the information we could in such situations (remember, both before and after there were many instances of widespread nocturnal attacks by the VC in various parts of the country) in order to obtain the most accurate stories possible. There are some [officials] who were critical later of this particular call-out on the ground that it led to more detail and color and drama than might have been the case otherwise and therefore intensified the negative impact of the story in the United States. I don't accept the criticism for a moment. The stories would have been just as sensational if I had not called out—perhaps more so since they might not have been as accurate.[1]

Wire-Service Coverage

The Tet attacks put the greatest strain on the wire services. With a 13-hour time lag behind Saigon, newspaper editors in Washington

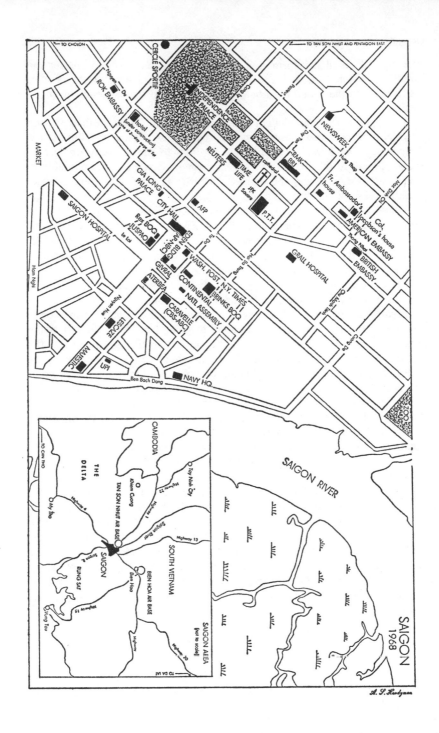

TO CHOLON

TO TAN SON NHUT AND PENTAGON EAST

CERCLE SPORTIF

ROK EMBASSY

Nguyen Du

MARKET

hotel (under construction) scene of 30-day siege of Tet

INDEPENDENCE PALACE

NEWSWEEK

REUTERS

TIME LIFE

cathedral

RMK BRJ

Hung Thap

Fr. Ambassador's house

GIA LONG PALACE

CITY HALL

JFK Square

Col. Jacobson's house

AFP

Rex BOQ USPAO

EDEN ARCADE

SAIGON HOSPITAL

AMERICAN EMBASSY

P.T.T.

Le Loi

BROD BLDG

WASH. POST, N.Y. TIMES

GRALL HOSPITAL

BRITISH EMBASSY

Ham Nghi

GIVRAL

CONTINENTAL

BRINKS BOQ

ATERBEA

NATL. ASSEMBLY.

CARAVELLE (CBS-ABC)

Nguyen Hue

LESCAZE

MAJESTIC

UPI

Ben Bach Dang

NAVY HQ

CAMBODIA

TO CAN THO

THE DELTA

TAN SON NHUT AIR BASE

Khiem Cuong

Tay Ninh City

Highway 22

Saigon River

My Tho

Highway 4

Highway 13

SAIGON RIVER

SOUTH VIETNAM

SAIGON

RUNG SAT

Saigon R.

Bien Hoa

BIEN HOA AIR BASE

Vung Tau

Highway 15

Highway 1

SAIGON AREA (not to scale)

TO DA LAT

SAIGON 1968

A. S. Hardy men

and New York were just back from lunch Tuesday EST when the news arrived. That left them enough time to get some sort of story in print in the 8:30 p.m. first editions, unless communications with Saigon broke down completely. Television producers in New York could not hope to get film of the communist attacks against the embassy on the 6–7 p.m. news shows; but they could use wire-service bulletins for the anchormen's scripts. The weekly news magazines had no deadline problems; *Newsweek* and *Time* did not "go to bed" until Saturday night.

Time's chief of correspondents, Richard Clurman, got an immediate taste of the Saigon atmosphere at 3:06 p.m. EST (4:06 a.m. Saigon time). William Rademaekers, his new bureau chief in Saigon, called New York on the direct Telex line from the *Time* office at 7 Han Thuyen Street—which was halfway between the embassy and the presidential palace, then both under noisy attack.

Rademaekers, listening to his first battle, wearing pajamas, and cradling an M-16 rifle, was on the Telex by candlelight:

DON'T RING THE TELEX ALARM BELL. WE MUST KEEP SILENT. PLEASE DO NOT TURN ON YOUR MACHINE. WE WILL CALL YOU.

Minutes later, he again opened the wire to report:

DICK RAD HERE. . . . THERE'S BOOM BOOM NOT FAR FROM DOOR [or so it seemed] AND CRACK. EYE HAVE CHILD AND FEW OTHERS AND PREFER TO WAIT UNTIL ALL QUIET TO TALK. . . .

In short, like his *Newsweek* competitor, Merton Perry, Rademaekers could wait until dawn came, and his apprehensions eased, before writing the story.

But for the wire services—with radio and TV clients, as well as newspaper clients going to press all over the world at various hours—the competitive and time pressures were tremendous.

The Associated Press. Zorthian's telephone call to AP helped get that bureau going, and it was first off the mark with a bulletin filed by Bureau Chief Robert Tuckman:

98: BULLETIN—VIETNAM
The Vietcong shelled Saigon itself early Wednesday in a stunning follow-up to its attacks on eight major cities.
CR220P 1/30[2]
99: SAIGON—ADD VIETNAM (98)
First reports said rocket or mortar shells landed near Independence

Palace, seat of the government in the heart of Saigon, other government buildings and the U.S. Embassy.
Small-arms fire was heard in the streets.
CR222P 1/30
101: SAIGON—ADD VIETNAM (99)
The attack started around 3 a.m., less than 24 hours after the series of Lunar New Year's Day attacks against seven provincial capitals and the key city of Da Nang, second largest city in South Vietnam.
One building near Independence Palace was set afire.
Allied planes took to the air and some dropped flares over the capital area to illuminate enemy positions.
CR236PES 1/30

Peter Arnett reacted more quickly than some:

I lived in Pasteur Street on an almost direct line between the first two Vietcong targets in Saigon: the U.S. Embassy and the southern gates of the Presidential Palace. When the B-40s started blamming, I got the message fast, shoving my wife and two kids into the bathroom (it has the thickest walls), and slipping down to the office once the nervous guards outside stopped firing their machine guns straight up the street. White, Tuckman, and Esper were already in the office when I got there. Time: around 3:45 a.m. A source (Barry Zorthian) phoned me that Mission Coordinator George Jacobson was besieged inside his house in the embassy grounds. I interviewed him by telephone,[3] then with Nance and Holloway drove around the city. We were waved off the embassy area by MPs, and later on, swinging towards the southern gates of the Palace, we were rudely stopped by a burst of AK fire from the half-built hotel where the Vietcong attacking the Palace had holed up.

We lay under our mini-jeep for 30 minutes before being rescued by some Aussie MPs. I returned to the embassy area just before daylight, phoning the office with developments from the RMK [Raymond-Morrison-Knutson, the big construction consortium that built U.S. bases] head office just along from the embassy. We bulletined each of the developments: I was exhausted running back and forth from the phone. Later in the morning I began writing the wrap-up on the whole embassy attack, correcting earlier statements from U.S. MPs that the Vietcong had actually got inside the embassy building. They hadn't. The MPs thought they were getting AK fire from the upper floors; actually, it turned out, this fire was coming from Vietcong shooting over the high walls.

But it was not immediately clear, even with Zorthian's telephone calls, what was going on, except that the Vietcong had come downtown. In the hours just before and after dawn, the only targets reachable by the newsmen were those in the downtown area near their offices. Most newsmen headed for the U.S. Embassy. And, in the darkness, it was not easy to see what was happening.

The 716th MP Battalion's own message log partially indicates the widespread nature of the attacks. This log, of course, was not available to newsmen:

0300: BOQ [bachelor officers' quarters] No. 3, a field-grade officers' billet near Tan Son Nhut, reports enemy action.

0315: U.S. Embassy under attack.

0316: Explosion at Phoenix City BOQ.

0317: Explosion at Townhouse BOQ.

0318: BOQ No. 1 under attack.

0319: McArthur BOQ under attack.

0321: Report of hostile attack at Rex BOQ.

0325: Explosion at BOQ No. 2.

0340: Automatic-weapons fire and attack at BOQ No. 3.

0341: MPs at U.S. Embassy request urgent ammo resupply.

0342: Heavy sniper fire at Metropole BEQ [bachelor enlisted quarters].

0350: Incoming mortars at Montana BEQ.

0358: Saigon port area reports small-arms and automatic-weapons fire.

0359: Mortars and rockets fired at U.S. Embassy; reinforcements requested.

0407: MP jeep C9A reports that 2½-ton truck carrying 25-man reaction team to BOQ No. 3 hit by rockets and claymore mines. Heavy casualties.

0408: Jeep C9A hit; both MPs killed.

0419: BOQ No. 3 pleads for ammo resupply.

0420: General Westmoreland calls; orders first-priority effort to recapture U.S. Embassy.

0430: Request armored vehicles and helicopters for embassy assault; reaction team appointed.

0449: Cleveland and Columbia BOQ request ammo and assistance.

0500: Three claymores detonated at Saigon motor pool. Booby traps discovered.

0516: Explosions and small-arms fire at Royal Oaks BOQ.

0535: Automatic-weapons fire at Butte BEQ.

0542: MP shot in attack on Denbigh BOQ.

0546: Claymore detonated at Flint BOQ.

0600: Camp Red Ball under attack.

0602: MP machine-gun jeep captured by VC.

0613: Claymores detonated at several BOQ.

0615:   Area near Ambassador Bunker's home hit by mortars and automatic-weapons fire.
0618:   Tent City B at Tan Son Nhut under attack.[4]

As Arnett noted, the situation at the embassy was confused. The chancery fronted southeast on four-lane Thong Nhat Street. As dawn broke, Arnett and most other newsmen were clustered, along with some distraught MPs, at the corner of Hai Ba Trung Street, a good 100 meters west of the embassy. They could get only an oblique view of the embassy's rooftop helicopter pad and upper floors. A TV camera crew ran along on the opposite side of Thong Nhat Street and filmed the embassy's front wall. But neither they nor the other newsmen could actually see whether the Vietcong were inside, or what was going on in the embassy yard behind the high wall.

Nor could the men of the 716th MP Battalion who were with the reporters. Most of the MPs, involved in combat for the first time, were confused, alarmed, and excited. Their jeep radios crackled with reports of attacks elsewhere, of comrades in trouble. They heard firing inside the compound and looked at the three blotches in the chancery's facade and at the hole to the right of the front gate. "They're in the embassy," an MP sergeant said, his eyes wild, "they're in the embassy."

Arnett later recalled that the sentiment among newsmen at that point was that "the situation was perfectly clear." Reporters, he noted, "were within a few yards of the fighting, as far up as we could get. After all, the MP captain did tell me with the utmost certainty when I asked him if the Vietcong were inside the embassy building: 'My God, yes . . . we are taking fire from up there . . . keep your head down.' "[5]

Although neither newsmen nor MPs were eyewitness to most of the action, the MPs were about all the reporters on the scene could use as an "official source." At 8:35 a.m. Saigon time, the "rescue" platoon from the 101st Airborne Division arrived by UH-1-B helicopters on the embassy roof. It was assumed that the paratroopers had landed to kick the enemy out of the embassy's lower floors. Actually, however, the fight was largely over by then, for it was only minutes later that the MPs broke through the front gate. As reporters and TV cameramen followed, George Jacobson was thrown a pistol and shot down the last VC in the bedroom of his house, just to the rear of the embassy. TV cameramen filmed the scene. The reporters, in short, only got in on the last act.

The AP bulletins, based on the alarmed talk of the MPs, began by *attributing* (to the MPs outside the compound) reports of the Vietcong's presence in the chancery. But an hour after dawn, just prior to first-edition deadlines for morning newspapers in the eastern United States, the AP was putting out leads that *flatly stated* that the Vietcong were in the chancery:

181: VIETNAM

Saigon (AP)—The Vietcong seized part of the U.S. Embassy in Saigon early Wednesday and battled American military police who tried to recapture it.

Communist commandos penetrated the supposedly attack-proof building in the climax of a combined artillery and guerrilla assault that brought limited warfare to Saigon itself.

One Marine guard was reported wounded in the early fighting for the building. . . .

GG707P 30

185: BULLETIN—VIETNAM (Tops 181)

Saigon (AP)—American military police supported by paratroopers moved into the U.S. Embassy compound near the heart of Saigon after daybreak Wednesday to wipe out Vietcong suicide guerrillas holed up inside the embassy building. . . .

GG721P 30

197: BULLETIN—VIETNAM (Tops 185)

Saigon (AP)—U.S. troops made a helicopter assault Wednesday on the American Embassy in Saigon, landing on the roof of the building and fighting their way down against the Vietcong suicide commandos holed up in the building.

GG821P 30

202: BULLETIN—VIETNAM (Tops 197)

Saigon (AP)—U.S. troops recaptured control of the American Embassy on Wednesday, wiping out Vietcong suicide commandos who had held parts of the building for six hours.

The Americans counterattacked on the ground and from the embassy rooftop helicopter pad where paratroopers were landed to put a squeeze on the Vietcong commandos.

GG825P 30

As late as 9 p.m. EST (10 a.m. Saigon time), AP continued to give the impression that the Vietcong had actually gotten into the embassy building, with some garbled details (later dropped) from one of its photographers, Dang Van Phouc:

By 8:55 a.m. the U.S. forces had secured the ground of the embassy and troops were working their way through the building to flush out the remaining Vietcong.

Associated Press photographer Dang Van Phouc, who got inside the building, reported bodies were strewn around the rooms. He said the Vietcong wore gray uniforms with cartridge belts and that some had red arm bands.

He said the Vietcong apparently poured into the compound and on into the building after firing a rocket that opened the hole in the outer wall.

Again, at 10:39 p.m. EST, about two hours after reporting that U.S. troops had secured the compound, the AP persisted:

A132WX—SAIGON-STATE DEPARTMENT 120

WASHINGTON (AP)—The State Department, quoting its reports from South Vietnam, said Tuesday night the Vietcong had been unable to penetrate the main U.S. Embassy building in their predawn raid in Saigon.

"They got inside the compound, but they didn't get into the building itself," a State Department official said.

News reports differed. *Reporters on the scene in Saigon said attackers seized a portion of the main building and fought U.S. troops rushing it.* . . .

The State Department said it had received cables directly from the embassy reporting the attackers had not been able to enter the main building.[6]

By 11:24 p.m. EST, the AP was reporting the reaction of General Westmoreland as he arrived and toured the embassy grounds with Zorthian and other officials:

Westmoreland told newsmen, "Obviously the enemy had been planning the assault on the American Embassy for some time. They chose the Tet Lunar New Year period for this assault. The enemy obviously assumed the security would be lessened during this period.

"The enemy had proclaimed a truce," Westmoreland went on. "This attack occurred at approximately 3 a.m. It started with an antitank rocket which blasted a hole in the outer wall of the embassy big enough for a man to crawl through.

"Through this hole, a platoon of enemy soldiers, disguised in civilian dress, came inside the embassy compound. They had infiltrated into the city and were armed with satchel charges and demolitions. With the demolitions, they tried to demolish it—the embassy.

"A . . . mortar round also came from the outside. There was superficial damage to the embassy.

"The next event that happened was that the embassy was surrounded by military police between 3 a.m. and 5 a.m. Some sniper fire was encountered. Finally the military police entered the compound and killed a number of the enemy who were in civilian dress."

Westmoreland's account seemed plausible to this reporter, who saw the chancery's unbroken front and rear doors and, through the windows, little damage except for the smashed reception desk. Moreover, several of the paratroopers who had come in via the roof and were milling around in the embassy yard said they had seen "nothin' " inside.

No one I talked to in the confusion *after* the compound was secured continued to claim the VC had been in the building. Much was unclear, especially since reporters were shooed away by mid-morning. We had suspicions, but no solid contrary evidence to Westmoreland's account.

Arnett's viewpoint differed. He continued to cite the earlier statements of the MP captain, outside the wall, to offset Westmoreland's account. "We left it up to the reader to decide, somehow indicating our own doubt in the General's statement." Considering the record over the years, Arnett said, "we had little faith in what General Westmoreland stated . . . often in the field we had reason to be extremely careful in accepting the General's assessments of the course of a particular battle."

Heavily committed to its early lead, AP did not back off easily. Two hours after the recapture of the embassy (approximately 11 a.m. Saigon time, 10 p.m. EST) and Westmoreland's arrival, it reported the General's version, but quickly added a qualification: "Visiting the embassy shortly after U.S. forces regained control, General Westmoreland said the Vietcong did not get inside the . . . building itself. However, dozens of persons *on the scene* said some of the Vietcong were in the lower floors of the main building. Vietnamese police sources also said *some* of them had made their way into the building."

Why did AP keep carrying the erroneous information? Arnett suggests that the bureau that day was ready to believe the worst—even if it came from normally suspect Vietnamese police sources: "We did get all manner of reports from our Vietnamese staff. They were calling the Vietnamese police, and the photographers (including Phouc) were bobbing around the embassy. This profusion of reports led to the statements that 'dozens of persons' had said the Vietcong were in the embassy."[7]

Arnett returned to the AP office to clear up the matter. But as late as 2:09 a.m., January 31, EST, in a story filed by Edwin Q. White, AP was still repeating the building invasion reports: "A Vietcong suicide squad blasted its way into the U.S. Embassy compound . . . and fought for seven hours Wednesday before being wiped out by American forces. Paratroopers swarmed out of helicopters that landed on the roof of the eight-story building to lift the siege. . . . Some sources, including a U.S. captain, reported some of the communist invaders got into the first floor of the big embassy building. But Gen. William C. Westmoreland . . . said the building was not penetrated. . . ." Finally, at 6 a.m. EST, the AP sent a wrap-up by Arnett indicating that the Vietcong attackers had failed to get into the embassy building, and that the battle was virtually over when the 101st Airborne's rescue platoon arrived.

Yet, even next day, despite Arnett's corrective story, in its second night lead from Saigon, timed 5:48 p.m., January 31, EST (6:48 a.m., February 1, Saigon time), the AP refused to clarify whether the Vietcong had entered the building (UPI had backed off the previous day). AP did not identify its "captain" or its "major": "Reports conflicted as to whether the commandos got inside the embassy building. Bunker said, 'The Vietcong were never able to enter the chancery building offices.' A U.S. captain at the scene said some penetrated the first floor. A major overruled him, saying they did not. General Westmoreland said they did not. Vietnamese police said they did."

Why did AP keep alive this doubt 12 hours after its own reporter had said the contrary? "Sloppy editing in New York," said Arnett.

As a result, in U.S. eastern morning newspapers, and in most of the country's other morning editions, the impression given by AP was that: (1) the Vietcong had seized the embassy itself and (2) Westmoreland was lying when he said they had not. Moreover, in initial late broadcast news, the impression was the same.

United Press International. Late Tuesday night (Saigon time) in his office at 19 Ngo Duc Ke Street, Eugene V. Risher, the UPI bureau manager, sent a message to the home office about his staff deployment and the previous night's attacks at Da Nang and in the Central Highlands:

TOYKO FOR ENNEX

SAIGON Jan. 30234 (UPI)—LOGANS 30102 THE SUPPLEMENTARY MACV COMMUNIQUÉ CONTAINED NOTHING WE DIDNT ALREADY HAVE.

THIS THING SHOULD NOT BE CALLED VC DEFEAT. FACT OF CO-
ORDINATED ATTACKS OVER SUCH WIDE AREA AND THAT THEY CAN
GET INSIDE EIGHT MAJOR CITIES AND RAISE HELL WOULD SEEM MORE
OF A VICTORY BUT I DONT THINK IT NECESSARY TO CALL IT EITHER.
INFORMATIVELY UPCOMING WITH CORPORA SIDER [sidebar story]
WHO NOW IN BAN ME THUOT. INFORMATIVELY [Alvin] WEBB, [Richard
V.] OLIVER IN DA NANG, [Robert] KAYLOR IN NHA TRANG, [Thomas]
CORPORA IN BAN ME THUOT, KATE [Webb] HEADING EARLIEST WEDNESDAY
TOWARD PLEIKU. [Thomas] CHEATHAM, [Daniel] SOUTHERLAND, AND
[Perry] YOUNG STANDING BY IN CASE SUCH HAPPENS HERE.

In short, UPI, like AP, was deployed widely at Tet. It was also one
of the rare occasions when UPI had almost as many reporters in Vietnam as did AP. But even Risher had no one in the Delta (IV
Corps) where, as it happened, some of the most severe Vietcong attacks (Vinh Long, Can Tho, My Tho) were to occur on January 30
and 31.

When the attacks against Saigon began, it would appear that
Zorthian's phone call got to AP before UPI, for UPI's first bulletin
on the action was 38 minutes behind AP's. In the United States, the
first UPI bulletin came out on the tickers at 2:58 p.m. EST (3:58
a.m., Wednesday, Saigon time), followed by others:

217A: VIET 1/30 NX—BULLETIN PRECEDE
Saigon (UPI)—Machine gun, mortar, and rifle fire broke out in several spots inside Saigon early Wednesday. U.S. military police reported
clashes with the Vietcong near Independence Palace and at several other
spots in the downtown section of the capital.
BA258PEST
218A: VIET 1/30 NX—BULLETIN
5th Day ld 102A by Eugene V. Risher
Saigon (UPI)—The Vietcong's greatest offensive of the war swept
into the heart of Saigon early Wednesday. U.S. military police reported
fights with the Vietcong near the Independence Palace.
(MORE)BA3PEST
219A: VIET 1/30 NX—URGENT
1st add 5th day ld Viet Saigon 218A XXX palace
The streets of the capital rocked to the sounds of machine gun, mortars, and rifle fire as the communists followed up an assault on eight other
major cities with forays into Saigon itself.
Clashes broke out near Independence Palace and at scattered spots in
the downtown section of the capital where American and allied troops
had been warned to expect communist infiltration.

(MORE) MF/BA302PEST
220A: VIET 1/30 NX—URGENT
2nd add 5th day ld Viet Saigon 218A XXX infiltration
Machine-gun and rifle fire erupted less than a block from the UPI bureau as banks of military police and Vietnamese police battled Vietcong
snipers.
One of the MPs reported a band of about 25 Vietcong guerrillas in the
area. They said scattered fighting had broken out throughout the
city. . . .
BA306PEST

After talking to Zorthian, UPI put out its initial report on the attack against the embassy, and New York relayed it:

233A: VIET 1/30 NX—BULLETIN
2nd night ld Viet 222a by Eugene V. Risher
Saigon (UPI)—Vietcong invaders struck into the heart of Saigon
early Wednesday, battled allied defenders in the streets, and attacked the
U.S. Embassy compound in a mortar and ground assault.
MOREWB409PES
236A: VIET 1/30 NX—URGENT
1st add 2nd night ld Viet Saigon 233a XXX ground assault
. . . Military police reported fighting swirled around the American
Embassy and Independence Palace.
The Vietcong raiders sent mortar rounds slamming into the embassy
and launched a ground attack. They penetrated the embassy compound
but did not get inside the building.
MOREWB420PES

At 6:36 p.m. EST (7:36 a.m. next day, Saigon time), after saying
the Vietcong had failed to get inside the chancery, UPI added some
color on the attacks downtown, mostly accurate, but including the report that "tracers crisscrossed John F. Kennedy Square in front of
Saigon's Roman Catholic Cathedral." At that point, reporters, nervous but unmolested, had been crossing John F. Kennedy Square to go
to and from the embassy on Thong Nhat Street, which ran across the
rear of the cathedral.

At first UPI was cautious about the embassy fighting. But at 8:08
p.m. (9:08 a.m., January 31, Saigon time) and at 9 p.m. EST, despite its earlier story, it put out bulletins asserting that Vietcong had
occupied the building. At 9:23 p.m. EST it passed along a State Department denial that the embassy had been occupied, but at 9:34
p.m. said the communists occupied the floor on which Bunker's office

was situated. At 9:48 p.m., reporting the reoccupation of the area, UPI imaginatively recounted a six-hour battle through "the carpeted offices of the chancery." (In a separate story filed at 10:31 p.m. EST, UPI reported accurately that, except for Bunker's office, the floors were of linoleum tile.)

At 12:28 a.m. EST (January 31), five hours ahead of the AP, but too late for most east-coast morning newspapers in the United States, the UPI pulled off the "Vietcong-are-in-the-embassy" with this:

326A: VIET 1/30
4th add 6th night ld Viet Saigon 318A XXX guards
During the heat of the fighting, United States *military men* said the terrorists had occupied five floors of the embassy. Later a spokesman said the communists did not penetrate the main building and the State Department in Washington confirmed this.

Risher, faced with a highly competitive situation, did the best he could. His immediate preoccupation was not with the embassy; the war seemed to be breaking all over the city:

I knew of the attacks on Saigon when Bill Snead, our photo chief, crashed through the door of my apartment and woke me up. He lived two floors above me and had been awakened by the attacks on the Navy headquarters in Hai Ba Trung Square, about 150 yards from our bureau, some 45 minutes earlier. He had tried to wake me both by telephone and knocking on the door but I slept through it. He went back upstairs, got his camera and started photographing the tracers going up and down the street. When a small-arms round came through the side of his apartment, he tried to wake me again and this time was successful. . . .

The UPI occupied two adjacent, store-front-type buildings, with the news and photo bureaus located on the ground floor and apartments above them. Snead and I went downstairs to the bureau and I filed an initial bulletin saying fighting had broken out in the center of Saigon. We started making telephone calls to MACV and Zorthian and were interrupted by two MPs who rushed into the bureau, dove behind a desk, and shouted for us to turn out the lights.

They had been leading a convoy from the dock area and had been taken under fire. We turned out the light in the front of the bureau nearest the street but kept the one at the back over the news desk on.

The MPs pulled closed the iron grate over the front of the bureau and took up positions behind it with their rifles, making a small barricade out of desks.

A short while later, when it became apparent that the fighting was at the end of our street and not in it, one of the MPs and I sneaked gingerly a few yards down the street to where his jeep had coasted into a tree, and retrieved his radio. This was our main source of information on what was going on in Saigon until sometime after dawn, when Snead and his photographers were able to get out into the streets and Southerland, Reilly and Cheatham managed to make their way into the bureau.

Cheatham stayed with me and Southerland and Reilly left in a jeep with instructions to find out what was going on. From monitoring the MP radio it appeared that widespread attacks were underway, but I did not at this stage consider the embassy to be the focus of them. I think I mentioned to Dan and Bill that they should particularly check the Independence Palace and check some of the U.S. billets that the radio indicated were being hit.

My recollection is that during the first several hours of the Tet offensive I communicated by telephone twice with Zorthian. Once was in the early morning hours when he told me that several places, including the embassy, were under attack. . . . In any event, he did not give me Jacobson's telephone number and I did not get the impression from our conversation that the embassy fighting was the most important center of the attack.

My second conversation with him was around mid-morning, when he called to say the VC had not entered the chancellery. . . .

Another very important source of information for us during the pre- and post dawn hours of that day was the radio net which we monitored at JUSPAO. Joe Fried of the New York *Daily News* got there early and fed us information. Sometime later, perhaps an hour or so, we got our own man over there who I think was Perry Young.

So virtually all our information on the attacks came from monitoring radios until well after dawn. I'm not sure what time Kate Webb got to the embassy but the fighting was all over before I knew she was there. She had been unable to find a telephone—or perhaps she thought we had somebody else there—and did not file anything until after Jacobson was freed and she was able to get back to the bureau. Unfortunately, she left shortly before Westmoreland and Bunker made their appearance in the courtyard and we were somewhat behind in reporting their remarks.

However, Snead and several photographers did make it back earlier and gave us some eyewitness detail.

It was after the Bunker-Westmoreland appearance that I talked with Zorthian the second time and this conversation prompted us to begin checking back and to pull back off the enemy-in-the-chancellery bit.

I do not recall precisely when we said the VC had gotten inside the chancellery. I do recall that in the first reports I stipulated that the attackers were only inside the embassy compound and that later—as information from the radios and initial reports from returning reporters began pouring in—I purposely fuzzed up whether they were actually inside or not.

In retrospect, this was a cheap way out and must have driven our domestic deskmen out of their minds but it also is an indication that at this stage of the unfolding story—with the fighting underway at Independence Palace, Tan Son Nhut, several billets, and our own little war at the Navy headquarters—I did not consider it of overriding importance.

I think the Saigon file will show that subsequently we labeled the source of some of the reports that the enemy was in the building and, finally, the evidence seemed so overwhelming we said it flatly.

Some of the evidence, as I recall it, was:

—Reports from photographers at the scene that they were receiving fire from above.

—Reports from several MPs engaged in the fighting that they were receiving fire from inside the chancellery. Several pinpointed the floor and I think we named at least one sergeant in our copy.

—A confirmation relayed to me by our monitor at JUSPAO based on information that he got off the radio. I don't know precisely what the information was but I'm quite sure that one of Zorthian's deputies who was monitoring the radio along with our man also thought they were inside because I talked with him on the telephone about it and got information on what offices were located on which floor.

—Radio reports that a Marine guard on top of the embassy was wounded and that a helicopter rescue team attempting to land atop the chancellery was driven away by fire.

These pieces of information convinced me that the enemy was indeed inside the building.

The line in our story about fighting through the carpeted halls of the chancellery was my doing and completely unforgivable. . . .[8]

In short, both AP and UPI finally passed on, without attribution, the information given them by the MPs; yet, to repeat, no reporter in the gray dawn on Thong Nhat Street could *see* the embassy battle behind those high walls prior to breaking in the front gate with the MPs after the fight was all but over. The wire reports did not indicate this uncertainty. UPI, apparently striving for what its foreign editor calls "words [that] popped out at the reader," leaped beyond even the available *mis*information.

The immediate result was gross exaggeration of what really happened at the embassy: a small but bold raid to seize the chancery that miscarried, apparently through Vietcong confusion and the quick thinking of a Marine guard, who closed the big front door. It is worth repeating that, to its credit, UPI—unlike AP—did not cling to the

"Vietcong were in the building" angle, once the situation was clarified.

But none of this post-mortem crept into the appraisal in the *UPI World Log* (February 3, 1968). As always, the accent, from headquarters, was on speed: "We trailed on early details of the fighting at the U.S. Embassy and on the assault by Vietcong into the compound itself. The opposition [AP] apparently got a staffer there before we did. We were unable to match for a cycle one remarkable story of the Colonel [Jacobson] trapped in a bedroom who caught a pistol thrown up to him and killed a Vietcong with it. . . ."

Newspaper Reports

For the newspapermen in Saigon on January 31, the situation was slightly different. They knew that their home offices would be alerted by the wire services, at least to the fact that the attacks were going on. In any case, it was impossible for the one- two- and three-man newspaper staffs to "match the wires" on a countrywide or even Saigon-wide story. Yet something had to be written and filed, if only to satisfy pride and prestige. The problem was putting together a coherent story in time for succeeding editions, allowing for what always happened in times of crisis—delayed communications.[9]

This meant that the stories had to be written on the run. Unlike the wire services, neither the Washington *Post* nor the New York *Times* had a rewrite man in the office taking dictation. This, plus the lack of direct communications of their own, resulted in a scramble for the reporters—running to Reuters to pound out a few paragraphs on the extra Olivetti typewriter there, then running back to the embassy.

The New York *Times* had its experienced stringer, Sidney White, in Reuters' office to catch up with MACV and other sources (and to see what Reuters was gathering), because the day's story had to embrace not just the embassy but also combat developments around the city and country. And all of this had to be put together in three to three and one-half hours.

But little of what was happening was immediately clear to newspapermen in the early hours of January 31. In the Caravelle and Continentale hotels, most newsmen slept more soundly than did Arnett, whose apartment was close to the action. The UPI staffers, also, were near the waterfront, where the Vietcong hit the Vietnamese Navy's headquarters. The *Post* reporters were far from the scene. Zorthian's predawn telephone calls proved most helpful, however. Lescaze of the *Post* recalls the morning's events this way:

The phone rang about 3:30 a.m., an unwelcome event since Becky [Mrs. Lescaze] and I had gone to bed late after I wrote a story on the attacks the day before in I and II Corps. It was John Randolph of the Los Angeles *Times* who said that Vietcong were attacking Independence Palace. I remember thinking this was unlikely and wondering what had caused John to interrupt my sleep, etc. From our bedroom, with the air conditioner on, the sounds of firing were very faint. But, awake, listening and standing in the living room, it was clear that something was happening close by in the city. . . .

I shaved (odd concern for appearances) and dressed. Then, I walked up Nguyen Hue Street to the AP bureau in the Eden Building.

On the street it was much easier to hear the shots (from, I guess, the embassy and the Palace). A couple of jeeps went by fast as I walked, but I saw no one walking and I doubt anyone saw me in the dark.

Peter Arnett, Horst Faas, and Robert Tuckman were in the AP bureau along with the telegraphers and several photographers of the AP Vietnamese staff. Arnett confirmed Randolph's report and broadened it to include the attack on the embassy and other parts of town. It was about 4 a.m. and AP had filed several (maybe ten) graphs of sketchy information. They had already talked to Zorthian at least once. About this time, 4–4:30 a.m., Zorthian called my apartment and spoke to Becky. He wanted to fill me in and to warn me (as he was warning other journalists) that he had no certain knowledge where the VC were and therefore how dangerous it was to walk about.

I walked along Le Loi Street to Tu Do and up to the Cathedral. From there, it was apparent that most of the (downtown) fighting (or at least shooting) was at the embassy and I ran into MPs who were taking cover behind trees and who were generally uninformative about what was happening. I walked along Thong Nhat Boulevard toward the embassy for less than 100 yards and ran into other MPs who told me to go back because any further advance would put me in a cross fire. This was probably untrue, but I was not reluctant to retreat and I walked back to Reuters and, after calling Zorthian, filed about four graphs at roughly 6:30 a.m. The Reuters office was dark but several people were awake and there—Jim Pringle, who lived upstairs, Bruce Piggott, telegraphers and perhaps some *Time* people or some British journalists. I called Braestrup. Buckley and Mohr arrived about dawn, which was about 7 a.m. as I recall.

With the daylight I walked toward the embassy taking cover behind trees and walls as the firing broke out sporadically. Journalists were now out in force and they were taking up as many observation posts along

Thong Nhat as the MPs. There was still quite a bit of automatic-weapons firing in the embassy compound and an occasional wounded MP was walked away from the compound wall by some buddies. The black Citroen with its dead driver and many bullet holes was stopped in the street roughly across from the main gate. An MP jeep that had been hit driving by was also stalled in the boulevard. As I remember, Braestrup appeared and we each ran a couple of bulletins back to Reuters. (I had filed about three takes after my first daylight look.)

About 8:40 a.m. I realized that the battle was over. I was in the compound along with Braestrup and maybe 12 other reporters for a start and about the same number of MPs. There were also a few Marine guards in civilian clothes, a couple of embassy security officers and, shortly, some of the paratroopers who had landed on the embassy roof.

It was over and Zorthian and Westmoreland arrived to talk about it.

This writer was less alert. Having filed my Khe Sanh and Da Nang copy, I drove home to bed at 1:30 a.m. The phone rang a couple of hours later.

"They're attacking the city," Lescaze said.

"What city?" I asked.

"This city," Lescaze said patiently. "Saigon."

"Ridiculous," I replied. "Just some incoming."

The cloudy night sky in the direction of Tan Son Nhut air base was full of orange flares. A couple of helicopters came low overhead. In the distance was the thump of artillery fire. Also the popping of Tet firecrackers. Nothing that wouldn't wait until morning.

The phone rang again at dawn. "They're fighting at the embassy," Lescaze reported.

"OK," I said. "I'll meet you at Reuters."

Tu Xuong Street, where I lived, joined Cong Ly, the main four-lane boulevard from Tan Son Nhut air base into downtown Saigon. As I dressed, I looked out my second-floor bedroom window and saw a column of dusty U.S. Army M-112 armored personnel carriers come roaring downtown past the pastel villas and walled gardens on Cong Ly. The hatches were open, but the gunners were alert in helmets and flak jackets, with .50-caliber machine guns loaded. That looked serious. U.S. troops in Saigon.

As I went out to my car, a rented 1959 Volkswagen, I saw my neighbor, a CIA man, getting into his Toyota sedan. "Better come with me," he said. "The police are putting up roadblocks."

It took a while to get the Toyota started. Then we started down tree-lined Cong Ly, past the police, who looked calm enough with

M-1 carbines. There was sporadic shooting out of sight off to the right—somewhere behind Independence Palace. The Palace looked unscathed but was swarming with ARVN troops. Across the park, the long, bare, narrow Reuters office at 15 Han Thuyen Street was full of reporters. The twin-spired red brick Saigon Cathedral blocked any view of the embassy. The Reuters men were running in relays between the embassy and their office, filing a paragraph or two at a time.

Counting cable transmission time, we would all be pressed to make late editions, especially those of us on east-coast morning newspapers. In effect, we would be almost as hard pressed as the wire services and would be filing in bits and pieces, which the deskmen at home would have to sort out into a coherent story. We exchanged rumors; snipers, action at Tan Son Nhut, a squad of VC holed up across from Independence Palace, the embassy "held" by Vietcong. The scale of fighting was hard to discern. No one then had any inkling that the Vietcong had put 11 battalions (3,000–5,000 men) into the city's western Cholon districts, Tan Son Nhut, and the suburbs. No one knew what was going down in the MPs' logs. The embassy fight was a militarily insignificant affair, compared to what else was going on; but to us, it was the whole story.

Lescaze had already filed a message to the *Post* and gone to the embassy. Given the communications problems (too much traffic, resulting in long delays), we had missed the first edition and probably the second. I hastened to catch up with Tom Buckley of the New York *Times*. We crossed Thong Nhat Street, skirting the massive brick rear of Saigon Cathedral. Were there snipers in the Cathedral towers? The square was empty. It was a bad time of day for nightowls anyway. Gray morning skies.

"This is the nadir," said Buckley, as we trotted across the street. "The absolute nadir."

Next to the green iron fence at the corner of Hai Ba Trong Street were Peter Arnett, Charles Mohr, Francois Sully, and others. Arnett talked of his earlier predawn look-around. We joked nervously. Nobody was in a rush to climb over the embassy wall. We watched from afar and waited for the MPs to move again.

Lescaze went back to file. Several television cameramen were across the street, facing the front gate. Around us were the excited MPs of the 716th Battalion. From inside the compound came occasional sounds of fighting: M-16 fire, grenades, explosions. At 8:30

a.m. we saw the Huey helicopters come down to the roof, and the paratroopers drop off and disappear.

Then a TV crew followed "our" MPs as they broke into the front yard (others joined by Marines had been skirmishing in the backyard). Dead Vietcong in blue and brown clothing with narrow red arm bands lay in the front yard around the concrete flower pots. (Later I saw a burlap sack of *plastique* explosive outside the wall next to the four-foot hole.) The MPs had thrown ID cards on the bodies. We edged up to the embassy facade. There was some final backyard shooting—Colonel Jacobson's final minute of travail—and then the press was wandering all over the place. We checked back with some 101st Airborne troopers. The MPs were intolerant; they had lost two of their own at the compound's vehicle entrance on Mac Dinh Chi Street. The newsmen were shooed out.

Lescaze and I, like Mohr, were running back and forth to Reuters to file our bits and pieces (none of these originals survive) until noon. Zorthian was on the scene by 9:30 a.m. (8:30 p.m. EST) and Westmoreland was inspecting things by 9:45, as AP reported. The statements by Westmoreland and by Bunker in the front-yard press conferences, however, were too late for the early *Times* and *Post* press runs.

The New York *Times*. The Late City edition of the New York *Times* had three page-one stories and a picture on the Vietnam offensive.

At Mohr's orders, Tom Buckley spent most of the morning at Reuters writing the lead-all (with bits of information supplied by Reuters, Sidney White, and Mohr). It left ambiguous the question of whether the Vietcong had gotten into the embassy building. Moreover, the State Department denial was not bracketed in the lead-all by the desk in New York. Well down in the story there was a reference to the early reports that the Vietcong had gotten into the building and to the denials by Marine guard officers. But General Westmoreland's account, quoted extensively (see above) by the AP, was abridged in the *Times* to a mere two sentences: "The enemy's well-laid plans went afoul. All the enemy in the compound have been killed."

A separate Mohr "embassy action" story had the Vietcong "overrun and then hold a section of the embassy's grounds," with "Marine guards fighting to keep the enemy out of the main chancery building," plus a reference to reports of VC occupancy.

Buckley's lead wrap-up, given a four-column heading, ran as follows:

FOE INVADES U.S. SAIGON EMBASSY
RAIDERS WIPED OUT AFTER 6 HOURS
VIETCONG WIDEN ATTACK ON CITIES

Ambassador Safe—Guerrillas Also Strike
Presidential Palace and Many Bases

SAIGON, South Vietnam, Wednesday, Jan. 31—A 17-man[10] Vietcong squad seized parts of the United States Embassy in the center of Saigon and held them for six hours early today.

The Vietcong, wearing South Vietnamese Army uniforms,[11] held off American military policemen firing machine guns and rocket launchers. Finally the invaders were routed by squads of American paratroopers who landed by helicopter on the roof of the building.[12]

Ambassador Ellsworth Bunker was taken from his residence about five blocks from the embassy to what was described as a secure area, the Associated Press reported. He returned to the embassy at 11 a.m., about two hours after the last enemy resistance was wiped out. Others of the embassy staff were also said to be safe. The American flag was raised in front of the embassy at 11:45 a.m., almost five hours later than normal.

Only scattered reports of American losses were available by midafternoon. The total was perhaps 40 men killed and twice as many wounded. The guerrilla forces were believed to number no more than 500. . . .

Elsewhere in the country, heavy fighting was reported in the capitals of the five provinces of the I Corps area, the northernmost section of the country, and in several district towns there and in the Central Highlands cities of Ban Me Thuot, Pleiku, and Kontum.

Targets Widespread

The raiders in Saigon, besides attacking the embassy, fought their way into the grounds of the Presidential Palace.

Waves of helicopters raked them with rockets and machine-gun fire.[13]

The palace houses the executive offices of President Nguyen Van Thieu and Vice President Nguyen Cao Ky. The United States Embassy said the President was safe at an undisclosed place. The whereabouts of the Vice President was [sic] said to be unknown.[14]

As the fighting raged, this correspondent was pinned down for 15 minutes behind a military police jeep as tracer bullets arched a few feet overhead.[15]

The bodies of at least two American military policemen lay perhaps 50 yards away. Vietcong and civilian dead also sprawled on the sidewalk.

Heavy fighting was also reported near the runway at Tan Son Nhut Airport, where an enemy company of about 100 men was making a suicide stand against a larger force of Vietnamese troops and American troops and American military policemen. The field was closed to all but emergency flights.[16]

A handful of commandos held out in the building housing the Saigon radio, only a few blocks from the embassy. Part of the structure was burning.

The attacks began at 3 a.m. today. Eleven hours later, only *fragmentary reports* could be obtained of many of the guerrillas' assaults that turned Saigon, a relatively secure island in a widening sea of war for the past two-and-a-half years, into a battleground.[17]

Despite public warnings by the Saigon police that a terrorist assault could be expected last night in the aftermath of the enemy's attacks on major cities, the raids seemed to have caught both the Americans and the South Vietnamese by surprise.

An American military police battalion and the Saigon police found themselves outgunned.[18]

Not until the arrival of the first helicopters at the embassy were any infantry troops, American or South Vietnamese, seen in the center of the city.[19] There were no tanks or heavy weapons to meet the enemy.

Safety Was Key Aim

The embassy compound, covering four acres, opened last September. The primary consideration in its construction was security—even down to the helicopter landing pad installed atop the chancery, the compound's main structure, so Ambassador Bunker *would not have to travel through crowds that might sometimes be hostile.*[20]

· ·

The downtown streets were quiet and deserted when the first mortar rounds exploded on the block-square grounds of the Presidential Palace.

New Assaults Reported

Small-arms fire crackled in a dozen places. As the cannonade continued, allied helicopter gunships swung overhead, sweeping enormous lights over the area.

The fresh wave of attacks was viewed by *some officers* as the start of a general offensive, intended to force the United States to the bargaining table or make it face the likelihood of a greatly expanded and more costly war.

The new raids came as coherent reports of yesterday's sweeping raids became available. . . .

In all the raids, the enemy displayed coordination and offensive strength without precedent in the war.

· ·

South Vietnamese losses were probably heavier [than American].

Although the enemy units generally achieved surprise, they took heavy casualties in the prolonged fighting that followed.

The figure may reach a total of more than 500 enemy dead. *Informed sources in Saigon*[21] *regarded this as a bargain price for the enemy to have paid for the enormous blow scored against government prestige.*

As Mohr later recalled, one of the main reasons for lingering uncertainty "on the important issue of whether the chancery building itself had been entered" was the quick expulsion by the MPs of the newsmen from the compound after the embassy was secured. Earlier during the fighting, Mohr had heard—along with other newsmen—the MPs assert that the foe was in the building. Once the yard was secured, one officer from the 101st Airborne contingent refused to enlighten him one way or the other.

"Our exclusion from the area so quickly made further conclusive inquiry difficult," Mohr recalled. So, in his own story, he wrote what he knew; that "a section of the embassy grounds" had been entered by the foe, and that there had been reports that the Vietcong had entered the chancery. Next day (February 1, Saigon time), Mohr wrote that the building had *not* been entered, when he "felt sure that this was true."

Westmoreland's account got skimped in the *Times* partly because Mohr was leaving for Reuters just as COMUSMACV arrived. "I chose to keep going on the grounds that the wire services would have his remarks, which I expected to be short, vague, and defensive. In retrospect, I think the *Times* should have wrapped in more of what he said. But further delay on my part might have meant no story at all in the *Times* for that day." Mohr, like other newspapermen, was harried by the thought of the pile-up of stories at Reuters.

Moreover, although he wrote a "conservative" story, Mohr recalls, "I was skeptical of quick official denials." The "credibility" of the Mission, due in part to its role in the Johnson Administration's autumn 1967 "progress" campaign, had been badly damaged, Mohr noted, long before Tet.[22]

Mohr concentrated on his own eyewitness story; he did not have time to cross-check Buckley's wrap-up, which took a less conservative line. Mohr's story focused on his old friend, George Jacobson:

U.S. AIDE IN EMBASSY VILLA
KILLS GUERRILLA WITH PISTOL

SAIGON, South Vietnam, Wednesday, Jan. 31—The Vietcong terrorist attack on the United States Embassy ended this morning with a gun battle between an embassy official and a guerrilla on a staircase.

Col. George Jacobson, retired, who holds the title of United States Mission Coordinator, had been trapped in his white stucco villa in a corner of the spacious embassy grounds throughout the fierce fighting, which raged in the compound from about 3 a.m. until 9 a.m.

Using a .45-caliber automatic pistol that had been tossed to his second-story window by an American military policeman, Colonel Jacobson turned and killed a wounded Vietcong rifleman stumbling up the stairs to get away from tear gas fumes filling the ground floor.

"I was very lucky," said Colonel Jacobson. "He got in the first shots and shot three times but missed. I didn't do much, because the military police and Marine guards had already crippled him and he couldn't shoot straight."

7 Americans Killed

At least five American military policemen and two Marine guards were killed in a wild night that saw the Vietcong terror squad overrun and then hold a *section of the embassy grounds,* against initial attempts by rescue forces to fight their way in.

Bodies of Vietcong littered the grass and graveled terrace around the modernistic eight-story chancery building.

An *initial count* by military policemen said there were 17 bodies of Vietcong after the fight ended.

In one of the strangest scenes of the Vietnam War, helmeted American troops ran crouching across broad Thong Nhat Boulevard to assault the gate of their own embassy at dawn today.

Seven American helicopters landed on the roof to discharge a platoon of American paratroops who raced down the stairways to come to the aid of Marine guards fighting to keep the enemy out of the main chancery building.[23]

Meanwhile, the rattle of gun-fire and explosions could be heard from the area of the nearby Independence Palace and numerous other parts of Saigon as the guerrilla commando units fought scatter actions late into the morning.

The pierced concrete grille that shades the windows of the chancery building was broken in three places with jagged holes left by Soviet-designed B-40 anti-tank rockets fired by the guerrillas in their initial assault.

A 3.5-inch bazooka rocket had also torn a hole in the high reinforced concrete wall of the grounds.[24]

Some guerrillas apparently crawled through this hole during the attack. Others shot their way through the gates guarded by United States Army Military Policemen. At the side gate of the grounds two young American soldiers lay dead, one of them shot in the face by a machine gun.

Many details of the embassy battle were unclear for the time being even though newsmen ran crouching with military policemen when the grounds were retaken.[25]

Some Killed by Guards

It *appeared,* however, that the Vietcong commando unit shot its way into the grounds at about 3 a.m. Some of them were killed by the small contingent of United States Marine guards in the building.

Instead of giving up the attack and trying to flee, the guerrillas set up defensive positions on the grounds. *Some of the attackers were said to have held the lower floors of the building itself for several hours.*[26]

When an American helicopter tried to land on the building's roof before dawn,[27] it was driven away by fierce automatic-weapons fire from the guerrillas.

Besides the guerrillas inside the compound, American military policemen converging on the chancery building had to deal with snipers firing from nearby roofs and other locations.

Two military policemen getting out of a jeep across the street from the main embassy gate went down in a hail of bullets about 8 a.m.

"Get those men and get that sniper," shouted a military police captain wearing a protective flak jacket emblazoned with the legend "In God We Trust."

While the Marine guard contingent held out in the main building, an American military police captain and a young private first class, Paul Healy, 20 years old, of Holbrook, Massachusetts, led the way in a rescue assault into the grounds at first light.

Throwing grenades and firing their automatic M-16 rifles, they killed the guerrillas who tried to keep them out.

"One VC threw a grenade at me," said Private Healy. "It hit the wall and fell down about two feet from me. I dived for cover and didn't get hurt. I killed that man with a grenade and later got three more with another grenade."

His grim face was twitching with emotion as he told his story and a major gently put his arm around the youth's shoulders.

Private Healy, other military police, and Marine guards fought their way across the flowered lawns to try to rescue Colonel Jacobson, the only embassy official who lives on the grounds.

"I saw raw courage tonight on the part of the Marine guards and military policemen," said Colonel Jacobson, his sleepy eyes drawn and haggard and his maroon sport shirt rumpled with sweat.

"I saw them advance straight into the direction of enemy fire and silence that fire. If you want to get more brave than that, I would rather not be around."

The first-floor foyer of the chancery building was a *smoldering* shambles. The reception desk with its elaborate pushbutton console telephone was wrecked.

Some of the bodies on the grounds—thought to be South Vietnamese —might prove to be those of embassy employees rather than Vietcong, since witnesses could see United States identification cards on two of the bodies.

An unexploded, live grenade and several Soviet-made rockets littered the grounds, presenting a demolition hazard.

One Vietnamese was riddled by American machine-gun fire near the embassy this morning when he failed to stop his ancient black sedan after an American command to halt.

The Washington *Post.* For the *Post* and *Times,* the normal technique on a running (deadline) story was akin to the practice of the wire services: One first filed a lead with as much detail as was then available, bearing in mind that "nuledes" (new lead paragraphs) would have to be substituted as events changed. Thus paragraphs toward the end of the story as first written would deal with earlier events and "firm" detail, and, presumably, would not have to be changed as time went on.

The idea was to organize the story in such a way that the harried foreign editor at home could simply substitute, as necessary, successive nuledes of three to ten paragraphs which would then be stitched to the firm copy further down in the story and rushed to the composing room for successive editions. In brief, one puts a new locomotive on the train for each of three or four editions.

At Tet, of course, this process was less than smooth. In the *Post*'s case, both Lescaze and I were typing the bits and pieces, with Lescaze handling the nuledes and I the supplementary material—all amid the pandemonium at Reuters and between running visits to the embassy. The *Times* had Buckley writing the ledes, with Mohr and Sidney White supplying added details. In both cases, this process put a heavy burden on the foreign desks at home, where editors had to patch it all together.

As indicated, both newspapers were slow to get much from their Saigon correspondents. One observer in the *Post*'s home office told how Harry Rosenfeld, the paper's assistant foreign editor, walked around, after the first wire flashes, muttering, "Where's Lescaze?" At that moment, Lescaze was trying to find out what was going on. (As for this writer, I was out on Tu Xuong Street, stubbornly asleep.)

In its first edition on January 31, the *Post* ran as its lead story a rewrite out of the wire services ("from news dispatches"), which had been put together in haste by the foreign desk. It carried an eight-column, page-one banner headline:

VIETCONG SEIZE PART OF U.S. EMBASSY

Building Retaken In Fight

SAIGON, Jan. 31 (Wednesday)—The Vietcong brought their largest offensive of the war to the U.S. Embassy in Saigon early today. Guerrillas seized part of the building and held it against attacking American military policemen and paratroops.

At least 10 of the policemen were killed and several more were wounded, U.S. officials said.

The Americans finally regained control of the building by launching an assault from helicopters they landed on the roof of the eight-story building. *Parts of the building had been held by the enemy for six hours. . . .*

At the embassy, opened only months ago and said to be proof against attack, *American officials said* they believed an enemy suicide squad of about 20 men were holed up in the compound on *part of the first floor of the building itself. . . .*[28]

At 7 a.m., according to the Associated Press, the fighting was still swelling around the building. *Reporters were being kept at a distance.*

Later, with fresh wire copy, the foreign desk rewrote the lead (but not the headline) to indicate that the embassy "complex," not the building, had been seized. But the story went on to cast doubt on Westmoreland's denial that the embassy had been entered:

SAIGON, Jan. 31 (Wednesday)—The Vietcong brought their largest offensive of the war to the U.S. Embassy in Saigon early today. Guerrillas invaded part of the complex and held it for six hours before attacking American troops took it back.

Paratroopers finally landed from helicopters on the roof of the eight-story main building in an assault that ended the battle. The bodies of 19

Vietcong—reportedly the entire attacking force—were later found on the embassy grounds. . . .

. . . .

But *dozens of persons at the scene said some of the communists had been in the lower floors of the building. Vietnamese police sources said the same. . . .*[29]

In the last edition (2 a.m. EST), the *Post* substituted this headline:

VIETCONG INVADE U.S. EMBASSY

Assault Crushed By GIs

It left little room for nuances. Lescaze's story—actually a composite of bits and pieces filed by both of us—ran below:

SAIGON, Jan. 31 (Wednesday)—The Vietcong invaded the U.S. Embassy compound and attacked Saigon's Presidential Palace early this morning in daring raids accompanied by about a dozen rounds of mortar and rocket fire which fell in various areas of the capital.

The attack at the embassy began shortly before 3 a.m. At 8:45 a.m. helicopters put U.S. troops on the roof of the eight-story main building inside the embassy complex and *they ended the battle.*[30]

The raids in Saigon came on the second day of communist attacks against major cities throughout South Vietnam. Can Tho, the principal city in the Mekong Delta, was reported attacked this morning. Bien Hoa Air Base, 20 miles northeast of Saigon, was shelled and the huge helicopter base at Marble Mountain outside Da Nang was taken under rocket and mortar fire.

The *heaviest enemy activity* appeared to be around the Central Highlands province capital at *Kontum.*[31] Official spokesmen in Saigon said Kontum was standing up to the 19th ground attack against the city since early this morning.[32] In the embassy fighting, one U.S. Marine guard was killed, five Marines were wounded and seven American military policemen were killed or wounded. Military officials believe four of them were killed.

Gen. William C. Westmoreland, the U.S. commander in Vietnam, said the enemy had "quite obviously" been planning the raid for some time.

Standing amid the *debris*[33] of the battle outside the door of the embassy building, Westmoreland said: "The enemy's well-laid plans went afoul."

He said the enemy had intended to destroy the building with explosives. "There appears to be no structural damage, contrary to the objective of the enemy," Westmoreland said.

All of the enemy who got inside the embassy compound apparently were killed.[34] Nineteen bodies were found on the ground around the building. Several of the dead carried U.S. Embassy identification cards in their wallets. It was not immediately clear if they had stolen the cards or were embassy employees who helped set up the raid.

Westmoreland said a platoon of enemy disguised in civilian dress entered the compound after blowing a four-by-four [foot] hole in the concrete wall surrounding the compound and crawling through.

All were armed with automatic weapons, antitank rockets, and a large quantity of explosives.

The embassy was opened only a few months ago. It was supposed to be secure against attack. One of the most graphic descriptions of the fight at the high-walled embassy compound came from George Jacobson, Mission Coordinator, who spent the night in his house in the garden in the rear of the embassy compound.

At about 2:45 a.m., he said, he was awakened by the sound of shooting and thump of B-40 bazookas—which made four jagged holes in the concrete facade of the embassy. "I was not armed," Jacobson said. "I watched from my upstairs bedroom as the MPs and Marine guards advanced against enemy fire." *The fight raged in the garden* of the embassy compound.

This morning, MPs from outside entered the garden about 8:30 while Marines reportedly held out on upper floors of the embassy[35] and were reinforced by seven helicopter loads—about 50 men—landed on the rooftop helicopter pad.

They threw tear-gas grenades into the ground floor of Jacobson's house. "They threw me a gas mask through the window and a pistol," he said.

A Vietcong, carrying an M-16 automatic rifle, came up the stairs to escape from the tear gas. Jacobson waited for him.

"He saw me first but he must have been wounded. He was a bad shot. I knocked him down with two .45 shots," Jacobson said.

After talking to newsmen, he embraced his two Vietnamese servants who had also survived, somehow.

"A miracle," he said.

American helicopters and flare ships circled over Saigon but there was *no evidence* that they had opened fire. Tracer bullets could be seen occasionally being fired up at the helicopters from within the city.

As dawn came this morning, a few Saigon residents appeared on their bicycles. They moved along Saigon's streets as military police jeeps honked them out of the way as they sped from the scene of one outbreak of fighting to another.

Meanwhile, sniper fire continued around the Independence Palace. One report said an estimated dozen Vietcong were spraying fire around the south side of the Palace.

Observers were puzzled that no sizable American or Vietnamese force was brought into the downtown area until the helicopter assault on the embassy roof. Warnings had been issued to Americans and Vietnamese that Vietcong terrorist acts were likely during the truce period. . . .

Unfortunately, appended to this brief conservative story was a "shirttail" containing a sizable residue of the earlier "from news dispatches" foreign-desk rewrite. The shirttail, largely AP, repeated the assertion that "dozens of persons at the scene" and "Vietnamese police sources" said some of the Vietcong had entered the embassy chancery.

The conflict between this and the Saigon bureau's story was one the bureau never did clear up. In its own dispatch, the bureau never cited any claims that the Vietcong entered the embassy. It accurately paraphrased, high in the story, part of Westmoreland's account of the Vietcong attempt to blow up the building. Later on, it stated that the fight took place "in the garden." Yet, nowhere does the bureau's story, as it appeared in the *Post,* say flatly that the Vietcong *were not* in the building, nor does it cite Westmoreland's flat denial. We were unaware of what the wire services had been filing: Rebuttal did not loom very large in our minds at the moment. Westmoreland's account seemed plausible, and, for all our suspicions, we did not then know or hear enough to be sure the Vietcong *had* entered the building. So we left it ambiguous, and, given the communications problems, there was no way that the *Post* foreign desk could ask us to make the point explicit.[36] (The *Times'*s Mohr nailed down the point in a story published February 2.) Moreover, the *Post's* final edition, oddly, failed to mention, in its Washington "reaction" story, the State Department's denial that the sappers had entered the chancery. Thus, the *Post* reader, if he read the late editions on January 31, was left wondering whether the sappers had occupied their objective or not.

Another striking feature is the scantiness of the information contained in the *Post's* main Saigon story—compared with those of AP, UPI, and the New York *Times*—about the battle elsewhere in Saigon. Busy running back and forth between the embassy and Reuters, Lescaze and I were unable to learn much about the broader picture. The *Times,* with Sidney White monitoring the Reuters file, had the edge. In addition, much of our output did not get into the paper. The *Post's* Reuters circuit was out of service for several hours; through a mix-up, when Reuters finally got the Braestrup-Lescaze copy moving, it came into Washington paragraph by paragraph without the normal identifying "slugs," senders' names, and time-date notations. Because the *Post* shared its Reuters circuit with the Los Angeles *Times,* similarly anonymous bits and pieces from William Tuohy and John Randolph came in on the same teleprinter, confronting the *Post* desk with a mixed pile of unidentified, unrelated paragraphs to be sorted out under deadline pressure.

Also on the *Post*'s January 31 page one was this writer's Da Nang story. Contrary to what the wires and TV carried, no enemy ground assault got into Da Nang proper aside from the small raid on I Corps headquarters; the big fight was in the Da Nang suburbs. Rockets had not knocked out the air base, as some sources reported. Indeed, the *Post* foreign desk hung onto its Da Nang story, filed January 30. Possibly because I had not been awakened in the pre-dawn hours at the Da Nang press center, but came from Khe Sanh well after sunup, my piece was almost blasé:

Gunfire Ends Da Nang's Holiday

. . . Aside from causing considerable alarm and confusion throughout Da Nang's thinly defended complex of Vietnamese and American bases, the daring Vietcong raid against the I Corps headquarters was no great military success. However, according to U.S. Marine sources, prisoners taken during the fight said it was only the first of a series of such attacks planned against Da Nang by the communists.

The raid, these sources said, was obviously planned to take advantage of South Vietnamese slackness during the Tet holiday, and was planned well before President Nguyen Van Thieu yesterday called off the 36-hour truce. . . .

Paired with this, and under a joint headline ("Concerted Attacks Leave Bloody Trail"), was Lescaze's January 30 story on the Central Highlands (see Chapter 2). Amid the foreign desk rush, it had been drastically trimmed and peculiarly subtitled ("Security Drop Seen in Areas").

Evaluating the performance. In summary, one might say that the *Times* and the *Post,* despite manpower shortages, deadline pressures, and communications delays, provided readers (of final editons) with less confusion on the embassy battle than did the wires. But there were some oddities, notably the following:

Both the *Post* and the *Times* stories complained of the slowness of U.S. infantry and armor to show up downtown. This was an understandable reaction—*we* were jarred, *we* wanted U.S. armored personnel carriers *downtown* where *we* were. Actually, extra troops were not needed at the embassy or palace. The infantry and armored forces in Saigon were in Cholon, to the west, including those U.S. mechanized forces I had seen speeding down Cong Ly after sunup. The enemy had put a half-dozen battalions into that area, a threat which demanded far more military attention than the embassy. But, of course, that was not generally known immediately.

Neither the *Post* nor the *Times* carried the Westmoreland embassy yard interview, which was shown on CBS News ("Special Report," January 31, 11 p.m. EST). The General again emphasized the north: "In my opinion, this [anti-cities attack] is diversionary to [the foe's] main efforts, which he had planned to take place in Quang Tri province from Laos towards Khe Sanh and across the DMZ." It was a viewpoint which soon aroused great skepticism among newsmen, especially those who had been at the embassy that morning. How could any effort against Saigon, especially downtown Saigon, be a diversion? The General did not revive this "diversion" theory in his briefing the next day.

The *Times,* including everything but Charles Mohr's embassy story in Buckley's wrap-up, gave the impression that the enemy "punch" had been "especially" strong at Da Nang, Vietnam's second largest city. The *Post,* as noted, retained its man's Da Nang story and showed, by inference, that Da Nang was in fact a minor affair compared to the other ground assaults. (Da Nang, however, got big play in the AP and on TV, because the reporters were there.) For its part, the *Post* gave undue prominence to Kontum.

The *Post* did not specifically warn its readers that all returns were not in yet, although the rewritten wire-service story mentioned the Saigon rumor mill. Both Mohr and Buckley had such warnings in their stories.

Both the *Post* (in its four separate stories, including the shirttail) and the *Times* (in Buckley's wrap-up) conveyed a rough catalog from MACV communiqués of the action upcountry, but not in the Delta. That news was not available early in Saigon, and neither paper had a man in the Delta.

The *Post* lead story ventured almost no generalizations. The *Times* wrap-up cited the view of "some officers" who, on the hectic morning of January 31, were said to consider the Saigon attacks as "the start of a general offensive intended to force the United States to the bargaining table or make it face the likelihood of a greatly expanded and more costly war." The *Times* also produced "informed sources" who regarded enemy losses as a "bargain price" for "the enormous blow [*sic*] scored against government prestige."

The embassy story, as we have seen, dominated the wire-service leads, got the big headlines, and, later, was featured on network TV shows—all in accordance with standard U.S. press traditions. The "terrorist-proof" embassy was "symbolic" (of what, take your choice), the battle was dramatic (Colonel Jacobson was good copy), and, most important, the newsmen were around to watch the action (or part of it). All the elements of an irresistible story were there— green choppers landing paratroopers on the rooftop helipad, the shouts of MPs, the dead VC sprawled around the flower tubs on the immaculate embassy front lawn. And all of it only blocks from the Caravelle Hotel. What more could readers and viewers want?

In retrospect, one wonders how much less misinformation would have been generated had newsmen not been able to get so close and yet so far. Certainly Zorthian passed the word promptly: He alerted the news bureaus by telephone, produced Westmoreland, and helped newsmen interview MPs and others after the battle was over. His own reports were accurate. But during the postdawn hours prior to Jacobson's liberation and the arrival of Westmoreland and Zorthian, newsmen had to rely on their own judgment. The wires, forced to file, let the drama run away with them, and TV was to follow suit.

Had the embassy, for example, been tucked away in an enclave at Tan Son Nhut air base, reporters could not have reached the scene of the attack before battle's end. By that time, the event would have been seen, perhaps, as what it was: a bold but abortive raid by 19 Vietcong sappers against a building that turned out, on this occasion, to be "terrorist-proof" as advertised, once the surviving guards managed to close the front door. The sappers did not "hold" anything for six hours; they fumbled their initial assault and thereafter, cornered, were engaged in a confused night fight in the yard with Marine and MP forces whom the reporters could not see. Hanoi did not regard the raid as a victory.[37]

Possibly, if they had borne in mind the 1964–65 Vietcong terrorism in Saigon, newsmen might have been less excited about the sappers' achievement in slipping into a curfewless Saigon on the Tet holiday. That the embassy was grossly and surprisingly underguarded was true enough; but that the compound could be *attacked* was no surprise. Yet some newsmen felt impelled to belabor the officials for allowing this to happen: it was "symbolic"; after all that optimistic "progress," it was, as Tom Buckley said, the absolute nadir.

As they read the wire-service accounts, the same feeling hit the editors back home. The roof had fallen in in Vietnam. The credibility gap had been shown to be as wide as the Gulf of Tonkin. The Vietcong *even* took over the *embassy!*

In fact, our very preoccupation with the embassy fight that first morning exaggerated the event's importance and "psychological effect." We were distracted from more significant battles (notably around Tan Son Nhut, where sappers got onto the runway, then were routed by the fortuitous arrival of U.S. armor). The embassy fight became the *whole* Tet offensive on TV and in the newspapers during that offensive's second day—and with the exception of the *Times,* newsmen did not warn their audiences that it was, in reality, only one, inconclusive part of the whole. Such warnings are not part of the journalistic response to breaking events. It seems clear they should be.

Reaction: Washington and New York. With the news of the January 30 (Saigon time) attacks (Pleiku, Ban Me Thuot, Da Nang, Nha Trang) already well in hand, and spot news of the embassy raid just becoming available, the next step was to get the official reaction. The situation, of course, was far from clear to officials and editors alike. Some reports warned the reader of the fog; others didn't.

At 10:39 p.m., January 30 (EST), time for late editions of the *Post* and *Times,* the Associated Press reported the State Department's (accurate) denial that the Vietcong had penetrated the chancery, but noted that "news reports differed":

WASHINGTON (AP)—The State Department, quoting its reports from South Vietnam, said Tuesday night the Vietcong had been unable to penetrate the main U.S. Embassy building in their predawn raid in Saigon.

"They got inside the compound, but they didn't get into the building itself," a State Department official said.

News reports differed. Reporters on the scene in Saigon said attackers seized a portion of the main building and fought U.S. troops rushing for it.

Americans recaptured the diplomatic complex after helicopters landed paratroopers on the embassy roof. The Vietcong suicide squad was wiped out, with 17 bodies counted after the fighting.

The State Department said it had received cables directly from the embassy reporting the attackers had not been able to enter the main building.

The AP, like the UPI, also reported on a White House meeting of top Administration figures apparently focusing on "the eight-day-old North Korean crisis triggered by communist capture of the U.S. intelligence ship *Pueblo*":

WASHINGTON (AP)—President Johnson kept in close communication with both military and diplomatic leaders in Saigon throughout the Vietcong showcase assault on the U.S. Embassy in South Vietnam Tuesday night.

The series of raids on the South Vietnamese capital were described by the White House as apparently "pretty serious" from the very start.

White House aides said the President received about 25 cables from Saigon during the eight hours after the attacks on the embassy and key South Vietnamese buildings began.

The cables included messages from U.S. Ambassador Ellsworth Bunker, who was moved from his home to a safe but undisclosed destination during the attacks, and from Gen. William C. Westmoreland, commander of U.S. forces in Vietnam.

Johnson also met late in the day with two top Republicans in Congress, Senate minority leader Everett M. Dirksen of Illinois and his House counterpart, Rep. Gerald R. Ford of Michigan.

The talks apparently focused on the eight-day-old North Korean crisis triggered by communist capture of U.S. intelligence ship *Pueblo*, but also touched on the war in Vietnam and the outlook for Johnson's legislation in Congress.

The President began the day with a similar meeting with Democratic leaders.

Secretary of State Dean Rusk, Secretary of Defense Robert S. McNamara, and Gen. Earle G. Wheeler, Chairman of the Joint Chiefs of Staff, attended both White House sessions.

The White House also said McNamara's successor, Clark Clifford, and the Central Intelligence Agency chief, Richard Helms, were at the Republican meeting.

Press secretary George Christian was asked by newsmen at the outset of the Saigon attacks whether he felt the communist offensive in Vietnam might be related to the seizure of the *Pueblo*. He said that would be a matter of pure speculation.

Both the New York *Times* and the Washington *Post* contained fuller, but more speculative, Washington reports.

The *Times* ran a page-one piece, without by-line, from its Washington bureau:

. . . During the attack, the President met for about an hour with his principal national security advisors—Rusk . . . McNamara, Secretary of

Defense-designate Clark M. Clifford, Wheeler, who is Chairman of the
Joint Chiefs of Staff, and Walt W. Rostow. . . .

The President also had briefings for the Republican leaders, Senator
Everett McKinley Dirksen and Representative Gerald R. Ford, on the situation at the embassy and on efforts to get North Korea to release the
Pueblo and her crew. During the meeting, he was given fresh reports
from General Westmoreland, Ambassador Bunker, and other American
officials in Saigon. . . .

Officials said that in terms of casualties or damage to the embassy
building, the attack was not so severe as the terrorist bombing on March
30, 1965, in which 22 persons were killed and 200 were wounded.

But today's raid was considered to have surpassed the earlier one as a
dramatic gesture.

The State Department and the White House maintained telephonic and
telegraphic communication with the embassy while the raid was in progress, the officials said. They denied press reports that some of the
Vietcong commandos had penetrated the embassy building proper and
seized control of part of it.

"Our information is that none got into the embassy building proper,"
one official said. "They got into the compound, but not the building."

Administration officials charged North Vietnamese and Vietcong forces
with "callous" violations of the holiday cease-fire at Tet, the Asian New
Year period. The timing of raids over the last 24 hours, the officials said,
indicated that they had been carefully planned "specifically" for the holiday period. . . .

But the government refused to interpret these moves as a sign from
Hanoi that it did not want to enter into peace talks.

Robert J. McCloskey, State Department spokesman, said he considered
it too early to judge the relationship of the military action to diplomatic
endeavors to sound out North Vietnam on its bargaining terms. His comment was made before the embassy raid.

There was not much to work with. The *Times* got into speculation
on "talks"—always a prime *Times* topic:

But during the Tet period, the Administration *appeared in effect to be
showing a possible pattern for compromise with Hanoi.* On the one hand,
Washington has informed North Vietnam indirectly through diplomatic
channels that "normal" levels of fighting and infiltration into the south
will not stand in the way of talks.

But, by bombing the southern part of North Vietnam and continuing
the temporary pause in the northern part, the Administration *seemed* to
be warning that this would be the pattern if North Vietnam engaged dur-

ing talks in intensified attacks or in major buildups of forces across the Demilitarized Zone in South Vietnam.[38]

On page two of the same edition, Joseph B. Treaster, a former *Times* man in Saigon, wrote a sidebar in New York on the embassy, saying in effect that events had proved the architect all wrong, and that the building was a waste of the taxpayers' money:

When the United States Embassy building . . . was opened last September, the architect, Frank J. Martin, proudly proclaimed: "Security is our primary consideration here."

"We'll be able to withstand just about any type of minor attack," he added.

The building was fitted with shatterproof Plexiglass windows, reinforced concrete walls, and a massive terra cotta sun-screen that was designed to double as a blast shield.

Construction workers toiled for two years under the sweltering Southeast Asian sun to erect the six-story building at a cost of $2.6 million, almost triple the original estimate.[39]

That day, a harbinger of things to come, the paper also reminded its readers that some New York editors and writers were joining university professors and student activists in the antiwar movement. Their leaders included Gerald Walker, a sub-editor of *The New York Times Magazine*. The headline (on page two) ran "Writers and Editors to Defy Tax in War Protest: 448 Say They Will Not Pay Any Rise Tied to Conflict—Assail Vietnam Policy."

In broad terms, James Reston, the *Times*'s Washington columnist and associate editor, discussed, mostly apropos of the *Pueblo* case, the limitations of the power of both America and its allies:

. . . In politics, as in physics, every force now tends to create an equal counterforce. Hanoi cannot impose its will on Saigon and Washington by force of arms. Saigon, even with the help of half a million Americans and their military machines, cannot compel the Vietcong and North Vietnam to surrender.

. . . Washington can smash North Vietnam, but China would inherit the wreckage. Moscow has the missiles to paralyze our airfields in South Vietnam and blow our aircraft carriers out of the water, but it dare not use them. . . .[40]

The *Post*, as was its custom, weighed in heavily with hasty analysis, from Washington and Hong Kong. From the British Crown Colony, Stanley Karnow, the *Post*'s veteran China-watcher, newly returned from Saigon, wrote a lengthy "interpretative," based on "sources close to the Vietnamese communists":

As North Vietnam and the Vietcong see it, their forces are now shifting into large-unit operations for the first time in the Vietnam conflict. The communists' version of their potential, not unlike official U.S. claims, is naturally colored by wishful thinking. In the opinion of qualified Saigon informants, however, there is a certain plausibility in the communist view of the present situation.

According to the communists, their strategy is a repeat of that which North Vietnamese commander Vo Nguyen Giap said was used to defeat the French in the Indo-China War. . . .

According to sources close to the Vietnamese communists, this shift began with the battles of Loc Ninh and Dak To last fall and is continuing at Khe Sanh.

The escalation, these sources indicated, is based on the conviction that the allies in Vietnam lack the manpower to respond to large operations and, at the same time, pursue their widespread logistical, defensive, and pacification programs.

To some extent, the large-scale operations are also apparently aimed, even at the risk of high communist losses, at inflicting heavy casualties on the American forces in order to create a psychological impact in the United States. . . .

The communists hesitate to spell out their eventual goal in so many words, but sources close to them imply that the objective of their military moves is to gain a favorable battlefield position for the possibility of negotiations.[41]

In Washington, Murrey Marder, the *Post*'s diplomatic man, added his own complex interpretation of his sources' interpretations—a traditional chore for State Department reporters which the *Times*'s Max Frankel once called digesting "spun sugar candy":

United States officials look upon the soaring communist offensive unfolding in South Vietnam as a multiple-shock strategy.

The most ambitious series of attacks ever mounted by the Vietnamese communists is regarded by U.S. planners as a literal execution of the military-psychological-diplomatic strategy which the communists themselves have proclaimed to their own forces. . . .

No one in Washington yesterday was minimizing the boldness of the communist thrust as it reached into the U.S. Embassy in the heart of Saigon.

As fighting exploded in the embassy compound, officials in Washington minimized that penetration as an isolated "grandstand" play; but they conceded that it enhanced just the impression of offensive power that communist strategists are striving to create.

What the Johnson Administration is banking on, officials underscored, is private assurance by Gen. William C. Westmoreland, the U.S. commander in South Vietnam, that his forces can handle whatever the communists throw at them.

Captured communist documents have labeled what is now taking place in South Vietnam as "the most important historical period for us." They have termed this "the winter-spring campaign" with the objective of "creating an honorable defeat" for the United States at a peace conference. The declared technique is the combination of military and political struggle to topple the present government of South Vietnam and form a "coalition" government that the National Liberation Front (Vietcong) would dominate.

The end result for the Vietnamese communists has been labeled "decisive victory." In communist usage it is a term that means less than total or complete victory, U.S. experts note.

For these reasons, and also because of information gleaned from private diplomatic soundings, U.S. planners generally regard the communists' current military lunge as only one phase of a sequence of actions. As a result, the diplomatic door that now stands ajar for secret probings of North Vietnam's intentions is being left in that position.

The hope on the U.S. side is that the communist offensive now being developed around Khe Sanh and other northern sectors—yet to be touched off—can be contained and hurled back along with the hit-run type of attacks displayed yesterday. Then, it is hoped, North Vietnam may be ready for what the United States would regard as serious negotiating.

It possibly could be argued that the Vietnamese conflict already is on the verge, or even in the midst, of the "fight and negotiate" strategy foreshadowed in captured communist documents. Neither Washington nor Hanoi, however, has chosen to apply this term to the secret diplomatic probing that continues over North Vietnam's December 29 offer for "talks" if the United States bombing of that nation halts "unconditionally." . . .[42]

Finally, although there was no time for *Post* editorial reaction to the embassy attacks,[43] there was a gloomy editorial-page elegy for Khe Sanh, whose siege had already begun, by Ward Just: "It will be our biggest battle. Perhaps the Americans will kill as many as 4,000 of the enemy—5,000 maybe, or if Hanoi flings divisions into the fight perhaps even 10,000 or more. . . . Of course if the ratio of enemy dead to ours holds as it has held for the past three years, we will lose one-third as many as they do. Take those figures above—4,000, 5,000, 10,000—and cut them by two-thirds. Those would be our losses. To defend Khe Sanh."[44]

Network Television

Their own correspondents' Telexed alerts, and the first wire-service stories, reached several networks on January 30 in time for the big evening shows—which would be the first source of news of the Saigon attacks for most east-coast Americans. Along with reading rewrites of the wire-service reports from Saigon, the network commentators also "projected"—or in other words, looked to the future.

Walter Cronkite of CBS apparently went on the air with his show wrapped up before the news of the Saigon attacks arrived. He focused on the earlier upcountry attacks (on which film had already come in) and on one angle: damage done to U.S. aircraft. The CBS film indicated that Da Nang air base was devastated and out of action. As the wires indicated, it was not:

Cronkite: The VC in their first series of attacks today destroyed or damaged 42 American aircraft. The loss was put at $25 million. One of the major targets was Da Nang, and we have a report from CBS newsman, Jeff Gralnick.

Gralnick (with film): That's Da Nang air base, under attack, seen here as it started from two miles away. The raid began at 3 a.m. on the first day of the Vietnamese New Year. The Vietcong and North Vietnamese celebrated in their way. They fired salvo after salvo of 122 mm. rockets and heavy mortars into the air base from the surrounding hills, as they have seven times before in the last months. Shells could be heard dropping in for about an hour. Fifty or so rounds in all. One storage house took a direct hit, burned fiercely as chemicals and electrical supplies went up.[45] Nearby, two Air Force sergeants wrestled with an unexploded or dud rocket which had dug itself into the ground. They were trying to get it away before fire reached it, causing it to go off.[46]

More up to date, NBC's Chet Huntley started a lengthy, albeit confused, wrap-up, including the wire-service-reported penetration of the embassy by Vietcong commandos:

The Vietcong seized part of the United States Embassy in Saigon early Wednesday Vietnam time. Snipers are in buildings and on rooftops near the embassy and are firing on American personnel inside the compound. Twenty suicide commandos are reported to be holding the first floor of the embassy.[47] The attack on the embassy and other key installations in

Saigon, at Tan Son Nhut air base and Bien Hoa, north of Saigon, came as the climax to the enemy's biggest and most highly coordinated offensive of the war. There was no immediate report of allied casualties in Saigon but they are believed to be high. The attacks came as thousands of civilians were celebrating the Lunar New Year, and at times it was impossible to distinguish the explosion of mortar shells and small-arms fire from those of the firecrackers the celebrants were setting off.[48]

Guerrillas invaded the grounds of the United States Embassy and some were still there toward daybreak. They wrecked the gates of Independence Palace, where President Thieu has his offices.[49] They raided headquarters of South Vietnam's Chiefs of Staff and Navy and struck officers' billets in the area around Tan Son Nhut Airport.

In Washington, a White House spokesman called the Saigon assault "pretty serious" and indicated it had not ended.

The enemy offensive began with an attack on Da Nang. At least $15 million worth of fighter airplanes were destroyed and many others damaged.[50] Then the enemy struck at Hoi An, Kontum, Pleiku, Tuy Hoa, Ban Me Thuot, and Nha Trang. Fighting still is going on in a half-dozen of those cities.[51]

Bob Young of ABC left it to Frank Reynolds, his White House man, to explain what had happened:

Young: The massive communist strikes in South Vietnam, coupled with the *Pueblo* incident, kept the lights burning at the White House for most of the night. ABC's Frank Reynolds reports on how the President's day has been.

Reynolds: As of now, on the basis of information available here, the fighting in Saigon is not considered a major military effort by the communists actually to seize the capital or topple the government. Rather, it is regarded as part of a nationwide campaign of terrorism and guerrilla warfare, all timed to coincide with the big push that is expected up north near Khe Sanh.

The embassy in Saigon has maintained communications with Washington, and there is no real fear at the White House that a first-rate disaster may be in the works in the Vietnamese capital. There is, however, a grim realization that the United States is in for a very rough time through all of Vietnam in the next few days and weeks.

The last report the President had directly from General Westmoreland was delivered early this morning. The General expressed his usual confidence that American forces are ready and will be able to take care of the situation. Nevertheless, there is *no point in denying*[52] the genuine concern here, not that American forces may suffer a major military defeat, but that the price that almost certainly will be paid may be very, very high.[53]

To recapitulate, the initial accounts of the Tet attacks against Saigon were about what one would expect. The U.S. Embassy bulked large in the stories produced by Americans because: (1) it was American, (2) it was close at hand, and (3) it was dramatic—the action, begun in darkness, lasted six hours before it was resolved.

As always, the wire services were under intense competitive pressure to be first with "hard," vivid accounts. Hence the willingness of, first, AP, then UPI, to throw caution aside, to convey to the reader (and the clients' news editors) at home a highly misleading sense of certainty about the available "facts," and to add a little artificial flavor (fighting through the "carpeted offices") in bulletin after bulletin. Possibly because it was first at the embassy scene, the AP was extremely slow to clarify its initial accounts, even after its man on the scene (Arnett) did so. The UPI was quicker to correct the first impression—in time for east-coast afternoon papers of January 31, if not the evening TV news shows of January 30.

The *Times*'s and *Post*'s sins were mostly those of omission. Each newspaper's deskmen at home failed to add the full version of Westmoreland's brief account of the embassy fight, as reported by AP, to the truncated versions hastily supplied by their own Saigon staffers. There was ample time to do so for final editions. The *Post*—in contrast to the *Times* and the wire services—also failed to publish the second "official" version of the embassy action, namely the State Department's denial in Washington that the chancery had been penetrated by the Vietcong sappers. Furthermore, the *Post* (unlike the *Times*) included no warning to the reader that all returns were not yet in. The *Times* (Mohr) explicitly set the record straight on February 2; the *Post* never did.

Arnett and other Saigon newsmen were later to argue that the Administration's focus on the question of Vietcong penetration of the chancery was overreaction to a minor wire-service error. Yet, it can also be argued that the very emphasis placed by the wires (and others) on the embassy attack put a premium on accurate portrayal of events there, and on prompt correction of first reports; there is a vast difference between seizing an objective and dying in a bold but abortive effort to do so. Hanoi did not claim a victory—psychological, symbolic, or otherwise—at the embassy. But American newsmen were quick to award Hanoi a major "psychological" triumph there, if only because they—the newsmen—and Lyndon B. Johnson had been taken by surprise. It was a portent of journalistic reactions to come.

4

Military Victory or Defeat for Hanoi?

As we have seen, there is fairly broad agreement among historians today that Hanoi suffered a military setback during the 1968 Tet offensive. The communists, after a half-year's planning and preparation, had switched their strategy, struck for the cities, and achieved tactical surprise against the holidaying South Vietnamese and the overconfident U.S. command. Yet, the resulting confusion, damage, and casualties among the allied forces and South Vietnamese civilians, while unprecedented, were not crippling. Moreover, it seems that Hanoi may have been even more badly informed and overconfident than the allies prior to Tet. The communist commanders made a sizable military commitment to the urban offensive. They not only utilized their local force battalions, but also surfaced key Vietcong cadres, exposing experienced, hard-to-replace guerrillas to heavy losses. But to little effect. The communist field commanders were unable to *exploit* either the surprise they achieved or local allied weakness (even at Hue). They failed to crack or cripple ARVN, to hold the urban centers, or to shake apart the Thieu-Ky "puppet regime."

The communists initially bombarded or attempted to invade 36 of 44 province capitals, 64 of 242 district capitals, and even such hitherto peaceful areas as Da Lat, Vietnam's mountain resort and site of ARVN's Military Academy.[1] To an extent that few newsmen realized on January 31–February 1, it was touch-and-go in a dozen places (e.g., Saigon's Tan Son Nhut Airfield area, Hue, My Tho, Vinh Long, Ben Tre, Kontum, Quang Tri), as Gen. Earle Wheeler was privately to note later.[2] U.S. troops were rushed to reinforce ARVN units fighting at half strength due to grossly ill-timed Tet holiday leaves. But by February 4, the enemy surge had ebbed except in greater Saigon, Hue, Da Lat, and Phan Thiet. By February 25, with the recapture of Hue, *the city fighting was finally over.* Thereafter, amid continued "insecurity" in the hinterland and along the highways, recovery slowly began. Only at Khe Sanh, the isolated Marine base close to Laos, did the enemy sustain his pressure, and even there he began to pull out in mid-March.

Thus, in its military aspects, is the Tet battle seen in retrospect. No one knows for certain what Hanoi's real—as opposed to announced—goals were. Historians have some strong indications in captured documents and defectors' statements that North Vietnamese leaders rapidly recognized the "Great Offensive's" failure to score decisive military successes. On February 1, COSVN (the communist command group for southern South Vietnam) ordered units to fight hard in "disputed areas" (e.g., Saigon's suburbs), but not to start new actions, and to avoid assaults on American positions. On February 21, COSVN ordered a pullback of the battered battalions still fighting close to the cities, and a switch to war on the cheap—harassing mortar and rocket fire and sapper raids. (Ironically, these last orders were issued just as MACV officers gave their most pessimistic briefings, and the spirits of newsmen in Saigon, still-embattled Hue, and encircled Khe Sanh were at their lowest ebb.)[3]

Westmoreland's Evaluation

The enemy's initial failure to exploit surprise in the cities was immediately perceived as irretrievable by Westmoreland (although he worried about northern I Corps and the possible threat from uncommitted enemy forces north of Saigon). He saw Hanoi's initiative—its rash decision to fight a conventional war in the open, on American terms—as an unprecedented opportunity for U.S. forces to inflict heavy, possibly irreplaceable losses on the communist forces. Already, on January 31, an hour or so after the U.S. Embassy compound had been secured, he said as much to agitated officials in Washington. Standing on the blood-spattered lawn of the embassy compound, as dead Vietcong sappers were being carried away, he repeated his assurances to newsmen: "The enemy exposed himself . . . and he suffered great casualties. . . . As soon as President Thieu, with our agreement, called off the truce, American troops went on the offensive and pursued the enemy aggressively."[4]

As Don Oberdorfer was later to recall, "The reporters could hardly believe their ears. Westmoreland was standing in the ruins and saying everything was great."[5] This writer was among those who listened politely, envying the General his *sang-froid*. We walked away, shaking our heads. To the newsmen, the sappers' raid on the embassy was a dramatic, humiliating blow at the symbol of the entire U.S. presence in Vietnam. How could Westmoreland persist in his old optimism?

Later, Gen. Bruce Clarke (USA-Ret.) visited Vietnam during the Tet offensive and wrote that the foe "took the battle down around the Caravelle Hotel and, so, from the standpoint of the average reporter over there, it was the acorn that fell on the chicken's head and it said 'The sky is falling!' "[6]

There is no question that newsmen, especially those correspondents whose prior exposure to gunfire was minimal, were shaken. And it was widely believed—or at least reported—that this "psychological" impact was shared by the average South Vietnamese. Moreover, quick claims of enemy failure by Westmoreland had been heard before, notably during the Administration's 1967 progress campaign. At Dak To, Con Thien, and Loc Ninh, the enemy had been "defeated," yet, somehow, the results were inconclusive: the NVA apparently absorbed its heavy losses and, after inflicting highly publicized casualties on the Americans, faded into the background and continued to fight the war.[7] Thus, at Tet, the sudden, unprecedented exposure of the Vietcong to U.S. firepower was not widely perceived as significant.

Newsmen's skepticism was fed also by two major public relations errors on the part of MACV. First, optimistic early descriptions at the "Five O'Clock Follies" of the combat situation in Saigon and at Hue (based on misleading field reports from U.S. senior advisors) denied the realities observed by newsmen on the scene. Second, the U.S. command gave soaring statistics on enemy casualties. Each day a cumulative total for the post-January 30 period was announced. MACV ended this practice on February 10 (having reached a cumulative total of 27,706); later, enemy losses were put at 30,000, and weapons captured for the entire month of February at 16,000.[8]

Westmoreland was later to defend the casualty estimates; he and other MACV officials habitually argued that, in any event, enemy losses due to U.S. air strikes and artillery were understated. However, especially at Tet, it was difficult for newsmen—familiar with the normal institutional tendency to try to "look good," and aware of the state of communications and of the particularly thick fog of battle in early February—to accept the MACV figures. Moreover, on the basis of past experience in the field, some reporters knew the pressure on U.S. company and battalion commanders for "body counts," and the cynicism with which such counts, often made up on the spot, were reported by radio to the next higher headquarters. Typical of the reactions in print was a New York *Times* story that commented: "The assertion today that more than 10,000 of the enemy had died in the outbreaks was viewed with reserve by some observers [i.e., newsmen]."[9] In the same day's issue, Tom Buckley reiterated the idea: "The enemy death toll for three days was tabulated at 5,800 men, as against 535 allied dead. If correct, the figure on enemy losses would equal the toll usually claimed for three weeks of fighting."[10] Lee Lescaze wrote in the Washington *Post:* "The casualty figures put out by the allies in the current communist offensive are thrown into question by the incredibly favorable ratios claimed and by the assertion of precise figures in battles for which even the most general of other details are lacking."[11]

In addition, at Tet as in the past, it was widely assumed by newsmen in Saigon (and Washington) that, in any case, *losses did not matter* to Hanoi, and hence did not affect enemy plans. *Newsweek* speculated that "while Hanoi could now afford to fight and talk simultaneously, the United States has too weak a hand to do so. Before Washington can even consider going to the conference table, in fact, it must first insure that its military position in Vietnam is not further eroded."[12] *Time* cited the enemy losses, but suggested they were in part a good investment: "Giap took losses that most other states' armies would consider unacceptable. . . . On the other hand, Giap scored some very substantial gains."[13]

In fact, however, as was observable at Tet, Hanoi showed a mixture of recklessness and extreme caution in expending troops. After the first wave of attacks on January 30–31 had passed, NVA/VC troops tried to hold their positions around many cities, notably Saigon, where fighting in the suburbs lasted three weeks. They tried to reach Da Nang until February 10. They were able to fire mortars and rockets at as many as two dozen towns in a single night, February 17–18, providing wire services with an opportunity to sound the alarm with a "second-wave offensive." They held on to Hue for three weeks. But they did not mount repeated "human-wave" ground attacks heedless of cost. Khe Sanh was no exception. And assaults on U.S. firebases or base camps elsewhere were rare at Tet. This caution was a marked departure from costly Vietminh offensive tactics during the latter years of the war with the French.[14] But few newsmen—and few of their middle-echelon American sources in Vietnam—perceived this. The focus was on what the "wily Giap" would do next.

The Official Appraisal

Totting up alleged enemy casualties, U.S. and South Vietnamese officialdom also claimed tactical military defeats for the foe. Their descriptions varied. There were both some realistic appraisals and some determinedly euphoric ones. Thieu, as translated by the AP, issued perhaps the most sweeping and euphoric of the early statements as he declared martial law: "The communists' general offensive attempt has been completely foiled."[15]

Westmoreland, discussing the embassy fight, said the enemy's plans had run "afoul" on January 31. At the JUSPAO auditorium next day (Saigon time), he outlined what he saw as the enemy's three-phase "go for broke" strategy. He said the enemy anti-city attacks "may be running out of steam,"[16] and claimed heavy enemy losses. But he did not claim "victory" or a "last gasp." He saw more heavy fighting. He predicted again that it would come in the north, although this time without citing the anti-city attacks as a "diversion" from northern I Corps, and got page-one headlines on February 2 in both the New York *Times* ("Offensive Is Running 'Out of Steam,' Says Westmoreland") and in the Washington *Post* ("Clashes Persist in Viet Cities; General Warns of DMZ Push").

There were also other official assessments in Saigon of the Tet offensive's military significance, as Zorthian and Brig. Gen. Winant Sidle mustered the MACV generals for press briefings. These briefings, it should be noted, concentrated on what was closest to newsmen's immediate interests: current and future "threats," not whether the anti-cities drive was a "victory" or "defeat." On February 1, following Westmoreland, Lieutenant General Weyand, widely respected among newsmen, described the enemy's moves in the Saigon area in detail, claimed an initial enemy military defeat, and suggested that the foe was paying a heavy price for any "psychological" gains. But Weyand was one of the few high-ranking U.S. officials who warned the public against quick final judgment, a warning that ran against all U.S. journalistic (or political) instincts. The warning, along with much of Weyand's detail, was ignored by the media, in part because there was just too much else to file that day. Said Weyand:

> My position . . . has been for the last month or two that we will not know what the true picture is possibly until May or June. . . . Have we hurt [the enemy] as bad as we think we have? We'll be able to see more clearly then—does he have the support of the people? Do these political or psychological attacks have a lasting effect upon the people? Or are they interpreting this as an act of desperation and further evidence of a form that they would reject? I just don't think at this point I really have the knowledge to give you anything worthwhile on that. If I can't do it by May or June, then I'll be disappointed.

Perhaps the most refreshing appraisal came on February 3 from Westmoreland's COC director, Brig. Gen. John Chaisson, who, while highly overoptimistic about clearing Hue "in the next day or so," told newsmen:

> It's been a week of surprises. I think the Vietcong surprised us with their attacks and I must confess I'm surprised to find myself up here this afternoon. We have been faced this past week with a real battle. There's no sense in ducking it, there's no sense in hiding it. . . .
> I've got to give 'em credit for having engineered and planned a very successful offensive, in its initial phases. It was surprisingly well-coordinated, it was surprisingly intensive, and I think in conducting it [the enemy] showed a surprising amount of audacity because he had put an awful lot of his goods up on the table in this battle. Now it's up to us to see what we can do about cleaning the table.
> Q.: You started off by saying this was a week of surprises. What was the intelligence?
> A.: Well, . . . I'm not the intelligence man, . . . but as I read the intelligence it did not indicate that we were going to have any such massive spread of attacks as this . . . we were quite confident that something would happen around the Tet period—documents and other reasons led us to believe that. . . . but . . . our intelligence at least never unfolded to me any panorama of attacks such as happened this week.

Next day (Sunday, February 4), Maj. Gen. Philip Davidson, MACV J-2 (intelligence chief), and the man blamed for the Tet surprise, told newsmen at yet another JUSPAO briefing how he had

At the United States Mission yesterday, a senior official assessed the enemy offensive in a news conference under "background" rules—meaning that he could not be quoted by name in news accounts. He suggested that the Vietcong had not only suffered a "substantial military defeat" but might also have failed in their objective of inciting a "general uprising" among the populations of the 35 cities and towns that were attacked. . . .

Although the senior official insisted that the week's events amounted to both a military and a political victory for the Saigon government, he acknowledged that *the victory* had created "some difficulties" and would "slow the pacification effort until security is restored."

The assessment of the engagements as an allied victory, the official went on, *was based on the comparative casualty figures.* These have been gathered for the most part by South Vietnamese officers and made public, contrary to custom, by the American command.

The tally, as of yesterday morning, was 12,704 enemy soldiers killed, or about a third of the total attacking force. On the accepted minimum estimate of two men wounded for each man killed, the casualty report would indicate that the entire Vietcong force had been put out of action.[18]

Here, at its most obvious, was the "carryover" effect of MACV emphasis on enemy loss, and of earlier U.S. optimism. Besides, newsmen asked, how did Bunker know so much, so soon? The Ambassador's assessment of enemy failure *in Vietnam* has since been echoed by most historians; but it was poorly timed in press terms.

The *Post* handled the Bunker briefing in a Lescaze piece from Saigon paired with a wire-service battle wrap-up. Well down in the story, the senior U.S. official was reported as citing heavy enemy losses. In addition it was noted that: "The senior U.S. Mission officials said that this week's attacks did not change their estimate that steady, unspectacular progress is being made by the allies in Vietnam. 'I don't think that because you have this kind of attack that you have a failure,' one said."[19]

In Washington, while the President and his subordinates also spoke up about the enemy's lack of military success, they made few "victory" claims. On February 1, at a White House Medal of Honor ceremony, President Johnson finally broke his 48-hour silence on the Tet offensive to say "the enemy will fail again and again [because] we Americans will never yield." Ever sensitive to the media, he called a surprise press conference (thus precluding TV) at the White House on Friday morning, February 2. He made no "blood, sweat and tears" speech, nor did he radiate optimism or confidence. He looked weary.

The President was occasionally defensive, with a jibe or two at the would-be military pundits, constant referrals to Westmoreland and the military as sources of his information, an indirect and misleading rebuttal of charges that MACV had been taken by surprise, and derisory remarks about Hanoi's claims of victory. The give-and-take showed Johnson's cautious mood:

Q.: Mr. President, do you believe, sir, their winter-spring offensive and their call for an uprising and their attempt to impose a coalition government is based on their belief that they are taking military punishment that they cannot sustain for a long time? In short, sir, are we still winning the war?

The President: I think I see nothing in the developments that would indicate that the evaluation that I have had of this situation throughout the month should be changed.[20]

I do think that the second phase is imminent. What we expected is upon us. We have gone through the first phase. If it comes out as expected, I think I can give you a better answer to your question when it is over with.

I don't want to prophesy on what is going to happen, or why. We feel reasonably sure of our strength. . . .

I am not a great strategist and tactician. I know that you are not. Let us assume that the best figures we can have are from our responsible military commanders. They say 10,000 died and we lost 249 and the South Vietnamese lost 500. That doesn't look like a communist victory. I can count. It looks like somebody has paid a very dear price for the temporary encouragement that some of our enemies had.

We have approximately 5,900 planes and have lost 38 completely destroyed. We lost 100-odd that were damaged and have to be repaired. Maybe Secretary McNamara will fly in 150 shortly.

Is that a great enemy victory?

. . . .

We have known for several months, now, that the communists planned a massive winter-spring offensive. We have detailed information on Ho Chi Minh's order governing that offensive. . . .[21]

AP disseminated two leads on the conference, differing considerably in tone. Its first bulletin focused partly on what Johnson did not say:

President Johnson reported today that the military phase of the communist offensives in Vietnam have failed but he avoided saying that *the war is being won.*

Johnson told reporters, too, that he does not believe the Vietnamese
Reds have racked up a psychological victory. . . .[22]

Its night lead was put out five hours later:

President Johnson portrayed as a failure Friday what he termed the
general uprising of Vietnamese communists. He said it may mean some
adjustments but no change in basic strategy for the United States and no
increase in combat troops at this time.

The President told a quickly called news conference he does not believe the communists have scored a psychological victory, either. . . .

The President got page-one headlines next day in the Washington
Post:

LBJ CALLS UPRISING FAILURE
VIETCONG HOLDING ON IN HUE;
THIEU ASKS MORE BOMBING
PRESIDENT SEES REPULSE OF NEW DRIVE

and in the New York *Times:*

PRESIDENT TERMS U.S. READY
FOR A PUSH BY ENEMY AT KHE SANH

Each newspaper also printed a full transcript of the conference.

Oddly enough, neither Westmoreland's promise, on February 1, of
more hard fighting nor Johnson's caution prevented critics from alleg-
ing that the Administration was claiming a desperate last push on the
part of the foe. One example was James Reston's statement in his
column that the "latest propaganda line [is] that we are now seeing
the enemy's 'last gasp.' "[23] Yet no Administration figure publicly
mentioned a "last-gasp" effort. Moreover, the President denied assertions that MACV had reported enemy morale to be on the decline.[24]

Meanwhile, Defense Secretary McNamara and Gen. Earle Wheeler
were on Capitol Hill on February 1 and 2 to testify before the Senate
Armed Services Committee. Interviewed by the press after the first
day's session, both were crisply optimistic:

Q.: Mr. Secretary, there's a great deal of unrest over the events of the
past few days, particularly the events in Vietnam. How can you explain
the apparent lack of preparedness out there for guerrilla attacks of this
nature?

McNamara [ignoring the question]: First, let me comment on what may be the enemy's objective in this current series of attacks in South Vietnam. I think they may be two. He may be trying to inflict on the South Vietnamese, the U.S., and allied forces a severe military defeat. We believe we are well prepared for that.

. . . Or, alternatively, in the event that such an objective eludes him, he may be seeking to achieve a substantial psychological or propaganda victory. . . . General Wheeler talked to General Westmoreland by telephone just an hour before we came to this Committee session. Perhaps he would like to elaborate on that.

Wheeler: General Westmoreland informed me that he estimated the objectives of the enemy were essentially as outlined by Secretary McNamara. He added that the enemy had engaged in what he characterized as suicidal efforts to gain objectives set for them, that their losses have been extremely heavy. He estimates, or his commanders estimate, that [the communists] have lost in the last three days some 6,200 men killed. We, too, have suffered some losses, but theirs have been ten times greater than ours.

Q.: What have ours been—600?

Wheeler: A little over 500. As of right now, [the] report on losses of U.S. men killed is 193. The enemy effort has not been successful. He has not forced General Westmoreland to draw troops from the critical Khe Sanh-DMZ area; he has not succeeded in overrunning and holding a major Vietnamese city; he has not succeeded in achieving a military success which in my judgment, or General Westmoreland's, is worth the cost to him.[25]

. . . .

Wheeler: General Westmoreland figures that [the communists] have the capability for keeping this up possibly for another couple of days with diminishing activity. . . .[26]

During a second interview the following day, McNamara commented: "We think it's quite unlikely that [the enemy] can achieve his first objective, which we believe to be the infliction of a severe military defeat on the South Vietnamese and allied forces." In the same interview, General Wheeler—far more optimistic at this point than anyone else—denied any "intelligence failure" and suggested that the enemy employed "desperation tactics" in the cities.[27]

At White House urging, McNamara and Secretary of State Rusk went on "Meet the Press" on Sunday, February 4, for another exposition of Administration reaction. McNamara was sharply challenged by newsmen Elie Abel and Lawrence E. Spivak, both apparently deeply impressed by the drama of the Tet attacks:

Abel: Mr. Secretary, are you telling us the fact that the Vietcong after all these years were able to temporarily at least *grab control* [*sic*] *of some twenty-odd provincial capitals and the city of Saigon,* are you telling us that this has no military meaning at all?

McNamara: No, certainly not. . . . [But] the North Vietnamese and the Vietcong have not accomplished either one of their major objectives, either to ignite a general uprising or to force a diversion of the troops which the South Vietnamese and the United States have moved into the northern areas of South Vietnam, anticipating a major attack. Vietcong and North Vietnamese have suffered very heavy penalties in terms of losses of weapons and losses of men in the past several days. They have of course dealt a very heavy blow to many of the cities of South Vietnam. . . .

Spivak: Mr. Secretary, one more question. The President described the recent attack against South Vietnam as a *complete* failure as a military movement. That's not the impression any of us get from the press reports. Would you describe that as a complete failure?

McNamara: Well, I think the President pointed out that this was but the first act of a three-act play. And we can't forecast the second and third scenes at the present time.

The following day, the lead of Peter Grose's *Times* story played up not what had been said about Tet, but Rusk's disclosure of U.S. "months-long diplomatic soundings aimed at starting peace talks," accompanied by a minor bombing curtailment around Hanoi. AP and the *Post* did likewise.

On February 5, General Wheeler was again interviewed on Capitol Hill. It is notable that he did not claim the pre-Tet situation had been restored:

Q.: Do you have the progress report—what is going on this morning —from Saigon?

Wheeler: I talked to General Westmoreland at about 9:15 this morning. . . . There was an attack last night by some 200–300 North Vietnamese against Hill 861, which is one of the outer defenses of the Khe Sanh perimeter. . . . It was repulsed by Marines there with substantial losses to the attackers. . . . In Saigon, General Westmoreland stated that apparently *some of the fragmented groups of infiltrators have congregated in the Cholon area,* which is the Chinese quarter of Saigon, and they are now being cleared out by the ARVN forces who located them. [Emphasis added.]

On February 14, Wheeler cautiously added things up, saying: "Well, there are pluses and minuses, as there always are in any military action. On the minus side, the South Vietnamese to date have lost something over 2,000 killed. . . . On the other hand they *have defeated the enemy*.[28]

On February 25, after the recapture of Hue, in the AP interview already noted, Westmoreland said in public what in essence he had been telling Washington all along: The enemy thrust was a go-for-broke effort, and Hanoi had suffered a "military defeat." The General said: "I liken the recent Tet offensive by the leadership in Hanoi to the Battle of the Bulge in World War II. By committing a large share of his communist forces to a major offensive, he achieved some tactical surprise. This offensive has required us to react and to modify our plans in order to take advantage of the opportunity to inflict heavy casualties upon him. Although the enemy has achieved some temporary psychological advantage, he suffered a military defeat."

In sum, the Administration's statements concerning overall enemy failure were less euphoric than some critics later claimed. However, Wheeler's translations of his Tet radio-telephone conversations with General Westmoreland, notably with respect to the enemy's "desperation" and his strength in Saigon, conveyed an optimism unjustified by the perceivable facts. Some of the MACV communiqués and the inflated enemy casualty figures in February were wide of the mark.

Lyndon Johnson's argument that U.S. forces had not been taken by surprise was a misleading half-truth. But most of the official spokesmen, including the President, prudently promised more fighting, more bloodshed. There were many claims of enemy "failure," but few of allied "victory"—an important distinction not made in most of the commentary published out of a shaken Washington.

Media Response

Initially, as we have seen, the media reported little on enemy military success or failure except in terms of "positive" statements by Washington and Saigon, "negative" statements by Hanoi, and speculation that the allied statements were irrelevant or overoptimistic. Thereafter, as February went on, U.S. reporters in Vietnam by and large let slide the thorny question of a Vietcong victory or defeat in the cities. Newsmen were not inclined toward retrospection. They were preoccupied with possible future enemy thrusts and with continuing hard fighting in Khe Sanh, Hue, and Saigon. When they finally had a first look at some of the cities that had been cleared, notably in the Delta, they were more impressed by the damage wrought by U.S. firepower than by the fact that the enemy had been bloodily ejected.

However, several detailed "after-action" reports, notably in the New York *Times* and Washington *Post,* described the "military" results of the fighting. The few other analyses that were published did not dwell on enemy losses and denigrated ARVN's role. On February 21, for example, AP passed along Peter Arnett's analysis covering many aspects of the Tet urban offensive ("three weeks of carnage"). It said: "Most Vietnamese fixed positions held out, with troops in many cities preferring to yield public buildings such as radio stations and provincial offices—rather than move out from their heavily defended bunkers. The Hue armory with its stock of 1,000 M-16 rifles and other weapons fell without a shot being fired, said Americans in that city. In most cities, U.S. firepower saved the day."[29]

Some newsmen were as loath as General Weyand to try to tot up a net score on any aspect of the Tet fighting, especially since MACV continued to warn of a possible "second wave" throughout February. Reacting to clippings sent from home, the *Post* Saigon bureau, for example, cabled the foreign desk on February 17: "DEFINITIVE PICTURE TET RESULTS YET TO EMERGE SO WARN AGAINST TAKING ANYBODY'S SCORECARD TOO QUICKLY."

Nevertheless, many did not wait: They told the U.S. audience that the worst was yet to come, that the enemy had won a major "psychological" victory among the South Vietnamese, a victory which by implication made military results irrelevant. It was not until the U.S. command *announced* the allies' week-old "Resolved to Win" offensive in the area around Saigon on March 15 that wire-service war wrap-ups and other accounts began to suggest that enemy pressure had eased around the cities, and that American and ARVN forces had regained the initiative.

Television "Specials": Portraits of Havoc

Initially, the networks cast doubt on official claims, but avoided rigid analysis. NBC presented a "special" on February 1 showing the impact of the attacks and dismissing enemy losses. Robert Goralski at the Pentagon concluded the broadcast:

Even the American military most grudgingly admired what the Vietcong were able to do and what they had seized. The *perfectly timed* attacks again will be remembered a lot longer than the less dramatic but hard-fought American victories of late.

Pentagon officials believe the Vietcong paid dearly for their acts of rampant terrorism, but surely the communist leaders *must feel they were worth it.* They do not appear to be final acts of desperation. . . .

. . . The communists may not be winning the war, as the Pentagon claims, but they don't seem to be losing it either.[30]

ABC commentator Joseph C. Harsch (who also worked for the *Christian Science Monitor*) in his February 1 analysis joined in the charges that the Administration was putting out a "last gasp" theory:

There's another side to the story, what government officials say in private bears little resemblance to the highly orchestrated public good cheer. . . .

For public consumption the enemy is short of manpower, near the end of his rope, and has risked the last desperate throw of the dice just before giving up. But in fact, best estimates here are that the enemy has not yet, and probably never will, run out of enough manpower to keep his effort going.

What this city yearns for is someone like a Winston Churchill, who would admit frankly the fact that after two years of massive American military intervention in Vietnam, the enemy has been able to mount and to launch by far the biggest and boldest and most sophisticated offensive of the whole war.

Maybe it is the last wild throw of the dice; let us profoundly hope so. But it is also the exact opposite of what American leaders have, for months, been leading us to expect.[31]

And CBS's Jeff Gralnick, reporting after a look at Hue from a spotter plane, said the battle showed that "the Vietcong proved they could take and hold almost any area they chose. An intelligence officer said . . . while it was still uncertain what, if anything, the Vietcong would do during this New Year period, that if they were in this for political gain rather than military victory, an attack on Hue, to take it and hold it for even six to twelve hours, would be a tremendous triumph. And this they have done."[32]

In New York, Walter Cronkite, on the "CBS Evening News," was quick to call the score for that network—largely from wire-service dispatches or official claims. He began on January 31, the day after the first TV reports of the attacks: "The tide apparently is turning in the Vietcong's stunning series of coordinated attacks on cities and military strongholds throughout South Vietnam, but the fighting still goes on." But the tide was not turning the evening of February 1, after the Westmoreland briefing to newsmen in Saigon. Said Cronkite: "The communists have carried their offensive against South Vietnam's population centers into its fourth day. Bitter fighting continues in many sections of the country." The next day, February 2, presumably referring to Thieu's statement about enemy defeat, Cronkite commented: "The allies proclaimed today that they have broken the back of the five-day-old communist offensive in South Vietnam, but dispatches out of that pathetic country tell a somewhat different story."

On his February 14 broadcast, made from Saigon less than a week after his arrival there, Cronkite quickly assessed the "impact of the recent communist offensive." He cited conversations with U.S. officials and "nongovernment Vietnamese," reporting that "first, and simplest, the Vietcong suffered a military defeat," while ARVN held up. But then, as later, he took a dim view of the South Vietnamese government, which, he suggested, might now be riven by *coups d'état.* "Such discord here in the south," he said, "would strengthen the resolve in the north, and put any hope of negotiations and the war's end further in the future. And that, perhaps, is the *real meaning* of the Tet offensive," Cronkite concluded, "military defeat" notwithstanding. [Emphasis added.]

This exclusive analysis was followed 13 days later—after Cronkite's return to the United States—by his much publicized half-hour CBS "special" on the war. He cast doubt on official estimates of enemy losses and civilian damage. He described the ruins of Hue and the refugees. He termed pacification a "casualty" of the offensive. He suggested that a prompt response by the South Vietnamese government could "salvage a measure of victory from *defeat,*" but said such reaction was unlikely. He summed up:

It seems now more certain than ever that the bloody experience of Vietnam is to end in a stalemate. . . .

On the off chance that military and political analysts are right, in the next few months we must test the enemy's intentions, in case this is indeed his last big gasp before negotiations. But it is increasingly clear to this reporter that the only rational way out then will be to negotiate, not as victors, but as an honorable people who lived up to their pledge to defend democracy, and did the best they could.[33]

In effect, Cronkite seemed to say, the ruins, the refugees, the disruption of pacification that came at Tet, added up to a defeat for the allies that would force President Johnson to the negotiating table. His hurried tour of Vietnam (Hue, Saigon) had shocked the commentator.[34] Only the darkest clouds hung over his show that night, and on most nights thereafter.

On March 10, NBC presented an hour-long Frank McGee special report entitled "Vietnam: A New Year . . . A New War." A counterpart to Cronkite's special report, it was a more dramatic show, focusing on Vietcong soldiers (who were presented, in contrast to the ARVN, as "ready and willing to die"), the ruinous aftermath of the Tet attacks, and the peril to Khe Sanh. Howard Tuckner, home from Vietnam, provided commentary: "Children knew fear . . . saw fighting . . . and murder in cold blood. Saigon was once a beautiful city filled with beautiful people . . . there's not as much of Saigon now as there once was." Who won the battle of Saigon? "Militarily the allies won," said Tuckner. "They held the city. Psychologically, the Vietcong won. They got into the capital in force."

McGee concluded with a jab at the Saigon regime:

The cities are no longer secure; perhaps they never were. We *don't know what has happened to the rural pacification program because the rural areas are under communist control.* We can only imagine.

But if security was to be the forerunner of loyalty, then loyalty is further away than ever. And if loyalty was to provide the strength of government, the [Saigon] government is weaker than ever, though it still exists. From all this, we must conclude that the grand objective—the building of a free nation—*is not nearer, but further from realization.*

In short, the war, as the Administration has defined it, is being lost. [Emphasis added.]

Essentially, Cronkite and McGee (particularly the latter) described the Tet attacks in the emotive terms characteristic of much TV Tet coverage: gunfire, destruction, vast numbers of refugees and wounded GIs—and all, as ever, matched against prior Administration claims of progress. McGee and Cronkite did not wait for the fog to lift: The allies were not "victors," they were not "winning" but "losing."

Ironically, Cronkite's appraisal went on the air three days after Hue, at long last, had been retaken. McGee's "special" appeared just as allied troops were preparing for the catch-all "Resolved to Win" offensive. Enemy troops were pulling back, and some newsmen in Saigon, making tentative sallies out into the hinterland, were reporting that all was not lost.

The Newspapers: Minimizing Enemy "Failure"

Both the *Times* and *Post* contributed to the early surge of stories minimizing the *military* significance of enemy action. Hanson Baldwin of the New York *Times,* for example, on February 1 reported Pentagon speculation that, while enemy losses had been heavy, the foe's objectives had been psychological, not military, and were "focused squarely on public opinion in this country." The foe's prime "military effort," hampered by U.S. bombing, Baldwin said, was against the Marine base at Khe Sanh. It was a Pentagon view that quickly changed.

On the same day, Charles Mohr also cast doubt on American claims of enemy failure, stressing Hanoi's apparent psychological goals:

American officials asserted that the Vietcong had suffered immense casualties and had failed in their general offensive. But since the attacks were apparently meant primarily to achieve psychological effect, there was debate about their effectiveness.

. . . .

But some other officials said privately that they feared that the Vietcong show of strength, unprecedented in the war, would undermine public faith in the government's ability to maintain security.[35]

In the *Post*'s February 1 issue, Ward Just, reporting in Washington, added a Dienbienphu angle:

Official Washington reacted to the Vietcong assault on Saigon and a score of provincial capitals, airfields and towns with public confidence and assurances that the American command in Saigon had "advance information" on the timing of the raids.

But privately the atmosphere was "pretty grim," to quote one knowledgeable official. Even the toughest of the pessimists here had not thought the communists could mount so many offensives, with so many men.

Senator Mike Mansfield (D-Mont.), the Senate Majority Leader and a frequent critic of the Administration's war policy, said that "they've evidently chosen their own target areas, and have been able to penetrate, initially at least, all of them. . . ."

Elsewhere in the federal establishment, among officials familiar with Vietnam, there was widespread dismay. "It is a fantastic achievement for the Vietcong," said one official. "Although we ought to remember that they did not penetrate the embassy. . . ."

The general [unidentified] had no doubt that the allies could hold Khe Sanh, but he said that the strategic parallel with the 1954 battle [of Dienbienphu] was too obvious to be dismissed. Elsewhere in the Pentagon, a senior officer declared that the attacks on Saigon and the other cities represented a considerable symbolic defeat. "We have a real psychological and political problem on our hands," he said. . . .[36]

The *Post* also ran a page-one wire-service wrap-up on Hanoi's and other foreign reaction ("Ho Cheers Vietcong 'Victory' "), as well as the commentary of Washington columnist Joseph Kraft:

"The war in Vietnam is unwinnable and the longer it goes on the more the Americans, already badly overexposed, will be subjected to losses and humiliations, even in the places of maximum security. . . ."

. . . Hard as it may be, the important thing now is not to pick up the challenge and charge in head down. On the contrary, the true national interest is to adjust the American position to the bleak realities. . . .

At this time, under pressure from the other side, it is harder than ever to recognize the realities, and make adjustments. But unless the adjustments are made, unless this country adopts its military and its public diplomatic position to its truly limited objectives, then what has lately been happening in Saigon and elsewhere will be only a mild foretaste of the humiliations to come.[37]

Few analysts directly addressed the question of enemy military failure. Joseph Alsop, however, quickly did so:

We are already engulfed in another spate of warnings that all is hopeless in Vietnam because of the attack on the U.S. Embassy and the other Vietcong efforts in Saigon and other cities.

In reality, however, this flurry of Vietcong activities in urban centers will almost certainly prove to have just the opposite meaning in the end. The nearest parallel is probably the fruitless Japanese use of kamikaze pilots in the Second World War's final phase. . . .

It is certainly idiotic to go on talking about a war "with no end in sight," as so many do in this country, when the other side so obviously thinks (or fears) that a rather early end is in sight.[38]

Joseph Kraft four days later was to describe the question of military victory or defeat as "absurd." What Tet exposed, he said, was a Saigon government with "corrupt military authorities" and an unworthy army. The urban destruction by U.S. firepower explained why "so few [South Vietnamese] are actively aligned with this country." The Saigon government cannot "enlist the support of the local population." All this "does not prove that the United States has suffered a

military defeat," Kraft concluded, but it showed that the United
States should hold firm—not escalate—and move down the path to a
"negotiated settlement." Tet had proved, according to Kraft, that
American military power in Vietnam was unable to produce "useful
political results."[39]

The same thesis—the irrelevance of the military question, the inca-
pacity of the Thieu-Ky regime, and the enemy's closeness to the people which permitted the Tet surprise—was reflected, albeit hazily, by
the later CBS and NBC "specials." It was a convenient thesis; it
required no analysis of the battlefield, assumed average South Vietnamese reactions were those of American commentators, and conveyed the notion that the foe's chief goal was to provoke air attacks
by the allies on Hanoi's own forces in urban areas.

The *Post* also uncritically published Sir Robert Thompson's much-
quoted analysis from faraway London.[40] Only 12 days after the attacks, the former advisor to Diem compared the Tet offensive's
"effect" to that of the German panzer thrusts that brought on the
1940 fall of France in World War II. Thompson saw enemy losses as
"acceptable" to Hanoi. His (apocalyptic) article deepened the gloom
of many in Washington, including Pentagon civilians.

The *Post*'s Saigon bureau held off on any quick military assessments, but cast doubt on Westmoreland's (accurate) prognosis that
the urban thrusts had slackened. One example was this reporter's reference, after Westmoreland's February 1 briefing in Saigon, to his
similar pre-Tet statement: "On January 17, Westmoreland was
quoted by news services as saying that the communists 'seem to have
temporarily run out of steam' but that heavy fighting could be expected soon in the northern I Corps sector including the 5,000-man
Marine outpost at Khe Sanh. He did not then mention the possibility
of prior generalized attacks against Saigon and other heavily populated areas."[41]

In fact, as quoted by AP, Westmoreland, while "pointing north,"
left open the possibility of a "resurgence" of communist "initiatives"
elsewhere around Tet—a "resurgence" of the early January anti-cities
attacks—even if he did not specifically warn against attacks on Saigon. In short, this writer's reference was shaded (through haste,
shock, and a conviction that Westmoreland was still overly attentive
to I Corps) to make Westmoreland look a bit more surprised by Tet
than the AP quote and its context would have indicated.

On March 8, C. L. Sulzberger, the New York *Times*'s Paris-based columnist, provided a long-distance view, leaning heavily on a French analysis. "In a purely military sense," he wrote, "there has been evident deterioration in the U.S. position . . . [Westmoreland] requires reserves immediately." If these reserves were not forthcoming, he said, the allies in Vietnam "may be exposed to further serious *prestige* defeats."[42] Thus, Sulzberger shifted in mid-column from military to "psychological" defeat.

Shortly before Sulzberger wrote, Hue had been retaken. Khe Sanh, Westmoreland was suggesting, was no longer the enemy's prime target. U.S. bases were being harassed but not crippled, and the U.S. military had begun to recover from the disarray of Tet. Moreover, having received in late February six additional battalions to flesh out his forces up north, the General had already told Washington on March 3, and Saigon newsmen on March 6, that a coordinated allied offensive was in the works.

The News Magazines: Avoiding a Final Appraisal

In Saigon, William Rademaekers, *Time* bureau chief, wrote on February 8: "The enemy was hurt and hurt badly. . . . If the events of the last week could be measured on a military ruler, there is little doubt that the allies would be considered the victors." *Time*'s first post-attack issue (dated February 9, with General Giap on the cover) assumed Hanoi's "psychological" gains, described Giap's "tour de force," but calmly concluded:

Allied intelligence had predicted that there would be some attempted city attacks during Tet, but the size, the scale, and, above all, the careful planning and coordination of the actual assaults took the U.S. and South Vietnamese military by surprise. In that sense, and because they continued after five days of fighting to hang on to some of their targets, the communists undeniably won a *victory of sorts.* "This is real fighting on a battlefield," admitted Brig. Gen. John Chaisson, Westmoreland's combat operations coordinator for South Vietnam. The communist attack was, he said, "a very successful offensive. It was surprisingly well coordinated, surprisingly intensive, and launched with a surprising amount of audacity. . . ."

In the end, however, the communist victory may be classed as Pyrrhic. The allied command reported nearly 15,000 of the attackers killed. Even if the total is only half that—and some observers think that that may be the case when all the combat reports filed in the swirl of battle are crosschecked—it would still represent a huge bloodletting of the enemy's forces in South Vietnam. . . .[43]

Many of the attacking units, like the one that hit the U.S. Embassy, were *avowedly suicidal;*[44] few of them, even when they did seize towns or installations, managed to hold them for long. Some were promised reinforcements within 48 hours—and never got them—or were given food and ammunition for only five days. . . .[45]

Time did not touch explicitly on the matter again.

On February 10 Rademaekers began noting the "demoralizing effects" of the urban attacks, notably in "eroding people's confidence in the government." Few other newsmen in Saigon *guessed* otherwise at the time. On February 15, in a file to New York headquarters, he said that the foe had gained "a substantial victory" largely because the VC got into the cities.

In short, the *Time* bureau chief, like many others, was casting about for indications of lasting enemy "success" or "failure" that went beyond the shock of the first days' attacks. As February dragged on, like his competitors on *Newsweek* and, to a lesser degree, like the analysis-writers on the *Post,* the *Times,* and the networks, Rademaekers was to focus not on the military outcome of the city battles, but on the damage and the dire possibility of renewed enemy attacks. "The same allied *apparatchiki* who talk about the enemy 'hurting,' and 'his desperation,' find no difficulty in warning about 'second wave' capability," he wrote in a file to *Time* on February 18. The foe was "threatening massively" in I Corps, making "ominous moves" around Saigon, and "pinning down" allied units around Hue, he wrote on February 28, in an interpretation of MACV officials' background discussions of enemy "capabilities."

Newsweek's February 12 issue directly challenged official claims of enemy failure:

> Westmoreland and his commanders were clearly caught short by the scope and intensity of the raids. . . . And they *insisted* on reading the communists' objectives in strictly military—rather than political or psychological—terms.[46] Thus, by this reasoning, the enemy's heavy casualties and failure to hold most of the urban objectives he seized spelled defeat. The other side of the coin was far bleaker. . . .
>
> In Hue and elsewhere last week, the Vietcong showed that they could still be *devastatingly effective*—a lesson not lost on the people.[47]

The following week, with General Westmoreland on the cover,

Newsweek again dismissed Administration claims of enemy defeat, citing the "punctured" optimism of past Administration claims:

Both in Vietnam and in America [the enemy attacks] aroused searing doubts about U.S. strategy in the Vietnamese war and about the man entrusted with its execution—Gen. William Westmoreland. These doubts, however, did not appear to extend to the Administration, most of whose members continued to insist publicly that the enemy had suffered a major defeat. . . .

Many Americans thought that it represented the sort of "victory" the United States could ill afford. For one thing, U.S. casualties—920 killed and 4,560 wounded—were a record high for the war. But even that fact, painful as it was, did not disturb the U.S. psyche as much as the puncturing of countless official claims, made over a period of years, that the United States was winning. . . .[48]

As February and March went on, *Newsweek* turned its attention to the urban damage, notably in Hue, and to Khe Sanh. At the same time, in a rare attempt by the media to examine in detail the enemy's anti-cities effort, *Newsweek*'s Washington and Saigon bureaus furnished the raw material for a two-page analysis of Hanoi's military successes and fumbles.[49] *Newsweek* cited an abundance of fumbles. Nevertheless, its writer in New York concluded that "despite the fact that the communists did not achieve most of their [military] objectives, their offensive was far from a failure." Why? In answer, the magazine leaned heavily on Tet's adverse effect on U.S. public opinion, and emphasized the imponderables in Vietnam—the possible impact of allied troop withdrawals to defend the cities, leaving rural areas open to "communist encroachments," and the alleged loss of "battlefield initiative" (a favorite topic) by U.S. forces. To clinch its case for enemy success despite military failures, *Newsweek* quoted an anonymous "U.S. intelligence expert": " 'Personally,' [he said] . . . 'I'm discouraged,' " and predicted that more enemy offensives were coming.

In fact, had they looked farther afield than Khe Sanh, *Newsweek*'s editors could have seen that, by this time, the "battlefield initiative" was either with the Americans (as in III Corps) or shared by both sides (as in I Corps). The battered cities were clear, and U.S. troops were hard at work in the upper Delta. ARVN—whose performance was not even cited in the *Newsweek* analysis—was recruiting and recuperating from heavy casualties; its senior commanders, worried about more raids on the cities, were being prodded by an optimistic

Westmoreland to sally forth alongside the Americans and fill the
"vacuum" left in the countryside. By early March, the foe had pulled
back from most urban areas; the exact status of much rural territory
remained unknown. But *Newsweek* concentrated on Khe Sanh, where
the "action" was.

In retrospect, given the information then available, no newsman
was in a position during February and March 1968 to render an independent judgment on the question of whether the enemy's apparent
losses and observable (but rarely observed) tactical failures together
constituted a *significant* military setback. Such a judgment, like so
many others made at Tet, required not only familiarity with military
matters, but also a knowledge of Hanoi's real capabilities (a matter
of dispute among U.S. intelligence agencies), and even of the future.
One could only try to report what was happening on the ground and
what the cautious specialists (Westmoreland and field officers) were
saying about it, and then point out the observable, corroborative
facts, the inflated casualty figures, and the contrasts (the long and
bitter battle for Hue, the relatively rapid cleanup in Saigon). Editors
and reporters had to be willing to wait and see, and some were.

At home, also, and to a lesser extent in Saigon, U.S. leaders and
subordinates made broad public assessments that were intended,
as such crisis assessments are, to calm a surprised and alarmed U.S.
public. Read with care, however, these assessments were seldom euphoric. But they ran head-on into a credibility gap which doomed
them to unsympathetic interpretation by the media.

Except at Hue and Saigon, there were few hard facts available to
dispute the Administration's early military appraisal of the urban attacks. Thus, unable to contradict McNamara and Wheeler directly,
yet deeming it their duty to rebut official claims, many a newsman
and commentator quickly resorted to other means. They turned to
"psychoanalysis" of the South Vietnamese—or speculation as to who
"held the initiative"—to explain to their audiences why, once again,
the Administration was "wrong" and Hanoi had scored a meaningful
success in South Vietnam. At best, this was overwrought instant analysis; at worst, it was vengeful exploitation of a crisis. Historically, it
proved unfounded.

5
North Vietnamese Performance

One of the odd characteristics of American journalists is their tendency, on occasion, to vastly overrate their country's enemies. This has been particularly true in the case of wars fought with Asians. In World War II, for example, the Japanese were commonly described as natural jungle-fighters; in fact, Japanese soldiers, coming from a northern climate, suffered no less hardship in the jungles of New Guinea than did the Americans. The Communist Chinese in the Korean War were depicted as operating in "hordes," possessing inexhaustible manpower and fanatically eager to die for Mao; later it developed that the Chinese were stopped in 1951 by heavy losses and forced to retreat, with more than 20,000 of them preferring captivity to a hero's death on the battlefield.[1]

At Tet, the same tendency was apparent. Characterizations of enemy performance were numerous, but superficial and brief. Here again, the U.S. press was extremely short of competent, let alone expert, judges of either military affairs or the rapidly evolving complexities of the two Vietnams. There were few incentives for any journalist in 1968 to make the semi-scholarly effort of a Hanson Baldwin or a Bernard Fall. Moreover, despite a U.S. involvement in Vietnam going back to 1950, the American academic community was little better endowed, as Professor John K. Fairbank of Harvard once complained; there was much talk about Vietnam in Cambridge and Berkeley, but very little scholarly research.

Essentially, this chapter deals with the media's explicit treatment of: (1) Hanoi's own statements about the Tet offensive and (2) the enemy's performance—his planning, leadership, strategy, tactics, weaponry, morale, manpower, resources, logistics, and general ability to wage the war. As for the first, one may say that U.S. print media treatment of the foe's official statements was generous, if not always illuminating. In the New York *Times,* for example, during the first two weeks of the offensive, statements from Hanoi hailing its own successes at Tet got page-one coverage twice,[2] while inside the paper were 19 other "Hanoi" stories, mainly on North Vietnamese descriptions of successes and goals. The Washington *Post* was less generous: one Hanoi story on page one,[3] seven stories inside. *Time* ran a cover story on General Giap on February 9 ("Days of Death in Vietnam"). *Newsweek* pictured "GIs Routing Vietcong from Saigon Embassy" for its Tet cover ("The Vietcong's Week of Terror") on February 12, but inside wondered if Westmoreland hadn't fallen into "Giap's trap."

On the second count, one searches in vain through most of the media descriptions of the foe, even well into March 1968, for indications that the enemy's planning, tactics, execution, zeal, and weaponry were less than flawless. His ability to achieve "another Dienbienphu," his "lethal" mortars and rockets at Khe Sanh and elsewhere, his "suicide squads" defending Hue, his "willingness to die," his alleged "political" shrewdness in attacking the cities, his omnipresence, his inexhaustible manpower resources (since "losses meant nothing" to him) were breathlessly depicted, particularly on TV, and drawn as a contrast to America's unworthy allies, the South Vietnamese.[4] In short, even as they described the flaws and problems of the allies, the newsmen in Saigon and Washington by and large failed to examine the North Vietnamese and Vietcong with the same critical eye.

Some of the exaggeration was fostered by the frank expressions by American officials of respect for their foes and frustration with their allies—a recurrent phenomenon in U.S. military history. Some was also doubtless a subjective reaction to the Tet surprise, and to the greater degree of personal risk involved in reporting combat operations thereafter. And, perhaps, as in other phases of the Tet coverage, there was a desire to say an emphatic "I told you so" to the Administration, after months of broad official assertions that the enemy's morale was slipping, his plans had been thwarted, and Hanoi was "no longer winning."

In addition, the initial preoccupation of most newsmen—in terms of enemy performance—was not with evaluation, but with the apparent (or surmised) effects of Tet on the *allies*. Later, after the opening attacks, their concern and that of their editors back home shifted to "What next?" Predictions are far more appealing journalistically than is a second look, however illuminating, at what has just happened. And at Tet, this traditional bias was reinforced by personal anxiety, especially when the newsmen's home base of Saigon was under threat. Finally, another factor inhibiting reporting of countrywide enemy performance during Tet was the narrowness of media coverage, which was confined largely to Saigon, Hue, and Khe Sanh, and then only during the confusion of the actual fighting.[5]

Happily for the allies in February 1968, however, the "wily Giap" was less than omniscient. His subordinates' battlefield performance was often muddled; damage wrought by his Soviet- and Chinese-supplied weaponry was costly, nerve-wracking, and headline-making, but nowhere decisive; and North Vietnamese and Vietcong troops (sapper squads aside) often backed away when faced with determined resistance. Indeed, it can now be argued that Giap himself, after gaining a rare degree of tactical surprise, failed to exploit it, committing just enough troops (an estimated 84,000) to make good targets for allied firepower—and far more than enough to make headlines—but not enough in any one place at any one time to score decisively on the ground.

This general analysis is far easier to make now than it was during the gray days of February 1968, when MACV spoke of an imminent "second wave" and, determined not to be caught short again, named a half-dozen possible targets for enemy attack. Yet it was possible after the Tet offensive's first month to spot flaws in the North Vietnamese performance: their artillery fire against Khe Sanh was erratic in volume and accuracy,[6] and the 2nd North Vietnamese Division was tardy, thus doomed, in its drive on Da Nang.[7] And even those 19 brave sappers who got into the U.S. Embassy compound were unable to complete their mission. The enemy, *Newsweek* was almost alone in pointing out, was "plagued by the confusion that is characteristic of all military operations."[8] One example was the 26-day battle for Hue —the longest urban engagement of the offensive. What struck this reporter (mostly after that battle) was not only how tenaciously the NVA fought, but how erratically Hanoi's commanders took advantage of the military opportunities open to them. The Americans' Perfume River supply route was never blocked, nor was Hue methodically sealed off from reinforcement by helicopter or truck convoys. Interdiction efforts were intermittent, if costly to allied units engaged. The Highway One bridges were not blown up until well after allied relief forces had crossed them. Even as MACV at first grossly under-estimated enemy strength in Hue, so did Hanoi, after overrunning most of the city in six hours, fail to follow up by massing its forces to eliminate remaining allied strongholds and, most important, by seal-ing off the city. During the battle, Hanoi apparently reinforced its eight-battalion initial assault forces to a total of 16 battalions,[9] but 11 were badly hurt.

At Hue, as in other Tet battles, initial NVA advantages were frit-tered away. Had Hanoi reinforced the city with a 10,000-man divi-sion from Khe Sanh, Gen. Creighton Abrams told the writer in Janu-ary 1969, "we'd still be fighting there." At Hue, the NVA fought a brave but badly directed battle, aided by poor flying weather, allied unpreparedness, and initial allied restrictions on the use of artillery in the city. Their comrades at Khe Sanh and along the DMZ failed to divert U.S. reinforcements, and the key bases at Da Nang and Phu Bai were not hit often enough or accurately enough by rockets or mortars to prevent allied reaction. But such failures went largely un-noticed by newsmen under stress and unproclaimed by a chastened MACV.

The Official View: A Restricted One

As we have seen, General Westmoreland on February 1 produced his own three-phase thesis of what the enemy's intentions were, with the accent on Khe Sanh. His director of the MACV combat operations center, Brigadier General Chaisson, accurately credited the enemy's initial onslaught with being "surprising" in its intensity, scope, and coordination, although he suggested that the foe might better have launched all his attacks on the same night (apparently Hanoi's co-ordination was not perfect). Westmoreland's J-2 (Assistant Chief of Staff for Intelligence), Maj. Gen. Philip B. Davidson, focused on enemy deployments and, defensively, on the question of "surprise." On the whole, however, neither Westmoreland nor his subordinates in Saigon, then or later, discussed enemy battlefield tactics beyond "infiltration." They emphasized the overall "effects," notably enemy losses and psychological objectives, as did the White House.

An exception was a background briefing on February 8 in Saigon by General Abrams, at which he gave one of the few official critiques of enemy tactics. While largely discussing ARVN performance, Abrams also cited enemy ambitions, such as bringing NVA tank personnel along for the capture of an ARVN armored school near Saigon, and NVA artillerymen to take over an ARVN artillery installation in the Central Highlands. He cited one example of enemy tactical miscalculation: a daylight attack across open fields against ready ARVN armored cavalry units near Ban Me Thuot. But these comments went almost unreflected in the media.

To a considerable degree, both shaken Administration officials and the military, in Saigon and Washington, were preoccupied with showing an alarmed American public that the enemy had failed to gain his strategic objectives—popular uprisings, control of some cities, disintegration of the ARVN. The official Administration view of enemy strategy was partly expressed by Gen. Leonard F. Chapman, Jr., commandant of the Marine Corps:

Yes, the enemy saw we were winning. And he began to see that he could not win in South Vietnam.

So he changed his approach to the war. The new communist strategy was announced by the Prime Minister of North Vietnam, Pham Van Dong. As the planning and the positioning of troops for the January assaults on the population centers were underway, he said:

"Our purpose is, through a program of all-out attacks, to cause many U.S. casualties, and so to erode the U.S. will that antiwar influences will gain decisive political strength."

In other words, the government in Hanoi is hoping to change our mind —to make us waver—to make us give up and get out. And he's still trying.[10]

As late as early March, few newsmen were asking officials in Vietnam to analyze enemy battlefield tactics, although one of their favorite sources, John Vann, the outspoken old Vietnam hand and deputy senior advisor for III Corps, was emphasizing that the enemy's own fumbles—not American brilliance—had cost him success on the ground. The foe, Vann said, was outfumbling the allies.[11]

Even as they reported (inflated) enemy losses, MACV spokesmen in Saigon were caught up by the fixations of the Saigon press corps: What was coming next? Under newsmen's questioning, they were determined not to be caught underestimating enemy capabilities a second time. So, intermittently, throughout the month of February, Westmoreland's information officers focused not on enemy limitations but on possible enemy targets and "second waves"—their speculations and warnings being transformed into predictions by the media. Westmoreland's suggestions that the enemy's anti-cities attacks might be on the wane (in his February 1 briefing) and that the foe was unable to launch another Tet-style offensive (on February 25) were contrasts. Thus MACV spokesmen in Saigon occasionally contributed in February to a general journalistic perception that no logistics, organizational, or manpower limitations inhibited the NVA's capacity, even after the "first wave," to strike anywhere at will ("No place was safe any more").

It was only by interviewing intelligence specialists, and by visiting U.S. and ARVN field units and asking basic questions about the foe, that newsmen in Vietnam could unearth more of the crucial details of enemy tactical performance. But manpower, energy, and interest were lacking for such immediate post-mortems, and the enemy remained, by and large, a menacing paragon of military efficiency throughout February and March.

The Wires: Reports from the Foe

The French news agency, Agence France Presse, had its own man, Bernard Cabanes, stationed in Hanoi. Of his claustrophobic experience, shared by European diplomats there, he was later to tell this reporter: "Six months in Hanoi is six months lost from your life."

The AP and UPI had no one in Hanoi. Both agencies, especially AP, routinely reported from Hong Kong, Tokyo, and other points, without comment, what Radio Hanoi—relaying National Liberation Front (NLF)[12] communiqués, as well as statements of the North Vietnamese or North Vietnamese diplomats abroad—had to say. One example:

TOKYO (AP)—The Vietcong reported Saturday that U.S. naval craft were sunk in the five-day communist offensive in South Vietnam.

A Vietcong communiqué said the unidentified American warships were sunk off Ben Tre during an American counterattack early Wednesday.

It also said "all the American and puppet troops" stationed at Phu Loc, a northern district town, were wiped out early Thursday.

North Vietnam's Vietnam News Agency relayed the Vietcong claims. . . .

In Hanoi, the presidium of the central committee of the Vietnam Fatherland Front, a coalition group that includes communists, said the Vietcong assaults "show that the people's war is invincible." . . .

Earlier, Radio Hanoi reported a new force had been set up in South Vietnam to overthrow the Saigon government and establish a new "revolutionary" regime. . . .

A Japanese-language broadcast said the national leadership of the new force issued an appeal to the South Vietnamese people last Wednesday calling on them to rise up and topple the government.

An English-language version said the appeal called on officers and men of the South Vietnamese Army and police force to surrender their weapons and side with the people. It gave the force's name as the Committee of the Alliance of National Democratic and Peace Forces.[13]

On another occasion, AP reported on what the NVA troops sang at Khe Sanh:

TOKYO (AP)—The Vietcong says that between battles in the strategic Khe Sanh Valley, its troops compose poems and plays about their victory.

Hanoi Radio broadcast this example today:

> The Yanks have modern B-52s
> Of which they make a bugaboo
> But woe to the GIs
> When we opened fire
> On the front of Highway Nine
> How they wept and cried!
> And us, clean-shaven,
> We asked them after each battle:
> What can cause more trouble
> Our cannon or your B-52?[14]

The wires also reported what President Johnson had to say about the enemy's morale on February 2:

. . . The matter of communist Vietnamese morale came in for some protracted attention on the basis of a question pegged to the psychological importance of the communist aggressiveness. Johnson said he hadn't read so-called reports that communist morale was way down.

"The fact that people's morale may be suffering and that they may be having great difficulty doesn't keep them from breaking glass windows or shooting folks in a store or dashing into your home or trying to assassinate somebody. That goes with it. That is part of the pattern," Johnson said.[15]

But discussions of Vietcong tactics (aside from enemy "suicide" squads, atrocities, and a second "Dienbienphu") were relatively rare in AP and UPI.

One notable piece was Peter Arnett's colorful "truckload of flowers" dispatch on how the Vietnamese infiltrated into Saigon, which landed on page one in the New York *Times* and the Washington *Post* and was lifted and rewritten into Tet accounts by the news magazines and TV commentators as well. It began:

SAIGON (AP)—The Vietcong commandos who stormed the U.S. Embassy Wednesday rode into Saigon concealed in a truckload of flowers.

Like the Greek soldiers who hid in a wooden horse to enter Troy, Vietcong employed deceit and surprise to launch their attack—two tactics as old as war itself.

. . . .

The past few days have shown that the communist underground is as effective and all-pervading in Saigon as in the most contested hamlets in the countryside.

. . . .

Police report that none of the prisoners captured so far has been able to give the location of houses where they picked up their weapons and ammunition. They were issued the weapons at night by the cell leader. The communists have lost many troops, but the underground remains in perfect shape in Saigon.

. . . .

The success of the communists in gaining easy access to the city and staying for at least three days also throws into doubt the effectiveness of the Vietnamese security in and around Saigon.[16]

Yet it later developed that much of the Vietcong underground (or "infrastructure") in Saigon, as in other cities, "surfaced" and was destroyed in the early fighting. Moreover, given the lax state of Vietnamese security (and prior allied indifference to urban defense), the surprising aspect of the Vietcong move into Saigon was not that infiltration occurred, but that it resulted in so many failures, such as the repulse of raids on Independence Palace and the headquarters of the Joint General Staff and the Navy. In brief (and in retrospect), Tet was less a demonstration of Vietcong efficiency than the result of a kind of mass escapism by the Saigon regime. But newsmen were shaken by the infiltration; and that Hanoi failed to exploit its opportunity was not then clearly apparent to many of them (including this writer).

Most of Arnett's story, he later related, came from his Vietnamese brother-in-law, "a Captain Chau, attached to the [Vietnamese] Joint

General Staff in the logistics division. He was also seconded to the CID [Criminal Investigation Division] in investigating some black-market cases, so when Tet took place he worked full time on security chores. In one of my rare trips to my in-laws' house in Tran Cao Van Street during the early Tet attacks, I encountered him and he told me how the [ARVN] had determined how some of the Vietcong had gotten in. From then on, it was just checking with the right people, plus visiting some of the cemeteries where the weapons had been buried and so on. In other words, I was lucky."[17]

On February 12 Arnett tried an analysis of enemy strategic intentions which pretty well summed up the speculation—and apprehension—around Saigon:

SAIGON (AP)—What did the communist high command hope to achieve in its attacks on 35 South Vietnamese population and administration centers? . . .

To what degree were the objectives attained and what has been the impact of the recent events of the war?

The answers to these questions and an assessment of the enemy's intentions in the Khe Sanh battleground in the northwest are being carefully examined and debated in Saigon.

For the first time, the U.S. command seems to be assessing the communists as tacticians, rather than just fanatical hordes pouring across the border to become cannon fodder for U.S. guns. . . .[18]

American officials say weeks may pass before the picture becomes clear. . . .

A major problem in assessing communist objectives is that the intelligence haul has been poor in recent days. No high-level Red cadre have been captured, documents have been vague and out of date.

The most *experienced observers* believe that the communists probably included part of each of the theories [put forth by U.S. officials] in their major objectives and that no one theory would apply. There seems little doubt that the communist high command would have welcomed a popular uprising against the government in Vietnam's major cities. Many prisoners have said they were told that the public could be expected to aid them.

Observers doubt, however, that the communists really expected the cities to fall as easily as that. The mounting of the major military campaign against the U.S. Marine Combat Base at Khe Sanh also seems to indicate that the communists expect more fighting. . . .

Experienced observers believe that whichever of the theories is correct, it will make no difference to the future communist military posture.

"Now that they have come at us in the cities once, they will come back

again and again, and each time harder than the previous time," a Vietnamese official commented. *Another Vietnamese* said: "I think they want
us and everyone to get the message—they are around us and can strike at
any time. I think they want to negotiate on their terms."[19]

It is noticeable here, and in a subsequent AP analysis, that Arnett,
like most newsmen in Saigon, did not discuss specific enemy tactical
successes or failures, even those in the capital area. The same was
true of a retrospective analysis on February 21, which dwelt largely
on the blood and thunder of the offensive:

. . . The communist infrastructure, those hundreds of outwardly loyal
citizens who comprise the hidden apparatus of the enemy, led to assembly
points the troops they had concealed.

The attacks were coordinated on a master plan. First, the sappers
launched suicide assaults against the most important buildings. Then
shock troops lashed at peripheral military installations. The battle was on
—at Saigon, at My Tho, in the Delta, the Highlands, the coastal plains.

The cities and towns not attacked in the first day were hit the second
or third day.[20]

Probably the most comprehensive single official American evaluation of the foe's intentions and objectives at Tet came from Douglas
Pike, the independent-minded USIA specialist on the Vietcong who
flew in from Hong Kong to question prisoners and read captured orders and documents. He put together a written analysis, distributed
by JUSPAO, of which AP, on Sunday, February 18, gave a lengthy,
cogent summary, slightly firming up Pike's admittedly speculative
findings:

SAIGON (AP)—An evaluation of the current communist offensive
by an expert on Vietnamese communism says Hanoi may have miscal-
culated the effects of its expanded military actions.

Douglas Pike, whose 1966 book, *Viet Cong,* is considered a definitive
study of the communist National Liberation Front, examined documents
captured recently and prisoner interrogation statements before writing a
report for the U.S. Embassy.

Pike, a Foreign Service officer with the U.S. Information Service, says
the communists expected their offensive to disintegrate the South Vietnamese Army, cause a popular uprising in support of the NLF, and
seriously damage the U.S. military machine in South Vietnam.

The embassy issued Pike's findings Sunday, but noted: "The paper
does not constitute an official assessment or policy statement by the U.S.

Mission, but is made available as an evaluation reflecting the thoughts of a leading expert in Vietnamese studies."[21]

The story did not get into next day's Washington *Post,* which instead ran a somewhat vague piece on page one by its China-watcher Stanley Karnow (temporarily in Saigon) on Giap the "mastermind." In the same issue was an Alsop column which stressed enemy tactical flaws ("Major Failure in City Battles Was Enemy's, Not the Allies'"). At the initiative of Assistant Managing Editor Howard Simons, however, the paper ran the full text of Pike's analysis in its Sunday "Outlook" section on February 25. On February 19, the New York *Times* also ignored Pike's evaluation, having already used a brief page-four interview story ("U.S. Aide Assesses Strategy of Giap, Says that General May Be Trying to Win by Spring") on February 13. On February 19, it ran a short, fairly specific piece ("Allied Command Divided on Foe's Aim in New Raids") by Gene Roberts out of Saigon on conflicting assessments not of overall enemy strategy but of the weekend's hit-and-run attacks, which the wire services had hastily described earlier as the Tet "second wave."

Why was Pike thus ignored? Several newsmen surmised, three years later, that the story was crowded out by competing official February 18 analyses of enemy Tet strategic intentions and results emanating from: (1) President Johnson's entourage during a visit to former President Eisenhower[22] and (2) Ambassador Bunker on "Face the Nation." In addition, Pike was well known in Saigon, but not to New York or Washington deskmen.

The AP's William Ryan, flown in shortly after Tet to do some of the in-depth analysis, cited the possibility, pushed by MACV, of enemy difficulties:

SAIGON (AP)—The Americans and their South Vietnamese allies, waiting for the Vietcong to drop the other shoe, are being kept jittery and to a certain degree off balance. The communists too have their problems, American sources say. . . .

There is . . . a possibility that the Vietcong is suffering from a severe manpower problem. The Tet offensive cost heavily and American officials are persuaded that the communists are hurting badly in this department.

If this is so, the communists also have their dilemma. Should they risk using up more manpower to follow up the momentum of the offensive with another, or should they risk losing that momentum by waiting to replenish their forces?

The extent to which the Vietcong has been losing troops has become manifest in the northern part of South Vietnam.

Most of the enemy forces from the 2nd Corps area northward are now North Vietnamese regulars. Americans say—to the extent of 75 percent in the 1st Corps area. In the 2nd Corps area there appears to be an even mixture of North Vietnamese and Vietcong. Only the 4th Corps in the south has forces which are almost entirely Vietcong. . . .

Whether there is, soon or eventually, another major offensive against the cities probably depends upon the communists' own assessment of their manpower problems and capabilities in the light of their losses.[23]

The following day, Ryan, on Giap, breathlessly stated the obvious:

SAIGON (AP)—The battle which finished the French in Indo-China began 14 years ago this month on March 13. Many here wonder if the architect of that victory will choose a time between now and May 7, the date of the French fall, to seek a crushing military and psychological triumph.

Gen. Vo Nguyen Giap may be planning just that, some Americans say —but not necessarily where the Americans expect it.

Giap is noted for deception, and this in itself arouses worry that his long-range target is Saigon.

The North Vietnamese commander and deputy premier has the Americans and South Vietnamese watching every place at the same time.[24]

From there on, aside from pointing out analogies between Dienbienphu and Khe Sanh, the AP in Saigon did not venture further into overall strategic analysis of the foe.

On March 29, JUSPAO put out a key captured document—a February 1 circular from COSVN—which described pluses and minuses in the communist performance as seen by COSVN. The AP gave it a respectable 500-word synthesis, beginning: "Two days after the start of the Tet offensive January 30, the *Vietcong high command* told all communist guerrilla units in South Vietnam they had *won an important victory but failed to achieve their main objectives*. A captured Vietcong circular warmly praised communist forces at all levels for their simultaneous attack on cities and military installations throughout the country."[25]

Such captured documents were not generally held in high regard by the Saigon press corps; they were old, often of uncertain authenticity or importance, and usually could be held to mean anything. During his twice-yearly visits to Vietnam, Joseph Alsop read them by the dozen, but few other newsmen had the inclination or time. There was wheat in the chaff, however—amid the usual rhetorical exhortations, what was bothering Hanoi often came through under the rubric of "self-criticism." In this particular case, the COSVN circular, like the January 5 pre-Tet document warning of an attack on Saigon, was apparently genuine, and thus important, if not conclusive.[26] It emphasized faulty coordination and liaison, and tactical shortcomings, and this emphasis tended to fit with what were (dimly) perceptible flaws in NVA/VC performance at Tet.

The New York *Times* took no notice of AP's story at all. Its own story from Saigon on March 30 was out of the embassy, and said that Ambassador Bunker was seeking a better job for Lt. Gen. Bruce Palmer, the "intellectual" USARV deputy commander in Vietnam, possibly as deputy to Abrams to "play a pivotal role" in a "revamping" of U.S. forces in Vietnam. The story remains a *Times* exclusive to this day; why it landed on page one nobody knows.[27] The Washington *Post* in Saigon (namely, its visiting Pentagon reporter, George Wilson) was concerned with the loss of an F-111 over North Vietnam ("Lost F-111 Could Be Technological Gold Mine for Reds"), but the home office also ran the AP story, in slightly abbreviated form, on the same page.[28] There was no coverage of the captured COSVN document on the evening television news shows whatsoever.

As part of its voluminous file from Saigon, the AP reported also the odds-and-ends of enemy performance: the enemy had good weapons in good supply, if not in abundance (March 1); the number of enemy defectors (following a month-old trend) was less than half the year-ago rate (March 4); the North Vietnamese attracted U.S. artillery fire with wooden tank decoys north of the DMZ (March 7); five North Vietnamese defectors claimed they had 24 hours' notice of air strikes by B-52s based on Guam, presumably alerted by the electronically-equipped Soviet trawler off the island, but said nothing about the B-52s based at Sattahip in Thailand, and MACV called it "preposterous" (March 19); communist mobility was the "despair" of allied intelligence (March 21).[29]

Finally, the old cliché of recent American wars, the story, at some point, that the diehard enemy has been "chained" to his machine guns, was not overlooked. Tet provided the occasion for the AP during the Hue battle, when Lewis Simons reported what a U.S. PIO advisor said he had heard from the ARVN:

. . . The determination of the communist leaders was indicated last week when allied forces overran an enemy position. "We found three of them chained to machine guns on the west wall," said Army Capt. George W. Smith, 27, of Meriden, Connecticut, an advisor to South Vietnamese troops. . . .

Smith also had a report that when a North Vietnamese commander was killed his replacement asked permission to withdraw. "He was refused permission and ordered to defend his position to the end."[30]

Reuters upheld the tradition, too, and its version of the chained-machine-gunners story landed on page three of the *Times*.[31]

Television: In Praise of the VC

Vietcong performance was not a major preoccupation of the television networks, and direct reports on enemy thinking and behavior were few. But George Syvertsen of CBS, talking to several prisoners captured during the Saigon fighting, got a notion of enemy pre-attack security measures and the nonsuicidal sentiments of the POWs:

Q.: Are you a communist?
A.: No.
Q.: What are you?
A.: A liberation soldier.
Q.: What were you told before you came to Saigon?
A.: Before we set out we were told that we . . . about an operation to conduct. But we were not told where we would go.
Q.: So you didn't know even that you were going to Saigon, is that right?
A.: No.
Q.: Did your men know where they were going or anything about the action?
A.: We were not told to go to Saigon until we approached the city. [Second Vietcong through an interpreter]: Before I started out for Saigon I was told by my commanders that I would be welcomed by people and other liaison officers and agents, but when [I] came into town, [I] just got lost.
Q.: How do you feel now that the fighting is all over for you?
A.: I just want to go home. I am homesick. [Third Vietcong through an interpreter]: I arrived here in August of '67.
Q.: What do you feel now that the war is over for you?
A.: Now that the fighting is over for me and all, what I am now thinking is that I would be allowed either to leave or die.
Q.: And you'd like to go home?
A.: It is the wish of everyone, not me alone. It is also the wish of any bird to fly to his own nest.[32]

In contrast, Sam Jaffe of ABC News, after showing his filming of a firefight, billed the Vietcong as "bitter-enders," and made some rather loose predictions, due no doubt to haste: "The Vietcong here in Cholon [in Saigon] are a stubborn bunch who do not give up easily. It will take months to force them out of this immense area."[33] In fact, Saigon-Cholon (in contrast to surrounding Gia Dinh province and the suburbs) was clear of Vietcong within a week.[34] Another extravagant prognosis was made by NBC's Garrick Utley, visiting the U.S. 9th Division in the Delta. He reported that the pacification program "had been set back perhaps for many years" and "the Vietcong are strong and are not running from a fight. That would be bad in any part of Vietnam, but especially so here, the most densely populated part of it."[35]

On February 2, reporting from Hue, Jeff Gralnick of CBS echoed a common early TV theme, saying: "The Vietcong proved they could take and hold almost any area they chose."[36] Later in the month, CBS did a "special" on the Vietcong, and Bernard Kalb waxed extreme in his admiration:

. . . Citizen of Saigon, Vietcong insurgent, and who can tell the difference about an enemy that has emerged as a traumatic question mark [sic].

The Vietcong live mostly in a jungle-camouflaged world that is bounded by tanks, air strikes, and napalm. They have been attacked, assaulted, ambushed, bombarded, rocketed, mortared. The arsenal of the strongest military power in the world has been directed against them—with the greatest concentration of firepower in history.

The U.S. Air Force. The Vietcong have no Air Force.

The U.S. Navy. The Vietcong have no Navy.

Helicopters. The Vietcong have no helicopters. And yet they have found a way of outwitting U.S. strategy. But they have taken terrible casualties. . . .

The startling thing is how very late in the war the United States began learning about its $30-billion-a-year enemy. The Vietcong say that if they are forced to eat with spoons and forks they will be defeated, but if chopsticks are used, the Americans are no match for the Vietcong. In other words, they will not cooperate with our strategy. The Vietcong are waging a revolution. The United States is waging a war.

The Vietcong use the word "politics" as an active verb [sic]; Americans use it as a noun. This is a war about politics and, most of all—people, even though the guns make the most noise.[37]

NBC was reduced to deriving its "insights" from a captured Vietcong propaganda film, run with a narration by Douglas Kiker, who had been in Vietnam less than two weeks. Chet Huntley led off:

. . . The sniper firing has subsided now in Saigon. Those Vietcong not killed or captured have presumably gone back to their villages where they can take refuge. One such village, according to the Vietcong, is Cu Chi, 20 miles northwest of Saigon.

We have obtained film made by the Vietcong more than a year ago of their activities near this village. A North Vietnamese English narration of the film seems to indicate that the villagers spend much of their time working in opposition to the South Vietnamese government.

Here with the film is a report by Douglas Kiker.

Kiker: At the beginning, the people of Cu Chi are sharpening spikes for booby traps.

Although some of the later sequences in the film appear staged, this portion is accurate. The guerrillas here are collecting abandoned weapons and bits of metal from a battlefield. They take them to a workshop in the jungle where some arms are repaired and where metal is melted down to make new weapons. Most guerrilla units carry a variety of Russian, Chinese, and American, and homemade guns.

This sequence, depicting life underground, is accurate in showing the elaborate tunnel networks the Vietcong build. It's doubtful these scenes were actually filmed in Cu Chi, since the village is not an enemy stronghold now and U.S. officials *insist* it was not last year when this film was produced.[38]

The film shows people described as Vietcong guerrillas working in rice paddies with rifles on their backs. This never happens. American airplanes fly over South Vietnam so frequently that the Vietcong hide their weapons to avoid being spotted, but the film makers apparently felt this would make good propaganda.

This man is described as a simple peasant named Ba Nhi. The narrator says Ba Nhi has shown a remarkable aptitude for blowing up American tanks with grenades and mines. Ba Nhi is shown supposedly carrying live mines on a stick like a peddler with pots and pans. Once again, this is propaganda not based on fact. Mines have to be buried with great care. If Ba Nhi really handled live mines this way, he would blow himself up.[39] A girl named Wa Ti Mo is seen pursuing the enemy. . . . By cutting the shot of a tank with a one-second shot of an explosion the film makers gave the impression that Wa Ti Mo blew up the tank. . . .

Huntley: While the film was made for propaganda purposes, there are elements of truth in it. The Vietcong are active in the villages and many South Vietnamese are on their side. The Vietcong were there before the American troops arrived, and so far, no *foolproof formula* has been found for rooting them out. While they remain, they pose a constant threat to the government and to American troops.[40]

CBS told an exaggerated story about Hanoi's supply lines to Hue, implying that the North Vietnamese were running trucks down a superhighway right up to the walls of the Citadel in the heart of the city. Needless to say, the NVA's trucks halted well short of Hue. Said Harry Reasoner: "The battle for the South Vietnamese city of Hue has entered its 18th day. . . . [An] American officer said one reason the communists have been able to hold on for so long is that they are getting supplies and ammunition from outside. The officer said North Vietnamese truck convoys, operating at night, have been moving down the A Shau Valley, then swinging eastward to Hue, finally unloading at communist-held entrances in the wall of the Citadel."[41]

Similarly inaccurate was NBC's Paul Cunningham on February 14, describing the (nonexistent) "encirclement" of Da Nang: "Easy as it is for the enemy to *mass troops* outside Da Nang, he probably cannot take the city. An all-out attack would be very costly to him. In the fashion of this guerrilla war *it is simpler for the enemy to infiltrate troops* into Da Nang and attack key points. Thousands of Vietnamese civilians come and go from the countryside and *it is impossible* to check out each one."[42] In fact, of course, it was not "easy" for the NVA to "mass troops outside Da Nang," as its abortive advance south of the city during the previous 10 days indicated. Nor was it "simpler" for the NVA to "infiltrate" Da Nang and "attack key points"—they never did it, although they got close. In fact, the NVA 2nd Division's abortive drive for Da Nang was semiconventional in nature, but without any "massing." Troops in Vietnam never "massed."

After the wounding at Da Nang's Navy hospital of Russ Bensley, associate producer of the Cronkite show—already hit at Khe Sanh—CBS's Donald Webster announced that the hated Cong were everywhere:

. . . Less than 12 hours after the report you just saw was filed, the communists demonstrated that under the new war in Vietnam *no place is safe*. Last night they attempted to rocket the Marble Mountain Base, the big Marine camp where so many helicopters have been damaged in the past. But one of the 122 mm. rockets hit the naval support activity hospital just across the street. It hit just outside the ward where Russ Bensley and others were asleep. Seven men were wounded, three hospital corpsmen and four patients. One of the corpsmen lost an eye, but Bensley was the most seriously wounded of all. Today in surgery, doctors removed his spleen, and he has a badly ruptured colon. It will be many months in the hospital, but, eventually, he will recover.

The irony of it is that for several weeks now we've been planning to do a report about the new war in Vietnam, the fact that the enemy now has *weapons every bit as good as the Americans* [have] . . . that the enemy now is attacking with a new boldness and daring like never before, and the fact now that Vietnam is a much more dangerous place than ever before.[43]

Hanoi, as prisoners and captured documents made clear, did not have "weapons every bit as good as the Americans" (e.g., the B-52 bomber, the 175 mm. gun, the helicopter gunship). Webster may have been referring to light infantry weapons such as the AK-47 rifle and the B-40 (bazooka-style) rocket. But he did not make this clear. Moreover, the enemy's "boldness and daring" had noticeably decreased by the time Webster spoke.

In a later broadcast, Webster described the 122 mm. rocket:

Some people think that the communists' recent attacks on South Vietnamese air bases are done by two or three men, sneaking out in the middle of the night.

This is a 122 mm. rocket, the best they have, and the United States has nothing like it. . . .

This is a very complicated weapon: definitely not for amateurs, used only by the NVA. . . .

We have mortars which are smaller and artillery which is larger, and both are more accurate, but for the communist guerrilla-type operation, this serves its purpose and the accuracy isn't so important. When you're aiming at a big air base like Da Nang or Tan Son Nhut, you're bound to hit something every once in a while.[44]

The assertion that "accuracy isn't so important" was belied at Khe Sanh and elsewhere, where, had enemy fire been more accurate, the allies would have been in a difficult situation. As it was, some 1,000 helicopters and fixed-wing aircraft were damaged or (more seldom) destroyed, many of them by NVA rockets and mortars, notably at Da Nang.

On January 31, CBS cameraman Vinh Dan was captured by the NVA at Hue and filmed their activities in the Citadel. CBS ran the film on February 22, with narration by Murray Fromson:

The communists thought these scenes in Hue were being filmed for their own propaganda outlets. . . .

Dan destroyed his identification and told his captors he worked for French television. They put him to work for them. Though apparently staged, the film provides a revealing close-up of the North Vietnamese. It shows the youth of their soldiers. It also demonstrates the *modern weaponry*, the Soviet-made AK-47 automatic rifles, and the equipment, like radios, that are at the communists' disposal.

In these scenes, the North Vietnamese wear short pants, pith helmets, and seem to have packs enabling them to move quickly, but from the moment they slipped into the old walled city of Hue, they have shown no inclination to withdraw.[45]

In fact, by the time CBS put this film on the air, the NVA had made a last counterattack (against the ARVN) and were pulling out most of their survivors. The "modern weaponry" cited and the "radios" were standard NVA issue.

The *Times:* The Enemy Was Almost Infallible

During February and March, the New York *Times* published four "Hanoi stories" on page one, including Hanoi's announced goal of crumbling the Saigon regime and the North's talk of peace.[46] Inside the paper, during the same period, there was a total of 43 stories on statements by Hanoi or its emissaries abroad—more attention than the *Times* accorded the Saigon regime. Yet, all told, the *Times* published few stories dealing entirely or in part with Vietcong or North Vietnamese military performance—the ethnocentric focus was on American performance. The Administration's few extended discussions of enemy performance (in contrast to its claims of enemy defeat) were given two stories on page one.[47] Moreover, *Times* commentators at home provided little analysis on this subject, compared to their extensive treatment of allied performance and prospects.

James Reston early discussed "North Vietnam's Strategy of Terror," but, unlike other commentators, did not assume that losses meant nothing to Hanoi:

. . . It is undoubtedly true that "military progress" is being made and that "our forces have won every major battle in which they have been engaged," but it is noteworthy that Secretary McNamara is not joining in the latest propaganda line that we are now seeing the enemy's "last gasp."

The Vietcong guerrillas undoubtedly lost some strength last year, but their raids on Saigon and elsewhere show little evidence of the "low morale" General Westmoreland talked about when he was home last November. The North Vietnamese regulars may have lost every major battle of the war, but they are now concentrating at the Demilitarized Zone for what promises to be the bloodiest engagement of the war.

This may be a "last gasp" effort, but more than likely if General Giap gets badly mauled at Khe Sanh, he will retreat as he did for years after the French defeated him in North Vietnam and adapt his tactics to the military realities.

For the moment, the enemy is *willing* to take 10 deaths to our one, but this cannot last, even among the Vietnamese. If his forces are decimated at Khe Sanh, he may negotiate, as officials here are saying, but more than likely he will retreat into the Highlands, where he has shorter supply lines and convenient sanctuaries in border countries.

Meanwhile, we can expect more terror in the cities. The Vietcong do not have to stage dramatic raids on the American Embassy and military headquarters in order to create chaos in the urban areas. These are open cities, where the Vietcong are indistinguishable from the South Vietnamese. Anybody who has ever been in Saigon knows how vulnerable that capital is to sabotage. The Vietcong have always had the capacity to make life almost intolerable in Saigon, but they have not done so until now, apparently because they thought we would retaliate by bombing Hanoi and Haiphong. As the bombing expands, however, this is obviously less of a restraint.[48]

On Sunday, February 11, the *Times*'s "News of the Week in Review" section ran an unsigned piece (by Max Frankel) on the President's "Cruel Dilemma," citing the critics' view that: (1) casualties didn't matter to Hanoi, and (2) the enemy, just by proving the Administration to have been overoptimistic, had scored a strategic success.

Beginning with the paper's early Tet reporting from Vietnam, it was hard to find any suggestion in the *Times* that the Vietcong were fallible human beings. On February 1, Tom Buckley did the first on-the-spot assessment, with no more information than his colleagues. The enemy's losses—a matter of dispute—were given short shrift, but Buckley did note, ahead of all others, that 50 percent of the ARVN were on holiday leave. In addition, he painted a heroic picture of the enemy as ready and willing to die, a common theme in the opening days of the offensive:

Among the points that the attacks may have demonstrated are these:

Despite official statistics to the contrary, no part of the country is secure either from terrorist bombs or from organized military operations.[49]

Even local guerrilla battalions, as distinct from the main force, still possess highly efficient communications, leadership, and coordination. Despite the prevalence of government informers and security agents, the battalions are able to carry out their preparations in secrecy. They have an arsenal of excellent weapons.

Most important, after years of fighting and tens of thousands of casualties, the Vietcong can still find thousands of men who are ready not only to strike at night and slip away but also to undertake missions in which death is the only possible outcome. . . .

. . . .

By and large, the South Vietnamese armed forces have not clearly demonstrated such an extreme dedication to duty. And the tactics of the American forces are calculated to keep casualties at a minimum.[50]

Appearing the following day, Charles Mohr's account of enemy courage and zeal echoed Buckley to some extent:

SAIGON, South Vietnam, Feb. 2—On Monday night, the eve of the Vietcong guerrillas' audacious attacks in Saigon and other cities in South Vietnam, a police official told a reporter here that incidents were expected.

The guard at the building of the Saigon radio was being reinforced heavily, he said. By dawn a relatively small group of Vietcong had shot their way into the radio station and it was burning. The reporter called back his police friend and asked: "How could this happen when you reinforced your guard?"

"The Vietcong are not afraid to die," said the official in a matter-of-fact manner.

The courage and motivation of the guerrilla units that struck Saigon, Da Nang, the provincial capitals, and many other towns and installations were important factors in the havoc they created.

One thing that has made the offensive against towns so dramatic—and embarrassing to the allied command—is that it has been so prolonged.

Tonight there may still be as many as a thousand guerrillas in Saigon itself—94 hours after the attack began—according to United States military sources.

The Vietcong found some of the best fighting conditions they had ever experienced in the course of the war: Artillery could not be used against them and air strikes on a large scale were not practicable in city streets, although both helicopter gunships and fighter-bombers have been used to some extent—with bad results for civilians.

The battle has tended to underline a fact often forgotten—that the Vietcong almost always fight without "supporting fire" from artillery and aircraft, and fight well. They do even better as the odds against them decrease.

The attacks also showed excellent planning and valuable support by communist agents within the towns and cities.

South Vietnamese intelligence officials ruefully believe that there were an unusual number of "funerals" in one Saigon cemetery recently. A larger-than-usual number of coffins, followed by weeping women and children, were buried there.

On the night of the attacks, one source said, some of the coffins were dug up by guerrillas who took from them well-oiled automatic and heavy weapons.

What the population thinks of recent events is not entirely clear. To some extent, guerrilla fighting has kept people holed up in their homes. To some extent they have taken cover because of refusal by trigger-happy troops and police to let them go to work, buy food, or resume some degree of normal life.

But the crisis has not apparently been met by any high degree of patriotic fervor or commitment by the urban population. The people of South Vietnam appear to be cynical and tired of this war.

When one Vietnamese was caught in the suburb of Gia Dinh during a successful Vietcong attack on a police station, he went from door to door asking for refuge. He was turned away at door after door by people who said: "We want no strangers in our house at a time like this."[51]

This story was followed, on February 4, by AP's vivid "truckload of flowers" piece (already noted), perhaps the most extensive description of enemy tactics printed by the *Times* ("By Bus, By Truck, On Foot, Foe Built Forces in Saigon"). Mohr ignored, as Buckley and the AP story did not, the contributing holiday laxity of South Vietnamese leaders, notably in lifting the curfew, which so greatly facilitated the enemy successes in some areas. He also made it appear that all Vietcong forces shared the zeal of the "special units" or sapper squads that hit the radio station, the U.S. Embassy, Independence Palace, and other points. Moreover, even as AP spoke of the Vietcong's "mastery of the small details that bring success," so Mohr spoke of "excellent planning," but left out the fact that the sapper assaults on the key points had, for the most part, failed. Yet Mohr's story, one should emphasize, was far less rash, and jumped to far fewer conclusions, than those filed by many others during the first three frightening, exhausting days of Tet.

As did the other media, the *Times*—in New York and Saigon—paid tribute to the enemy's weaponry. But the *Times* tended to equate the older weapons—AK-47 rifles, 82 mm. mortars, B-40 antitank rockets, conventional artillery used along the DMZ since early 1967, and 122 mm. rockets used against U.S. air bases since mid-1967—with the newly arrived ones—light PT-76 tanks employed at Lang Vei near Khe Sanh, and the 107 mm. rockets used north of Saigon. What was new about enemy weaponry at Tet was not so much the types of heavy weapons, but the more intensive (although still oddly sporadic) use of them by the foe, and the tactics involved.[52]

On February 23, after the February 17–18 NVA attacks by fire on 47 cities and towns, Gene Roberts described the enemy's tactics in using light, simple rockets and mortars, particularly mortars, on the battlefield to harass allied positions. Roberts reported that "with the help of detailed maps and information, enemy mortarmen are often accurate with their first round, and do not have to adjust their aim, enabling them to slip away before helicopters can arrive." The foreign desk in New York played up this angle with the headline "Foe Giving Warfare Lessons With Simple Mortar." Mortars, however, as this writer knows from experience, are not precision weapons, but smooth-bore "area weapons." The first round, even if fired in daytime by a crew that can see the target, seldom lands right-on. There are variations in ammunition and in tube angle. The Vietcong usually fired at night and in a hurry. Rockets were far less accurate. As a result, the Vietcong wasted most of their rounds in their hit-and-run attacks against cities.

Ripe targets for the Vietcong abounded in the Saigon area—Tan Son Nhut airport, U.S. and Vietnamese bases at Bien Hoa and Long Binh, Westmoreland's headquarters—but these points suffered remarkably little damage, given their lack of physical protection and the scores of rocket and mortar rounds expended against them. Da Nang air base and, above all, the adjoining Marble Mountain helicopter base suffered perhaps the most from rockets at Tet. But for all the noisy enemy fire and, occasionally (and unnecessarily), costly aircraft losses inflicted, no allied base had to suspend operations.[53] Because they did not fire in a *sustained* fashion, as the Chinese did during the Korean War, the communists could not exploit the full potential of their weapons. Even Khe Sanh, under direct enemy fire, continued to receive big C-123 transports on its airstrip throughout the 77-day siege. Few newsmen noticed.

Early in March, Hanson Baldwin contributed two pieces to the *Times* on enemy armament. The first was a detailed photo essay[54] in which Baldwin contended that enemy weapons had: (1) turned "the guerrilla war . . . into a conventional war," a statement that could only truly be made about the DMZ area and Hue during the February battle; (2) enabled the foe to "outgun" the poorly armed ARVN, a fact occasionally noted by other writers and apparent two years earlier to Westmoreland, if not to his Pentagon superiors;[55] and (3) given the enemy parity in ground firepower with U.S. units along the frontiers and the DMZ, "where the enemy enjoys artillery support."

U.S. estimates of the number of enemy "tubes" in the latter areas varied widely. But even in the light of what was *then* told to newsmen, Baldwin overstated his case. Nowhere, except possibly in the vicinity of Khe Sanh, did the number of enemy artillery pieces come close to the local U.S. total and, in any case, enemy fire was highly sporadic and well below capacity. During the Khe Sanh siege, U.S. artillery at or supporting Khe Sanh fired nearly 1,500 shells a day—or five to ten times as many rounds as were "incoming."[56]

In his second piece, in "News of the Week in Review" next day, Baldwin repeated the same themes, adding that only "U.S. air superiority and artillery support" enabled the allies to outgun the foe in the South.[57] In the same section was an analysis from Saigon by Tom Buckley which showed that the shock of Tet and the media's awe of the enemy had not yet worn off:

SAIGON, South Vietnam—The war in Vietnam has come to resemble a surrealistic chess game played on a board 500 miles long.

On one side, the United States, South Vietnam, and their allies have four times as many pieces as the other player, and all the major ones— helicopter knights, air-strike queens, even a fleet. The Vietcong and the North Vietnamese have nothing but plodding pawns. . . .

How has it been possible for an enemy force which totaled no more than 250,000—half of them lightly armed local guerrillas—and which, according to allied counts, lost 15 percent of this strength in the last four weeks, to continue to hold the initiative against nearly 1.2 million?

Perhaps the most important point is that, for all practical purposes, the plodding enemy pawns have the power to make themselves invisible. Moving by night, adept at the arts of camouflage, hidden among the paddyfields and in the thousands of hamlets, infiltrated in all likelihood into South Vietnamese government intelligence services, they can mass their forces, strike against one or many weak points, avoiding the allies' strength, and then disperse.

Even now, within rocket range of the capital, thousands of enemy troops are finding places to hide.[58]

The "wily Giap" syndrome came through in a *Times* "Man in the News" profile written in New York (March 8) to accompany "Khe Sanh and Dienbienphu: A Comparison" by Charles Mohr, who saw only two major, albeit important, differences between the two situations: U.S. air power and Khe Sanh's proximity to potential relief forces. Oddly enough, Giap was described in the profile as one of the world's foremost experts "on" modern guerrilla warfare, rather than as a practitioner. The profile also did not mention that Giap, like most successful generals, had had military disappointments, such as his abortive offensive against the French in 1951. The *Times* saw Giap in the context of Dienbienphu, and that was all.

In its further coverage of enemy performance, the *Times* duly reported official assessments of enemy strength, his recruiting in the Delta, and his casualties.[59] In addition, its use of dispatches from AFP's Cabanes in Hanoi, while fairly undiscriminating, was helpful to those interested in North Vietnam's changing propaganda emphasis. Also, on occasion, these dispatches disclosed some of Hanoi's problems.[60] Overall, however, there were few hints in *Times* analyses or battlefield reporting that the foe was anything but shrewd, tenacious, ascetic, infallible, and menacing, and in this the paper had plenty of company.

The *Post:* A Closer Look

The Washington *Post* paid far more attention to the foe than did the other media. It used statements from Hanoi less frequently than did the *Times,* in part because, not having AFP's Hanoi correspondent to draw on, it had to rely instead on wire-service monitoring of Radio Hanoi, on U.S. Hanoi-watchers, and on Foreign Broadcast Information Service (FBIS) in Washington, Hong Kong, or elsewhere.[61] However, the *Post* was far heavier than the *Times* on conflicting analysis (from outside Vietnam) of Hanoi's goals, strategy, and achievements as ranged against those of the allies, and particularly of the Administration.[62]

During the first week after Tet, the *Post* ran no less than five staff-written analyses—one from Washington[63] and four from its veteran China-watcher, Stanley Karnow, in Hong Kong.[64] In Washington, like the *Times,* the *Post* had State Department, CIA, and Defense Department officials to draw upon, mostly in the lower and middle echelons. Given their disparate views of a still foggy situation, it was not surprising that the journalism based on these sources was often fuzzy. In Hong Kong, journalists had access to Pike, then stationed there, as well as Radio Hanoi and reports from the U.S. Embassy in Saigon. As Pike was to note, however, even he changed his mind about enemy intentions and strategy after he got to Vietnam and studied the POW interrogation reports. His original supposition had been simply that the enemy had propaganda goals; he later decided that Hanoi had the serious military and political objectives already noted.

In any event, the difficulties of hasty, long-distance analysis are apparent in this *Post* piece out of Hong Kong, published 48 hours after the Saigon attacks:

The Vietcong attacks against Saigon and other population centers in South Vietnam have multiple, interrelated purposes, according to analysts of the Asian communist scene.

Their judgment is that Hanoi is trying to demonstrate a military capacity to carry out both large-scale operations and hit-and-run harassment at the same time, while simultaneously engaging in both a diplomatic offensive and internal political maneuvers aimed at winning uncommitted South Vietnamese support.

As these experts see it, the communists are counting on this impact to provoke different but complementary reactions in South Vietnam and the United States that will serve to strengthen their positions *either* for eventual negotiations or for continued war.

This capacity to pursue an array of related tactics underlines the reality in the communist doctrine, often expressed in Hanoi and Vietcong propaganda, that "coordination between the military struggle and the political struggle is a law of revolutionary struggle." . . .

Only time will tell the answer. But so far the communists have shown that if they lack the *strength* for a *clear-cut victory*, they are *dynamic* enough to stave off defeat. That may prove to be their trump card at a conference table.[65]

The enemy's Tet tactics were further described by the *Post* as "commando raids"—a considerable understatement—plus vague "internal political maneuvers aimed at winning uncommitted South Vietnamese," both made largely possible by the Saigon regime's "lack of credibility" among the people. (There was no mention of Thieu's lifting of the curfew or of the ARVN on holiday leave as factors in the initial attacks.)

To its credit, however, the *Post* (thanks to Karnow and Murrey Marder) provided far more comprehensible reporting of what Hanoi was *saying* in the early days than did the *Times* (which tended to print the AFP stories without explanation). But there was a danger with Hanoi-watching as with Peking-watching: The flow of broadcast material and Hanoi announcements was so vast and contradictory that selection tended to be highly subjective.

There was a second pitfall for newsmen in Washington. Being civilians, they tended to seek out civilians in the government, whether in the Pentagon or State Department, to discuss Hanoi's intentions. Civilians were more talkative and took a broader point of view than the military. They also tended to focus on the political aspects of Tet. Moreover, there was a vague general journalistic bias, possibly due to the high priority given domestic American politics, in favor of the political angle, which, it was repeatedly asserted, was always being neglected in coverage from Vietnam; the Vietnam conflict, according to this way of thinking, was a "political war," well understood as such by Hanoi if not by Washington. The result was a focus in Washington analyses on the psychological repercussions and presumed political strategy of the enemy, while the military side of his performance was seldom explored in detail.

Later analyses by *Post* staffmen in Washington and elsewhere outside Vietnam dwelled largely on U.S. performance and prospects in Vietnam, with enemy performance cited only in passing. But on occasion, the *Post* did take a view from afar, presumably through the gloomy eyes of its lower-echelon sources at State. One such occasion came after Rusk's announcement on February 14 of Hanoi's rejection of President Johnson's terms for talks. In a news-analysis piece, Marder made Washington sound more frightened ("a near-state-of-siege climate") than Saigon. He brushed aside the public Administration assertions that the first stage of the Tet offensive had been thwarted and that the foe might be "unprepared" to launch a second wave. He wrote that the Administration's "most discerning experts cannot now provide it any assured 'scenario' [*sic*] for what happens next." Rusk's words, he said, "plunged Washington even deeper into a defensive position, leaving all initiatives in the hands of North Vietnam." He went on:

> The combination of communist options is conceded to be *almost limitless*. . . . What is privately dismaying many lower-level officials in Washington is what they regard as the far too military-centered estimate of the present challenge by top officials in Washington and Saigon.

Hanoi's strategy is *hydra-headed,* they warn, combining simultaneously military-political-psychological-diplomatic thrusts, interlaced to achieve a political, not a military goal: the destruction of the South Vietnamese government and forces, and the U.S. will to sustain them.[66]

By February 29, the "interlaced thrusts" had vanished. The *Post,* in another story by Marder, told its readers that Hanoi's policy now was to "build a base for a 'provisional government' in the 'liberated' countryside . . . and to encircle its cities and allied bases." In fact, most of Marder's article was a highly useful chronology of Hanoi's public "de-escalation" of earlier claims of victory and "general uprising":

> U.S. officials are studying this evolution of communist strategy with interest and apprehension. It represents a de-escalation of the original grossly exaggerated communist claims for having achieved a "general uprising." But American experts agree it also projects a grim, more realistic forecast of communist ability to pursue the challenge. . . .
>
> Instead of the "general uprising" the communists originally boasted they had touched off, Hanoi now refers to the "rapidly rising general-uprising wave." In place of the original emphasis on smashing the allied-held cities and bases, at least equal communist stress is being given to "liberation" of "the rural regions around the towns and cities." . . .[67]
>
> . . . .
>
> "In the coming days" [one Hanoi] broadcast taunted, "what area will the Vietcong attack—Khe Sanh, Dak To, Chu Lai or Da Nang? . . . Now it is Khe Sanh's turn. Is this a feinting blow or a real blow? What will happen if a feinting blow becomes a real blow, in the face of a lack of concentration of troops to mount a defensive?"[68]
>
> This goading nerve-warfare, some U.S. experts ruefully note, plus the at least partially valid boasts of communist gains in the countryside, amount to a claim that the allied forces now have been driven into an "enclave" defense posture.[69]

As the Washington *Post's* own home-based analysts concentrated largely on the diplomatic and political aspects of enemy Tet performance, its syndicated columnists were far-ranging and, in terms of their intermittent focus on the subject, about evenly divided between orthodox pessimism (Joseph Kraft, Marquis Childs) and optimism (Joseph Alsop, Roscoe Drummond, William S. White).

On February 2, Alsop, for example, argued that "Red Raids on Cities Are Sign of Weakness Not Strength," i.e., that the foe, due to attrition and morale problems, had to abandon "protracted war" in favor of a "final or semi-final effort," thus exposing himself to heavy losses—a thesis later partly (and less aggressively) echoed by Pike and adopted by Walt W. Rostow of the White House.[70] A few days later, Kraft told his readers that the United States had reached "the limits of its military power."[71] But there was no analysis of enemy strategy and tactics this time, and, as we have noticed, henceforth Kraft, like most other analysts, concentrated on allied performance and prospects, when he discussed the action inside Vietnam at all. It was Alsop, almost alone among Washington newsmen, who continued to discuss the enemy situation.[72] After General Wheeler's trip to Saigon on February 25, Alsop echoed the Joint Chiefs' plea that more troops be sent.[73] Thereafter, however, he gave less attention to enemy problems, and more to Westmoreland's.

The *Post*, as always, to the dismay of its own staff specialists, relied heavily (sometimes blindly) on outsiders for interpretive comment. On February 11, as already noted, it published, from London, Sir Robert Thompson's paean to the North Vietnamese generalship. In the "Outlook" section of the same date, "Vo Nguyen Giap of North Vietnam" was profiled by the London *Observer*'s Dennis Bloodworth as a "stocky, muscular pocket Clausewitz." Bloodworth noted, as the *Times*'s Giap profile on March 8 did not, Giap's 1951 tactical disasters against the French. But, Bloodworth asserted, the Tet offensive "must be read *solely*" as an attempt to thin out allied forces as, he said, Giap allegedly did prior to Dienbienphu,[74] since "wars of liberation are not won by terrorist tactics in toughly defended cities." Bloodworth's history was no less fuzzy on this point than others', notably the AP's. On February 21, the *Post* ran another London *Observer* piece, which also found no flaws in the Vietcong.[75]

As we have seen, the *Post* was the only U.S. publication to publish the text of Douglas Pike's on-the-spot analysis, on February 25. In deed, Pike did a good deal of speculating about enemy strategy-making in Hanoi, but one thesis stands up pretty well: that Hanoi had made a serious *military* effort against the cities.

In sum, the *Post* did better in reporting early in Washington what the enemy said his goals were, and how those goals changed, than did anyone else. But it is noteworthy that Alsop was the only writer appearing in the *Post* who showed much consistent interest in the subject. Reading *Post* home staff analyses in March 1968, one would not have been aware that Hanoi's battlefield tactics had changed since mid-February.

In Saigon, the *Post* bureau concentrated largely on the effects of the Tet attacks and on allied problems and performance; critiques of MACV's early estimates of enemy losses, which were unaccompanied by any official claims of Hanoi's short-range exhaustion; and official speculation on the enemy's next moves.[76] It should be noted, however, that in battlefield reporting, the *Post's* references, few as they were, to enemy flaws and fumbles were more numerous than those in the *Times,* whose Saigon writers tended to give the enemy more credit than was his due.

From Da Nang on February 7, this writer, after asking Marine officers why the foe had not been able to secure Hue, reported:

. . . As for their assessment of the enemy, the U.S. field commanders note several puzzling tactical failures by the North Vietnamese.

At Hue, after successfully slipping into town from mountain bases to the northwest, the North Vietnamese occupied most of the Citadel and attacked the U.S. military advisors' compound on the south side of the Perfume River. But the enemy occupied neither the adjacent helicopter landing site—to block off resupply—nor the Hue University buildings overlooking the site.

As a result, Marine helicopters were occasionally able to bring in supplies and evacuate wounded despite heavy fire.

Nor did the enemy cut off South Vietnamese 1st Division headquarters from reinforcements by seizing its helicopter landing site, at the northwest corner of the Citadel. Not until Monday did the North Vietnamese blow up the 100-foot bridge on the city's southwest.[77] This cut the Route 1 truck route from Phu Bai base to the Marines now fighting on the city's south side.[78]

However, the *Post's* first extended insights into enemy "planning" from Saigon came on February 13, with two stories. In the first, Stanley Karnow reported on summaries of interrogations of captured Vietcong, secured from U.S. intelligence sources:

. . . This evidence, drawn mainly from prisoner interrogations, indicates that about half of the Vietcong force went into battle unaware of a general strategic goal, while some 40 percent believed their action would trigger a response from the urban population.

Only about 15 percent, most of them officers, appear to have been told that the offensive was designed to result in the formation of a communist-dominated coalition government in Saigon. Whether any of the directives issued to the troops really reflected the thinking of the communist high command is still not known.

Therefore, analysts submit, it is too early to say if, in terms of their own aspirations, the communists' drive was a partial success or a partial setback. . . .

Apparently without knowledge that other Vietcong units were engaged in the same assault, and evidently unaware of the overall communist strategy, Hoa's [one of those interrogated] squad opened fire on the Palace at 3 a.m. on February 1. But the Palace was too well guarded. By dawn, the Vietcong team was down to eight members, and Hoa himself was wounded.

They retreated to nearby buildings, holding out until 9 a.m., when they surrendered with only 30 rounds of ammunition left. Hoa said that by then he was scared and hungry.

In contrast, another Vietcong soldier, 23-year-old Le Van Tung, told interrogators that he had gone into action in Saigon persuaded that all of South Vietnam was in communist hands and only the capital awaited "liberation."[79]

In the second story, Lee Lescaze reported on Pike's press conference on February 12:

A leading authority on Vietnamese communists said today that he thinks the Tet offensive was aimed at demoralizing the South Vietnamese Army rather than at triggering a general uprising.

Douglas Pike, author of *Viet Cong*, a history and analysis of the National Liberation Front . . . has been working with interrogation reports, captured documents, and transcripts of communist broadcasts in an attempt to discern "the degree of ambition" behind the Tet offensive.

Secretary of State Dean Rusk, Vice President Hubert H. Humphrey, and Gen. William C. Westmoreland have pointed to the absence of a popular uprising as proof that the communists failed to achieve their objective in the city attacks. . . .

The thrust of the enemy pre-battle indoctrination was that the operation would be a cakewalk, Pike said. He believes that Giap thought the South Vietnamese Army could not and would not fight and that this was the major miscalculation of the offensive.[80]

Both of these pieces ran at greater length than anything published on the same subject by the New York *Times*. In addition, on the same day, the *Post* ran another lengthy piece (along with Karnow's) that was primarily concerned with poor enemy coordination and the tardy, abortive, fierce, and largely overlooked thrust of the NVA 2nd Division for Da Nang. Based on a one-day session with the 1st Marine Division G-2 (intelligence) and G-3 (operations), the story as published omitted some significant information, such as the report

that, prior to Tet, the enemy had infiltrated a "shadow administration" ready to take over Da Nang. But this point was made:

. . . At Da Nang as at Hue, the communists apparently made some
mistakes which helped their opponents.
The initial well-coordinated ground attacks were launched solely by
local Vietcong forces.
As reconstructed by U.S. specialists from prisoner interrogations and
captured documents, the enemy had infiltrated refugee-crowded Da Nang
with key cadres. The Vietcong cadres' task was to pave the way for a
ground attack and, most important, "a general uprising" by the inhabitants against the Thieu-Ky regime and the Americans.
According to one captured Vietcong officer, the Vietcong local forces
jumped off 48 hours too soon. The 2nd North Vietnamese Division
(consisting of the 1st, 3rd, and 21st Regiments) was not in a position to
support the Vietcong forces. But the Vietcong forces did not get—or heed
—this information. They went ahead.[81]

Similarly, brief allusions to enemy tactical imperfections got into
the *Post*'s post-mortem stories from Hue concerning the enemy's failure to seal off the city or readjust its forces to knock out isolated
ARVN garrisons; from Quang Tri city, north of Hue, where enemy
Tet planners "apparently" failed to reckon with the presence of the
1st Air Cavalry Division's newly arrived (but well-advertised) brigade; and from Khe Sanh citing the "surprisingly erratic and sporadic" enemy fire against the base.[82] But in none of these cases was
enemy strategy or performance the chief *Post* topic. In the total copy
flow from Saigon, the subject cropped up only in bits and pieces. The
paper's full-blown analyses, aside from reports of Pike's views, were
done far from the scene, in Washington and elsewhere, with mixed
results.

The *Newsweek* Analysis

Of the two major weekly news magazines, *Newsweek* provided by
far the more extensive look at Tet enemy performance.

In its first post-Tet issue, *Time* presented the Tet attacks as demonstrations of "Giap's genius," the communists' "split-second timing"
and "resiliency" of communications and command, the "quality" of
their weapons, and their ability to "strike at will" anywhere in Vietnam.[83] It also picked up Arnett's "flower truck" story, and focused
on Khe Sanh as the ultimate goal for Giap, who was portrayed as a

man insensitive to casualties. Later, however, the magazine did not discuss enemy battlefield performance in any detail, although enemy weapons were described as devastating and ultra-modern,[84] and the enemy infantry as tenacious and stubborn.

Newsweek, throughout the February–March 1968 period, was to refer, in passing, to the "wily" Giap, "tough" North Vietnamese regulars, "ominous" enemy activity, and, in general, to a foe without setbacks or flaws. Nevertheless, as noted, it also conducted the only independent post-mortem of any significance on the enemy's Tet performance. The magazine sounded a note of realism: "At first glance, the attack appeared to be a faultless military triumph. Impressive it was. But recently, U.S. intelligence has compiled stacks of captured documents and transcripts of prisoner interrogations which suggest that the communists—for all their success in battle—were still plagued by the confusion that is characteristic of all military operations."[85]

To varying degrees, the article echoed Pike's speculative analysis, Alsop's arguments, and Westmoreland's contention, reflected later in his *Report on the War,* that North Vietnam's leaders *had* to try for "victory in the shortest possible time." Hanoi was "alarmed," *Newsweek* asserted, by the "devastating losses" inflicted by "U.S. firepower"—an implicit salute to Westmoreland's 1965–67 "attrition" efforts.[86] Indeed, *Newsweek* went on, a "secret delegation of communist military experts" from North Korea, Cuba, and China concluded that Hanoi "could not hold out many months longer"—a viewpoint not shared in 1967 by the U.S. media or, indeed, by the U.S. command in Saigon. This insight into secret communist thinking remains a *Newsweek* exclusive.

If the pseudo-intimate accounts of high-level pre-Tet communist thinking bordered on the fanciful, a number of points *Newsweek* made about North Vietnamese battlefield performance did not. Facts other newsmen could also have discovered but did not seek out were: (1) the foe's lack of battlefield coordination resulted in an inability to reinforce success; (2) "bold schemes" to seize the Saigon radio station and capture South Vietnamese armor went astray;[87] (3) key bridges were not blown; (4) local Vietcong commanders failed to quickly commit major units, thus letting the attacks' early momentum die.

Other points made by *Newsweek* remain debatable, notably that the Vietcong were "badly surprised" to find that the allies would use

firepower against them in populated urban areas. And *Newsweek*
alone made the assertion that "So confident were the communists
. . . that they placed an order at a renowned Chinese restaurant in
Cholon for 400 meals to celebrate their victory."

In concluding, the magazine drifted back toward orthodoxy: "Despite the fact that the communists did not achieve most of their objectives, their offensive was far from a failure . . . it caught the [al-
lies] by surprise and made a mockery of numerous allied claims that
the enemy was too weak to stand up and fight[88] . . . it forced thousands of allied troops to withdraw to the defense of the cities and laid
bare the South Vietnamese countryside to communist encroachments." Most important of all, *Newsweek* said, "by launching their
Tet offensive, the communists seized the battlefield initiative from
half a million U.S. troops and raised serious doubts in the minds of
millions of Americans . . . about the future course of the war."

Having depicted Hanoi as staging the Tet attacks in desperation,
as having had setbacks in Vietnam (if not in the United States),
Newsweek then implied that the foe still held that "battlefield initiative" it had gained at Tet. Except at Khe Sanh, this was observably
no longer true; by March 2, U.S. troops were moving out and enemy
forces were cautiously reverting to harassment and road interdiction,
especially in the Delta. Yet, elsewhere in the same issue, *Newsweek*
described the U.S. command as being forced "to shift its tactics from
search-and-destroy missions to the defense of fixed positions."[89]

In sum, only the *Post* and *Newsweek* paid much critical attention
to enemy performance; the New York *Times* tended either to print
Hanoi's statements without much comment or analysis, or to compare the Vietcong and the ARVN in a manner unflattering to the latter. So also did AP and the television networks. The overall impression in all media was that the initial round of Tet attacks left the
allies with nothing but problems and the foe looming larger than life
—omniscient, shrewdly holding the "initiative," and ready to out-
general the allied commanders again.

6

Civilian Deaths and Urban Destruction: How Much and Who Caused It?

It became necessary to destroy the town to save it.

—AP, quoting an anonymous U.S. major in Ben Tre, capital of Kien Hoa province, February 7, 1968.

Aside from the fighting around Independence Palace and the U.S. Embassy on January 31, nothing was more immediately obvious to newsmen in Saigon than the destruction and distress among South Vietnamese city-dwellers brought about by the Tet offensive. In Saigon reporters could view the smoke of burning buildings from the Hotel Caravelle roof garden, and in Cholon itself see city-folk streaming out of the fighting areas as from a natural disaster, while firemen fought the flames amid gunfire and other South Vietnamese paused to watch. Fires, destruction, crowded hospitals, and schools turned into refugee camps, all could be seen firsthand without much danger—and dominated much of the early reporting. It was true that the fighting and damage in the capital were mostly limited to the suburbs and to Cholon, as the *Times* and *Post* were to point out. But the sudden destruction and new sense of danger shook up many newsmen, including this writer, accustomed to thinking of Saigon as a privileged sanctuary from the war.

Keyes Beech, an old Far East hand, was among those newsmen to arrive from Bangkok via a special Air Force C-130 transport. His reactions to Saigon's changed scene were more restrained than many others. Beech was struck by the "normal" as well as the "abnormal":

"Keep your bags out of the aisle in case we have to get out of here fast," instructed an Air Force military policeman. He wore a helmet, a flak jacket, and carried an M-16 rifle.

"There are still snipers around," he said. "Anybody on the streets after 5 p.m. gets shot."

"Except correspondents," someone objected.

"That's your privilege, sir," said the MP.

"There's an 8 a.m. to 2 p.m. curfew for all Vietnamese," the MP said, "anybody on the streets after then gets shot."

In 14 years of arrivals and departures to and from Saigon, this was the fastest trip I ever made from the airport downtown. It took 10 minutes where it usually takes 20 to 30.

The streets were virtually barren of traffic. Nearly 3 million people were living behind shutters. Except for a few children and military vehicles loaded with gun-toting men, nothing moved. In the cool of the evening the scent of flowers was mixed with the odor of rotting garbage piled high on the sidewalks.

We pulled up in front of the Caravelle Hotel, that nine-story citadel of luxury in the heart of Saigon. A dozen Americans were sitting in the lobby watching the Cotton Bowl game on television. I asked who was playing.

"Alabama and Texas A. and M.," said one spectator, without taking his eyes off the screen.

A notice on the elevator door said, "In view of the existing situation" only a fixed menu will be served in the dining room, laundry service is "closed indefinitely," running water is rationed to half-hour intervals three times daily.

"The management deeply regrets for [sic] the inconvenience caused by the existing situation," the notice concluded. . . .

Night falls swiftly and without warning on Saigon in January. I stepped out on my balcony and brushed aside the bougainvillea to watch the war. A thin sliver of moon hung in the velvety night sky.

Flares, trailing plumes of smoke, ringed the city with light. From Cholon, the Chinese sector, there was the thump of mortars and the crackle of automatic weapons. Somewhere in the distance a siren wailed.

Directly below me two tired "white mice"—Saigon policemen—sat on the steps of the old French opera house that now serves as the National Assembly. They paid no attention as a Frenchwoman walked quickly past them taking her poodle for its evening stroll. It was nice to know that some things hadn't changed.[1]

But, like typhoons, hurricanes, or ghetto riots in the United States, the Tet destruction and the pathos of the refugees fit superbly into the conventional preferences of picture editors and TV producers. Before and after Tet, the wounded GI was the easy picture; at Tet one could add scenes of urban devastation, hospital wards, and fleeing civilians. Indeed, there were virtually no films shown or photographs published during this period of *undamaged* portions of Saigon, Hue, or other cities.[2] All Vietnam, it appeared on film at home, was in flames or being battered into ruins, and all Vietnamese civilians were homeless refugees. As newsmen recognized at the time (and some noted in dispatches), this was not the case in Saigon, Can Tho, or even Hue, where the fighting lasted three weeks. Had the overwhelming visual portrait of Hue or Saigon accurately reflected the realities, urban recovery could never have occurred.

Who was to blame for it all? Civilian deaths were blamed overwhelmingly by newsmen on U.S. or ARVN firepower, either flatly or by implication. It was not an unreasonable assumption; the allies had far more firepower than the foe. A few stories of Vietcong culpability —mostly rumors or South Vietnamese police reports—got into the first fortnight's reporting in *Newsweek, Time,* and the wire services. But by and large, the invading Vietcong were seldom described in February as prone to killing noncombatants or causing the exodus of refugees.

There were several factors in this exoneration of the Vietcong. One was that Americans were not terrorist targets in 1967 in Saigon or other cities, as they had been earlier. Also, it was widely believed by American newsmen that the Vietcong exercised "restraint," using "selective terrorism" in Saigon because they: (1) feared retaliatory U.S. bombing of Hanoi and (2) did not want to alienate the urban masses or "world opinion." Prior to Tet, the U.S. Mission's lengthy periodic reports of government officials slain, hostages taken, civilian marketplaces blown up, and enemy rural terrorism rarely got into print or on television. These countrywide summaries were based on South Vietnamese police reports, and thus were suspect to newsmen. None was issued during the confusion of February 1968. Furthermore, Vietcong terrorism was seldom dramatic—in journalistic terms —unless it happened in Saigon. Most "incidents" took place far from there, since the city's Vietcong terrorist network, never large except in some American imaginations, had been slowly decimated in 1967 by the capital police's Special Operations branch. But few newsmen had lengthy firsthand exposure to the realities of the guerrilla war in the hamlets. One could fly out by helicopter to photograph ARVN mistreatment of "suspects," the callous pileups of enemy corpses, the ruined hamlets or bomb-pocked rice paddies, and the expressionless peasants watching as big American GIs searched their homes for Vietcong weapons; but newsmen did not see or feel the effects on civilians of the other side's tactics. Lastly, there was a resistance to any official statements which smacked of old-fashioned "atrocity propaganda"—part of the general Saigon skepticism toward official statements from either side in the war.

These factors may also have accounted for the failure of most newsmen, with some honorable exceptions, to follow up official announcements in late February and March of the discovery of the first mass graves of civilians slain during the NVA occupation of Hue, which turned out to be the largest single toll of civilians inflicted by either side during Tet. At Tet, far more attention—in the ethnocentric American tradition—was paid to the Vietcong murder of U.S. medical missionaries in the Central Highlands than to the Hue massacre or any Vietnamese civilian losses inflicted by the Vietcong.[3]

During the first week after the Tet attacks, the news stories of the plight of the cities in the Washington *Post,* the New York *Times,* the wire services, and the news magazines largely paralleled the pictorial and TV coverage of Saigon and Da Nang, in kind if not in degree. They reflected "Tet shock" and, often enough, a rewrite man's traditional taste for disaster. However, unlike the pictures, the reporting also took account of the government's initial attempts at refugee relief, the tactical problems, and the return, here and there, to normalcy.

During the second week, as the U.S. Mission cordially flew groups of newsmen out to hard-hit Delta cities (including Ben Tre), a new rash of *retrospective* reporting and filming of urban destruction appeared. The destruction continued to bulk large in the print media until three weeks after Tet, focusing on Hue, and in TV film and news photos until March.

Interestingly, Vietnam-based newsmen traveled *more widely* in Vietnam during February to cover refugee or destruction stories than to cover any other facet of the offensive, notably including military operations and pacification. Thereafter, such urban coverage slackened even as did editorial interest at home in happenings in Vietnam, with far less space being devoted to recovery or the lack of it. Destruction was a "story"; recovery was not:

The very tactics of the allied counteroffensive in the days and weeks following Tet reinforced the mood of pessimism in Vietnam. Residential areas were blasted by rockets from helicopters and conventional artillery. The civilians who survived were jammed into impromptu refugee centers, and the South Vietnamese government foundered in bureaucratic chaos in attempting to combat this new crisis.

There was little public attention paid to the way the Saigon government eventually did resume functioning, the less than disastrous impact of the offensive in the rural areas, the staggering loss of life suffered by the enemy. These developments were reported, but the public now had little stomach for news from Vietnam.[4]

Saigon

In Saigon, JUSPAO chief Barry Zorthian met with newsmen every afternoon during the Tet period, in his paneled, map-lined office next to the Rex Hotel, to answer questions, cite recovery efforts by the National Committee on Reconstruction, and issue sketchy statistics on such matters as civilian casualties, refugees, and destruction of homes. None of the figures was claimed by Zorthian to be accurate amid the post-Tet confusion.

At the regular "Five O'Clock Follies" on February 4, Peter Heller of USIS did the best he could:

. . . Now let me come to refugees. . . . We have no reports on refugees from I Corps at all—the source of this is the Corps' refugee organization. We have reports on an estimated 9,400 from II Corps, but this includes reports only from Pleiku, Binh Dinh and Phu Yen provinces and the city of Da Lat. From III Corps area—we have an estimate of 20,000; only Bien Hoa, Gia Dinh, and Phuoc Tuy provinces are reporting, plus the city of Vung Tau. IV Corps area—they estimate 125,000 with only Ba Xuyen, Chau Doc provinces and the cities of My Tho and Can Tho reporting. The city of Saigon—there is an estimate at the moment of 20,000 of whom 1,000 are in the Vietnamese Red Cross compound. Approximately 5,000 at the Gia Dinh cathedral, some 2,000 at the Newport Catholic high school, an unknown number at two Cholon hospitals. Now, as far as relief is concerned, voluntary agencies have set up three medical aid stations for refugees—one at Gia Dinh cathedral, one at the intersection of the Bien Hoa highway and the Gia Dinh road, and a third elsewhere along the Gia Dinh highway—I do not have a location. The GVN has set up 22 emergency relief centers for refugees . . . 1 million piastres from each province for refugee relief, and is sending relief teams to

Saigon districts 1, 3, and 5. The trucks carrying supplies are being escorted by army guards.

Eugene Risher (UPI): Peter, are these figures based on the number of people who've showed up in the refugee centers?

A.: They're estimates, Gene, this is not positive stuff. . . . I asked about the supply. . . . And they said "fair." They're moving them off to the center—they're setting up aid stations; they're setting up relief; they're sending out quite a relief team of supplies and people.

Q.: Saigon?

A.: No, outside Saigon. . . . The chief of USAID public health division was very complimentary about the way the Vietnamese Ministry of Health is responding to this emergency. They said they have organized a campaign to inoculate all displaced persons. And that the Minister of Health is personally visiting his patients in hospitals in the capital area. They said the water line breaks have been repaired in the Saigon district, pumping facilities are in good condition, water pressure is near normal, and a spot check in four areas this morning disclosed that the chlorine residual is adequate by United States standards. A food distribution plan is now in operation and 10-ton trucks are busy distributing rice, wheat, and cooking oil. More trucks are scheduled to go into distribution service tomorrow morning.

USAID also reported that power supply in Saigon is approximately 75 percent of normal at the morning—it's going up. The ARVN is working very closely with the Ministry of Health in the disposal of bodies which has posed quite a problem in the last few days; there are many in inaccessible locations and . . . not all of these are civilians of course. . . .

After hearing Heller, AP's Barry Kramer filed this story:

SAIGON (AP)—Reports on how civilians suffered in the recent heavy fighting are filtering back slowly to Saigon, and they indicate that again the people are taking the brunt of the war. . . .

Most of the (174,000) refugees have been created within the cities— 20,000 in Saigon alone. The war already has made more than 2 million persons flee their homes in South Vietnam.[5]

Recent refugee reports have arrived from only eight of South Vietnam's 44 provinces and from six cities. Most of the new refugees are in the populous Mekong Delta, where 125,000 fled their homes last week, according to official U.S. figures.

Reports were even less complete on civilians killed or wounded in the massive Vietcong offensive launched in most major cities last week. . . .

In Saigon, government soldiers were disposing of bodies, many of which were buried under tons of rubble.[6] Officials say that at present there is no major health problem. . . .

The city's water and electrical systems have remained in operation during the fighting except for minor disruptions. Electrical production was reported at 75 percent of normal and water pressure was near normal.

Officials said medical supplies are being distributed to hospitals and there was no shortage.

One of Saigon's largest hospitals, Cho Ray, in the Cholon section, was operating at reduced efficiency because hundreds who fled their homes sought shelter there and are living and sleeping in every available space. Patient care and surgery continued, however.[7]

On February 10, AP reported a conflict between Zorthian's statistics and Thieu's:

SAIGON (AP)—Official U.S. estimates of civilian losses in recent fighting across South Vietnam are trailing those of the Saigon government.

American authorities said Saturday incomplete reports to the U.S. Mission showed 1,606 civilians had been killed and 345,000 were refugees.

President Nguyen Van Thieu said Friday preliminary figures showed 3,071 civilians had died in the fighting since January 30 and at least 350,000 were living in official shelters. . . .

Ambassador Robert W. Komer, assistant to Gen. William C. Westmoreland for civil operations, said early accounts of civilian casualties were exaggerated.

"As we are getting more sober reports, the numbers are going down," he added.

But the Mission's figures appeared low.[8]

Later, after many a "numbers" story, AP's William Ryan filed a summary refugee report based on official estimates, conjecture, and a visit to the An Quang Pagoda area:

SAIGON (AP)—From 7 to 14 percent of South Vietnam's people are homeless today and the government, in the midst of a costly war, faces a staggering refugee problem.

Just how staggering a problem it is can be imagined if, for example, from 15 to 30 million people were homeless in the United States. . . .

"This is the biggest challenge yet for a government which has not had much of a record for meeting challenges," said one American official. . . .[9]

The Americans reflect worry that another offensive with the force of the Vietcong's January 31 assault in the Cholon area of Saigon could generate a chaotic refugee situation.[10]

Most newsmen, including AP's, emphasized "color" and pathos:

SAIGON (AP)—Six days of fighting in Saigon have thrust the reality
of war upon a city population that for years escaped the horrors that
occur every day in the blood-stained countryside of South Vietnam.

This was the face of Saigon Sunday afternoon: A Vietnamese doctor
shrugged his shoulders beside the bed of a dying 3-year-old boy lying
sightless, his body a raw scar from stomach to forehead. The
flamethrower that had scorched him killed his mother and father.

A nervous policeman raised his rifle at a dozen Vietnamese families
that wandered to the . . . front of the National Assembly building in the
center of the city.

The weary men and women picked up their babies and bundles and
straggled up the street toward the central market—homeless nomads in a
city paralyzed by the war. . . .

The homeless wander the city seeking shelter and food. The fearful
crowd the grounds of hospitals, churches, and pagodas.

Some already are trying to rebuild on the ruins. A shopkeeper who had
lost everything was one of the few people in a block-long scene of destruction. He was trying to flatten the twisted tin roof on his house and
replace it on the charred walls. The destruction that surrounded him was
as total as in Berlin in 1945.[11]

The AP described another possible victim of a flamethrower in a
story from Da Nang: "Big American cargo planes, transporting
wounded from Hue Saturday, were half filled with South Vietnamese
civilians being taken to hospitals in Da Nang. . . . At Hue-Phu Bai
Airport they were a pitiful sight. One man had a horribly burned face
—evidently caused by napalm or a flamethrower."[12] The *Post*'s foreign desk, combining AP reports into a condensed page-one war
wrap-up, removed all doubt: "Big American cargo planes were ferry-
ing the wounded to Da Nang. The Hue-Phu Bai Airport was a pitiful
sight. One civilian had a horribly burned face, the victim of a
flamethrower."[13] Such "hardening" of wire-service reports from Saigon often occurred in the home offices of the newspapers, the networks, and the wires themselves.

The newspapers' own staff accounts of the Saigon destruction
tended to "explain" it to a greater extent than did the wire-service
stories. The staff-written accounts also provided a notion of the battlefield pressures on allied commanders and the civilian losses caused
by allied firepower. For example, as the *Post*'s Lescaze reported, initially there was some hesitation to use bombs (as opposed to helicopter gunships) on Vietcong battalions holed up in the city areas:

SAIGON, Feb. 1—The battle with Vietcong infiltrators in this city appears to be largely over, although fighting continued throughout the day in several outlying districts and a few scattered pockets.

Americans in sport shirts sipped cool drinks on the roof garden of the 10-story Caravelle Hotel and watched for signs of the occasional clashes.

Vietnamese Air Force A-1E Skyraiders occasionally swooped low over areas where Vietcong resistance continued. But they dropped no bombs and did not strafe.[14]

In another story, he also noted: "There is . . . no doubt that large numbers of civilians have been killed and wounded. American civilians in Saigon have suffered very few casualties but the Vietnamese here in the capital and across the country have been caught in cross fires and hit by artillery and air strikes in many cases."[15] Again:

. . . In Saigon and Gia Dinh alone, at least 15,000 refugees were driven from their homes by the fighting, according to the Minister of Social Welfare and Refugees, Nguyen Phuc Que.

Many of their homes were destroyed by allied artillery and air strikes called in to drive out Vietcong holed up in the neighborhood. Saigon and the other cities have suffered this week as villages and hamlets have throughout the war.

The Vietcong infiltrate and they do considerable damage. When the government troops or the Americans arrive to fight the Vietcong, the battle damage is sometimes enormous. Minister Que announced over the government radio tonight that about $8,400 would be given to each of Vietnam's 44 provinces to help refugees. In Saigon he said that 66,000 pounds of rice have been distributed to the homeless and hungry Saturday.[16]

For the *Times,* Charles Mohr reported:

. . . In one sense the Vietcong have been responsible for civilian deaths by launching the urban attacks. American officials say they are sure that the population will be bitter about the guerrillas because of their "callous disregard for human life."

But allied troops, trying to protect themselves in the extremely hazardous business of street fighting, have also killed civilians. And, Vietnamese sources said, there has been some resentment about the use of armed helicopters and even Skyraider fighter-bombers in populated areas.[17]

On February 3, both Mohr and Lescaze inspected suburban destruction and the effects of allied "area weapons." Reported Mohr:

SAIGON, South Vietnam, Feb. 3—The Saigon suburb of Nhonxa, which lies less than a mile from the city airport, looked like Stalingrad with palm trees today.

A battalion of South Vietnamese Marines tried all day to take the flattened town but could not drive out the Vietcong guerrillas holding it.

Row after row of concrete houses have been destroyed by the battle that has walked back and forth over the town since early Tuesday.

A United States Marine colonel who viewed the scene called the damage incredible and said the place was a shambles. It seemed likely that many Vietnamese civilians had died or been wounded in the largely Roman Catholic area. . . .

Almost all the civilian inhabitants of Nhonxa had fled their wrecked homes. The allied force did not hesitate to use their heavy firepower on the stubborn Vietcong units facing them.[18]

Said Lescaze:

SAIGON, Feb. 3—Shortly after noon yesterday the first U.S. helicopter gunships began strafing near the Binh Hoa crossroads in Gia Dinh province about 1,500 yards from the Saigon boundary.

During the morning, residents of the heavily populated area had stayed indoors listening to the small-arms fire as Vietnamese Rangers and national police fought an estimated 50 Vietcong.

The first rockets from the helicopters struck near an American storage area where a small group of guards had gathered for lunch. Two were wounded. . . .

After about 30 minutes, the gunships stopped firing their rockets and machine guns and a helicopter crew began telling residents over a loudspeaker to leave the area.

Most of the people were already in the street walking past three towers of black smoke rising from three service stations hit by rockets.

Nguyen Van slipped out of his house and made his way to a riot police camp about 50 yards away. Some 100 civilians had already taken refuge in the camp.

One woman told Nguyen her four children were killed by one of the helicopter rockets.

She was wounded slightly in the groin and carried two of the children into the camp with her, but they died on the way.[19]

Mohr noted that "there were many incongruities" in the urban battles, a fact that failed to get across elsewhere: "While relatively small clashes disrupted the central area of Saigon, Americans and South Vietnamese went about the streets on errands. Some French residents walked their dogs on downtown sidewalks. . . . But in some places in the city and suburbs the destruction is almost total. Allied forces were resorting to bombing and shelling rather than risk the lives of troops in street-to-street assaults."[20]

On February 23, as fighting ebbed, the *Times*'s Gene Roberts visited the refugee camps:

. . . Just how many have become refugees as a result of the Vietcong's Lunar New Year offensive is a matter of confusion, although both South Vietnamese and United States officials agree the number runs into hundreds of thousands. . . .

. . . .

At least 42,000 houses were destroyed in provincial towns and cities, and thousands more in the Saigon area, although studies here are still incomplete.

To relieve the housing shortage, the government has promised to build 10,000 to 12,000 units for refugees in Saigon on a 20-year loan plan and says it will provide free building materials for those in the provinces.[21]

The news magazines, in their initial coverage of the Tet attacks, did not dwell on the details of destruction in Saigon. When they did take up the subject, both *Time* and *Newsweek* put the onus on the Vietcong. On February 9, *Time* said:

. . . They also brought bullets and bombs into the very midst of heavily populated areas, causing indiscriminate slaughter of civilians caught in the cross fire and making homeless twice over the refugees who had fled to the cities for safety. . . .

Two- and three-man teams went from door to door, like census-takers, asking for the names of local police and government officials, the addresses of ARVN and government families. Those they got—or found —they killed on the spot. . . .

At week's end, Saigon was still a city shuddering with the roar of bombs and the splat of bullets.[22]

Newsweek writers described the scene this way on February 10, when the battle for South Vietnam's cities, except in Hue and Saigon's Cholon and suburban districts, was in fact already over:

For the second week in a row, the cities of South Vietnam shuddered under the devastating blows of war. Day after day, thick columns of smoke from burning homes cast a black pall over the urban landscape, and thousands of panic-stricken refugees spilled into streets reeking with the bittersweet odor of rotting corpses. At night, the helpless huddled in the shelter of churches and in dusty pagoda courtyards, while air strikes and artillery fire split the darkness with thunderous flashes. And with each dawn, there still seemed no end in sight.

Thus the blood-drenched battle for control of South Vietnam's major cities ground on.[23]

The Saigon damage and destruction was a prime staple of television early in February. Wire-service accounts from Vietnam were transformed into the sober would-be omniscience of news anchormen. For example: "The only shops doing any real business in Saigon are the coffin-makers. As more and more civilians die, the hammers and saws of the coffin-builders are busy far into the night. There is still no official count of the *huge* number of civilians killed in the fighting. And in the streets and back alleys of Saigon hundreds of Vietcong and North Vietnamese bodies lay where they fell, for them there were no coffins, only mass graves on the outskirts of the city."[24]

This was a direct but embroidered lift from AP's Peter Arnett, whose February 2 lead began: "The only shops open in Saigon today were the coffin-makers. Business was brisk. . . . The artisans worked busily to meet the demand resulting from the devastating battles that have swept across the suburbs."[25]

On the networks, the destruction in the suburbs was occasionally portrayed as occurring in "downtown Saigon"—an error of some importance to a viewer's notion about urban devastation in the capital. Here is a CBS report with Don Webster and Walter Cronkite:

Cronkite: One of the tragic aspects of the Saigon battle is that many of its victims are those who have fled to the capital thinking they would be safe from war. . . .
Webster: The allied forces have just held an air strike at the end of this street, right in downtown Saigon.[26]
Among the things burning, apparently, is a gas station, and the black smoke can be seen all over the city. On every street . . . stream thousands of refugees, residents of the area, many of them have no idea at all whether the fire will spread to their homes. It's not quite clear exactly why there had to be an air strike, almost any building could be struck from the ground,[27] but there have been several in the last few days in Saigon.
. . . The government has been trying to give warning to citizens to evacuate before an air strike is held. Sometimes by using the government radio, other times by using loudspeakers attached to helicopters. But still there are all these masses of refugees, who wait until the air strikes actually hit before they flee.[28]

On February 6, ABC's anchorman, Bob Young, declared:

. . . Vast sections of Saigon are now in ruins. Entire neighborhoods have been reduced to rubble in bitter house-to-house combat.

Thousands of residents have been driven into the streets looking for somewhere to hide.

ABC's Lou Cioffi describes one such battle.

Cioffi: The death and destruction caused by the fighting in Saigon can best be measured by the faces of its people, faces that reflect fear. For the second straight week now, the city has been in the grip of terror brought on by a greatly outnumbered force of VC troops. Although allied officers estimate that the total number of guerrillas is relatively small, it might as well be an army.

The very nature of the city with its narrow, winding alleyways makes the job of digging the guerrillas out difficult and dangerous, and in this kind of fighting the inevitable victim is the civilian population. Frightened, confused, they have been driven from their homes by the fighting, shot at by both sides. They have taken the heaviest casualties. And although they run, there is practically no place in the city that can be called safe. . . .

Young: Saigon food supplies continue to dwindle. Many people are going hungry, and food prices continue to rise. Our ABC correspondents who live at the Caravelle Hotel in Saigon say that prices have now soared to $8 per meal and they're expected to go even higher.[29]

In Saigon, as elsewhere, television crews went out to find and film the rubble and the plight of the refugees:

Paul Cunningham (film clip): In a section of Gia Dinh where two VC battalions tried to block U.S. troop reinforcements to Tan Son Nhut airfield, this is what civilians living there came home to: blocks of smashed, burned-out rubble.

By day there are hopeless attempts to fashion some kind of shelter. At night it's a place where sporadic firing breaks out, impossible to live in.

Most of the people of this Gia Dinh section, about 2,000 of them, have sought shelter, and more important, food, at a nearby Catholic church and school, one of dozens of refugee centers set up around the city. . . .

Wilson Hall (film clip): Hospitals in Saigon were always short of beds. After the past week's street fighting, they're desperately short.[30]

And, as late as March 10, NCB's Frank McGee "special" on Vietnam attributed Saigon's losses solely to an allied military decision to "kill or maim some of the people" to protect the rest. Said Howard Tuckner: "South Vietnamese and American military leaders decided that in order to protect most of the . . . people, they had to kill or maim some of the people. . . . The only real losers were the people, and in this war there's nothing new about that."[31]

None of the media devoted much effort in Vietnam—or gave much "play" at home—to correcting first impressions. On February 10, JUSPAO secured a helicopter to take newsmen over Saigon at 1,500 feet. Photographer John Nance of AP found the damage limited:

SAIGON (AP)—Patches of ash and rubble scar Saigon like footprints of some giant wearing hobnailed boots.

Roughly 95 percent of the city appears relatively unharmed. The destruction is widely scattered. But where it is bad, it is awesome.

On the fringes, smoke billows from a half-dozen places hit by dive bombers and rocket-firing helicopters.

This was Saigon as seen from the air today after 11 days of fighting. Most major damage within the capital appears to have come from fires.

There are small slashes of wreckage in almost every sector. A half-dozen large, ugly holes gaping from the city floor each cover a cluster of blocks where there had been houses [and] shops. . . .

In the heart of the city, the dots of traffic move haltingly past the police and military sentries at the Presidential Palace, the embassies, and government grounds.

There are no great patches of devastation there, but the streets look strangely empty.[32]

Nance's story did not get used on TV or by the Washington *Post.*

Charles Mohr of the New York *Times* was also along on the flight, and he explicitly noted the difference between seeing destruction on the ground and seeing it from the air, giving some perspective to prior reports and to both television and still photos:

SAIGON, South Vietnam, Feb. 10—This city has so far escaped general or even widespread destruction despite almost two weeks of fighting in its streets.

The greatest amount of destruction in the city has resulted from South Vietnamese air strikes and artillery attacks which, in turn, grew out of Vietcong attacks on government patrols.

The largest single area of destruction is only about two miles southwest of City Hall, sandwiched between the National Vien Hoa Dao Buddhist Pagoda and Ming Manh traffic circle.

From the ground this area seems like the flattened German city of Dresden, destroyed in World War II. From the air, however, the devastated area appears to measure about 500 to 700 yards square.[33]

Mohr did not make page one.

During the period under study, no other such bird's-eye views—pinpointing the damage done to specific cities—were provided by the media. The damage was striking and picturesque in parts of many towns and cities; more helicopter surveys by newsmen might have led to an accurate description of its true extent. We now know, with Mohr and Nance, that destruction was a good deal less than total; it was sometimes magnified in reports by local officials anxious to obtain maximum relief aid.

Devastation in the Delta

There was relatively little examination of the damage wrought at Tet beyond the Da Nang suburbs and the Saigon area until February 5, when JUSPAO obtained air transport for the first of several one-day press trips to the Delta (press seats on the regular military aircraft to the area had been pre-empted by higher priority needs during the previous week). It was a shock to see this flat, green, rice-growing region hit by the conflict. Like Hue, it had been largely considered immune from the "big war" that, prior to Tet, had dominated South Vietnam's frontier areas. Many newsmen had traveled by air and car through the Delta during the 1967 fall election campaign, enjoyed good food at riverside restaurants, and marveled at the peaceful hustle-bustle of the market towns. Barry Kramer of AP, who usually covered Saigon politics, was one of them. After seeing Can Tho and My Tho at Tet, he wrote:

CAN THO, Vietnam (AP)—The communists attacked 11 of the Mekong Delta's 13 province capitals in their big offensive and as a result of the fighting estimates Monday were 1,230 civilians killed. More than 3,000 wounded and from 80,000 to 120,000 homeless.

An American general said in some areas the Vietcong used civilians as shields to make their advances. In other cases there was evidence the communists refused to let civilians leave areas they knew would come under U.S. and South Vietnamese counterattack.

Thus some of the civilian casualties resulted from allied assaults. There are peasants of the Mekong Delta, long a Vietcong stronghold, who blamed the Americans and their own government for their plight.[34]

My Tho, the Delta's second largest city, with 70,000 population, about 40 miles northeast of Can Tho, was half destroyed. Most of the damage came from U.S. and South Vietnamese bombs, artillery, and rockets. The Vietcong had moved inside My Tho with the objective of seizing the headquarters of South Vietnam's 7th Division. To stop them the allied forces had to attack them in the positions they had taken in homes and other buildings. It was a necessity of war.

But the looks the people of My Tho gave Americans Monday appeared to be angry looks. At last count, 63 civilians were dead and more than 680 wounded.

In Can Tho, a U.S. . . . official said, government loudspeaker trucks warned about 20 civilians for six hours to leave a residential area taken over by the communists. For some reason they didn't leave before U.S. forces attacked with napalm. The American official received evidence the Vietcong would not let the civilians out and 17 of them were killed.

About 50 civilians in all were killed in Can Tho. The official estimate is that 10 to 20 percent of the 300 wounded civilians in Can Tho resulted from U.S. military action. The others were killed or wounded in fighting between the South Vietnamese and Vietcong.[35]

Lescaze of the *Post,* a veteran Delta hand, described My Tho with one of the first (and few) coherent reconstructions not only of the Vietcong attack and damage but also of South Vietnamese response:

MY THO, South Vietnam, Feb. 5—A third of My Tho is destroyed.[36] Perhaps 50 percent of this prosperous Mekong Delta city's people have lost their homes.

No one is sure how many civilians have been killed. About 300 are known dead, some killed by allied bombing, others by the Vietcong or after being caught in a cross fire. More than 1,000 wounded have been treated in the provincial hospital.

Rue Pasteur on the west side of the city is a dusty line between piles of broken brick and a few standing walls. Twenty-one . . . burned-out buses stand where they were parked last Tuesday night, before three Vietcong battalions, operating from a command post in the bus station, opened the battle for My Tho at 3 a.m., Wednesday. . . .

. . . .

Initially, Vietnamese officials have responded quickly to the problems of reconstruction. Seven committees have been established and the 5,000 to 7,000 homeless are being taken care of in schools and churches. The majority of the estimated 40,000 whose homes were destroyed have been taken in by family and friends.[37]

Unlike Kramer and many another correspondent, Lescaze warned that it was "too early to tell what the people of My Tho were thinking," apparently failing to spot those "angry looks." He cited the view of the American pacification officials there—that the popular reaction was mixed anger and respect vis-à-vis the Vietcong—but did not pretend to render a judgment after a one-day, two-city junket.[38]

On February 7, another press visit to the Delta was organized, this time to Ben Tre (population 35,000), capital of Kien Hoa province, one of the Delta provinces where the Vietcong were strong, and where the enemy had committed an entire regiment, perhaps 2,000 men, with severe street fighting lasting two days, as Lescaze also reported. He and Bernard Weinraub of the New York *Times* made the trip. So also did Peter Arnett, who later recalled:

The week prior to the Tet attacks, I had been down in Ben Tre on a pacification story and met all the Americans in the MACV compound plus the civilians [USAID and CORDS personnel]. I got to know them pretty well in the four days I was there. No trouble, then, when I returned [on the press trip]. . . . While [the other newsmen] were getting the grand tour, I was out on my own, first interviewing an Air Force major who told me how he directed bombs on the city, then with others, including the three Army majors in the compound.[39]

This version of Arnett's story from Ben Tre appeared on the AP wire on February 7 in the United States. It included the quote of a U.S. major that was destined to become an enduring cliché of the war:

BEN TRE, Vietnam (AP)—At what point do you turn your heavy guns and jet fighter-bombers on the streets of your own city? When does the infliction of civilian casualties become irrelevant as long as the enemy is destroyed?

The answers to both these questions came in the first few hours of the battle for Ben Tre, a once placid Mekong Delta river city of 35,000.

"It became necessary to destroy the town to save it," a U.S. major says.

The destruction of this provincial capital was drawn out over 50 hours.

Ben Tre was one of 35 population centers attacked by communist forces in the upsurge of fighting last week. A reinforced regimental-sized enemy force of approximately 2,500 men invaded the city and its environs, U.S. advisors report.

They were eventually driven from the city. All important government installations had held out. But the civilian death toll was high as the Vietcong was driven from the center of the town and its suburbs.

U.S. advisors said today that this firepower probably contributed largely to the deaths of at least 500 civilians and possibly 1,000.

"We will never know for sure," said Lt. Col. James Dare, from Chicago, commander of U.S. Advisory Team 93.

"Many families are buried permanently under the rubble."

Allied firepower included 500-pound bombs, napalm, rockets, various types of antipersonnel bombs and 105 and 155 mm. artillery. The decision to use this firepower was not taken lightly, U.S. advisors asserted.

"They are our friends out there," one American said, pointing out of the U.S. advisory compound to the smoking city. "We waited until we had no choice. The Vietnamese Chief of Staff had to bring in an air strike on the house of his neighbor."

The Ben Tre defenders said the Vietcong attackers had overrun most of the city, and were containing the Vietnamese and U.S. forces, getting ready to overrun them, when the heavy firepower was sent in.

"We had to argue with our corps headquarters at Can Tho," a U.S. captain said. "They didn't like the idea. But they were convinced when we explained that it was rockets and bombing, or the end for us."

Fighter-bombers splashed napalm on a 3,000-yard-long river bank opposite the U.S. military compound that was cluttered with thatch-roof homes. The flimsy structures were reduced to ashes.

Armed helicopters made dozens of passes at the rambling marketplace in the center of the city, smashing its walls and leaving the roof a mass of twisted steel girders.

Two- and three-story concrete homes and business houses around the marketplace became gaunt shells of blackened concrete. The Ben Tre radio station, occupied by Vietcong who began broadcasting to the population, was taken out in a bomb attack by U.S. fighters. . . .[40]

Various versions were edited on the AP desk in New York. One of them put the major's quote in the lead. The story earned Arnett special mention in dispatches. Said the *AP Log* for the period February 4–10: "One of the most graphic of the week's stories was Arnett's account of the destruction of Ben Tre 'to save it,' and his photos added to the story's impact: grim civilians, the bullet-riddled arch over the central market." In the same issue, ironically, the *Log* chided AP's New York bureau because it "was slow hitting the human misery angles in the Gotham [New York City] garbage strike."[41]

Arnett himself said:

When I left Ben Tre with the others early in the afternoon, I had that quote tucked away in my notebook along with much other information that the others just didn't have: particularly from the Air Force major who had agonized over having to bomb the town. I quoted him fully in the story, which, by the way, got a big ride all over the place. Now what about The Quote? Who said it? I will tell you this much: Two of the majors were together when one of them came out with it. The perpetrator is still in the military, now a lieutenant colonel the last time I heard, having survived an intense MACV investigation of the quote. (The first helicopter into Ben Tre after the story appeared was filled with colonels from MACV bent on discovering who had made that quote. Peter Kann of the *Wall Street Journal* was present when the MACV brass flew in. . . .) So I will keep my silence until I run into him again and get his clearance.[42]

UPI's Dan Southerland, Arnett's competitor, was also in Ben Tre, and also quoted a U.S. soldier, but by name:

BEN TRE, Vietnam (UPI)—As an American soldier who lived through the fighting put it, the war has "pretty well chewed up" this once beautiful Mekong Delta city.

"The Vietcong were holed up in a lot of buildings and there was no way to get them out but to shell and bomb them out," said Air Force Sgt. John M. Todd.

More than 2,000 Vietcong last week swarmed through this province capital, 45 miles southwest of Saigon. They held it for 42 hours except for a few strong-points such as the Vietnamese Army and province headquarters and the U.S. military compound.

American jets bombed the center of town to drive them out. Helicopters rocketed the business district. And U.S. Navy River Patrol Boats flattened a village across the river because they were "getting fired on from almost every house over there."

The Vietcong outnumbered the Vietnamese Army force in the town six to one. Half the soldiers were away from their posts celebrating the Lunar New Year holiday. . . .

But more civilians than soldiers were killed and wounded in the battle of Ben Tre just as they had been in the fighting at My Tho city 10 miles north of here, and many other places throughout South Vietnam.

Authorities said as many as 1,000 civilians were killed—double the combined dead of communist and allied forces—and 1,500 wounded out of Ben Tre's population of 35,000.[43]

Bernard Weinraub's Ben Tre story focused on the people and the effects of battle:

BEN TRE, South Vietnam, Feb. 7—On this warm, languid day in Ben Tre, children picked through the smoldering rubble in the market place, American soldiers patrolled shattered streets, South Vietnamese troops scoured empty blocks for bodies, and Mrs. Dieu Thi Sam sat stunned in the bombed wreckage of her home and wept.

She pointed to the sky. "The first bomb landed on the next house," she said in Vietnamese. "I ran down the street and began to cry. My house exploded. I keep crying. I cannot stop."

. . . Nearly 1,000 South Vietnamese are believed to be dead after one of the bitterest battles of the week's Vietcong offensive.[44]

But the *Times* foreign desk could not resist the AP's anonymous major, and it shirttailed Weinraub's story with the quotation and a stronger rewrite of the AP's second paragraph: "He was talking about the decision by allied commanders to bomb and shell the town regardless of civilian casualties, to rout the Vietcong."

Neither Arnett nor the major in Ben Tre could have read the *Times*'s James Reston, whose Washington column on February 7 cited a vivid AP report that "large sections of Saigon and Hue lay in smoldering ruins," and then asked: "How do we win by military force without destroying what we are trying to save?" And, later, "How will we save Vietnam if we destroy it in the battle?"[45]

Arnett's quote passed quickly into the overheated rhetoric of the Vietnam debate back home. It was cited, paraphrased, reshaped, misattributed, and used for years as an all-purpose description of the war. *Time* picked it up on February 16 to explain, as did Arnett, the battle: "It was the Vietcong's decision to bring the war into the midst of the cities, and the initial damage was wrought by communist guns and mortars. But the bulk of the actual destruction occurred during the allied counterattacks . . . these posed a grim dilemma that was summed up bluntly—and injudiciously—by a U.S. major involved in the battle for Ben Tre. 'It became necessary to destroy the town to save it,' he said."[46]

Senator Albert Gore restated it: "Apparently the Vietcong have taken to the cities as their jungles, and here we find guerrilla fighting in its most vicious form. I have not thought that military victory in its traditional sense was in the offing in Vietnam at any time in any manner. A military victory can only be achieved by the destruction of what we profess to seek to save."[47]

ABC applied it to the battle of Hue: "The Marines crossed the Perfume River in assault boats last night and today in the face of heavy fire; the going is rough and Marine officers concede that it may be necessary to rip apart, destroy the beautiful Citadel in order to save it."[48]

Drew Pearson used it: "The problem boils down to the fact that we are supposed to be the saviors of Vietnam, yet we were not able to save, and the only way we can restore our police power is by shattering buildings and killing civilians with bombs and artillery. In other words, to save Vietnam we must almost destroy it."[49]

The New Republic reworked the quote, and attributed it to Major Brown: "North Vietnam also has Soviet bombers able to pound the allies if they wish. North Vietnam, however, prefers leaving that sort of destruction to the Air Force which did its best to wipe out Ben Tre, 50 miles below Saigon. Helicopter and bomber attacks on Ben Tre were directed by Maj. Chester L. Brown of Erie, Pennsylvania, who said to the Associated Press that 'it became necessary to destroy the town in order to save it' and 'a pity about the civilians.' "[50]

Time, discussing the Vietnam debate at home, said: "Aside from the outright pacifists who object to all wars, there are many who protest because they feel that the United States is destroying Vietnam in its determination to save it."[51]

In 1971, *The New Yorker,* by then increasing its political commentary, recalled it:

. . . In the winter of 1968, when an American officer explained the bombardment of the city of Ben Tre, in South Vietnam, by saying, "It became necessary to destroy the town to save it," it was almost immediately obvious that, with unwitting, insane brilliance, he had penetrated to the very heart of what was then the Vietnam War. . . . Furthermore, to judge from the tepid response in our country to the *growing danger of war with China,* we can no longer see the threat of even the biggest deal of all—what would truly be the last war, for everybody. Like the war in Indo-China, that war would be fought for nothing. And if we reach that dread pass, and if any Americans survive, there may well be one among them who will say, "We had to destroy the world in order to save it. But don't worry. It wasn't any big deal."[52]

Meanwhile, newsmen in Vietnam in early February 1968 proceeded unaware of Arnett's coup. The initial rash of destruction and after-action battle stories from the Delta during the first half of that month (four from AP from four cities, paralleled by one from UPI,[53] three in the Washington *Post,* and three[54] in the New York *Times*) was followed in late February and early March by a few other reports on the slowness of recovery and the reaction to destruction in the hardest-hit cities. For example, UPI's Arnold Dibble wrote from Can Tho:

CAN THO, South Vietnam (UPI)—American money built the University of Can Tho, the first school of higher learning ever established in the Mekong Delta—Vietnam's food basket.
American bombs, shells, and bullets destroyed it.

The university, constructed on a pleasant, palm-lined campus, opened a year ago to 1,500 students embarking upon a brave new world.

Early in February, American-made artillery, American-made gunships, and finally jets unroofed, sieved, and ultimately leveled the school after Vietcong holed up there during the first stages of the Tet (New Year) offensive.

The construction and destruction of the University of Can Tho provided yet another paradox within a paradox in a paradoxical war. The questions it raised are, in essence, the story of the Vietnam War: (1) Was the bombing necessary? (2) What is its effect on the "war to win the hearts and minds" of Delta residents whose loyalties to the Saigon government are shaky at best?

No one knows for sure how many Vietcong were in the buildings. When there was nothing left but rubble, less than 10 bodies were found. Unofficial estimates ranged from six to two.

There are those here who believe the university could have been saved and secured if South Vietnamese troops had gone in and rooted out the enemy. This the South Vietnamese forces could not or would not do, although they had sealed off the area, an operation some feel that ultimately would have caused the enemy to run out of ammunition and food supplies.[55]

The *Post*'s Lescaze made his own visit to Can Tho, writing: "In city after city, they complain to a visitor that it was not necessary to knock down their houses, because only a few Vietcong were nearby. Whether or not they are right does not matter. They believe the damage was unnecessary and they know most of the damage was done by South Vietnamese troops and Americans."[56]

Lescaze also visited the hamlet of Bung Trop:

The Vietcong moved through Bung Trop on their way to attack Ba Xuyen's province capital, Soc Trang, and again in their retreat. About 80 percent of the hamlet was destroyed by American helicopters. . . .

The people of Bung Trop have sought out their district chief and asked him to promise that helicopters will never be used against the hamlet again. . . .

The American military, and probably the Vietnamese provincial officials, are not willing to let Vietcong shell the air base (or Soc Trang itself) without retaliation. If the shells come from Bung Trop, about 1.5 miles away, Bung Trop will be raked again. . . .

The people say their hamlet was struck for 12 straight days following the Tet attack on Soc Trang. They believe that three or four Vietcong were killed in Bung Trop.

Most of the rockets hit after the enemy had left the hamlet, they say. About 10 civilians were said to have been killed.[57]

The news magazines continued to concentrate on Saigon and Hue. But on February 16 *Time* reported: "In the Delta, Vinh Long was 25 percent destroyed and burdened with 14,000 new refugees. Ben Tre . . . was one of the hardest-hit towns in all Vietnam: 45 percent destroyed, nearly 1,000 dead, and 10,000 homeless. *Many sections of Saigon were heavily damaged and 120,000 people left homeless.*[58] Estimates of the damage to Hue ran as high as 80 percent. *One out of five* of Da Lat's 82,000 people was without a roof over his head."[59]

Newsweek's Merton Perry said the word in the Delta was "disaster," adding: "According to the doctors at the hospital, when the fighting started about 50 percent of the civilian casualties were caused by the Vietcong and about 50 percent by the United States and South Vietnamese. But as the United States began counterattacking with its immense firepower, it also began accounting for almost all of the casualties."[60]

Television also continued to be preoccupied with Hue and Saigon, but the anchormen repeated the Delta wire reports. Said Walter Cronkite: "Saigon today received its first detailed report from the communist attacks in the Mekong Delta last week. And they said that in major battles in 11 provincial capitals there, more than 1,200 civilians were killed and 100,000 left homeless. Hardest hit was the major Delta city of My Tho, where at least 25 percent of the buildings and homes were destroyed. Most of that damage was caused by allied air and artillery strikes."[61]

NBC's Howard Tuckner elaborated on My Tho:

This was a lovely city—a week ago. Now, a sizable part of this provincial capital in the Mekong Delta is almost completely destroyed. . . . Much of the destruction was caused by Vietcong and South Vietnamese Army troops firing rockets and mortar shells at one another, but much of it also was caused by U.S. bombs. About 10,000 South Vietnamese lived in this area. Hundreds were killed. At least 1,500 civilians were wounded by the air strikes and by the troops firing on the ground. The wounded have been told that the South Vietnamese commander had to order the air strike to keep the city from being overrun. Most of the wounded do not believe this. Through interpreters they said, "The air strikes were ordered not so much to save the city, but to save the South Vietnamese civilian headquarters in My Tho. . . ."

Many were wounded when the Vietcong used them as shields, ad-

vanced behind them, even the children. Government troops fired through
the civilians. The wounded say the government troops shot up the civilians . . . even when no Vietcong were nearby. . . . South Vietnamese
commanders often had to beg their troops to stop firing.

The U.S. AID doctor in charge of the My Tho hospital says many of
the more than 1,500 wounded are not expected to live, even those who
were already treated. Dr. Jenkins also said none of the five South Vietnamese doctors were in the city when the attack occurred, that they were
all off holidaying during the Vietnamese Lunar New Year though they
feared an attack would come. All the surgery has been performed by
Dr. Jenkins and a few relatively inexperienced South Vietnamese interns.
About 50 South Vietnamese troops died in the fighting, yet only two persons attended the public burial. The burial party had to be there. Before
the attack, government troops got along very well with the people of My
Tho. In the past, every time a South Vietnamese soldier died in combat
many My Tho civilians attended burial services without being asked.
Now things have changed in My Tho, and this woman knows it. Things
will not be easy for her in My Tho from now on. She is the wife of one
of the slain soldiers . . . and she continues to say, "Why did you leave
me?"[62]

Tuckner implied that the widow knew she would be the target of
civilian retaliation for wild firing by ARVN troops. However, he put
more blame than most on the Vietcong for civilian casualties. It is an
emotive account, and the accompanying film showed only destruction.

During February, of the 16 Delta province capitals, newsmen visited four—Can Tho, My Tho, Vinh Long, and Ben Tre. These were
the worst hit (although a fifth, unvisited city, Chau Doc, was also
badly damaged in street fighting). Almost no one, including this
writer, thought it worthwhile to visit and describe other, unscathed
Delta towns during Tet, even as air transportation improved. There
were higher priorities. Manpower, again, was scarce. The "recovery"
—or lack of recovery—stories in early March were few, and limited
largely to the *Post, Time,* and the wire services. In all, the networks'
weekday evening news shows in February aired three film reports
from the Delta (two on CBS, one on NBC) and another three in
March (one each on CBS, NBC, and ABC). All echoed the earlier
Delta themes.

Hue: The "National Shrine"

No city got more press attention during Tet than Hue, or the "ancient imperial capital," as it was commonly described by the media.[63] There were sound reasons: the city was accessible; it was known, however superficially, to old Vietnam hands in the press, and the fight for its control lasted 25 days, from January 31 to February 24. During their relatively limited exposure to Vietnam, several generations of newsmen had found Hue a welcome, picturesque oasis in the war.

The AP, three days after the Hue battle began, set the scene:

The ancient imperial capital of Hue, its royal splendors and old pagodas already ravaged by time and wars, was the scene of a fierce battle today as allied troops tried to drive communist forces from the Citadel.

Vietcong flags flew from crumbling stone battlements. Gunfire echoed among royal tombs and along the banks of the gently flowing Perfume River.

Hue, with its lush lotus ponds and timeless ruins, was one of the last outposts of placid charm in the chaos of the Vietnam War. But [the 1965–66 Buddhist] demonstrations, shellings, and now a major battle have changed all that.[64]

The city was "old" by American, not Asian, standards, and certainly not "ancient." Besides a small military airfield, cream-colored, tile-roofed villas and schools, tall pagodas, and humbler residential areas, the Citadel contained the moated Imperial Palace. Hue University across the river was opened in 1957, after independence. The oldest relics were the "emperors' tombs"; these were located outside the city and emerged relatively unscathed from the 1968 battle. For all its historical significance, the "ancient imperial capital" of Hue was not Vietnam's "soul"—as it was sometimes described—any more than Boston is the "soul" of America.[65] Newsmen often described, but by and large did not and could not *know,* what Hue really signified to South Vietnamese elsewhere in the country, or what the damage done to the city meant psychologically—i.e., in terms of public support for the Thieu regime.

Time's David Greenway, one of the two newsmen (the other was ABC's Bill Brannigan) to cover the ARVN's bitter Citadel fight in early February, described the military problem (and Brigadier General Truong's reaction, which did not see print) in a February 9 report to New York: "The 1st Division commander, Ngo Quang Truong, was also getting frustrated. When asked if the palace itself were not a national monument too important to bomb, he said: 'You exaggerate. It is good for tourists, but if we meet heavy resistance we will use air strikes, artillery, everything.' "

Of necessity, during the battle, newsmen's views of the physical damage and casualties in Hue were limited. Reporters and TV cameramen focused on the sites of the U.S. Marines' toughest fighting: the blown bridges, the destroyed An Cuu market, and battered houses along Highway One coming from Phu Bai into Hue's south side; Le Loi Street paralleling the south (right) bank of the Perfume River (including the hospital, province chief's house, and the *Cercle Sportif*); the few blocks around the MACV compound, also on the south side of the river, including part of Hue University; and, on the city's north side, the devastation along the Citadel's thick northeast and southeast walls, including a much-photographed shopping district between the Citadel wall and the main bridge. These, of course, were not the only hard-hit Hue neighborhoods; they were the neighborhoods where newsmen were on hand.

Another factor affecting Hue reporting was the allied use of firepower. Bad weather and official restraint initially limited the amount and area of allied bombing; primary reliance by the Marines was on men firing 106 mm. recoilless rifles, 90 mm. tank guns, and other relatively accurate "direct-fire" weaponry at "point" targets they could see themselves. As the battle went on, however, parts of the Citadel walls and neighboring houses, in particular, were hit by "area weapons"—bombs, eight-inch howitzers, and naval gunfire. To the uninitiated or imaginative observer on the ground, it suggested Seoul or Stalingrad. *Time,* for example, likened the Citadel to the "ruins of Monte Cassino after allied bombs had reduced it to rubble."[66] Actually, Hue got off fairly lightly by World War II or Korean War standards for three-week urban battles.[67] But neither newsmen nor Hue's inhabitants knew or cared. In the United States, Hue became the symbol of cities "destroyed" by U.S. firepower to "save them." The fact that the NVA chose to make a stand in strength in Hue was not always mentioned, especially in "aftermath" stories.

How much battle damage was, in fact, done to Hue? Estimates vary. Three days after the battle was over, Robert Kelly, Hue's top U.S. AID advisor, told me he had no precise figures; he expected to get the city functioning again in a month. The Australian advisor for the Citadel district, Maj. Neville Wilson, also estimating roughly, said that perhaps "40 percent" of the housing was uninhabitable.[68] The official news agency, Vietnam Press, reporting on President Thieu's March 9 visit to Hue, said 6,174 families (45,340 persons) were "victims of the Vietcong attacks" (refugees) in Hue itself, but if the environs were included the total came to 86,429 persons and "16,000 houses destroyed."[69] Aside from the estimated 3,000 persons executed by the Vietcong, "some 944 civilians were known killed and 784 wounded" in Hue, by South Vietnamese count, out of a population of 140,000.[70]

Later, for purposes of determining relief payments, this balance sheet of housing units destroyed[71] was forwarded to Saigon:

Totally destroyed	4,456
Damaged "more than 50%"	3,360
Damaged "less than 50%"	2,757
Total	10,573

If one accepts the South Vietnamese estimate that these houses accounted for "some 80 percent" of Hue's housing, one finds that roughly 40 percent of the housing, mostly the wooden or stucco houses of the poor in or near the Citadel, was destroyed.[72]

At first, reporters were pinned down to the environs of the MACV compound, with no firsthand knowledge of the battle or its effects in the Citadel. AP's John Lengel, who accurately described allied troops as "battling more to maintain their positions than to oust the enemy" (contrary to erroneous official word in Saigon), saw aircraft strafing and rocketing the Citadel, which he—or a rewrite man—described as a "pile of ruins."[73]

On February 10, after the Marines had more or less cleared the south side of the Perfume River, Lengel wrote this story, before seeing the rest of the city:

HUE, Vietnam (AP)—In the rubbled wake of roaring street fighting between communists and U.S. Marines in Hue, the chief impression is that things cannot be the same again. . . .

One could not envision the slender Vietnamese men and women in white shirts and native dresses working under the slow ceiling fan again in the Finance Ministry. The building is a classic war ruin.

The roof has been burned off a high school. Power and telephone lines are tangled like spaghetti.

The riverfront Sports Club (Cercle Sportif) looks like the aftermath of a night-club fire.

At Hue University, bullets chewed into the electronic console in the American-donated language laboratory. Expensive microscopes stand like pop sculpture in a sea of meshed glass. Marines doze in the old wicker seats of a lecture theater.

It is still impossible to gauge the breadth of the damage. After 11 days the Vietcong flag still flies from the ancient imperial Citadel on the north bank. Little progress is being made by Vietnamese troops and the inner city of the Citadel is still a no man's land.[74]

Can the devastation of Hue be compared to a bombing of Kyoto or a shelling of the Acropolis?

The city means much to Vietnamese, though relatively few people outside of Vietnam have heard of it.

The Citadel, built by Emperor Gia Long in the 1800s, stands as a symbol of Vietnam's few breaths of independence and unity.

Hue University faculty members were *keystones* in intellectual circles. . . .

The war brought to the 140,000 people of Hue and the surrounding area a wave of vicious fighting, executions, tanks, machine guns, artillery, and tear gas.

But few seasoned observers see the *devastation* of Hue backfiring on the communists. They see as the greatest hope a massive and instant program of restoration underlined by a careful psychological warfare program pinning the blame on the communists.[75]

It is hard, however, to imagine expertise on such a broad scale in this land.[76]

This reporter initially shared the impressions of generalized devastation. Thus he was surprised on February 8, while accompanying units of Lt. Col. Ernest Cheatham's 1st Battalion, 5th Marines, to see how little damage there was: holes blown by Marines in garden walls, some broken windows and bullet-chipped walls, but no ruins or rubble. This was the scene in the middle-class Phu Cam area on the south side of Hue, along Nguyen Hue Boulevard. The reason was that the Vietcong and NVA forces were no longer making a bitter house-to-house fight here. There was considerable damage elsewhere, but it was in patches. The chief damage in Phu Cam was caused by looting by ARVN troops. Possibly because I was more interested that day in the people—Marines, South Vietnamese civilians, and rescued Americans—this fact did not get into my day's story.[77]

UPI, covering the Citadel fight, emphasized the unseen ruins—possibly on the rewrite desk in New York—as it described a "suicide stand" by the North Vietnamese "in the rubble of Hue's former Imperial Palace grounds." "Massive orange fireballs rolled up above the once-sacred shrines," said UPI, as Marine pilots dumped "500-pound barrels" of napalm on "the ruptured palaces of Vietnam's one-time kings."[78]

In its early wire-service wrap-ups on Hue, the *Post* said that Lt. Gen. Hoang Xuan Lam, the South Vietnamese I Corps commander, had given permission for the attackers to "use every weapon in their arsenal. The Roman Catholic cathedral in the center of town was among the buildings said to have been heavily damaged."[79] A rewrite of an AP report from Da Nang, this story was not strictly true, as newsmen in Hue were well aware. Lam gave such permission later—bombing began February 12—but the Imperial Palace, inside the Citadel, was off-limits.

On February 18, the AP wrote that the U.S. command had decided a week earlier to "use all the firepower needed" at Hue, and accept "bad publicity" as unavoidable.[80] On February 24, however, as reporters for the New York *Times* and the London *Times* accompanied South Vietnamese troops on the final victorious sweep through the Imperial Palace, they did not find the reputed massive devastation. Wrote Charles Mohr of the New York *Times:*

. . . For the diverse Vietnamese people, the palace comes as close as possible to a national shrine, although many Vietnamese from the Mekong Delta or from North Vietnam would regard it as of only slight importance.

Damage in the palace area was relatively minor despite sporadic artillery and mortar shelling by South Vietnamese troops in recent days.

The 100-by-600-foot throne room was only slightly damaged and the red-and-gold lacquered throne, on a three-tiered platform, was untouched by battle.[81]

The AP reported:

Elsewhere in the Citadel, which measures a mile and a half on each side, *the devastation was almost total.* Much of it was in residential areas jammed with small stucco, tile, and thatched-roof houses.

It was a scene of crumbled walls, damp, decaying bodies, burned vehicles, and trees shattered by shells. . . .

The thick walls surrounding the Citadel, built by French engineers in the 19th century, escaped major damage in most areas, though they were pitted foot-by-foot with machine-gun bullets, and the artillery left some scars.

The inner wall surrounding the Imperial Palace was more fragile and was damaged severely. The ornate gates, decorated with Chinese dragons and oriental sculpture, were badly shot up.[82]

Hue "aftermath" or recovery stories later were numerous, with human interest added. It was still not clear, as AP's John Lengel indicated, how badly hit Hue actually was, aside from the ARVN looting:

HUE, Vietnam (AP)—They scratch in the rubble for what they can find. They elbow each other for a ration of rice. They gather tree branches for firewood.

After 26 days of fighting, the people of Hue live from minute to minute.

Le Quang Phu, a clothing merchant, poked through the rubble of his bomb-blasted store Monday and found only a jumbled pile of sandals.

"I cannot ever have a store here again," Phu said. "I am trying to get to Saigon."

Phu has an exit pass to leave the city. They are hard to get. . . .

. . . After 26 days of fighting this city of 140,000 seemed 80 percent destroyed. Skirmishing continues just outside of the city and no one rules out the possibility that the communists might return.

Electricity has been partly restored. Civil servants are going back to work, but even the simplest jobs are complicated.

Only about 150 of 3,000 government workers are on the job.

"You tell a girl to type a letter," says one official, "and she doesn't have a typewriter, paper, or a place to work."

All the records were taken or destroyed by communist troops, in such public buildings as the province headquarters and Hue University. . . .

It is estimated that 2,500 civilians were killed and 1,200 more wounded in Hue during the fighting.

"Hue will never really be the same," said an American advisor. But he said it might be back in "working order" in 90 days.[83]

Next day, quoting "U.S. officials," AP said that "60 percent of the buildings are damaged" or destroyed, and "civilian casualties are estimated at 1,300 killed and 3,000 wounded."[84]

In early March, the UPI painted a picture of near-normalcy, but also noted the general air of insecurity:

HUE, Vietnam (UPI)—Sampans now drift lazily down the Perfume River and aged fishermen pass their nets where just a few weeks ago U.S. Navy gunboats feared to venture.

Pretty Vietnamese girls in their pastel-colored *ao dais* stroll the Trinh

Minh The, the park where earlier communist snipers ruled the Citadel from the fortified wall beneath the flag of the Vietcong.

Nearby, little children with laughing eyes and bright smiles toss stones into the algae-covered moat surrounding the Imperial Palace which North Vietnamese regulars earlier controlled for 25 days.

In spite of these scenes of gaiety and tranquility, much of the city of Hue remains in ruins.

Mostly because of governmental delays and red tape, only small portions of the city have had water and electricity. Fully two-thirds of Hue's 70,000 refugees have returned to their homes. Little has been done to repair and rebuild the homes, shops, and offices that were left damaged by the siege.

. . . .

Moreover, according to U.S. senior province advisor Robert Kelly, before they were beaten out of Hue the communists told a number of civilians they would return and capture the city again.

Thus, one of the biggest problems facing the allies in Hue is trying to restore some of the sense of security the people had prior to the outbreak of fighting January 31.[85]

From the start, television emphasized the pathos. CBS accused the Marines of creating more refugees by firing mortars downtown. Said Don Webster (in a film clip):

There are refugees all over Vietnam, but nowhere is the sight so appalling as here in Hue, where almost every resident is a refugee. This used to be the showplace campus of Hue University, the Department of Education; now it's a shambles. . . .

A decorative fountain, just across the street from the university, has become a community washbasin. These women wash their clothes in it. Others, their babies or their dishes. And just a few yards away the war goes on. Some of these mortar rounds may hit enemy North Vietnamese, but firing right into the downtown area, almost all of them will hit homes, creating permanent refugees. . . .

There's little doubt these U.S. Marines are winning the military battle in Hue. The hope is that the Vietnamese people will blame the communists rather than the Americans for whatever damage is being done.[86]

In fact, as the film shows, the Marines had set up light 60 mm. mortars next to the fountain, which was itself in the downtown area, to fire in support of troops moving on the urban outskirts in the soccer stadium area. This writer was there with Webster. The danger was not of creating more refugees, but of possibly attracting retaliatory Vietcong fire to this crowded area around the mortar site.

Walter Cronkite, who briefly toured the south side of Hue, not the Citadel, reported:

I'm standing on the south bank of the so-called Perfume River. The city, of course, is devastated, and now the fight here is as bloody, as vicious as it's ever been.[87]

NBC's aftermath story was to be rivaled only by *Newsweek*'s in hyperbole. David Burrington narrated (in a film clip):

American officials in Hue admit that the city is demoralized and almost without hope at the moment. According to official estimates, more than three-quarters of the people are now homeless. The initial estimates say that 80 percent of the buildings in Hue have been mostly destroyed. Underneath the rubble, many of the dead still lie, and more than 2,000 civilians are believed dead. In fact, more civilians apparently died than soldiers.

Looting is widespread. Vietnamese servicemen have been the worst offenders. Some were caught, but they were not strongly disciplined. People in the city protest bitterly. They say that the North Vietnamese did not loot during their occupation. American officials admit they have no evidence of enemy looting.

Order is still maintained only by martial law. There is almost no government. It was smashed like the provincial headquarters. So far, there's not even a tentative plan for rebuilding the city. People have been too busy to even think about it. Everyone, including the government staff, is too preoccupied with survival.[88]

Time magazine paid attention primarily to the tactical aspects of the Hue battle. However, on February 9 it made brief reference to damage by allied bombing:

. . . [General] Lam and U.S. Marine Lt. Gen. Robert E. Cushman, Jr., knew how to get [Hue] back fast, but only at the cost of reducing it to ruins, and turning much of Vietnam's heritage to crumbled stone. So the Skyraiders, wheeling and diving over Hue in support of the allied counterattack, at first used only guns and rockets no larger than 2.5 in. in order to protect the city's buildings and royal tombs and monuments. When after four days the communists still held more than half the city, heritage was reluctantly sacrificed to necessity and the bombs loosed on the Citadel. The United States, however, insisted that the South Vietnamese do the bombing themselves.[89]

Again, in its next issue, *Time* went further, saying: "Gradually, the battling turned the once-beautiful city into a nightmare. Hue's streets were littered with dead. A black-shirted communist soldier sprawled dead in the middle of a road, still holding a hand grenade. A woman knelt in death by a wall in the corner of her garden. A child lay on the stairs, crushed by a fallen roof. Many of the bodies had turned black and begun to decompose, and rats gnawed at the exposed flesh."[90]

Newsweek was behind *Time* in covering the Hue battle, but compensated with some overheated descriptions of the after-effects. It reported early restraints in allied bombing, but gave a still-exclusive insight as to the reason: "Though allied planes strafed communist positions, they were reportedly under orders not to drop bombs for fear of adding to the already large number of civilian casualties. Another likely reason for the restraints placed on the use of air power: Somewhere in the city, it was assumed, the province chief and 10 American civilians were being held captive by the communists."[91]

The magazine's aftermath story was entitled "The Death of Hue," and it set up some straw men—such as "a triumphal parade"—and then knocked them down with an abundance of anonymous quotations and old-fashioned appeals to the emotions:

For 25 days, the huge red and blue Vietcong flag fluttered over the once-picturesque city of Hue. But last week as U.S. and Vietnamese troops occupied the city after some of the bitterest fighting of the war and hauled down the enemy banner, there were no smiles, no kisses, no tossed flowers for the conquerors. Americans walking the streets of Hue drew impassive, sometimes hate-filled stares.

Occasionally, when an American went by, a Vietnamese would spit on the ground. "We understand why you had to do it," a citizen of Hue told *Newsweek's* Maynard Parker, "but we can never forgive you for it—for all the destruction and death you caused."

Parker's report:

. . . It was not a triumphal parade. On all sides, as the Marines marched along, all they could see was destruction. No one knows how many bombs, how much napalm was dropped on Hue. But it was enough. "We used everything but nuclear weapons on this town," recalled a Marine. And what the bombs did not destroy, the soldiers and Marines— both U.S. and Vietnamese—finished off in a week-long binge of looting. "There ain't much left of Hue," said another U.S. Marine.

Treasures: When the battle began, the U.S. and South Vietnamese commanders hoped to spare Hue's many treasures: the gilded temples, the Purple Forbidden City, the priceless collections in the museum. But in the end everything had to go. As one U.S. officer told me: "At first, the Vietnamese said we couldn't bomb this temple or that house. But when both of us started to take such heavy casualties, there were no arguments. We knocked down everything we wanted to."

Newsweek also took note of Vietcong "execution squads":

Ordeal: In the 25 days of fighting, Hue's 140,000 citizens suffered some 2,500 dead, either in the fighting or at the hands of Vietcong execution squads. More than half the buildings in the city were destroyed. But the statistics do not begin to tell the story of a populace shattered by the ordeal of three weeks of combat. In dozens of Hue's families, the Vietcong kidnaped the sons of fighting age as they retreated. Store-owners have no goods to sell. . . .
Not until almost a week after Hue was taken could an armed food convoy get through. The 230 trucks brought 2 million pounds of food, much of it for the 60,000 homeless who wander the city. . . .

The magazine concluded, prematurely: "It is unlikely that the old city of Hue will ever come back to life." The story closed with a spinoff on the AP's Ben Tre quote: " 'We cannot blame you. It was either you or the Vietcong,' one student told me. 'There was no other choice but to bomb the town. We had to be sacrificed to destroy the Vietcong.' "⁹²

In its last issue of the Tet period (written March 30), *Newsweek* went back to Hue and found the "prostrate" city "a shadow of its former self." It accurately depicted a demoralized citizenry:

. . . In the onrushing course of events hardly anyone bothered to recall that many of South Vietnam's major cities had not yet begun to recover from the first shock of the Tet assault. *Yet few facts about Vietnam today have more significance than that.* From the shattered city of Hue last week, *Newsweek* correspondents Francois Sully and Kevin P. Buckley filed this report.
. . . Six weeks after the communists were finally driven out, in fact, Hue still lies completely prostrate, a shadow of its former self. Of the city's pre-Tet population of 140,000, at least 4,000 civilians were killed, 30,000 have fled, and yet another 30,000 have expressed a desire to leave.
"Before the fall," as one American official puts it, there were 17,134 houses in Hue; today, fewer than 7,000 remain. The apparatus of civil government, too, has collapsed and the military have taken over. . . .⁹³

Curiously, moreover, few of them point an accusing finger at the North Vietnamese. "When the NVA were here," said one student, "they were polite and well-disciplined, totally different from the government troops, the Americans, or even the Vietcong."

The *Newsweek* account made the Hue killings sound like isolated affairs:

Even the bonds of family—the almost mystic force that holds Vietnamese society together—were sundered during Tet. On the first day of the fighting, for example, a pretty, wellborn schoolteacher by the name of Ton Tu Ngoc Nhuan opened the door of her family mansion to find her two elder brothers dressed in the khaki uniforms of the North Vietnamese Army. Behind them stood a detail of gun-toting guerrillas. "Where is Uncle Than?" (the former police chief), one of the brothers asked. Their grandfather replied that Uncle Than was absent. Mercilessly, his grandson killed the old man on the spot. And when Nhuan's father-in-law reproached them, he too was silenced, with a bullet through his mouth. Then his wife was murdered. At that, Nhuan fainted. When she awoke several hours later, she found every other member of the household—ten blood relatives—lying dead in the garden.[94]

Hue was not the only city hit at Tet, but the worst-hit city; and it was the only city on which *Newsweek* was to focus (twice) in March 1968.

The Massacre

The Hue massacre was, as we have noted, largely overlooked; news reports cited "Vietcong terrorism" without any information as to its scope.

The first U.S. newsman to begin to uncover what life was like in Hue under enemy occupation was George McArthur of the AP, who in early February filed this report, echoed much later, in substance, by other investigators:

HUE, Vietnam (AP)—The communist forces that all but overran Hue one week ago came with complete dossiers and photographs of enemies to be executed or arrested. . . .

The troops and the commissars in the initial days were exceptionally polite and tightly disciplined, many refugees reported. . . .

Many Americans, both civilian and military, were known to have been taken prisoner. Several refugees reported that, at least at first, the Americans were treated well, though kept under strict guard in several areas. . . .

. . . .

Cadres would knock on the door or burst inside, asking for American or South Vietnamese soldiers. If no soldiers were present, the communist troops immediately became polite.

"We do not molest civilians," they would say. "Stay inside. Keep your
doors closed and do not be afraid."

. . . .

The communists were harsher on the north side of the Perfume River,
almost totally defended by South Vietnamese troops, than on the south
side, where the fighting was being done by American Marines.[95]

McArthur was one of the few newsmen to not only look at Hue's
civilians, but ask about their experiences, primarily through several
French-speaking priests in Hue. His story cited the blacklists of local
officials marked for arrest and execution, but gave no numbers. The
full extent of enemy executions was not then known; the battle was
still going on.[96]

On February 11, the AP cited the Hue mayor's report—the first
official mention of a massacre:

HUE, Vietnam (AP)—Communist troops in Hue executed 300 civilians and buried them in a mass grave south of the city, the province chief
said today.

Lt. Col. Pham Van Khoa, province chief, mayor of Hue, and military
overseer of the Hue district, said those executed were province officials,
technicians, policemen, and others who had been long marked for death
by the communists.

He said the executions took place Friday when the communists were
being pushed from the south side of the city by U.S. Marines.

Khoa said the mass grave was several miles southeast of the city, an
area not yet reached by allied forces. He said, however, that his reports
of the executions were precise and unquestionable.

At the same time, a Vietnamese civilian reported seeing from 125 to
150 Catholics being led from the city as captives Saturday.

Where the captives were being taken was unknown to the civilian, who
witnessed the scene from a hiding place near Hue's southern boundary.

Two other executions were reported Sunday by civilians who said two
police officers were marched before a communist firing squad as the communists withdrew. . . .[97]

The Washington *Post* ran a six-paragraph version of the story inside the paper. The New York *Times* story, by Thomas A. Johnson,
ran on page one.[98]

On February 28, the UPI ran a Saigon story citing government
spokesmen reporting the discovery of 100 bodies of "soldiers and civilians," some with their hands tied behind their backs, in a common
grave.[99] The UPI on March 3 further reported from Saigon:

SAIGON (UPI)—Ninety-five South Vietnamese civilians found buried in mass graves in Hue were killed by the Vietcong because they refused to fire at American planes during the battle for the old imperial capital last month, it was reported Sunday.

South Vietnamese government sources said survivors of the atrocities told of seeing victims forced to dig their own common graves and begging for mercy before they were cut down by guerrilla firing squads. . . .

. . . .

The bodies of the massacred civilians, discovered several days ago, were being exhumed Sunday. Wailing women and children looking for relatives watched as workmen opened the fresh graves in dry paddy fields and a school yard on the outskirts of Hue.

First reports of the mass executions came last month during the height of the fighting for Hue and the Citadel.[100]

On February 29, Bernard Weinraub of the *Times* described despair, ruins, and refugees in Hue, and also cited a "mass grave" where some bodies of "missing civil servants" were found.[101]

On March 6, the AP's William Ryan visited "the wreckage of what was once a city of legendary beauty," a city "which has bled to death." He devoted most attention, as did other newsmen, to American frustration, government corruption and sloth, what he termed a "massive psychological defeat" for the allies, and fear, misery, and despair. Only in passing did he note that "about 1,000 civilians have died . . . many were executed by enemy forces—mass graves have been found." Ryan did not visit them.[102]

On March 9, the U.S. Embassy issued a press release raising the number of bodies found in three mass graves outside Hue to 400, and said the Vietcong had made a systematic effort to track down specific persons. The *Times* ran a brief Reuters dispatch on page two ("Foe Killed 400 Hue Civilians"). The *Post* ran this story inside the paper:

SAIGON, Mar. 9—The Vietcong killed about 400 civilians—including women and children—during the 25 days they occupied Hue last month, the U.S. Embassy said today.

The latest of three mass graves found amid the rubble of the war-shattered city contained 10 victims, some of whom had their hands tied behind their backs.

An embassy official said Vietcong prisoners admitted during interrogation that their commanders ordered the execution of almost 400 civilians around Hue. The victims included Catholics and government officials.

So far three mass graves containing more than 100 bodies have been found near the city.

An embassy spokesman said almost 12,000 South Vietnamese were victims of Vietcong terrorism this year. Some 5,831 were killed and 2,783 kidnaped, while the remainder disappeared without trace, he added.

At least 300 persons lost their lives to Vietcong execution squads in the Catholic neighborhood of Phu Cam . . . the spokesman said.[103]

That was the end of it, for both the wire services and the newspapers. Neither the mass graves nor executions were mentioned in another *Times* story on Hue published March 23.[104] One of two *Post* stories by Lee Lescaze, also in late March, accurately cited ARVN looting, governmental chaos, 2,500 civilian deaths, ruins, Buddhist-Catholic animosity, anti-American sentiment, and indiscriminate government arrests; and a "former government official" was mentioned as saying "the communists were relatively selective in their arrests and executions."[105]

To recapitulate, AP did four stories focusing on Hue executions, UPI two, the *Times* four, and the *Post* three. *Newsweek,* as we have said, cited the "execution squads," but did not cite or follow up the embassy announcement. The television networks, as far as our records show, made only one brief passing mention of the massacre (see page 356) and showed no film reports on the subject.

In late March, *Time,* which had paid little attention to Hue's post-battle plight, picked up the account by a London *Times* reporter of his investigation of the massacre, apparently the only such investigation by any newsman in the entire press corps:

The communists executed hundreds of civilians during their Tet offensive, but the slaughter was particularly marked in and around Hue, where estimates of those put to death range from 200 to 400. British journalist Stewart Harris, who opposes U.S. policy in Vietnam and declares that "my instinct is not to sustain it by writing propaganda," recently visited Hue and vicinity to investigate the executions. Last week he reported his findings in the *Times* of London. [Harris's story follows:]

The North Vietnamese Army and the Vietcong executed many Vietnamese, some Americans, and a few other foreigners during the fighting in and around Hue. I am sure of this after spending several days in Hue investigating allegations of killings and torture. I saw and photographed a lot for myself, but inevitably I relied on many civilians and soldiers, Vietnamese, Americans, Australians, and others. All seemed honest witnesses, telling the truth as they believed it. . . .

Summing up all this evidence about the behavior of the Vietcong and the North Vietnamese Army in Hue, one thing is abundantly clear and ought to surprise no one. They put into practice, with their usual efficiency, the traditional communist policy of punishing by execution selected leaders who support their enemies. In Hue, as elsewhere, they were unable on the whole to capture and execute the more important officials, because these men were careful to protect themselves in heavily fortified compounds, defended by soldiers and police. In Hue, as elsewhere, the more defenseless "little people" were the victims—the village and hamlet chiefs, the teachers, and the policemen.

Already most of these positions have been filled again, and I find it impossible to write adequately about the courage of men who succeed the executed.[106]

What Harris learned was only the beginning. The first discovery of Vietcong victims had come in the Gia Hoi High School yard on February 26. Eventually, 170 bodies were recovered there. In the next few days and months, 18 additional grave sites were found, and in 1969 and 1970 the search continued. As of mid-1970, a total of 2,810 bodies had been found, scattered in mass graves in nearby mountains, in coastal sand flats, and around the imperial tombs southwest of Hue. And a total of 1,946 persons were still unaccounted for.[107]

Why was so little attention paid to this subject by other newsmen? In retrospect, and after discussions with press colleagues, these points come to mind: (1) the initial word on the executions, which made page one of the New York *Times* on February 12, came from Lt. Col. Pham Van Khoa, Hue's incompetent mayor, who was later to become suspect to newsmen and a target of criticism by U.S. advisors for going into hiding during the battle; (2) U.S. advisors in Hue, and Khoa's able successor, Lt. Col. Le Van Than, were preoccupied in March with the plight of the living, not the fate of the missing or dead, and so were most newsmen who visited the city; (3) the embassy announcement on March 9 was widely ignored or shrugged off as atrocity propaganda, and was not "pushed" hard by JUSPAO; and, finally (4), there was nothing in March 1968 to raise suspicions of a massacre in Hue—no mass funerals, graveside ceremonies or demonstrations. The visual evidence was all on the other side; the Vietcong were thought to practice only "selective" terror. In a sense, newsmen and their editors may have been as mentally unreceptive to reports of the Hue massacre as was much of the U.S. public later to reports in 1969 of the My Lai massacre. In any case, we missed the unfolding of one of the crucial psychological stories of Tet. The Hue massacre, ignored in America, was not ignored in Vietnam.

As Douglas Pike, who investigated the scene for the U.S. Mission, later observed, "In the chaos that existed following the battle, the first order of civilian business was emergency relief—then came the home rebuilding effort. Only later did Hue begin to tabulate its casualties." Pike's hypothesis was that the killing began with a deliberate effort to purge those officials and "natural leaders" on blacklists. This was the effort cited by the U.S. Mission on March 9. Then, believing they could hold the city, local Vietcong cadres decided on a purge of all persons, including students and intellectuals, who were a *potential* threat to a new communist order. Finally, in the last week, with the realization by the Vietcong that the battle was lost, came the largest number of killings—the killing of those who had been arrested for "indoctrination" and who had seen (and could identify) the local Vietcong who had "surfaced" during the communist occupation. Virtually all the executions, by Pike's findings, were done by Vietcong, not by NVA troops or other outsiders. These were systematic executions, not random acts of anger or panic. Moreover, the communists made a major effort to hide their work.[108]

In sum, the broad picture of "near-total" urban devastation and despair in South Vietnam was overdrawn in February 1968, especially by the wire services, the television networks, and *Newsweek.* The Americans, by their heavy use of firepower in a few cities, were implicitly depicted as callously destroying all Vietnam in order—in the phrase that became common—to save it; while the Vietcong's indiscriminate use of their own firepower, as well as the Hue killings, were largely overlooked. When individual newsmen, notably Mohr and Nance, provided a more precise measure of the extent of the damage, their reports—in contrast to other reports and to still-photo and TV film "disaster" treatment—got little play.

Was this heavy stress on what AP called the "human misery angle" peculiar to Tet? Not at all. It was, in part, a conventional journalistic reaction to calamity, whether tenement fire or Central American earthquake, with a keen sense of impact on the audience. At Tet, this reaction was reinforced by genuine shock: Many reporters were confronted with their first extensive view of war's random destructiveness and waste, while media editors and managers in Washington and New York viewed what they had misperceived as a low-level "jungle-war," when it emerged in an urban setting, as something akin to World War II. The result was, at best, a kind of compassionate sensationalism. Especially on film, this treatment tended to blur, or even obliterate, the other realities, notably the military outcome and the resilience of the South Vietnamese.

7

Performance, Morale, and Leadership of U.S. Troops

At Tet, as in other crises, most newsmen did their best work reporting events which they could see. But at Tet, eyewitness reporting of combat, including combat by U.S. forces, was limited. The fact that there were sizable numbers of newsmen in Vietnam did not, as we have previously noted, insure broad geographical coverage. Because of competition among rival news organizations, most of these newsmen flocked to the same places and watched the same events, albeit with varying degrees of perception. Nowhere was this more apparent than in battlefield reporting. With respect to eyewitness coverage of U.S. forces in combat during February and March 1968, the result of this "herd journalism" was striking: Roughly nine out of ten firsthand newspaper stories, wire-service dispatches, and TV reports from the battlefield were from Saigon, Khe Sanh, and Hue.

These three battles were important (although Saigon was primarily an ARVN fight, and at Khe Sanh the expected climax did not occur, with the early February infantry fighting on the hill outposts being inaccessible to reporters). They involved, however, only about 15 of the 100 U.S. maneuver battalions deployed and about 20 percent of the U.S. casualties suffered during February–March 1968. The recapture of Hue finally freed some newsmen in the larger bureaus (AP, *Time,* UPI, the networks, the New York *Times*), but none made serious efforts to catch up on military operations elsewhere, possibly due in some cases to sheer fatigue. After Hue, attention shifted to Khe Sanh.[1]

The net result, in terms of media treatment, was that the fighting in

Saigon, Hue, and Khe Sanh became the whole war, a war in which, seemingly, no or few ARVN forces fought, and U.S. forces were particularly hard pressed. The overall—and inaccurate—impression given, especially on film, was that, well into March, the outcome on the Vietnam battlefield was very much in doubt. Left in obscurity was the less dramatic war fought by the other 85 U.S. battalions, the 150 understrength ARVN battalions, and the Koreans, Australians, and New Zealanders. After the first week of city fighting, this unseen war raged in the Saigon "exurbs," in the upper Delta, below Da Nang, in the coastal lowlands around Quang Tri, along the Marines' Cua Viet River supply line south of the DMZ, and in the Central Highlands. These actions were episodic but costly, as U.S. forces locally recovered the initiative from an enemy who bravely held out, here and there, before finally pulling back.

The unseen war was the province of the daily war wrap-up stories by wire-service and New York *Times* rewrite men in Saigon. They depended largely on the Five O'Clock Follies and the twice-daily MACV communiqués. In turn, MACV briefers and communiqué-writers depended on the scanty, fragmentary spot military reports from the field. Thus, even when not being defensive about "bad news," the briefers could supply little context for the ground actions sketchily described in the communiqués, and this was particularly true during the first week after the Tet attacks. On February 2, Major Conrado, the ground-action briefer, was candid about his ignorance before a tense and suspicious audience in the JUSPAO auditorium:

Conrado: Good afternoon. [Laughter.] I have nothing to add to the release. [Laughter.] With one exception. And that's to give a slight explanation as to why you see us relatively void of additional ground information this afternoon. That's because there just isn't any available at this time to plug the holes in the existing situation, with the exception of those we've already closed in the past. And there are no casualty updates. I look forward to additional casualty updates—tomorrow morning's release. I'll answer as many questions as possible, keeping in mind that there are many numerous, many acts taking place all over the area and it's almost impossible to keep a running account of everything that's going on. So I'll attempt to shuffle through as many papers here and recount what I already know about some of them.

The briefers could not report what individual U.S. units were attempting to do, or what the enemy had been up to in a given area. The military reporting system was not geared to providing back-

ground for newsmen. When the communiqués cited ground action in
Hue or Saigon (in the early days of Tet), or a rocket bombardment
of Da Nang or Saigon's Tan Son Nhut airfield, the wire services could
embellish (or correct) the MACV version with reports from their
own men in the field. But in most other cases, the harried rewrite
man in Saigon, with his bundle of multigraphed handouts, was dependent on his own memory and experience; at Tet, such assets ran
demonstrably thin. Yet it must be emphasized that MACV provided
what the wires wanted: the raw ingredients for repeated daily "hard
news" stories.

The resulting war wrap-ups and "war leads" did not—and, unas-
sisted, could not—convey a coherent picture of the course of the war.
Written in Saigon, they were rewritten with brio in New York, on a
highly competitive basis, to catch the eyes of busy, jaded telegraph
editors and network news producers around the country. They were
twice deformed—by the MACV reporting system and by wire-service
embellishment. AP clients complained on occasion. But it was this
"hard news" story, supplied by its own Saigon man, that the *Times*
put on page one every day; and it was the AP or UPI version of the
same story that the *Post* foreign desk rewrote for its own editions,
and that TV writers reshaped yet again for the evening news shows.
News editors relied on the war wrap-up to bolster the front page, especially on weekends, when other "hard news" was scarce.

On the 10 days during the Tet offensive when enemy actions assumed a synchronized, nationwide pattern (the January 31–February
8 and February 17–18 periods), the war wrap-up was the obvious
choice for page one. There was no alternative. Yet on most other
days, the wrap-up at its very best conveyed little about U.S. combat
performance or the overall state of the battlefield.

In Vietnam, periodic "pooling" efforts among reporters to catch
up with the military situation around the country, especially after the
recapture of Hue, might have yielded a clearer picture. For its part,
the AP might have done better to issue its concise, undramatic, area-
by-area daily "map summary" as its war wrap-up on most days; the
Times and *Post* might have done better to print it—or a similar UPI
summary—with a map, inside the paper, while giving more prominence to firsthand military reporting or other aspects of the Vietnam
story on their front pages. But the conventions of reporting, and competitive pressure, kept the much-processed war wrap-up the "big" Vietnam feature.

Hue: A Comprehensible Battle

The differences in accuracy and comprehension in firsthand, secondhand, and third-hand reporting of events are illustrated by much of the Tet coverage. But in terms of U.S. combat performance, two military operations make the point most graphically: the three-week battle of Hue and, an extreme case, the March 16, 1968, sweep by "Task Force Barker" through the then obscure hamlet of My Lai 4 in Quang Ngai province, when the "My Lai Massacre" occurred.

Perhaps the best individual journalistic performances during Tet came out of the eyewitness coverage of the U.S. Marines' role in the recapture of Hue. (The ARVN, which suffered the most casualties in the battle, got little coverage, for various reasons.) The Hue reporting upheld a proud tradition in Vietnam among the handful of genuine war correspondents there: The newsmen went to the battlefield, exposed themselves, however briefly, to almost the same hazards as the "grunts," and, with varying degrees of comprehension, recorded the action. There was no other way to get at certain realities; truth began at battalion level.

The circumstances at Hue were not ideal, but the battle was comprehensible: Two (later three) understrength Marine battalions were trying to help ARVN retake parts of a small, European-style city, and there were definable boundaries, obstacles, and objectives. The Marines faced a foe whose tactics here were conventional. The city was accessible—by helicopter or, despite ambushes, by truck convoy from Phu Bai. The action was sustained, unlike most prior actions in the war. One could learn. Reporters could move with the assault platoons (as did Don Webster of CBS, Lee Lescaze of the *Post,* John Lengel of AP, David Greenway of *Time,* Alvin Webb of UPI, and Charles Mohr, Tom Johnson, and Gene Roberts of the New York *Times,* to name only a few).

Moreover, Hue had a "name." For a good many American newsmen, particularly those with 1966 experience of the Buddhist agitation in the city, there was a sentimental attachment to the place—a feeling shared by the American civilians and 300 advisors who lived comfortably in the Hue MACV compound, a converted three-story hotel on the city's south, or European (French), side. In 1966–67, as in certain Delta towns before Tet, the war seemed far away; the nearest U.S. base was at Phu Bai, eight miles to the south on High-

222

way One, and the 1st ARVN Division headquarters was tucked away
off in the east corner of the Citadel. As Ward Just wrote: "During
the Buddhist rebellion in 1966, Hue scarcely seemed a part of South
Vietnam at all. In the evenings you bicycled past seditious banners
calling for the overthrow of the government and expulsion of the foreigners, past the sound of martial music and shouted slogans, to the
north side of the slowly flowing Perfume River. The sampans were
moored there, up-river beyond the town center. For two hundred
piastres ($1.50), you rented a sampan to sleep in."[2]

Hue was also, of course, one of the few cities in Vietnam that bore
traces of the distant past—the restored Imperial Palace and the emperors' tombs on the southern and western outskirts, with their elaborate tiled eaves. And, it would appear, President Thieu, at least,
regarded Hue as South Vietnam's most important *regional* center in
political terms.

What few newsmen, especially on TV, were to remember or explain to their audiences during the battle was that Hue—by its location—was also important to the allies in a *military* sense. Here a railroad bridge and a Highway One bridge crossed the Perfume River on
the main supply route from Da Nang to allied forces below the DMZ.
No less important, Hue was the unloading point for ammunition,
fuel, and other bulk supplies which were brought up the Perfume
River in U.S. Navy landing craft after being unloaded at Tan My, the
small U.S. base at the river's mouth, from larger Navy coastal vessels
traveling from Da Nang. This water supply route (and two others to
the north, at Cua Viet and, later, Wunder Beach) were essential to
support Westmoreland's growing concentration of troops (the 1st
Cavalry, 101st Airborne Division, and 3rd Marine Division) north of
Phu Bai, as well as the ARVN 1st Division and the installations
around Phu Bai itself.

For the North Vietnamese, as newsmen could see, Hue was a particularly convenient place to attack on January 30–31, 1968. The
city was only about five miles from the nearest mountains and about
12 miles from the North Vietnamese Base Area 101, thus easily rein-
forceable if seized. Moreover, Hue was only lightly defended and,
outside the Citadel, unfortified. Its ARVN garrison could easily be
cut off from allied reinforcement: The Perfume River, winding up
from the sea, was in no place more than a half-mile wide, with a nar-
rower shipping channel easy to mine or cover by recoilless cannon on
the river bank; Highway One from the south crossed the Phu Cam

canal on the An Cuu bridge, easy to blow up; there was only one helicopter landing site close to the MACV compound—on an exposed
riverfront park within sight and light mortar and machine-gun range
(1,000 yards) of the Citadel. On the north side of the river, the 1st
ARVN Division helicopter strip off the eastern corner of the Citadel
was almost equally vulnerable.

What is striking, in retrospect, is how the North Vietnamese,
achieving tactical surprise against a weak headquarters garrison,
failed to exploit their initial success. They ultimately put 16 battalions (perhaps 6,000 men) into the fight; but the 1st ARVN Division
headquarters troops held on to their compound, as did the U.S.
advisors, until relief forces broke through. Thereafter it was a bitter
house-to-house fight, with bad weather; the reinforced ARVN forces
faced the strongest enemy units in the high-walled Citadel, but lacked
heavy weapons for city fighting; the Marines had to help. The Citadel
was finally cleared February 24–25.

Hue was the longest sustained infantry battle of the war to that
time and, by Vietnam standards, losses were high: The ARVN
suffered by far the greatest allied losses—384 killed and 1,800
wounded; the three understrength Marine battalions involved lost
142 dead and 857 seriously wounded; enemy losses were claimed to
be 5,113 killed and 89 captured.[3]

The battle—as far as the Marines were concerned—had two successive phases: (1) January 31–February 10, when five companies of
Marines (2nd Battalion, 5th Marines and 1st Battalion, 1st Marines) cleared the unfortified, relatively open south side of the city,
hoisted the American flag over province headquarters, and secured
the Highway One approach from Phu Bai; and (2) February 11–24,
when two, then three, companies of 1st Battalion, 5th Marines
crossed the Perfume River to join the ARVN effort to retake the Citadel, moving slowly against heavy resistance along the northeast wall
toward the Citadel's east corner.[4]

From the start, the fog of war swirled thickly at the MACV
briefings in Saigon concerning Hue. On February 2, for example,
Major Conrado announced:

> The city of Hue continues to contain areas of enemy resistance. How-
> ever, there has been considerable reinforcement into the area in the last
> day and a half or so and we are making—the progress is good because
> . . . we managed to recapture the area which was their command post in
> the city. . . . And now ARVN forces are right in the middle, eastern

portion. However, the enemy still has pockets of resistance in the north-western portion. . . . There was an indication that there were many automatic weapons surrounding those areas and I assume, because it's no longer mentioned, that we have fought our way through the automatic weapons. . . .[5]

Q.: Was the 1st ARVN Division headquarters attacked?

A.: I don't ever remember seeing a report on the division. I know that the [U.S.] compound [on the south side] has stood its ground and has always been in our hands.

Q.: Where are the American planes bombing, if not the Citadel area, Major?

A.: Well, I have no information that American planes are bombing.

Q.: There was a report that came out of I Corps that the Citadel areas were held by the North Vietnamese; that ARVN troops, armor, and tanks took, retook part of the Citadel; that communists are being squeezed in a pocket in the Citadel and that light bombs are being used to minimize damage in the Citadel.

A.: Well, I have to agree with the possibility of air strikes in the area and the possibility of aircraft. I just don't know where U.S. planes were bombing in the Citadel.

Q.: They may be other kinds?

A.: Well, what's the difference really?

Q.: If you're not aware of these basic things they're putting out there, how can we follow what you. . . .

A.: (Interrupting) You directed the question to me that U.S. planes were bombing. I don't have any information that U.S. planes were bombing.[6]

In Saigon, MACV, despite considerable rebuttal from the press, described the Hue fighting with great optimism as "mopping up" for more than a week. On February 4, for example, the evening communiqué said: "As of last evening the northwest and southwest portions of the Citadel at Hue had small pockets of enemy forces present; mopping up continues; as of noon yesterday two enemy companies were attempting to flee the Citadel and could not break ARVN contact." On February 7, the rosy tone continued: "At 11 this morning it was reported that a small pocket of enemy resistance still existed along the wall in the extreme southwest corner of the Hue Citadel. The enemy forces in the Citadel are being mopped up by ARVN elements."

On February 10, however, more realism began to creep into the MACV summaries of action in Hue, and thereafter during the battle there was little mention of "mopping up."

The Wires: The Real Story

The initial AP reports of the battle were a corrective both to MACV and to the optimism (born out of ignorance) of Brig. Gen. Foster LaHue, commander of the Marines' composite "Task Force X-Ray" headquartered at Phu Bai, eight miles from the battle. According to Richard Oliver of UPI, LaHue, in an interview, said: "Very definitely, we control the south side of the city." Oliver continued: "LaHue, commander of Task Force X-Ray and U.S. Marines in Hue, also said, 'I don't think they [the communists] can sustain. I know they can't. I don't think they have any resupply capability, and once they use up what they brought in, they're finished.' "[7]

LaHue said what he had apparently already told MACV headquarters—the South Vietnamese I Corps commander, General Lam, was at that point equally blasé—leading to a February 3 prediction by Brigadier General Chaisson to newsmen in Saigon that the battle would be over shortly.[8] Naturally, this was reflected in MACV communiqués.

John Lengel was the first AP man in Hue (John Schneider, a red-bearded free-lancer for CBS, had already gotten in with the first Marine rescue force). Three years later, Lengel recalled how he reached the embattled city on February 1–2 from Phu Bai, the U.S. base down Highway One:

I got to Phu Bai [from Da Nang] alone to match the "scattered islands of resistance" story [Richard] Oliver filed on his way back to Da Nang. He just happened to be in Phu Bai when [the Hue attack] started and the information he got there apparently was upbeat enough that he walked away from the story. I just thought I was going up for a hard day's interviewing. But I couldn't get into Hue. The Marines weren't on the road. That was bad. Though Schneider was supposed to be up ahead, he had got in with the first company. Another convoy formed the next morning by the training grounds outside the wire. We were getting mortared just standing there and I could see the situation was more serious than anyone popularly thought. . . . [Rick] Merron [an AP photographer] drove up about noon, I guess, just as a pilot was waving me aboard an ammunition resupply CH-46. Then any doubts I had fell away. [En route to Hue] the chopper was jinking [dodging], skimming in ways the Marines seldom flew. It was chill, gray, low overcast as it was to be the whole month. We took at least one hit, the gunner said, beneath the rear rotor.

I swear we pulled a G coming around sharply into the landing zone, the mike boat ramp near the bridge. The ramp went down and the trouble was sealed when the LZ Marines tumbled in, waved us out past the wounded. We flopped behind that two-foot terrace there. The chopper was gone in seconds and we had some popcorn AK fire and I guess some recoilless coming down the street along the river side of the university. It took us a half-hour to make the MACV compound a block away.

The compound was the Alamo. The government and the Marines were the scattered islands of resistance the Marines in Phu Bai had been talking about.

. . . I had important, establishing eyewitness stuff; I believe the first that came out of Hue. I was anxious over what to do with it. Leave for Phu Bai to file? Give up my vital position? Go through the frustration of getting back in? Idly I tried a telephone. It was in my mind that they would never work. It did and I had some of the best communications I ever had in Vietnam. The signalmen at the switchboard near the dispensary were very good to me for the whole story. . . .[9]

Dictating to Saigon from the MACV compound, Lengel filed this story, which got on the wire back home early on February 2:

HUE, Vietnam (AP)—Four battalions of communist troops control most of the streets of Hue, Vietnam's ancient imperial capital. They are resisting allied forces with machine guns, mortars, and rockets.

The enemy fire was so intense today that two U.S. helicopters attempting to run the gauntlet to collect wounded were shot down over the city.

U.S. Marines and infantrymen and South Vietnamese troops are battling more to maintain their positions than to oust the enemy.

The Vietcong-North Vietnamese force deployed through the city holds a major part of the old walled Citadel, formerly the seat of kings but now a pile of ruins [not so, but no one then knew the difference], and the headquarters of the South Vietnamese Army's 1st Infantry Division.

South Vietnamese troops hold a small part of the Citadel. The Americans are fighting from a half-block-square compound that houses U.S. advisory headquarters.

The city is now in its fourth day of virtual siege. Refugees have poured in, swelling the normal 40,000 population enormously. Civilian casualties are believed to be extremely high.

The allies also control the bridge across the Perfume River that joins the city.

The communists burst upon Hue four days ago, and both the province chief, Lt. Col. Pham Van Khoa [survived and was fired], and a senior American civilian advisor for pacification [killed] may be in enemy hands, Americans at this compound believe.

A platoon of U.S. Marines fought its way to within sight of the American advisor's house three days ago but Vietcong soldiers were surrounding the building.

American and South Vietnamese planes strafed and rocketed communist positions in the heart of Hue today. There were reports they had been ordered not to drop bombs because of the civilians.

At one point during the afternoon, American Marines and U.S. Army advisors were directing huge volumes of fire onto the street from this three-story building on the western edge of town. They were trying to cover the dash of four armored trucks to evacuate wounded Americans at a boat ramp at the edge of the Perfume River.

In addition to the senior pacification advisor, concern is also felt for nine other American civilians in the city.

Some of the U.S. Marine companies have reportedly suffered heavy casualties. At least 10 Marines are known to have died and another 108 have been wounded.

There have been heavier casualties among the South Vietnamese troops, U.S. advisors say.

No one really controls the city.[10]

Lengel did not stay in Hue for the entire fight; he came and went, as did most other correspondents. But he dictated reams of copy to Saigon:

. . . I filed everything I could get my hands on. The first obligation was a factual assessment of the progress being made. Assessments were opinions of commanders, sergeants, officials on what had been done so far. I think everything I saw got into my copy one way or another: three days of a Marine squad; the damage, the visible plight of the refugees coming our way; every kind of quote; the follow-up and discounting of enemy use of gas in the Citadel; the reluctance of a squad to go through a fence hole into a field of fire and the abandonment of the plan; the young acting sergeant leading a platoon who got a letter from a Missouri stockbroker, disabled leading the same platoon through Seoul; Khoa, the fugitive province chief; the Marines' commandeering of cars; the small things I saw them take; the big things the ARVN took; the NVA dead I saw and my own casualty count with estimated body counts from the battalions; how a recoilless rifle team found they could collapse some houses with one shot, if you hit above the main doorway; Marines heating their rations on university Bunsen burners; the Marine tankers routinely on their way to Dong Ha who fought for weeks with their four battered machines; and it goes on and on; the escaped Jesuit; the mayhem. . . .[11]

Soon Lengel had company. AP's George McArthur reported (as did no one else except Don Oberdorfer of Knight newspapers) on

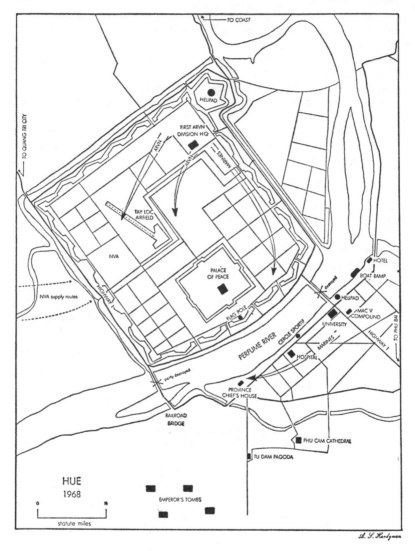

HUE
1968

EMPEROR'S TOMBS

A. S. Hardyman

what happened to Hue's civilians under Vietcong rule. Several other AP reporters and photographers, including Robert Ohman, also joined in. UPI's Alvin Webb was also there, and wounded during the battle. His most vivid reporting, in the UPI tradition, coincided with the 1st Battalion, 5th Marines' bitter Citadel fight. Here is one example:

(Editor's Note: The following dispatch from Alvin B. Webb, Jr., was carried out of Hue's walled Citadel by a fellow correspondent at a time when Webb, who had been covering the battle from the start, had no communications.)

HUE CITADEL, South Vietnam (UPI)—This is getting tough and terrifying. I don't mind admitting I'm scared.

I wish I knew what was going on on the outside. This is written the time of night when you get morose. I hope this stuff is getting out.

If any UPI staffer comes in, please bring water and cigarettes—filters and preferably mentholated.

It is nine blocks from where I am sitting on the south gate of the wall around the Citadel.

It may become the bloodiest nine blocks for the men of the United States Marine Corps since that other war in Korea when they fought and died in the streets of Seoul.

"Seoul was tough," an old top sergeant who was there told me a few minutes ago. "But this—well, it's something else."

There is a kid Marine on a stretcher about 10 feet from me. There isn't much left of his left leg.

I stopped writing this report long enough to help carry the wounded Marine to a truck. It was a delicate business. "He has a messed up back," a corpsman told me.

"I've seen too much of this," a Marine said to me. "We've got to get some help. They're going to annihilate one-five (1st Battalion, 5th Marines)."

Some of the wounded died. One took two slugs in the stomach, another was shot through the head with a round from a .45-caliber pistol. The first had just come back from Hawaii where he spent a week's leave with his wife and two children. The Marine with the bullet in his head never saw his baby daughter.

On Wednesday, Maj. Robert Thompson of Charlottesville, Virginia, commander of the one-five, had figured to be all the way down to the Citadel's south wall.[12]

The truth is that at the moment North Vietnamese and Vietcong remain in solid control of just about the southern half of the Citadel.

The nine blocks ahead of us to the wall are defended by what seems like a small but fantastically well dug-in and well-supplied communist force.

"Five snipers," Capt. Scott Nelson of Jacksonville, Florida, said. "That's all it takes to tie us down completely."

You can hear the whine of the snipers' bullets and the eerie whoosh of

B-40 rockets and feel the thunder of mortar rounds chewing up houses.

. . . .

The beauty of the place is one of the problems for the Marines and South Vietnamese troops.
The North Vietnamese are holed up in the sacred bastions.[13]

. . . .

We move forward. We sweep into a building facing Nguyen Dieu Street behind a blistering blast of M-16 fire and thunderous belches from tanks.
We took the building, and found a body inside. The man was wearing a khaki North Vietnamese Army uniform and carried two hand grenades made in Communist China. He lay face down in a pool of darkening red.
I looked at him. A Marine interrupted my thoughts.
"You remember where you were sitting five minutes ago?" he asked me.
"Absolutely."
"Well, they just put four mortar rounds in on us—right where you were sitting."[14]

The Saigon UPI bureau was not to be left behind, even as the battle neared its end, with two successive leads designed to perk up the reader's attention. The first:

SAIGON (UPI)—U.S. Marines fighting *foot by bloodsoaked foot* today captured a Vietcong watchtower on the southeastern corner of Hue's old Imperial City and ran up the American flag in a signal that the end was near for the *diehard* communist defenders.
The Leathernecks—reinforcements who arrived by helicopter Wednesday—charged this final 150 yards through the *suicidal* Vietcong defenders on the heels of bombing runs that *bathed* their last enemy holdout area in flaming napalm and the smoke of 500-pound bombs. . . .

. . . .

The advance in this *bloodiest battle* of the Vietnam War was costly.[15]

In the next version, certain phrases are retained:

SAIGON (UPI)—U.S. Marines attacking behind a *wall* of flaming napalm today virtually *sealed off*[16] the suicidal band of Vietcong who have held the Imperial City fortress in Hue for 23 days in bitter fighting that helped raise American dead to a record 543 last week.
The Marines raised the American flag on a watchtower at the southeast corner of the ancient Citadel, secured the Nguyen Hoang Bridge across the Perfume River to other Marines on the south bank, and *vowed* to rip

down the Vietcong flag that still fluttered defiantly over the communist redoubt.

The Vietcong defenders were hemmed in by South Vietnamese on the north and west and on the east by the Leathernecks who drove through the southeast corner of the walled city *foot by bloodsoaked foot* against heavy fire that persisted despite bombing and napalm attacks.[17]

The wire service still photographers and picture editors focused on the usual dramatic subjects: the wounded, the refugees, the ruins, a Marine flag-raising. There were no pictures in *Life* or elsewhere of exuberant Marines driving commandeered Hondas, or panel trucks inscribed "Hotel Company Kicks Plenty of Ass," or refugees returning to *unscathed* homes (later to be looted by Vietnamese rear-echelon soldiery), or young American pacifists (engaged in missionary work) being rescued by grinning Marines. The photographic traditions persisted at Hue.

Hue on Film: Drama and Despair

The television crews did extensive work at Hue. All told, the networks presented 18 film reports from the city from February 1 to February 25.[18] CBS's Don Webster, who had already worked hard in Saigon, with his Vietnamese cameraman caught some vivid film vignettes of the fighting on the south bank, marred slightly by Webster's hasty commentary. CBS presented this from Webster on its February 7 evening news:

For days now, they've been fighting their way, bloody inch by inch, down Le Loi Street. And all that time they could see down the street a flagpole, and on it was a Vietcong flag. Much is left in shambles as the Marines advance building after building, the North Vietnamese retreat building after building, giving up nothing without a fight. . . .

In the front ranks of the Marines, a man is suddenly wounded. He's been hit in the eye by shrapnel from an enemy B-40 rocket. Despite the obvious pain, doctors later told him he will not lose the eye, and although the sound of the blast punctured his eardrum, he will not lose his hearing. But all the time the Marines have had their eyes on that enemy flag. It's flying on a pole in front of the province capitol building. . . .

Finally, the assault. They're approaching what used to be the most important government building in the province. Now, with no province government at all, it has *no significance* at all, except for the flag in front. . . .[19]

With fighting still going on just a few yards away, the Marines have risked their lives to pull down a symbol (sound of guns, shouts). No one is quite sure where the American flag came from in the middle of the battle. Like so many things, when you need something, someone just happens to have it. There was no bugler, and the other Marines were too busy to salute, but not often is a flag so proudly raised.

Then suddenly, a surprise. . . .

Rimming the edge of the courtyard, someone noticed small holes, camouflaged. In almost every one there's an enemy soldier, a few dead from the day's shooting, but some still alive. Others are not so lucky. Marines fire into the holes. Another one is lucky; he stuck his arms out of the hole in surrender as a Marine approached, and he's pulled out alive and uninjured. . . .

Sometimes these prisoners can be very useful, giving valuable intelligence information, but in this battle in Hue, it's been going on for so long now and there are so many prisoners, *there's really nothing left to be learned.*[20]

For one of the few times in the Vietnam War, the U.S. Marines are really in their element in this battle in Hue.[21] Right now this province headquarters is the front line, and they're holding an assault, much like those that made them famous in other wars, and to a great extent this assault is being won or lost on the basis of sheer courage, and there's no shortage of that in the Marines.[22]

Again from Webster, on February 10, was this:

The North Vietnamese have blown up four major bridges in Hue this week, including this important one—but this trip may backfire on them, and they even had to fight to prevent U.S. Marines from blowing up another one. . . .

About 50 yards in front of those tanks is the end of Le Loi Street. There's a bridge there, and the main railway station is just across the bridge.

When the VC blew up the other bridges, they thought it would stop the Marines; but it hasn't at all. Helicopters and boats have been bringing all the supplies they need. Now that the Marines are advancing, the North Vietnamese may be trying to escape, and they may regret having blown up some of those bridges. The U.S. [forces are] going to knock out this bridge to trap the enemy on this side of the city.[23]

The whirl of firing back and forth is almost deafening. . . .

Suddenly, one of the Marines is hit by enemy fire. Getting aid for the wounded man and fighting the communists have equally high priority. While they're waiting for the Marine ambulance to arrive, a hospital corpsman works on the wounded man. He was hit by shrapnel and a lot of it.[24]

The Hue battle became a nightly topic on the network shows in February, and the men who rewrote the wire copy to provide scripts for the anchormen sometimes got confused. Here is Chet Huntley, for example:

> After two weeks of stalemate caused, at least partly, by the United States's reluctance to join in an attack on *artistic and architectural treasures*, the Marines today entered the walled Citadel in Hue on the left bank of the Perfume River. Five hundred men crossed the river in assault boats and executed a wide flanking movement, entering the Citadel from the northwest to join up with South Vietnamese troops[25] fighting their way toward the Imperial Palace and the southeast corner of the Citadel, which the enemy still holds.[26]

The Marines' first, or south side, phase went relatively swiftly; indeed, on some days, there was little opposition once the Marines spread out to the southwest. But the Citadel phase, which began on February 11, on the north side of the river, was hard going. For troops and newsmen accustomed to the relative roominess of the rice-paddy battlefield, where maneuverability and firepower could be brought to bear, it seemed especially endless, fearsome, and frustrating. UPI made the Citadel sound like Flanders in 1917 or Cassino in 1944 (the Marines advancing "foot by bloodsoaked foot"); it was hard to notice that only three understrength companies of Marines were being reported on. Television was not to be left behind in magnifying the battle drama. Here is Harry Reasoner with Robert Schakne:

> Reasoner: United States Marines advanced about 200 yards inside the walled Citadel of Hue on this, the sixteenth day of the battle for the South Vietnamese city. The advance was made only after communist positions came under a concentrated attack from jet fighters, Navy guns, and land-based artillery. One of the strongpoints taken today was a stone tower, which had given the communist snipers an excellent field of fire. Prior to the introduction of massive firepower, the allies had made little progress against the enemy forces. CBS News correspondent Robert Schakne reports on Tuesday's action.
>
> Schakne: This is the nastiest kind of street fighting, through the maze of alleyways, houses packed along the old *medieval* wall around the Citadel. What remains of an old tower fortress, built more than a century ago, again is put to combat use. That's the North Vietnamese strongpoint.

That's where the snipers are; that's where the rocket firing had been coming from. Now the Marines were trying to silence the firing with grenade launchers. A medieval battlement turned out to be a formidable strongpoint against 20th-century guns. A tank is no more successful than the grenades or the artillery or the infantry. Charlie is still in there.

What was to have been the final assault on the tower is suddenly turned back by a burst of machine-gun fire from the other flank. A hidden communist gunner in the house opposite the wall. A dead squad leader cut down by the machine gun. And three other Marines wounded. And this is only the beginning. No one can estimate the cost in lives of the battle for Hue.[27]

NBC echoed the despair theme:

Chet Huntley: The situation in Hue has become so critical that today the city's mayor, Col. Pham Van Khoa, said he plans to execute a number of Vietcong prisoners in public.

An unidentified American advisor reportedly is encouraging the mayor. He was quoted by UPI as saying, "There will be summary executions of VC and hopefully some of the infrastructure." By infrastructure he meant enemy leaders.

The Defense Department late today told NBC it has no information at this time on the report.[28]

David Burrington (film clip): American Marines are so bogged down in Hue that nobody will even predict when the battle will end. Weather is one big factor. Monsoon clouds prevent air support. Helicopters have to fly so low they constantly get shot at—so they seldom fly. When they do make it into a safe corner of the Hue Citadel, casualties are waiting. Some of the wounded here have waited more than 18 hours. More than 500 Marines have been wounded and 100 killed since the fighting in Hue began. Most of the casualties have come in the Citadel battle. The battalion here is now at half-strength.

The price has been high and it's gained the Marines about 50 yards or less a day in a heavily populated part of the Citadel. Still, nothing is really secure. The journey through the friendly zone is a wild race past enemy snipers.

At battalion headquarters, where there are still remnants of the Vietnamese New Year never celebrated, officers admit their unit is in trouble. They say they don't have enough men now, that they're not getting enough support along their flanks, and that their tanks have no mobility in the city's narrow streets.

The North Vietnamese, on the other hand, are apparently still getting fresh troops, they have plenty of ammunition, and they show no signs of quitting. . . .

This is Delta Company on the far left flank along one of the Citadel's walls. Ahead, a squad is trying to inch ahead under covering fire.

The one favorite weapon is the Russian AK-47. When the men capture one, they use it.

These men have fought like this for a week now. They have lost about half the company and they admit it's slow going. . . .

The streets are loaded with debris and bodies. It may be weeks before they can be picked up. Up ahead are some American bodies.

Most of the city is now in rubble. This is a middle-class section. Some of Vietnam's best known intellectuals live here. Now, the war has finally come to them.

The palace, considered Vietnam's spiritual capital, is expected to be destroyed, and many Vietnamese say the fight really isn't worth it now that their city is dead.[29]

CBS also snatched failure from the jaws of hard-won success. For example, John Laurence reported that "The American flag flies on the Citadel wall, *but there is no breeze to blow it,* and the job is far from done for Delta Company."[30]

The networks at Hue, as at Khe Sanh and Saigon, were under the usual competitive pressures for "action" film, and for getting it home in the fastest possible time. The strain began to tell. This writer had to restrain one highly courageous TV correspondent from rushing aboard a helicopter with his bag of film ahead of a wounded Marine.

Reporters in Combat

The New York *Times* ran 19 staff-written stories from Hue during the battle, most of them the best of their kind. Gene Roberts got into Hue from Phu Bai by truck on February 2, and covered the south side fighting in low-key reporting that contrasted with the blood-and-thunder tone of television and much of the UPI copy. (The *Times* used only six wire-service stories from Hue.) Roberts cited the strain on the Marines, and at the same time their humor:

HUE, South Vietnam, Feb. 4—United States Marines stormed into enemy-held houses, throwing canisters of tear gas and nonpoisonous nausea gas today, but enemy forces donned gas masks and held onto most of the city.

Some officers said that the stiff resistance by the enemy meant that the battle for Hue could drag on for days, perhaps even weeks.

At nightfall, the Marines held eight blocks of the city, a gain of five from yesterday. They suffered more than 20 casualties, bringing the total for five days to about 150. Enemy losses were described as heavy.

The action came as fresh intelligence reports showed that the enemy held 10 strategic positions and scattered sniper posts in Hue, once the seat of Vietnam's imperial government.

"What we need is sunny weather and air strikes and more air strikes," one officer shouted over the roar of cannon and machine-gun fire. . . .

"That crazy dog!" a tank commander shouted from his turret. "If he had any sense he wouldn't be in this damn place!"

No one knows where the dog came from. Like the goose that waddles around the door of the compound mess hall, he simply showed up after the battle began.

Weary Marines grinned at each other over coffee at dawn today, pointed their rifles at the goose, and warned the mess sergeant, Frank Crum of Valley Station, Kentucky, that they would have the goose for dinner if he did not stop serving them C-rations.

At lunch, Sergeant Crum served them steaks that had come in with a supply convoy. He told them that he had cooked the steaks only because he wanted to save the goose.

The steaks were the first cooked here in five days.[31]

Roberts' description of the trip from Hue to Da Nang by Navy landing craft on February 10 was one of the better pieces of newspaper copy filed out of Vietnam:

DA NANG, South Vietnam, Feb. 10—The only thing that seems worse than staying in Hue is trying to leave it.

With the skies above the battle-scarred city still overcast, helicopters whir in only sporadically, and then just to evacuate critically wounded soldiers.

The last truck convoy that tried to reach Hue to bring in supplies and take out American civilian refugees—was ambushed. Twenty Marines from the convoy lost two armored vehicles, seven trucks, a jeep, and a trailer before turning back.

Two days ago, desperate to leave the booming guns in Hue, foreign refugees formed around the boat landing to seek passage on one of the Navy landing craft that still ply the Huong River, bringing supplies to the Marines who are fighting against Vietcong and North Vietnamese battalions.

Navy crewmen warned the refugees that it might be safer for them to remain in the American compound in the city. The compound has high walls, bunkers, and sturdy concrete buildings to minimize the danger of mortar and rocket fire.

The boat landing, on the other hand, is unprotected. But more than 50 refugees, plus newsmen and wounded Marines, gathered there to wait in the rain for a landing craft to clear her decks of 150 tons of ammunition. An enemy mortar crew fired at the landing. A Filipino mother, the wife of an advisor to the South Vietnamese government, gathered up her 5-year-old son and jumped behind a crate of C-rations.

"We've been through so much these last nine days," she said in a low voice, "it wouldn't seem fair if something happened to my son now."

"The only thing we can do now is hope the bastards are lousy shots," one wounded Marine said to another as he leaned against a packing case and puffed casually on a cigarette. "There ain't no place to hide."

The mortar men were lousy shots. Two shells fell in the river, kicking up small geysers of water. A third one hit a packing crate, well away from the landing craft and the waiting passengers.

While the shells were falling, the Marines kept working, driving onto the landing craft with fork-lifts, picking up crates and hauling them ashore.

When the last crate was hauled from the craft, the passengers rushed aboard. The women, children, and the stretcher cases were taken below the main deck. The others, including wounded Marines who could still walk, squatted on the deck in the rain.

It was a strange cargo. There were two priests, who had been held captive by the Vietcong; the bodies of six Marines in green plastic bags; and a group of teachers who had found themselves trapped for nine days in Hue while artillery and mortars boomed around them.

There were also three Canadians, three Poles, and six Indians, representatives of the International Control Commission who were trying to work for peace amid war, and South Vietnamese physicians who were searched carefully by the ship's crewmen on the alert for explosive charges.

"If you've got weapons, you ought to get them ready," one crewman told the passengers. "It will be a miracle if we don't have to use them."

There was no miracle. Ten minutes out of Hue, Vietcong troops ran along the river bank firing rifles and rockets at the lumbering landing craft. The wounded Marines rushed to the ship's railings, firing steadily.

Pfc. Calvin Reigle, an 18-year-old Marine from Buffalo, tried to shoot but could not pull the trigger of his rifle. He gave it to another Marine, who could shoot despite bandaged fingers.

Bright red tracer bullets zipped over the cabin of the landing craft, a rocket shell struck a river patrol boat that had come along for protection.

One of the neutral workers of the International Control Commission crouched low on the deck and said, "Is this boat moving at all?"

A half-an-hour later, when the shooting had subsided, one of the Canadians reached under his coat, pulled out a bottle of Ambassador Scotch and passed it around to the Marines. They emptied it in four minutes. The Canadian passed around another bottle, then another, as the landing craft lumbered out of the Huong and into the 10-foot swells of the South China Sea.

A Pole lurched over to the Canadian and asked whether he had any seasick pills; the Canadian said no. The Pole made his way to the ship's railing and hung his head over the side.

One man on the deck turned to a newsman and grinned.

"I could've given him some pills," he said, "but let him suffer. He's pulling for the other side."

At 11:15 p.m., seven hours after the 57-mile voyage had begun, the landing craft pulled into Da Nang.

The Filipino woman lifted her son onto the wharf, hugged him, and laughed. "We're here!" she kept saying, "we're here!"[32]

Tom Johnson (in Vietnam on temporary assignment to do, as noted, a *Times* series on the black GI), came from Da Nang to relieve Roberts, and Charles Mohr followed. Johnson accurately covered the start of the bitter, slow Marine effort in the Citadel and also conveyed some notion of what the much-ignored South Vietnamese forces had been up to.[33] But perhaps Johnson's best vignette of the Hue fighting and of the young Marines involved in it came in his later Negro GI series:

A young Negro Marine in war-ravaged Hue typified the "grunt's" bravado, his eagerness to fight, his disbelief that he can be hurt or killed. . . .

"Put me in your paper," the Marine told a correspondent.

"What can I say about you?" the newsman asked.

"You can say Lance Cpl. Raymond Howard, 18, better known as 'Trouble,' from Bay Minette, Alabama, squad leader, Second Platoon, Delta Company, First Battalion, Fifth Marine Regiment, is going 'cross the river to kick him a few behinds."[34]

Charles Mohr narrowly escaped being hit on February 19 when he and several other newsmen, including David Greenway of *Time* and Alvin Webb (both wounded), were pulling a wounded Marine to safety in the Citadel area. Mohr covered the Marine action and the final assault on the Imperial Palace by the South Vietnamese.

The Washington *Post* relied on the wire services for four of its 16 on-scene Hue stories, but other wire copy was sometimes rewritten on the foreign desk, as were the war wrap-ups. Once more, errors resulted, but the *Post* had only two battlefield reporters, Lee Lescaze and this writer, in Vietnam. There was little choice, given the number of battlefields to cover. To bolster its own reporting, the *Post* also drew on the Hue dispatches filed by William Tuohy of the Los Angeles *Times* and, with less happy results, on the reports of the London *Times* on the February 24 assault on the Imperial Palace. The *Post* used eight Hue stories of its own, versus 19 for the New York *Times*.

Essentially, Lescaze and I split the Hue assignment. This reporter went first, to cover the last few days of the Marines' south-side fighting (after trying in vain to get to the ARVN on the north side of the river—Bill Brannigan of ABC was the only U.S. reporter to make it there early). For transportation, I tried the 1st Air Cavalry Division helicopters operating out of Camp Evans, northwest of Hue. Early in February, together with David Greenway, I dined with Maj. Gen. John Tolson, the Air Cavalry's commander, and heard and saw how the bad weather was hampering his newly moved division's logistics buildup and its efforts to move down on Hue. Only about half of the helicopters were ready to fly, and transport for us directly into Hue Citadel proved impossible. (Like Greenway, I did not file on Tolson's difficulties, for security reasons, but used the information indirectly in a subsequent Hue story, noting that bad weather and insufficient troops made it difficult for the allies to cut off the NVA.)[35] Two days later, another try for Hue with Greenway, this time from Phu Bai, was interrupted when our Army CH-47 helicopter, flying under the overcast at 300 feet, made a forced landing near the Cau Hai lagoon after being struck by AK-47 fire. The pilots got the ship aloft again, and back to Phu Bai, where I boarded yet another helicopter for Hue, arriving—finally—unscathed. Such travel problems were common during the Hue battle, with more than 100 newsmen[36] entering, then leaving the city, by means of helicopters, landing craft, or the truck convoys that ran through ambushes down Highway One to Phu Bai.

One morning, I decided to collect material for a long story on the Marines' south-side battle—chronology, problems, tactics, morale—and, after talking with Marine and Army officers at the MACV compound, joined Greenway in heading for the battalion (2nd Battalion, 5th Marines) scheduled to attack that day southwest of Le Loi Street. Like the TV correspondents and photographers, Greenway wanted to go straight to the platoons leading the assault; I insisted instead that we go down the chain of command—first to Lt. Col. Ernest

Cheatham's battalion headquarters, then to company and platoon—
both to get information and avoid getting lost. Despite the usual
alarms and some bitter clashes, it was a relatively "light" day for action. Marines had time to talk. The resulting story, slightly cut by the
foreign desk for space reasons, set forth *how* the Marines (and
enemy) were fighting in the waning days of the south-side battle.[37] It
also included a passing description of the "much-vaunted" pacification program "torn to shreds" in the Hue-Quang Tri rural areas
by Tet. The phrasing was essentially this reporter's taunt at Ambassador Komer, the pacification chief, and his pre-Tet optimism. The
facts, as perceived by weary AID officials in Hue, might better have
been reported flatly, without the gratuitous stab. As it turned out,
pacification had been set back but not "torn to shreds."

Lescaze's turn in Hue came on February 15. Like everyone else,
he had trouble reaching the city from Phu Bai, and instead wisely decided to fly a spotter plane from Da Nang and get a bird's-eye view
of the battle. He produced the first general notion of where the city
was damaged and where it was not, as well as an inkling of the lack
of coordination among U.S. Army and Marine and South Vietnamese
troops—one of the problems Westmoreland's newly dispatched deputy, Gen. Creighton W. Abrams, was then trying to sort out in Phu
Bai.[38]

Lescaze, along with Tom Johnson and Charles Mohr of the *Times,*
Alvin Webb of UPI, and John Lengel of AP, filed on the ordeal of
the Marines (1st Battalion, 5th Marines) engaged in the Citadel
fight. The fighting was a good deal more dangerous there for newsmen and Marines alike than it had been on the south side (after the
first four days). As Michael Herr of *Esquire* later wrote:

> Between the smoke and the mist and the flying dust inside the Citadel,
> it was hard to call that hour between light and darkness a true dusk, but
> it was the time when a lot of us would open our C-rations. We were only
> meters away from the worst of the fighting, not more than a Vietnamese
> city block in distance, and yet civilians kept appearing, smiling, shrug-
> ging, trying to get back to their homes. The Marines would try to menace
> them away at riflepoint, shouting, "Di, di, di . . . go on, get the hell
> away from here!" and the refugees would smile, half-bowing, and flit up
> one of the shattered streets. . . .
> On the worst days, no one expected to get through it alive.[39]

Like other newsmen, Lescaze wrote of the understrength Marine
units,[40] whose plight aroused considerable sympathy. Indeed, on

February 21, Lt. Gen. Robert Cushman, Jr., said he would replace the Marine battalion in the Citadel, commenting that "the steam has gone out of them." He also said that the Hue fighting could go on for several weeks, and noted that 100 Marines had been killed and 60 helicopters hit.[41] Unlike TV and some of the wires, however, Lescaze noted, when the battalion was relieved, that it was "exhausted, undermanned, but undaunted."[42]

Some of the newspaper reporters, like the TV correspondents, overstated the Marines' plight. The Los Angeles *Times*'s Tuohy, for example, said "resupply for the battalion is precarious," indicated that Navy supply boats on the Perfume River were "prime targets for enemy guns" (without noting how few were hit), and, oddly enough, criticized the allies for not surrounding the Citadel, "although its perimeter is *not more* than eight miles in all."[43] As newsmen in Hue and Da Nang were well aware, the 1st Air Cavalry was then slowly moving four battalions toward the Citadel's northwest side, against stiff opposition from the NVA; in any event, sealing off an eight-mile perimeter would have demanded far more troops (two battalions per mile) than were available. Had the 1st Air Cavalry and 101st Airborne Divisions been in position when Tet struck, Hue probably could have been encircled. But Tet caught both units still in the process of shifting into the Hue area.

Restricted as they were—first by circumstances, then by their own conviction that the Marines were the only story, and always by manpower—AP and newspaper reporters did well in covering the U.S. Marine performance at Hue. AP's George McArthur and the Knight newspapers' Don Oberdorfer branched out into other themes, notably the fate of Hue's civilians under NVA rule (although the early South Vietnamese allegations of the Hue massacre were not explored in detail after the battle). Only Bill Brannigan of ABC and David Greenway of *Time* managed to describe the early days of the ARVN fighting in the Citadel. No newsmen accompanied the slow-to-get-started 1st Air Cavalry thrust from the north at the enemy's rear. In short, the Marines were covered; the battle as a whole was not.

Later, discussing the race back to Da Nang to file (and rest), Herr wrote:

> We lucked out on our connections. At the battalion aid-station in Hue we got a chopper that carried us and a dozen dead Marines to the base at Phu Bai, and three minutes after we arrived there we caught a C-130 to Da Nang. Hitching in from the airfield, we found a Psyops [Psycho-

logical Operations] official who felt sorry for us and drove us all the way
to the press center. As we came through the gate we could see that the
net was up and that the daily volleyball game between the Marines assigned to the press center was in progress.

"Where the hell have you guys been?" one of them said. We looked
pretty wretched.

The inside of the dining room was freezing with air conditioning. I sat
at a table and ordered a hamburger and a Remy Martin from one of the
peasant girls who worked the tables. I sat there for a couple of hours, and
ordered four more hamburgers and at least a dozen brandies. (I had no
idea of it until the check came.) It was not possible, it was just not possible to have been where we'd been before and to be where we were now,
all in the same afternoon. One of the correspondents who had come back
with me sat at another table, also by himself, and we just looked at each
other, shook our heads, and laughed. I went to my room and took my
boots and fatigues off, putting them under the bed where I wouldn't have
to look at them. I went into the bathroom and turned on the shower. The
water was hot, incredibly hot, for a moment I thought I'd gone insane
from it, and I sat down on the concrete floor for a long time, shaving
there, soaping myself over and over. I was using up all the hot water, I
knew that, but I couldn't get interested in it. I dressed and went back to
the dining room. The net was down now, and one of the Marines said
hello and asked me what the movie was going to be that night. I ordered
a steak and another string of brandies. Then I went to bed and smoked a
joint. I was going back in the morning, I knew that, it was understood.
But why was it understood? All of my stuff was in order, ready for the
five o'clock wake-up. I finished the joint and shuddered off into sleep.[44]

The News Magazines: Both Accuracy and Error

Time's first story on Hue (in its February 16 issue) was basically a
solid report from the scene by David Greenway; in this case, the
Time rewriter in New York followed closely Greenway's file. A comparison is interesting. Here, in part, is Greenway's original story:

> The battle for Hue was well into its second week and still a tattered
> Vietcong flag hung limply over the Citadel's main gate. Across the Per-
> fume River on the south bank the U.S. Marines continued their house-by-
> house fight among the ruins of the once beautiful city. Thousands of refu-
> gees were packed into the modern buildings of the Hue University, facing
> the river, and small children ran in and out among the parked tanks as
> women cooked over small fires in the fitful rain—the "crachin" that blan-
> kets much at [I] Corps this time of year. . . .

Further on down the street the *Cercle Sportif* . . . sat forlornly, pock-marked with bullets and all its windows smashed in. Inside, gay colored streamers, probably for a Tet party, still hung from the ceiling, but billiard tables were covered with plaster, and broken tennis rackets, bottles and loving cups lay about the floor.

Other buildings were completely gutted—their red tile roofs smashed in by heavy explosives. And everywhere lay dead bodies. "There are so many corpses lying around town it's unreal," said one medic. "If somebody doesn't get this place policed up, there is going to be an epidemic." . . .

"There has been a definite pattern to the fighting," said Col. Ernest Cheatham of Long Beach, California, the . . . commander of the [2nd Battalion, 5th Marines]. . . .

"The North Vietnamese will fight like hell defending these buildings. But once we get men actually inside the building, they fall back."[45]

By mid-week the Marines had cleared all the area along the riverfront to where the Phu Cam River (really only a small canal) cuts into the Perfume River. There they doubled back along the canal towards the Cathedral. But there was always the danger of snipers slipping in behind them in the night. So even in areas previously cleared, shots would ring out from ruined buildings sending Marines scuttling for cover as the bullets followed them along the wall. In the courtyards of captured buildings mortar crews started setting up their tubes in order to bring death down through the roofs on the next block. One crew, in the garden of the province chief's house, "liberated" a skeleton from the medical school and had it sitting atop their mortar pit.

But if the Marines were making progress on the south side of the river, the ARVN were making very little inside the Citadel. The cooks, clerks, and bottlewashers manning the 1st Division headquarters managed to hold out against the initial attack, and were later joined by the fighting battalions garrisoned outside the city. . . .

But by Thursday, February 8, the entire southern half of the Citadel, including the palace, was [still] in enemy hands; U.S. advisors laughed bitterly when they heard Radio Saigon announce that the Citadel was nine-tenths captured.

The ARVN had first tried to attack using armored personnel carriers, but the streets of the Citadel are long and straight and the NVA could sit back and knock them off with rocket launchers and recoilless rifles straight up the road from half a mile away. Also, the ARVN troops failed to deploy the APCs properly and sent them out ahead of the infantry. As a result, all but three of their 12 APCs had been knocked out by Wednesday.

Also, some of the units were down to 40 percent strength, due not only to casualties, but also the high number of Tet time leaves. All week long the bad weather had curtailed resupply, and the ARVN were hurting for ammunition.

Within the Citadel there was not the high degree of destruction as on the south bank, but the ARVN were fighting the same house-to-house fight as the Marines—albeit less aggressively. . . .

ARVN soldiers fired long bursts of machine-gun fire at [the enemy's] suspected positions. But although the ARVN were putting in air strikes by mid-week, there was obviously a reluctance to use heavy ordnance within the Citadel itself.

Often, as the ARVN forces set up a machine gun in someone's back yard, the family would come out to bring the soldiers some tea and cakes. They seemed genuinely glad to see the government troops, but it was equally clear that some of them had helped hide North Vietnamese troops and ammunition in the weeks before the uprising. For when the blow was struck on the morning of the 31st, there was a strong NVA force already within the Citadel itself.[46]

The ARVN had an additional problem as well. The NVA were well entrenched within the huge, 12-foot-thick, 18th-century walls that surround the Citadel itself. Dug into these vast, medieval-looking stone redoubts, the enemy troops are invulnerable to all but the heaviest artillery. One airborne company tried to assault one of these redoubts three times before finally giving up the attack. "It would take the battleship *New Jersey* to get them out of those walls," said one frustrated American advisor. . . .

. . . .

The NVA, in an amazing feat of arms, sent frogmen down the Perfume River and neatly dropped the center span of the last bridge over the river, despite the fact that the allies had both bridgeheads. . . .

Because of the bad weather, helicopter pilots had to make the dangerous run into Hue a couple of feet off the deck with runners brushing the rice in the paddies and taking fire all the way. By mid-week, helicopter resupply had almost come to a standstill and most of the ammunition had to come by boat up the Perfume River.

Here is the New York rewrite:

Almost uniquely in Vietnam last week, it was possible to follow clearly the progression of one battle: the block-by-block struggle of the allies to recapture the city of Hue from the North Vietnamese units that swept into it two weeks ago. The North Vietnamese had arrived to stay, and students from the University of Hue acted as their guides, in some cases donning the uniform of Vietcong regulars. As the ancient capital of Vietnam, Hue was a prime piece of captured real estate for propaganda purposes, and the NVA fought for every inch of it against ARVN troopers and a battalion-size force of U.S. Marines that moved in from the south.

At first, the Marines found the going not only tough but unfamiliar, since they had to retake the streets almost house by house. "The first two days, it was a matter of learning this sort of thing," said one Marine commander, Col. Ernest Cheatham. "The Marines haven't fought a fight like this since Seoul, back in 1950." As more and more blocks fell to the Marines, they commandeered brightly colored Honda motorcycles, small buses, and cars, to ferry themselves back and forth in the action.

Gradually, the battling turned the once beautiful city into a nightmare. Hue's streets were littered with dead. . . .

Every so often the Marines came across pockets of American civilians, some of whom had been successfully hiding out for nine days. When they liberated the Thua Thien province headquarters, the Marines tore down the Vietcong flag, one of dozens the communists had planted throughout the city, and raised the Stars and Stripes. Their commander had told them to run up the South Vietnamese flag, but two Marines had died taking the building; they were not about to be denied the satisfaction of raising their own flag (though it later had to be lowered to conform with South Vietnamese law).

Meanwhile, the ARVN forces were making slower headway against the NVA defending the thick-walled battlements of the Citadel. They first tried to use armored personnel carriers to spearhead their attack, but the long, straight streets of the old quarter enabled communist gunners to knock them out from half a mile away. With only three of their original 12 APCs still operative, the ARVN troopers started the same house-to-house combat as the Marines on the other side of the fetid Perfume River.

In a predawn bit of derringdo, communist frogmen swam down the Perfume and neatly dropped the center span of the last remaining bridge over the river, despite the fact that the allies held both bridgeheads. Boats thus became the main means of evacuation and supply, and each boat ran a gauntlet of NVA sniper fire. But at week's end the NVA pockets of resistance were slowly shrinking, and all of the city except a part of the Citadel had been seized by the allies.[47]

The concluding sentence of the New York version—which did not stem from Greenway's file—hinted at a quick finish. In fact, the Hue battle only ended two weeks later. The map *Time* ran with the story was somewhat confused and optimistic (as were most published maps of the Hue situation): Most notably, it showed the western and southern approaches to the city—NVA escape and reinforcement routes—as cut off by the U.S. 1st Air Cavalry Division, which at this point was still well out of range. Unmentioned in the *Time* story were: (1) the bad "crachin" weather cited by Greenway, which hurt helicopter and air support, (2) the serious difficulties of the ARVN, and (3) the undermanned U.S. forces.

Time's story the following week veered into cliché and error:

Writhing [*sic*] in the agony of prolonged battle, once lovely Hue remained the only city in South Vietnam where the Vietcong flag still flew. Ten days of bitter street fighting cleared—at least temporarily—the modern residential section south of the Perfume River, but the battle raged with full fury in the rubble-strewn Citadel, the early 19th-century imperial fortress that holds much of Vietnam's architectural and cultural treasure. As thousands of refugees huddled under a gray pall from count-less fires, 1,000 U.S. Marines crossed the river to help the 2,500 South Vietnamese infantrymen and Marines fighting to recapture the formal royal enclosure, once known as "the Forbidden City." . . .

. . . .

Rocky Debris. Finally, all restrictions were lifted last week, and jet fighter-bombers, artillery, and naval gunfire began slowly shattering the walled complex into rocky debris. Even so, progress could be made only yard by bloody yard.[48] "It's just like Iwo Jima," said Marine Capt. Myron Harrington, 29. . . .

Renewed fighting flared in Hue's southern section at week's end, when some 700 enemy troops suddenly appeared in an area thought secure. How they got there was a mystery, since allied officers had declared the city sealed off.[49]

In their third Hue story, *Time*'s writers in New York—possibly influenced by the television coverage—gave way to vivid exaggeration, even as the battle ended:[50]

The U.S. Marines were now engaged in what a company commander called a *"brick-by-brick* fight" to drive the North Vietnamese forces from the Citadel. Finally, when allied troops had shrunk the communists' ground to three fortified pockets, South Vietnamese soldiers, flanked by a company of Black Panther Rangers, shelled a hole in the wall guarding the most important redoubt—the Imperial City—and swarmed in.

They found only a handful of defenders left.[51]

Thus came the allies' all-but-decisive blow to recapture the scene of the fiercest and *most costly battle* of the Vietnamese War to date, a battle so unlike any that had gone before it in the war that allied forces had to learn by doing. During the four weeks that they had clutched the city, over 2,000 North Vietnamese soldiers and Vietcong had holed up hard behind the foundations of crumbled buildings. . . .

Against this strong opposition, the allies waged a *relentless* two-prong attack—U.S. Marines southbound on the east, ARVN Marines headed the same way on the west. . . .

Helicopters *sprayed napalm* across the ponds and courtyards of the Imperial Palace. . . .[52]

From a crescent-shaped position along the west wall,[53] the enemy was able to keep a steady stream of supplies and reinforcements flowing into the Citadel. . . .

The most important advance came when low-crouching U.S. Marines swept onto the long *south* wall overlooking the Perfume riverbank, a position that finally gave the allies sturdy positions on each wall of the Citadel. The Marines celebrated by triumphantly running up the Stars and Stripes. . . . The death toll was among the most expensive of the war: nearly 450 allied dead, including some 100 U.S. Marines, and so many casualties that the *5th Battalion's 1st Regiment*[54] was finally left at half-strength.

Still, the allies moved on toward the imperial city.[55]

Newsweek covered Hue a week later than *Time* did, in its February 26 issue. It blended UPI material and cliché prose, written in New York, to present a conventional Hue battle story, accompanied by an inaccurate map showing allied "thrusts" from the southwest rather than from the northeast:

. . . Perhaps because of its *symbolic* value, the Vietcong and the North Vietnamese chose Hue for the most determined stand of their Tet offensive. So tenacious was their grip on the old city, that early last week the U.S. Marines, who had cleared most of its southern part, were thrown in to assist the South Vietnamese assault on the Citadel.[56]

Initially, the Marines made an attempt to do as little damage as possible to the Citadel. But in their first full day of fighting there, despite heavy casualties, the Leathernecks gained only 100 yards. And with that, they resorted to all-out attack.[57] U.S. and South Vietnamese planes swooped in to paste the Citadel with bombs, while from the South China Sea several miles away, the five-inch guns of U.S. destroyers supplemented a barrage by land-based artillery. *Growled* one American officer: "We're planning on blowing the walls down if that's what it takes to get Charlie out of there."

By the end of the week, it appeared that it might take just that. Despite the bombardment, North Vietnamese soldiers still clung to strongly fortified positions along the southeastern wall. And as they fought on, Hue's *architectural treasures* were steadily crumbling into debris.[58] There was, moreover, a grievous human toll as well; caught in the cross fire and deprived of fresh water, sewer service, and electricity, the 140,000 residents of Hue were falling victim to hunger and disease.[59]

Included in the story was this, cabled from the battered city by *Newsweek*'s Robert Stokes:

The guns and planes are still chewing up the Citadel, and already entire blocks elsewhere in town have been flattened.[60] Dead North Vietnamese soldiers, their bodies blackened by decay, sprawl in doorways: The stench makes one want to vomit. The dormitory of Hue's university has been turned into a refugee center, and there the smell is not of death but of filth, stale food, and urine. Already three deaths from cholera have been reported.

The story continued:

In the streets where Vietnam's most beautiful women once strolled in graceful *ao dais*—ankle-length dresses slit to the waist over billowy pantaloons—beggars now scrounge through heaps of garbage. And along the banks of the river, where university students used to hold outdoor seminars, wounded U.S. Marines now wait numbly for evacuation. Nearby are neat rows of *grisly green rubber bags*—each containing the corpse of a young American, each bluntly labeled: "Dead."[61]

In its final report on the battle, *Newsweek* wrote:

. . . In large part, the record U.S. casualty list reflected the fierce battle for control of the ancient imperial capital of Hue. Now reduced to little more than rubble, Hue shuddered under the explosions of bombs and artillery as South Vietnamese troops and two U.S. Marine battalions[62] sought to dislodge a force of North Vietnamese troops entrenched within the city's walled Citadel. With casualties in some Marine companies running as high as 50 percent, the Leathernecks' progress was painfully slow. Explained one Marine officer: "We don't have enough men, enough air support, or enough artillery to do this thing quickly."[63]

Once Hue was recaptured (February 24–25), battlefield reporting declined. The daily search-and-destroy encounters of U.S. battalions in the rural and "exurban" areas emerged in the military communiqués—once more—as just so many isolated reports. In fact, however, U.S. troops were fighting hard, bitter, but unpublicized battles around the country, and the casualty figures showed it. What puzzled some editors in the United States was that, although the major city fighting had ended, these American casualties continued to run so high. The *Post*, for example, queried its Saigon bureau on March 15:

"NOTE CASUALTIES THIS WEEK OVER 500 FOR THIRD WEEK IN ROW AND FRANKLY WE SKEPTICAL EXPLANATION THESE HIGH CASUALTIES RESULTING FROM MINOR BUT FREQUENT ENGAGEMENTS. IS THIS NOT WORTH PURSUING PAST OFFICIAL STATEMENTS SO FAR MADE?" The answer, of course, was not that fraud was being deliberately perpetrated by MACV. Rather, the *Post* editors, among others, were not getting a clear picture of the battlefield either from their own reporters or from the wire-service wrap-ups.

The Victory at "Pink Village"

Perhaps the most extreme example of journalistic dependence on the MACV communiqué, combined with inaccurate military reporting from the field to MACV, was the treatment of what became known in 1969 as the "My Lai Massacre," led by Lieutenant William Calley, of several hundred villagers near Quang Ngai city.

The Army unit involved was a lone, composite, battalion-sized "Task Force Barker" (named after its commander) assigned to a routine search-and-destroy operation 40 miles south of its parent outfit, the 11th Brigade at Tam Ky, and some 20 miles southeast of the next higher headquarters—the Americal Division at Chu Lai. Although the Americal's units were frequently involved in severe fighting, its sector—coastal Quang Ngai and Quang Tin provinces—was, ironically, off the beaten track. The Americal was in a modified coastal "enclave" posture, and its widely dispersed units were involved essentially in shielding its surrounding, populated area by seeking out nearby NVA and Vietcong main force units, and dispersing or destroying them. Because Quang Ngai and Quang Tin embraced perhaps the most heavily "pro-Vietcong" population in South Vietnam, as well as strong NVA-Vietcong forces, they were among the provinces hardest hit by U.S. firepower. Rural devastation there approached that inflicted in 1950–53 on areas of Korea.

The Americal, neither "glamorous" nor conveniently accessible to newsmen, was largely ignored. During all of 1968, for example, no *Times* man was recorded as visiting the division. Even a visitor was in no position to check current operations beyond what was being reported from the field, and no massacre was reported. To have known a massacre had occurred at My Lai, the press would have to have been there.

In Saigon, the MACV communiqué on the Americal that day was

detailed and—as the subsequent (1969) exposure of the massacre of more than 100 Vietnamese civilians showed—completely misleading. The evening communiqué indicated that a severe fight had occurred and that action was "continuing":

OPERATION MUSCATINE (QUANG NGAI PROVINCE)—Thus far, 128 enemy have been killed in an engagement between elements of the Americal Division's 11th Light Infantry Brigade and an enemy force of unknown size. The action is taking place in an area [six miles] northeast of Quang Ngai city.

This morning at 0750, a company from the brigade made contact with the enemy force when the company entered an area that had been subjected to artillery preparatory fire.

Another company from the brigade, also involved in the search-and-destroy mission, was inserted into the area at 0910 approximately [two miles] east-northeast of the point of original contact. As the companies moved toward each other sweeping the area, they engaged the enemy in sporadic contacts throughout the day.

During the course of the engagement, the infantrymen were supported by Army artillery and helicopter gunships.

At last report the contact was continuing. . . .

The later U.S. Army, Vietnam, Daily Summary of March 17, 1968, said this:

Elements of the Americal Division's 11th Light Infantry Brigade reported killing 128 enemy soldiers Saturday during an assault against a Vietcong stronghold some six miles northeast of the I Corps city of Quang Ngai. The "Jungle Warriors" were supported during the day by artillery and helicopter gunships.

A company of the brigade's 1st Battalion, 20th Infantry conducted a heliborne combat assault early yesterday morning west of the village of My Lai. During this initial phase of the operation the infantrymen killed one communist soldier, while supporting gunships killed another six.

The infantry company, led by Capt. Ernest Medina, Schofield Barracks, Hawaii, engaged and killed 14 Vietcong while moving toward the village. They also captured three M-1 rifles and detained 10 suspects. One of the suspects told an interpreter that 35 Vietcong had moved into the village two hours earlier.

As the U.S. infantrymen moved through the marshes one mile west of the village, they counted the bodies of 69 enemy soldiers killed by supporting fire from a battery of the 6th Battalion, 11th Artillery. The 105 mm. battery, commanded by Capt. Steven Gamble, Portsmouth, New Hampshire, was positioned three miles to the north.

A platoon from the 4th Battalion, 3rd Infantry was then airlifted into a position south of My Lai. The infantrymen, led by 2nd Lt. Thomas K. Willingham, Clark, New Jersey, made contact with an enemy force along the beach one-half mile south of the village. The U.S. soldiers killed 30 Vietcong in the ensuing fighting.

In the afternoon the platoon members observed Vietcong soldiers attempting to hide in a tunnel complex. The enemy were engaged and eight were killed. The Americans also captured a quantity of enemy equipment and ammunition.

U.S. casualties in the several engagements were two killed and 10 wounded.

We have no record of what questions, if any, were raised at the Five O'Clock Follies about the action.

The AP in Saigon added color to the story, putting out this lead:

SAIGON (AP)—U.S. infantrymen, in a hide-and-seek fight through rice paddies and sand dunes along the central coast, killed 128 Vietcong guerrillas today, the U.S. command said.

A spokesman said a company of the 11th Light Infantry Brigade, sweeping into an area that had been bombarded minutes earlier, tangled with guerrillas this morning.

A second company was dropped by helicopters two miles to the north an hour later and heavy fighting broke out as the guerrillas tried to escape the tightening vise.

Helicopter gunships and artillery supported the advancing U.S. infantrymen in the running battle six miles northeast of Quang Ngai city and 330 miles northeast of Saigon.

American casualties were not given since the forces were still in contact, a U.S. spokesman said. . . .[64]

UPI gave the story a vivid first-person touch, apparently after a telephone call to the Americal's PIO:

SAIGON (UPI)—An American assault team carried into battle aboard helicopters trapped Vietcong with their backs to the South China Sea Saturday and reported killing 128 in an infantry-artillery vise 330 miles north of Saigon.

Units of the 11th Light Infantry Brigade, one of several outfits forming parts of the U.S. Americal Division, scored the impressive victory along the seacoast near My Lai—a town so heavily dominated by communists that GIs call it "Pink Village."

The Light Infantry troops moved in behind a curtain of artillery, surrounded the village, and began blazing away at its Vietcong defenders.

A platoon led by 2nd Lt. Thomas K. Willingham of Clark, New Jer-

sey, came under almost immediate guerrilla fire when it landed on the
sand dunes just outside My Lai.

Willingham asked for and received support from helicopter gunships,
and he said the firepower from his men and the choppers killed 30 guerrillas by body count before the Vietcong broke and ran for tunneled hiding places.

First contact in the My Lai fighting came at 7:30 a.m. Saturday. It was
all over by 2 p.m., front reports said.[65]

A later UPI version, based on an Army handout, read:

On the northern coast, units of the Army's 11th Light Infantry Brigade
scrambled from helicopters that pounced on the sand dunes just outside
"Pink Village," My Lai. U.S. artillery gave them covering fire.

But 2nd Lt. Thomas K. Willingham of Clark, New Jersey, leader of
one of the first assault platoons, reported his men came under almost immediate guerrilla fire from the fortified village. American helicopter gunships swung in low and peppered the communists.

Willingham's platoon charged. The Vietcong broke and ran for their
hide-out tunnels. Six-and-a-half hours later, *"Pink Village"* had become
"Red, White and Blue Village."[66]

In fact, there were no sand dunes and no resistance at My Lai it-
self, and the vivid UPI version was apparently based on what Army
PIOs in Chu Lai put together. The Army's own PIO correspondent,
Ronald Haeberle, on the scene, mentioned no massacre.[67]

The New York *Times* ran the My Lai story, written out of its
Saigon bureau from the MACV roundup, on page one:

SAIGON, South Vietnam, Sunday, Mar. 17—American troops caught
a North Vietnamese force in a pincer movement on the central coastal
plain yesterday, killing 128 enemy soldiers in day-long fighting.

Two American soldiers were killed and 10 wounded, according to an
American spokesman.

The fighting erupted six miles northeast of Quang Ngai in an area of
sand dunes and scrub brush between Highway One and the South China
Sea. . . .

About 150 men of the Americal Division encountered the enemy force
early yesterday. A second company from the same unit was dropped in
by helicopter two miles to the northeast to provide a squeeze on the
enemy troops.

The United States soldiers were sweeping the area, where numerous
clashes had been fought in the last year and a half, but which had been
relatively quiet in recent months, with the exception of the Lunar New
Year attack on the city of Quang Ngai itself.[68]

The operation is another American offensive to clear enemy pockets still threatening the cities.[69]

The area was heavily shelled by artillery at dawn yesterday before troops moved in on foot.

While the two companies of United States soldiers moved in on the enemy force from opposite sides, heavy artillery barrages and armed helicopters were called in to pound the North Vietnamese soldiers.

The American command's military communiqué said fighting continued sporadically through the day. The action ended at 3 p.m., when the remaining North Vietnamese slipped out and fled, according to the communiqué.

It was not made clear how many of the enemy had been killed by the artillery and helicopter attacks, and how many were shot down by the American infantrymen.[70]

The *Post* had no page-one news from Vietnam that day, but used a desk-edited version of the AP My Lai story inside the paper.[71]

And then the story was forgotten—another remote fight, another wire-service "action lead."

Summary: A Deficient Picture

Several points seem worth noting about the coverage of U.S. battle performance. First, most eyewitness combat reporting, rare and restricted as it was, showed up better in February than the MACV communiqués or the communiqué rewrites in Saigon. However, in February, even the wire services lacked the manpower to cover the major Tet battlefields aside from Hue, Saigon, and Khe Sanh, and the newspapers, television networks, and news magazines were even worse off in this regard. Thus the media were dependent on the communiqués, and picked from them what seemed most desirable for their purposes. But major battles—such as the Marine fighting south of Da Nang, the repulse of the enemy at Quang Tri, and the continuing action on the outskirts of Saigon and in the Central Highlands—were scarcely covered by the communiqués, and so went largely unreported. After the fall of Hue, the major bureaus did not redeploy in March and seek out the new battle actions elsewhere—actions which developed into a disjointed but vigorous U.S. counteroffensive. Newsmen turned from Hue to Khe Sanh, from one localized drama to another.

Second, there was the usual tendency by television producers and wire-photo editors to run easy cliché shots. At Hue, it was possible to film episodes that had some continuity and provided context, since the Marines were trying to take ground. But repeatedly, informative TV film was marred by sloppy, sometimes simple-minded narration.[72] Most of the explanatory commentary was overblown—partly because TV correspondents had lacked time to probe to any degree into the meaning of filmed material. The idea, as always, was to get "good" film first.

Moreover, it was as clear here as anywhere, other factors aside, that as "processing"—rewriting and editing—increased, accuracy tended to decrease. Least processed (if often cut) was the copy of the newspapermen. Most processed were news-magazine stories and TV anchormen's scripts.

On another level, it should be added, very few newsmen were sufficiently experienced, interested, or informed to "explain" the battle scene in its larger context. Here and there, written in Washington, New York, or Saigon, were muddled, usually misleading, pseudo-learned comments on such matters as search-and-destroy tactics, clear-and-hold operations, and "enclave theories." But by and large, neither the newsmen nor their editors thought it important to examine the Army's leadership, tactics, or organizational performance in Vietnam in any detail after three years of war. The interest was in action and drama, not military concepts or systems. Concepts—discussed in public by Westmoreland—made little impression on the press. The Army system, good and bad, was there to see, but we did not know what to look for.

As a result, even as they portrayed the "little picture" well at Hue and Saigon, newsmen in Vietnam neglected the obvious flaws in U.S. command performance at Tet: Westmoreland's failure to fully complete his troop shift north before Tet broke, or to see beforehand the psychological importance of a "no-risk" military policy (later adopted) for the defense of the capital; his failure, before and after Tet, to discipline Army field commanders and Air Force spotters for the occasionally indiscriminate use of air power and artillery fire in rural areas, especially where no friendly troops were "in contact" with the foe; and the lack of joint planning and coordinated ARVN-U.S. Army staffwork for the defense of the cities (such arrangements for Saigon did not come until after the second attacks in May 1968).

There were still other deficiencies: the inattention paid by MACV to the refugee problem *until* Tet; the excessive comfort of the rear echelons; the short, one-year tours served in Vietnam by most career officers, resulting in inexperienced leadership and probably higher U.S. losses; the failure to provide sufficient protection against bombardment for expensive U.S. aircraft on the ground; and the failure to equip U.S. (and ARVN) troops with sufficient heavy direct-fire weapons (such as the Marines' 106 mm. recoilless rifles) for fighting in cities. The latter circumstance left the infantry dependent for fire support on helicopter gunships, air strikes, and howitzer fire—all of which were far less accurate, and more destructive of civilian life and property.

By the same token, Westmoreland's accomplishments before and during Tet also got little attention. Among these were the prescient logistical buildup in the north; the sheer size and the careful dispersion of U.S. bases; the deployment of enough troops, before Tet, to the north to deal with Khe Sanh, Hue, Quang Tri, and a sizable enemy penetration in the adjacent coastal area; the quick reaction (and redeployment) of U.S. troops to help ARVN in the cities; the orchestration of the B-52 raids around Khe Sanh; the dispatch of General Abrams to straighten out the Hue battle, and the creation of a flexible new command for Hue and the DMZ; and Westmoreland's personal support of pacification and reconstruction.

In sum, Westmoreland—his real flaws and virtues—did not emerge clearly in the Tet coverage, in contrast to, say, the Marines' performance at Hue. Moreover, Westmoreland's problems got little attention, notably the link between White House curbs on U.S. strategy (e.g., no ground moves against the foe's bases and supply lines in Laos and Cambodia that were so important at Tet) and Hanoi's crucial long-term strategic advantages in its war against the South. Again, newsmen and their bosses had other preoccupations.

8

Khe Sanh: Disaster in the Making?

No event during the Tet period was to stimulate more sustained journalistic output, particularly in terms of TV film, still photographs, and "news analysis," than the NVA's 77-day siege of the U.S. Marine Combat Base at Khe Sanh, in the mountainous northwest corner of South Vietnam. Khe Sanh was the most important continuing story during Tet. Almost to the end, it was a story heavily flavored with the suggestion of impending disaster—a disaster comparable to that suffered by the French garrison of Dienbienphu at the hands of General Giap in 1954.

The disaster did not occur. Indeed, North Vietnamese ground attacks, after several fierce but abortive tries at Khe Sanh's outposts in late January and early February, were limited to one push at the main perimeter on February 29 and a few probes thereafter. Despite enemy shelling, aerial resupply and reinforcement and casualty evacuation continued. Marine losses at Khe Sanh were only a small fraction of those suffered by U.S. units elsewhere. In terms of the Vietnam War's military pattern, the siege was an aberration, giving MACV a rare opportunity to focus its B-52 bombers for a sustained period on a small area.

AP took the lead, television followed, and newspaper editors fell in line in concentrating on Khe Sanh, especially after the recapture of Hue on February 24. Yet, Khe Sanh was not that significant in the overall Tet picture; it was the only place, after the first few days of the battle of Hue, where U.S. forces were still on the defensive in Vietnam following the initial Tet attacks. This was a point seldom made in the media. To the contrary, by emphasizing Khe Sanh so heavily, many in the media appeared to believe (and suggest) that the foe was still exerting heavy military pressure throughout Vietnam long after that pressure had in fact eased. Moreover, Khe Sanh itself was depicted well into March as being in a state of peril even as enemy shelling slackened and clearing weather helped U.S. air power.

By our count, Khe Sanh was the subject, during the 60-day period of February–March 1968, of: (1) 25 percent of all Vietnam film reports on weekday TV evening network shows (for CBS the figure was 50 percent); (2) the lead paragraphs and headlines of New York *Times* war wrap-ups (written in Saigon) on 17 of the 60 days, of the *Post* on 13 days, and of AP on 12 days; (3) 18 percent of all Vietnam pictures in the *Post* and *Times;* and (4) 38 percent of all AP Vietnam stories filed with datelines outside Saigon (Hue got almost equal AP attention, accounting for 37 percent).

There was considerable reaction to this emphasis at home. Early in February, for example, Senator Eugene McCarthy, a peace candidate for the Democratic nomination, set off a two-week Congressional tempest by speculating that the military thought Khe Sanh's defense would require nuclear weapons. As time went on, CBS's Walter Cronkite presented the siege as a "microcosm" of the whole war. So did *Newsweek*'s editors, who ran the "Agony of Khe Sanh" as centerpiece for a mid-March issue, calling for a negotiated peace. In the Washington *Post,* historian Arthur Schlesinger, Jr., urged the prompt evacuation by air of the entire Marine garrison (a tactical impossibility). Robert Kennedy, running for the Democratic Presidential nomination, began to cite Khe Sanh as a symbol of the folly of U.S. involvement in Vietnam.

Whatever its military or political significance, Khe Sanh filled a *journalistic* need. It had inherent dramatic values. It seemed like a simple, easily defined story: more than 5,000 isolated Marines (and 300 South Vietnamese Rangers), surrounded by large concealed numbers of North Vietnamese troops, bombarded as never before in Vietnam by rockets and artillery, dependent on airlift for supply, bedeviled by bad weather, seemingly at the mercy of hidden enemy artillery observers in the surrounding mountains—the "eyes" of General Giap, the victor of Dienbienphu, who, it was rumored (and widely reported), had "taken personal command" of the siege. What an ominous predicament for U.S. forces (and, above all, for Lyndon Johnson), already surprised by the Tet attacks against the cities! If enemy "initiative" had faded elsewhere, Hanoi certainly had the "initiative" at Khe Sanh.

No less important, Khe Sanh was a *sustained* contest, filling the news vacuum left by the end of the Hue battle. It was not just one of a series of intermittent, bloody, but seemingly inconclusive one-day firefights. The siege was like the Dak To and Con Thien hill battles in 1967, only more so—a story newsmen could count on day after day.

Yet, Khe Sanh was an oddly obscure story. The hill outposts of the base (Hills 881 South, 861, 861 Alpha, 558, 950), where most ground action occurred during the siege and where life was dirty and most dangerous, were largely inaccessible to newsmen. The B-52 strikes were also largely invisible to the press. But the sprawling main base on the Khe Sanh plateau, with its aid station and metal air strip, provided sufficient visual color and drama: enemy shelling, fearsome fires and explosions, wounded Marines, trenches, smashed bunkers and aircraft, close-in U.S. tactical air strikes, "Americans under stress." There was precious little quick information, but plenty of good pictures by conventional standards. It was a hell of a place.

Khe Sanh: Explaining Why

The January 21–April 7, 1968, siege of Khe Sanh began in earnest with bad weather, the timely defection of an NVA lieutenant who disclosed the enemy's initial plan, and a nip-and-tuck defense of the Marine outpost on Hill 861. It ended with good weather, a Marine push-out, and the April 1 launching of Operation Pegasus, the lightly opposed relief expedition by the Marines and the U.S. 1st Cavalry Division.

Using light Soviet-built PT-76 tanks, the NVA assaulted and took the isolated Lang Vei Special Forces camp on the Laotian border (manned by 24 Americans and 500 Montagnards) near Khe Sanh on February 7. By U.S. estimates, the enemy's encircling divisions fired a daily average of some 150 rockets, mortar shells, and artillery rounds at the base and its surrounding hill outposts.[1] He made three major assaults against these outposts and one abortive push against the main base perimeter itself, on March 1, and then, except for probes, began to back off in early March, under unprecedented U.S. air bombardment.

Marine casualties at Khe Sanh (Operation Scotland) totaled 205 KIA and 852 wounded (evacuated) from *November 1, 1967,* to

March 31, 1968, with 65 dead in March alone.[2] Even if one assumes *all* these casualties occurred during the 77-day siege period, they came, on the average, to three killed per day and 12 wounded—considerably fewer losses than comparable U.S. 6,000-man units suffered elsewhere during the same period. And both the flow of replacements and evacuation of casualties continued throughout the siege.

Aircraft losses were minor. A total of four U.S. transport fixed-wing planes were destroyed on the ground or shot down: three twin-engine C-123 Providers and one four-engine C-130 Hercules (in contrast to 62 aircraft lost by the French at Dienbienphu).[3] A spotter plane and two fighter aircraft (an F-4 and an A-4) were shot down. The exact U.S. helicopter loss at Khe Sanh is elusive, but one Marine historian put the toll at 17, with perhaps twice this number receiving serious battle damage.[4]

All these figures, except the total helicopter losses, were either published in MACV communiqués or available to newsmen during the siege.

The Marines were to claim 1,602 enemy bodies along the perimeters, but this figure obviously did not reflect any NVA losses suffered from the 100,000 tons of bombs dropped and the 158,000 rounds expended by Marine artillery (nor did it take into account losses from shells fired by the Army's long-range 175 mm. guns from Camp Carroll). Westmoreland was later to estimate total enemy losses of 10,000 to 15,000 killed,[5] but this was accepted, at best, as no more than a guess. Nevertheless, most newsmen were ready, after a tour of the bomb-cratered moonscape around Khe Sanh following the siege, to concede that the foe had suffered more agony than had either Khe Sanh's defenders or visiting newsmen.

The Administration did not add to public understanding of the battle. Because of White House political worries, legitimate security concerns, and verbal sloppiness, the official U.S. rationale for defending Khe Sanh was never spelled out convincingly during the Tet period.

A former Special Forces outpost, guarding a major gap in the Annamite Mountain range, Khe Sanh had been taken over by the Marines in September 1966 as the western end of a planned, but never completed, network ("Dyemarker") of strongpoints and electronic sensors designed to curb enemy infiltration below the DMZ. Its airstrip was defended by the Marines in a series of bloody hill battles in May 1967; later the strength of its garrison fluctuated, shrinking to as little as one company as Marine units were deployed to meet crises elsewhere. Reinforcements came after a fresh NVA buildup in nearby Laos was spotted in mid-December 1967. This threat was reported by *Post* columnist Joseph Alsop, after talks with Walt Rostow and others, on December 15 and December 18, but no one else paid much attention until mid-January 1968.

Moreover, as Neil Sheehan of the New York *Times* reported on February 23 ("Khe Sahn: Why U.S. Is Making a Stand"), Khe Sanh was also privately seen by "military leaders" (Westmoreland) as an ace in the hole—a staging point for possible thrusts along Highway Nine into the Ho Chi Minh Trail area in southern Laos. In fact, such thrusts from Khe Sanh were proposed by Westmoreland to McNamara during the latter's visit to Saigon in July 1967. They were part of a secret proposal for a new strategy and the major 200,000-man troop buildup which was turned down in mid-1967 by the White House as politically unpalatable (only to be partly revived by Gen. Earle Wheeler at Tet). But this rationale for Khe Sanh's defense, understandably, was not discussed in public during the siege. (Khe Sanh finally played its staging-point role during the unhappy venture by ARVN along Highway Nine into Laos in 1971.)

In mid-January 1968, Westmoreland indicated he expected action in the north, but—as newsmen often failed to grasp—involving not just Khe Sanh, but also the entire Quang Tri-Thua Thien two-province area, including the DMZ. He discussed this enemy threat for the first time in the press in his interview with AP on January 17, 1968.[6] Again, on the "Huntley-Brinkley Report" (picked up by AP) of January 22, 1968, he pointed out an enemy buildup in the northern part of I Corps, south of the DMZ, and in the direction of Laos.[7] But no specific military rationale was then offered by Westmoreland—or none at least was published—for the commitment to Khe Sanh specifically. Nor was the Khe Sanh defense discussed in detail by the General at his post-Tet February 1 briefing in Saigon. Westmoreland said then only that he expected an attack at any time.

In Saigon, MACV spokesmen's discussions of Khe Sanh were reflected only vaguely in the media before Tet. Khe Sanh, it was said, *blocked* enemy infiltration routes—a clearly impossible claim and a prime example of official verbal sloppiness. This claim was repeated in Washington by General Wheeler in early February. The impression was given to laymen that Khe Sanh was supposed to bar *all* the northwestern approaches to the heavily populated coast, not just hamper a sustained push by NVA regular forces, with their artillery and trucks, toward Quang Tri city and the lowlands.

Westmoreland and Lieutenant General Cushman, commander of III MAF (and thus of Khe Sanh's defenders), had other reasons for choosing to hold a static position at Khe Sanh: (1) in January 1968 the Marines lacked sufficient helicopters—and sufficiently good weather—to conduct a "mobile" defense of the Khe Sanh gap in the Annamite Mountains (tactics later adopted); (2) it was preferable to try to tie up—and decimate with B-52 strikes—a major enemy force far from the populated coast; (3) the effectiveness of the systematic use of massive air power and electronic sensors to frustrate enemy attack had been demonstrated in the defense of the smaller exposed outpost at Con Thien the previous autumn; and (4) Khe Sanh appeared important to the enemy, according to captured or defecting NVA officers, and hence should, as with air power and a fairly small (four-battalion) U.S. ground commitment it could, be denied to him. Whatever their merits, these arguments were not advanced early in public, apparently for military security reasons.[8]

In their Saigon press briefings following the initial Tet attacks, Brigadier General Chaisson, Westmoreland's tactical "man Friday," and Major General Davidson, his intelligence chief, did not discuss the tactical significance of Khe Sanh, but the enemy buildup against the base. Newsmen in Saigon at that point were not interested in rationales. Said Davidson: "The strength of an NVA division is supposed to be 10,000 men, but it very seldom is. They're quite flexible in their tables of organization and equipment and I would say, particularly with the new ones that came down, that we could figure about 8,000. So you can see we probably have somewhere between 30,000 and 35,000, maybe 40,000 [in the Khe Sanh-DMZ area]."[9]

For his part, Lyndon Johnson exposed his private nervousness about Khe Sanh in his talk to the 27th Marine Regiment departing for Vietnam as reinforcement. He attributed, as was his wont, all assessment of the military situation to the military: "This is a decisive time in Vietnam. The eyes of the nation and the eyes of the entire world—the eyes of all of history itself—are on that little, brave band of defenders who hold the pass at Khe Sanh and the area that is around it. . . . General [Lewis W.] Walt, who is here with me tonight, who has flown across the land with me today, tells me that he has walked every mile of I Corps. And General Walt believes it can be defended."[10]

Thus, the "why" of Khe Sanh remaining cloudy to laymen, including the President and newsmen, the door was opened to speculation. In Vietnam, accurate reporting of Khe Sanh was also seriously impeded by a combination of other factors: competition for scarce seats on flights to the base; once there, hazardous and abbreviated visits; and, back at Da Nang, the base of journalistic operations for Khe Sanh, a serious lapse in Marine command attention to "information" and "press problems." All of this was further complicated by a mob scene resulting from the U.S. Mission policy of liberal press accreditation.

The "Dienbienphu Syndrome"

By far the most popular journalistic exercise of Tet was comparing the Khe Sanh siege to the ill-fated 56-day defense—from March 13 to May 8, 1954—of Dienbienphu by the French that climaxed the 1946–54 French Indo-China War. This game was inflamed by pre-Tet "backgrounders" in Washington by Walt Rostow, the President's national security advisor, concerning a probable enemy effort to score "a Dienbienphu" at Khe Sanh, and by similar talk at MACV and in the Pentagon, where, however, the speculation also included the rest of northern I Corps as a potential enemy target. Rostow and the worried President called for data on Dienbienphu; Westmoreland asked his own staff for a study (completed February 11, 1968) of the French battle and enemy tactics employed there.[11]

In Saigon, as Herr noted:

It was about this time that copies of the little red British paperback edition of Jules Roy's *The Battle of Dienbienphu* began appearing wherever members of the Vietnam press corps gathered. You'd spot them around the terrace bar of the Continental Hotel, in L'Amiral Restaurant and Aterbea, at the 8th Aerial Port of Tan Son Nhut, in the Marine-operated Da Nang press center, and in the big briefing room of JUSPAO in Saigon, where every afternoon at four-forty-five, spokesmen conducted the daily war briefing which was colloquially referred to as the Five O'Clock Follies, an Orwellian grope through the day's events as seen by the Mission. (It was very hard-line.) Those who could find copies were reading Bernard Fall's Dienbienphu book, *Hell in a Very Small Place*, which many considered the better book, stronger on tactics, more businesslike, with none of the high-level staff gossip that made the Roy book so dramatic. And as the first Marine briefings on Khe Sanh took place in Marine headquarters at Da Nang or Dong Ha, the name Dienbienphu insinuated itself like some tasteless ghost hawking bad news. Marines who had to talk to the press found references to the old French disaster irritating and even insulting. Most were not interested in fielding questions about it, and the rest were unequipped. The more irritated they became, the more the press would flaunt the irritant. For a while it looked like nothing that had happened on the ground during those weeks seemed as thrilling and sinister as the recollection of Dienbienphu. And it had to be admitted, the parallels with Khe Sanh were irresistible.[12]

How valid was the comparison? Certainly, there were some gripping similarities: The looming, dark green mass of Dong Tri Mountain to the north of the Khe Sanh airstrip made many a newly arrived newsman think of the mist-shrouded hills pictured in the histories of Dienbienphu. Indeed, while working for the *Times,* this writer, after his first visit in 1966 to Khe Sanh, saw it as resembling a "miniature Dienbienphu"—an allusion blue-penciled by the *Times* foreign desk, presumably because it was too unfamiliar to the average *Times* reader.[13] The *Times,* and others, made it up to the readers later.

In cold statistical terms, there were major differences between Khe Sanh and Dienbienphu, differences which were perceivable by comparing Fall's data with the U.S. information then obtainable, by visiting Khe Sanh, by obtaining MACV or Pentagon statistics (incoming artillery rounds, casualties, sorties flown), or by consulting the map:

	Dienbienphu	*Khe Sanh*
Distance from friendly bases	100 miles plus	12 miles (Rock Pile)
Airfield status	Unusable	Usable (for C-123s)
"External" artillery support	None	175 mm. guns (Rock Pile, Camp Carroll)
Available daily tactical combat aircraft	100	1,500
Average incoming rounds (daily)	2,000 plus	150
Aircraft losses	62	6–7 (excluding helicopters), with 18 damaged
Aerial resupply (daily)	100 tons	161 tons plus (excluding helicopter support)
How replacements arrived	Parachute	Helicopters and fixed-wing aircraft
Evacuation of wounded	None	Helicopter
Enemy efforts after first ground action	Continuous	Four assaults through March 1, then probes

	Dienbienphu	Khe Sanh
Average air combat sorties (daily)	22	300
Average heavy bomber sorties (daily)	None	45–50
Passengers air-landed/evacuated via cargo aircraft	0/0	2,676/1,574 (not including helicopter passengers)

In short, the major differences between Khe Sanh and Dienbienphu that were observable by newsmen in Vietnam during the siege concerned logistics, materiel, distance to friendly forces, besiegers' efforts to take ground, and the relative intensities of the fire of both sides. It should be noted that the highest recorded daily total of enemy incoming mortar, artillery, and rocket fire at Khe Sanh totaled 1,307 rounds, on February 23, less than the daily *average* for Dienbienphu. Marine casualties were also far lower than those of the French, although exact comparison is difficult.[14] In sum, Dienbienphu was a high-intensity siege; Khe Sanh was not, despite some intense early moments, and continuous heavy strain on U.S. aerial resupply.

As Herr noted, the busy Marines were not keen on discussions of Dienbienphu. This caused some head-shaking among newsmen who had done a quick read of Fall or Roy. On occasion, as we will see, Col. David Lownds, the commander of the 26th Marine Regiment at Khe Sanh, or Lieutenant General Cushman would deal fleetingly with the chronic question. "Air power" and "proximity to friendly forces" were usually the military's shorthand explanation of why Khe Sanh was "different." It was a shorthand dimly understood and often rejected by civilian newsmen who ventured to Khe Sanh aboard heavy-bellied two-engine C-123s, bucking down through the overcast, and then stumbling to cover, while the plane taxied under mortar fire for take-off. Newsmen could not see the B-52 strikes, the ground control radar, or most of the tactical air sorties; on their brief visits, they could only see the mountains, talk to junior Marines, view enemy trenches, and sweat out the "incoming."

Back home, among editors and Washington newsmen, as well as politicians, Dienbienphu became a subject of fascination—if not of profound study—because of Khe Sanh's possible political impact on President Johnson's personal fortunes and his war policy as a whole. Should Giap overrun Khe Sanh,[15] so the reasoning went, it would deal a major psychological blow to the Administration's war policy, as Dienbienphu did to French war policy in 1954. (Some historians have noted that France had already begun negotiations well prior to the Dienbienphu siege.) As the siege went on, there were two page-one studies of Khe Sanh-Dienbienphu in the New York *Times*[16] from Washington—a striking example of editors turning hungrily to long-distance analysis to fill what was viewed as a gap in on-the-scene reporting from abroad. Other parts of the media joined in the over-kill, notably the networks.

The "Dienbienphu syndrome" spurred a major journalistic exercise, as will be shown. But there was another theme popular among newsmen, especially right after Tet: The North Vietnamese buildup around Khe Sanh—deliberately or not—served to divert or "immobilize" major U.S. forces away from the cities. *Life* said that most of the "45,000 troops" sent to back up the Khe Sanh garrison had been pulled away from "critically important pacification duties"—a half-truth repeated elsewhere. *Newsweek* informed its readers that the siege was immobilizing not only the base's own 5,000-man garrison, but also "close to 10,000 other U.S. troops who are being held in reserve."[17] Sir Robert Thompson also, in his already noted analysis, saw Khe Sanh as a "military diversion," keeping "the best part of two U.S. divisions tied down."[18] The New York *Times* published a similar analysis, which stated that "only time will tell whether what was apparently a well-advertised movement by two North Vietnamese divisions into the hills around Khe Sanh was a diversion."[19] It was widely written, by Sir Robert and others, that the foe: (1) had ample trained combat manpower available and (2) would and could expend it, heedless of loss, at Khe Sanh or elsewhere. Hence, any diversion of *Hanoi*'s troops to Khe Sanh was irrelevant.

A little more study of the situation by newsmen might have precluded undue stress on the "diversion" thesis. If Hanoi had, in fact, simply intended a cheap diversion of U.S. forces from urban areas, it did not turn out that way. As of January 25, the NVA's two divisions (18 battalions) in the Khe Sanh area equaled about 20 percent of NVA main-force battalion strength in South Vietnam and about 40 percent of NVA strength in I Corps.[20] Westmoreland's four battalions at Khe Sanh were equivalent to 10 percent of his I Corps "maneuver battalion" strength and 5 percent of his 97 battalions in all Vietnam. These crude data were available at Tet to newsmen in Washington and Saigon, and no doubt to Hanoi.

Westmoreland, worried about the DMZ as well as Khe Sanh by Tet time, had rushed three more Army brigades into northern I Corps (from the 101st Airborne Division and the 1st Air Cavalry Division); they were not at Khe Sanh, or "tied down" in reserve, as variously stated in *Times* and *Post* analyses, but operating actively on the coastal plain, near long-exposed, populated areas (Hue and Quang Tri city). These cities, as it turned out, were to come under far more serious and sustained attack at Tet than the areas (Bong Son and Bien Hoa) where those units had been stationed earlier.

In net terms: By his troop shifts, designed primarily to back up Khe Sanh and the DMZ, Westmoreland vastly strengthened northern I Corps populated-area defenses, as it happened, over what they had been on January 1, 1968. Thus, fortuitously, battalions of the 101st Airborne and 1st Cavalry, however surprised, were on hand to smash a major attack on Quang Tri city, and to push against enemy-occupied Hue from the north. No such sizable U.S. forces had been available in these areas before.[21] And, happily for the ARVN, a South Vietnamese Airborne Task Force was on hand to help out at Hue. Had these troop shifts not taken place, the thinly spread Marines and ARVN would have been hard-pressed to cope alone with the heavy enemy urban attacks that did occur.

The changing enemy intentions vis-à-vis Khe Sanh remain a mystery.

According to the 26th Marines' unit diary (March 23), two battalions of the 29th NVA Regiment, a unit of the besieging 325C Division, were sent to Hue in February to reinforce success there. But the enemy also made four bloody attacks in the Khe Sanh area against outposts (Hills 861 and 861 Alpha, Lang Vei Special Forces camp, and a small platoon position) and one abortive, night regimental push, crushed by B-52 strikes, against the ARVN sector, on February 29–March 1. Then the foe backed off, except for probes and declining rocket and mortar fire. He dug trenches up close, but he never attempted to seize the key Marine platoon outpost, observation point and electronic sensor relay station atop Hill 950, on the western nose of Dong Tri Mountain, which seemed to loom so closely over Khe Sanh from the north. He did not assault the exposed Marine outposts on Hill 881 South or Hill 558 on the west side. Nor did he use 37 mm. antiaircraft guns (employed later against U.S. helicopters at A Shau) as reported by AP and *Time,* or mass .50 caliber weapons off the runway. Had this been done, the aerial resupply of Khe Sanh would have been precarious.

His artillery fire, however noisy, was sporadic and inaccurate, given the easy target. He did not *surround* the camp with artillery. He prudently kept his heavy weapons in or close to Laos, west of Khe

Sanh. If the conservative Marine estimates of his strength are correct, he initially massed too many men and guns around Khe Sanh just to "isolate" it. Yet, it may be, as Westmoreland later contended, that as time went on, with the U.S. bombing (100,000 tons, equal in destructive power to five Hiroshima-type atomic bombs) continuing and the Marine outposts holding firm, the enemy commander did not want to risk enough additional troops or expose his artillery in an effort to overwhelm Khe Sanh by sheer force, heedless of losses.

The NVA troops began to thin out in mid-March. They stopped repairing their siege trenches on March 10. In retrospect, the NVA commander (or his superiors in Hanoi) appear less than decisive about Khe Sanh.[22] Had the NVA shifted one whole division from Khe Sanh to Hue in early February, Gen. Creighton Abrams was to observe in January 1969 to this writer, "we would still be fighting there [at Hue]."

Like much of the enemy's piecemeal tactical performance elsewhere during Tet, his behavior at Khe Sanh remains a mystery. But much journalistic imagination was devoted to explaining it—telling the reader what the wily Giap, victor of Dienbienphu, had in mind.

The Press at Khe Sanh

The III MAF press camp, on the Da Nang riverfront, was a former French-owned motel, upstream from downtown Da Nang. It consisted of four long, low, tile-roofed, whitewashed buildings arranged in a hollow square which was used as a parking lot for Marine vehicles and the white-painted network and AP jeeps. The Marines had added a central press shack on the riverside, named in honor of Dickey Chapelle, a free-lancer killed in Vietnam. In the front room here, under a sloping, sound-proofed roof, were a series of telephones contacting with "Parchment," "Tiger," "Da Nang," and other military exchanges tied to Saigon. In the back room were 1:50,000 scale maps on sliding panels showing the location of III MAF battalions in I Corps; in addition, for newsmen who had missed them, tapes of past briefings by senior Marine officers were available. There was also a restaurant and bar (served by Vietnamese), a nightly movie, and a certain pecking order: The Vietnamese and American network and wire-service staffs had rented their own cluttered, air-conditioned bunk rooms on the north side of the compound; on the south side, *Time-Life* leased three beds (hung with mosquito netting), with AFP in another room; *Newsweek* had one bed; the New York *Times* rented one bed; and the other newspapers had no reserved places, but bunked where they could. On the west side of the quadrangle were two unair-conditioned rooms, with noisy ceiling fans, for the overflow and the transients: German TV crews, Japanese photographers, French magazine writers, energetic processors of "home-town" news items about GIs, and a Brazilian who went everywhere, even to Khe Sanh itself, with a plaid suitcase.

Even prior to Tet, the press camp was crowded. John B. King, then a Marine PIO staff sergeant and escort (and visitor to Khe Sanh, Hue, and Con Thien), later described the fringe element:

There is the wife of a TV news commentator who hasn't written a line of news since her college days and who admits that was many years ago; the newsman who lived in Da Nang press center and operated two cheap bars downtown; the college boy whose dad financed a trip to the Orient to give him a glimpse of the war; the divorcée who loafed around I Corps and never wrote a line; the merchant seaman who jumped ship and borrowed a camera to become a free-lance photographer; the retired Swedish army officer who just wanted to see what was going on; the sob sister from the *Village Voice* who staged a sit-in strike and had to be carried out of the Americal Division's press camp. The list seems endless.[23]

In those days, the center, guarded by an aged Vietnamese with a carbine, was a peaceful enclave. It had a fine view of the red-blinking radio towers on Monkey Mountain and a distant view of Marble Mountain, the Marine helicopter base. During the 1966 Buddhist "struggle movement," newsmen sallied forth aboard the network jeeps to cover the near-civil war a few blocks away. By late 1967, they also went to the crowded market to buy black-market uniforms, boots, and packs, or to China Beach for a swim, or to hear the regional commander and political boss, Lieutenant General Lam, hold forth in polished zippered boots at the ARVN I Corps compound, or to interview Marine staff officers at III MAF headquarters.

The latter worked in an old park-like French compound, shaded by Aleppo pines, across the river by Navy launch from the "White Elephant," a hotel converted into U.S. Navy headquarters in downtown Da Nang. A regular Navy minibus service—gray Dodge station wagons—ran irregularly through the Da Nang area, along with the bigger buses. There was a whitewashed museum, guarded (during Tet) by amiable militiamen who had strung hammocks from the adjoining trees. Next door was an ARVN supply unit, and on the other side an LST ramp used by the Korean Navy. Nevertheless, the war seemed far away during the day, especially to newsmen newly returned from Hue or Khe Sanh. At night, the steady thump of outgoing artillery and the orange flares only provided background and atmosphere.

CBS's Bernard Kalb wrote about arriving at the place:

You always can tell when your aircraft is approaching the big U.S. Air Base at Da Nang, on the coast. The South China Sea is a glittering dish of blue. It all looks like an aquatic playland. Jamaica, anyone? Close to shore you fly over a long curve of beach, and it's a Sunday, and the sands are heavily populated. It looks as though the whole town is out today. The sun gilds it all, South Vietnam on a calendar, a kodachrome for a travel agency selling tours to the "Orient." That is the view from the right side of the Air Vietnam DC-6.

The view from the left is war.

A surging column of flame and smoke from a fuel storage tank smudges the porcelain sky. NVA rocket? Sabotage? Da Nang attacked while we were flying up from Saigon? But the runways are business as usual, as busy as O'Hare International, the U.S. Air Force will tell you, even busier, the busiest in the world, about 2,000 landings and take-offs a day, sir, except that the passengers are bombs and rockets and napalm. . . .

The civilian air terminal at Da Nang is a crowded, shattering mélange of generations—elderly Vietnamese gentlemen in plastic pith helmets and Ho Chi Minh goatees, matriarchs in traditional ao dai high-necked gowns and pantaloons, boys in tight trousers, teen-age girls self-consciously conspicuous in toreador slacks and above-the-knee psychedelic prints copied from the patterns in French and American fashion magazines. There are the chewing of betel and the smell of perfume; peasant women using their conical straw hats as fans and picking their bare feet; city ladies in silks, their painted toenails showing in their spike-heeled shoes. Two babies are being breast-fed, and a doll-like three-year-old girl is playing with the circles of gold that pierce her ears.

It is all cozy and intimate and unreal, as though we are checking into a resort, not a war. . . . It is only when we arrive at the press center half an hour later that we are able to get the official story. An announcement on the bulletin board says: ". . . the fire, which was believed to have been started by a star-cluster flare, not, repeat not, dropped by an aircraft, was confined to one of the 11 tanks on the farm. . . . Measures had been taken to prevent the fire from spreading."

Next to it is a mock travel poster you see at many U.S. military installations throughout South Vietnam—FLY FAR-FAR EASTERN AIR-

WAYS, THIS VACATION VISIT BEAUTIFUL VIETNAM—and underneath a drawing of GIs, shells exploding around them, firing away.[24]

A combat veteran of World War II, Col. Karl E. Faser, a pint-sized North Carolinian, was in charge of the press center. He had not sought the job. He abhorred it. His able predecessors and successors had prior press experience. Faser had none. He had been simply reassigned from a billet in III MAF's finance office by Lieutenant General Cushman.

Colonel Faser found it painful to deal with the polyglot crowd of "hippies" and vagabonds he was obliged to assist, house, and feed. Not always without cause, he privately raged at much of what he read of his lodgers' output. On occasion, in this writer's hearing, Faser, goaded beyond endurance by unreasonable demands or disparaging remarks by newsmen, exploded. "You and your damn DeGaulle," he shouted one night at a long-haired crew of French television folk. To a certain degree, he took refuge in housekeeping: the press club bar and dining room sprouted brick facing, paneling, soft lights, Armed Forces television, and the obligatory captured AK-47 rifle mounted on the wall like a trophy swordfish. Faser led daily volleyball games for all Marines.

And, except for the first days after Tet, war or no war, the nightly outdoor movie was shown on the riverside terrace to a half-military, half-journalistic audience, and Faser was always there in his folding chair. Tired reporters trying to dictate combat stories to Saigon over the tortured military phone system from the press room next door during movie time had difficulties making themselves heard over the sound track.

When Tet came, it also became clear, "Faser's Zoo" had an enormous load to carry: As many as 128 newsmen in one week (February 11–17) were escorted to Hue or Khe Sanh, many of them newcomers to both war and Vietnam. With only 20 transient beds, the press center was crowded. Transport, communication, and tempers were strained. "The confusion," Sergeant King later recalled, "was appalling."

Thus, during Tet, Da Nang was not an ideal place in which to gain a clear picture of the military situation. In the field at Hue or Khe Sanh with Sergeant King, Sgt. Bill Smith, and other professional PIO escorts, the situation was far more comprehensible. Several of Faser's staff officers, without much encouragement from superiors, tried to keep themselves informed sufficiently to brief new arrivals on the tactical situation. But Cushman's headquarters across the river was usually too busy—or too cautious—to give Faser's people much help.

Bad tempers were further aggravated by the "quota" system, necessary in military terms. No more than 10 newsmen were allowed at Khe Sanh at any one time, and six places were allocated automatically to the three wire services and three television networks, with the rest of the horde waiting in line for the other four places. This led to considerable frustration, since no one in Da Nang could be sure when those at Khe Sanh would return, opening up space for the next in line. The pressure waned somewhat after mid-February.

Faser and his deputies made an effort to keep newsmen informed, but only after Tet was well under way. Interviews were obtained for newsmen with the III MAF G-2 chief, Colonel Houghton, on February 12, and a combination G-2-G-3 briefing was held for newsmen with Brig. Gen. Carl Hoffman (later a newsman's favorite) and Colonel Houghton on February 15. A briefing was held by Lieutenant General Cushman on February 21. Cushman and Westmoreland held a news conference in Phu Bai on March 10, with Cushman following on March 11 and March 26, and with another G-2-G-3 briefing at Da Nang on March 14 and March 29.

These briefings were not without their severe moments. Michael Herr, whose semi-surrealistic reminiscences of Hue and Khe Sanh portray better than most the newsman's view, described one early session. His account is not to be taken as a literal transcript:

"What about the Marines at Khe Sanh?" someone asked.

"I'm glad we've come to that," the general said. "I was at Khe Sanh for several hours this morning, and I want to tell you that those Marines there are *clean!*"

There was a weird silence. We all knew we'd heard him, the man had said the Marines at Khe Sanh were clean ("Clean? He said 'clean,' didn't he?"), but not one of us could imagine what he'd meant.

"Yes, they're bathing or getting a good wash every other day. They're shaving every day, every single day. Their mood is good, their spirits are fine, morale is excellent, and there's a twinkle in their eye!"

Braestrup stood up.

"General."

"Peter?"

"General, what about the defenses at Khe Sanh? Now, you built this wonderful, air-conditioned officers' club, and that's a complete shambles. You built a beer hall there, and *that's* been blown away." He had begun calmly, but now he was having trouble keeping the anger out of his voice. "You've got a medical detachment there that's a disgrace, set up right on the airstrip, exposed to hundreds of rounds every day, and *no* overhead cover. You've had men at the base since July, you've expected an attack at least since November, they've been shelling you heavily since January. General, why haven't those Marines *dug in?*"

The room was quiet. Braestrup had a fierce smile on his face as he sat down. When the question had begun, the colonel had jerked suddenly to one side of his chair, as though he'd been shot. Now, he was trying to get his face in front of the general's so that he could give out the look that would say, "See, General? See the kind of peckerheads I have to work with every day?" Braestrup was looking directly at the general now, waiting for his answer—the question had not been rhetorical—and it was not long in coming.

"Peter," the general said. "I think you're hitting a small nail with an awfully big hammer."[25]

Lieutenant General Cushman was a tough, stocky, rather stolid man, who lacked enthusiasm for encounters with laymen. But, as time went on, he patiently subjected himself to newsmen:

DA NANG, Vietnam (UPI)—Marine Lt. Gen. Robert Cushman today said the battle for surrounded Khe Sanh is a "titanic firepower struggle" which he is convinced the allies can win.

The Marine commander in Vietnam put his feelings to newsmen in one sentence: "I don't think the enemy can take Khe Sanh. I think we can hold it." . . .

"Khe Sanh is still getting about 150 incoming rounds a day and I am not fooling myself that he [the enemy] has the capability of stepping it up if it suits his purpose. The communists don't invite destruction from the air by revealing too many of their gun positions.

"They are still capable of conducting an attack against Khe Sanh. However the price would be very high indeed. The enemy is digging trenches and using other tricks of the trade which he learned at Dienbienphu," he added.

[In response to repeated questions] the General told the news conference there was a possibility the Reds might try something at Khe Sanh on March 13, the 14th anniversary of the start of the battle of Dienbienphu.

He noted that the communists occasionally commemorate such anniversaries, but that he *had no indication* whether they would on this one, the anniversary of France's landmark defeat in Indo-China.

The Marine General said troops in the I Corps . . . had been on the offensive since the Tet attack began and had been killing an average of 250 communists a day.

"[The enemy] has been avoiding us. But we have been able to find him. . . . I would say in round figures we have killed 20,000 in the past few weeks, which is more than we killed all last year." . . .

In discussing the decision to hold Khe Sanh, Cushman said, "A very deliberate decision was given to hold on. I believe it should be held and I so recommended. And General Westmoreland agreed with me.

"There were several reasons that went into the decision, like how many troops that you tie up, the sacrifices that are involved if you give it up, in terms of their ability to move their units closer to the cities," he continued.

The General said the two North Vietnamese divisions at Khe Sanh would be on their way to Hue and Da Nang if they had not been occupied at Khe Sanh.

He said the communists are capable of attacking anywhere in the I Corps area and "in our opinion we are strong enough to stop them."[26]

Lacking at Da Nang—as at Saigon—was readily available, current, comprehensive information. This was particularly true about the tactical balance at Khe Sanh, notably U.S. ability to provide close-in radar bombing even in bad weather and at night; the relative significance of tactical events (e.g., an ambush); importance of the hill outposts; the various geographic assets and liabilities of the Khe Sanh positions; and cumulative statistics on casualties, incoming artillery fire, and bombing tonnage.

This broad picture was rarely available in Khe Sanh itself, either, especially given the shelling and the in-and-out journalistic traffic. The commander, Colonel Lownds, and his staff were busy with the defense. Moreover, Lownds was reluctant to dwell on tactical detail during his afternoon sessions with an ever-changing polyglot cluster of strangers. His crowded underground command post was off-limits. Some insights were available from the hard-pressed staff at 3rd Marine Division headquarters at Dong Ha, the next highest command echelon for Lownds. But most newsmen, with only limited time, and awaiting their allotted seat, went to Khe Sanh direct and "blind" from Da Nang.

This by-passing of the chain of command also helped to lead to severe gaps in knowledge about Khe Sanh. None of the newspaper maps were accurate. Nor were most descriptions in prose. This reporter was not aware, for example, until March 5, after talking to helicopter pilots, that Hill 558, blocking a valley approach northwest of the base itself, was also held by Marines, making a total of five hilltop outpost positions. Its existence was cited early by AP; it was not mentioned in map briefings by Faser's aides, possibly because they did not know of it. Nor was anyone in Da Nang available early for evaluation of the initial enemy assaults—or indeed any of the enemy assaults—on Khe Sanh or its outposts.

Such evaluations were badly needed. For example, a tall, blond Swedish correspondent, three days after his arrival in Vietnam, confronted this reporter at Da Nang in vacation attire: sandals, corduroys, a blue sports shirt. He announced that he was going to Khe Sanh. I asked him if he had obtained boots, military garb, and a helmet. "Oh, no," he replied, "I thought I would buy such things at Khe Sanh." A Briton in Saigon told me that he was headed for Khe Sanh because it had "the smell of a rotting corpse" and he wanted to be in on the finish.

For most journalists, the most nerve-wracking part of the Khe Sanh story was the oft-described flight by C-130 or C-123 transport in and out of the place. What we did not then know was that the 3rd Marine Division's commander, Maj. Gen. Rathvon McC. Tompkins, a genteel South Carolinian, flew from his headquarters at Dong Ha into Khe Sanh by helicopter almost daily.[27] But for most newsmen, two or three round trips were enough.[28]

As far as can be determined, no newsman except John Wheeler of the AP became a Khe Sanh "regular," a resident, with attendant increase in knowledge. Wheeler made Khe Sanh "his story" for sound professional reasons, anticipating an enemy effort to overrun the place. He sojourned there long enough to get some perspective on the base and to know its geography, its hazards, and the garrison's various elements. His feature stories usually reflected this knowledge. AP, as Arnett noted, wisely let Wheeler stay put in Khe Sanh for days at a time, without demanding daily "spot" stories.

For most of the rest of us, a combination of unusual press load, the information gap, unusual restrictions on movement, and, no less important, the professional urge (or requirement) for quick in-and-out reporting led to highly unfavorable conditions for accurate and impartial firsthand coverage of the Khe Sanh siege. In Saigon and in the United States, speculative excess, fed by ignorance, bloomed as a substitute.

AP: A Reliable Witness

John Wheeler of AP was a husky, crewcut veteran of more than two years of reporting in Vietnam when he assigned himself to the Khe Sanh siege. "More than any of us, Wheeler was a proprietor in Khe Sanh," wrote Don Sider of *Time,* another newsman who covered the entire siege. "We would come in and out—three or four days at Khe Sanh, and three days or a week away. But he *lived* at Khe Sanh. It was his story and his home." Wheeler flew out on occasion, too, to deliver copy, to enjoy steaks, cognac, and hot showers at the Da Nang press center. But he gained an intimacy with the Marines' situation and the Khe Sanh perimeter that few others could match. And, by all accounts, he displayed an enviable calm under pressure. Sider recalled (in a September 1975 letter to this writer) that after the Lang Vei battle, he and Wheeler were surprised by a few mortar rounds at Khe Sanh while riding with some Marines in a jeep. Everyone but Wheeler got into a bunker. After the shelling stopped, Sider found Wheeler outside. Why, Sider asked, hadn't Wheeler scrambled for cover? " 'I stopped to pick up this,' Wheeler said, handing me my notebook [which contained all Sider's precious notes on Lang Vei]. 'You dropped it getting out of the jeep.' "

Wheeler filed at least 13 by-lined pieces (out of 53 datelined AP stories in our file from Khe Sanh in February–March 1968). None of them had the apocalyptic tone that so often characterized television "voice-overs." Khe Sanh, Wheeler made clear, was not a picnic, but he also conveyed the Marines' sustaining group esprit.

His "Life in the V Ring," about the ordeal of Marines of a reconnaissance company in one of the main base's chief impact areas near Lownds' command post and an ammunition dump, began:

KHE SANH, South Vietnam (AP), Feb. 12—The first shell-burst caught the Marines outside the bunkers filling sandbags. More exploding rockets sprayed showers of hot fragments. The Americans dived for cover.

"Corpsman! Corpsman!" came a shout from off to the right. "We've got wounded here!"

"Corpsman! Corpsman!" The shouts now came from the distance. Men were dragging a bleeding comrade toward cover.

Inside the bunkers the Marines hugged their legs and bowed their heads, trying to make themselves as small as possible.

But Wheeler also noted: "The anguish is bottled up within tolerable limits . . . the survivors of the reconnaissance company, although frightened, are uncowed. When the call for stretcher-bearers comes, the young Marines unhesitatingly begin wriggling out to help."[29]

Wheeler also described—as few others did—the serious burden placed on the hill outposts, although he did not then fully explain their importance to Khe Sanh's defense:

KHE SANH, Vietnam (AP)—The combat complex of Khe Sanh is coming under increasing pressure of raids and bombardment and the cruelest punishment of all is being taken by the U.S. Marine protective outposts on the hills surrounding the main base. . . .

Only the night, with its protective cloak of darkness, gives the Marines enough cover to repair trenches and bunkers wrecked by shellfire and to improve their positions.

A sign—and symbol—of the jauntiness of the hilltop Leathernecks can be found on 881 South, where daily a tattered American flag is raised and a bugle plays "To the Colors." The Marines stand at attention and salute during the rapid ceremony, and then dive for cover. They have it timed so they will be prone in their trenches by the time the North Vietnamese mortar shells begin falling again.[30]

Profiting from his lengthy exposure to the place, Wheeler covered more of the significant aspects of the siege than anyone else. Most of the AP's other dispatches from Khe Sanh (by visitors John Lengel, George McArthur, Peter Arnett, Lewis Simons) also supplied "context." For example, Simons reported that the heaviest single day's shelling—1,307 incoming rounds of artillery, rocket, and mortar fire on February 23—produced "comparatively light casualties" (10 killed and 19 seriously wounded), considering both the volume of fire and the garrison's size.[31] But it was the AP war wrap-up (and UPI's) that got the most play in newspapers and that provided the raw material for the nightly television commentary.

Just before Tet, Khe Sanh had begun dominating AP war leads, following the January 21 attacks on Hill 861 and the announcements by MACV of what were obviously heavy B-52 strikes in the area.

On January 25, AP picked up MACV's estimate of two NVA divisions in the Khe Sanh area, then threw in the other NVA units along the DMZ—as MACV sources also did rather loosely.[32] Enemy bombardment was described by AP as continuing *despite* B-52 strikes; no U.S. official claimed enemy bombardment would cease, but enemy "success" is inferred. A kind of prototype of the Khe Sanh story *as written in Saigon* and edited in New York—by AP and others—was the result:

SAIGON (AP)—American bombers pounded North Vietnamese gun and troop concentrations threatening U.S. Marines in the Khe Sanh Valley for the sixth straight day today in one of the biggest air campaigns of the Vietnam War.

Despite nearly 8,000 tons of bombs and record air attacks against the dug-in North Vietnamese, enemy guns continued to hit the Khe Sanh base and the three[33] strategic hills the Marines control just to the northwest.

By noon today, the North Vietnamese had dropped another 20 mortar and rocket rounds on the Marine positions protecting the northwestern approaches to South Vietnam 16 miles below the Demilitarized Zone.

The day's barrage[34] followed perhaps 300 rounds of heavy artillery, rockets, and mortars that communist gunners *slammed* into the combat base and the adjacent peaks last night, killing seven Marines and wounding another 77. Of the 77 wounded, 37 had to be evacuated.

The North Vietnamese fired their 152 mm. guns, their biggest artillery, at Khe Sanh for the first time. . . .

U.S. commanders predict a major North Vietnamese offensive along the northern frontier with the big push on Khe Sanh either just before the Lunar New Year, January 30, or just after it. With at least three North Vietnamese divisions and possibly four deployed through the frontier region, two of them in western Quang Tri province around Khe Sanh, *it could develop into the biggest conventional-style confrontation of the war.*

This last paragraph—or variations of it—sustained many a Khe Sanh story on a dull day. The story continued:

The first barrage last night came in as the mist was closing in on the Khe Sanh airstrip, indicating that the communist gunners had timed the attack to take advantage of weather that would hamper American planes from striking back.

Red artillery shells scored at least two direct hits on Marine bunkers but none hit the airfield. Early today a C-130 cargo plane *landed with a load of logs* to reinforce the bunkers. . . .[35]

U.S. headquarters . . . reported that American air strikes and artillery set off 29 secondary explosions six miles northwest of Khe Sanh, indicating they hit enemy gun positions or ammunition dumps.

A record *798* strike sorties—a sortie is one attack flight by one plane—were flown in South Vietnam yesterday, and more than *half (475)* were in support of Khe Sanh. In addition, eight-engine B-52 Stratofortress bombers struck *four* times at suspected communist positions in the area, pushing to *26* their total number of *multiplane* missions in the Khe Sanh area in the last *10* days.[36]

The Marines have reported 25 of their men killed and 164 wounded at Khe Sanh since last Saturday.[37] The Leathernecks have killed 303 North Vietnamese troops, the U.S. command says.[38]

The AP duly totaled the number of enemy rounds fired, but it took careful reading to see how apparently little damage the 300-round barrage actually inflicted—for example, hitting two bunkers (out of scores) and not hitting the airstrip. Presumably the incoming rounds hit other targets, as MACV reported, if seven Marines were killed and 77 wounded. But, as was the case throughout the siege, the inaccuracy or sporadic nature of enemy fire was rarely conveyed to the lay reader.

Colonel Lownds's afternoon sessions with newsmen usually took place by a sandbagged corner near his underground command post. The turnover of press personnel meant that the same questions were asked anew by the latest arrivals: Will the North Vietnamese attack? Will the Marines hold? Why hadn't the Marines dug in better? Would there be another Dienbienphu? Did the Colonel think morale could hold up? Lownds politely left to higher-ups the rationale for holding Khe Sanh, was vague on the fine points of Dienbienphu, and declined to be articulate about possible catastrophes. As Herr observed:

Interviews with . . . Col. David Lownds seemed to reveal a man who was utterly insensible to the gravity of his position, but Lownds was a deceptively complicated man with a gift (as one of his staff officers put it) for "jerking off the press." He could appear as a meek, low-keyed, distracted, and even stupid man (some reporters referred to him privately as "The Lion of Khe Sanh"), as though he had been carefully picked for just these qualities by a cynical command as a front for their decisions. When confronted with the possible odds against a successful defense of Khe Sanh, he would say things like, "I do not plan on reinforcements" or "I'm not worried. I've got Marines." . . .

His professional ignorance of Dienbienphu drove correspondents crazy, but it was a dodge. Lownds knew very well about Dienbienphu and what had happened there, knew more about it than most of the interviewers. . . .

He was also growing tired of reporters and of the criticism which most of the questions addressed to him implied, and I couldn't help but feel sympathy for him. There were policies and attitudes at Khe Sanh that were getting grunts killed, but I doubted that they were the Colonel's. He was really sort of a grunt himself, he had been there for a long time now, and it was beginning to tell on his face. The stories published about him never bothered to mention his personal courage or the extreme and special caution with which he risked the lives of his men.[39]

The AP ran a profile of Lownds on February 5. The New York *Times* covered him in its "Man in the News" profile on February 12. The AP portrait ran heavily to drama:

KHE SANH, Vietnam (AP)—The defender of Khe Sanh combines the caution of a banker and the zest of a hardened combat man who is sure he can win his toughest fight.

Col. David E. Lownds and his reinforced 26th Marine Regiment are surrounded by two divisions of North Vietnamese troops—more men than Hanoi has committed to one battle so far in the war.

The communists have artillery, heavy rockets, and *deadly accurate* mortars. All are *zeroed in* on the Khe Sanh base camp and take a daily toll of Marines.[40]

Neither AP nor the *Times,* however, conveyed what comes through in the official Marine history of Khe Sanh (Shore's *Khe Sanh*) or, indeed, in the Herr article: Despite considerable nervousness at higher levels, Lownds (and his staff) played a cool, complex, professional game which kept Marine losses low. They used a variety of kinds of U.S. firepower to reduce enemy fire and break up enemy ground attacks before those attacks could gain momentum. It would have taken a longer time than most newsmen spent at Khe Sanh to grasp what the game was all about. It is a measure of newsmen's interest in Lownds that, among all the photographs taken at Khe Sanh, virtually no pictures of the Colonel appeared in the press during the siege. *Life* photographer David Douglas Duncan's portfolio, however, did show Lownds at work.[41]

Throughout the siege, the Dienbienphu theme got an AP workout, especially in early February and on the eve of the March 13 anniversary of the 1954 battle. One example came on February 2, just after the anti-cities attack broke:

(*Editor's Note:* Khe Sanh, in northwest South Vietnam, has been described as the *cork in the bottle holding back the communist tide.* From Gen. William C. Westmoreland on down, the opinion is widespread that it will be a major target in Phase III of the Red plan which Westmoreland said Thursday is now unfolding Phase II. Here is how it is right now at Khe Sanh.)

KHE SANH, Vietnam (AP)—Burrowed into a thickly jungled valley astride North Vietnam's *shortest invasion route* into South Vietnam, some 5,000 Americans in the fortress of Khe Sanh are playing a desperate game they call "the big wait."[42]

The battered camp resembles a Western cow town waiting for the big shootout. Powdery red dust billows from the cratered road that passes for a main street. No man ventures out without a gun and a flak jacket. . . .

. . . .

. . . The grimly beautiful valley inevitably recalls Dienbienphu, the French fortress that fell in 1954, but Lownds discounts the similarities. When the airstrip at Dienbienphu was closed by Gen. Vo Nguyen Giap's artillery, the base was doomed. Lownds says Khe Sanh could be maintained without the airstrip, as it was last fall when monsoon rains made it useless for more than a month.

When outposts Gabrielle, Beatrice, and Hugette fell, Dienbienphu was in an impossible squeeze. The Marines' camp is already squeezed into a scarred red dustbin measuring only two square miles, defended mainly by the 26th Marine Regiment and a small force of South Vietnamese Rangers and Green Beret Special Forces. . . .[43]

The subsequent fall to North Vietnamese tanks of the Lang Vei Special Forces camp, four miles from Khe Sanh, on February 7—in Lownds's eyes actually irrelevant to Khe Sanh's defense—prompted AP's Saigon bureau to declare that the loss of the camp opened a "gateway on the Laos border" for the NVA. A Dienbienphu reference was also thrown in for good measure: *"Perhaps ominously, the capture of the outpost showed signs of the tactics of North Vietnamese Gen. Nguyen Giap, the victor over the French at Dienbienphu 14 years ago. . . . Giap . . . is believed to be directing personally the action against Khe Sanh and other frontier bases, possibly from a forward jungle headquarters."*[44]

On February 9, citing Bernard Fall, AP did a balanced comparison, citing Khe Sanh's advantages in air power and the "friendly forces within striking distance":

KHE SANH, Vietnam (AP)—Fourteen years after the decisive French defeat in Indo-China, U.S. Marines at Khe Sanh wait for battle in an outpost that looks like one synonymous with debacle in Vietnam—Dienbienphu.

The topography is similar, the same North Vietnamese general commands the communist troops that surround the stronghold, and initiative is with the enemy.

U.S. military officials say there is a major difference—the American command's ability to supply its men with firepower, materiel, and virtually unlimited air support.

The absence of these factors during the 55-day siege of Dienbienphu is considered the decisive factor that made possible the Vietminh attack which overwhelmed the garrison May 7, 1954. Two months later, France was ready to leave Vietnam.

The Marine base at Khe Sanh, just south of the Demilitarized Zone near the Laotian border, is defended by 5,000 to 6,000 men. The French sent some 15,500 to their fortress about 180 miles northwest of Hanoi.[45]

As the anniversary of Dienbienphu drew near, AP sent out a March 8 "Dienbienphu Special Report" by William L. Ryan, its special analyst, who flew to Saigon from New York after Tet. Ryan remembered his 1954 experiences and found little change:

SAIGON (AP)—By day, from a military plane, there was little to see but the dark green, mist-shrouded hills brooding over a seemingly empty land.

By night, the earth spat fire.

A ring of death surrounded the fortress. Planes no longer could land there. It had to be supplied and reinforced by air. That was Dienbienphu toward the end of the road for the French. . . .

The war was seven years old when it ended. If, as most Americans do, one dates the U.S. war in Vietnam from 1961, this one is seven years old, too. And many in Vietnam wonder: Is Gen. Vo Nguyen Giap, the military mastermind of that 1954 battle, seeking another Dienbienphu for precisely the same reasons he sought the first victory at a frightful cost in human life?[46]

As the siege waned, on March 22, AP reached for another Dienbienphu angle: the reported deployment of communist 37 mm. antiaircraft cannon at Khe Sanh—just like those that crippled the French aerial resupply effort in 1954. It helped enliven the war wrap-up: "*U.S. officers* considered the presence of the 37 mm. antiaircraft guns north and south of Khe Sanh serious. These guns knocked down French planes trying to supply Dienbienphu in the battle of 1954 that drove France out of Indo-China. About seven of these guns have been destroyed, *battlefield accounts said.* The Americans consider them a grave threat not only to supply planes but to fighter-bombers."[47]

"U.S. officers" and "battlefield accounts" were not much of a source. There was no claim in MACV or Air Force communiqués that the much-feared 37 mm. guns had been destroyed around Khe

Sanh. But pilots flying over Khe Sanh, especially transport pilots, repeatedly reported "suspected 37 mm. sites" in February and March; I noticed such "suspected sites" marked on a map at Marine helicopter operations rooms at Quang Tri and Phu Bai in early March. No G-2 confirmation was forthcoming; no aircraft were reported hit or damaged by 37 mm. flak at Khe Sanh in subsequent Air Force accounts. AP did not mention this "grave threat" to Khe Sanh again. However, it was picked up, without attribution to AP, by ABC and CBS in their March 22 evening news shows. The *Times* also used the dispatch, and it was included in the Washington *Post*'s March 23 war wrap-up.[48] It was a good story for a slow day.

UPI: A Continuing Drama

The United Press bureau in Saigon was less interested in Khe Sanh than in Hue. In our UPI files, which are incomplete, we see a total of 14 Khe Sanh datelines versus 53 for the AP. Nevertheless, Khe Sanh got much attention from UPI, especially in its Saigon war wrap-ups.

On the whole, UPI, faithful to its New York rewrite tradition, tended to exaggerate both sides of the story in highly colored prose. On the capture by the North Vietnamese of Lang Vei, it said:

SAIGON—The first communist tank attack of the war today overran a U.S. Army Special Forces camp near the North Vietnam border but *pilots* said the Green Berets were fighting on in *underground* bunkers.

U.S. spokesmen said at least nine Soviet-built T-34 tanks rumbled in from nearby Laos under cover of darkness and crashed through the Lang Vei Camp's barbed wire defenses, with *800 North Vietnamese running alongside shooting flamethrowers.*[49]

A few hours later, another UPI story prolonged the battle a bit and even had the Green Berets recapture the camp:

SAIGON—Doggedly fighting U.S. Green Beret defenders knocked out five Soviet-made tanks today and regained control of their Lang Vei Special Forces camp from flame-throwing North Vietnamese. . . .

. . . .

While the Special Forces battle raged, communist gunners launched a heavy bombardment of the main Khe Sanh base, menaced by a *giant* North Vietnamese force surrounding the *tiny* Marine fortress America has vowed to defend.[50]

Next day, UPI told its readers that Lang Vei was "critical," and, singularly prone to exploit reports of enemy armor, no matter how qualified, did so here:

SAIGON—Heavy fighting engulfed wide areas of South Vietnam's three northern provinces today. North Vietnamese troops were reported moving more *modern Russian tanks*[51] into the embattled Lang Vei-Khe Sanh area.

The U.S. command said the loss of the "Green Beret" camp at Lang Vei was "critical" for *control* of the Laotian border area and Highway Nine, a vital east-west route *linking* Lang Vei to the U.S. Marine fortress at Khe Sanh *four* miles away.[52]

The "critical" quote stemmed not from an official spokesman, but from a Saigon "backgrounder" by Gen. Creighton Abrams. Asked if the loss of Lang Vei was critical to the defense of Khe Sanh, Abrams said: "It is not critical to, I wouldn't say, to the defense of Khe Sanh —it's critical to us in the sense that we want to be able to control the borders." It seems clear that he was referring to the general function of the Special Forces camp–border surveillance. Nevertheless, like most of the other media, UPI linked Lang Vei and Khe Sanh.

On February 9, having decided that Lang Vei was "critical," UPI reported that the enemy was pouring through "the gaping hole in U.S. lines" (such "lines," of course, did not exist):

SAIGON—*Communist field commanders, taking advantage of the gaping hole in U.S. lines at Lang Vei, today poured troops, ammunition, and food across the Laotian border for the building battle of Khe Sanh. American forces at least partially plugged the flow with fearsome artillery and air attacks. . . .*

The Khe Sanh Valley in South Vietnam's extreme northwest corner resembles the nearby U.S. fortress at Con Thien just below the Demilitarized Zone where U.S. Marines crushed a month-long communist siege in early October.[53]

All signs Friday pointed to a Con Thien-type siege against Khe Sanh, and some U.S. generals feared an all-out offensive on the sprawling[54] *Marine fort in the valley* by as many as 20,000 North Vietnamese troops. More than 6,000 Marines defend Khe Sanh and its environs, and American commanders have vowed to hold it at all costs.' . . .

The U.S. command has said Khe Sanh *could be* the capstone of the big communist offensive which has *spread* the flames of war from one end of South Vietnam to the other in the past 11 days.[55]

By February 29, UPI was relying on the standby—the reporter's description of his trip into Khe Sanh—but noting, as AP and TV did not, low U.S. losses:

> KHE SANH (UPI)—Anyone who believes that "getting there is half the fun" has never made the trip to the Marine combat base at Khe Sanh. It's a rough ride that culminates in sheer terror. . . .
>
> They have shot down only one C-130 Hercules transport and have not yet managed to bring down a 123, but they score hits frequently. Two air crewmen have been wounded this week and the sound of bullets punching through the metal is a distinctive one.[56]

In its later war wrap-ups, however, UPI was even-handed in reporting enemy fire coming in, U.S. bombs going out: "The communist activities around Khe Sanh proceeded despite attacks by B-52 bombers within three miles of the base today and jet fighter-bombers and helicopter gunship attacks. The North Vietnamese kept up *sporadic* gunfire into the Khe Sanh perimeter."[57]

On March 1, UPI reported the enemy attack on the Khe Sanh sector held by ARVN, and determinedly brought in Dienbienphu. Like AP, UPI did not neglect comparisons with that 1954 battle. It was more crude about it than AP, however, especially as the Khe Sanh situation in March remained largely static:

> SAIGON (UPI)—Allied defenders with B-52s dropping bombs just ahead of them Friday repulsed the first *major ground attack* by North Vietnamese troops against the surrounded U.S. Marine base at Khe Sanh. A wave of 500 *charging* communists reached the base's barbed-wire perimeter before being driven back in fierce fighting. . . .
>
> Khe Sanh, *just south* [15 miles] *of the Demilitarized Zone border,* has become *a focal point of the war since the U.S. Joint Chiefs of Staff* guaranteed President Johnson in writing the base would not fall as did Dienbienphu to the communists in a similar strategic situation 14 years ago.[58]
>
> The North Vietnamese who launched the attack Friday were driven off by a battalion—about 350 men—of South Vietnamese Rangers. Anticipating the assault, the defenders had called in air strikes by the eight-engined B-52 Stratofortresses.[59]

On March 2, UPI again saw the North Vietnamese "closing in" on Khe Sanh: "U.S. B-52 Stratofortresses bombed within a half-mile of Khe Sanh early Sunday to help hold back thousands of North Vietnamese closing in on the Marines' fort on South Vietnam's northern frontier, military spokesmen said."[60] Nor was Dienbienphu omitted in that day's vivid night leads. According to one: "A UPI dispatch from Khe Sanh said intelligence reports had identified one of the North Vietnamese battalions in position around the Marine base there as the 304th—a veteran unit of the battle of Dienbienphu."[61] Another dispatch echoed the theme: "North Vietnamese troops are steadily tightening the ring around the U.S. Marine bastion of Khe Sanh in what appears to be a repetition of Dienbienphu."[62]

On March 11, having uncovered a "high-speed" road 35 miles to the south, UPI quickly linked it to the Khe Sanh siege:

SAIGON (UPI)—Battlefront reports Monday said communist troops armed with loudspeakers had tunneled to within 100 yards of Khe Sanh and were urging South Vietnamese infantrymen to abandon their American comrades at the fortress and surrender. . . .

The *proportions* of the battle for Khe Sanh *escalated sharply* Monday with a report from informed U.S. military sources that communist armies were putting the finishing touches on a new *high-speed* supply road into South Vietnam's northern sector from Laos.

UPI learned the road, an extension of the Ho Chi Minh Trail, enters South Vietnam through the A Shau Valley 35 miles south of Khe Sanh and winds eastward over jungle mountains to the strategic coastal plains just south of Hue.[63]

Route 547 was in fact an unpaved dirt road and, in any case, had nothing to do with Khe Sanh. Instead, its development was seen by Westmoreland as tied to an enemy buildup in the A Shau Valley, threatening Hue. But Hue was no longer in the news.

On March 12, UPI did not omit a Dienbienphu anniversary story, striking a philosophical note:

SAIGON (UPI)—Fourteen years ago this week, in a large valley in Southeast Asia, some 11,000 French Union troops waited, anxiously but confidently.

For weeks they had been waiting in their bunkers and foxholes, in the same way as some 5,000 U.S. Marines now wait in a battered brown valley outpost a few hundred miles to the south. . . .

Those who do not understand history, it is said, may be condemned to repeat it.

But not wanting to repeat it, the American military command has compared Khe Sanh and Dienbienphu and, citing several significant differences, has declared Khe Sanh to be eminently defendable.

No one comparing the situation at Khe Sanh and that at Dienbienphu 14 years ago, however, can fail to note certain important similarities.[64]

In another story that day, reporting U.S. B-52 bombings, the theme was repeated:

SAIGON (UPI)—U.S. Air Force B-52 Stratofortresses today pounded North Vietnamese ringing the Marine fort of Khe Sanh on the northern border of South Vietnam. Military sources said the jets dropped a new type delayed-action bomb capable of smashing communist attack tunnels.

U.S. spokesmen said the Strategic Air Command bombers struck six times in the past 24 hours. The sources said each wave used the bombs fitted with fuses to explode after landing and destroy tunnels more than 20 feet below ground.

In Khe Sanh, intelligence sources said Gen. Vo Nguyen Giap, North Vietnam's defense minister and mastermind of the landmark French defeat at Dienbienphu 14 years ago, is in next-door Laos directing the assault on the Marine bastion.

Giap launched his battle against Dienbienphu on March 13, 1954, and Khe Sanh's Leathernecks were braced for the possibility the long-anticipated attack against them would begin Wednesday because the communists have a tradition of kicking off campaigns on anniversary dates.[65]

Next day, UPI reported the bombing of the A Shau Valley "high-speed" road, persisting in the tie to Khe Sanh:

SAIGON (UPI)—B-52 Stratofortresses dumped tons of blockbusters Wednesday on a newly discovered jungle road across South Vietnam being used by North Vietnamese commanders to pour troops and guns toward Khe Sanh and other American outposts. . . .

Reports [sic] from the Khe Sanh front described the 16,000-man North Vietnamese army surrounding the fortress as in an "eerie silence" Wednesday. It was the 14th anniversary of the beginning of the epic siege of Dienbienphu.[66]

On March 18, UPI wrote:

SAIGON (UPI)—Dienbienphu tactics failed the communists today at Khe Sanh. Overwhelming U.S. artillery and fire by South Vietnamese Rangers smashed the third North Vietnamese attempt to break into the surrounded northern border fort even before the 400 attackers reached the barbed-wire defenses.

Using the strategy that helped bring them victory against the French 14 years ago, a North Vietnamese battalion surged out of zigzag trenches and dashed for the fort American generals have vowed never will fall.

The communists had unleashed their heaviest barrage in a month Sunday to prepare the attack. The Leathernecks in the Khe Sanh area said the shells, rockets, and mortars fell on them at a rate of one every three minutes—more than 500 throughout the day.[67]

As we have seen, "Dienbienphu tactics" could mean anything. According to Fall, they meant overwhelming infantry masses sent against a single point, not, as here, a 400-man probe against a 6,000-man garrison. According to the 26th Marines' journal, probes against the ARVN sector were recorded on March 4, 13, 15, and 18.

On March 20, UPI reported NVA troop withdrawals—perhaps the most significant wire-service scoop of the Tet period:

> SAIGON—U.S. military and intelligence sources said today the communist siege of Khe Sanh has failed. They attributed this to "fantastically high" communist casualties and to an end of monsoon rains that hampered U.S. air power. . . .
> U.S. Air Force Capt. Charles Rushworth . . . a forward air observer [over Khe Sanh] . . . said there were indications up to two regiments (2,400 men) of North Vietnamese had moved away from Khe Sanh. Other pilots agreed. . . .
>
> . . . .
>
> [UPI correspondent Richard V. Oliver] said military experts at Phu Bai believed the communists might continue to harass Khe Sanh with shelling and occasional probes, but most of the experts said they believed their ability to overrun the entrenched base camp in the northwestern corner of South Vietnam was lost with the shift of the wind and the change of the monsoon weather.[68]

The story was somewhat confused in later versions, with a "top U.S. intelligence officer" being quoted by UPI as saying the enemy forces were moving *east* from Khe Sanh toward Quang Tri city on the coast, not west toward Laos.[69] But, in fact, the 26th Marine Regiment's S-2 officer at Khe Sanh "began noting an exodus of major NVA units," notably two regiments of the 325C Division, in mid-March toward Laos.[70] Later, Defense Secretary Clark Clifford was to say that the enemy pullback began March 12.[71]

However, on March 20, UPI's report was greeted by newsmen with suspicion. The Washington *Post* foreign desk cabled its Saigon bureau on March 22: "UPI REPORTING WITHDRAWAL OF TWO COMMUNIST REGIMENTS FROM AROUND KHE SANH ON BASIS UNNAMED MILITARY SOURCES AND WHILE MUTED APPRECIATE FURTHER READING SOONEST, AS THIS NOT FIRST RED WITHDRAWAL REPORT."

Saigon's answer is missing. But this reporter recalls being highly skeptical and inclined to await the outcome of the pending effort to relieve Khe Sanh. The *Post* did not run the UPI story. Neither did the New York *Times*. AP in Saigon pressed Brig. Gen. Winant Sidle for some word; he denied the UPI story on March 21. There was no indication, he said, that the threat to Khe Sanh had increased or decreased of late. AP knocked down UPI, albeit without an outright denial of a withdrawal:

> Brig. Gen. Winant Sidle, the U.S. command's information chief, says the threat to Khe Sanh has neither lessened nor increased and "there has been no significant movement of North Vietnamese troops either way—pulling out or reinforcing." . . .
>
> There were some reports of movement of units away from Khe Sanh, but a high U.S. source earlier warned that, with Hanoi's mobile tactics, whole regiments could be moved 17 miles a day over secret trails.
>
> Most of what is known about enemy movements in the mountains in the Khe Sanh Valley area comes from jet reconnaissance planes with highly sophisticated sensing gear. An Air Force officer said, "There is constant movement in the Khe Sanh area but we can't associate it with any withdrawal."
>
> It may be that combat troops are replacing engineers charged with preparing the battlefield with trenches, bunkers, and tunnels. Another guess is that the lessened pressure is designed to draw the Marine garrison out from behind its barbed wire and mines on offensive sweeps in territory where ambush would be easy.[72]

Sidle afterward told this writer that MACV G-2 were waiting for some prisoners to confirm the Marine reports before accepting them as well-founded. Some ever-suspicious newsmen in Saigon, also, argued much later that MACV on March 21 did not want to make it seem that the impending Operation Pegasus—then being planned—would be anticlimactic.[73] Pegasus, as noted, met light resistance, against newsmen's expectations.

On March 26, UPI continued to suggest a possible easing-up at Khe Sanh, reporting a fresh appraisal by Lieutenant General Cushman. Cushman noted renewed Marine patrol activity and light casualties, points not picked up by others, notably the *Post* and *Times:*

> Cushman said fighting in his area during the past few weeks has been light, particularly around Khe Sanh. . . .
>
> "Khe Sanh certainly is the more nerve-wracking and we can't fight out against it," he said. "And, therefore, it makes a different situation psychologically."
>
> The communist shelling of Khe Sanh tapered off Monday with only 50 incoming rocket, mortar, and artillery rounds that inflicted light damage and casualties.

Leathernecks at the base have begun patrolling outside the perimeter for the first time since the communist encirclement was completed late in January.[74]

Then, on March 30, the UPI gave an account of the successful, highly coordinated Marine company raid on an enemy ridge south of Khe Sanh, making it sound like a random patrol action. It was, in fact, the first Marine infantry attack on the besiegers, another sign that the siege was easing, not a "resurgence of heavy combat":

SAIGON (UPI)—An outnumbered U.S. Marine *patrol* pushing into jungles around Khe Sanh ran into a North Vietnamese battalion Saturday and fought a bitter hours-long battle only 1,000 yards from the fortress. The Marines reported killing 40 enemy before pulling back with "moderate" losses.

The fighting marked a resurgence of heavy combat around Khe Sanh and came at a time when communist shelling of the base had been dropping off to the point where only 50 rounds fell Friday and *some U.S. intelligence officers said the big threat to the base was over.*

UPI correspondent Raymond Wilkinson, reporting from Khe Sanh, said the North Vietnamese battalion of perhaps 400 men fought from deep bunkers and trenches as the *smaller Marine patrol* pushed through tall elephant grass. . . .

Wilkinson said the Marines held out as long as they could, then pulled back to fortifications within the main Khe Sanh perimeter with the North Vietnamese on their heels.[75]

The Networks: Speculation and Projection

As a group, network television correspondents were perhaps the least informed about Khe Sanh and the quickest to jump to conclusions. They spent the briefest time on the ground at the base, and they were tied to their cameras and the search for "marketable" film.

Rarely, for example, did TV correspondents—in contrast to the newspapermen and to AP's John Wheeler—report that the positions under heaviest pressure were not at Khe Sanh Combat Base itself, but on three of its five hill outposts to the west. As long as these outposts remained in friendly hands, the garrison on the Khe Sanh plateau was shielded from direct fire and from an assault along the enemy's easiest avenue of approach—from the west and northwest. Two outposts were attacked early in the siege, and it was here that life was most grueling, and that most of the helicopters lost were shot down, medical evacuation was most difficult, and the supply lines were tenuous.

Usually, television crews could not film the outposts, and instead concentrated on the "threat" and the Dienbienphu image. Even before Tet, in accordance with TV news tradition, they projected the specter of Dienbienphu and emphasized heavy losses:

Ron Nessen (film clip, Khe Sanh Marine Base): The commander of the 26th Regiment . . . is Col. David Lownds. . . . Over the background noise of artillery and jet planes attacking the North Vietnamese surrounding his position, Colonel Lownds talked to newsmen.

Lownds: Trying to compare it with *Dienbienphu?* Oh, I think there's lots of things. You just heard some of them. As I read it, and I'm not a student of Dienbienphu at all, air power plays an important part, also artillery plays an important part.

I have considerable artillery and I have considerable air at my disposal.

Nessen: Colonel Lownds's troops use simpler language and expressed more personal feelings about the fighting and dying they must do, but seemingly, to a man, they shared their commander's confidence that they will win the battle. . . .

Every day, more dead and wounded Marines were flown out of Khe Sanh. If North Vietnam hurls its thousands of troops against Khe Sanh, as expected, a terrible battle will be joined, and *there will be more such cargoes.*

The Marines think they will win, another Iwo Jima or Pork Chop Hill. *The North Vietnamese think they will win,* another Dienbienphu. Whatever result is written into history, it will be written in blood.[76]

Lieutenant General Cushman focused less exclusively on Khe Sanh than did his questioners. He had the entire DMZ and I Corps to worry about.[77] Here he was interviewed by Robert Schakne:

Schakne: . . . There's been talk about the impending action; if indeed it does come at Khe Sanh, it's possibly the biggest conventional war battle that has been fought in Vietnam. Is it building up to that degree, as far as you can see now, as the biggest land battle?

Cushman: Oh, I don't know. There were almost as many forces around Con Thien last September—hard to tell. This, of course, lies with the enemy's intentions, and I would be a fool to try to guess what he's thinking. Rather, I address myself to what he's capable of.

Schakne: And what is he capable of?

Cushman: He's capable of an attack against Khe Sanh in considerable strength, along with attacks at several other places in considerable strength—places of even more significance. Consequently, my forces are disposed with that in mind.[78]

Even after Tet began, nothing—following the first few days of fighting in Saigon and Hue—so captured the imagination of network TV producers and picture editors in New York, and particularly of the management at CBS, as did the siege of Khe Sanh. According to CBS correspondents in Vietnam, New York ordered them, by turn, to staff Khe Sanh. Overruled were protests from the hard-pressed Saigon bureau, headed by Daniel Bloom, that Khe Sanh was too "static" a story to justify a fixed commitment of scarce staff manpower and that, journalistically, it did not justify the constant risky travel in and out of the airstrip by CBS correspondents.[79]

The network's New York office, however, did not grasp the realities of "staffing" Khe Sanh. CBS's Murray Fromson, for example, arrived at the base on one occasion after a day's delay in getting a ride. Loaded down with three 400-foot rolls of TV film and other gear, as well as his own field pack, he stumbled and fell as he hopped off the moving plane on the airstrip, injuring his knee. He stayed for three days, longer than most visitors, before taking a helicopter to Dong Ha, the 3rd Marine Division headquarters. There, he had to wait for another day to get to the U.S. headquarters and airfield at Phu Bai, south of Hue. At Phu Bai, he found another plane to Da Nang, from where, finally, the film—containing three stories—could be shipped to Saigon.

Like all newsmen at Khe Sanh, Fromson was completely out of touch with Da Nang, Saigon, and the home office. Moreover, he had to bring out his film himself. "You couldn't just give it to some pilot, or another reporter," he noted. When he got back to Saigon for a breather, he recalled later, Bloom informed him that New York "wondered why you came out of Khe Sanh?"

Only after the wounding at Khe Sanh of Russell Bensley, a co-producer of the Cronkite show (an incident that was duly filmed and presented March 4), did CBS allow its Saigon bureau to staff Khe Sanh on a voluntary basis. All told, Khe Sanh accounted for almost half (20 of 46) of the CBS film reports appearing from Vietnam on weekday evening television shows during the Tet period.[80]

It was a difficult and unsatisfactory story for all the media, but even more so for television. As Ron Nessen of NBC recalled later, "You got off the plane, ran to cover, and tried to get some sort of a story together, and then got out." Of all the film reports from Khe Sanh, only three were filmed outside the "downtown" and adjacent perimeter area close to the airstrip, and only one was filmed on any of the hill outposts. In terms of breadth of coverage of Khe Sanh itself, TV could not match David Douglas Duncan of *Life*. An ex-Marine, and a still photographer, Duncan, not subject to the same technical pressures as the AP photographers and the networks, managed, over a six-day period, to put together a comprehensive portfolio of the Khe Sanh experience.[81]

Television, as its own correspondents noted, was too limited. Within its narrow focus, the cameras, for the most part, pointed at the visual clichés—the wrecked planes, the wounded, Marines scrambling on and off aircraft under mortar fire, close-in jet strikes on the hills to the north, and an occasional "Are you scared?" interview with the troops, or an "Are they going to attack?" session with Colonel Lownds. One looks at the pictures by Duncan and remembers Khe Sanh. One views most of the film footage, especially those nervous standups, and remembers one's own fears, those of a civilian suddenly thrust into an isolated, unfamiliar battleground amid strangers and unpredictable dangers. The Khe Sanh garrison comes through on TV film as an assemblage of apprehensive, unorganized, even hapless, individuals—like the exhausted reporters—not as a group of trained Marines, organized into fighting units, with friends, local knowledge, training, and a special esprit de corps to sustain them through the fearsome, unpleasant business of digging in, shooting, and waiting under enemy artillery, rocket, and mortar bombardments that ranged from sporadic to heavy. Unconveyed on TV was the crazy gallows humor, considerable professionalism, and camaraderie of the Marines.

In composing their explanatory "voice-overs," sometimes scribbled out and taped without knowing exactly what the cameraman had filmed, or in their standups, the TV reporters, by and large, were caught in a dilemma. Their reports had to be on-scene ones. Unlike the newspapermen, they could not go back to Da Nang, think, compose, fill in some of the gaps. There was no coherent "action" or sequence to describe at Khe Sanh, only disconnected events: the air strike, the incoming mortar burst, the evacuation of the wounded. Ducking shells, TV newsmen saw thin Marine defenses but rarely the handicaps of the enemy or his risks. For them, there was no difference between the impact of 300 rounds of incoming fire and

1,500 rounds. They were "stuck"—with a hazardous scene, and an important story that *hadn't happened yet*—and under severe time pressure, they had to "project."

Some did so with a vengeance.

One of the special sub-themes in the TV coverage, for example, was that Khe Sanh was totally at the mercy of the North Vietnamese. The first evening film report from Khe Sanh after Tet began came from Don North of ABC.[82] He pointed out the enemy's vulnerability —in assault—to B-52 strikes (a vulnerability demonstrated during the abortive NVA attack against the main perimeter February 29–March 1). Then he noted the weather problem for the B-52s and, ignoring U.S. artillery and all-weather radar bombing, indulged in speculation:

> There is open ground between Khe Sanh and the surrounding mountains where the North Vietnamese are now dug in. U.S. air strikes could take a heavy toll of enemy troops crossing that open ground; the North Vietnamese would like to see air bases throughout Vietnam crippled by rocket attack when they make that dash across the open ground.[83]
>
> A second factor they hope for is bad weather, [but] so far the northeast monsoon around Khe Sanh has been amazingly light. In the clear skies U.S. planes bomb at will. There's no road into Khe Sanh; all ammunition, including supplies, are brought in by air and they're at the mercy of the weather.
>
> The next time bad weather closes in on Khe Sanh, it may trigger an all-out assault in every city and hamlet of this country with Khe Sanh at the center of the storm.[84]

Murray Fromson of CBS, after discussing the importance of the hill outposts, asked Colonel Lownds if the enemy was really trying to take Khe Sanh; Lownds said yes. Then Fromson addressed the TV camera:

> The mountains that surround the Marines look foreboding. The weather slows down their own resupply efforts and prevents fighter-bombers from hitting mortar and artillery positions. One staff officer put the situation this way: They're getting ready to smack us hard. If the airfield is knocked out and the weather stays bad, we're in bad trouble. This is one place where the Americans cannot claim they have the initiative in Vietnam. *Here, the North Vietnamese decide who lives and who dies. Every day, which planes land and which ones don't,* and sooner or later *they will make the move that will seal the fate* of Khe Sanh.[85]

In another report broadcast by CBS on February 15, Peter

Kalischer called Khe Sanh a "trap"; worrying about the defensibility of the place, he talked to Marines building bunkers:

Kalischer: . . . The Marines are long on courage and short on dug-in positions. How much of the day's work is this sandbag stuff?
Marine: Just about a full day—a long, long time.
Kalischer: How come you fellows haven't got a thicker cover of this stuff? You got about two layers here.
Marine: Oh, we got about, I think about the fourth or fifth layer we got right now, besides the fuel mat which is made out of steel.
2nd Marine: No, this is the sixth layer.
Marine: Sixth layer, excuse me.
Kalischer: What will that keep out?
Marine: Right now it should stop a small mortar.
Kalischer: What about a big one?
Marine: I hope so. I'm not sure though.
Kalischer: American military commanders say that *Khe Sanh is no Dienbienphu,* but for the Marines here it's *just as badly situated.* The enemy looks down their throat 360 degrees; while they'll tell you that Khe Sanh is no battlefield of their choosing, they're anxious for the North Vietnamese to launch their all-out attack. Khe Sanh is a trap, but for 5,000 Marines, or for three North Vietnamese divisions? On that answer many lives, many military reputations, and perhaps the outcome of this war depend.[86]

Don North of ABC filmed the airplane wrecks along the Khe Sanh runway, failing to mention that air losses had been minimal. However, he noted heavy U.S. firepower:

. . . Waiting tensely beside the strip are Marines who have served their time at Khe Sanh. They are veterans of this war at the age of 18, and have seen thousands of the enemy's incoming rounds at Khe Sanh. Their main aim in life here was to become 19—a final dash across the runway into the empty cargo planes for a flight back to the world. *Along the runway are the skeletons of cargo planes* that didn't make it out of Khe Sanh.
The expected enemy assault against Khe Sanh is yet to come. Meanwhile the battle of Khe Sanh is *largely a logistics battle* with both sides trying to cut each other's supply arteries[87] and at the same time building up their own supplies. Meanwhile the Marines continue to dig in and wait for the major enemy attack at Khe Sanh. So far only *brief skirmishes*[88] have taken place. Heavy U.S. air and artillery bombardment of the enemy positions *may be keeping* the North Vietnamese off balance.[89]

ABC put on David Douglas Duncan, who discussed the airlift into Khe Sanh: "When enemy fire comes in, the guys run for it. When planes come in, they try to shoot a landing so fast the enemy gunners can't knock them down with either rockets or machine-gun fire. The big C-130s, *sometimes they make it, sometimes they don't.* Here one has just been hit by incoming rockets." Actually, only one C-130 was knocked down, but it made a good picture.[90]

On February 29, Walter Cronkite, just back from Vietnam (having visited Hue, but not Khe Sanh), introduced a film report by Jack Laurence. Cronkite commented:

Cronkite: Khe Sanh seems to be a microcosm of the whole war.[91] There is just not very much that is rational about it. It isn't even of any major strategic value at the moment, as Jack Laurence points out.

Laurence: *Khe Sanh waits.* It has been waiting for an anticipated attack for months. Digging in, building up, reinforcing for *what will undoubtedly be the most significant battle of the war.* The question is "Will the attack come?" and if so, "Can Khe Sanh hold?"

. . . .

. . . Reconnaissance patrols have stopped. And Khe Sanh is no longer an effective *roadblock against the enemy.*[92]

From the North Vietnamese point of view, Khe Sanh is an easy target for its mortars and rockets. *A convenient place to bleed the Marines.* And what may be most crucial, *tie down and isolate 6,000 American troops,* and *about 20,000 reserves far from the protective coastal plain.* For twenty years, *General Giap has used the same tactics.*[93]

Cronkite concluded:

Three weeks ago, President Johnson demanded and received from the Joint Chiefs of Staff the assurance that Khe Sanh could be held. In Vietnam, no one to whom this reporter talked, including the highest officials, were so certain. All without exception hedged on such an assurance.[94] And among lower echelons there was great and admirable certitude, but one sensed little conviction.[95] Since its usefulness as a *roadblock* and a forward base has been so vastly diminished, it can be assumed that Khe Sanh *now is mostly a symbol.* But of what? Pride, morale, bravery, or Administration intransigence and military miscalculation?[96]

CBS's Don Webster on March 1 managed to report an infiltrating North Vietnamese soldier without claiming he was the advance guard of a horde:

This is the first line of defense at Khe Sanh. Seven strands of barbed wire forming the outer perimeter. But now the North Vietnamese have gotten so bold that one soldier has actually penetrated all seven strands and the mine fields and actually entered the Marine base at Khe Sanh. He didn't get very far—gunned down just a few feet inside the perimeter, but it is the first time a North Vietnamese actually entered the base. Besides the 5,000 or so U.S. Marines at Khe Sanh there are about 300 South Vietnamese troops guarding the perimeter at one end of the runway. It was here the North Vietnamese launched their attack.[97]

On March 6, another CBS report from Khe Sanh showed the by then-familiar aircraft wreckage at the base, but again without mentioning total announced losses. Webster narrated:

Getting in and out of Khe Sanh is even more dangerous than just being there, and the metal airstrip at Khe Sanh shows why. The runway is *now littered with the wreckage of airplanes and helicopters.* Some were hit on take-off, others on landing, some while standing on the airstrip, and others while flying over. The North Vietnamese on the surrounding hills now have the airstrip well zeroed in with their mortars.

When a plane does land, much of the activity stops while everyone watches to see if the plane makes it. This is all *that's left of a C-130* that landed loaded with gasoline.[98] It burned and exploded when hit by enemy fire. Some inside escaped; others did not.

This is the residue of a *CH-53 helicopter,* the biggest the Marines have. About the time this was being filmed, another helicopter was being shot down just a few miles from Khe Sanh, killing all 22 Americans on board.[99]

On March 14, in another vivid report on the flight into the base, CBS's George Syvertsen referred to the "graveyard of twisted wrecks" along Khe Sanh's runway and filmed one of three C-123 transports hit by enemy fire:

. . . A well-placed round sets the left wing tank afire and this tired old aerial workhorse casts a pall of smoke and gloom over the defenders of Khe Sanh as it dies. But the workaday business of supplying Khe Sanh goes on even while it burns. . . .

Two C-123s in one day is a pretty good bag for the communist gunners and from now on it's going to take even more courage for an Air Force pilot to fly into Khe Sanh.[100]

ABC's anchorman in New York came up with this exclusive on March 15 (as enemy forces were beginning to withdraw): "U.S. Marines at Khe Sanh report the communists have dug trenches at the end of the only landing strip, *putting 1,000 yards of the field out of use.* It is also a growing feeling that the enemy may have also tunneled under the airstrip to plant mines."[101]

The same UPI report was picked up by NBC's Chet Huntley the same day, with a bit of high-level strategy and finance thrown in by David Burrington:

> Huntley: . . . The Marine base at Khe Sanh was shelled again today, and reports from there say that the North Vietnamese have dug trenches so close to the base airstrip that it is practically unusable in that portion.
>
> Burrington: One high commander admits privately now that the Khe Sanh outpost, isolated in its mountain valley, has *no purpose, no mission, no goal,* except to stay alive.
>
> A few months ago, Khe Sanh was a key base for surveillance of nearby infiltration routes, but as the North Vietnamese move closer to the camp, and their trenches are now up to the wires, the reconnaissance patrols were eliminated. Now, if the patrols went out only a few hundred yards, they wouldn't come back. So, all effort here is now geared simply to survival.
>
> The cost of survival gets higher as the enemy moves closer. Air strikes, some only a few yards from the base perimeter, cost millions of dollars a day.[102]

CBS brightened a bit on March 18, but still gave the enemy credit for "devastating accuracy." Said Jeff Gralnick:

> It is nine weeks now that the Marines have been encircled at Khe Sanh, and by now a routine of existence has developed at the combat base. The Marines [are] going about the business of keeping Khe Sanh despite the North Vietnamese in the surrounding hills, and despite some 300 incoming mortar and rocket rounds that pepper the base daily.
>
> Supply for the Marines and replacements comes in now almost solely by helicopter. They sneak in under the North Vietnamese guns, touch down, and get off as quickly as possible, before gun crews, staring down at the base, observing it from the surrounding hills, can line up their guns and fire, as they have with devastating accuracy at the big cargo planes that once landed here regularly and now cannot.[103]

ABC also sounded more hopeful on March 19. Bob Young began:

> America's B-52s flew five saturation raids around the Marine outpost at Khe Sanh, one of the heaviest bombing strikes of the war in that area. A virtual air armada continues to provide Khe Sanh with its only link with the outside world. ABC's Don Baker reports now on one type of American sky plane and its mission at Khe Sanh:

Baker: The garrison at Khe Sanh is heavily dependent on American air superiority. . . .
The weather's improving around Khe Sanh, and there's been no letup in the supply flights. There's more optimism now about this beleaguered garrison. It just could be that all that air power will win the battle of Khe Sanh.[104]

Shortly afterward, however, CBS renewed the Dienbienphu theme, after receiving an AP report on 37 mm. antiaircraft guns around Khe Sanh. Harry Reasoner gave a quick military analysis in New York:

One of the wire services [UPI] quoted some U.S. intelligence sources this week as saying that the communist siege of Khe Sanh had failed, primarily because the enemy has lost too many troops from American air strikes. That report subsequently was knocked down by an American general [Sidle].
And today it was disclosed that Khe Sanh may be in *greater danger than ever.* The reason is that the North Vietnamese, for the first time, have moved a highly mobile antiaircraft gun, the 37 mm., *into positions* encircling Khe Sanh. . . .
Comparisons can be carried too far, but it was noted that the communists used the same guns to knock down French planes trying to supply the men of Dienbienphu.[105]

On March 28, CBS again projected fear, even as the foe was pulling back and forces were gearing up for Operation Pegasus, as all newsmen knew. Building on a perfectly ordinary interview with a Marine captain on a front-line duel with enemy gunners, Jeff Gralnick generalized: "The North Vietnamese [are] out there only 200 yards or less away. They are in those bomb craters and trenches, behind those piles of dirt, what appears to be a machine-gun barrel, poking out of one hole. From out there, the communists *shoot at and hit almost every helicopter and cargo plane that flies into or over Khe Sanh.*"[106]

Next day Gralnick again reported from Khe Sanh, against a background of ruins. He conducted a traditional TV "Are you scared?" sequence:

Gralnick: Khe Sanh, into its third month of siege now, fogged in this morning as it is one day in three. It has been since January 21 a target range for the North Vietnamese in the surrounding hills. They have flattened virtually every building, blown away every tent, with a constant rain of rockets and mortars, some days a hundred or less, other days as many as 600 or a thousand. No rhyme or reason, apparently *just a reminder* that they are out there.

The two square miles of this combat base are a shambles now of ruined rolling stock, *smashed cargo planes and helicopters.*[107]

For the most part, living at Khe Sanh has moved underground, into bunkers 10 feet and more down, a kind of security where life goes on. This, the *Seabees' bunker,* probably the best at Khe Sanh, an indication of how well Seabees build anything.

. . . .

Gralnick [addressing Marines]: *Do you ever worry that you won't get out of here?*

Halvorson: I've thought about it. I just try not to let it bother me too much, and I can live with it then, I guess.

Gralnick: Do you ever worry you won't get out of here?

Preston: Oh sure. Hell, yes. That's something that's on your mind all the time. It does make you a bit shaky, especially if you get close rounds. The guys on the equipment have it real bad, because they can't hear 'em coming in at all. The noise of the machinery drowns out the whine and the noise coming in.

Gralnick: *Do you figure you're doing any good here?*

Preston: Well . . . I'm a builder and we're not going to build anything, because Charlie's just going to blow it away. We build bunkers occasionally. The main mission here is the airstrip, keeping it open, which is the equipment operators' and steel workers' job mainly. Everybody helps when it's real bad, though, as a rule. . . .

. . . .

Gralnick: All the bunkers, though, are not as plush as the Seabees'. This one, pieced together out of logs, metal runway sections, and dirt-filled ammunition boxes. A direct hit probably would kill every man in here. What do you think of the place?

3rd Marine: Hell of a place to be; I ain't kidding.

Gralnick: Is the *incoming* the worst, or is the *waiting* the worst?

3rd Marine: I couldn't say really. I hate both of them.

Gralnick: *So there really is no end in sight.* The North Vietnamese in the hills out there beyond the fog show no inclination to pull back or attack. U.S. commanders show no inclination just yet to drive them back. So for the Marines and the Seabees and the rest here, there is nothing to do but sit and take it, just to wait, and hope they'll rotate out, leave before they join the roster of wounded and dead here.[108]

It was a fitting television ending to the siege with "no end in sight." Next day, in fact, the Marines began pushing out into the surrounding ground, as the ARVN had done before them. On April 1, Operation Pegasus began—against light opposition.

On the relatively few occasions when the TV newsmen did not try to foretell the future, they produced some fairly sensible journalism, depicting, for example, the day-to-day life of the Marines and the ARVN 37th Ranger Battalion, which bore the brunt of enemy ground pressure in March.

Tom Streithorst of NBC, for example, visited beat-up Hill 861, explaining, on March 25, the outpost's importance, while the accompanying film showed the Marines under much greater pressure than they were experiencing at the main base. One saw air strikes and helicopters coming in. The helmeted U.S. Marine commander, a captain, pointed out how close the enemy was, commenting, "They're pretty good." Streithorst added that the Marines complained that one-third of the napalm cannisters dropped by U.S. planes failed to detonate.

On March 26, Don Webster noted that: "Every time Khe Sanh takes a lot of incoming rounds, it gets a lot of publicity. What sometimes is overlooked is that it's not a one-way street; the Marines at Khe Sanh are putting out a lot of fire, too." Then he went on to call attention, belatedly, to the fact that the ARVN was at the base, too: "Not far away, there's another casualty, this time a South Vietnamese Ranger there, guarding one of the four sides of the Khe Sanh perimeter. The communists know this, and both of their recent assaults on the base have been on the South Vietnamese side of the perimeter."[109]

ABC's anchorman, Bob Young, also put in a plug for the ARVN Rangers, on March 8, and NBC's Chet Huntley the same day noted that the ARVN had "decisively repulsed" an NVA probe against the eastern edge of the perimeter.

Only one film report dealing specifically with the 37th ARVN Ranger Battalion at the Khe Sanh siege was shown on an evening news show. It was by CBS's George Syvertsen, on March 9, who also noted—in a rare TV comment—the high morale of all hands:[110]

The Rangers have among the most hard-pressed sectors of the Khe Sanh perimeter. They've sustained more ground attacks and probes than any other unit here. The enemy is close during the day, even closer by night.

By night the enemy digs. His trenches, like this one, the line of reddish-brown earth, have now reached the first strands of the perimeter wire. It's a source of pride to the Rangers that they hold the most exposed positions and that the American Marines are behind theirs. Also, once darkness falls, the Rangers are not permitted to enter the Marine perimeter, even if they're being overrun.

Capt. Walter Gunn of Greenbriar, Tennessee, the Rangers' advisor, says that's the way the Vietnamese want it.

Gunn: They will stay in the hole and fight to the last man if it has to be, and I've gone around here and listened to some of the troopers talk, and they accepted it.

Syvertsen: But despite their isolation, the Vietnamese troopers know they have powerful support, as these air strikes only a couple of hundred yards away from their perimeter demonstrate.

One of the most remarkable things about Khe Sanh is the fighting spirit of the troops. They're just itching for the enemy to make his move, the sooner the better. And nobody here seems as eager for the fight to begin as the Vietnamese Rangers.[111]

Syvertsen, as he remarked later to this writer at Da Nang, had been surprised, in the light of his own apprehensions, to find that the Marines and ARVN saw things differently than newsmen did. In this broadcast, he may have overcompensated. Infantrymen seldom "itch" for a fight; at most, they may simply want to "get it over with."

A subject that aroused considerable network attention was Lyndon Johnson's famed query to the Joint Chiefs of Staff about the feasibility of holding Khe Sanh.[112] Reporting Gen. Earle Wheeler's remarks on the matter on February 5, ABC gave the General's explanation of why he thought Khe Sanh could be defended:

Wheeler: If lost, [Khe Sanh] would permit North Vietnamese troops to advance deep into South Vietnamese territory, come very close to the heavily populated coastal regions, and thereby exacerbate the fears of the South Vietnamese that the North Vietnamese will be able to take over the two northern provinces of South Vietnam, a long-time objective of theirs.

Now, as to why I think it can be defended. In the first place, we have a sizable garrison there. General Westmoreland has ample fire support in the form of artillery, air support, both B-52 and tactical aircraft, and he has mobile reserves which can be helicopter-lifted or fixed-wing-lifted into the area at need.

I believe that all military preparations have been taken to foresee what the enemy may do and to frustrate his attack on the area.

Reporter: There will be no Dienbienphu, then?

Wheeler: We do not plan to sustain a Dienbienphu.[113]

ABC's commentator, Joseph Harsch, its house dove (to offset hawk Howard K. Smith), followed Wheeler's remarks with another long-range "diversion theory" analysis of the tactical situation:

An uncomfortable suspicion has been spreading around this town today that the American command in Vietnam has already had its Dienbienphu, but in reverse.

Our side has been preparing at Khe Sanh for an enemy attempt to turn it into another Dienbienphu. The Marines have repeatedly been reinforced there. The President has been anxious; he called in his Joint Chiefs of Staff, made them sign a paper that Khe Sanh can and should be defended.

General Wheeler has just given us the reason why it should, but if it fell, the North Vietnamese could go deep into South Vietnamese territory. But they're already deep into South Vietnamese territory. The Marines at Khe Sanh have not prevented General Giap's battalions from going where they please. Our generals have assumed that the attacks in the South were diversions to pave the way for a massive attack on Khe Sanh. That is what happened in the case of Dienbienphu, but latest battle reports show ample North Vietnamese activity, ranging from the DMZ to the Delta, but only minor jabs at Khe Sanh, perhaps just enough to keep our troops concentrated where they can have the least influence on the outcome of the campaign.

Perhaps our generals are prepared for the wrong battle.[114]

Next day, NBC's Chet Huntley was less pessimistic on radio, if not on the evening TV news. He cited air power as the crucial difference between Khe Sanh and Dienbienphu:

When the French were engaged in their climactic battle, from the 20th of November, 1953, to the 8th of May, 1954, they flew a total of 10,400 air missions on behalf of their beleaguered forces. Today our Air Forces have the capability of flying more than that in a single week. . . .

If the North Vietnamese do intend to strike at Khe Sanh, the attacks must come soon. The monsoon season is in its last days. When the monsoons end, American air power will increase in effectiveness. . . .

. . . captured enemy documents also reveal a strong suggestion that the enemy is not capable of organizing operations on this scale with frequency. There is even a hint that Khe Sanh could be their Dienbienphu.[115]

Deeply depressed was Marvin Kalb, CBS's State Department reporter, who had been talking to equally depressed State officials in Washington:

The events surrounding Khe Sanh, the isolated American fortress near the DMZ, are, if not the same, then very similar to the events surrounding Dienbienphu.

There is a haunting quality about Dienbienphu, a historical ghost, casting a long shadow across Washington at this time. There are few officials who like to discuss it. How could they? It raises doubts, naturally, about the course of American involvement in Vietnam, as though any foreign Occidental power must of necessity get trapped in the same complexities of the Vietnam jungle and end as the French did, in a kind of Dienbienphu, having made the same mistakes, the same miscalculations, the same bad judgment.

This is a deeply depressing thought, but it is one which pops up with terrible frequency these days.[116]

On the same day, Walter Cronkite in New York told a CBS radio audience that "the words of professional optimists are being brushed aside," "the name Dienbienphu is heard," and "the parallels [with Khe Sanh] are there for all to see."[117]

The Dienbienphu theme diminished a bit over the next few days, but Jack Laurence of CBS, in a radio clip from Saigon, revived it—although rather left-handedly—noting that, to the Marines at Khe Sanh, the Con Thien battle the previous autumn seemed more analogous than did Dienbienphu (as well as being within recent Marine experience). He said: "There have been a number of comparisons between Khe Sanh and Dienbienphu, but the Marines don't see it in anything but the mountainous terrain. . . . But for Khe Sanh for now, some veteran Marines are saying, 'The closer you get to the rear, the worse it looks at the front.' "[118]

Another radio report, not from Saigon, by Lew Wood of NBC, agreed with Wheeler's estimate of why Khe Sanh had to be held, but vaguely observed that American thinking was "much like" the French in 1954. Wood concluded:

. . . there are some who see a parallel with the battle of Dienbienphu 14 years ago.

The positions of the opposing forces are similar. *The strategic approach of the Americans is much like the French thinking in that other recent war.* On the communist side little has changed. A crafty, some would say even a brilliant military tactician, Vo Nguyen Giap, is commanding their forces as he did in 1954.

The big difference—and it could be the vital difference—is air power. . . .

The French *were confident before Dienbienphu.* The Americans insist they have reason to be confident today.[119]

NBC's Tom Glennon stressed the dubious Giap-in-charge angle amid other Dienbienphu "similarities" on March 4:

The enemy artillery positions surrounding the American entrenchments here is [*sic*] effective and entrenched, and some of it looks down the throat of the Americans below. The French garrison faced precisely the same situation.

In 1954 the French commanders depended upon air power to neutralize enemy positions and disrupt their supply lines. The small French air arm couldn't even begin to do the job. Today forthright American pilots admit it's very difficult to knock out well-concealed and well-emplaced enemy guns; they wipe out enemy gun crews but these troops are replaced.

There's another similarity. The man who commanded the Vietminh forces against the French at Dienbienphu is the same general who directs the tens of thousands of troops surrounding Khe Sanh. He is General Vo Nguyen Giap.[120]

David Burrington of NBC discussed Dienbienphu twice, first commenting:

There's a lot of concern here at Khe Sanh that the North Vietnamese are not only just outside the base, but that they're underneath it as well. Several tunnels have been found. . . .

At Dienbienphu such tunnels were actually used to blow up the top French command bunker, and there's concern that this, too, could happen here.[121]

Later, with Frank Blair:

Blair: The Marines fear now that the enemy has some strong hidden artillery positions in the Khe Sanh area, and may call them into use suddenly with devastating effect. . . .

Burrington: . . . Nobody can know whether the enemy artillery is in these hills or not, because it's never been fired, it's being saved as a surprise, as a secret weapon, presumably for the big attack. That's how it was done 14 years ago at a place called Dienbienphu.[122]

CBS capped it all with its Dienbienphu anniversary effort on March 12: a Hanoi film of the communist victory in 1954, followed by *Newsweek*'s François Sully (who did not set foot in Khe Sanh during Tet) and Army Lt. Gen. William Rosson's dry rebuttal. Don Webster presided:

Sully: The first time I went to Khe Sanh, I was traveling in a small plane. The weather was bad, the airstrip was fogged in, the hills were shrouded with haze. I saw the tiny airstrip . . . and in the background the rugged mountains of Laos, and I thought to myself, oh, my God, Dienbienphu all over again.

Webster: What mistakes do you think the Marines are making at Khe Sanh based on your experience at Dienbienphu?

Sully: Of course, the first mistake is to be there. In this country you don't block an infiltration route with a static position. And the second mistake is, since you have to be there, since it has been decided that you should be there, is to limit themselves to a defensive position. You should go out, you should seek the enemy, find prisoners, disrupt the enemy communication lines, but they shouldn't stay in there building their bunkers, filling sandbags. And third, the third mistake is that they don't reinforce the perimeter strong enough. They have a one-line defense, they should have two or three.

Webster: In what ways is Dienbienphu different than Khe Sanh today?

Rosson: Don, I see several principal difficulties, or differences, rather. In the first place, it was a very deep basc in relation to the friendly positions. You may recall that the principal French bastion in North Vietnam at that time was in the Red River Delta, and Dienbienphu was something in the order of 175 or 180 miles west of that. The French had nothing to compare with the air power that we enjoy today, in, in any category, really, strike, reconnaissance, or air lift, and then there was certainly a difference as it relates to Khe Sanh, in that we have artillery within range of that position, and a rather substantial amount of it, whereas the French, of course, over the great distances involved had nothing to compare with that.[123]

Douglas Edwards of CBS News read his UPI file and gave his own anniversary commentary, including an interview with Lieutenant General Cushman:

The Marines were on special alert at Khe Sanh this past day, just in case the communists decided to observe the anniversary of the start of the attack on Dienbienphu, 14 years ago, but nothing happened.

The enemy's silence was described as eerie [by UPI].

General Cushman, the Marine commander, has this estimate of the situation.

Cushman: . . . He is still capable of conducting an attack against Khe Sanh; however, the price would be very high indeed. He is digging trenches and doing other tricks of the trade which he learned to do at Dienbienphu, and we're shooting at him. That's about the situation there. You might say no change.

Edwards: There has been one change, however, and maybe General Cushman didn't know about it when he made that estimate.

The Air Force has discovered a new communist road below Khe Sanh, and they bombed it today with B-52s.[124]

Thereafter, the "Dienbienphu syndrome" on the networks began to fade. As Michael Herr noted, for a time it had been "irresistible." All in all, on weekday network evening news shows alone, the Dienbienphu analogy crept in some 11 times in 31 "combat" film reports on Khe Sanh, or in the introductions thereto, without counting spot news items from Vietnam and Washington.[125] Only twice were the dissimilarities between Dienbienphu and Khe Sanh cited, either by the reporter or by U.S. military commanders.[126] In short, Dienbienphu was largely used as a convenient "scare" word.

The Newspapers: Limited Firsthand Coverage

In Vietnam, despite some reinforcements, the New York *Times* and the Washington *Post,* especially the latter, were too undermanned at Tet to match the AP's almost daily reporting from Khe Sanh. Their reporters got to the base in late January as the siege began, wrote competent stories, and departed. They did not try to follow up with frequent visits: Khe Sanh, as they saw it, was a "static story" until such time as the foe launched his "big push." After the Tet attacks, the *Post* and *Times* Saigon bureaus focused on a variety of other more pressing matters: fighting in Saigon and Hue, urban recovery, the performance of the Thieu government. In terms of the action on the ground, there was no other choice: Khe Sanh was not yet Dienbienphu. In terms of what interested the home offices, the dearth of staff coverage of Khe Sanh left a large hole in current information and "context." Khe Sanh was perceived in New York and Washington as a running story whose potential drama continued to fascinate busy journalistic managers more than anything else happening in Vietnam at Tet. Both *Times* and *Post* editors sought to fill this hole with wire-service copy and, uncritically, with secondhand news and often contradictory analyses of Khe Sanh from Saigon, Paris, New York, Washington, and London.

The result was an odd mix of relatively level-headed (if limited) on-scene reporting with some extraordinarily imaginative scenarios of future disaster, especially by the *Times,* and repeated analogies to Dienbienphu. Khe Sanh became a journalistic game that anyone could play. The *Times* and *Post* editors and reporters may not have succumbed to the speculative fever that swept the networks, but their temperatures, on occasion, ran very high.

In Vietnam, before Tet, following the general trend, both the *Times* and *Post* got off to a good start. Both sent two men apiece on trips to Khe Sanh. The *Times*'s Charles Mohr first reported the U.S. buildup on January 17. Joseph Alsop had already reported the enemy buildup in mid-December.[127] But most newspaper reporting of the base came after the opening January 21 bombardment and the fierce but abortive NVA attack on the Hill 861 outpost.

The *Post* home office cabled Saigon on January 25 asking that a close eye be kept on Khe Sanh: "KHE SANH LOOKS FROM HERE LIKE MOST SIGNIFICANT CONFRONTATION OF WAR AND FIRST-CLASS COVERAGE BY LEE [Lescaze] HAS WHETTED OUR APPETITE. IF YOU BOTH AGREE AND PROMISE KEEP HEADS DOWN WE WOULD LIKE CONTINUE EYEWITNESS TOUCH WITH STORY. ALSO WONDER WHY OR IF NORVIETS HAVE NOT ACCOMPLISHED ONE OF MAJOR OBJECTIVES BY FORCING US TO TAKE TROOPS FROM PACIFICATION AND ELSEWHERE TO REINFORCE KHE SANH."

Newsmen and civilian officials in Washington were already discussing the diversion theory cited earlier, that Hanoi, active as in the past along the DMZ, was trying to relieve the pressure on the guerrillas to the south. It was a thesis which both this writer and others in Saigon found plausible, in the light of past history and of the new northward move of part of the 1st Cavalry Division from Binh Dinh province in II Corps. However, this writer, preparing to go to Da Nang, had also been told by MACV staff officers that there was concern for the whole northern sector, not just Khe Sanh. Moreover, the Marine base had thus far been subject only to the single ground assault against Hill 861. Hence this cable went back: "AM HEADING NORTH SUNDAY MAINTAIN COVERAGE KHE SANH WHICH IS POTENTIAL NOTNOT ACTUAL CONFRONTATION AND NOTNOT SOLE CAUSE REDEPLOYMENT EXPACIFICATION AREAS."

After his visit to Khe Sanh, Lescaze concluded that, considering our lack of manpower, frequent *Post* visits to the base were a waste of time. "You get out there, and nothing happens except the incoming. So you spend your time ducking, not reporting." This writer agreed, following his own trip to Khe Sanh, a trip which coincided with the short-lived Tet truce on Monday, January 29. It was still possible, then, to work in relative tranquillity. Without undue apprehension, one could fly to Hill 861, aboard a Marine CH-46 supply helicopter. One could tour much of the main base perimeter, observe the shallow trenches and wrecked "hootches" (huts), talk to Marines and ARVN Rangers, and listen to Lownds's polite but uninformative comments.

On January 30, the *Post* home office received—thanks, no doubt, to the cease-fire and the temporarily good weather—a detailed, relatively calm "situationer," which, slightly trimmed, ran (undated) on February 5. It failed to mention one Marine outpost, Hill 558. It did not spell out the intensity of the U.S. air effort or describe the enemy shelling. It began conventionally enough, disposed quickly of the Dienbienphu angle, and described the ARVN:

KHE SANH, South Vietnam—How many North Vietnamese would it take to overrun the isolated Marine garrison at Khe Sanh?[128]

Leaning against the sandbagged edge of the trench, Col. David E. Lownds, commander of the 26th Marine Regiment, looked thoughtful for a moment.

"I should like to hope they don't have enough," he said matter of factly. "Anyway, we're here to stay. As fast as they come up on the barbed wire, we are going to kill them."

Judging from talks with many of the Marines here, few disagree with their Colonel. Indeed, one squad leader put it this way: "You know, I think those North Vietnamese are nervous."

. . . Few Marines appeared daunted by the Dienbienphu analogy. On the perimeter trench, Pfc. Clarence Hunter, 20, of Philadelphia, helped his friend, Lance Cpl. Jerome Foster, fill sandbags while a scratchy portable record-player sounded strains of The Miracles singing "I Love You Baby." Several yards in front of their trench was a man-high black radio booster box.

Within the perimeter trench, the base looked like a shanty slum on the outskirts of Manila. Everywhere were smashed hootches and trash, but here and there flew unfamiliar flags—state flags sent to Khe Sanh chauvinists from home, Confederate Stars and Bars, red Marine Corps banners, even a Canadian maple leaf ensign. Everywhere, waving above the sandbagged bunkers and smashed tin roofs, were radio antennae, resembling at first glance a grove of TV aerials. . . .

Somewhat downcast by Marine C-rations instead of their traditional rice, the Rangers were nevertheless as cocky as the Marines with whom they fraternized. Indeed, 1st Lt. Trong Thuoc had inked over his breast pocket the identifying legend: "Supervisor of Guards of Marine Security."[129]

This was the *Post*'s longest staff-written story out of Khe Sanh. Tet broke, and Saigon, Hue, Da Nang, and the Delta preoccupied the two *Post* reporters. The foreign desk did not press its men further on Khe Sanh coverage.

Mostly as a gesture, the *Post* visited Khe Sanh overnight once again during Tet—in bad weather under light shelling in mid-February—with indifferent results. Most of this writer's time was spent ducking. The trip resulted in a trimmed feature story on the manic humor of a doughty Marine ammunition platoon in whose sturdy bunker I slept (the Navy Seabees' stout shelter was another much-publicized newsman's favorite).[180]

Coupled with time-consuming visits to Dong Ha and Da Nang, the Khe Sanh visit also occasioned a hybrid second article, much of it all too typical of many written about the siege.[181] It was a brief, matter-of-fact description of Khe Sanh's "sporadic" daily shelling, low Marine casualties, hazardous but adequate aerial resupply, "unspec-tacular" recent enemy activity, and somewhat improved base de-fenses. It also mentioned Hanoi's failure to exploit earlier opportunities, stout Marine morale, and the fading of some of the earlier Marine "ebullience." The intensity of allied outgoing fire-power, especially bombing, was not understood and not cited, except obliquely as a possible deterrent to enemy gunners. The NVA's un-successful early February assaults were erroneously belittled as "probes." The four-engine C-130s were described as still managing to land; in fact, only the smaller two-engine C-123s were allowed to risk landings after February 12. The C-130s dropped supplies by par-achute.

Then, tired, and having little more to say about Khe Sanh itself, this reporter went on to relay the speculation he had heard (and *sought*) in interviews or mess talk with four Marine G-2 and G-3 staff officers at Dong Ha and Da Nang. The speculation was not wild. But it concerned the worst *possibilities:* diversionary enemy moves against other Marine bases, timed to coincide with "D-Day" at Khe Sanh; "natural targets" for enemy attacks (the Khe Sanh-supporting artillery base at Camp Carroll); possible enemy efforts to dig in more artillery for a Dienbienphu-style effort; the apparent need for more U.S. manpower in hard-pressed I Corps "if Khe Sanh is to be suc-cessfully defended in a showdown." (The battle of Hue was still dragging on; the Marines were worried about the DMZ area; that week was, perhaps, the psychological low point of the February–March period for the allies.)

Many contingencies were, naturally, under discussion at various staff levels. But Marine officers I talked to were not predicting enemy moves, only suggesting, in response to my queries, that certain moves seemed "logical" and that the enemy seemed capable of making them. My story, like many others, blurs this distinction. The officers' speculation, for the reader's sake, should have been expressly labeled as such, and framed with appropriate caveats. Moreover, as I view it in retrospect, I should have conveyed my awareness that: (1) in practical terms, Marines had to "expect" an assault on Khe Sanh and be prepared, militarily, for the worst, and (2) following the January 30–31 Tet surprise, few U.S. staff officers were willing to *rule out* any enemy move, at least in talks with newsmen.

In sum, this story represented, in relatively mild form, a common but dangerous reaction to a chronic journalistic problem at Tet and in other crises: Faced with a scarcity of "news," of fresh (or obtainable) information concerning what was happening, one turned to what *could* happen. News magazines and television, as we have seen, were especially prone to this solution. But none of the media was immune.

Both *Times* and *Post* editors were to make Khe Sanh page-one news throughout February–March. Like the *Post,* however, the *Times* did not insist that the base be "staffed" by its own reporters, who also had to keep up with other Tet developments.

In essence, the *Times*'s staff coverage paralleled that of the *Post:* The only *Times* reporter to visit Khe Sanh overnight during February and March was Gene Roberts, the new bureau chief, who went there for the first and only time in mid-February after surviving a convoy ambush and providing daily coverage of the Marines' fight for Hue's south side.

Roberts wrote a feature on stout Marine morale.[132] He was back in Saigon when his second Khe Sanh piece—on page one—appeared. It reflected a common, partly subjective reaction among newsmen, including this reporter, who visited the Khe Sanh camp in mid-February—that some of the trenches were too shallow and the sandbagged bunker roofs too thin for protection from bombardment.[133]

CBS's Peter Kalischer (see pp. 293–94) had focused on the problem, as did *Time* and *Newsweek.* I had brought it up at a press conference with Marine staff officers. Roberts wrote: "Even the most confident Marines . . . are not boasting about their defenses as they steel themselves against a possible enemy attack that could result in the largest battle of the war."

Roberts noted that there was only one concrete (underground) bunker at the camp (Lownds's command post) built by the Army (Special Forces) in 1966. The Marines did not "follow through on the Army's plan for concrete bunkers," or spend much effort on protection. Some Marine officers said that Khe Sanh had not been intended as a "major defensive fortification." Roberts quoted Army officers as saying Marines felt digging was demeaning.

All this was largely true. Marine historians note another reason for the protection problem: Prior to mid-January, the Khe Sanh base had never housed more than one battalion; suddenly, enough timber, steel matting, and other supplies had to be brought in by air to build bunkers under fire for four Marine battalions, supporting units, and the ARVN 37th Ranger Battalion. No bunker could be built strongly enough in the flat Khe Sanh plateau to withstand anything heavier than the common 82 mm. mortar round—the rockets and heavy artillery were impossible to stop with the material the 26th Marines had on hand.[104]

In any event, Roberts reported: "Marines reply that weaknesses in their defenses can be overdramatized, and that they have firepower plus air support . . . [and] the enemy would be making a mistake if he thought of Khe Sanh as another Dienbienphu." What Roberts failed to note was what struck this writer only on his second trip to Khe Sanh: The flawed defenses on the main base (as opposed to the deep trenches on the hilltop outposts) were not being subjected to constant barrage (as reported by the wires), but to "sporadic" fire, with "relatively light" casualties.

Viewed with the benefit of hindsight, what this writer, Roberts, and others did not emphasize was that, while Khe Sanh's defensive flaws existed, their gravity remained a matter of speculation, depending on the enemy's future ability (and intention) to mount an intensive, Dienbienphu-style bombardment and assault.

Not long afterward, in his syndicated column, S. L. A. Marshall, the veteran combat historian, cited contradictions between low casualty totals at Khe Sanh and wire-service descriptions of enemy fire as "murderous"; mocked the (Times) map showing "three or four solid North Vietnamese divisions perched on the hills just outside Khe Sanh"; and derided another (AP) story for saying "all resupply" is by airdrop. Marshall observed that "every correspondent on the spot appears to be haunted by Dienbienphu . . . so persistently somber is the mood, so persistent the tone, that the poor devils composing the condemned garrison have little or no chance to come smiling through."[135]

It was about the only such caveat voiced in the media at home until the second half of March. But there were some protests. On March 5, AP cited Senator Harry Byrd's defense of post-Tet censorship by MACV, noting the revelations published by the media on Khe Sanh's defenses:

WASHINGTON (AP)—Sen. Harry F. Byrd, Jr., D-Va., told the Senate today it "makes sense" for the American command to withhold information on damage inflicted by the enemy on fixed targets in Vietnam. . . .

The problem is compounded, Byrd said, "by the fact that the Administration—and the Department of Defense in particular—has attempted to manage the news so often that it makes the American public hesitant to endorse or even accept Vietnam censorship."

Byrd said he thinks that some correspondents "have gone beyond the call of duty in discussing the state of morale among the men awaiting attack at Khe Sanh, in reporting the strengths and weaknesses of the defenses there, and suggesting enemy plans of attack that might succeed in overrunning the outpost."[136]

Right after Tet, both *Post* and *Times* editors were fascinated by the Dienbienphu angle. They asked for major "comparison pieces" from Saigon. The overworked *Post* bureau put the request low on its list of priorities, not realizing that such comparisons were being made almost daily at home. The *Post* editors used a fairly balanced AP story which, however, said "intense shelling—*like that now aimed at Khe Sanh"—eventually crippled French resupply.*[137]

The *Times*'s Charles Mohr, on March 8, wrote an extensive, highly speculative "anniversary" piece, likening the static situation at Khe Sanh to the period *prior* to the 1954 siege. He noted that MACV no longer considered Khe Sanh the foe's prime target: "Senior military officers in Saigon [Westmoreland] indicated yesterday that they believed that Hue, rather than Khe Sanh, would be the next major enemy objective. Others disagree." Then, with far more precision than anyone else, he described the chilling possibility that Giap might repeat his Dienbienphu tactics and triumph: "Both the methods of the siege and the terrain bear at least some resemblance to Dienbienphu. There are those here who believe that the enemy might attack Khe Sanh on the anniversary next Wednesday in a symbolic gesture."

Mohr implicitly rejected the U.S. military claims that air power and proximity to friendly forces (within artillery range) made Khe Sanh "different." Giap, Mohr noted, derided French air strikes; the failure of U.S. air power at Khe Sanh to "silence" enemy mortars and antiaircraft machine guns may have given Giap confidence in success here also. Mohr quoted heavily and judiciously from Bernard Fall, but omitted Fall's contention that 100 U.S. B-29 heavy bombers could have saved Dienbienphu.

Mohr also suggested that the North Vietnamese "delay" in staging an all-out effort against Khe Sanh or its outposts was deliberate, part of the same slow, strangling tactics used against the French. He likened Dienbienphu's outlying strongpoints—which fell—to the Marine outposts, but then did not mention the abortive January–February assaults against those outposts. Nor did he cite the frustrated February 29–March 1 night attack against the ARVN sector of Khe Sanh's main perimeter. Mohr had not been to Khe Sanh since January. In effect, he all but predicted that the worst was yet to come. What did the story show? It showed that even Mohr, when it came to analysis, could flop as badly as anyone else, if with more grace.

Mohr ended: "Most important of all, General Giap believes that 'men not weapons are decisive in war.' His troops around Khe Sanh are estimated at 20,000. 'With a sufficient concentration of forces on the principal point of effort we are assured of being able to press home the attack to our advantage no matter how strong the enemy defense is,' he wrote." The *Times* put the story on page one,[138] and inside added a New York-written "Man in the News" profile of General Giap. Under his photograph, the caption read: "Trying for Another Dienbienphu?" As an "expert on modern guerrilla warfare," the *Times* said, Giap ranked "with Mao Tse-tung and Ernesto (Che) Guevara." (Giap may not have found the latter comparison flattering.)

Two days later, the Sunday *Times* in its weekly news analysis section published Gene Roberts' discussion of the U.S. "defensive" posture throughout Vietnam. Roberts noted Westmoreland's suggestion on March 6 that Khe Sanh was apparently no longer the foe's prime target, but added that "many" who had studied Giap's writings and "other accounts" (presumably Fall's) thought there was still a "remarkable parallel" with Dienbienphu. "And at week's end," Roberts wrote, possibly with tongue-in-cheek, "these students of military history began saying 'I told you so,'" after enemy troops were reported slain "tunneling" close to the Khe Sanh perimeter.[139]

On March 17, the *Times* printed another Saigon feature story, requiring little legwork, on Khe Sanh. It reported Hanoi's apparent "surge" of propaganda about the base, vowing destruction of the Marine garrison; this, unnamed U.S. officials in Saigon were quoted as saying, "presumably" meant "some type of move up there."[140]

The fascination with the story was still there, and the reporters in Saigon knew it, if only by noting what their editors were printing. Had the *Times* and *Post* reporters joined Merton Perry of *Newsweek* during his early March visit to Khe Sanh, they might have sensed how things had changed, notably the weather, whose improvement permitted a doubling of fighter-bomber sorties in March.

The *Post* bureau managed to avoid mentioning Dienbienphu in two subsequent stories about Khe Sanh. One was a report on the Marine CH-46 helicopter squadron at Quang Tri, north of Hue, which ran supplies to Khe Sanh's hill outposts.[141] The other was the *Post*'s only staff-written Khe Sanh "action" story on page one during Tet. It described a three-hour flight over the Khe Sanh-Laos area (Highway Nine) aboard an Air Force spotter plane and cited the accurate U.S. bombing that day, which appeared to help make enemy bombardment of Khe Sanh "surprisingly imprecise and erratic." The story failed, however, to mention the sheer volume of the bombing or the improving weather, or to cite the disadvantages to the enemy of "motorizing" his logistics. It was a feature that could have explained far more.[142]

The *Times*'s Gene Roberts, writing from Da Nang, a few days later quoted senior officers as declaring that air power—80,000 tons of bombs dropped—had made Khe Sanh a "disaster" for the enemy, who had tied up two divisions there that could have been used against the cities. The enemy's big push, a spokesman for Westmoreland (Sidle) was reported as saying, had been pre-empted by the U.S. bombing. Then Roberts discussed the Dienbienphu analogy again, with senior officers calling it erroneous and citing Fall's conclusion that 100 U.S. bombers would have saved Dienbienphu. Unnamed foreign military attachés in Saigon, Roberts wrote, "remain unconvinced" that the analogy was invalid, suggesting that the enemy's delay in attacking was deliberate.

In essence, Roberts was the first newsman to report the details of the intensity of U.S. bombardment, and Westmoreland's conclusion that air power had won at Khe Sanh, even prior to the relief expedition. (UPI had, of course, accurately cited an NVA "withdrawal" a week earlier, but Sidle had denied it.) In contrast to Mohr's earlier, pessimistic (March 8) page-one analysis, Roberts' story was on page two.[143]

The last mention of Khe Sanh by a Saigon-based New York *Times* staffer was again by Roberts. Printed three days later, the story seems to have been written much earlier. With a Dong Ha dateline, Roberts dealt accurately—in light of available information—with life among the troops, the 1968 U.S. troop buildup in northern I Corps, the abundance of local allied operations, and potential enemy targets. But, oddly enough, in view of the by then widely known impending Operation Pegasus, Roberts pictured U.S. troops in that area as waiting for the enemy to attack, as if the story had been filed a fortnight earlier but held by the New York desk:

. . . the enemy is steadily moving closer to Khe Sanh with his network of zigzag trenches, despite a major United States bombing effort that has pounded him with more than 80,000 tons of explosives since January 22. . . .[144]

. . . American intelligence officers suspect that the North Vietnamese are using the same tactics the Vietminh used to conceal supply movements from the French during the siege of Dienbienphu 14 years ago—tying the tops of trees together to shield their roads.[145]

In brief, these points can be made about *Times* and *Post* staff coverage of Khe Sanh. In terms of available information, the correspondents did their best work laying out the situation in January, as the siege started.[146] Then, finding the situation largely unchanged in mid-February, both bureaus, but most notably the *Times* bureau, resorted to secondhand, speculative reporting about the future. This speculation, not always clearly separated from prediction, and usually attributed to anonymous sources, did not occur in a vacuum. The *Times* and *Post* reporters set the framework. They sought out the available officers, asking them about certain specific possibilities and not others, and introducing the Dienbienphu question. The results, if interesting, were hardly conclusive, and too incomplete to warrant the space and "play" repeatedly given them.

In the war wrap-up department, the *Times* scored well ahead of the *Post,* the AP, and even the UPI with the "Great Bomber Threat" story of February 11.

In its customary briefing, MACV reported Saturday, February 10, in Saigon that "two and possibly three" obsolescent Soviet-made Ilyushin-28 "Beagle" bombers had been sighted on the ground and strafed by raiding U.S. Air Force jets at Phuc Yen air base 18 miles *northwest* of Hanoi. The AP reported it more or less as announced.[147] The UPI lead, however, without any encouragement from MACV spokesmen, quickly linked the "Russian-made jet bombers" to Khe Sanh, 325 miles away, saying that the aircraft were "within 30 minutes flying time" of the Marine base. "The report," said UPI, "further escalated the potential scope of the developing battle for the American fortress."[148]

The page-one *Times* war wrap-up, written in Saigon, escalated "the potential scope" even further. It conjured up not only the UPI prospect ("Red Bombers Hit Khe Sanh") but added a second specter: a "jungle strip" in "eastern Laos" providing a base for modern MIG-21 fighters to exert a "decisive effect" in "a North Vietnamese final assault on the stronghold." The *Times* said that the hunt was on for the "jungle strip," not mentioning that any MIG runway would have to be 10,000 feet long, and thus difficult to conceal. Although there was no reference to Dienbienphu, the paper here provided the most imaginative newspaper story of the Tet period. It remains an unchallenged New York *Times* exclusive:

SAIGON, South Vietnam, Sunday, Feb. 11—Twin-jet bombers have been sighted at the Phuc Yen air base 18 miles northwest of Hanoi, an American military spokesman said today. The air base is within striking range of the United States Marine stronghold at Khe Sanh.

The Air Force said several months ago that the North Vietnamese might have six of the planes. . . .

The sighting of two, or possibly three, of the IL-28 bombers caused *little apparent concern* to the American command even though the Marine base at Khe Sanh is only 325 miles to the southwest of Phuc Yen.

The IL-28, it was explained, is too slow to have much chance of avoiding interceptors that would be in the air moments after Air Force and Navy planes with side-scan radar picked up the take-off.

Of somewhat greater concern, according to a senior United States officer, is the *possibility* that the North Vietnamese have hauled enough steel matting down the Ho Chi Minh Trail to a point in eastern Laos within 100 miles of Khe Sanh to build a runway that would be used by MIG-21s.

It was emphasized that no such site was known to exist, but the officer said a search was being pressed by reconnaissance planes and *probably by long-range commando units.*

The use of even a small number of MIGs in support of the assault on Khe Sanh *could be serious.* Their bombs, and napalm or air cover for the tanks that the enemy forces are expected to use at Khe Sanh, could have a decisive effect in a final assault on the stronghold. The enemy used tanks in overrunning the outpost in Lang Vei Wednesday. The MIG-21s have a range of about 750 miles. From a jungle strip they would have a chance of hitting Khe Sanh before American planes could arrive. . . .

An intensive rocket, artillery, and mortar bombardment, which would precede a ground assault on Khe Sanh, would no doubt knock out the airstrip and all supplies would have to be parachuted in. Senior officers are said to accept this probability. . . .

At Khe Sanh, only scattered shelling was reported at the base and its outpost to the northwest. But this was described by a *source* at the United States command as "the lull before the storm—and it could begin any minute."

The Marine garrison of more than 5,000 men and two brigades of helicopter-borne troops of the 1st Cavalry Division (Airmobile), in reserve about 50 miles away on the coast, appear to be *waiting* for the on slaught.[149]

The *Post* editors, like those of the *Times,* liked the bomber story and put it on page one. The foreign-desk rewriteman, faced with the conflicting AP and UPI IL-28 stories, hedged on the Khe Sanh angle in his fourth paragraph: "From Phuc Yen, [the bomber] could reach the beleaguered U.S. Marine Base at Khe Sanh in about half an hour [UPI], but U.S. officials made no suggestion that the planes would be used in South Vietnam."[150]

These bomber reports were a one-day wonder. The Beagles and the Laotian "jungle strip" were not heard of again.

Had the *Post* foreign desk been able to query its Saigon bureau by direct Telex, the home office might have been quickly persuaded that the Beagles' existence was interesting, but irrelevant to Khe Sanh or the larger course of the Vietnam War. However, throughout Tet, as in other war crises, U.S. editors manifested a stubborn fondness for "airplane stories," relevant or not. Perhaps war planes—exploding, bombing, dog-fighting, or merely "poised"—represented something familiar, akin to the domestic airline crashes and hijackings that contributed to the traditional daily news menu.[151]

The *Post,* keen on feature material about Khe Sanh, ran one of the rare published pieces about individuals there performing with heroism. It was a story by John Randolph of the Los Angeles *Times* about a conscientious objector, serving as a Navy medical corpsman, who was killed in action. Randolph began: " 'It was the saddest thing of all—to have to cut his new boots off,' said Lt. Donald J. Magilligan, standing on the bloodsoaked floor of the underground medical bunker and shaking his head slowly."[152]

The *Post* also ran a lengthy, dramatic, but error-studded piece by a newcomer to Vietnam, David Leitch of the London Sunday *Times,* who had made the standard in-and-out trip in mid-February. The headline was: "Khe Sanh Is Quite Takeable." The *Post* preceded the article with this note: "This dispatch was written 10 days ago. Both the weather and the American position have deteriorated since."[153]

Leitch was highly imaginative. He apparently also was blessed with superb eyesight: The North Vietnamese besiegers, he wrote, were "brisk, eager little men in jungle kit going about their jobs with frightening impassivity." The Marines were both uneducated and "muddy, frightened men," waiting for the "coup de grace"; the U.S. bombers took "suicidal risks"; and the only Marines leaving "are the dead ones in rubber bags or the wounded on stretchers."

It did not take a military expert to see that Leitch was overexcited. Nevertheless, the *Post* gave his apocalyptic impressions more space than any other story it printed about the siege.[154]

Both the *Times* and the *Post* intermittently used AP features from Khe Sanh to fill in the gap left by their Saigon reporters. The *Times* selected seven. None of them were features showing Marine morale holding up. On February 9, the AP described the confusion at Khe Sanh over how to handle the refugees from the Montagnard settlements and also dealt with the Special Forces outpost at Lang Vei, and John Wheeler wrote a story on the Marines' "high spirits." The *Times* used the refugee story. Similarly, on February 22, the *Times* chose to run Wheeler's story (of the previous day) about a vain effort to rescue a wounded man, not that reporter's piece about the flag-raising ceremony held by Marines daily on Hill 881 South amid shellfire.

The *Post* also ran seven AP features, four of them also used by the *Times.* The *Post* put one of them, "Khe Sanh Marines Use Divining Rods" (to detect suspected North Vietnamese tunnels), on page one; the *Times* put it on page three. Both papers used an AP story on Marines battling rats at Khe Sanh, on March 27. Again, the *Post* used none of Wheeler's morale stories, nor his accounts of the key role played by the outposts. The *Post* used one Wheeler report: "Foe Tightens Ring Around Khe Sanh," accurately describing development of enemy approach trenches, but failing to note the sporadic nature of enemy bombardment.[155]

At home, even prior to Tet, Khe Sanh was a major subject of analysis, speculation, and discussion in Washington and New York—initially prompted in part by the widely rumored worries of the beleaguered President, the predictions of "confrontation" by officials at the Pentagon, and the news reports from Vietnam. Even with the onset of the *Pueblo* crisis on January 23, there was a good deal of Dienbienphu talk, which increased thereafter.

In the *Times*, four days after the siege started, Hanson Baldwin wrote an unsigned article detailing friendly and enemy troop dispositions in and around Khe Sanh, and saying that "the largest battle of the war appeared to be impending around Khe Sanh and the Demilitarized Zone."[156]

The *Post* ran Joseph Alsop's column on January 29 describing Khe Sanh not only as a "major test of strength," but as the "climactic episode" to Hanoi's "winter-spring offensive," with "some pretty hairy moments" in store for both sides. Alsop, like Westmoreland, linked Khe Sanh to a "major effort" elsewhere by the foe, without spelling out the details.[157] Until he visited the outpost, on March 31, Alsop was to worry aloud about Khe Sanh, even as he became bullish about the Tet offensive against the cities, and the *Post* also carried these reports.[158]

The *Post*'s Ward Just wrote an editorial-page analysis erroneously reporting that "15,000" more men had been sent to defend Khe Sanh. He argued that Khe Sanh was a "classic example" of Westmoreland's attrition strategy, that an alternate "line" could have been established in the lowlands "in territory favorable to the Americans," and that it could cost the Americans up to 3,000 dead "to defend Khe Sanh."[159]

In the same day's paper, columnists Rowland Evans and Robert Novak cited high-level worry about Khe Sanh as a "diversion" from the Central Highlands, saw a U.S. failure to anticipate "outright invasion" across the DMZ, and noted the "grim prospect of high U.S. casualties." *"Anything less* than throwing the enemy back with huge losses in an undisputed U.S. victory, *as Westmoreland predicts"* could give Hanoi "new muscle in its talk-fight policy" and force an "agonizing reappraisal" by Washington.[160]

On February 1, columnist Joseph Kraft said Khe Sanh was divert-
ing U.S. troops, "leaving the populated places more vulnerable than
ever." He mocked military thinking that the enemy might be trying
for a Dienbienphu as just another case of U.S. "self-delusion."[161]

After Tet, this pattern of bold long-distance analysis continued.
Khe Sanh was something that Vietnam commentators could get their
teeth into. Indeed, the New York *Times,* during the siege, ran no
fewer than six analysis or explanatory pieces from Washington or
New York in the daily paper,[162] together with Sunday maps and their
error-prone captions. On one occasion, when a *Times* Saigon writer
failed to mention Dienbienphu in his Khe Sanh "weekender," the
Sunday editor filled in the gap with a two-paragraph boldface summary of the 1954 battle entitled "Specter of Dienbienphu."[163] The
analysis pieces were accurate in many respects, but left out *knowable*
key factors about the current situation: sporadic enemy fire, light
U.S. losses, early abortive enemy attacks (not mere "probes"), and
the intensity of U.S. artillery and air bombardment.

After the successful North Vietnamese tank attack at Lang Vei on
February 7, the *Times* ran a page-one story by its Pentagon correspondent, William Beecher, saying that the PT-76 tanks used by the
enemy there were "modern." He quoted a Pentagon source as saying
Westmoreland was ready for tanks with mine fields and "concrete
bunkers."[164] As General Abrams was to report on February 8, and
AP to report subsequently, the tanks were old thin-skinned machines: The Marines' primary reliance at Khe Sanh, as Abrams said,
to stop further armored incursions was on 106 mm. recoilless rifles
and five M-48 tanks, for which the PT-76 was no match. There were
no concrete (fighting) bunkers. This did not mean that Beecher was
faking it, only that he was checking on details with Pentagon informants far from the scene.

The *Times's* Hedrick Smith, an old Vietnam hand and State Department reporter, wrote a lengthy piece not only describing Administration worry over Khe Sanh, but also describing in detail the geography and situation on the ground around the base, which led him,
inevitably, into errors. For example, he said Marine defensive tactics
on the outposts were simply to hide in their bunkers when the NVA
assaulted, call in artillery on their own positions, and then emerge to
find the enemy dead. This did not happen; as was known in Vietnam,
the fighting was hand-to-hand.[165]

On February 23, from Washington, Neil Sheehan in the *Times* noted the "doubts" in "this nervous capital" about Khe Sanh. He cited both the President's request for assurances against a second Dienbienphu and the Pentagon's public rationale for holding Khe Sanh as a blocking position. Raising the question of how the Administration came to decide to defend Khe Sanh "at all costs," he offered the suggested answers of "senior military observers": the "inertia of events," "prestige," a "strategy of static defense" below the DMZ, and "finally, there is the unfulfilled hope held by American military leaders that Khe Sanh might serve as a staging point" for thrusts into southern Laos to block the Ho Chi Minh Trail.[166]

On March 13, the anniversary of Dienbienphu, Hanson Baldwin accurately reported the continued "uneasiness" of senior Marine officers in Washington over the commitment of four Marine battalions, trained primarily for offensive warfare, to the static defense of Khe Sanh. (He and they, of course, did not then know that the besiegers had already begun to withdraw.) Baldwin's Marine sources cast doubt on the Dienbienphu analogy, conceded the enemy ability to dig in, and expressed their preference for bolder U.S. offensive action, including forays into North Vietnam above the DMZ. Baldwin's *Times* piece did not attempt to go into detail on events at Khe Sanh, except to suggest that U.S. countermortar radar, however prone to breakdown, was helping to reduce enemy shelling. It was a proper Washington "reaction" story, limited in scope, not trying to explain what was happening on the ground 12,000 miles away.[167]

None of these written-at-home *Times* pieces were grossly exaggerated or unrealistic, but, with the exception of Baldwin's, they all tended to go beyond "reaction" or "policy" and include detail that could not help but be more error-prone or incomplete than if provided by newsmen on the spot. But New York insisted on running such Washington stories.

As before Tet, the *Post* offered the worries of syndicated columnists Joseph Alsop,[168] Evans and Novak,[169] and Jack Anderson.[170] The *Post* outdid the *Times* in printing foreign analyses of Khe Sanh, with Sir Robert Thompson's already noted observations from London that the "confrontation" was a clever "diversion" by the victor of Dienbienphu, and with a widely-published pickup from the London Sunday *Times* in Paris covering the response of three senior French Indo-China War veterans to the question: "Is Khe Sanh a second Dienbienphu?" (The three answers were "no," "no," and "maybe.")[171] Its last contribution was the S. L. A. Marshall column chiding newsmen for excessive gloom and offering, without endorsing, a more optimistic view by Marine Lt. Gen. Lewis W. Walt.[172]

During February, both the *Post* and the *Times* in Washington covered the various other official vibrations: Johnson's early prediction of a successful defense, *Time*'s reference to his request for assurances by the Joint Chiefs on Khe Sanh, and Administration denials that atomic weapons were contemplated for Khe Sanh's defense.

The *Post*, however, did not venture to assess Khe Sanh in special articles by its own Washington-based military and State Department specialists. There were only fleeting references, some of them indicating how "nervous" Washington was. For example, in a story reporting "officials'" speculation about Hanoi's "hydraheaded" strategy, Murrey Marder said: "The combination of communist options is conceded to be almost limitless [a common assumption that lasted longer in Washington than in Saigon] . . . while the bulk of U.S. attention is fixed on . . . Khe Sanh . . . there is growing doubt among some U.S. officials that the communists literally plan to reproduce the Dienbienphu attack."[173]

In March, the *Post*'s interest in Vietnam declined as its editors' abiding favorites—Washington debate and domestic politics—blossomed. On eight days that month no stories at all *from* Vietnam appeared on page one.[174] But Khe Sanh retained its appeal: about one-third (10) of all the *Post*'s 32 Vietnam stories in March that did make page one were about Khe Sanh. In March, the *Times* published 47 page-one stories from Vietnam; about one-fourth (12) concerned Khe Sanh.

Viewed collectively, neither newspaper's outpouring of "analysis" and repetitive descriptions from Vietnam and elsewhere added much of substance to the initial "situationers" written by its reporters at Khe Sanh in late January. In essence, the editors' day-to-day perceptions of what was "news" in South Vietnam during Tet—and this was especially true of the *Times*—differed from those of their men in Saigon, who did not "staff" Khe Sanh.[175] This divergence was not resolved by either orders to intensify Khe Sanh coverage or a shift in editors' story preferences. Instead, the newspapers' prime advantages over television (more space than the networks had time) and over the wires ("sophistication" and "context") were often wasted in the rush to publish (or encourage) secondhand reporting and speculation on Khe Sanh. The amount of "hard" information and "context" on Khe Sanh supplied to the reader was not commensurate with the space and "play" the newspapers devoted to that story in February and March 1968. Indeed, there was distortion: Other important matters, such as pacification, the role of the ARVN, the military situation elsewhere, were left in the shadows, while the spotlight was on a story that was potential, not actual.

In summary, the accompanying table shows how great was the number of Khe Sanh stories that got into the *Post* and, especially, the *Times* during February and March 1968:

	Times	Post
FROM VIETNAM		
Khe Sanh—as headline or as war wrap-up lead	17	13
Stories from Khe Sanh	14 (2 staff)	13 (3 staff)
Other Khe Sanh-related stories	26 (19 staff)	10 (4 staff)
Total	57	36
Total on page 1	23	19
FROM WASHINGTON		
Administration statements	3	2
Analyses/reaction (not columnists)	6	2
Columnists	0	4
Other Khe Sanh-related stories	3	0
Total	12	8
Total on page 1	8	1
FROM ABROAD		
Hanoi statements	3	0
Other	1	4
Total	4	4
Total on page 1	1	0
Total Khe Sanh stories	73	48
Total on page 1	31	20

In addition, the Khe Sanh photographs printed by each paper amounted to almost one-fifth (18 percent) of its total Vietnam picture coverage during the Tet period. Ten of the 25 *Times* Khe Sanh photographs showed U.S. troops wounded, dead, ducking fire, or surveying enemy-inflicted damage; four showed them in noncombatant poses; and only one picture showed Marines firing back. There were eight photographs of air strikes close to the perimeter or of air transports landing or parachuting supplies under fire. The *Post* ran 30 pictures of Khe Sanh, with roughly the same breakdown by category. But the *Post* had fewer shots of GIs ducking (one) and more (four) of Marines firing back. The *Post* also ran one photograph of a South Vietnamese Ranger.[176]

The News Magazines: "Agony" at Khe Sanh

Like the other media, *Time* and *Newsweek* discovered Khe Sanh before Tet began. *Time,* for example, in its issue of February 2, prepared a week earlier, published a Khe Sanh map that was slightly less inaccurate than others, identified Marine-held Hill 950 as communist-held, said (like AP) that Giap was reliably reported to be personally directing the Khe Sanh siege,[177] and spoke of the enemy's "enormous" firepower but "intermittent" shelling. The Marines, said *Time,* were waiting "for the inevitable moment" when Giap "makes the ultimate test of Khe Sanh's defenses."

After the opening Tet attacks, Khe Sanh (and Hue) became the chief focus of combat reporting in both magazines. *Time*'s editors—divided, as we have noted, in their views on the war—took a semi-official, chins-up view of Khe Sanh in their first post-Tet issue on February 9:

Circular Reasoning. Westmoreland sees the assault on Khe Sanh as the capstone of a three-phase campaign devised by Giap last September to win the war. . . .

Those U.S. analysts who believe that Khe Sanh will be attacked are convinced that Giap envisages it as a second Dienbienphu. . . .

In topography, Khe Sanh looks like a smaller version of Dienbienphu, but the terrain and underbrush are far worse for an attacker. The communists must go downhill through terrible maneuvering grounds,[178] cross the ravines, then climb the plateau on which Khe Sanh sits—all in the face of intensive artillery fire and air attack that the French at Dienbienphu did not have. . . .

Symbolically Vital. Khe Sanh is eminently worth holding—and defending. It is a major point on the DMZ defense line, the barrier that U.S. forces have sought to string from the sea below the DMZ to the Laotian border. It now blocks off the easiest supply line that Giap has into South Vietnam. . . .[179]

. . . .

The U.S., slightly apprehensive, was ready for an attack—and even hopeful that Giap would strike.[180] As for Giap, he no doubt was calculating the gains and losses of his big week in South Vietnam, deciding whether he could afford another bold venture.[181]

Three days later, summarizing developments, *Newsweek* said:

. . . And, by U.S. official accounts, the attacks on the Vietnamese cities were all but certain to be followed by a mammoth battle at Khe Sanh, overlooking the Ho Chi Minh Trail, where 6,000 Marines face perhaps 40,000 tough North Vietnamese Army regulars—a battle that some believe the communists hope to turn into another Dienbienphu. . . .

Their inclination—shared by many in Washington—was to write off the offensive as a diversionary gambit to weaken the American effort at Khe Sanh. And they insisted on reading the communists' objectives in strictly military—rather than political or psychological—terms. . . .

. . . By this analysis, the Laos incursions, the *Pueblo* seizure, the Tet offensive, and the Khe Sanh siege are all elements in a carefully staged communist show of strength before coming to the bargaining table—an updated version of the fight-and-talk strategy used by Ho Chi Minh against the French.[182]

One of *Newsweek*'s two young $50-a-day stringers in Vietnam, Bob Stokes, supplied a quick touch of color to the account:

. . . Khe Sanh, perched precariously on a laterite plateau in the northwest corner of South Vietnam, is besieged by some 40,000 communist troops hidden in the lush folds of the surrounding hills. And since the enemy started shelling Khe Sanh on January 21, more than 30 Marines have been killed there and 180 wounded bad enough to require evacuation. . . .

Survival, as *Newsweek*'s Robert Stokes learned last week during a visit to the Marine fortress, is something you have to concentrate on at Khe Sanh from the moment the wheels of your plane touch down on the metal matting of the camp's airstrip. Stokes's report:

. . . Khe Sanh's commanding officer, Colonel Lownds, a tired man who looks much older than his 47 years, gave his daily briefing about twenty minutes after the second shelling. He talked for almost half an hour—but he didn't say very much. Questions about tactics or strategy were carefully parried. But it was apparent that Lownds's Marines were playing a waiting game. All patrolling outside the camp has been discontinued, probably because the outnumbered Marines are afraid of getting sucked into a major battle outside the base's boundaries.[183]

The next week, following the loss of the Lang Vei camp and the NVA's vain attack on Hill 861 Alpha, *Time*'s sang-froid was shaken.

BIG STORY

It led off by saying Westmoreland's reputation rode on the "impending struggle for Khe Sanh," which held the nation in "complete thrall":

That is a gamble Westy was willing to take because . . . control of Khe Sanh, U.S. commanders insist, puts the Marines in a blocking position across the natural route into the northern provinces. . . .

Nonetheless, there are analysts who fear that Westmoreland may be falling into a trap set by North Vietnam Defense Minister Vo Nguyen Giap, hero of Dienbienphu and strategist of the current offensive. Indeed, there are *some chilling* parallels between Giap's winter-spring offensive in 1954 and the current Red strategy. While the communists built up their strength at Dienbienphu to 40,000 men—the estimated force now around Khe Sanh—they *simultaneously launched assaults against the French throughout Indo-China.*[184] The Tet offensive was a similar widespread assault by the communists which may have been aimed, at least in part, at pinning down U.S. troops in cities far from Khe Sanh.

Westmoreland and the Joint Chiefs of Staff, who unanimously approved his strategy, are counting on U.S. air power, firepower, and troop strength to make the difference. Unlike the French, who had few warplanes and were able to mount only 10,400 air missions to Dienbienphu in five months, the United States could equal that number in a few days with the 5,900 planes and helicopters it has in Vietnam.

"The enemy has got his blade on our Achilles' heel at Khe Sanh," says a Pentagon intelligence specialist. "He's sawing away—and we're committed to hold." The blade is also poised above Westmoreland. His reputation—and much more—is riding on the ability of that barren, hillgirt outpost to stand.[185]

A third battle story followed: "Fall of Lang Vei." It is interesting to compare the *Time* and *Newsweek* accounts—both partly gathered from survivors. Here is *Time*'s story:

The week's *only successful* communist stab was made at Lang Vei, a hilltop U.S. Special Forces camp four miles southwest of Khe Sanh on [Highway Nine]. Basically a post for interdicting communist movement into the South and for overseeing allied patrols into nearby Laos, Lang Vei was defended by some 400 South Vietnamese and Montagnard irregulars and 23 Green Berets, operating out of a deeply dug bunker made of three feet of reinforced concrete and two-inch steel plate, complete with its own ventilation system.[186] As much as any place can be in Vietnam, *it seemed an ideal outpost, immune to artillery attack* and so situated that ground troops would form a carpet of corpses if they dared attack up its hillside.

But Giap had a surprise for Lang Vei: nine Soviet light tanks, equipped with thin armor but powerful guns, the first communist use of tanks in the entire war. The tanks deployed in classic fashion east and west of the outpost, then rolled right through the camp's wire and up onto the bunker roofs, followed by North Vietnamese infantrymen. . . . Its loss did not materially affect the defense of Khe Sanh itself, said a top U.S. officer [General Abrams], but "it is crucial to us in the sense that we want to know what's coming over the Laotian border." And he added: "We thought we could hang onto it."

During the attack on Lang Vei, communist gunners poured nearly 1,500 rounds inside Khe Sanh's perimeters as a diversion—some six shells a minute in the heaviest NVA bombardment of the war.

Giap also launched probing artillery and ground attacks on Marine outposts on *surrounding Hills 861 and 558,* both supporting positions of the Marines at Khe Sanh. His men were beaten back twice, suffering 106 dead the first time and 124 the second.[187]

In the same issue, *Time*'s Don Sider drew one of the calmer, more comprehensive pictures of Khe Sanh, noting a record communist 1,500-round bombardment on February 7 which "caused no deaths," and also mentioning "outgoing Marine fire and air power" and the cumulative casualty rate of 10 percent. Sider's (or *Time*'s) chief omissions were the garrison's size and the presence of ARVN Rangers.[188] *Time* did not mention Dienbienphu.

The worst moment at Khe Sanh, Sider later recalled, came that week on February 7, after the loss of Lang Vei. It was a grim, foggy day with plenty of NVA "incoming." He and John Wheeler ran into David Douglas Duncan, the photographer, who had spent the night in Lownds's underground command post, listening to the radio as Lang Vei was overrun. "They told me to get out," Duncan told the reporters. "If any planes come in today, they told me to get on one." Colonel Lownds himself was undaunted. Some of his staff were convinced that the big attack on Khe Sanh itself would come that night. "By tomorrow morning," one of the pessimists told Sider, "we'll all probably be eating rice [as prisoners of the NVA] or we'll be dead." Sider asked Duncan if he planned to leave. Duncan, a veteran of World War II and Korea, was a Marine reserve officer. "I can't leave them," he said. That settled it for Sider. "As *Time*'s guy, I couldn't leave either," he later recalled. "I don't think leaving ever entered Wheeler's head." Duncan and Sider went to what was left of a mess shack. "We found a pot of soup on the stove, so we scrounged a couple of cans of C-rations and ladled ourselves a hot lunch. We sat on the dusty steps of the broken-down shack slurping soup from our cans and made jokes about living like a couple of bums in a hobo jungle. The soup was delicious, and so was that moment." After interviewing the newly arrived Green Beret survivors of Lang Vei ("bloody, filthy, vacant in the eyes") and dodging increasingly numerous NVA rockets, Wheeler and Sider joined some Marines in a company command post on the perimeter. "If we were going to be killed, it might as well be in a good seat," Sider recalled, "and somehow that reasoning seemed to make sense. Finally, about 4 a.m., we drifted off to sleep, listening to the radio net. That night was like the peak of a high fever. When we awoke in the morning, and found that no ground attack had come, we knew that it was over. Khe Sanh was going to make it."

Newsweek, in its issue of February 19, speculated with a vengeance in an assessment of Lang Vei and the overall situation:

Top U.S. strategists believe that Giap is preparing his *pièce de résistance* at Khe Sanh. . . .

Repeatedly, North Vietnamese units staged determined assaults against strongpoints around the camp in attempts to probe the Marines' defenses. And in one of their most successful operations of the war, the North Vietnamese used 15 Soviet-made PT-76 tanks to overrun a U.S. Special Forces camp at Lang Vei, only four miles west of Khe Sanh. *Ominously,* Soviet-made jet bombers turned up for the first time; at least two of them were spotted on an airfield near Hanoi.[189]

Despite the fall of Lang Vei, U.S. commanders *cling* to their intention to defend Khe Sanh "at all costs."[190]

U.S. strategists think Khe Sanh is worth fighting for. . . .

This opinion of Khe Sanh, however, is not shared by all observers. To begin with, critics argue that Khe Sanh's value as a western anchor is questionable, and that this was recognized long ago by the United States when it approved a South Vietnamese contingency plan to abandon the two northernmost provinces of Thua Thien and Quang Tri and regroup behind the protective barrier of the mountains near Da Nang.[191] What's more, they point out that the communist threat against Khe Sanh has lured more than one-third of General Westmoreland's available ground forces into the area—thus stripping other provinces of much-needed protection. Finally, some experts question whether Giap intends to hit Khe Sanh. . . .

If the communist siege of Khe Sanh was planned simply as a diversion for the offensive against the cities, it may well raise some agonizing problems for General Westmoreland.

For with so many U.S. troops already committed in the northern provinces, he does not have sufficient mobile reserves to beat down *instantly*[192] a second wave of attacks on the cities.[193]

Newsweek also had a lengthy story on Lang Vei:

Of all the furious actions fought in South Vietnam last week, perhaps the most *dramatic* was a *clear-cut defeat* for the United States. That was the fall of Lang Vei, a small Special Forces camp four miles west of the Marine bastion at Khe Sanh, and like many military reverses, it came as a brutal surprise. . . .

The tiny camp was *not designed for defensive fighting;* although honeycombed with protective bunkers, it operated primarily as a base for reconnaissance patrols probing Laos and the Ho Chi Minh Trail. . . .[194]

The tanks were *modern* PT-76 Soviet light amphibians that mount a 70 mm. gun. . . .[195]

The *great steel monsters* ground irresistibly forward. . . .

The camp was not important to the defense of Khe Sanh, though it did serve as a valuable watchtower. . . .[196]

The enemy's use of tanks was an *ominous* note, even though U.S. officers believed that the rugged terrain around Khe Sanh would limit their usefulness there.

Most unsettling of all was the fact that the small camp, inundated with refugees, had not been abandoned or reinforced while there was still time. . . .

And, *rightly or wrongly*, the fact that the United States had not been able to hang onto Lang Vei *could not fail* to raise doubts about the impregnability of Khe Sanh itself.[197]

Newsweek used several pet phrases in this issue; for example, "most unsettling of all" was the fact that Lang Vei had not been "reinforced." In another story ("The View from Abroad"), "most unsettling of all" was the surge of "shock and disbelief that swept Australia." Similarly, the tanks at Lang Vei were "ominous," just as were the "Soviet-made jet bombers." *Newsweek,* it might be said, merchandized the jitters.

The following week, *Time* did its best to come up with a Khe Sanh-Dienbienphu story again:

Khe Sanh, the imperiled northern position where some 6,000 U.S. Marines are surrounded by 40,000 NVA regulars, waited wearily through another week for what General Westmoreland still believes will be the largest battle of the war. Though the big enemy push failed to materialize on several predicted dates, the massed communists were indeed closing in. "I see no reason to believe that they'll stop now," said Khe Sanh's commander, Col. David E. Lownds, 47. *With new NVA bunkers spotted only 300 yards from Marine lines, corpsmen with stethoscopes knelt on Khe Sanh's red clay to see if the enemy had tunneled underneath, as occurred around Dienbienphu.* So far, they have heard nothing suspicious. Trying to discourage an all-out attack, U.S. warplanes pummeled the foggy hills around Khe Sanh in the most concentrated bombing campaign of the war. More than 7,500 fighter-bomber sorties and 100 B-52 strikes have unloaded at least 120 million pounds of bombs around the besieged base in the past three weeks—more explosive force than the two A-bombs dropped on Japan. They triggered more than 2,000 secondary explosions, signifying direct hits on ammunition or fuel dumps. But North Vietnamese artillery, mortars, and rockets still *peppered* Khe Sanh at a rate of at least 100 rounds daily, killing an average this month of two Marines a day and wounding many others.[198]

Whether the NVA masses will ever attack Khe Sanh became a matter of growing doubt and *deepening divisions.* Some ranking officers wondered if the enemy buildup there was only a diversion for the urban offensive further south or for a by-pass thrust at Quang Tri or Da Nang. There was also a *dawning realization* that, for all President Johnson's warning against another Dienbienphu, Khe Sanh could be overrun by overwhelming human-wave attacks. . . .[199]

To preclude one such possibility, intelligence officers spread the warning among U.S. bases that North Vietnamese MIG-21s may strike Khe Sanh or other places in I Corps and that Hanoi might even try to send its handful of Russian IL-28 jet bombers as far south as Saigon. *For several months, Giap is known to have been considering the use of warplanes in the south.*[200]

That concluded *Time*'s feature reporting from Khe Sanh, although both *Time* and *Newsweek* continued to describe the siege or cite its importance.

The following week, *Newsweek*'s national lead article was devoted to the war, and was as relentlessly gloomy as Administration spokesmen were "relentless optimists." *Time* and *Newsweek* were in harmony this week. Said *Newsweek:*

Lyndon Johnson's Administration seemed as besieged last week as the lonely U.S. Marine outpost at Khe Sanh. With the military situation in Vietnam looking more *precarious* by the day, the pressures intensified on every Presidential flank. . . .

Even official Washington's most relentless optimists found it hard to brighten the military picture. Only after three weeks of ferocious combat did the Marines finally seem to be routing the communists from Hue's Citadel. The enemy was building up around Saigon. Khe Sanh came under heavy artillery fire and a new barrage of questions about the quality of its defenses.[201]

Newsweek's Robert Stokes reported from Vietnam:

. . . No one on the U.S. side can say for sure why the North Vietnamese have not yet launched a major assault against Khe Sanh. . . .
Many of the trenches are still shallow, there is a shortage of barbed wire, and most of the bunkers lack adequate overhead protection. And communist guns constantly probe these weaknesses; late last week, in the enemy's biggest bombardment of the siege, 1,300 shells slammed into the base in a single day. . . .[202]
In addition to the NVA troops already in South Vietnam, two or three enemy divisions are *lurking* just north of the Demilitarized Zone.
All these units could be flung at Khe Sanh, but the gut feeling of most American officers is that the enemy forces in the DMZ area will aim to seize the two northern provinces—Quang Tri and Thua Thien—and then try to hold the ground. American commanders are relying on their planes and guns to chew up the attackers.[203]

Time, reporting events of the same week (ending February 24), after citing the 1,307-round bombardment (but not the resultant damage), described the siege as "tighter than ever," as "the NVA crept closer and closer."[204] *Time* indicated that, in effect, all U.S. installations in northern I Corps were now under similar pressure—a considerable exaggeration. The magazine also paid attention to the air war, describing the Khe Sanh bombing and resupply efforts and their limitations, and noting light U.S. plane losses. Then *Time,* well ahead of AP, said that the North Vietnamese were adding "37 mm. flak" (a rumor), and that "flyers even fear that SAMs and MIGs may soon be used around Khe Sanh." This week, *Time* cut down the number of besiegers from 40,000 to 30,000.[205]

The following week, *Time,* echoing the apprehension at home about Khe Sanh, reported:

Nearly half the 10 U.S. combat divisions in Vietnam are jammed into I Corps . . . facing a potent concentration of communist regulars. . . . There is growing concern that the 5,000 Marines at the besieged outpost of Khe Sanh can be overrun by the North Vietnamese infantry divisions that are *inexorably* tightening the circle around them. Warned Senate Armed Services Committee Chairman Richard Russell: "I am afraid this position may be difficult to defend. I hope we will be able to reinforce our troops there sufficiently." Even South Vietnam's President Nguyen Van Thieu is *said* by associates to believe that the Americans should *evacuate Khe Sanh*[206] rather than risk a defeat that could curdle U.S. opinion about the war.[207]

On March 11, *Newsweek* also succumbed:

The signs of a tightening communist siege of the U.S. Marine fortress at Khe Sanh were unmistakable, traced as they were in the zigzag pattern of North Vietnamese trenches worming their way through the red soil toward the shallow American perimeter. . . .

. . . it became harder than ever for U.S. copters to land at Khe Sanh. Machine guns peppered the transports as they dropped down to the metal landing strip; one C-123 was shot down and almost every incoming plane was hit. And if the skies were *perilous,* the lush terrain around Khe Sanh was even more *deadly.* A platoon-size Marine patrol that ventured less than half a mile from the base was chopped to pieces in an ambush, and a second platoon sent to its aid was not even able to recover all the dead. Meantime, a different kind of *terror stalked* the men inside the bastion; under an *incessant, nerve-shattering artillery barrage,* the 5,000-man Marine garrison has taken painful losses—1,200 casualties (mostly light wounds) in six weeks. . . .

Yet all the Marines could do was dig in and wait in impotent rage for the North Vietnamese to launch a ground attack.

Late last week, it seemed for a moment that the showdown had begun. Three platoons of North Vietnamese sappers crept through a predawn mist to plant the thin tubes of explosives known as bangalore torpedoes under the wire along a part of the defenses manned by a 500-man battalion of South Vietnamese Rangers.[208]

. . . a flight of giant B-52 bombers dropped their heavy bombs only 750 yards in front of the Ranger positions.

"I thought this might be the big attack," said the base commander, Col. David Lownds, "but it was just another probe."[209]

The shelling, of course, was "nerve-shattering," especially to reporters, but not "incessant"; the losses were "painful," like all losses, but relatively light. *Newsweek* failed to note that replacements arrived to fill the ranks.

After Westmoreland, on March 6, suggested that Hue, not Khe Sanh, was now the prime enemy target, *Time* scooped UPI on NVA troop movements and "truck convoys" away from the siege, reporting: "North Vietnamese Army units along the DMZ appear to be shifting eastward, away from Khe Sanh, toward Quang Tri city or Hue. The 304th NVA Division, which was south of Khe Sanh, has been moving with truck convoys through the A Shau Valley toward

Hue.[210] If Hue rather than Khe Sanh is the enemy's big target, that will not bother the allies."[211]

No troop movements away from Khe Sanh were mentioned in *Newsweek* on March 18 (the issue deadline was March 9). Westmoreland's suggestion that Khe Sanh was no longer the main enemy target was quickly brushed aside with: "The truth of course is that neither Westmoreland nor anyone else can be certain of enemy intentions." The magazine also came out against the President's Vietnam policy; "More of the Same Won't Do" was the lead article, and the "Agony of Khe Sanh" was the label on the cover: a color photograph of a Marine ducking a spectacular explosion at the base. That week, Khe Sanh was *Newsweek*'s "symbol" of the whole war.

There was an odd juxtaposition in the same issue. The sheaf of articles written in New York depicted the Khe Sanh garrison as "tortured," an easy target for the "brilliant" Giap, and suffering what to lay readers might seem heavy punishment. Pictures showed Marines mostly dodging fire, dying, getting wounded—doomed. But a firsthand report from Khe Sanh by Merton Perry, without minimizing the danger and discomfort (a "miserable place"), found the "agony" not so agonizing. He reported the March weather improving, the casualties lower, and the Marines displaying "high" morale:

> The North Vietnamese are busy all around Khe Sanh. Borrowing from their own military history, they have begun to dig trenches that zigzag up to within a hundred yards of the Marine lines. So far, there are only a few trenches—nothing like the intricate, spidery maze dug by the Vietminh at Dienbienphu—but the Marines suspect that the communists have also started to tunnel down toward the base from the back slopes of the ridges that surround the Khe Sanh plateau. . . .
>
> . . . The greatest danger, however, comes from the daily barrage by NVA mortars, rockets, and artillery pieces. . . . The constant shelling is . . . enough to make the men who live there wonder constantly about what is coming next. And the wonder and the waiting inevitably tauten the nerves of the 5,000 Marines who crouch inside Khe Sanh.
>
> . . . .
>
> Despite their isolation the vast majority of the Marines at Khe Sanh—from the lowliest, tiredest grunt on up to Col. David Lownds . . . remain totally confident. A major factor behind this optimism is the awesome firepower of the U.S. forces.[212]

The pessimism originated mostly in New York.[213] The Khe Sanh cover story was *Newsweek*'s biggest effort of the Tet period. It is worth citing as an indication of how high the Khe Sanh-Dienbienphu "fever" could run, even as the situation in reality was easing; and of how far *Newsweek* had gone in taking over *Time*'s old role as an "advocacy" magazine on the Vietnam issue. Along with the "Agony" story, the *Newsweek* editors also ventured into mathematics:

. . . U.S. commanders have sought to maintain four-to-one combat superiority. But in the aftermath of the communist Tet offensive, that advantage has virtually vanished. Today, for the first time in the war, the United States and its allies face their enemy on a one-to-one basis. . . .

. . . Military men in Saigon have been forced to revise their estimate of the enemy's order of battle to include a total of 235 maneuver battalions—which is almost exactly the number of allied battalions.[214]

During the rest of the Tet period, *Time*'s interest in Khe Sanh (and Vietnam) waned. *Newsweek* did not return to the base in print. However, it ran a brief feature as a follow-up to its "Agony" effort: It described the pain and fortitude of the Marines wounded and flown in from Khe Sanh (and elsewhere) being treated at "Delta Med" (Company D, 3rd Medical Battalion) at Dong Ha.[215] There, at least, the agony was real.

If *Time*'s editors could be faulted for their earlier unrealistic view of the Vietnam War, Don Sider noted in 1975, they also deserved credit for a "sensible approach to Khe Sanh," resisting "easy comparisons to Dienbienphu and the temptation to overdramatize." He added that it was always tempting to improve the story with "some drama." At siege's end in early April, for example, Sider walked the perimeter with Colonel Lownds. "In the sunset, Lownds stood very tall, looking out, for the first time, the master of all he could see. It had to be his supreme moment, I thought. He had survived and won. I asked him what he was thinking, expecting a properly heroic victory statement—something out of Douglas MacArthur, or maybe John Wayne.

" 'I've just been wishing,' Lownds said softly, 'that I could meet with the man who was running their side. I'd like to compare notes with him.' "

9

South Vietnamese
Performance

The following story was carried by the Associated Press on February 16, 1968:

ROCHESTER, Mich. (AP)—Professor John Kenneth Galbraith of Harvard University today predicted that important units of the South Vietnamese Army will either disappear into the woods or join the Vietcong within the next few months.

Galbraith said the defections will occur as part of what he described as "further collapse" of the South Vietnamese government.

"It's been an open secret for a long while," Galbraith said, "that important units of the South Vietnamese forces up in the 1st Corps area or [in the] 25th Division south of Saigon have a close working relationship with the Vietcong and will either disappear into the woods or join the Vietcong."

Galbraith is chairman of Americans for Democratic Action, which endorsed Senator Eugene McCarthy of Minnesota last week as a peace candidate challenging President Johnson for the Democratic Presidential nomination.

He gave his views in an interview today before speaking at Oakland University in Rochester, about 30 miles north of Detroit. . . .

Galbraith said his conclusion of imminent collapse of the South Vietnamese government and army is based on a "careful reading" of news accounts of the war.

The one unassailable truth about the South Vietnamese performance at Tet is that, contrary to the expectations of Galbraith and others of similar opinion—and notwithstanding the fears of Washington officials—there was no "collapse." The Thieu government and its armed forces muddled through, abetted, then as in 1972, by U.S. help and by Hanoi's own mistakes and miscalculations. Holding up during February and March of 1968 represented neither a shining victory for Saigon nor a sudden political regeneration. But the unexpected resilience of the South Vietnamese had major implications for Americans: Among other things, it helped to undercut military arguments in Washington for a major U.S. troop increase and led, instead, to "Vietnamization" as a way out for the Johnson Administration and its successor. As for the long-suffering South Vietnamese, the Tet experience forced President Thieu to begin to shape his regime in response to the war's demands, although he was never to resolve the conflict between the needs of his country and what he perceived as the practical necessities of his own political survival.

Yet, Professor Galbraith's predictions should not now be judged with undue severity. The overwhelming *journalistic* fact about the South Vietnamese performance at Tet was that it was rarely reported firsthand. Moreover, the few firsthand reports there were, received little prominence in the United States. This "dim-out" contrasted with the attention given to South Vietnamese flaws in secondhand Tet commentary and analysis from Saigon, New York, and Washington and in the growing election-year debate back home.

Old journalistic habits were at work here, as well as the already noted general unfamiliarity of the American press corps with Vietnam and the Vietnamese. Newsmen in Saigon, for example, covered the Thieu regime's response to Tet much as most of their colleagues at home covered the Johnson Administration in Washington: they reported pronouncements; reaction statements; plans, such as those for full mobilization; hazy official statistics, such as refugee totals; and votes and debates in the legislature. Crucial pre-Tet decisions by Thieu, notably his popularity-seeking orders lifting the Saigon curfew and granting the ARVN a 50 percent leave for the Tet holiday, were given little prominence in press explanations of South Vietnamese failures at Tet. Instead, under pressure to explain Hanoi's ability to achieve tactical surprise, a good many newsmen, especially at home, dredged up Saigon's old sins. They cited, as they had since the mid-1960s, such things as official corruption, political favoritism in the Army, and failure to carry out land reform. Had Thieu been "popular," or had the South Vietnamese people possessed the "will to fight," so the argument often went, the Tet surprise would not have occurred. Less instant analysis and more aggressive firsthand reporting would have led to other, more mundane explanations. This chapter is divided into two parts. First, we shall deal with the coverage of the South Vietnamese military and police forces during Tet. Then, we shall consider the more conventional reporting of the Thieu government's reactions to the crisis.

South Vietnamese Military Forces at Tet

As Tet broke, the South Vietnamese military, to American audiences, were almost as "faceless" as the North Vietnamese and Vietcong. Rare had been the television or print feature on the ARVN GI or officer, the description of the South Vietnamese soldier's life in the field or garrison. As we have noted earlier in this book, the ethnocentric emphasis placed by U.S. newsmen on American GIs reflected, above all, the wants of their editors at home. It also resulted from the relative ease of access to American units and their commanders. And, in more substantive terms, this journalistic emphasis matched the takeover in 1965–67 by American units of the so-called "big war" against communist main force battalions and regiments. In short, there were few incentives for newsmen to accompany even the elite ARVN units on operations or to study at firsthand the overall ARVN performance in the war.

In the wake of the Tet attacks, the South Vietnamese military in Saigon, for its part, did nothing to soften its reserved attitude toward newsmen—an attitude common to most Asian regimes. In Da Nang, the U.S. Marine information advisor at the ARVN I Corps headquarters produced useful battle chronologies and background data as February wore on. Lieutenant General Lam, the military commander (and war lord) of I Corps, genially received the press, even if his judgments occasionally clashed with reality. But in Saigon, where the war wrap-ups were written, the Vietnamese Joint General Staff did not ease its polite reticence—partly, newsmen suspected, because slow ARVN field communications left the JGS, and Thieu himself, in the dark about fast-breaking Tet events. MACV spokesmen at JUSPAO briefings conveyed some notion of ARVN activity, but not much.

The result was that, at Tet as earlier, U.S. reporters (including this one) usually got their impressions about ARVN secondhand from U.S. Mission officials, Vietnamese reporters, or U.S. advisors at base camps or province headquarters, and rarely observed ARVN troops on combat operations. Even post-action or between-action interviews by newsmen with U.S. combat advisors, or with ARVN officials who spoke English or French, were uncommon during Tet.[1] Yet the ARVN performance, good and bad, was as significant as anything that happened during Tet in Vietnam.

Out of a total allied force of about 1.3 million, the South Vietnamese armed forces numbered 643,116 on December 31, 1967. Regulars (Army, Navy, Air Force, Marine Corps) accounted for 342,951; Regional Forces (RF), 151,376; and Popular Forces (PF), 148,789. (An increase to 685,000 men had been publicly promised by then Premier Ky on July 27, 1967.[2]) At Tet, the losses among these forces continued to exceed those of the Americans, as had been the case since the United States lost its first serviceman in Vietnam in 1961. Somehow, despite its much publicized mediocre or corrupt leadership; its high desertion rates; its substandard logistics, weaponry, and training; and its neglect by MACV and Washington (implicitly acknowledged even by Westmoreland), the ARVN stayed on the line in January–February 1968.

At Tet, the ARVN and South Vietnamese militia were deployed in pacification areas and in and around the towns and cities—Hanoi's chief targets—while more mobile U.S. forces were largely oriented toward enemy main force units in the woods, hills, and on the borders. Few U.S. installations outside the Saigon-Bien Hoa area were targets of enemy ground attacks at Tet. But ARVN compounds and headquarters were badly hit. ARVN suffered the lion's share of the allied losses in Saigon and Hue; and at Khe Sanh, the little 37th Ranger Battalion was the target of the only NVA assaults against the main base perimeter. South Korean, Australian, or U.S. relief forces saved the day in at least a dozen places, notably Saigon, Hoi An, Quang Tri city, Hue, Tan Son Nhut air base, and Vinh Long. American helicopters and fighter-bombers flew almost everywhere; U.S. air and naval transport moved ARVN reinforcements and supplies. But, with their U.S. advisors, the undermanned ARVN and the local militia did the ground fighting alone in most of the rest of the 36 (of 44) province capitals, 64 (of 242) district capitals, and 50 hamlets initially assaulted at Tet.[3] The South Vietnamese units' performance varied widely under the shock, but, overall, their stout resistance was an essential factor in Hanoi's military failure.

What was the media's reaction to this South Vietnamese performance?

The overall role of the ARVN during the Tet period was given only fragmentary emphasis in war wrap-ups; but there was far more indication of ARVN's battlefield existence in this category of news story than in features, analyses, or pictures.

The AP and UPI generally cited "allied" (American and South Vietnamese) troops as reacting to the initial Tet attacks on January 30–31. In February and March, all told, AP published 53 omnibus leads (for a.m. newspapers) on the Tet fighting which indicated that "South Vietnamese" or "allies," not just Americans, were involved in the action. Our UPI files are incomplete, but a roughly similar proportion appears. Here is one example:

SAIGON (UPI)—South Vietnamese paratroopers supported by U.S. jet fighter-bombers fought a fierce battle Sunday with a large Vietcong force equipped with antiaircraft weapons at the edge of the U.S. Tan Son Nhut air base outside Saigon.

The Vietcong, who had bombarded Tan Son Nhut with mortar and rocket shells in the past week, held a heavily fortified position 1.3 miles west of the perimeters of the giant U.S. base. They had at least two .51 caliber machine guns and fired them at low-flying aircraft.[4]

The Washington *Post,* in its daily war wrap-ups, usually rewritten from the wires, put "South Vietnamese" or "allies" in the lead 22 times, but in the headlines only 11, in 60 days. The *Post* ran six other stories or analyses primarily devoted to ARVN or Regional or Popular Forces, and none got on page one.[5] Out of 30 *Post* pictures of troops in combat, only eight dealt with South Vietnamese soldiers or police.

The New York *Times,* in its war wrap-ups, put "allies" or "South Vietnamese" in the lead paragraphs 20 times, and 20 times in the headlines. The *Times* ran only four other stories in two months devoted to ARVN, and none went on page one.[6] Out of 15 *Times* pictures of troops in combat, only three were of South Vietnamese soldiers or police. Only one photograph, the February 1 execution of a Vietcong prisoner by Brig. Gen. Nguyen Ngoc Loan, director of the national police (see below), got on page one.

Television anchormen, reading, as usual, rewritten wire-service reports, often mentioned "allies" or South Vietnamese forces on the evening news shows under study. CBS, for example, did so on 31 nights. But the proportion of film reports from Vietnam in which South Vietnamese troops or police were shown in action at all was small: 18 out of 118 (12 in Saigon, one in Hue, five elsewhere).

Seven of these were devoted *largely* to depicting ARVN performance: three on ABC, two on CBS, and two on NBC.

Neither *Time* nor *Newsweek* devoted a single story to ARVN per
se, and both magazines commented only sparsely on ARVN performance.

The Officials Ignore ARVN

In broad terms, the U.S. government, in its vast flow of Tet pronouncements, said very little about ARVN performance at Tet, and
what it did say did not excite news editors.

Earlier, on January 19, 1968, Lt. Gen. Lewis W. Walt, Assistant
Commander, USMC, and former commander (1965–67) of III MAF
in Vietnam, told a Denver audience that the ARVN "are not as
proficient as our forces. They haven't had the training they should
have and they do not have strong leadership throughout, but I think
that these things are understandable. They really started building
their military forces in 1954, and they have been fighting a war ever
since."[7]

Also shortly before Tet, Eugene V. Rostow, Undersecretary of
State for Political Affairs, said:

It is not unnatural that Americans want to learn what Americans are
doing in that distant war. It is not unnatural to see headlines about major
battles, at which a hundred or more of our boys lose their lives. We understand this. We understand, too, that perhaps the hundred Vietnamese
militiamen and soldiers who, at the same time, lose their lives in a hundred small engagements protecting their wives and children in a hundred
hamlets throughout the country don't make as good copy. But they are
there, fighting and dying just the same.[8]

Defense Secretary McNamara also discussed the ARVN in his
gloomy "posture statement" in the Senate on January 22 (released
February 1). Reports of the statement were carried in both the *Post*
(on page one) and the *Times,* but without McNamara's comments on
the ARVN.

Then came Tet. On February 10, Secretary of State Dean Rusk,
addressing a New Jersey group, laid down the line: "With very few
exceptions, South Vietnam troops fought with courage and persistence. Their record in the last 12 days should lay to rest once and for
all the myth that the South Vietnamese troops won't fight."[9] This
remark was omitted from wire-service accounts of Rusk's speech.

On February 14, General Wheeler, Chairman of the Joint Chiefs, had this to say when questioned by the press:

Q.: There have been severe dislocations—both socially, economically, politically, and militarily—in Vietnam as a result of the guerrilla raids. What's the outlook for the future now?

Wheeler: Well, there are pluses and minuses, as there always are in any military action. On the minus side, the South Vietnamese to date have lost something over 2,000 killed. This, of course, has eroded the strength of their units. Moreover, a number of their men were on Tet holiday leave, some of them have not been able to get back to their units because of the difficulty of travel. These are the minuses. On the other hand, they have defeated the enemy, and troops that defeat the enemy usually have their morale go up. General Westmoreland told me this morning on the telephone that yesterday (last night our time) he visited the ARVN 51st Infantry Regiment, up in the northern provinces [south of Da Nang], and found that their morale was extremely high because they had a most successful battle with North Vietnamese regular forces [the 2nd NVA Division, which tried and failed to reach Da Nang].[10]

This statement got no play in the media either.

On March 1, President Johnson added his bit:

The South Vietnamese are drafting this month all their 19-year-olds. In June, they will get their 18-year-olds, although our average draftee is 20.4 years old.

If we had drafted as many men according to our population as they have drafted, instead of our having a little over 3 million in our service, we would have 9 million.

If we had lost as many men according to our population as the South Vietnamese have lost—you hear all of these ugly things about it—it wouldn't be 19,000—it would be hundreds of thousands.[11]

It was quite clear that, in terms of what they talked about most in public, the Administration and the military in Washington were as ethnocentric as U.S. officials and newsmen in Vietnam. During Tet, harried public figures were largely responding to perceived political problems rather than attempting to sort out the overall situation in Vietnam for the public. One has the sense that, to the Administration, in February 1968, the ARVN was a worrisome but unknown enigma.

In Vietnam, oddly enough, General Westmoreland did not mention ARVN performance during his initial press briefing on February 1, but dealt primarily with the foe. Nor did his subordinates publicly

342   BIG STORY

discuss the ARVN in any detail. Indeed, newsmen asked Generals
Davidson, Chaisson, and Weyand and other officers no questions
concerning ARVN performance. The focus was on the enemy, American tactics, and the question of what was coming next. Ambassador
Bunker, however, on February 3, told newsmen (who reported it
without attribution) that the ARVN had held up well (i.e., no units
had defected) and that no popular uprising had occurred—two basic
U.S. Mission gauges of enemy failure.[12]

The one command-level evaluation of ARVN by MACV came on
February 8 from Gen. Creighton Abrams, then Westmoreland's deputy with special responsibilities for advising ARVN. Abrams was
fresh from a rapid tour of the eight ARVN division headquarters,
each with its American advisors, in the three corps zones south of I
Corps. Along with a discussion of enemy tactics and possible Tet objectives (such as seizing and using ARVN artillery, airfields, and
armor in the Saigon, Bien Hoa, and Central Highlands areas),
Abrams spoke highly of some ARVN division commanders' performances and cited no command flaws. But, by implication, he made
clear that other commanders had fumbled, and that the 18th and
25th ARVN Divisions around Saigon were hardly outstanding. (Har-
vey Myerson, author of *Vinh Long,* a firsthand account of pacification in the Delta, and one of the few journalist-authors in Vietnam to
spend any length of time in one place, learned, on his return to the
Delta after Tet, that General Tan, the commander of the 7th Division
at My Tho, had gone into a state of shock during the Tet attacks.
Similarly, at Can Tho, I was later told, Col. John Hill, the deputy
U.S. advisor to ARVN's IV Corps [the Delta], in effect took over
operational command on January 30–31, as Maj. Gen. Nguyen Van
Manh, the Corps commander—later sacked—retreated to his home
and remained there during the enemy attacks.) With the exception of
the 22nd ARVN Division at Ban Me Thuot and the Airborne and
the 5th Ranger Group around Saigon, Abrams also reported, the
ARVN commanders, in line with President Thieu's orders, had
granted Tet leaves which cut the operational strength of their battalions to 50 percent or less—150 to 250 men. This disclosure of the
leave figure was picked up by the AP—six days after the fact had
been cited by Tom Buckley in the New York *Times* and three days
after UPI had it.[13] Yet, this crucial reduction in fighting strength in
the middle of a war—a bizarre case of gross negligence by Thieu in

the face of advance warnings—was not necessarily a gauge of ARVN *ability* or willingness to fight.

On February 24, Ambassador Komer held a news conference to discuss the as yet vaguely measured impact of the offensive on pacification. Komer, three weeks after the initial attacks, was worried about the "defensive-mindedness" of the regular ARVN commanders, who were remaining close to the cities and towns; he said that only 35 of the 51 ARVN battalions assigned pre-Tet to support pacification were back in the countryside.[14] This point got into wire reports as well as the *Times* and the *Post*.

On February 25, in his lengthy interview with AP General Manager Wes Gallagher, Westmoreland gave a "chins-up" view of ARVN's performance, but cited none of Abrams' specifics:

Q.: What is your view of the performance of the South Vietnamese Army, since it was expected that it hold the cities? It is understood that the Vietnamese in a number of places were able to hold their compounds but unable to drive the Vietcong out without the help of the American forces.

Westmoreland: In general, the South Vietnamese Army performed well, indeed. As an example, all 11 of the Vietnamese division commanders were at their posts at the time of the attack and commanded their units effectively.

As I've already pointed out, the cities were attacked from within by the enemy who had infiltrated into them under the cover of crowds and the noise of Tet firecrackers.

Few cities of Vietnam are organized as fortresses. However, certain key [ARVN] installations within the cities are protected by fortifications. Therefore, these compounds were, in most cases, able to hold out, but reinforcements in many cases had to be brought in from outside to drive the enemy out of the cities. These reinforcements were both Vietnamese and American.[15]

On March 6, in his next major session with the press at MACV, Westmoreland (not for attribution) cited ARVN's Tet losses to date as 4,000 dead compared with 2,000 for the United States. He showed graphs to illustrate ARVN losses by division, and discussed the crucial "battle of the rebuild"—South Vietnamese efforts to get their units back up to strength and their bases and training facilities back in operation:

As far as ARVN is concerned, they're working hard to recover their losses. Vietnamese ground forces suffered almost 10,000 casualties, but so

far they have been able to provide over 14,000 replacements. These are
figures that have been gathered by my staff or me. . . .

You'll note the 1st Division suffered very heavy losses, because they
bore the brunt of the battle in Hue. But they have been able to provide
over 2,000 replacements for them.

. . . .

As far as the RF-PF [militia] are concerned, my figures, or I would
say our reports from the field, which are not conclusive, are that most of
the RF companies are intact and on their posts. And they have in general
fought very well. But 66 percent of the Popular Forces are at their posts.
Some are still in provincial towns and cities. Some of the posts were overrun and members killed or captured. About 60 percent of the RD [Revo-
lutionary Development] cadre are reportedly at their posts.

Most of Westmoreland's briefing, however, was devoted to discussion of enemy intentions against Hue, Khe Sanh, and Saigon, and, at
newsmen's insistence, of activation of a new Army-run "Provisional
Corps Vietnam" command at Phu Bai under overall Marine command. The General's remarks about the ARVN largely escaped notice in the resulting page-one dispatches. This reporter saved the
ARVN detail for a subsequent wrap-up piece four days later.[16]

All told, very few substantive details on ARVN performance were
volunteered (or *sought by* newsmen) in official U.S. briefings in Saigon or in press conferences at home. Nevertheless, newsmen in Saigon had these available "official" facts by the end of February 1968:
(1) the ARVN had been on 50 percent leave at Tet (Abrams); (2)
no ARVN unit had defected to the foe and few units had been overrun (Bunker); (3) few ARVN installations had been lost to enemy
assault, but the ARVN, manifestly, was taken by surprise and failed
to shield the cities; (4) ARVN troops and RF-PF lost twice as many
men killed as the Americans (weekly casualty reports); (5) ill-
prepared ARVN troops had borne the brunt of the city fighting at
Hue and Saigon, as elsewhere, but U.S. troops had to intervene in
Saigon, Hue, Ben Tre, and a dozen other places to help drive the
enemy out (Abrams, MACV communiqués); (6) ARVN commanders varied widely in effectiveness once the battle began
(Abrams); (7) ARVN commanders, having "resecured" the cities
and towns, were reluctant in late February to redeploy their garrisons
to the hinterland, fearing another thrust at the cities (Komer).

These "official" facts stand up well in retrospect. However, they
got relatively little attention from the media. What was reported

about the ARVN varied in accuracy, quality, and relevance, and seldom went beyond the clichés of the past.

The Wire Services: Action Stories

An early sidebar by AP's Peter Arnett on the civilian Americans who fought in Saigon included a jibe at the South Vietnamese:

SAIGON (AP)—The tall young American civilian crouched behind the high concrete wall, a pistol strapped to his thigh and a high-powered rifle in his hands. His clothes were dirty and he hadn't shaved for two days.

Ron Fleming, 26, a Harvard graduate, was defending his Saigon home. Like scores of other Americans in the embattled Vietnamese capital, he had discovered that law and order [sic] had broken down in many places and it was every man for himself. . . .

. . . .

The Americans have seen *no Vietnamese police or troops* since fighting erupted around their compound early Wednesday morning. At daylight Wednesday *they decided to defend themselves.*

One of them commented: "If the Vietnamese won't defend their capital, what will they defend?"[17]

AP's Lewis Simons found himself in Ban Me Thuot in the Central Highlands when the enemy hit on January 30, and filed a lengthy piece. Following standard journalistic practice, Simons was not with the ARVN defenders, but with his own countrymen—in the compound of the U.S. advisory team to the ARVN 23rd Division—and he got only a dim, distant view of South Vietnamese troops:

BAN ME THUOT, Vietnam (AP)—This peaceful mountain town had been basking on the outskirts of the war in Vietnam until Tuesday.

Then about 2,000 [North] Vietnamese soldiers and Vietcong struck with savage fury against a government force of about the same size, plus 200 U.S. advisors.

. . . .

. . . Wednesday, two government armored personnel carriers smashed through the wall on the far side of the soccer field. They were supposed to station themselves there and hold the line against the communists. But, *a few minutes later, they rumbled off, leaving a gap in the wall.*

When darkness came Wednesday night it was through this hole that communist machine-gunners and riflemen aimed their bullets at the bungalow [in the U.S. compound]. Cracking and whining, the rounds thudded into the wooden building, splintering walls and forcing the Americans to dash for cover.

. . . .

When the sun came up Thursday, burning the chill out of the air, the U.S. compound had held.
The South Vietnamese troops also appeared to be holding.[18]

Eddie Adams, the AP photographer, filed a short vignette on February 2 which actually showed the ARVN in action:

SAIGON (AP)—A group of Vietcong troops were eating soup at a sidewalk Chinese restaurant in Saigon this morning when the South Vietnamese Rangers caught them.

"The restaurant was their base of operations. We caught them at breakfast," said a Ranger officer with a grin.

The battle that started at breakfast in northwest Saigon was still going in the middle of the afternoon. At stake was control of an area of squatters' shacks, refugee camps, and an occasional concrete house owned by wealthy Vietnamese.

The residents fled Thursday after the Vietcong moved into their homes during the series of attacks in South Vietnam's capital.

The Rangers called in four helicopter gunships. The helicopters came in, spurting rockets and gunfire. . . .

The battle was vicious and at close quarter. The tough little Rangers with their steel helmets and camouflage uniforms slipped from house to house.[19]

Another description of the ARVN in action came from Arnett:

SAIGON (AP)—From the seventh tee of Saigon's only golf course you could drive a two-iron shot Saturday into the headquarters of a Vietcong infantry company.

The communists are clinging tenaciously to a cluster of homes in the bamboo shrubbery adjoining the course. The battle of Saigon has moved out here inch by inch as U.S. and Vietnamese troops attempt to dislodge enemy infiltrators in house-to-house fighting.

Late Saturday afternoon the Vietnamese 8th Paratroop Battalion fought a sharp, vicious clash with the communist company in the bamboo. Flanked by enemy snipers, the paratroopers moved back to regroup and re-attack Sunday.

"This might take us several days," commented the senior U.S. advisor with the paratroopers, Capt. Wesley Taylor. . . .[20]

AP did not report the 50 percent ARVN leave in Arnett's widely published "truckload of flowers" story on February 3, but ascribed enemy success in penetrating Saigon to lifting of the normal curfew. It went on, saying that this success "throws into doubt" the *generalized* "effectiveness" of Vietnamese security around Saigon since the departure of the Americans' 199th Light Infantry Brigade in December. AP also added a bit of nonhistory, quoting an anonymous veteran of the French Indo-China War, who ascribed France's defeat to "the time when they were forced to use French troops to defend the cities." In fact, the parallel was false, for the French always used their own as well as Vietnamese troops to garrison the cities.

But no portrayal of the South Vietnamese military and security forces had the impact of Eddie Adams' photographs—and ABC's and NBC's film—of Brig. Gen. Nguyen Ngoc Loan executing a captured, mufti-clad Vietcong officer near the An Quang Pagoda.

The *AP Log* of February 3, 1968, carried this account, entitled "Pictures at an Execution":

At the height of the battle for Saigon, Vietnamese Marines captured and disarmed a Vietcong officer. As they led him away from the battle area, Eddie Adams, AP staff photographer newly back for his third tour of duty in Vietnam; Howard Tuckner and cameraman Vo Su of NBC-TV; and a Vietnam Army photographer watched the developing tableau.

As the Marines and the prisoner neared the group, South Vietnam's national police chief, Brig. Gen. Nguyen Ngoc Loan, came up.

"The shooting occurred so quickly that I got the picture through reaction," Adams relates. "Loan gave no indication that he was going to shoot the man. I was about five feet away and had my camera with a 35 mm. lens ready when Loan strolled up. As Loan's hand holding the pistol came up, so did my camera—but I didn't expect what happened. I just shot by instinct.

"Impassively, Loan put his pistol in his holster and walked over to where we were standing. He said softly in English, 'They killed many Americans and many of my men.' Then he walked away."

Adams' radio-photoed set of pictures on the execution was given smash play around the world. The key shot showed the instant the bullet slammed into the victim's head, his features in a grimace. Previous Adams photos of the Vietnam War and of civilian suffering figured in his being named the New York Press Photographers' Association "Photographer of the Year" for 1967.

The AP filed a short "balancing" story to go with the pictures:

SAIGON (AP)—The chief of South Vietnam's national police executed a Vietcong officer captured in a fight near the An Quang Pagoda today.

The chief, Brig. Gen. Nguyen Ngoc Loan, fired a revolver bullet into the head of the officer, a tousle-haired Vietnamese in civilian garb who had been seized by government Marines.

"They killed many Americans and many of my people," Loan said.

Communist bands, in addition to gunning for allied military personnel, had staged several executions since the outbreak of the fighting here Wednesday. Wives and children of Vietnamese officers were among the victims.[21]

The *Times's* page-one display of the picture on February 2 came under the headline: "Street Clashes Go On in Vietnam, Foe Still Holds Parts of Cities; Johnson Pledges Never to Yield." Underneath Adams' photo was another of an ARVN colonel holding his child slain by the Vietcong—to provide "atrocities-on-both-sides" balance. However, the *Times* also printed the whole three-photo sequence of the Loan execution on page twelve.

At the *Post* home office there was some argument over whether to pair the photos of Loan and of the bereaved ARVN colonel on page one. The decision was taken not to pair. There was only one other page-one picture of a Vietnamese officer in the *Post* during the entire Tet period—of Maj. Gen. Nguyen Duc Thang, ARVN commander in the Delta.

Was the prominence given to the Loan photographs by newspapers a conscious effort, as the *Times's* picture editor, John Morris, suggested, to show the "horror of war," and of the Vietnam War in particular? What *information* did the photographs actually convey? That a brave but overwrought South Vietnamese police director, with a history of emotional instability, inexcusably shot an enemy taken in civilian clothes in the heat of battle? That our South Vietnamese allies were atrocity-prone? That Asians value life cheaply? That South Vietnam was a brutal police state?

My subsequent conversations with news editors and photographers, and my reading of the *AP Log,* suggest that little ideology was involved. Even the hawkish New York *Daily News* put the picture on page one.[22] In most places, one may assume, the decision to feature the Loan story stemmed simply from among the oldest journalistic instincts: Not every day do newspapers get a close-up picture of one man shooting another at "the instant the bullet slammed into the victim's head, his features in a grimace," as the *AP Log* noted.

UPI's coverage of South Vietnamese forces included a scoop on February 5 on the 50 percent ARVN holiday leave, which AP did not report until after Abrams' briefing three days later. But the New York editors, in recycling Eugene Risher's morning-paper story from Saigon for the evening editions, decided, as was usual wire-service practice, to give it some extra drama. In the eighth paragraph of his original story, as published on page one of the Philadelphia *Inquirer* on February 6, Risher wrote: "On the night the [Tet] truce started, and a few hours before the attack, newsmen who were trying to get information from the Vietnamese Joint General Staff complained that no one was there and that 'a corporal was running the war' on the Vietnamese side." The reworked story dropped the allusion to "newsmen," and said flatly, in the second paragraph: "A corporal was in charge at General Staff Headquarters in Saigon."[23]

Risher's original story reflected fairly well what was known or thought at the time about ARVN among the U.S. military, albeit with a bit more "color":

SAIGON, Feb. 5 (UPI)—The biggest communist offensive of the war caught much of the South Vietnamese Army with cannon covered, tanks parked, officers on holidays at beaches and mountain resorts, and enlisted men on furlough with families.

Despite warnings from the U.S. Military Command that large-scale attacks were imminent, up to 50 percent of the men in many units had left their posts to spend the Lunar New Year holiday, Tet, with their wives and children in Saigon. . . .

. . . .

High-ranking American officers did little Monday to hide their disgust at the performance of the South Vietnamese Army, although they had praise for individual units that bore the brunt of the fighting after they got started. . . .

. . . .

"The attack came during the Tet truce, at a time when the Vietnamese had their guard down," one ranking U.S. political officer said.

A high-level officer on Gen. William C. Westmoreland's staff, when asked to assess the performance of the Vietnamese in battle, said: "They did very well once they got started and I think General Westmoreland would say the same."[24]

The Networks: Better Than Most

Coverage by the networks of the ARVN performance reflected the wire-service raw material on which they so heavily depended. The focus was primarily on American and enemy forces. However, in the initial Saigon fighting at least, network television did better in *showing* the ARVN in action than anyone else. Moreover, it can be argued, television did better than the other media in terms of firsthand coverage of ARVN outside the capital.

As noted, Howard Tuckner of NBC was one of those who (quite by luck) found himself on hand with a cameraman when the Loan execution occurred. His report was introduced by Chet Huntley:

Huntley: A pall of smoke lay over Saigon where American and South Vietnamese forces struggled to eliminate stubborn pockets of Vietcong resistance. The Americans even battled the enemy near the Saigon home of Gen. William C. Westmoreland, the American commander. There was fighting in the Cholon section where the city's Chinese live, but the conflict was sharpest at the An Quang Pagoda, near the Saigon racetrack. Here via satellite is a report from NBC News correspondent Howard Tuckner on the battle for Saigon.

Tuckner: In this part of Saigon, government troops were ordered to get as much resolved as they could. Fighting was only a block from the An Quang Pagoda, a Buddhist church the Vietcong had been using as their headquarters with the reported approval of the militant Buddhist monk, Thich Tri Quang. An hour earlier, the Vietcong flag had flown from the rooftop. Now snipers were up there and government troops tried to locate their positions. [Words lost in fire.] South Vietnamese Marines considered all civilians potential enemies. No one was above suspicion. [Sounds of crowd, screaming, gunfire, etc.]

The Vietcong were working their way to the An Quang Pagoda [obscured]. . . . The Vietcong were now firing from the pagoda, and from the roof came [gunfire]. . . . For a half hour it was like this, the Vietcong had fled to the back of the Buddhist church, but all the others were there [screams, gunfire]. They were undoubtedly Vietcong sympathizers. Some undoubtedly were merely religious Buddhists who thought the temple was the best place for them to be at times like these in Saigon. The bullets had wounded at least 20 of them. The government believed that the night before, here, Vietcong commandos had held a meeting and that the Buddhists cheered when they were told the Vietcong were in the city to liberate Saigon.

Government troops have captured the commander of the Vietcong commander unit. He was roughed up badly, but refused to talk. A South Vietnamese officer held the paper taken from the enemy officer. The chief of South Vietnam's national police, Brig. Gen. Nguyen Ngoc Loan, was waiting for him [single loud shot].[25]

ABC, also present, had this report by Roger Peterson:

While scattered snipers are still being hunted down, Saigon remains a city besieged both from without and within. Occasionally helicopter gunships are used to discourage snipers, a rocket will either kill or drive away some of the remaining Vietcong in the area, and soon quiet returns momentarily. During those quiet times, those surviving looked after those not so lucky. . . .

A terrified dog breaks from his hiding place and searches for safety but doesn't really know which way to run. People are running too, heading for the open country to get away from death in the streets. Some had once fled to Saigon for safety.

This Vietcong terrorist was captured; the troops lead him to the front of the An Quang Pagoda, headquarters for the militant Buddhist faction, and there Brig. Gen. Nguyen Ngoc Loan, the embarrassed and angry man in charge of police and defending the capital, executes him. When the snipers are all killed or have left, the frustration behind Loan's revenge will remain, as the government tries to figure out how to regain the slight confidence the people once had in it.

The ABC cameraman who filmed that story is a South Vietnamese. As you noticed, he got film before and after the execution but not at the actual moment of execution. Asked about that he said, "I'm afraid of General Loan."[26]

Ten days later, NBC's Tom Glennon, on the Huntley-Brinkley show, reported on General Loan during a "running fight" in Cholon (Loan had also been active in the fighting across from the Independence Palace on January 31–February 1, and, later, in May, he was to be badly wounded while leading his men during the enemy "second-wave" attacks against Saigon): "A man appeared who two VC prisoners seemed to fear: Gen. Nguyen Ngoc Loan. General Loan's last public appearance was February 1, when he publicly executed a prisoner. He asked the captured Vietcong how many weapons they carried. Two apiece, was the answer. He then drew his stone-handled pistol and placed it to the head of the prisoner; he said, 'If you are lying, I will kill you.' The prisoner said he wasn't. General Loan hesitated, then put his pistol back in the holster."[27]

CBS's Jeff Gralnick was on hand, too, but did not report General Loan's interview with the POW. The introduction was by Harry Reasoner:

Reasoner: Saigon today was quiet except for a few clashes on the edges of the city. Over the past few days, most of the fighting has been concentrated in Saigon's Chinatown, the Cholon section. We have a report from CBS newsman Jeff Gralnick.

Gralnick: It is the 12th day of the Vietcong offensive in Saigon and they are here, in this burning square block of the Cholon district. . . .

Gen. Nguyen Ngoc Loan is here too. Director of the national police force, he has ordered his troops to clear the Vietcong from Saigon this weekend, *a job many consider impossible.* He works with the firemen, first directing them, then taking over. And once the fire is under control, he sits back in a military police jeep, enjoys a cigarette with one of the American troops. . . .[28]

In a weekend broadcast following the Tet attacks, NBC's New York commentators leaned heavily on the AP "flower truck" story. They mentioned the lifted curfew in Saigon, but also said that "much of the communists' effectiveness was due to their determination. As in *the rest of the war, they fought harder and were more willing to die than our Vietnamese.* . . . South Vietnamese troops have been responsible for guarding the cities, and U.S. troops might not have let the communists get away with as much as they have."[29]

On the same program, Robert Goralski, NBC's Pentagon man, without mentioning the holiday leave problem, said ARVN's failures meant added demands on the United States for manpower:

The original concept was to have the allies push out from the population centers and establish greater control over the countryside. American and South Vietnamese government forces held the cities, towns, and larger villages. The communists generally occupied the rest of the country. American troops were charged with running most of the search-and-destroy missions, trying to seal off the porous borders. South Vietnamese units, for the most part, served as rear-guard elements for defense of the cities and pacification. *As was shown this week, the South Vietnamese can't carry their load.*

. . . .

. . . High-ranking generals are now saying that a million Americans might be necessary, double the present force. If General Westmoreland asks for them, and if the Administration agrees, a call-up of many reserve units and National Guardsmen would be inevitable.[30]

On February 6, Merrill Mueller on NBC-Radio expanded on part of Risher's rewritten "corporal-in-charge" story as printed in the Washington *Evening Star:*

It was revealed today that [Westmoreland] warned all the commanders in South Vietnam, in writing, to expect the communist offensive on the cities the night of January 30. That means his warning went out at least a few days and probably one week before the attacks struck.

Part of his intelligence information came from a South Vietnamese division which itself had 16 days' warning of the battle plans. Nevertheless, that division was overrun, but partly because the Saigon government closed the city down for six days of Tet holidays, sent half the military and police units on leave, and left the supreme headquarters in the command of a corporal, after leaving standing orders.[31]

On February 14, Walter Cronkite, then on a flying visit to Vietnam, reported that "the Vietnamese Army reacted better than even its most ardent supporters had anticipated. There were no defections from its ranks, as the Vietcong were also believed to have expected."[32]

But Martin Agronsky in a radio broadcast a few days later from Saigon indulged in what was a frequent feature of Tet news analysis— "straw-man" journalism:

In the front of speculation about the current state of the war here, there are few islands of solid fact upon which to build any certain conclusions. In a way, what is needed is a more kind of dictionary of military and political definitions.

One good example of that need can be seen in examining the *claim* here that at last the South Vietnamese Army has proved it's a dependable, first-class fighting force. When that claim is analyzed, what emerges is *merely* that the Republic's troops did not disintegrate in the face of the enemy attacks.

As far as can be learned from reliable reports of the action, this is true, yet it never seems to occur to any of the claimants that there is anything curious in their holding that an army defending its own country would be described as having scored a victory because, instead of running away, it fought.[33]

No one, however, was claiming that the ARVN had "proved [itself] a dependable, first class fighting force." Agronsky implied that Westmoreland and other U.S. officials were making such claims. But, as Cronkite, Risher, and others had already indicated, U.S. officials were at best privately expressing relief to newsmen that the ARVN had held together and, in some cases, done rather well. The next day, February 18, on CBS's "Face the Nation," filmed earlier in Saigon, even Ambassador Bunker, who of all U.S. officials took the most favorable public view of the South Vietnamese performance, stopped well short of what Agronsky alleged was being said. Declared Bunker: "I think the Vietnamese armed forces . . . have demonstrated their capability. I think they've turned in an excellent performance. I think they've gained confidence in themselves. I think the people have gained confidence in them." ("Excellent" was excessive, and Bunker also diplomatically left much unsaid, notably not mentioning the Tet leave. Neither did he say what "capability" had been demonstrated—one for defensive fighting?)

Television crews filming the Saigon fighting apparently considered the ARVN at least passable. On February 19, for example, NBC broadcast a film report by Jack Russell on a fight between ARVN Marines and Vietcong at Binh Loi village outside the capital. Russell called the Marines "seasoned [fighters], South Vietnam's elite combat troops who are ready and waiting." He also noted that they had held their fire until civilians could escape.

On February 29, ABC presented this report on the Saigon police, introduced by anchorman Bob Young:

Much of Saigon is again suffering a case of jitters, anticipating a further enemy ground attack. ABC's Sam Jaffe went to the U.S. Embassy to see what measures its defenders have taken to prevent another Vietcong assault there. He found Marine guards had changed pistols for heavier weapons, but the Leathernecks remain critical of the Saigon police, who still man a post near the embassy. Here's Jaffe's report:

Jaffe: Now that the heat of battle has died down and the damage to the American Embassy is being repaired, Washington is asking U.S. officials here in Saigon why they were caught off guard. The Marine guard here agrees, practically to a man, that it was the Vietnamese police who let them down the night of the attack.

Guard: I call them a barbaric bunch of people because they never moved. You can clock the situation. When you see them moving, you can sense something is coming. Fifty yards away was a precinct with approximately 300-and-some policemen. None rallied to the defense of that embassy. I tried in vain all night to do so and couldn't get any help from them.

Jaffe: What'd they say?

Guard: They didn't say anything.

Jaffe: I talked to the MPs who were on duty the night of the attack and to the five State Department security men who oversee the embassy's security. Most of them agree. We lack proper intelligence; we lack support from the Saigon police who are responsible for the security outside the embassy.[34]

This account, by the Marine guards, of the Saigon police's failure-refusal to aid the embassy forces is an accurate one. The police presumably were preoccupied with their own survival problems.

During the Hue battle, the overall network emphasis was on the U.S. Marines. Paucity of coverage of the ARVN at Hue, by all media, has already been mentioned. This continued even after February 11, when it became possible to get—without extreme difficulty—from the south side of the city across the Perfume River to the Citadel on the north, where the ARVN was fighting. Bill Brannigan of ABC managed to reach the north side earlier, and on February 8 ABC broadcast his film report. Even here, however, the focus was mainly on the U.S. Marines on the south side. In a later ABC report, Sam Jaffe, describing the painful progress of the Marines on the Citadel, said: "The only main complaint our troops in Hue have is that *they are not getting the support from the South Vietnamese* who originally were supposed to take Hue by themselves. Many just stand around or play cards, *the Marines say*."[35]

Jaffe did not go to see the ARVN 1st Division troops nearby in combat.

On the same day, Chet Huntley said that it might be several weeks before U.S. Marines took all of Hue—he did not mention the ARVN. Six days later, ABC's anchorman Young passed on a wire-service report about Hue which concentrated exclusively on South Vietnamese flaws, real or alleged:

Most of the 1,000 South Vietnamese soldiers on leave in the city when it was hit wound up not as a fighting force but in a refugee camp where they stayed for 21 days. Two South Vietnamese doctors were caught trying to escape in a U.S. Navy boat and were ordered to return and aid the wounded. Lt. Col. Pham Van Khoa, the province chief, hid in civilian clothes for a week. One American advisor reportedly asked, "Why are their Vietnamese, the communists, so good, and our Vietnamese frequently so bad?"[36]

A similar report was broadcast on CBS the following day, but Steve Rowan, reporting from Hue, and moving with ARVN troops, countered with a different view of ARVN:

The battle isn't over yet; the fighting continues outside these walls to the south and west and to the northeast. But the walled Citadel of Hue is relatively secure. The Marines had praise for the South Vietnamese soldiers. . . .

. . . Using a 106 mm. gun to blast their way through the well dug-in communist troops, the South Vietnamese finally got through to the palace and found their fellow-soldiers wounded in the initial battle more than three weeks ago.

The Vietnamese soldiers continued to pursue the North Vietnamese and Vietcong troops from house to house, bunker to bunker. Today, their morale was high, their spirits boosted to some extent by some American bourbon they had liberated. The second highest ranking U.S. officer in Vietnam, Gen. Creighton Abrams, paid a visit to Hue, then talked about the situation.

Abrams: The performance of the troops here, I think—when it's all surveyed after a few months have passed, you'll find that this is one of the heroic beginnings of the modern Vietnamese Army.[37]

At battle's end, NBC presented an aftermath film report from Hue ("City Without Hope") by David Burrington which, for the first time on TV, hinted at the Hue massacre with this statement: "Hundreds of government workers were killed and thrown into temporary graves." However, it gave more attention to the looting by ARVN soldiers, fleetingly showing several of them picking up whiskey bottles, and declared: "The North Vietnamese Army did not loot."[38]

By MACV count, the ARVN 1st Division and the Saigon command threw 11 battalions into the fight (compared with three U.S. Marine battalions and, in the outskirts, four 1st Air Cavalry battalions), losing 384 men killed out of total allied dead of just over 500. Yet, in media eyes, Hue was a Marines-only fight, with ARVN shown on film only at the end, and not very favorably at that.

At the siege of Khe Sanh, TV anchormen recognized ARVN's presence only when the 37th ARVN Ranger Battalion became the target of the enemy's only ground probes and attacks against the main perimeter. At other times, film reports largely ignored ARVN at that battle. There were three exceptions, all on CBS. On the March 1 "CBS Evening News," a report by Don Webster, primarily about a North Vietnamese trooper getting into the base perimeter, also included an interview with the Rangers' U.S. advisor, Army Capt. Walter Gunn, and cited the Rangers' role in the fighting. Rangers could be seen on camera in the background. On March 9, George Syvertsen also did an evening news film report on the Rangers, pointing up their exposed positions: "A good portion of Khe Sanh's defenses are manned by the South Vietnamese Rangers. . . . The Rangers have among the most hard-pressed sectors of the Khe Sanh perimeter. They've sustained more ground attacks and probes than any other unit here. The enemy is close during the day, even closer by night." Finally, on March 26, on the "CBS Morning News," Don Webster, reporting on the wounded, included a Ranger, saying:

"There's another casualty, this time a South Vietnamese Ranger, guarding one of the four sides of the Khe Sanh perimeter. The communists know this, and both their recent assaults on the base have been on the South Vietnamese side of the perimeter."

That night, Dob Webster was on the air again, with an interview of Sidney Roche, an obscure former pacification official in Saigon. Roche received attention for a day on television and radio with his criticisms of the way the allies were running the war:

Roche: Well, as you know, the American Army has been here for several years now, training the Vietnamese Army, and in my opinion it's getting worse instead of getting better. Its equipment is essentially World War II type equipment, its leadership is extremely poor, and it's been performing very poorly in the field in the past year or so.

Webster: How did they perform during the recent Tet offensive?

Roche: Well, during the Tet offensive, by and large, the RF and the PF, that is, the Regional Forces and the Popular Forces, blunted the Vietcong attacks against the cities. Now, there were cases where the ARVN failed to go to the assistance of district towns which were under serious attack from Vietcong forces. . . .

Pacification chief Robert Komer provided a rebuttal:

Frankly, [Roche] has had nothing to do with the advising of the Vietnamese Army for a long, long time now. I'm not a military man either, but I see a lot more of the ARVN than he does, and I also know that most of the American military advisors . . . are confident that the ARVN is getting considerably better.[39]

On March 6, ABC's Bill Brannigan touched upon another facet of the ARVN performance—the mobilization of troops:

The crucial test of the government's new mobilization comes later in the month. That's when the volunteer phase ends and drafting begins in earnest. In the past, bribery, forgery, and outright favoritism had made the draft in South Vietnam something of a farce, something which the "Saigon cowboys," as draft dodgers are called here, have easily managed to escape.

There's no doubt that the government can fill its quota of new trainees. There's been a steady swollen stream of volunteers at induction centers in Saigon ever since the Vietcong offensive. The new mobilization plans announced last October weren't really taken too seriously before the Vietcong attack.[40] Now, the young men and veterans subject to the new call-up are pouring into army posts. Their outlook is fatalistic; like many draft-eligible youngsters in the United States, they feel they'll have to go anyway, and by volunteering they stand a better chance of choosing units and jobs.

New recruits are needed to fill holes in Vietnamese ranks left by the Vietcong offensive. Besides the killed and wounded, there are still a number of soldiers who have yet to return from holiday leave, maybe as many as 50,000 men. Some were probably killed or captured. Others may have joined local units when the fighting broke out, and there's bound to be some who simply deserted or even defected to the other side, particularly in areas that were overrun.[41]

With MACV's announcement of the allied "Resolve to Win" offensive on March 16, "the biggest allied offensive of the war," TV crews began going out with ARVN as well as U.S. troops in the Saigon hinterland. ABC's Roger Peterson was with ARVN Rangers and U.S. armor in a report broadcast on March 18. On March 19, NBC showed Tom Glennon's filming of U.S. armor and ARVN infantry in Hau Nghia province. Said Glennon:

The Vietcong was here. The ARVN 25th Division and the American 11th Armored Cavalry hunt them.

[The American] K Troop made contact with the enemy. They were about 150 yards away. The tanks and armored vehicles with the machine guns were firing tracers. The ARVN troops were both on line in front of the armor, or alongside it.

The Vietcong unit, and it was a strong one, returned the fire with machine guns and rockets.

The American cannon continued firing to further soften up the positions. The battles being fought here daily are much bigger and more savage than the ones before Tet. Fifty allied battalions are involved. The ARVN units constitute the overwhelming majority of these forces. In five or six days of fighting, more than 580 enemy soldiers have been killed. ARVN and American losses have been described as light.[42]

By and large, one interesting trend emerges from the network coverage: Those few TV newsmen who actually covered ARVN troops in combat were a good deal less disparaging in their broadcasts than their colleagues who did not.

The Newspapers: Scant Coverage

The February 4 (Sunday) New York Times ran AP's "flower truck" story, with its rather broad indictment of ARVN as a fighting force. The story reflected, it will be recalled, on the questionable effectiveness "of the security offered by South Vietnamese units."[43] It contained no mention of the ARVN leave, although the *Times* had already reported that information.[44]

In the same day's "News of the Week in Review" section, the Saigon bureau noted that "the Vietnamese police issued a warning 12 hours before the commandos arrived. Cautionary notices were posted at American billets. Even so, fewer than half of the relatively small number of Vietnamese troops stationed in the city were in their barracks, [and] 50 percent of the police force was home for the holidays."[45] Then the *Times*'s Saigon commentator added this: "From South Vietnamese sources . . . there were statements that large formations of Vietcong troops had simply marched down Highway One from the Bien Hoa area while [South Vietnamese] militia units looked the other way." This remains a New York *Times* exclusive.

Elsewhere in the section, Senator Edward Kennedy, newly returned from a three-week trip to Vietnam to examine the refugees' plight, was interviewed by John Finney of the *Times*'s Washington bureau. The questions were less than probing, the answers less than specific:

Q.: Do you feel this [South Vietnamese] corruption is accompanied by a lack of dedication and commitment to the war effort?

A.: I think it is, for these reasons: First, there have been examples where corps commanders have been assigned to certain units, and who are participating in the whole area of corruption. . . . I think this has brought about a demoralization among the fighting men in a number of units among the people of South Vietnam. . . . And, obviously, we realize that the ones that are making up the difference are the American fighting men.[46]

However, in contrast to the commentators, Charles Mohr was with the Vietnamese Marines in combat near Tan Son Nhut on February 3, and he noted the stubbornness of both sides. His eyewitness piece appeared on page five:

. . . American jets and South Vietnamese Skyraider propeller-driven planes attacked the area several times during the day.

"Love those 500-pound bombs," said a United States Marine advisor as the powerful crump of explosions was heard.

. . . .

None of this seemed to flush the guerrillas. At 1 p.m. all incoming fire was from the north, but by 4 p.m. bursts of enemy fire were coming from the west.

"This is bad," said a United States Marine captain, Ron Ray of Louisville, Kentucky. "We're moving and they're dug in. You are bound to lose people this way and have nothing to show for it. We'll take this village eventually, but so what?"

Captain Ray is the advisor to Maj. Pham Van Thang, the serenely calm commander of the 1st Vietnamese Marines, who moved from shattered house to shattered house with his radio.

There was no sign that the guerrillas were fleeing. In fact, they had obviously driven the South Vietnamese Marines back 100 or 200 yards by afternoon.[47]

Not until February 25 were South Vietnamese troops again shown in action by the *Times* firsthand—and again by Mohr—as they ended the battle for Hue by occupying the Citadel's Imperial Palace. It was the second and last such firsthand *Times* story of ARVN in combat during Tet:

In deference to the Vietnamese, the United States command ordered that "under no circumstances will Marines enter the palace itself." The palace was occupied by 150 men of the elite Hac Bao or Black Panther Company of South Vietnamese troops and 300 men of the 2nd Battalion, 3rd Regiment, of the South Vietnamese 1st Division.

The 2nd Battalion troops had taken the main southern tower of the outer Citadel wall, from which a Vietcong flag had flown since dawn on January 31. They pulled down the battle-tattered banner and hoisted a bright new South Vietnamese flag—a field of yellow crossed by three red bars.[48]

Lt. Gen. Nguyen Duc Thang, who took over as Delta commander at Tet, and was always a favorite with Americans, held a March 9 press conference in Can Tho and got page-one coverage in the *Times* the following day for saying that the foe had made up his losses, albeit with untrained recruits. The story was by Gene Roberts:

General Thang said today only that he considered the losses to be severe. "But," he emphasized, "we have got to say they [have gotten] replacements already." . . .

He took over the job only 10 days ago, but already has won praise from United States officials working in the Mekong Delta.

One of his first acts was to speed the construction of new bunkers in Can Tho, the largest city in the Delta. The step is expected to make it possible for fewer men to defend the city and to free others to pursue the enemy.[49]

Recalling his February experience outside Tan Son Nhut, Mohr wrote a "News of the Week in Review" piece for the March 10 paper:

SAIGON, South Vietnam—In the early stages of the battle for Saigon last month, a battalion of South Vietnamese Marines stubbornly attacked entrenched Vietcong troops in the rubble of a suburb only a mile from the Tan Son Nhut airport, a large military-commercial installation.

An American advisor with too much experience to be starry-eyed or mindlessly optimistic said last week: "These guys are part of the strategic reserve. They get moved all over the country to fight and are away from their families 10 or 11 months a year, year after year.

"They are all volunteers," he added. "When people say the South Vietnamese won't fight, they shouldn't include units like the Vietnamese Marines."

The performance of the Army and the stability of the Saigon government have come under new scrutiny and questioning as a result of the communist offensive. The problem now is whether both can recoup the losses they have suffered and prove they are effective instruments against the communists. . . .

No unit defected as a unit to the enemy or broke and ran in the face of fire. Although eight of the 10 divisions had given 50 percent of their men Lunar New Year furloughs, no sizable unit was overrun or destroyed.

Some Western analysts believe that North Vietnamese generals had counted on the partial disintegration of ARVN and had been convinced that it was "an Army that won't fight."[50]

Other *Times* reporters, who had not seen the ARVN in action, cited different views, but without a balancing mention of ARVN's role in the fighting. This piece by Peter Grose is an example:

WASHINGTON, Mar. 16—Senator Robert F. Kennedy charged today that the Administration's policies had "glossed over with illusions" the realities of the war in Vietnam.

He summarized the main points of his own position as he challenged President Johnson for the Democratic Presidential nomination. . . .

Basically, he said at his news conference, "I'm in favor of de-escalating the struggle. . . .

"I'm basically in favor of the South Vietnamese taking over more of the effort. . . ."

While Administration officials accept this in principle, the practical demands of the military situation have led United States commanders to rely on American combat units.[51]

The same day, Hedrick Smith of the *Times*'s Washington bureau reported an unnamed Administration official as saying of the South Vietnamese Army, "All they do is talk and make plans. What we need is action."[52] Similarly, Tom Buckley of the Saigon bureau, also on March 17, commented:

. . . The performance of the South Vietnamese Army continues to be of some embarrassment to the American command. For the record, the old refrain—"They're improving all the time"—is repeated.

Nevertheless, with the exception of some of the Paratrooper, Ranger, and Marine battalions, it is privately acknowledged that the showing during the Tet offensive was nothing to write home about.[53]

Like the network men, those *Times* reporters who actually accompanied the ARVN into battle were less prone to quick judgment than those who did not.

The Washington *Post,* like the *Times,* ran the "flower truck" story on page one ("How VC Infiltrated Saigon") on February 4. The next day, in discussing the briefing by General Davidson, Lee Lescaze wrote, without by-line: "Davidson made no reference to the readiness of allied units when the attack came. Other senior officials have acknowledged that government troops were understrength because of the Tet holiday and that the Vietcong caught the allied defenses at their weakest."[54] In short, the *Post,* like the *Times,* had made clear by February 5, through its own staff reporting, that one major factor in the failure to prevent the Vietcong incursions was the ARVN's holiday in the midst of war.[55] Again like the New York *Times,* the *Post* repeated the story of the ARVN Tet leaves after the Abrams briefing:

SAIGON, Feb. 9—Although there were scattered bits of intelligence early last month that the enemy might try an offensive during Tet, the South Vietnamese Joint General Staff authorized commanders to give as many as 50 percent of their men leave for the holiday.

In some units more than 50 percent of the men were absent when the Vietcong hit.

At My Tho, the battalion of the South Vietnamese 7th Division stationed in the city had less than 200 men present for duty at 3 a.m., January 31, when the attack began.

At Ben Tre . . . about 400 South Vietnamese troops were present in the two battalions defending the city when the Vietcong attacked with about 2,000 men. . . .

With or without Tet leave, however, nowhere did South Vietnamese soldiers or police stop advance elements of the Vietcong from infiltrating the nation's major cities—in many cases bringing substantial supplies of weapons and ammunition. . . .

Information on the series of battles is still incomplete, but it appears that the South Vietnamese defenders reacted fairly well to the attacks, given the first surprise, according to U.S. military sources.

In cities where they were being overrun, like Ben Tre and My Tho, air strikes, artillery, and American troops were called for. But elsewhere in the Delta, at Ban Me Thuot and in some of the battles in the III Corps area—Baria and Xuan Loc—the South Vietnamese carried the fight themselves, without U.S. ground troops and with less use of air and artillery on the cities.[56]

What the gross lapse of the Tet leaves signified in terms of ARVN's nationwide ability to bear up, or of its "willingness to fight," was not then generally known to Saigon newsmen. Nevertheless, some had made up their minds anyway. To repeat, Ambassador Bunker's February 3 encomiums for the ARVN were not accepted as the final word; and there was remarkably little said about ARVN by Davidson, Weyand, Chaisson, and others in JUSPAO briefings at week's end.

The following day, in describing post-Tet changes in Saigon, Lescaze noted, as among the "bad signs," that "Vietnamese soldiers and police have looted furniture and foodstuffs from damaged homes and shops."[57] This was a complaint later voiced to me by U.S. advisors at Hue.[58]

As already described, during the first week of the battle in that city, this reporter tried and failed to get to the ARVN fight in the Citadel, but wound up instead on the south side with the Marines. However, in an effort to catch up with the ARVN performance, I filed two post-mortem stories based on interviews with U.S. advisors and ARVN officers. Both sources voiced pride and relief in the ARVN performance, the Americans even more than the Vietnamese. The stories focused on the much-praised all-volunteer Hoc Bao ("Black Panther") Reconnaissance Company, the 1st ARVN Division's only infantry unit in Hue when the attack came; and on U.S. advisors' contentions that the understrength run-of-the-mill 3rd Regiment did just as well as the vaunted elite units.[59] Many details were lacking; no one, for example, was citing ARVN flaws. (AP's John Lengel later insisted that, in covering the Marines in the Citadel fight, he saw ARVN units on the Marine flank failing to keep up.) Moreover, the two stories undoubtedly reflected my own relief that Hue was finally no longer a dangerous place to work. Nevertheless, later, the 1st

ARVN Division and its skinny, phlegmatic commander, Brig. Gen. Ngo Quang Truong, became widely recognized as the best of ARVN. After the recapture of Hue on February 24, both *Post* reporters made a deliberate effort to view Tet's effects on pacification in the countryside. There, we got a fleeting look at the ARVN, as well as the militia. Lescaze, concentrating on the Delta, cited looting by government troops, Rangers "seen changing into civilian clothes" during the battle, and questionable morale. He also noted that "throughout the Delta, government soldiers and police found themselves outgunned by the Vietcong during the Tet fighting."[60]

In Saigon, Lescaze also reported an item of concern to the U.S. Mission:

SAIGON, Mar. 1—About 10 percent of the South Vietnamese Army is unaccounted for a month after the Vietcong offensive.

The Tet attack caught many South Vietnamese Army units with 50 percent of their men on leave.

"Many soldiers are undoubtedly having a hard time finding transport back to their units," one source said today.

However, the percentage of missing soldiers is about the same as it was a month after Tet last year, when there was no Vietcong drive against the cities.

In past years, the Lunar New Year leave has been unilaterally extended by considerable numbers of government soldiers—many of whom returned to their bases later.[61]

Reflecting the feverish atmosphere in Washington, and possibly also some of the Joint Chiefs' efforts to persuade President Johnson to send massive reinforcements to Vietnam, one *Post* analyst, Chalmers M. Roberts, noted:

As President Johnson ponders how many more troops to send to Vietnam, the critical question is whether he is facing the reality of a choice. . . .

Today the South Vietnamese forces are concentrated in the cities and towns. Even there American troops have had to be added. In short, the South Vietnamese have demonstrated what more and more has been the fear in Washington: With some exceptions, *they lack aggressive will to fight* for their country.[62]

The story was an example of the ignoring of what one's own colleagues were reporting from the field, especially when those reports contradicted the current conventional wisdom in the capital. It was a

rare lapse for Chalmers Roberts, but one all too common in Washington before and after Tet.
Following General Westmoreland's briefing on March 6, and drawing on earlier interviews with U.S. advisors and ARVN officers, as well as reports from *Post* stringer Nguyen Ngoc Rao, I put together a pluses-and-minuses piece on the ARVN. It was far from all-inclusive. Yet, as far as I can determine, it was the only such relatively detailed ARVN story produced by wire services or newspapers during the Tet period:

SAIGON, Mar. 9—Vice President Nguyen Cao Ky, bareheaded, wearing olive drab and his usual lavender scarf, rose today to praise the "bravery and professionalism" of the South Vietnamese soldier in meeting the communist Tet offensive. . . .

In the eyes of many Vietnamese, the ARVN did, in effect, win a victory. It was not necessarily a victory over the Vietcong—the long-term effects of the Tet offensive are still being debated—but over American critics who had contended that "the ARVN can't fight."

One hears little such criticism now. To the surprise of many, the ARVN battalions, notably at Hue and Quang Tri city, did not dissolve under heavy attack. So far as is known, there were few surrenders by isolated ARVN compounds and no panic-stricken retreats by major units. Perhaps 100 of the 2,000 Popular Forces militia outposts were abandoned or overrun; perhaps 40 to 50 hamlets were attacked or overrun as communist columns, striking for the cities and towns, ran into them.

The ARVN took heavy casualties—9,754 killed, wounded, or missing. . . . Among the regular ARVN units, the 1st Division (Hue and Quang Tri) lost most—2,611 men, or about a fourth of its effective strength. . . .

The official preoccupation now is with the "rebuilding process." As of March 1, a total of 14,400 replacements had been sent to field units to fill depleted ranks. Courses at some training centers were cut temporarily from 13 to nine weeks, deserters and other defaulters assigned to special penal battalions were amnestied and sent to regular units. Military jails were emptied. . . .

. . . the Thieu government's call-up of reservists and its pledges to crack down on draft dodgers produced a flow of manpower. In the Saigon area alone, according to Vietnamese sources, young men are now reporting at the rate of 1,200 a day—more men than the training centers can handle. . . .

Having been caught by the Tet offensive with 50 percent of its manpower off duty, the ARVN now takes the war more seriously. In the Saigon area, for example, officers and enlisted men must stay on duty or in barracks 24 hours a day: Only two- or three-hour passes during daylight are permitted on rotating basis. At night, the clerks and cooks man listening posts or patrol their perimeters. . . .

Serious headaches remain, aside from the demonstrated ability of the Vietcong and North Vietnamese to renew their strength and strike again.

Reaction to the Tet crisis has brought no fundamental changes in the Army's class-conscious promotion system. There has been no purge, as long promised, of corrupt and incompetent officers. Training centers . . . may not be adequate to handle a promised 65,000-man Army increase by June.

. . . problems of tactics and psychology remain. . . . Ironically, the Tet attack, which left hamlets relatively unscathed, has scared militia platoons into a more passive posture. . . .

Despite the enemy's Tet success in night infiltration, the ARVN (and it should be added, the U.S. forces) have made no noticeable move to step up night patrolling and shield civilians from Vietcong night incursion. Like their U.S. allies, the ARVN still tend to button up for the night. . . .

In terms of armament, the average ARVN rifle company still fights at a disadvantage.[63]

In retrospect, the piece assumes greater importance: In effect, it said that the ARVN, for all its flaws, had survived and was not in a state of psychic collapse. Hence, contrary to the assertions in Washington of hawks and doves alike, the United States did not have to "take over the war" with massive injections of new manpower to stave off defeat.

The same day, the *Post* ran Lee Lescaze's story on General Thang's Can Tho press conference:

Since Tet, the Vietcong have been in or near the principal cities of the Delta and have shown no reluctance to fight. And, according to several sources in the Delta, the government troops have been reluctant to pursue the enemy after having secured the cities. . . .

Thang is determined that his army will attack quickly and often and that the people will respond with support for the government.

He is confronted with the record of 10 years' war in the Delta in which neither side has made remarkable progress. . . .

Thang, who is respected for his energy, candor, and bravery, faces an enormous task.

He will not surround his own house with a regiment of troops and virtually disappear from the scene under pressure, as did his predecessor, Maj. Gen. Nguyen Van Manh, during the Tet attack on Can Tho.

Throughout the Delta, many officials are cheered by his appointment to the Corps command. "If he can't do it we've had it," one said recently.[64]

In terms of attention, ARVN got short-changed. After the end of the Hue battle, *Post* editors began to focus on domestic issues—the Vietnam debate at home, and election-year politics. None of the catch-up stories from Vietnam on ARVN status made page one. Indeed, as we have noted, there were no stories at all from Vietnam on page one of the *Post* on eight of the 31 days in March,[65] not even war wrap-ups. But Vietnam-related stories originating in Washington or on the political hustings made page one daily.

In sum, the *Post* reporters in Vietnam paid more attention to ARVN, albeit mostly secondhand and after the fact, than did the *Times* staffers there. At the same time, home-based commentators of both papers seemingly ignored the reports out of Saigon on the ARVN, sketchy as those reports were. The Tet attacks were quickly regarded both in the United States and among some Saigon newsmen as final proof of ARVN's "unwillingness to fight," rather than as evidence of a gross lapse of leadership by Thieu. It is also possible to wonder, given only the conspicuousness of ARVN's perceived failures in the post-Tet domestic debate, why *Times* and *Post* editors did not: (1) press their Saigon men for closer examination of ARVN performance, particularly in March, and (2) give greater prominence to what scant reporting they did receive. The answer, again, seems to have been that ethnocentricity begins at home.

The News Magazines: Poorest Coverage

As Tet began, the accent in *Time,* as in most other publications, was on American military problems. But by the second week, the magazine ventured an optimistic generalization of ARVN, presumably based partly on the accounts of its reporter, Hugh Greenway, in Hue, and partly on the more glowing assessments of General Abrams. However, none of ARVN's problems—its losses, inadequate weaponry, and disrupted training—were cited. Said *Time:* "Although nearly half the ARVN soldiers were away from their posts throughout the country on four-day Tet leaves, those on duty fought bravely and well—and in fact bore the brunt of the subsequent battles in the streets and took the majority of allied casualties. There was not a single instance of an ARVN unit surrendering or going over to the invaders."[66]

A week later, *Time* discussed the Loan execution:

That picture is lodged in people's memories. Taken during the recent communist assault on Vietnam's cities, it showed Brig. Gen. Nguyen Ngoc Loan . . . cold-bloodedly executing a guerrilla suspect—a thin, frightened, but stubborn-looking man in plaid shirt . . . who had been seized by soldiers in a Saigon street. In no mood to ask questions, the spindly General whipped out his snub-nosed .38 revolver and remorselessly blew the suspect's brains out. "Many Americans have died recently," Loan told TV newsmen later. "So have many of my best friends. Buddhists understand—do you?"

Loan's act caused little stir in Saigon, where for two years the government has waged a ruthless, successful campaign against street terrorists. His fellow-student in pilot-school days and long-time sponsor in government, Vice President Nguyen Cao Ky, dismissed the incident with little more than a shrug. But the execution aroused . . . world opinion, and raised a question that has concerned the United States since it took on the Vietcong: How should prisoners in a guerrilla war be treated?[67]

By the end of February, the magazine had still not caught up with ARVN's activities, except to express apprehension:

In the countryside, the communists are *busily reaping the harvest so painfully wrested from them* over the past two years in allied operations; propagandizing the peasants, collecting rice and taxes and, above all, *recruiting fresh soldiers* for their depleted ranks—even *impressing into their ranks some ARVN soldiers caught home on Tet leaves.* About half of the South Vietnamese Army was on leave when the communists first struck nearly four weeks ago, and *many ARVN soldiers have not yet returned to their units.* The government's hope is that many of the missing offered their services to the nearest headquarters when the crisis began and are still serving in these areas. *But no one knows for sure.*[68]

By mid-March, *Time* was reporting merely that the ARVN was taking part in the offensive around Saigon alongside the Americans:

For the first time since Tet, the allies last week swept out on the offensive, launching their largest operation of the war. Code-named "Resolved to Victory," the drive aimed at breaking the ring of three enemy divisions menacing Saigon. It employed more than 50 battalions formed from the U.S. 1st, 9th, and 25th Divisions and the South Vietnamese 5th and 25th Divisions, plus task forces of Vietnamese Marines and paratroopers. The nearly 50,000 troops fanned out through a five-province belt around the capital.[69]

Following the White House's March 22 announcement that West-moreland was to leave Vietnam to become Army Chief of Staff, *Time* commented: "Strategy aside . . . his clearest single failure was not to have built the South Vietnamese Army into a respectable fighting force."[70]

Newsweek was particularly impatient with ARVN, during Tet as before. For its first post-Tet issue, the magazine was apparently caught with a story written and scheduled in advance of the attacks:

One reason why U.S. troops are spread so thinly across the tortured face of South Vietnam is the limited effectiveness of South Vietnamese troops. In an effort to remedy this situation, U.S. authorities in Saigon have put increasing emphasis on improving the caliber of the 50,000 regulars in the Republic of Vietnam Armed Forces (RVNAF)—and with some success. Thus, the South Vietnamese 1st Division, which was thoroughly demoralized only a year ago, now is rated by U.S. officers an excellent fighting unit. Last week, however, on top of all the other blows the United States suffered in Vietnam, came discouraging evidence that further progress in reforming the South Vietnamese Army was probably going to be slow and painful.[71]

The same week, discussing the press in Vietnam, *Newsweek,* in passing, indicated that the ARVN was involved in the Hue counterattacks, a point it did not stress elsewhere:

CBS cameraman John Schneider was in Da Nang when the VC overran most of Hue. No one was able to get into the besieged city, and so Schneider hitched a ride with a forward air controller on his way to direct air strikes. Since the VC held the Hue airfield, the plane had to land at Phu Bai, also under attack. Hitchhiking and walking, Schneider reached Hue in time to shoot 900 feet of exclusive film showing ARVN troops starting their counterattack.[72]

The following week, *Newsweek* spoke of U.S. troops being "committed to aid the lagging efforts of the South Vietnamese forces" in Saigon.[73] "Lagging efforts" was gratuitous; no newsman who observed ARVN fighting in Saigon suggested then or after that the ARVN "lagged" any more than U.S. troops. It was hard, slow work for everyone. Furthermore, the ARVN did not have 10 battalions inside the city, as *Newsweek* reported; the big effort was in the suburbs.

The United States moved one battalion and one company into Saigon to relieve shot-up ARVN troops there (two Ranger battalions).

In the same issue, the psychological angle was emphasized, with "suspicion" and rumors:

> The psychological impact of the communist offensive was most telling on those South Vietnamese who had publicly aligned themselves with the Saigon government. In an obvious effort to underscore the fact that supporting the government was risky business, Vietcong terror squads roamed through Saigon last week executing the families of Vietnamese Army and police officers and killing policemen on deserted street corners. Already, there was some suspicion that certain South Vietnamese units in the capital had worked out a modus vivendi with the Vietcong. And even Saigon officials admitted that they did not know whether many of the troops who were on leave at the time of the Tet attack—fully 30 percent of South Vietnam's regular armed forces—*would return to their units or wait to see which side emerged the victor.*[74] In the face of this crisis, South Vietnam's President Nguyen Van Thieu concluded that the time had come to try to enforce his nation's general mobilization law.[75]

By mid-March, *Newsweek* was writing:

> Somehow, the political support which the United States has given to the government of President Thieu and Vice President Ky has not had the intended effect either. The two generals in mufti have been unable to galvanize their troops or their people, and few indeed would be so rash as to predict that anything lasting can be built on their government. . . .[76]
>
> This is the dismal balance sheet at the moment. It can be argued that it is too pessimistic an accounting; but the reports of the Administration have always been too optimistic—a habit that still persists.[77]

In the same issue, *Newsweek* went on:

> A report recently leaked to the press by a U.S. official in Saigon asserts that "corruption is permeating all echelons of government and society. . . ."
>
> . . . in fact, inefficiency and corruption render most organs of state power in South Vietnam painfully ineffective. A striking case in point is the Army of the Republic of Vietnam (ARVN). American officers maintain that the ARVN fought well during the New Year battles, and this apparently was true in many, if not all, cases. But that was a matter of self-defense. In the post-Tet effort to clear the communists out of the cities, South Vietnam Army units have frequently displayed a distinct lack of aggressiveness.[78]

Newsweek did not mention ARVN again, except for this in its "Periscope" section: "There may have been less than meets the eye in the recent allied 'Quyet Thang' (Determined to Win) offensive around Saigon. Quyet Thang actually was no more than a series of search-and-destroy operations—but to bolster the sagging morale of the South Vietnamese troops, it was referred to in the communiqués as one big battle and given a South Vietnamese name."[79]

In sum, the news magazines paid less heed to ARVN than did any of the other media, and dealt with it largely in generalities. *Newsweek* evidenced a commitment to past views of ARVN, reinforced by an internal decision to take a formal stand against the war. The magazine did not separate, but closely welded, fact and opinion. Often, in the overflow of information in the United States, the news magazines fill in some of the holes; with respect to ARVN, they merely added to that fighting force's invisibility.

Vietnamese Politics and Government: A Variety of Themes

The performance and politics of the Thieu regime in February and March 1968 received fuller newspaper and wire-service coverage than did ARVN, although they were subjects rarely treated on TV film. Here, American reporters, as they had in the past, depended largely on daily memoranda supplied by their Vietnamese stringers, who watched the National Assembly debates, translated official decrees and Thieu's radio speeches, and traded gossip with their sources within the government and noncommunist opposition. As February ended, some American newsmen, no longer so preoccupied with the battlefield, began to discuss the Thieu regime's mixed reactions to Tet with U.S. Embassy officials, who were pressing the South Vietnamese for stronger mobilization measures.

Developments were described from Saigon in conventional terms by most print newsmen (including this writer). We reported such events as the early formation by Saigon politicians of "unity" fronts; the arrest and "protective custody" of Thich Tri Quang, the militant Buddhist, and other radical Thieu foes; Thieu's speeches and decrees; the discordant comments of Vice President Ky; and the imposition of martial law. Such "announcement news," almost as easy to garner in Saigon as in Washington, dominated the wire-service reports on the GVN. However, it sometimes became blurred in translation, and it conveyed few of the realities in the hinterland. Yet, as

James Reston was to observe in late March, some of these "announcements" were highly significant, for Tet and U.S. prodding forced Thieu into making some major public commitments. Most important, he began lowering the draft age and mobilizing more men, steps he had apparently been reluctant to take earlier for domestic political reasons, including legislative opposition.

Oddly, Thieu's crucial Tet errors of lifting the Saigon curfew and granting ARVN a 50 percent leave, although reported, did not get page-one headlines or enter into the rhetoric of the swelling post-Tet Vietnam debate in the United States. Instead, the Tet surprise, as already noted, was linked by TV and newspaper analysts to old themes: military rule, corruption, unpopularity, "lack of will," and other defects. To some of these impatient American analysts, such flaws "caused" Tet; and the GVN's failure, amid the post-Tet shock, to take corrective action seemed to confirm that government's unworthiness as a U.S. ally.

One early product of such hasty media analysis was the thesis that the Vietcong could not have brought troops through the countryside and into the cities without the acquiescence of the population. The implication was that the Thieu-Ky regime "lacked support." It was a thesis that soon faded in reporting from Saigon, but hung on longer in the United States. The notion popped up quickly in Washington in a *Post* story by Ward Just:

> . . . officials here continued to ponder with amazement the swiftness and ferocity of the communist attacks. There was general agreement among knowledgeable specialists that the enemy had to have at least the acquiescence, if not the actual aid, of substantial numbers of South Vietnamese, including members of the armed forces.
>
> There also was general agreement that real [sic] intelligence on the raids had been nonexistent. The population, which almost certainly knew of enemy troop movements into Saigon, had not told the allied authorities.[80]

Again, three days after the Saigon attacks, a dispatch from Stanley Karnow in Hong Kong said: "The experts contend there is probably considerable plausibility to the communist thesis that the Vietcong raids could not have been possible without widespread support, particularly in cities and suburban areas."[81]

The idea was rebroadcast by Senator Eugene McCarthy, among others, as reported here by Marjorie Hunter from Washington:

The Senator, a candidate for the Democratic nomination for President, said that the wave of terrorism in South Vietnam during the last few days indicated "that we are in a much worse position than we were two years ago.

"The Vietcong are clearly getting protection from the population, and the so-called pacification program must be largely a sham."[82]

Even at the end of February, the New York *Times* raised the point in a Saigon bureau Sunday article on enemy tactics: "The allied troops would be better able to find the Vietcong mortar squads—who must often move into villages to set up their weapons before striking —if more peasants were willing to inform on enemy movements. But informers have been few."[83]

Newsweek also thought it was a point worth raising: "It was . . . *obvious* that the Vietcong could not have done what they had unless much of the South Vietnamese population—whether out of fear, apathy, or some genuine sympathy—*had lent at least passive support.*"[84] Again, in support of its thesis that the government "lacked support," *Newsweek* said:

. . . the attitude of the majority of South Vietnamese was strongly suggested by their failure to alert U.S. or government officials to communist preparations for the Tet offensive. . . .

The central problem plaguing the Saigon government, according to a U.S. psychological warfare expert, is that it "has no cause it can express in terms that mean anything to its own peasantry." . . . In their commitment to constitutional democracy and in their efforts to establish it in South Vietnam, American officials have, in effect, converted the Saigon government into a sacred cow.[85]

On February 16, Martin Agronsky, visiting Saigon from Washington, and Peter Kalischer video-taped an interview with Ambassador Bunker for CBS's "Face the Nation":

Agronsky: Is it not true, however, substantially, that before this attack came, when there were these large movements and concentrations of the Vietcong all through this country, there was no warning given to the government by its—
Bunker: Well; no, I'm—
Agronsky: Isn't that true, sir?
Bunker: No, I'm not sure that that is true or not. I think there was a general knowledge that trouble might start around this time. There was no specific pinpoint of the actual specific time.

Kalischer: Yes, sir, but just one point. The thing that we would like to get to is the fact that the man on the corner, in the corner shop, the little fellow in the thatched house outside the village who noticed 300, 400 strangers—and you can't hide those people who are preparing to filter in —he never went around to the corner cop and said, "Hey, there are strangers here."

Bunker: Well, you don't know how they moved. They moved mostly at night, of course, they moved in disguise, in their infrastructure, the VC infrastructure throughout the country, in all the cities, and it is not surprising to me that there was an element of surprise, given the timing of this thing.[86]

Kalischer's question, if nothing else, reflected a remoteness from rural Vietnam and a lack of familiarity with Vietcong tactics, common to many Americans. Bunker's answer was correct, if incomplete. First, anyone who had flown by helicopter over the swamps, woods, and canals surrounding Saigon could comprehend the ease with which Vietcong troops, moving swiftly from jungle base camps in small groups by night, could by-pass scattered militia outposts and hamlets to concentrate for attack on the city's edge. (Oberdorfer notes in *Tet!* that the premium placed on secrecy by the Vietcong-NVA leadership prior to the attacks contributed to the tactical surprise achieved, even as it led to some crucial breakdowns in Vietcong coordination.) Second, the Vietcong normally did not move in groups. of "300 or 400" in the lowlands; their movements were not "large." Third, any field-experienced Vietnam hand knew that a peasant, seeing Vietcong troops and deciding to ignore the risk of reprisal and to inform, would be unable swiftly to contact "the corner cop," because there were no police in the hamlets. Fourth, as was well known, Vietcong agents and sapper teams stayed out of sight, in their own "safe houses." Fifth, and finally, allied intelligence services, like the FBI in America, did not rely for information on the average citizen, but on their own agents and informers, as well as on interception of Vietcong radio messages, interrogation of deserters and prisoners, and captured documents.

As Oberdorfer has pointed out, we now know there were many timely warnings from these intelligence sources, but Thieu, among others, refused to heed them.[87] In brief, the Vietcong did not *need* popular acquiescence in order to penetrate the cities, nor did the allies depend on the populace for advance notice. Tet was not a referendum on Thieu's popularity.

Largely overlooked in the reporting on the GVN was the immediately relevant question: How well did the administrative structure survive and cope with the equivalent of a great natural disaster—524,000 new refugees and sizable urban destruction—in the middle of intensified, semi-conventional warfare throughout much of the nation? Even as the city fighting ebbed in late February, journalistic manpower shortages in Saigon, the priority on reporting on Americans in action, and the lack of editorial demand at home limited the possibilities of finding answers firsthand, although some newsmen tried.

Moreover, even prior to Tet, the South Vietnamese government was not particularly popular among newsmen. Thieu lacked "flair" and he was also press-shy. Vice President Ky was at least a vivid personality; his propensity for emotional, off-the-cuff comments to newsmen made him quotable, and thus "newsworthy" (even if the more prudent U.S. newsmen warned home offices not to take his statements too literally). Although both men, after being pushed and cajoled by their fellow military officers, had run on the same ticket in the 1967 elections and won with 34.8 percent of the vote, it was no secret that—like most Vietnamese politicians—they did not get along. Thieu was a cautious central Vietnamese Catholic. Ky was a northern Buddhist. Starting with their collaboration in mid-1965, theirs was a marriage of convenience, designed to hold intact the hawkish Catholic and "military vote," as, to Thieu's chagrin, Ky often made obvious in public.

Acting as prime minister was a man whose name seldom got into U.S. newspapers: Nguyen Van Loc, a colorless, bespectacled Saigon lawyer and political associate of Ky. He is mentioned in *The Vietcong Tet Offensive, 1968,* the ARVN's own official Tet history, as trying (like Thieu) to give "the common people as normal a Tet [holiday] as possible," authorizing them to celebrate by setting off firecrackers for a four-day period ending February 2. Loc was replaced on May 18, 1968, after considerable acrimony in the Vietnamese parliament, by Tran Van Huong, a grandfatherly French-trained former premier and schoolteacher from My Tho. Huong was a veteran nationalist (who had broken with the Vietminh in 1946), and the fourth-ranking vote-getter in the 1967 Presidential elections. With the exception of the weary, widely respected Foreign Minister, Tran Van Do, who represented South Vietnam at the 1954 Geneva conference (and refused to sign the famous accords), the rest of the Vietnamese cabinet was a blank to most newsmen. Direct contacts with the Vietnamese Administration in 1966–67 were not extensive. We were largely limited to dealings with the polite, rather efficient people of the official Vietnam press center, where one could get accredited in one day; the infuriatingly slow immigration officials at Tan Son Nhut Airport; the "white mice" (gray trousers and hats, white shirts) of the Saigon police department; the fairly reliable post office; and occasional English-speaking district chief or refugee director; and province chiefs or ARVN commanders of the four corps areas. Thus, American newsmen had very little firsthand information in Saigon on which to base any quick evaluation of the South Vietnamese government at Tet in political or administrative terms. In addition, the same ignorance of Vietnam's language, history, and culture that hampered coverage of other Vietnamese aspects of the war also restricted coverage of the GVN.

Corruption—shakedowns, profiteering, or bribes involving officials —permeated much of the Administration and its low-paid officialdom, especially under the inflationary impact of U.S. spending in Saigon. Examples were often reported by U.S. advisors, as well as condemned by Vietnamese leaders and cited in the U.S. media. In this, wartime Saigon was not unique, however; easy comparisons are Naples in World War II or Seoul in 1950–53. In any case, as far as this reporter is concerned, having already experienced the hand-me-down French administrative process in Laos and North Africa, I found Vietnam remarkably efficient by comparison, with underpaid local functionaries less prone to overt bribe-demanding than those of Thailand or India.*

* In January 1970, after the first U.S. troop withdrawals from Vietnam, the Nieman Fellows in Journalism at Harvard held a "Vietnam Night" symposium at the Faculty Club. On hand were this writer and some of the toughest Vietnam journalist-critics (Frank McCulloch and Wally Terry of *Time*, Ward Just of the Washington *Post*, and Hedrick Smith of the New York *Times*). Their audience included John Kenneth Galbraith and other Harvard faculty members who had been in the forefront of the peace movement. The old Vietnam hands variously scored Johnson, McNamara, the 1965–67 Administration "progress" line, the war's disproportionate burden on blacks, and superficial media coverage. Then a professor asked: "Wouldn't the most *moral* thing now be to simply pull out and end the war?" To the audience's considerable surprise, the newsmen disagreed. Ward Just argued that, just by going into Vietnam, the United States had incurred a moral obligation not to abandon those Vietnamese whom Washington had encouraged to stand up and resist. "Thieu

Less readily perceived in 1967–68 than the *fact* of wartime corruption was corruption's generalized impact on the South Vietnamese people. It seems clear, however, that the big influx of money, while it made Saigon a boom town, added to the erosion of traditional Vietnamese values and of civic trust and faith. Indeed, to varying degrees, newsmen contributed to this process by selling American dollars for Vietnamese piastres at the black-market rate—roughly 190 piastres, versus the legal rate of 113 piastres, per dollar. The transaction was usually carried out by the discreet, apprehensive Indian money-changers in the Eden Building, known as the "Bank of India." Prices in Saigon for goods and services sold to foreign newsmen—hotel rooms, rent, restaurant food, car rentals, and, during the 1967–68 porcelain-collecting craze, pottery and "Hue blue"—reflected the black-market (or "free market") rate. Some newsmen made a killing from their expense accounts by charging the home office in piastres at the legal rate but paying in cheaper black-market piastres. Others, like this reporter, charged the home office in honest dollars, but, to conserve bureau funds, paid some expenses in black-market piastres (a practice ordered stopped by the Washington *Post* in 1969). CBS and *Time,* to my knowledge, had an absolute ban on buying or using black-market piastres; most other bureaus left it up to individual newsmen. In 1966–68, several newsmen were charged with alleged black-market currency dealings, but the Vietnamese did not crack down in earnest. Moreover, in 1966–67, MACV would not (or could not) allow the sale of Army jungle garb, packs, or boots to civilian newsmen; but these items were readily available in the thieves' market in Saigon, presumably after being stolen on the Saigon docks. Of course, some of the same newsmen involved in such dealings were often puritanical in their condemnations of the same black market and of Vietnamese corruption generally.

Partly as a professional reflex, U.S. newsmen often took notice of another negative aspect of Thieu's performance: political censorship or suppression of Vietnamese newspapers (radio and television were

---

and Ky," he said, "can take care of themselves. But there are hundreds of thousands of little people—schoolteachers, district officials, hamlet chiefs—who face reprisals if we leave them in the lurch. We shouldn't have gone in, but we can't just 'pull out.'" As was clear that night, there was a considerable gap between the perceptions of the South Vietnamese by, on the one hand, the newsmen, who remembered individuals, good and bad, and on the other by academicians, who viewed the GVN from afar as an abstract "military dictatorship" and saw Hanoi as a "liberating" force.

government-controlled, with U.S. advisors). By U.S. peacetime standards, the government was intolerant if erratic. White spaces regularly appeared in the Saigon *Daily News* and other papers prior to the August 1967 election campaign. Even so, by Southeast Asian (or Third World) standards, or by wartime standards anywhere, the Saigon press was remarkably free to criticize or report the criticisms of the regime's noncommunist foes during the 1967 election period. After the elections, censorship was first relaxed, then renewed. Yet the January 1968 manifesto calling for a negotiated peace got into the Saigon *Daily News,* which also carried the complaints of columnist Van Minh (actually Nguyen Ngoc Rao, then the *Times*'s stringer). In any event, the 40-odd Saigon papers had important problems in addition to censorship. There were too many of them, and none was strong enough financially to survive a shutdown or do much reporting. Also, most were, in the French pre-World War II tradition, merely mouthpieces for one or another of the Saigon political cliques, and quick to seize on rumor and scandal.

Police suppression of dissent, notoriously well-organized in the Diem era, was less consistent under Thieu prior to Tet. Considering the deadly complexities of what was at least partially a civil war, Saigon was hardly a city ruled by terror. While it is true that Thich Tri Quang, who tried to overturn the 1966 government, was occasionally sequestered in a police villa, he was also allowed to lead abortive, bloodless protests in 1967 in downtown Saigon.

Draft-exempt student leaders railed in public against the military (without attracting much following) and French-speaking intellectuals complained over coffee in the Café Pagode. Later, some politicians, out of war-weariness or fear, moved to Paris. Hundreds of other people, suspected of Vietcong sympathies (or simply victims of official grudges), wound up in the prison cages of the Con Son Islands. But, in 1967, newsmen had no problem locating and interviewing the government's noncommunist critics, most of whom were largely left unmolested, possibly because of U.S. Embassy pressure or possibly because most of them represented little more than themselves.[88]

The legitimacy of the Saigon regime was also a chronic media issue prior to Tet, notably with regard to the September 1967 elections, in which Thieu and Ky won out over 10 rival "civilian" slates. Charges and countercharges were many, and the losers declared the elections had been "rigged." The runner-up, an energetic, surprisingly wealthy,

English-speaking lawyer-businessman, Truong Dinh Dzu, the self-styled "peace candidate," went to jail on a fraud charge soon thereafter; he appeared a martyr to some in the United States, if not in cynical Saigon.

Just prior to the 1967 elections, President Johnson sent a group of 22 VIPs (including senators, governors, mayors, clergymen, businessmen, and civil and labor leaders) to certify as to the legitimacy of the Vietnamese election process. Saigon bureaus received orders to "cover" the visitors, for names make news. The resultant reporting appeared on page one, and Johnson gained in support, as intended. But few U.S. specialists in Saigon were prepared to say how "clean" or "dirty" the voting had been, or by what standards. The New York *Times* bureau in 1967 made a special effort to investigate voting fraud charges by Thieu's foes, but few irregularities turned up. In this writer's view, the election was "rigged" well before election day. Through the parliamentary process (using Thieu's patronage and money power), the candidacies of Maj. Gen. Duong Van Minh ("Big Minh"), then in exile in Bangkok, and Au Truong Thanh, the former economics specialist and another "peace candidate," were ruled out. That, and the proliferation of candidates, were sufficient—a wholesale vote fraud was not necessary.

All these factors were part of the "conventional wisdom" about the Thieu regime prior to Tet. But they did not explain what happened in January, February, and March 1968, nor did they explain why most South Vietnamese apparently did not prefer Hanoi's rule to that of Saigon.

As already noted, after the onset of Tet, the Saigon regime decreed general mobilization, started to add 135,000 men to the armed forces, and, in perhaps its most significant political move of the Tet period, began the unprecedented arming of the civilian population. These long-overdue steps were highly important to Johnson Administration policy. In fact, coupled with enemy losses and ARVN's sacrifices, they helped make it unnecessary for the United States to send massive troop reinforcements to Vietnam to hold the battlefield "initiative," and they permitted "Vietnamization" to begin in mid-1969 without military setbacks.

Yet this crucial aspect of Thieu's post-Tet performance—however uneven and mediocre—did not receive commensurate attention in the U.S. press, although it was reported by AP's Barry Kramer and UPI's Daniel Southerland, particularly after mid-February. Far more "play" was given to the "negative"—accurate reports of the collapse of individual Vietnamese officials under Tet stress (notably at Hue by George McArthur of AP and in the Delta by Lescaze of the *Post*); the arrests of Thich Tri Quang and other antigovernment figures; legislative quarrels with Thieu; and the old corruption and other charges. Moreover, nothing that the Thieu government or the ARVN did or said at Tet got the sensational treatment accorded the AP pictures and TV sequences of General Loan's execution of a Vietcong prisoner. AP photographs of Thieu visiting Hue after the battle (February 25) did not make *Time, Newsweek,* or page one of the *Times* or *Post,* for such photos lacked drama.

In brief, the *Times* published only four front-page stories on South Vietnamese politics or GVN reaction and performance in February and four in March, out of 107 page-one stories from Vietnam; the *Post,* always more interested in "politics," published slightly more: seven in February and six in March, out of 95 page-one stories from Vietnam. Neither newspaper did a wrap-up on the GVN's "muddling-through." The *Post* devoted equal page-one attention to the regime's arrests of its political foes and to Thieu's mobilization plans. Also, during the same period, both papers printed stories out of Washington citing State Department and Congressional impatience with the GVN failure to carry out prompt major reforms amid the Tet crisis.[89]

The Administration Said Little

In contrast to the official, somewhat paternalistic optimism emanating from the White House and State Department before, during, and after the 1967 elections in Vietnam, very little was said in public in Washington about the GVN performance during the Tet period. In his February 2 press conference, President Johnson remarked only:

The biggest fact is that the stated purposes of the general uprisings have failed. Communist leaders counted on popular support in the cities for their effort. They found little or none. On the other hand, there have been civilian casualties and disruption of public services. Just before I came into the room, I read a long cable from Ambassador Bunker which described the vigor with which the Vietnamese government and our own people are working together to deal with the problems of restoring civilian services and order in all of the cities.

One finds no subsequent mention of the Thieu regime (as distinct from the "South Vietnamese people") in President Johnson's plentiful public statements prior to his climactic March 31 speech, when he cited Thieu's readiness to bear a greater burden in the war.

Defense Secretary McNamara, whose enthusiasm for Asian management methods was limited, in his gloomy January 22 "posture statement" (released February 1), uttered his much quoted statement that the war depended on "the will of the South Vietnamese people to survive as an independent nation." His remarks on current GVN performance were brief:

Although the political structure is still very fragile, the first essential steps in the evolution of a viable South Vietnamese state have been taken. Furthermore, over half of the entire adult population of South Vietnam (including those adults working or serving with the Vietcong) participated in the electoral process through which these new institutions were brought into being. Political evolution, moreover, has not been confined to the national arena. Some of the hamlet and village councils recently established by popular election represent a structure that over the long run could outweigh in importance the more widely publicized advances in the national government. But at all levels of government, continued progress toward stability and responsiveness requires a determined attack on basic social ills, including the problem of corruption. The fate of the government rests on its success in surmounting obstacles to the prompt development and introduction of the economic and political programs that will gain and retain wide popular support.[90]

On "Face the Nation," Undersecretary of State Nicholas deB. Katzenbach emphasized the U.S. Embassy's "opportunity" theme:

They [the South Vietnamese government] don't always do everything that we would like to see. Things don't always go as fast as we would like to see them go. That happens. It even happens within the United States from time to time. They have trouble getting tax legislation; we have trouble getting tax legislation. It is not an unusual situation. But I would say that right now, at this moment, there is a great opportunity for the South Vietnamese government. Immediately following all these attacks they have a great opportunity to move into the situation, to move into it effectively, and efficiently, and to take hold. It was significant that the people did not join the VC in any large numbers. It is now encumbent on the South Vietnamese government to see if they can use this opportunity to improve their government services as they are trying to do, to make various reforms that they want to make and that they ought to make, and to see if right now they can gain the loyalty of considerable numbers of the people.[91]

In passing, Dean Rusk noted the Central Recovery Committee's existence in a speech on February 10: "The South Vietnamese government has set up a task force under Vice President Ky to deal with refugees and other urgent problems. The Lower House has designated a member to serve on it and other groups will be represented. More than 70 refugee centers are already operating in Saigon, and food is being distributed throughout the city."[92]

In Saigon, as always, Ambassador Bunker was the chief defender of the GVN, even as he privately prodded Thieu on mobilization, reforms, and release of political prisoners. Perhaps Bunker's most bizarre duty as ambassador during Tet was to go on television on February 2 to rebut Vietcong radio claims, widely believed by the Saigonese, that U.S. forces were cooperating with the VC to set up a coalition government.

The Wire Services: A Narrow View

Both UPI and AP—in Saigon as in Washington—provided an abundance of "announcement news," with some of it getting on the evening television news shows and into the New York *Times* and Washington *Post*. Neither wire service, however, sent much beyond the "announcements." Our UPI files, again, are incomplete, but what is on hand does not reflect great differences from the treatment accorded the GVN by the AP.

AP covered Thieu's first public appearance after the opening Tet attacks, noting that he "claimed" the GVN was not taken by surprise:

Thieu said emergency measures would go into effect, probably Saturday, to cope with mounting health and sanitation hazards and to rebuild dwindling supplies of food in Saigon and other cities. The President claimed the government and the South Vietnamese Army were not taken by surprise by the attacks.

"On the contrary," he said, "several months ago we captured a document which indicated such an offensive would take place as the first phase prior to sitting down to peace talks."

Why then, the President was asked, were the communists able to make headway in attacks on numerous cities?

Thieu replied he did not believe the government army was prepared to cope with such widespread fighting and still maintain its role in the pacification program and other efforts.

Thieu said government censorship of the press, dropped last year during the political campaigning, will be resumed when newspapers start publishing again after the Lunar New Year holidays.

"I believe freedom of the press and freedom of speech at this time would foster speculation and false information and would be helpful to the Vietcong," he added.[93]

AP also noted the "execution stakes" in central Saigon:

SAIGON (AP)—Six execution stakes at Saigon's central market were removed Sunday, leading to speculation that the U.S. Embassy had urged the South Vietnamese government to be less harsh in its handling of captured Vietcong.

The posts had been put up after the Vietcong began nationwide attacks and raids on Saigon six days ago. The stakes were never used, but there have been reports of on-the-spot executions of captured Vietcong on the city's streets, and even executions without trial of Vietcong in Saigon's prisons.

The embassy apparently also was aware of worldwide reaction to a photograph showing the South Vietnamese national police director, Gen. Nguyen Ngoc Loan, shooting a captured Vietcong in the head at point-blank range on a Saigon street.[94]

Even as it reported damage, however, the AP repeatedly noted that the recovery effort was being made: "The government has set up a high-level national recovery committee which has budgeted $5 million for refugee relief and reconstruction of the damaged cities. Ambassador Ellsworth Bunker has ordered a full mobilization of U.S. Mission resources and manpower in support of this effort, the Mission announced."[95]

From Washington, the problem of diversion of U.S. aid to Vietnam into communist hands was reported, pointing up chaotic conditions and implying local police corruption:

WASHINGTON (AP)—Communists are on the receiving end of some U.S. commodities sent to Vietnam, says a top official of the Agency for International Development, because stopping such diversions completely would be "impossibly expensive."

. . . .

A strict control program with police inspectors was tried, [AID Deputy Director Rutherford] Poats said, adding:

"We came to the conclusion it doesn't work. It had limited utility and some police preyed on the people, collecting shakedowns."

Besides, he said, it simply isn't always possible to say whether a village to which materials are being shipped is or is not under Vietcong control. A village's political leanings can change markedly after dark, he said.[96]

George McArthur reported U.S. advisors' adverse views of the GVN in an aftermath story on Hue which described the particularly bad performance of local officials there:

HUE, Vietnam (AP)—When communist forces virtually overran Hue four weeks ago, the city's official structure vanished like a punctured soap bubble.

The conduct of the city's officialdom was the despair of American advisors as Hue was slowly freed.

"They are leaderless and gutless," one harried American exploded after a day of frustrations.

. . . .

A doctor from neighboring Quang Nam province was vacationing in Hue when the communists struck. His own house never fell into communist hands and he was untouched. Yet, with thousands in the city needing medical care, he never treated a patient. It wasn't his job, he said.

. . . .

Not for 17 days did the province chief, Lt. Col. Pham Van Khoa, issue orders to shoot looters.

"By then everything had already been stolen, sometimes twice," an American official said.

. . . .

Had it not been for the American presence, the situation would have sunk to chaos. It was American rice which kept more than 60,000 refugees from starvation, and American medical teams which administered the thousands of shots which warded off disease.

It was more than three weeks before Khoa began to get the shaky government machinery moving at all. He had been missing for the first seven days, hiding in civilian clothes in part of the city overrun by the communists.

. . . .

The question was re-raised in Hue, and elsewhere: Why are "their Vietnamese," the communists, so good, and "our Vietnamese" frequently so bad?

Seasoned American officials consider that, given the present circumstances—20 years of war and the limpid popularity of the Saigon government among other things—to expect more of the population is useless.

Such understanding, however, makes the tragedy of Hue no less painful.[97]

The AP consistently reported "march North" stories, although it was quite clear that ARVN could no more invade North Vietnam than Chiang Kai-shek could invade mainland China without a major (and unlikely) U.S. commitment. What Thieu and Ky thought on this subject was irrelevant, and the press knew it. But on March 22 they had urged a movement northward, and, because they said it, it was "news." Here, Thieu and Ky were linked to a Saigon newspaper's call for escalation against Hanoi:

SAIGON (AP)—A Saigon newspaper known as the voice of the South Vietnamese Army has called for an invasion of North Vietnam.

An editorial Friday in *Tien Tuyen* urged a step-up in bombing of the North, including the dikes of the Red River Delta, and a landing of troops in the North. . . .

Much of the South Vietnamese military leadership, including President Nguyen Van Thieu and Vice President Nguyen Cao Ky are known to favor escalation of the war against the North.[98]

Finally, Barry Kramer wrote a balanced wrap-up of the GVN's post-Tet performance, largely on the Saigon policy level:

SAIGON (AP)—The Saigon government has moved into action in many directions in the wake of the Tet offensive, leading one American observer to suggest: "It's amazing what a little panic will do."

President Nguyen Van Thieu is acting to increase his armed forces and has launched an attack on corruption and incompetence. He has pushed his military commanders to get their troops out of the cities, emphasizing a return of pacification teams to the countryside.

The list of objectives is long. Most observers agree they are the most aggressive and far-reaching moves proclaimed by any Vietnamese government in so short a period.

But they are for the most part only objectives and not yet accomplishments.

"Considering that this is an underdeveloped country, with a war going on, and with a poorly developed bureaucracy, it's really amazing that they've been able to do this well," an American official says.

"But, you know, the South Vietnamese government has gotten a very bad press. Most politicians back in the States are convinced that Saigon just can't make it.

"They've done a lot, but with the political situation back home, I wonder if it's enough. I wonder if it isn't too late."

Another American comment: "Thieu has done pretty well, but a Magsaysay he ain't." The late Ramon Magsaysay, President of the Philippines, was a dynamic leader who had the ability to rally his people.

Thieu is indecisive, his critics say, although in recent days he has shown increasing determination and aggressiveness. Feeling between Thieu and Vice President Nguyen Cao Ky has precluded strong cooperation by the two most important men in the government, however.

A Vietnamese journalist, usually critical of the Thieu government, commented: "I think the most important thing in the last two months is not what the government is doing or says it is going to do, but the fact that there is political stability."

This stability, in contrast to former days of coups and countercoups, is impressive to Americans, too. . . .

Thieu has ordered a net increase of 135,000 in the armed forces by the end of the year. The United States has agreed to equip them, but manpower experts say it will be difficult to bring a net increase of 135,000 unless there is a decline in casualties and desertions.

U.S. officials also say they are worried that the increased draft calls, with recall of reservists and veterans, will weaken seriously the government's already thin executive crust as well as essential utilities and industries.

Nineteen-year-olds are being drafted and 18-year-olds will be called starting in May. The number of volunteers in February, 10,084, was two and a half times the number during the same month last year.

Thieu says 10,000 weapons have been given to self-defense groups, many of them in Roman Catholic parishes and hamlets which tend to be anticommunist.

. . . .

Several measures fall into this category [of reform], chief among them the naming of 12 new province chiefs. Thieu also has replaced two of the four corps commanders, and plans to overhaul the relationship between Saigon and the provinces.[99]

The Networks: Mostly Familiar Charges

GVN performance was hard to portray on film, and thus was even farther from the grasp of network journalists than of other newsmen. Mention was scant, and came mostly in anchorman commentary or reports on the speeches of U.S. politicians or Administration spokesmen.

On February 1, for example, CBS's Walter Cronkite noted Defense Secretary McNamara's words about "the will to survive," saying that "one of the main problems of the war is the South Vietnamese themselves." Next day, NBC's Chet Huntley, on radio, aired as expert the views of Senator Edward Kennedy, just returned from a pre-Tet two-week visit to South Vietnam:

... Senator Kennedy reports that the effort of the South Vietnamese is still halfhearted. In many instances he found South Vietnamese asserting that this was not their war, that it was, in their opinion, a war between the United States and the Chinese Communists, so why should they have any part of it. The Senator found that the graft and thievery and favoritism go on unabated. He reports that in some cases 50 percent of our aid goes into private profits in the form of graft and thievery before it ever reaches the people for whom it is intended.

Still, American supplies are stolen off the docks of Saigon. Still, South Vietnamese landlords live it up in Saigon and collect their exorbitant rents from the peasants in the countryside. Still, South Vietnamese military officers are running bars and bordellos in the capital. The elected and appointed officials of the new South Vietnamese government have never had it so comfortable, and here, as Senator Kennedy says, there is an incentive in behalf of keeping the war going as long as possible.

Senator Kennedy has proposed an attitude of new toughness on the part of the United States. He recommends that we must serve notice to the South Vietnamese that they must bear their part of the burden and they must make a more determined effort. Eighteen-year-old South Vietnamese youths still lounge about on the streets of Saigon while 18-year-old Americans are dying fighting. . . .

. . . .

Senator Kennedy suggests that if this be the true character of the South Vietnamese, then by what sort of judgment are we going through this agony to save them?[100]

The first major television analysis of the GVN's performance or prospects came from Walter Cronkite on February 14, only a few days after his arrival in Saigon. Cronkite spoke with firmness, but at times it was not clear which government he was analyzing. He cited the "credibility gap" and "hope for peace"—both preoccupations in Washington, not in Saigon: "If the government does not respond well to this challenge, if it cannot close the credibility gap and restore that elusive hope for peace, a clamor [sic] will rise again for another change of government, and not necessarily through constitutional process. Such discord here in the South would strengthen the resolve in the North and put . . . the war's end further in the future."[101]

NBC's David Brinkley commented on corruption in Vietnam which "is deep and profound, at almost every level." The announcement of the 19-year-old draft did not make CBS; instead,

Cronkite noted that Senator Ernest Gruening, a pre-Tonkin Gulf dove, planned to investigate "Saigon corruption." On the same show, Cronkite editorialized about Thieu's austerity measures, noting: "President Thieu said today that South Vietnam has now entered a critical period of its national history, quite an understatement."[102]

NBC's Douglas Kiker, also a post-Tet visitor to Vietnam, saw the GVN's "stability" threatened by the foe's weak mortar and rocket bombardments (and also a few ground assaults) on February 18–19, almost three weeks after the opening Tet attacks: "Officials might say now that this second wave of attacks was less severe. . . . And maybe they would be right. But nevertheless the effects of these attacks on the stability of the government of South Vietnam and the progress of this war is going to be profound."[103] Kiker continued his political analysis in Ban Me Thuot three days later:

> It's a tortuous vise the South Vietnamese are caught in. Between the Vietcong . . . who do not hesitate to use force and terrorism . . . and a national government *headed by generals* which so far has given these people *only* insecurity, corruption, and little or no evidence that it is a government which will act in their best interests. . . . Most of them [the South Vietnamese] have little or no motivation to accept responsibility or to participate in political affairs. They're tired of *military rule*, they're weary of this war.[104]

This was an "old sins" analysis. Kiker was a good deal quicker than most of his colleagues to sum up the GVN's Tet liabilities.

On March 5, ABC, quoting Bill Brannigan in Saigon, reported that 18- and 19-year-olds were now being drafted (actually, only 19-year-olds at that point). The next night Brannigan's film clip got on the air with views of Saigon draft centers. Then, having given the devil his due, Brannigan on March 7, like Kiker, repeated the well-worn charges. Land reform, he said, "creeps at a snail's pace"; there were bribery, kickbacks, and a black market, while the United States spent "$3 million an hour" in Vietnam. Small wonder, he commented (as did Kiker), that the peasants continued their "neutrality," caught between "continued injustice and corruption under the neo-mandarins or the one-party rule of the Vietcong."[105]

Thieu's March 11 ouster of six province chiefs and the mayor of Hue made the wire services, and thus was cited on all three networks by anchormen as a blow against corruption. Two days later, that old wire service stand-by, a threatened "march North" by the South Vietnamese, made both NBC and CBS.[106]

ABC White House correspondent Frank Reynolds discussed Johnson's speech of March 21 in which the President praised the South Vietnamese people's will to fight. Said Reynolds:

> The major nightmare that haunts [the Administration] about the war in Vietnam is the fear that one day the American people might decide the South Vietnamese themselves are not doing enough to fight their own war. The Administration is deeply concerned about charges that the government in Saigon is apathetic toward corruption and that the people of Vietnam do not really care who wins the war just so long as the fighting stops. . . .
>
> [Johnson] believes there will be no peace until the North Vietnamese decide the American people won't quit, and in order to make sure that does not happen, he must also convince the American people that the South Vietnamese are willing to fight on. *That is a large order for anyone, perhaps especially for a President whose own credibility is under fire these days.*[107]

The same night, ABC and CBS anchormen reported Thieu's announced plan to increase the South Vietnamese armed services by 135,000 men; NBC did not.

The Newspapers: Conflicting Reports

Those in the home offices of the New York *Times* and Washington *Post*—who were furthest from the scene, and closest to the domestic Vietnam debate—were the most prone to repeat the conventional charges against the GVN as explanations of the initial enemy success at Tet. An early example came on February 4, when the New York *Times* Sunday editor published an interview with Senator Edward Kennedy. It was one of the longest single accounts published during the Tet period by the *Times* concerning the GVN's performance.

Kennedy's justified concern was with refugees—the 904,000[108] who fled U.S. bombings and the ground fighting in 1965–67, mostly in the northern half of the country. His familiarity, during his brief Vietnam visit, with other aspects of GVN activity was necessarily limited. Moreover, that the Senator's firsthand experience did not cover the Tet period was a fact nowhere cited in the *Times*'s account:

> WASHINGTON—Senator Edward M. Kennedy, Democrat of Massachusetts, recently returned from a visit to South Vietnam and leveled

charges of corruption in that war-torn country. He discusses his views in the following interview with John W. Finney of the New York *Times* Washington bureau.

Q.: Senator, did you come back with the impression that corruption is increasing in South Vietnam?

A.: I traveled first to Vietnam in 1965 and again in the beginning of this year. I would say that the increase in corruption in all levels of government and in governmental programs with which I am primarily concerned, such as refugees, has increased dramatically.[109]

Kennedy's charges of corruption (perhaps less to the point than a charge of "neglect") were much publicized. They helped AID officials and others in Saigon who had sought greater U.S. efforts to help prod Thieu and Ky on the "refugee" problem prior to Tet. But for Kennedy to go further, and suggest, as he did, that major reform and "broadening its popular base," rather than military security, could or should preoccupy the Thieu-Ky government, four days after a major enemy assault on its cities, was simply pre-Tet oratory, and might have been recognized as such by the *Times*.

The U.S. Mission's thesis that the Thieu-Ky government had gained an "opportunity" (as cited by Undersecretary Katzenbach) was accurately reflected in a *Times* Saigon bureau story by Bernard Weinraub a week later. It included a summary of what, in fact, Thieu had been doing and saying, and a realistic U.S. Mission assessment of the prospects for reform amid battle:

SAIGON, South Vietnam, Feb. 10—There is a growing feeling in this tense city that the South Vietnamese government must react swiftly to cope with the confusion and disappointment that have swept the country since the Vietcong staged daring raids on Saigon, Hue, and other major cities.

"There is an opportunity here to be seized or lost," an American official said today. "If the government moves with decision, they'll wind up in a strong position. If not, they're in trouble."

"The government now has a chance to move into a vacuum," said another official.

Yesterday President Thieu said he was prepared to step up mobilization and start drafting 18-year-olds by July. He also asked the legislature to give him authority to rule by decree for the next year on economic and financial matters.

Although American officials indicate that martial law is necessary, there appears to be growing uneasiness among South Vietnamese politicians, intellectuals, and students that the constitutional process may suffer as a result. . . .

Reforms in corrupt practices and in nepotism will probably not be pressed because the emphasis over the next few months will be on the military clean-up of the Vietcong.[110]

In a February 11 *Times* column entitled "Illusions and Deceptions," Tom Wicker saw the United States fighting on in Vietnam to contain communism despite "the failure of will and effort of the South Vietnamese people." Two weeks later, citing the "considerable setback" in pacification, Ambassador Robert Komer, in a press backgrounder in Saigon, put the burden of recovery on the South Vietnamese government—an effort to prod Saigon via the press. Mentioning only a "high official," the *Times* quoted Komer as saying: "The real question now is who will fill the vacuum in the countryside. It depends how fast the South Vietnamese government moves in—and how aggressive and how fast the enemy will be."[111]

As it turned out, of course, the GVN moved very slowly to restore its already frail pre-Tet administration outside the district and provincial towns, especially in the Delta and I Corps; but, as John Paul Vann, chief U.S. pacification advisor in I Corps, observed to this reporter in early March, the enemy did not move any faster to fill the "vacuum." To an extent not appreciated at the time, the foe had been hurt and disorganized by Tet losses.

The same day, but further back in the paper, the *Times* ran an account of the coming takeover of the Delta command by General Thang, who had resigned as Minister of Revolutionary Development (pacification) just before Tet:

The husky, tough, and outspoken officer has long been a favorite of the American command because of his honesty, energy, and dedication to social reform. . . .

"It is one of the most encouraging steps the Vietnamese have taken in a long time," one American official said. . . .

His resignation took effect on January 27, only two days before the Vietcong's Lunar New Year offensive began.

In a brief speech on his resignation, General Thang said: "There are deficiencies that we have not been able to detect because of our incompetence. There are others that I personally realized but have been unable to correct due to my lack of means or power."[112]

Also, on the same day—the day that Hue fell to the allies—the

Times carried an AFP story, well inside the paper, on the government's arming of civilians:

SAIGON, South Vietnam, Feb. 24 (Agence France Presse)—An informed source said here today that weapons had been distributed to 600 South Vietnamese civil servants and that 700 other civilians had begun military training.

Self-defense groups are gradually being set up throughout the country, the source said, adding that some 12,500 civilians, mostly officials, had joined the "People Under Arms" program that Vice President Nguyen Cao Ky announced just after the start of the Vietcong Lunar New Year's offensive.

Civil servants are given top priority for weapons, the source said. They would use them to defend government buildings.[113]

Joseph Treaster followed up this story in a page-one report a week later, noting complaints that "so far no weapons have been distributed and the neighborhood militiamen complain bitterly of this. They also complain that the government is not taking sufficient steps to protect the people against what they consider to be an inevitable second major enemy attack."[114]

As a U.S. Senate debate on Vietnam brought a renewal of scathing attacks on the Thieu-Ky government, Charles Mohr, in a Saigon story primarily devoted to "pacification," reported the U.S. Mission view that the ARVN did "relatively well" during Tet. Then he went on to comment:

The long period of inaction and inertia that had seemed to mark the Thieu government was thus giving way to more encouraging action. But it was still too early to tell if the government would show continued vigor . . . the government is functioning in most towns, [but] an ominous problem is that the government is not really functioning in much of the rural countryside because so much of the countryside has been abandoned for the time being.[115]

The *Times*'s Saigon bureau two weeks later analyzed Thieu's tardy purge moves. Wrote Tom Buckley:

SAIGON, South Vietnam, Mar. 16—The enemy's Lunar New Year offensive has given President Thieu an opportunity to carry out one important election promise.

That was to reduce the power that had made the country's four corps commanders virtual monarchs [*sic*].

If it had not been for the enemy attacks, it is regarded as doubtful that the President could have done anything about achieving this reform, at least not without many more months of the patient maneuvering for which he is well known.[116]

In the same issue, Senator Robert F. Kennedy, an avowed Presidential candidate, made news with his attacks on the South Vietnamese. In a rare instance, the *Times* reporter, Peter Grose, noted that some of Kennedy's facts were debatable:

"I'm in favor of our making it quite clear to the South Vietnamese that their corruption should end, that they have to have a general mobilization, and that they have to draft 18-year-olds and 19-year-olds," Senator Kennedy said.

The Administration has reacted with impatience to this line of criticism in the past, for American officials say this is exactly what is already taking place. Extensive efforts to eliminate and punish corruption have long been made, they insist; the South Vietnamese have already decreed the drafting of 19-year-olds, and a draft of 18-year-olds is now being urged by the American Mission in Saigon.[117]

For the most part, however, the *Times*'s Washington bureau was not heeding the reports of its Saigon staff. In what was apparently a reflection of the Administration debate on Vietnam, Hedrick Smith wrote this State Department "inertia" story, which also appeared in the same issue:

WASHINGTON, Mar. 16—United States officials are disappointed at the pace of recovery by the South Vietnamese government from the enemy's sweeping Lunar New Year offensive against the cities six weeks ago.

These officials have privately expressed fears that the Vietcong and the North Vietnamese are capitalizing on Saigon's inertia by recruiting replacements for their recent combat casualties and consolidating their hold on wider areas in the countryside. . . .

From Washington's view, it was also necessary for the South Vietnamese government to move rapidly to increase its draft calls, to get the disrupted administrative machinery functioning again, and to reassert the government's authority in as wide an area as possible.

It is in these matters, many American officials suggest, that Saigon has so far moved too slowly or, on occasion, even in the wrong direction.[118]

Indications that Thieu was moving ahead continued to get into the *Times,* although they were virtually unnoticed by the domestic debaters and given little prominence by *Times* editors. On March 24, for example, Thieu's anticorruption plans were reported:

SAIGON, South Vietnam, Mar. 23—President Nguyen Van Thieu, who dismissed seven provincial chiefs last week, will oust six more shortly in a growing effort to curb corruption and inefficiency in the countryside, sources close to the Saigon government said tonight.

. . . .

Several American officials have said that they would reserve judgment of the importance of the changes until they had learned the names of the new provincial chiefs and then had waited months to see what they had accomplished. . . .

Several American officials are dismayed by the slow economic recovery of the cities in the aftermath of the enemy's Lunar New Year offensive. Part of the blame, they insist, rests with the Saigon government, which has reacted slowly to American suggestions on the relief effort.[119]

On the same day, James Reston, after talking with higher Administration officials, gave some accurate indications of what President Johnson's "Vietnamization" policy (to be unfolded March 31) would be:

. . . the recent speech by President Thieu of South Vietnam, calling for the conscription of an additional 135,000 South Vietnamese soldiers, may be significant. . . .

This is the kind of talk Washington wants to hear, and the White House took some pains to alert the press to what President Thieu said. Talk, however, is not policy, but it could be the beginning of a new policy or at least a new emphasis on the primary responsibility of the South Vietnamese. . . .

All this is very fuzzy for the moment. It is nothing more than a new element in the discussion of policy, forced by military, economic, and political events, and could be overwhelmed by the enemy's future actions on the battlefield, but it is important nonetheless.

Maybe it is beyond their [the South Vietnamese] capacity. Maybe they can't prevail unless we continue our search-and-destroy policy that is now in serious dispute in Washington, but at least the debate on all these things is now going on in Washington and the Saigon leaders know it.[120]

The *Post,* as we have already seen, devoted more attention to Saigon politics than did the *Times.* An early example came on February 4, with Lee Lescaze quoting U.S. Embassy "officials" in Saigon: "There is a very great chance for the Vietnamese government to turn the whole thing to their advantage," the officials added. If the people react with anger to the Vietcong attacks during their Tet holiday cease-fire, and the government moves quickly to help them rebuild their homes and lives, this potential is present, officials believe.[121]

Two weeks later, Stanley Karnow, in a page-one speculative piece, wrote:

SAIGON—Many South Vietnamese feel that the communists' Lunar New Year offensive scored political and psychological gains for them that *may have significant consequences* in the months to come.

At the same time, judging from local opinion, President Nguyen Van Thieu's Administration has suffered a severe loss of prestige that *could* lead to the kind of internal political instability that has plagued South Vietnam in recent years.

These attitudes, some based more on emotion than reason, stem both from renewed respect for communist capabilities in launching the offensive and dissatisfaction with the Saigon government's performance in meeting the challenge.[122]

Karnow's speculations, which he shared with Walter Cronkite, remained just that. But he reflected official U.S. anxiety over the Tet "challenge."

In a discussion of Vietnamese views, Lescaze reported in the March 3 *Post:*

The Vietnamese officials are also well aware of the Vietcong Tet offensive's political impact in the United States. . . .

"The Vietnamese people are now ready to accept a general mobilization," [a source] said at an informal press conference. . . .

The source was speaking of the government decision to increase its armed forces by about 125,000 men by June. As late as three weeks ago, the target was a 65,000-man increase.[123]

The *Post*'s able Vietnamese reporter, Nguyen Ngoc Rao, wrote this Saigon wrap-up on Thieu's status in mid-March:

The uneasy relationship between the President and Vice President Nguyen Cao Ky still simmers, but there are no indications that it is nearing a breaking point. American sources say the chief result of Thieu's suspicion of Ky has been to further delay government decisions. . . .

Meanwhile, Thieu's government is muddling along better than most outsiders had expected. It is moving vigorously to increase its armed forces by 65,000 men by July 1. There are plans to add about 65,000 more troops in the second half of the year. . . .

All male civil servants, university professors, and students 18 years or older must undergo military training.

Meanwhile, Thieu seems determined to stamp out corruption in government.[124] Officials say he plans to dismiss other province chiefs after having fired eight this week. Army officials are being trained to replace them.[125]

Indirectly, in other stories (its post-mortems on Hue and the Delta and its forays into pacification), the *Post*, like the *Times*, conveyed some flavor of GVN performance in the hinterland. But the emphasis of these stories was on "people" and "security," not administration, such as it was.

The News Magazines: Two Contrasting Views

Time and *Newsweek* gave a more generous share of their total Vietnam space to the Thieu-Ky regime than did the other media. And perhaps on no other subject were the two news magazines so divergent in their views. *Time*, with one exception, was extremely charitable toward Thieu—more charitable than its Saigon reporters. *Newsweek* ignored Thieu's Tet holiday errors, and attributed the foe's Tet success to basic weaknesses in the GVN itself. The magazine saw the Thieu-Ky regime as being in ruins and deservedly so. In its second issue after the January 30–31 attacks, reporting on U.S. domestic reaction to Tet, *Time* wrote:

. . . Bobby Kennedy told his Chicago audience: "Enormous corruption pervades every level of South Vietnamese official life." Washington's Democratic senator, Henry Jackson, a staunch Johnson supporter, demanded that "the Saigon government get off its duff and get moving."
Nothing, naturally, would please the Johnson Administration more. The fact is, however, that *unless the U.S. wants to undertake a full-fledged colonial venture in South Vietnam*, its leverage in dealing with an independent and touchy Saigon government is severely limited.[126]

In the same issue, its New York writers and editors went further:

The crisis also brought about a stepped-up mobilization, which the U.S. military command has long encouraged. President Nguyen Van Thieu announced that henceforth every able-bodied man over 17 years of age would receive military training. . . . The measures would add some 65,000 men to the 650,000-man ARVN. Thieu also announced that the nation's taxes would be raised. . . .
For bringing such destruction into civilian areas, the Vietcong lost more people than they gained. But the South Vietnamese government undoubtedly was tarred by the same brush. Saigon was blamed for not being able to keep the Vietcong out of the cities in the first place—and then for

having to devastate wide areas to get rid of the enemy. Who lost the more remains to be seen. "It depends," says the I Corps U.S. commander, Marine Lt. Gen. Robert E. Cushman, Jr., "on how fast the government provides assistance to rebuild homes, offices, roads, and bridges."
The government is moving to do just that. . . .
Vice President Ky's National Recovery Committee was allotted $5 million to begin to heal the wounds of the enemy attacks.[127]

Two weeks later, editors of *Time*'s "Nation" section viewed the GVN performance less charitably—reflecting the shock in the State Department and among Pentagon civilians. Optimism was suddenly declared a "casualty" by *Time*'s New York writer, possibly referring to its fate among his superiors:

Optimism is a sturdy soldier, frequently able to survive even against overwhelming odds. Last week in Vietnam *it joined the list of casualties. Not since the early months of 1965, when the communists were on the verge of overrunning South Vietnam just before the U.S. buildup, had the mood and prospects of the allies looked so totally grim.*

. . . officials were still trying to find something comforting in the recent communist Tet offensive despite all of the evidence to the contrary. Vice President Hubert Humphrey declared that the Saigon regime "if anything has been strengthened by the attack," and on TV the U.S. ambassador, Ellsworth Bunker, in effect, agreed. Despite some qualifications made by both men, such statements sounded absurd.

In contrast, middle- and lower-echelon officials at the State Department, the Pentagon, and U.S. headquarters in Saigon voiced *profound pessimism.* They were dismayed by the uncertain performance of the South Vietnamese government, dejected by the *demoralization of a populace suddenly feeling even less secure than before,* disappointed by the failure of U.S. intelligence in anticipating the scope of the communist move at the time when attacks clearly should have been anticipated.[128]

Time also noted a "growing feeling of fatalism" and a "violent new period of doubt" in South Vietnam about the regime, and wrote:

In one area, the government acted with alacrity, and not much to the liking of the United States. In a series of arrests throughout the country, the national police picked up *as many as 500* South Vietnamese lawyers, professors, labor leaders, monks, and intellectuals that they feared could constitute or help form a coalition government with the communists. Among them were militant Buddhist leader Thich Tri Quang, runner-up Presidential candidate Truong Dinh Dzu and former Economics Minister Au Truong Thanh. As a counternote, the government approved the formation of a front of its own called the "Front for the Salvation of the

Nation," to "face and combat the NLF." Headed by former Lt. Gen.
Tran Van Don, the Salvation Front includes several of the other defeated
Presidential candidates and representatives from South Vietnamese reli-
gious and political organizations.[129]

The following week, the editors changed their thinking again about
the GVN:

One thing that survived the communists' Tet offensive largely intact
was South Vietnam's lively political arena. In the center ring, of course,
President Nguyen Van Thieu and Vice President Nguyen Cao Ky continue to maneuver for paramount influence. . . . Many pro-government
political leaders, as well as those who oppose the government, are displaying a fresh critical spirit that begins with the realization that the government has to reform and renew itself. . . .

Last week the government responded to a reform long urged by the
United States by finally doing something about the blatant corruption that
has traditionally attached to the powerful and tempting "warlord" posts
of the corps commanders. . . . And in an effort to remove some of the
temptations of leadership, Thieu last week decided that henceforth province chiefs would report directly to Saigon rather than to their corps commanders. . . .

Thieu discovered, though, that not everything could be accomplished
by decree. He had asked the National Assembly for special powers to
rule the country's economic sphere by fiat for one year. By a surprising
vote of 85–10, the House of Representatives turned Thieu down. Explained one representative, Nguyen Van Nheiu: "Special powers lead to
dictatorship." Thieu still has a chance to have his way if the Senate ap-
proves the measure and sends it back to the House.

But if nothing else, the exchange demonstrated that the fledgling constitutional rule begun last fall amid such high hopes was still alive and functioning despite all the havoc wrought by the communists in the last
month.[130]

Time also took the trouble to publish excerpts of interviews with
Vietnamese political leaders on future policy. However, they said
very little:

Vice President Nguyen Cao Ky: "It's possible that the majority of the
people of South Vietnam don't really like or support our government. But
if they had to make a choice between us and the communists, there is no
doubt who would win. Our program must be: (1) reorganize the armed
forces, (2) get more people into united-front organizations, and (3)
get popular support."

. . . .

Trinh Quoc Khanh, leader of the Hoa Hao sect and President Thieu's first choice as his running-mate last year: "I have met many Americans who say that they have no right to get involved in our internal affairs. But in fact they are involved. And if they are sincere, they must get even more deeply involved and help South Vietnam remedy past political mistakes. The Americans cannot let government leaders damage their anticommunist goals. They must look at Vietnam much like a business. If you invest money in a firm, you have some say about who should manage it and how he runs it."

Senator Ton That Dinh, one-time Army officer who helped overthrow Diem: "There is a real need to reform the government. But at the same time something must be done to motivate the people to fight the communists. We, like the communists, are fighting a people's war."[131]

In mid-March, Thieu's reform promises received skeptical notice in *Time:*

. . . Last week, responding to strong urgings from the United States and from within its own ranks, the government of President Nguyen Van Thieu finally showed some signs of doing something about its endemic, pervasive wrongdoers. It replaced six of South Vietnam's 44 province chiefs on grounds of corruption and incompetence. . . .

Thieu was merely taking a first step. Like their predecessors, his six new men are all lieutenant colonels or colonels, and as military men may still find it difficult to challenge the generals who are corps commanders. Thieu has embarked upon only a limited war against corruption.[132]

The following week, *Time* cited Thieu's March 21 television message:

It was, in effect, a hard-hitting post-Tet State of the Union message, promising many of the sweeping reforms that the United States has been urging over the past two months. The program, beamed to 170,000 TV sets within viewing range of 76 percent of the country's population, would, if carried out, go far toward solving the worst of South Vietnam's problems. Among President Thieu's major concerns:

Mobilization. "We must make greater sacrifices because this is our country," said Thieu. "I have decided to increase the armed forces by 135,000." The President said that the new troops would be created mainly by mobilizing 18- and 19-year-olds and by recalling veterans under 33 with less than five years of military service.[133]

. . . .

Refugee Rights. To help ensure that corrupt officials do not dip into the aid for the refugees of the communists' Tet attacks, Thieu spelled out exactly what each refugee family was entitled to get. In Saigon it was $83, 10 large iron sheets, and 10 bags of cement. In Hue the aid was the same except that, because of the excessive damage, each family should get 20 iron sheets. Elsewhere, each family was due $41.50, 10 sheets, 10 bags of cement. Thieu reported that the refugee rolls had already been reduced from the initial 700,000 created by Tet to 405,000.[134]

The vehemence of *Newsweek*'s negative views of the GVN stemmed partly from its New York editors' penchant for sweeping generalizations and partly from the personal outlook of its veteran French political specialist in Saigon, Francois Sully.

In its initial account of the Tet offensive, *Newsweek* wrote: "In an attempt to avert total chaos, President Nguyen Van Thieu declared a state of martial law." Martial law that week was an exclusive *Newsweek* obsession. Elsewhere in the same issue, Thieu's act was seen in a unique perspective:

More important, the communists succeeded in undermining whatever *small claim* the Saigon government once had that it could *control* its own country. And by forcing President Thieu to declare martial law—a step which temporarily at least permitted South Vietnam's generals to step back into their former positions of unchallenged power—the communists *wiped out* months of hard-won constitutional progress. This, in turn, *all but swept the foundation of legitimacy* from under Saigon's feet.[135]

Contrary to the predictions of U.S. officials that the Vietcong attacks would alienate the South Vietnamese from the communists, the *opposite* seemed to have occurred. Many South Vietnamese, in fact, seemed to place the greatest blame on their own government—and the United States —for failing to provide them with protection. "Our generals," said Nguyen Gian Hien, a Catholic leader recently elected to the upper house of the South Vietnamese legislature, "knew that the Vietcong were planning to attack Saigon. The public knew it. I knew it. And still, the generals did nothing. They were playing cards or dancing. This country still badly needs some real leadership."[136]

Still in the same issue, the theme of Thieu's martial law was taken up again, and this time justified. It now appeared that the tragedy that befell the South Vietnamese had yet to reach its "fullest proportions." Wrote Everett J. Martin:

Given the state of open warfare throughout Vietnam last week, it was, of course, necessary that President Nguyen Van Thieu declare martial law. But in the heat of events, it should not be forgotten that the *one thing* that might restore the shaken faith of the Vietnamese people would be to see representative government finally begin to function.

It is an open secret in Saigon that many in the military junta would much prefer to go back to their old method of ruling by decree with complete suppression of opposition opinion. . . . If any attempt is made to return to military rule as a permanent system of government, then the tragedy that befell the South Vietnamese last week will have reached its fullest proportions.[137]

Newsweek, like *Time,* quoted Defense Secretary McNamara's year-end report and commented:

. . . where once he used to set target dates for the beginning of an end,[138] McNamara this time clearly expected a long and costly struggle. . . . And most of all, McNamara stressed his main-theme message that South Vietnam needs to do more—"much more." "This total effort," he said, "is . . . one in which the people of South Vietnam must play the primary role. We and the other free-world nations who have come to South Vietnam's assistance can only help."[139]

In its late February reporting, *Newsweek* took another look at the Saigon government facing its "supreme test," and saw failure ahead:

"The supreme test now," said one top U.S. official, "is how Saigon performs." To meet that test, the South Vietnamese government established a "National Recovery Committee" whose chairman is Vice President Nguyen Cao Ky. Each morning at 8, Ky and 13 other ranking Vietnamese officials gathered in Saigon's Presidential Palace to plot the strategy of reconstruction. By last week, the committee had set up 77 food-distribution centers in the capital and laid plans to replace thousands of destroyed homes with urban-housing projects. Declared Deputy Ambassador Robert W. Komer, the perennially optimistic chief of the U.S. pacification program: "I am most impressed with the speed and decisiveness with which the [government] has organized itself."

Not everyone, however, was as impressed as Komer.[140] True, *hard-driving* Maj. Gen. Nguyen Duc Thang, who had buried his disagreements with the Thieu Administration . . . to take day-to-day charge of the recovery program, was working practically round-the-clock. But Thang faced enormous obstacles in carrying out his plans. For one thing, hundreds of civil servants were unable to travel to their jobs because of the strict military curfew; as a result, their understaffed ministries stumbled under the mounting work load. For another, communications were still so badly disrupted that it took days just to relay messages between Saigon and provincial capitals.[141]

. . . despite an unaccustomed display of solidarity among top South Vietnamese officials, many key politicians[142] throughout the country seemed frozen into inaction by the emergency.[143]

The following week, *Newsweek's* Saigon bureau took a look at that city's Chinese population, with its wealthy Chinese businessmen, and told readers that the Thieu-Ky regime needed Chinese support "if it is to survive at all." Most Saigon newsmen and their Vietnamese reporters would have suggested, rather, that the regime needed the Chinese businessmen considerably less than the Chinese businessmen needed the regime.[144]

Newsweek's major statement on the Thieu-Ky regime came, after an internal decision to condemn Johnson's war policy, in a feature entitled "Vietnam: A Reappraisal." It amounted to a lengthy series of editorials which did not pretend to separate fact from opinion:

> . . . Even if the United States were to win a clear-cut military victory in South Vietnam—a prospect that now seems remote indeed—it would be a hollow and ephemeral triumph unless the people of South Vietnam demonstrated the will and ability to govern themselves effectively.
>
> At the moment, there is scant cause for optimism on this score. From top to bottom the government of South Vietnam is torn by bitter rivalries. Its *titular* chief, President Nguyen Van Thieu, a cautious, colorless man, presides over an Administration that is not really his own. All the important officials—the only ones with authority—owe allegiance to Vice President Nguyen Cao Ky.[145] For although Ky came out second best in last year's struggle for the Presidency, his forceful personality still enables him to look and act like a winner. . . .
>
> Recently, in the wake of the Vietcong's Tet offensive, neighborhood groups in Saigon and other cities formed vigilante organizations to defend themselves against future raids. But this promising development has been thwarted by the deep-rooted antipathy between native South Vietnamese and immigrants from the north. . . .[146]
>
> The whole story of South Vietnam since the Tet offensive, in fact, has been one of missed opportunities. . . . South Vietnam's generals used the occasion to make a bid for *something like* a return to military rule. With martial law in force, more than 50 opposition politicians were taken into custody and held without formal charges. . . .
>
> Reasonably enough, the members of South Vietnam's parliament have sought to combat this *semi-coup*.[147] Last week, echoing a previous vote by the House of Representatives, the Saigon Senate refused to grant the Thieu regime emergency economic powers. And at the same time, a group of House members was circulating a petition which, in effect, called for a vote of no-confidence in Premier Loc and his Cabinet.[148]

Having raised, then befogged, the images of "military rule" and greedy generals, *Newsweek* went on to condemn the South Vietnamese legislators for obstructionist "bickering":

Throughout the recent crisis, South Vietnam's legislators have played a purely negative role. . . .
Such internecine bickering results in staggering inefficiency in even the simplest government functions. A Filipino technician who works for a U.S. construction firm recently had to wait two months for an extension of his residence visa; the buck had been passed all the way up to Interior Minister Linh Quang Vien.[149] Similarly, Vietnamese industrialists whose factories were damaged in the Tet fighting are still awaiting word from the Economics Minister as to whether they should *keep the plants closed or* expect the government to help in reopening them. Given this lack of leadership, it is scarcely surprising that ordinary Vietnamese so often resort to a process known as *xoai-xo*—literally, "turn around and pick up what suits me."[150]

. . . The countryside fares even worse. Land reform, a vital element in any effort to win the loyalty of the peasantry, has not been tackled seriously.[151]

It is difficult, once again, to fathom *Newsweek's* logic. Surely, neither *Newsweek* nor the Vietnamese peasant expected the regime to tackle land reform seriously in the aftermath of Tet. However, *Newsweek* was not alone in its approach. Its writers in New York, like journalists elsewhere, were seeking and offering instant explanation and measurement of disaster—telling the reader more than the writers themselves knew, or could know. For *Newsweek*, as for others, the South Vietnamese, faceless to most Americans, offered a convenient scapegoat for the Tet surprise—and the war's frustrations.

10

Did Tet Destroy Pacification?

Pacification is a very slow and painstaking process. Even after an area has been essentially "cleared" of main force elements, a free-world military presence must be maintained to cope with residual guerrilla units. In fact, we have found that it is very difficult to clear, completely and permanently, any area in which the guerrillas were once well established. Even where we have been conducting clear-and-secure operations for several years, guerrilla hit-and-run attacks still occur. . . .

In the final analysis, the ultimate success of our entire effort in South Vietnam will turn on the ability of the government to reestablish its authority over its territory so that peaceful reconstruction can be undertaken.[1]

Perhaps no effort undertaken by the U.S. Mission in Vietnam was as much debated by Saigon newsmen in late 1967 as the pacification program. With the belated merger of the U.S. military and civilian pacification advisory efforts into the single CORDS organization, General Westmoreland was assigned overall responsibility for the American share of the program in May 1967. Robert W. Komer, his deputy, ran CORDS as a subsidiary of the larger military command structure, MACV.

Part of the argument was over Komer himself—his public salesmanship, his use of computerized statistics, and his optimism. Part also stemmed from the deep skepticism, transmitted from earlier generations of Vietnam reporters and field officials, that the new attempt at pacification would prove any more fruitful than the erratic, much-publicized efforts of the past. Almost no one except Komer was optimistic about pacification, and even Komer was wary about publicly claiming any "turning points."

What Was "Pacification"?

"Some call it chiefly a matter of providing protection or continuous local security in the countryside," Komer told newsmen on December 1, 1967. "Others call it the process of 'winning hearts and minds.'"

The rhetoric changed often in 1965–67. It was called "the other war" by Lyndon Johnson to distinguish the rural economic-political-security effort from the war against communist main force units fought mostly by Americans. It was called "revolutionary development" in 1966. And Komer called it "pacification," a French term familiar to Vietnamese (and to veterans of France's 1954–62 war in Algeria). This changing phraseology reflected uncertainty, particularly in official Washington, over what "the other war" could be expected to accomplish.

Pacification had been blessed by President Johnson as a kind of extension of the Administration's domestic "Great Society" program to Vietnam. It was to embrace refugee resettlement, education, IR-8 "miracle rice," land reform, good roads, health care, hamlet elections, even rural electrification. From Maj. Nguyen Van Be's training center at Vung Tau, initially under CIA auspices, came thousands of black-pajamaed Revolutionary Development cadres to work in 59-man teams in newly cleared hamlets—the GVN's answer to the Vietcong cadres. Visiting their graduation ceremonies, replete with slogans, songs, and torchlight, was a VIP "must." Program was piled on program, on overworked, underpaid Vietnamese administrators.

As Komer was always quick to point out, the translation of all these efforts into the spread of government "authority," one of the ultimate allied goals, depended on local security: lightly armed, ill-paid Regional Forces and Popular Forces militia, who in turn depended on allied regular forces to evict the enemy's main force battalions. But McNamara noted that in 1967 enemy guerrillas persisted even then. Newsmen did not have to travel far to find Vietcong-controlled hamlets; some were in Long An province, within a half-hour's drive of downtown Saigon.

To advise, supply, and cajole the Vietnamese Administration, Komer operated a parallel administration of his own (see Chapter 1) in the hinterland: At a cost of $350 million, it embraced 2,700 military men (mostly on 12-month tours), and 1,200 civilians (State, USAID, CIA, USIS) operating in the four corps headquarters and the 44 province and 222 district capitals. In addition, the South Vietnamese, by Komer's count, had about 513,000 people assigned to the "slow and undramatic process" of pacification: 51 ARVN battalions (one-third of ARVN line strength), 152,000 Regional Forces and 148,000 Popular Forces militia, 74,000 national police, 41,000 of the over-publicized RD cadre members (who were in only 700 of 12,700 hamlets at any one time), 60,000 civil servants (in the provinces), 2,700 in "Armed Propaganda teams," and 6,000 "Census Grievance cadres."[2]

To keep track of events, Komer had a reporting system. District advisors' monthly checkoff lists for the Hamlet Evaluation System (HES, instituted by McNamara in 1966) were fed into CORDS computers to produce pacification ratings for each hamlet, district, and province and for the country as a whole. Komer and his executive assistant, Col. Robert Montague, used HES as one of several ways to spot regional problems, such as upsurges of enemy terrorism, or a slackening of government effort, and to see nationwide trends. It was not devised to assess Vietnamese "hearts and minds" or to draw from inexperienced, non-Vietnamese-speaking U.S. captains and majors anything but concrete, objective data: a school built and operating, a well dug, an enemy sniping attack. The best hamlets were evaluated as "A" hamlets (both "secure" and "developing economically"). "A," "B," and "C" hamlets were grouped together as only "relatively secure"; "D" and "E" hamlets were "contested," and others were flatly labeled "Vietcong."

However, Komer—and, most notably, Administration officials in Washington in 1967—also used the figures publicly to show "progress," to convince the public that "the other war" was not standing still. Here Komer ran smack into an already endemic journalistic suspicion (justified by past events) of statistics, computers, and "progress" reports.

In private, with newsmen or colleagues, Komer often mixed enthusiasm with jokes and candor about pacification's serious hurdles. To the few newsmen, even critics, who showed interest in the complexities of CORDS, Komer and Montague responded quickly. Komer's judgment (or neglect) of Vietnamese politics and society drew criticism from such old Vietnam hands as Gerald Hickey, the Rand anthropologist (and author of *Village in Vietnam*). He was also criticized by private American welfare groups (e.g., the International Voluntary Service, led by Don Luce) for not giving higher priority, pre-Tet, to help for refugees. But within the CORDS organization, as far as this writer and other reporters could tell, Komer was respected by his field people as an energetic, adroit manager (a rarity in Vietnam). He was admired for his encouragement of "in-house" critics and innovators, for his willingness to "stand up to the generals," for his eagerness to help solve the problem of a far-off district advisor or take issues to the Vietnamese. Sometimes, however, in a rare press conference or background session, Komer seemed to be something else: a fast-talking McNamarian promoter, conceding problems here and there, qualifying his progress reports, but emphasizing the "upward trend" in the statistics.

In effect, Komer was using the press, he later told this writer, primarily to keep pacification before the eyes of the Washington bureaucracy, and thus to make that bureaucracy more amenable to Komer's requests for men and money. A veteran of Washington struggles over policy and priorities, he knew that CORDS was a "stepchild"; unlike State, USAID, CIA, or the military, it had no bureaucratic advocates of its own back home. Thus, Komer felt he had to show, via the press, that CORDS, too, was worthy of support. If "progress" reports helped the Administration politically during its 1967 efforts to shore up domestic support, that was an added advantage.

CORDS and the Press Corps

No senior U.S. official in Saigon was more accessible to the press than Komer; but this very accessibility made him suspect to some. Many newsmen shrugged off Komer's public enthusiasm; others resented his efforts at the December 18 and January 24 press conferences to use the media for propaganda purposes. Komer was commonly described in print as "ebullient." Few newsmen exploited his willingness—or that of his junior aides—to explore pacification's problems in private. Few, on the other hand, developed any expertise of their own.

As Merton Perry of *Newsweek* noted later, there was "nothing to put your finger on" in terms of independent alternatives to Komer's nationwide statistics. Nor was there enough geographical exposure among newsmen to provide them with a "feel" for the countrywide situation or with a sense of change. Referring to his Vietnam experience in 1967, Robert A. Erlandson of the Baltimore *Sun* wrote, "Yardsticks for measuring progress or lack of it are difficult to find. Officials deluge newsmen with reams of statistics and briefings designed to convince them that all is well. Then reporters take to the field, find their own examples of the reverse, and report them."[3]

It was not hard to get at these examples, at least from an American viewpoint. In the field, CORDS personnel included young State Department officials and Army captains and majors. To Komer's credit, they felt freer to talk than did the U.S. Embassy officials or most senior officers of U.S. tactical units and Westmoreland's staff; although senior civilian CORDS officials at corps level tended to toe the "progress" line more than did their juniors, a trait shared by their military contemporaries advising ARVN units.[4]

The most energetic newsmen ventured out to key areas such as Binh Dinh, Long An, Phuc Yen, and Kien Hoa. They interviewed U.S. pacification advisors frustrated by Vietnamese officials' apathy, corruption, and incompetence, or simply by non-American approaches to problem-solving. Without attribution to the interviewees, these complaints found their way into print. A hamlet described officially as "relatively secure" was found not to be sufficiently "secure" for its chief to sleep there. A district chief diverted cement meant for refugee camps to his own home or to military projects. Militia sentries slept on the job. There was plenty of grist for other "horror stories" about pacification, like reports of tacit local truces between militia and Vietcong guerrillas, of Vietnamese preoccupation with survival at all costs, and of impatient U.S. preoccupation with "progress" despite the realities of the situation.

Komer himself used to show, to those few newsmen who inquired, an up-to-date list of the "ten best" and "ten worst" provinces, while, however, emphasizing that the "overall trend" was what counted. But few newsmen, again, were interested in the conceptual approaches, good or bad, that guided Komer. For example, one of Komer's basic propositions was that, in an underdeveloped, war-shaken country like South Vietnam, the United States could not hope for "quality": The "pacifiers" had to crowd out the Vietcong by systematic application of vast quantities of men (militia, administrators, armed civilians) and materiel (roads, arms, schools, economic aid). In time, Komer told this writer in October 1967, the sheer weight would tell;

Vietcong influence would recede. This basic notion never saw print. Yet it guided U.S. policy.

R. W. Apple, the *Times* bureau chief in Saigon, wrote a lengthy mid-1967 piece on the war, giving considerable emphasis to pacification. He included both "horror stories" and Komer's own statistics, to show that the program had reached a stalemate with neither side in a position to move decisively against the other (Apple did not know that Hanoi was planning the Tet campaign). His thesis provoked considerable rebuttal from sensitive officialdom in Saigon and Washington. Possibly because of this, the "Apple stalemate piece" became one of the newspaper stories clipped and kept by newsmen arriving in Saigon for the first time.[5]

Prior to Tet, however, even on the part of the New York *Times* and Washington *Post*, there was little market for pacification stories back home in terms of page-one attention. *Time* and *Newsweek*, also, had "cover stories" on combat, but not on pacification. As ABC's Bill Brannigan later recalled, with specific reference to television:

. . . the audience simply wasn't there. Incomprehensibility is built into a situation where an urban Judeo-Christian society is being told about an agricultural, Confucian society. And there were any number of people staffing news desks here in the United States who had difficulty grasping the significance of dispatches arriving from Saigon. A hell-for-leather firefight taxed no one's imagination, nor required a specialist's knowledge. "Pacification," however, was too often dismissed with an attitude expressed in an obscene slogan that enjoyed a certain vogue in U.S. military ranks: "Grab them by the b——, and their hearts and minds will follow."[6]

A few reporters—notably the *Times*'s Mohr and Apple and the *Post*'s Lescaze—examined pacification repeatedly in the field in 1967, and understood its concepts even as they noted its flaws. But for most newsmen, the complexities, ambiguities, and lack of interest at home made pacification a low-priority concern, despite its obvious importance and Komer's accessibility. Thus, in terms of occasional reporting of national trends in pacification, most newsmen were reduced to citing CORDS statistics, in simplified form, and then casting doubt on them by citing local contradictions—although the contradictions did not necessarily reflect the countrywide situation with any greater accuracy than did the official statistics. As Merton Perry indicated, pacification reporting was not a satisfactory exercise for journalists in a hurry.

Who Controlled the Countryside Now?

On January 24, 1968, six days before the Tet attacks, and after the well-reported (preliminary) enemy forays in Hau Nghia and Binh Dinh, Komer held a press conference to discuss "why . . . pacification [was] going better in '67." It was a basic lecture for newly arrived newsmen, an admission of "fairly unrealistic goals" for 1966 (prior to Komer's arrival), and a jibe at press reports of bad tidings from the field: "I think [1967] was a year of forward movement. . . . It's pretty hard to measure pacification results. It's easy enough to go out to one or two or three hamlets, and if they look good, to say pacification is doing well. It's equally easy to go out to a couple of hamlets, and if pacification is doing poorly, well, that's easy enough to see, too. . . . So you've got to look at averages."

The only man with the averages was Komer. The year-end reports, he said, on 12,722 hamlets showed that, partly as a result of a refugee influx to the cities, "about 67 percent of total population—some 11.5 million people out of the 17.2 million that we're carrying as the total population of South Vietnam—are now living either in the secure cities and towns or under reasonably good security conditions in the country." It was an (extremely modest) increase of 4.8 percent, Komer said, over January 1967. "I don't see how we can fail to do somewhat better in '68," he added. However, he warned, "we still have a long way to go."

Komer was not sharply questioned, despite the common knowledge that pacification was under severe year-end pressure from the foe in Hau Nghia, northwest of Saigon, and in Binh Dinh, in central Vietnam. No newsman at the Komer session, it would appear, had been keeping close tabs on pacification, and Komer's briefing got little play. Although reported on the wire, it was ignored by the news magazines and by the *Post*. CBS and the *Times* carried only brief reports.

The shock of Tet convinced many a newsman and editor (and many a stunned Washington bureaucrat) that Komer's declarations of January 24 and earlier Administration statements (as condensed and highly simplified by the press) bordered on delusion. The Vietcong had come through officially "pacified" countryside to attack the cities. It seemed that Komer's computers and Komer's trends had been all wrong. In Saigon, many junior officials were shaken, and did not hide these feelings from reporters. One could write "I told you so" with a vengeance.

Yet, there was a journalistic problem: During early February 1968, few newsmen (or officials) were in a position to know what had happened in the countryside, even on a localized basis. As has already been pointed out, their geographical exposure was limited. Air transport was scarce, and journalistic interest and manpower were focused on Hue, Saigon, and Khe Sanh. Komer's people, for their part, were preoccupied with the massive task of urban recovery. Komer ordered CORDS headquarters not to venture any "guess-timates" to newsmen on pacification's setbacks for two weeks, pending reports from the harried district and province advisors on their situations. Komer himself postponed any specific public discussion, with one exception. On February 5, he was interviewed on CBS by Robert Schakne:

Schakne: . . . American officials publicly still take a hopeful view. [Here is] Ambassador Robert Komer, the head of the pacification program, who had been reporting that two-thirds of the country's population was under government control.

Has there been any reassessment of whether or not we are making progress?

Komer: There will have to be, of course, a major reassessment. Once again, I think we are much too close to the battle to be able to tell very clearly how much damage has been done and how much reassessment required. Certainly we will reassess. But the important thing is this. We've taken all the damage. We've gone through a bad week. They had a lot of initial success in getting into most of the cities and towns, but what has it cost them and why did they do it? First, it cost them an awful lot, more than 15,000 killed, we think. More than 4,000 prisoners taken, and these figures will mount as we finish up the mopping up operations. The important thing is the longer term. It's where we stand a month from now, two months from now, three months from now, now that their initial attempt has failed. Are we going to end up with this country more secure or less secure? I'm not so sure that it's going to be a lot less secure. I do know that the figures in the Hamlet Evaluation System are going to go down substantially for the month of January, and probably February, too.[7]

Komer's warning to wait for long-term results went unheeded, even by Schakne.

In Saigon, in response to newsmen's desires, the military briefers concentrated on the fighting, the civilians on urban disaster. For example, at the Five O'Clock Follies on February 4, Peter Heller, the

USIS spokesman, cited the fragmentary nature of available information:

> Let me start out by saying that we had a situation similar to that that you have when you cover a national election and your first returns are coming in. We've got a return from one place and one from another and [they] don't at once add up to a complete picture. We'll give you what we have. I can tell you we do not have the two things that we've been looking for all day—and all yesterday—namely an overall estimate of civilian casualties and an overall report on refugees—those are the two things that we've been after. We do not have [them]. I do not apologize for it, because I know you know the reason why. We keep trying to get some information for you.

Thus almost any quick generalization about "who now controlled the countryside" was based largely on conjecture. Realizing this, many Saigon newsmen—in contrast to some at home—did not discuss the countryside in dispatches during the first two weeks of Tet. It became known that some once secure suburbs were suddenly full of Vietcong; that many main roads were suddenly "insecure," notably in the Delta and around Hue—for example, one could no longer drive unescorted from Saigon to the beach at Vung Tau, and Highway Four from the Delta was repeatedly cut; that the Vietcong was out in force around the cities; and that some ARVN battalions and the militia had been pulled in to defend province capitals from a "second wave" or to evict the "first wave." But the state of affairs in the hamlets themselves remained unknown.

Wire-service dispatches on the countryside situation—written from Saigon—were rare and conjectural during this period. On February 8, AP's Barry Kramer accurately reported the diversion of pacification resources to refugee relief, despite a GVN spokesman's claims that recovery would not "disrupt" present programs. "Seasoned observers," Kramer went on, "are likely to be wary [sic] of the government's new attempt to win over its people. . . . Pacification officials claim that, since the recent attacks have been concentrated in the cities, there won't be a great effect on the pacification program in the countryside. [This "claim" remains an AP exclusive.] But much of the pacification effort is based on popular confidence in the Saigon government. This confidence *undoubtedly* has been shaken since the government has shown itself unable to prevent attacks even in the relatively secure cities."[8]

Unable to be specific concerning the current situation, Kramer veered off, like so many others, into speculation about the "psychological" impact which the Vietcong attacks might have on the Vietnamese peasants. In short, Kramer, like everyone else, was guessing. Television and radio said little about Tet's effects on the pacification program until after Komer's February 24 report. What little they said earlier was equally as conjectural as what came later. Walter Cronkite commented that "it removes the starch from a lot of civil servants and potential leaders through the countryside who again are, or feel, open to communist retaliation. Pacification, only by which South Vietnam ever can run its own affairs, may have been set back by years, certainly by months."[9]

Martin Agronsky, newly arrived in Saigon, supplied a "news analysis" for CBS radio on February 17: "In the front of speculation about the current state of the war here, there are few islands of solid fact upon which to build any certain conclusions." So saying, Agronsky hopped off the "islands of fact," and conjectured himself into the hamlets:

In evaluating the damage done to the U.S. and South Vietnamese pacification program in the countryside, it is the same topsy-turvy kind of reasoning applied. The pride of the American pacification and the Revolutionary Development directors in the provinces is the Binh Dinh and Tai Phuoc area in the central coastal district 250 miles north of Saigon. This has been repeatedly cited as a prime example of the success of U.S. Ambassador Robert Komer's pacification efforts. Eighty percent of the area was listed as being under the firm control of South Vietnam, and yet after the Tet attack, it was clear that the Vietcong cadres had been able to move at will throughout that province, concentrating on places of their own choosing and doing all of this without any of the *supposedly patriotic* South Vietnamese people of the hamlets ever betraying these communists. Moreover, when the communists launched their attacks in this area, the *villagers left all the fighting to the South Vietnamese and U.S. troops.* There is no *known instance* of the people turning anywhere against the communists, even to the extent of revealing the enemy's locations to the South Vietnamese and American forces who fought on their behalf.[10]

On February 20, CBS's Peter Kalischer interviewed an expert at Ben Tre—an *agricultural* advisor, William Janssen, who said U.S.-aided farm progress had not changed Vietnamese political sentiments, and added, "I don't see how we can reach a military solution."[11] That was the only "pacification" interview done in the field by TV during the first three weeks of February.

The quickest, broadest journalistic analysis of the effect of Tet came in the Washington *Post* on Sunday, February 4, four days after the Saigon attacks. In a page-one rewrite of wire-service battle stories for the first edition, the *Post* foreign desk wrote: "Reports indicated that the pacification program to rally the people to the government's side was a shambles."[12] Neither AP nor UPI had ventured such a flat assessment. A *Post* editor altered the text to this in the third edition: "How badly the assaults disrupted the pacification program, designed to rally the people to the government, was also uncertain."

However, in the "Outlook" section, Ward Just, a Vietnam combat correspondent for the *Post* in 1965–67, and in 1968 a national staff writer, wrote an instant analysis, telling the reader that pacification was "killed dead":

. . . When the Vietcong flags are finally taken down from the score or more cities where they flew, including, for three days, the ancient Citadel of Hue, the capital of central Vietnam—its American analogy would be Boston—the bodies counted, the damaged buildings reoccupied and the constitution unsuspended, it will come time for the assessment, for the after-action reports and the "lessons learned."

This will almost certainly be that the raids, audaciously conceived, and executed with extraordinary ferocity, have as a practical matter killed dead the pacification program—and most of the assumptions that went with it.[13]

A week later, the already cited analysis of London-based Sir Robert Thompson appeared in the *Post*. It included this: "The nation-building and pacification, the years of work, are now in ruins. To start again from scratch with a new approach in a time frame of at least 20 years is not exactly an attractive prospect."[14]

In the same issue, reporting from the scene, Lee Lescaze was not so final in his pronouncements:

The pacification effort is one of the casualties of the Vietcong offensive. It is not yet clear how badly it has been hurt. There will be no computer map for the Hamlet Evaluation Survey this month. If there were, officials say, it would certainly show a sharp deterioration of security throughout the countryside.

But it does not follow automatically that the Vietcong took control of remote hamlets as they took temporary control of parts of many cities. In Kien Hoa province, the capital of Ben Tre came close to being taken by the Vietcong and was heavily damaged in the battle, while the priority pacification area of Ba Tri, near the coast, was hit by some mortar rounds that did small damage.[15]

The New York *Times*'s Washington bureau was only a week behind Ward Just's "killed dead" analysis with a similar one of its own. On Sunday, February 11, in a look at President Johnson's Tet problems, an anonymous bureau member wrote that Hanoi had already "proved over the past year that the allied forces could not pacify the countryside."[16] Tom Wicker, the Washington bureau chief and columnist, mocked the Hamlet Evaluation figures (as part of a rebuke to Bunker and Westmoreland for their role in the 1967 Administration progress campaign), and said exposure of the statistical deception was unnecessary, because the anti-cities attacks showed that not "any part of South Vietnam is truly under Saigon's control."[17]

In Saigon, the *Times* reporters stayed clear, as did their *Post* colleagues, of firm assessments of pacification. There was an exception or two. Tom Buckley on February 2—three days after the embassy attack—cited what amounted to little more than alarmed Saigon journalists' speculation, saying that "despite official [pacification] statistics to the contrary, no part of the country is secure either from terrorist bombs or from organized military operations." The attacks, he wrote, were a "reflection on American assertions that large sections of the country are 'pacified.' "[18]

Wicker and Buckley were typical of most newsmen (and some Administration spokesmen). They oversimplified the complex official statistics. Komer on January 24 had said that A-, B- and C-rated hamlets—comprising 67 percent of the population—were "relatively" secure. On December 1, 1967, in describing how the HES statistics were arrived at, he said they reflected the overall net situation over the previous month, noting that a single act of terrorism, or a mortar attack, on a given hamlet would affect that hamlet's "security" rating. In short, HES ratings for individual hamlets could and did shift up and down from month to month, as they did in February–March 1968. "Relative security" was not claimed as a *permanent* condition by Komer, although it must also be added that he did not stress this point on January 24. He anticipated "progress," not a "setback" and a "vacuum." Neither he nor anyone else predicted the Tet offensive.

In retrospect, Komer, under pressure from the media, might have been wiser to warn newsmen explicitly against describing hamlets as "government-controlled" or "safe"—words with *absolute* connotations misleading in a semiguerrilla war. A more realistic shorthand would have been "67 percent of the people live under some form of continuing GVN administration and allied military presence."

Bernard Weinraub was more cautious in a news story on February 11:

> The impact of the Vietcong's urban campaign on the pacification program in the countryside remains cloudy. The program seeks to wrest control of hamlets and villages from the Vietcong.
>
> "Nobody really knows what happened yet in the countryside," said one high American official [Komer]. . . .
>
> "What we think they did was sneak right through and not touch the hamlets," the official added. "What they did on the way out, when they exfiltrated, we just don't know and we won't know for another week."[19]

In the same day's *Times* "Review" section, a Saigon bureau writer (without by-line) began his short piece with an anonymous contrary quote: " 'The VC have changed the rules,' said one American official. 'No one talks about pacification anymore.' . . . Most officials remained uncertain of the impact on the pacification teams. . . . But some officials said privately that the pacification program in the countryside appeared, at least for the moment, irrelevant in the face of the attacks on the cities."[20]

The *Times* did considerably better three days later. Charles Mohr provided the first view from CORDS sources of the "extremely serious" but imprecisely known effects of Tet on pacification. He cited the withdrawal of the RD cadres and of "most" of the 51 ARVN battalions, saying that the government "in effect has temporarily abandoned" the countryside. He noted that the Vietcong "by-passed" rural areas en route to the cities. He suggested that a "four-week suspension of the program would no doubt cripple it." It was doubtful, Mohr wrote, whether province chiefs would go back to the rural areas, as ordered, by February 28. He said that "one important American official" (Komer) had forbade subordinates' discussions with the press. This circumstance led to considerable vagueness in the details of Mohr's story and, possibly, to the omission of any mention of the 300,000 Regional and Popular Forces militia, who had mostly stayed in place.[21]

Two days later, the *Times* carried Joseph Treaster's accurate, low-key "headquarters" story, written from Da Nang, on pacification in I Corps, the worst-hit sector at Tet. Treaster noted official admissions that pacification progress was at a "virtual standstill," and cited the lack of information on how many of the region's hamlets had fallen under enemy control. He did not mention the all-important militia's status or that of the ARVN, quoted the belief of officials that the RD teams were not the enemy's main target, and concluded that it "seems likely that a long and tedious recovery process" lay ahead.[22]

Later, the *Post* and *Times* reporters in Vietnam were preoccupied, as we have noted elsewhere, with the battle action and urban devastation. However, the *Times* did spare one of its seven men[23] for a look at pacification in coastal Binh Dinh province and its capital, Qui Nhon. Binh Dinh was one of the most heavily populated and Vietcong-oriented provinces in Vietnam. Bernard Weinraub reported:

QUI NHON, South Vietnam, Feb. 20—A month ago the villages and hamlets near this coastal capital were considered relatively secure and were the focus of a massive American and South Vietnamese effort to "pacify" the vital province of Binh Dinh.

Although the final impact of the Vietcong's Lunar New Year offensive on the pacification effort remains unclear, there are renewed indications from provinces stretching from the northern region to the Mekong Delta that the drive to wrest rural areas from the Vietcong has suffered a severe setback.

In the five northern provinces, for example, the program has been termed a holding action. . . . This "showcase" province—the pilot area for pacification—has suffered what high officials view as an 18-month setback. . . .

"We'll overcome the physical damage, no problem about that, but the psychological effect on the people is something else," added the official, who is close to the pacification effort. "It's all pretty nebulous at this point. . . ."

Possibly the key problem in Binh Dinh province is finding a security force to protect the teams. Guarding them had been the job of the Regional Forces and the local militia. After the Vietcong attacks, however, the troops moved into districts and towns to provide security, and there is no immediate indication when they will go back to the rural areas.

Most American officials here were gloomy.

"It has all gone down the drain," one of them said. "You work like hell here, and then in one night it's all lost, all that work—gone."[24]

Weinraub and Treaster provided the *Times*'s only on-the-spot hinterland pacification stories during the first three weeks of February. The other media, however, did not do much better.

The *Post*'s Stanley Karnow arrived from Hong Kong shortly after the January 30–31 attacks to cover Saigon for two weeks while Lescaze and this writer covered the fighting. Karnow talked to Komer and others at CORDS, and on February 16 the *Post* published his view—half "policy" story, half "survey"—of pacification. It began accurately with: "The rural pacification program . . . is virtually paralyzed as officials here try to determine whether to defend population centers or continue efforts to secure the country's hamlets." Then, in the best Washington tradition, Karnow went on to cite "officials." He noted "officials'" (i.e., Komer's) anxiety about filling the "vacuum" in the countryside caused by the pullback of "over half" the ARVN battalions and RD teams to the cities and towns, and, on the other hand, South Vietnamese leaders' reluctance to reexpose the urban areas by returning forces to the countryside. Wrote Karnow: "Some officials believe no ground has been lost. . . . Other American officials reject this assessment as uninformed and overly optimistic. They speculate that a number of hamlets formerly counted as secure are now in Vietcong hands." He also said that the 300,000 men in the crucial RF and PF militia were assumed to be "still largely in place," but that "they lack hard information on this." Finally, Karnow cited "sources" who raised the question of whether the allies had sufficient manpower to "carry on pacification while meeting the communist military challenge."[25]

One problem with this story, as with so many others written out of Saigon (and Washington) during Tet—by this writer as well as other reporters—is that the reader is left in the dark as to the relative importance, knowledge, or authority of the "officials" or "certain officers" quoted. None is identified as "senior," "junior"—or "drinking companions."

The *Post*'s only page-one pacification story during the entire Tet period leaned heavily on the semantics of a statement by Vice President Hubert H. Humphrey to the AFL-CIO in Florida on February 19. The story began:

[Humphrey] conceded here today that the communist Tet offensive "did stop" the pacification program in South Vietnam.

He did so, however, in claiming that the [enemy] had failed completely in their major objectives. . . .

Other Administration officials have admitted that the communist offensive hurt the pacification program. . . . But Humphrey is believed to be the first to say publicly that it has actually stopped the program.[26]

The news magazines were faced with the usual pressure to explain everything the first week. *Time* initially gave a cautious appraisal:

Some psychological success could hardly be denied the attackers. In the raid on the poorly defended U.S. Embassy in Saigon, they embarrassed and discomforted the United States, still coping with the stinging humiliation of the *Pueblo* incident. They succeeded in demonstrating that despite nearly three years of steady allied progress in the war, the communist commandos can still strike at will virtually anywhere in the country. *Though the smoke must clear before any realistic assessment can be made, the slow process of pacification* has probably suffered a major setback.[27]

The following week, *Time* noted only that pacification "will be inevitably set back by the immediate priority of reconstruction."[28] However, pacification got a little more attention three weeks after the initial Tet attacks, but apparently too late for the magazine to take note of Komer's February 24 briefing: "The U.S. effort has been set back by months and *perhaps years.* . . . With the countryside wide open to Vietcong soldiers, recruiters, and tax collectors, the crucial rural pacification effort is at a standstill."[29] In the same issue, *Time* painted a bleak, overwritten picture, not based on widespread travel:

Pulling in to defend the cities, the allies have been forced to cede large areas of the countryside to the communists. Except for the *largest population centers,* for example, the rich Delta is now almost entirely in Vietcong hands. There is not a Delta road *safe* to drive on, by day or night. *Massive* quantities of supplies are moving through the Delta for the enemy buildup around Saigon, and U.S. reconnaissance planes now sight *piles of enemy artillery shells* flagrantly stacked out in the open. But people and goods cannot move in the Delta; fish rot where they have been caught, rice molders unharvested. In Soc Trang, the cost of food has risen 30 percent; in Vinh Long, the price of rice has soared tenfold.[30]

Newsweek was quick to assert in its first Tet issue that the attacks had made "a mockery of claims by Deputy Ambassador Robert Komer . . . that 67 percent of South Vietnam's population lives in secure areas."[31] In New York, Everett Martin, the former *Newsweek* bureau chief, drew on his memory to suggest that pacification depended solely on the much publicized Revolutionary Development cadre teams—and hence was a failure even before Tet.[32]

The following week, *Newsweek* went further, saying that pacification "had been dealt a blow from which it would recover only slowly

—if ever."[33] In the same piece, the magazine declared that "guerrillas are *certain* to take advantage of the vacuum created in rural areas."[34] (The guerrillas did not, as it turned out.) And by Saturday, February 17 (deadline for the *Newsweek* issue dated February 26), anonymous "officials" were again at work: " 'The countryside,' said one U.S. official, *'has again gone to the Vietcong,* mostly by default.' And even Komer, when asked how long he thought it would take to get the pacification program back in operation, admitted: 'I haven't a clue and I don't think anyone else does either.' "[35]

Later Evaluations: Some Caution, Much Conclusion-Jumping

A little more than three weeks after the Tet urban attacks began, Komer finally gave newsmen some hard information. On February 24, he held a "not for attribution" press conference to discuss "best estimates" of civilian losses and urban damage, the allied relief effort, and the "considerable setback" in pacification. It was perhaps the most candid confession of any senior U.S. official in Vietnam.

In essence, Komer said that "a partial vacuum [had] developed in the countryside." The enemy was "still oriented on cities, disruption of lines of communication, or self-preservation" and "avoided relatively secure hamlets during the attacks." He provided statistics: 100 small outposts had been "overrun or abandoned"; 18 of 51 ARVN battalions formerly stationed in the countryside were withdrawn to urban areas, and it was not known when the 18 would return; half the RD teams were withdrawn. In 13 (of 44) provinces, Tet's impact was "serious," in 16 "moderate," in 15 "slight." He did not attempt to say what percentage of the population was now in secure areas; the February HES reports would normally not be available until mid-March.

The wire services accurately condensed Komer's briefing, as did Bernard Weinraub of the *Times* in a story which appeared on page one:

SAIGON, South Vietnam, Feb. 24—The United States Mission conceded today for the first time that the allied effort to pacify the countryside had suffered a "considerable setback" as a result of the Vietnamese offensive.

"There has been a loss of momentum, there has been some withdrawal (of security troops) from the countryside, there has been a significant

psychological setback both on the part of pacification people themselves
and the local population," said a high official of the Mission.[36]

In a second *Times* article related to pacification that same day, another Saigon bureau reporter referred obliquely to Komer, and then
supplied an anonymous quote to undercut him: "A high American
official acknowledged today that the recent attacks by the Vietcong
had badly hurt pacification. Another specialist put it more bluntly:
'We're right back where we were in 1963.' "[37]

The *Post*, whose two reporters were both out of Saigon, ran an abbreviated Reuters account of Komer's remarks inside the paper.[38] Its
two page-one Vietnam stories that day were a speculative piece by
UPI on the talks between General Westmoreland and the visiting
General Wheeler in Vietnam, and a major battle story from Hue.[39] In
terms of stories out of Vietnam, pacification never made page one in
the *Post* during February and March 1968. However, Murrey
Marder and Chalmers Roberts did give Komer's figures a long analysis on February 26:

> The new American computer in Saigon is no longer producing a print-
> out picture of the South Vietnamese countryside edging toward "pacifica-
> tion." At least a third of the Revolutionary Development teams and 18 of
> the South Vietnamese Army's 51 battalions have pulled back to urban
> centers. Yet these teams and troops were to be key elements in the "other
> war" to "win the hearts and minds of the people." Today Washington has
> dismayingly little comprehensive information on who-controls-what in the
> countryside and on whether the Tet offensive has convinced the farmers
> that the Vietcong are the wave of the future.[40]

To a large degree, what Komer told newsmen was what he had
been reporting to Washington, where official spokesmen later repeated his figures in public statements. William P. Bundy, for example, Assistant Secretary of State, got into this exchange on February
25 on NBC's "Meet the Press":

> Q.: There is an unidentified American official in Saigon who was
> quoted as saying there had been a considerable setback to the pacification
> program. So what is in process here?
> Bundy: I think you are in the middle of a tough fight. . . . They did
> shake people's faith in the government's ability to maintain security in the
> cities which hitherto have been immune, and there have been about a
> third of the provinces where the protective forces—mostly South Viet-
> namese—had to be withdrawn to defend the cities, and that is what has
> caused this disruption of the pacification program to a significant degree

in about a third of the country, and to some degree in another third of the country, particularly in the Delta and in the northern areas.[41]

In his March 11 testimony before the Senate Foreign Relations Committee, Dean Rusk made these statements on pacification:

There was a serious disruption in the pacification effort in about a third of the provinces. There was significant disruption in about another third of the provinces and very little effect in another third.

Seventeen of the 51 battalions of the South Vietnamese Army who were on pacification work were pulled back into the towns and cities as a part of the resistance to that Tet offensive. . . .

There has been disruption in communications. There was some over-running in some of the hamlets that were involved in the rural development program and a good deal of work has been concentrated in getting back out into the countryside.

The South Vietnamese forces have rapidly been replenished with re-placements for the casualties. They started drafting the 19-year-olds on March 1, and will be drafting the 18-year-olds on May 1.

Both the South Vietnamese and the allied forces are returning to the initiative in most parts of the country. And we would like to see, of course, as is evident, the countryside restored. But there was some serious setback in some areas to the pacification effort that you asked about, sir.[42]

Komer was heard again officially, on NBC-TV, just before he flew back to Washington with General Wheeler, who was secretly readying a massive 206,000-man troop request for White House approval. Komer was reminded of his January 24 estimate that 67 percent of the population (NBC said "hamlets") were "relatively secure." He said:

. . . Now the 67 percent was just the summary of a summary of a summary, and we did make very clear that we were just accepting the urban population as reasonably secure, and indeed up until the Tet offensive it was reasonably secure, and now after the Tet offensive it's again reasonably secure, but it certainly wasn't during Tet.

The most important thing is that the enemy's attacks on the cities by-passed the countryside. He didn't attack the hamlets, probably for very good reasons, that it would have given us the alert if he'd knocked off a whole series of hamlets on his way into the cities.

So, the pacification program wasn't really the target of this series of attacks on the cities.

What has happened, however, is that as we have pulled in perhaps a third to a half of the Vietnamese local security forces to help protect the cities and to help direct recovery efforts, this has left a vacuum in the countryside to a considerable extent, and I think that it is possible that if we don't get back out into the countryside quickly and show the flag and reassume control and show the GVN presence, it's possible that we might have a very substantial setback in the countryside. As of the moment, I think it's up for grabs.[43]

In short, Komer's estimate (as he had already stated on February 24) was that a "vacuum"—not a Vietcong takeover—had occurred in much of the countryside. History tends to substantiate that generalization; in any event, newsmen, once more, had no independent information to dispute him as to the nationwide picture.[44]

On February 27, Ambassador Bunker, on the Walter Cronkite "special" after the latter's return from Vietnam, said essentially what he had said to newsmen in Saigon on February 3: "They have certainly disrupted the pacification effort for the time being. For how long, I don't know. We haven't yet full reports on the situation. They have interrupted . . . and interdicted lines of communication which are now being opened up again. Whatever effect they may have had I don't know on the population."[45]

Although Komer on February 24 was hardly optimistic, some newsmen, once again, could not resist the temptation to imply that he was glossing over a catastrophe. Some, who had dismissed his "progress" statistics as illusory prior to Tet, now seized on his figures when they showed setbacks, reporting them without attribution as a springboard for far more sweeping conclusions.

UPI, however, did a restrained pacification story the next day:

SAIGON (UPI)—At the end of 1967 the U.S. agency in charge of the pacification program in South Vietnam—the program to "win the hearts and minds of the people"—issued a progress report. . . .

By computer, the agency said, it had determined and was able to announce that 67 percent of the people of South Vietnam, or 11,237,000, now live in areas secure from the Vietcong. . . .

Today, this "count" of areas and people made secure from the communists has little meaning. It was negated, and the whole program stopped, by this year's Vietcong offensive. . . .

There has been no official inclination to minimize the disruption of the pacification effort by the communist Lunar New Year offensive. Vice President Hubert H. Humphrey told the AFL-CIO Executive Council in Miami Beach, Florida, on February 19 that the communist onslaughts "did stop the pacification program." . . . It was postponed to give priority to "Operation Recovery," the government program to rebuild areas in Saigon and other cities wrecked in the Vietcong attacks, and to care for the half-million new refugees and thousands of civilian casualties.

. . . .

Whatever may be the long-term effects of the communist offensive on the pacification program, there is no question it has been seriously set back. At this stage the picture is unsettled and uncertain, adding to the controversy that always has surrounded the pacification effort.[46]

Although the *Times* and UPI were cautious about the future of pacification, the networks were not. A few days after Komer spoke, CBS's Robert Schakne visited Binh Dinh province, and noted the withdrawal of local pacification teams, which, he said, "more than anything [are] the symbol of the setback in pacification." He interviewed a U.S. advisor, Capt. Donald Jones, asking, "Are you discouraged?" Jones's answer: "Yes." Schakne then followed with a standupper: "No matter how fast they [the pacification workers] get back to their posts now, much of the damage has been done. The mere fact that they were called in from the hamlets in the first place gave the lie to the government's pledge they would stay. A pledge on which the people have depended when they risked Vietcong retaliation to cooperate with the central government. This is the real meaning to the setback to the pacification program."

Schakne echoed the fears of many lower-echelon pacification advisors. But, without attribution, he converted their conjectures into a firm explanation ("the real meaning")—a frequent device on television where time was short. Then Schakne concluded by giving his Binh Dinh trip a pseudo-link to Komer's trip to Washington. Komer, Schakne said, "likely" was in Washington with Gen. Earle Wheeler to ask for more American troops, not just to fight the North Vietnamese, but "to help get the Vietnam pacification program back on the road." In short, the United States would now have to take over the whole war, including the permanently damaged pacification program, because of Saigon's failures.[47] Schakne's attribution of this argument to Komer remains a CBS exclusive, unsupported by any evidence in the Pentagon Papers and flatly denied by Komer (March 1972) as "made up out of whole cloth."

Walter Cronkite used the same argument almost verbatim, but with an even stronger conclusion, in an earlier news analysis of his own, on the same day, on radio:

Gen. Earle Wheeler has made his preliminary report to President Johnson on the problems we face in Vietnam. Despite the officially optimistic quality of such high-level reports, it's reasonably certain the General also had grim news for the President. But the most disturbing news of all is likely to come from the man who returned to the United States with Wheeler, Deputy Ambassador Robert Komer. He's in charge of what's left of the battered pacification program in Vietnam.

The American boss for pacification is Ambassador Komer. This fast-talking, joke-cracking, glib salesman of democracy brought such efficiency to his job he even computerized the stage of pacification of each of the nation's thousands of hamlets. And his computers over two years kept punching out a story of success in village after village. Now, Komer sees much of his program in shambles, left by the Tet offensive against the cities.

Today, *presumably, Ambassador Komer told a sad tale to President Johnson.* That the Tet offensive against the cities also had dealt a serious setback to pacification in the country. That, in a third of the country's provinces the impact was serious, and in another third was moderate. Half of those Revolutionary Development teams were withdrawn from the hamlets to protect the cities. Those forces still are in the cities, and while the American military advisors urge their quick return, and the Vietnamese government acknowledges the urgency, they aren't moving quickly enough.

But no matter how fast they get back to their post now, much of the damage has been done. The mere fact that they were called in from the hamlets in the first place gave the lie to the government's pledge they would stay, a pledge on which the people had depended when they risked Vietcong retaliation to cooperate with the central government.

This is the real meaning of the setback to the pacification program, and it seems *likely that today Ambassador Komer asked President Johnson for more American troops* so that we can permanently occupy the hamlets and fulfill the promise of security to their residents, a promise the Vietnamese alone apparently cannot honor.[48]

The Schakne-Cronkite analysis, was a triumph of editorial "processing," if not of accurate journalism.

Marvin Kalb, CBS State Department correspondent, also commented on Komer, revising the Ambassador's statistics in the following fashion:

In recent weeks, as more and more information becomes available, officials are first beginning to realize how major a setback the allies had suffered. Pacification has stopped. A full third of the once pacified area is back in enemy hands. Another third is still open every now and then to the allies, meaning, effectively, two-thirds of the area is now communist controlled. The major cities are still in allied hands, but the provinces around the cities, at least many of them, are under communist control.[49]

On March 5, NBC's Garrick Utley at Can Tho, covering General Thang's takeover of command of the Delta, filmed some hospital scenes and said that the Vietcong attacks had "crippled the pacification program. . . . Before the Tet offensive, pacification was making good progress. Now it is at a standstill. Only half the pacification or [Revolutionary] Development teams are still in the field. . . . Officials hope to revive a limited pacification program this year, but, at best, it will be in only eight of the Delta's 16 provinces. . . . For now the Vietcong hold the initiative in the Mekong Delta." His conclusion: "The pacification program has been set back, perhaps for many years."[50]

As was so often the case, especially on television and in the news magazines, the "facts" were often accurate. But, to give the piece a strong "conclusion," the commentator had leaped a good deal further than the facts warranted. It was like adding up 2 plus 2 plus 2 and reporting a total of 98.

On the same day, in New York, Howard Tuckner of NBC radio cited without attribution the "vacuum" in the countryside and Komer's statistics on the GVN pullback, and added, "U.S. intelligence officials say the vacuum is being filled by the Vietcong." Indeed, he went on, "Some U.S. officials in Vietnam say it will take at least 18 months to get pacification back to where it was."[51]

Also on March 5, Schakne, on CBS radio with Douglas Edwards, was depressed:

> The word "security" no longer has any real meaning in Vietnam. The enemy has the capability of going almost anywhere, right into the cities. . . . We lost control of the countryside. We lost the principle of establishing security, wanting to prove to the Vietnamese people that we could secure areas and keep the Vietcong out, and it's been established we can't do that. Our whole pacification program has been thoroughly set back. Even the assumption we could not lose this war is open to question.[52]

On March 10, in NBC's "special" on the war, Dean Brelis in New York ignored the reporting from Vietnam and summarized: "Well, the cities are no longer secure; perhaps they never were. We don't know what's happened to the rural pacification program because the rural areas are under communist control. We can only imagine."[53]

In short, there was only a brief flurry of interest in pacification on the part of the networks after Komer's February 24 briefing; even so, TV and radio commentators went far beyond the available information to imply the dramatic worst.

The AP's only major pacification story came on the wire on March 7, describing the loss of "hard-won gains" in the Delta pacification effort since Tet, but predicting no timetable for recovery. Vietcong forces, the AP said, "roam the countryside almost at will." The AP correspondent, George McArthur, visited Can Tho, My Tho, and Vinh Long, but none of the other 13 Delta province capitals.[54]

In Saigon, following Komer's briefing, *Newsweek* continued to give its attention to Hue (even after its recapture), Khe Sanh, and U.S. troops in action. *Time,* on the other hand, made a conscious effort to see what had happened to pacification—and not merely urban recovery—in the hinterland. With a week to work in and relatively ample, experienced manpower, *Time* deployed its correspondents throughout the four corps regions, and provided one of Tet's few overall views of the country. It was clear that, as always, the situation varied greatly from area to area, and that pacification, while "set back," was not "dead." Despite a sizable pacification file from Saigon, the emphasis in the published material was heavier on urban than on rural recovery:

> Vietnam's northernmost [I] Corps, unwilling host to some 55,000 North Vietnamese invaders, is less a pacification prospect than an open battlefield. . . . The existing refugee ranks of 250,000 were swelled by an additional 107,000, some 90,000 of those from Hue alone[55]—out of the city's pre-Tet population of 130,000. Three-fourths of the 12,000 houses destroyed and the 10,000 heavily damaged were in Hue; destruction was made easier, of course, by the fact that . . . houses are often primitive and fragile structures. . . .
>
> . . . .
>
> The civilian dead in II Corps total 1,100, the wounded 4,000, the new refugees 103,000.[56] Some 12,000 houses were destroyed. . . . The security of the corps road network is about the same as pre-Tet, but that is not saying much; even then, an armed convoy was needed to traverse all major roads. Sixty of the 252 RD teams assigned to hamlets are still out of position, unable to go back because security cannot be guaranteed them. . . . One area abandoned: the coastal strip just north of Qui Nhon. "The '68 pacification program has been set back," admits Maj. Gen. William R. Peers, acting commander of Field Force I, "and we'll

have to take another look." Nevertheless, as another U.S. official put it: "My heart went up into my throat when the Tet offensive came. But now it appears that we did not get hurt as badly as we first thought."

. . . .

[In III Corps] . . . "We're still in a state of flux concerning recent losses or gains," says CORDS Deputy John P. Vann. "We're not sure what resulted from drawing in over 6,000 RD cadre and some of the Regional and Popular Forces to province and district towns." But the estimates are that communist real estate and population gains will be small in III Corps. . . .

. . . .

Estimates of damage and casualties in the Delta are spottier than elsewhere, because even pre-Tet the government's control was a sometime thing. Of the 5,274 hamlets in IV Corps, 2,000 were under Saigon's rule, 2,000 under that of the Vietcong, and the rest neither quite one nor the other.

. . . .

. . . The attacks closed the Delta's schools, pulled most of the 10,000 pacification workers into the towns. There is no doubt that the Vietcong have added to their extensive Delta holdings, and will dig in.

. . . Some 70 percent of the RD workers have returned to their posts but, in some provinces, such as Kien Giang, Phong Dinh, and Kien Phong, there is no chance of a return. The Vietcong pressure is just too heavy.[57]

The New York *Times* was more casual about its post-Tet investigation of pacification. Following Weinraub's February 25 report on Komer's briefing, the *Times* editors ran only one page-one story from Vietnam *thereafter* which dealt mainly with pacification. It concerned the protest resignation from CORDS of retired Army Lt. Col. Sidney J. Roche, who expressed, in a mixture of fact and fancy, his dissatisfaction with Komer and with South Vietnamese corruption.[58] The few other *Times* stories on pacification, inside the paper, were written mostly from secondhand sources. On March 3, for example, Charles Mohr, quoting "qualified sources," reported a hesitant shift back into the rural areas. It was significant news, especially since radio and television were still talking in terms of disaster:

SAIGON, South Vietnam, Mar. 2—South Vietnamese rural pacification teams are beginning to return to hamlets that had been abandoned for a month to take up again the flagging program to win the allegiance of rural families.

Qualified South Vietnamese sources said today that the administrative chiefs of the nation's 44 provinces had been ordered to resume pacification efforts. . . .
In effect, the South Vietnamese government temporarily abandoned its own countryside. To some observers, this was the most disturbing result of the Vietcong offensive, and basically more important than the destruction in the cities.
The orders to return to the countryside by March 1, which were issued in mid-February, have not yet been fully implemented, informed sources said. . . .
As many as 80 percent of the pacification teams have returned to rural duty in the Central Highlands and central coast, they said. In the provinces surrounding Saigon, the figure was put at 70 percent.

· ·

In the Mekong Delta area, there had been 15 army battalions—about 6,000 soldiers—assigned to protect pacification teams before the offensive.
Six of the battalions were left in place after attacks, but the nine others were withdrawn to urban areas. A month later, they were still there. . . .
One United States expert said that the progress described by the South Vietnamese in the northern and central provinces was apparently correct. But he expressed doubt that as many as 70 or 80 percent of the pacification teams had gone back to work around Saigon or in the Delta.[59]

A week later, the *Times* ran the AP's quick roundup on the Delta from Vinh Long,[60] but also noted, in a later story from Can Tho concerning Gen. Nguyen Duc Thang's press conference on taking over the Delta command, that:

In another act that delighted Americans, the General abolished the traditional late-morning-to-early-afternoon siesta among his 170,000 troops.
"Now that we are in time of war, there is no time for siestas," he said.
The big, muscular commander also declared that he was speeding efforts to return all rural development, or pacification, teams to villages and hamlets. At the present, 120 of the teams are in the field and 70 are in the cities.[61]

On March 29, the *Times* editors, with no staff stories on the current pacification situation out of Saigon since March 3,[62] published a pacification status report from the Washington bureau.[63] It was yet another example—if not a horrifying one—of newspaper willingness to indulge in Washington analyses of complex situations on the ground in Vietnam. However, the one-column story, by Hedrick Smith, a for-

mer Vietnam hand, was not irresponsible. Smith reported the information "officials" had received from Komer: the reluctance of the
South Vietnamese Army to redeploy to the hinterland, the fact that
recovery was slow in the Delta and near the DMZ but better in the
Central Highlands and around Saigon, and incomplete but fresh hamlet and urban damage statistics. He focused on the return of most of
the Revolutionary Development teams to the countryside. Almost
half the story was devoted to recording the continuing debate among
Administration officials over pacification's post-Tet status. This was
the most useful part of the piece, although Smith did not identify the
protagonists. The Pentagon Papers, published in 1971, disclose that
newsmen were not the only ones panicked by Tet into wild guesses
on pacification. Komer was to recall in 1970 to this writer that the
U.S. Mission lost all "credibility" in Washington official circles in the
post-Tet shock. The Pentagon civilians tended to believe the information provided by the media, whether it was firsthand from Vietnam or
secondhand from Washington.

Overall, in covering pacification, the *Times*'s performance was
highly uneven; Mohr, Treaster, and Weinraub supplied sound information, but interest at home was lacking, and their stories did not
make page one. The same can be said of the *Post*. After the recapture
of Hue, the paper's Saigon bureau, outmanned two-to-one by the
Times, nevertheless undertook a checkup on the countryside. Lee
Lescaze visited the Delta and Hue areas; this writer went to look at
the militia in III Corps and the ARVN near Quang Tri city, just
south of the DMZ. The arrival of George Wilson, the *Post*'s Pentagon
man, in early March freed us for a few days of pacification reporting.
The result represented perhaps that part of the *Post*'s Tet coverage
which was the least duplicated by the *Times* or other media: a dozen
localized stories examining rural security as well as urban recovery.[64]
We did not seek or collect enough material to write a single,
lengthy pacification wrap-up; deadlines, manpower, and the need to
cover other stories made it impossible to match *Time*'s overview.[65]

At home, the *Post* foreign desk found space for pacification stories
hard to come by; most of the Saigon bureau's output on this topic
was held over for a day or two after it arrived in Washington. None
of the pacification material got on page one; it was the victim of the
general switch in attention to burgeoning domestic politics and of the
continuing prominence of the battlefield story.[66]

A Complex Story, Badly Told

All in all, the media performance on pacification—a particularly important but complex story—was extremely weak during as before Tet. In Vietnam, some of the facts began to be apparent at the end of February; but there was neither enough manpower nor enough interest to properly pursue this crucial aspect of the Tet offensive. In addition, as we have seen, the intermittent analysis and commentary at home was particularly hasty, uninformed, and apocalyptic, even by Tet 1968 standards.

The wire services omitted much of the story. They failed to reallocate their relatively abundant manpower to cover pacification in the provinces in late February and March. (AP's Barry Kramer and UPI's Dan Southerland were assigned to cover *both* Saigon politics and pacification in the hinterland—a built-in contradiction.) Several wire-service veterans of Tet echoed the remarks of Bill Brannigan, cited earlier in the chapter, that pacification was too hard for client editors to understand as a "story" back home. According to this view, all the statistics and rhetoric about "hearts and minds," and the semantics of "security" and "government control," had confused editors (as well as politicians); they did not understand what the allies were basically trying to do: extend a degree of security, "normalcy," and government "presence" over an ever-wider area in a long, fluctuating, localized struggle for dominance with the Vietcong. Pacification was not a clear-cut dramatic "story," as were political coups, battles, and the Saigon black market.

Television and radio were perhaps the least well equipped to deal with pacification—given their constraints of time, accent on the obvious and visible, and shortage of Vietnam expertise even more acute than that of many other newsmen in the other media. Yet, as we have seen, they persisted in the most far-reaching speculation and the thinnest reporting in the guise of analysis well into March.

The *Post* and *Times* were quick to print hasty, overblown commentary in early February. As the on-scene reporting, however intermittent, improved, it was shunted inside the paper; the attention span at home was limited and, especially in the *Post* Saigon bureau, there were conflicting demands on scarce manpower. (It was not until October 1968 that the *Post* bureau provided a full-length report on pacification's problems and progress. It took three weeks' reporting. No other medium followed suit that year.)

Newsweek's efforts were hampered by a similar manpower shortage (two old hands, one newcomer, two stringers), a managerial penchant for drama, and an editorial decision to come out against Administration war policy—a decision which gave little incentive to the magazine's Saigon reporters to discover that all was not lost in early March. *Time* editors (divided on the war) and its Saigon bureau chief used their experienced manpower to good advantage in early March, and produced, as we have noted, the only relatively comprehensive overview of the Tet period.

As it turned out, Ambassador Komer's February 24 analysis of the rural "vacuum" was largely vindicated by events. The Vietcong, striking for the cities, disrupted pacification but did not attempt a wholesale occupation of the hamlets. (Possibly Hanoi felt it had too few men to do *everything*.) It took not "years" but seven months (encompassing two weaker subsequent enemy offensives) to bring the HES figures back to pre-Tet levels: 67 percent of the population in "relatively secure" hamlets. Enemy losses, greater U.S. realism, and belated South Vietnamese general mobilization helped the recovery. An accelerated pacification campaign—essentially a plant-the-flag effort—began in November 1968. By the end of 1969, the HES showed 92.7 percent of the population as "relatively secure," and in 1970 the *Post*'s bureau chief, Peter Jay, could drive unescorted in daylight 450 miles from Saigon to Da Nang. In 1972, when Hanoi launched its Easter offensive across South Vietnam's borders, with tank-supported regular NVA troops, the ARVN had little trouble from Vietcong guerrilla action (ambushes, sabotage) in the rear areas, except in Binh Dinh and Quang Ngai provinces and some provinces in the Delta. Finally, in April 1975, as the Thieu regime collapsed, the North Vietnamese, not the National Liberation Front (or Provisional Revolutionary Government) were the victors who marched proudly into Saigon.

This history seems to indicate that the Tet offensive dealt pacification a setback but no mortal blow. The point, journalistically, is not that Komer was "right" and the pessimists "wrong." The point is that the broad assessments of disaster in February 1968 were based not on understanding of pacification or on firsthand information, but on a keen sense of drama and "retribution." When some of the facts became clearer, the drama was no longer there, and the editors and commentators had lost interest.

11

Reinforcement and Escalation

This page-one headline in the New York *Times* of Sunday, March 10, 1968, in terms of impact on the Washington political scene, proved to be one of the most explosive of the Tet period:

WESTMORELAND REQUESTS 206,000 MORE MEN, STIRRING DEBATE IN ADMINISTRATION

FORCE NOW 510,000

Some in Defense and State Departmants Oppose Increase

The story was written by Neil Sheehan and Hedrick Smith. The *Times,* so it seemed, had unearthed the full, "inside" word on Administration policy-in-the-making, and highly controversial policy at that. The March 10 story appeared to shed some light on a question which always intrigues Washington newsmen in times of crisis: "What is the President going to do next?"

Journalistically, of course, times of crisis in Washington are dangerous. Reporters become especially vulnerable to manipulation by "leak." In the heat of competition, editors give prominence to speculation, generalizations, and prediction which, in calmer times, would undergo much stricter scrutiny. When the Administration's own answers to the "what next" question, at least in public, are vague or delayed, the competitive journalistic pressures for the "inside" story are intense. When the Administration's private search for answers, seldom a tidy process, is also complicated by rival bureaucratic claims, befogged by intra-Administration secrecy, and accompanied by election-year cacophony on Capitol Hill, the Washington political temperature rises further.

Such was the situation, an extreme case, in Washington in February and March 1968, after the shock of Tet. Some of the journalistic conjecture was devoted to the diplomatic front: another U.S. bombing halt, new peace approaches to Hanoi (an idea inflamed by a round of peacemaker diplomacy by U.N. Secretary General U Thant), a negotiated Saigon coalition government, a "compromise" peace?[1] But, as time went on, the "big" speculative story in Washington involved the answer to this politically (and economically) crucial question: How much more manpower was the President, who took an unyielding, firm line in public, going to put into Vietnam in response to the Tet crisis? What were the numbers?

The Administration on Reinforcement

Throughout the Tet period, the Administration in public tried to evade the issue of "more troops." Little over a week before the Tet attacks, Secretary McNamara noted in his annual posture statement that:

Last year we budgeted for a total of about 470,000 men in South Vietnam by June 1968, but last summer General Westmoreland requested and the President agreed to provide additional forces. Thus, by December 31, 1967, we had about 485,000 men there, and this number will grow to a total of 525,000. (Total allied forces in South Vietnam increased from 690,000 in June 1965 to 1,298,000 in December 1967 and are scheduled to grow to about 1,400,000 by June 1968.) The U.S. ground forces in December 1967 included 102 maneuver battalions[2] (79 Army, 23 Marine Corps). The ground forces are now supported by about 3,100 helicopters, and this number will continue to grow.[3]

In his initial post-Tet press conference, President Johnson stayed clear of predictions:

Q.: Is it possible that these developments in Vietnam that you had outlined, plus the imminence of this major offensive, could lead to deployment of additional American combat troops to Vietnam?

Johnson: I would not want to make predictions. Of course it is possible. The answer is yes. I wouldn't want your lead to say, "Johnson predicts possibility of troops," because that is not anticipated. We see no evidence of that.

. . . I must emphasize to you that lots of things would be considered, but so far as adding additional men, we have added the men that General Westmoreland has felt to be desirable and necessary.

There is nothing that has developed there that has caused him to change that estimate. We have something under 500,000. Our objective is 525,000. Most of the combat battalions already have been supplied. There is not anything in any of the developments that would justify the press in leaving the impression that any great new overall moves are going to be made that would involve substantial movements in that direction.[4]

Two days later, McNamara was on "Meet the Press" with the same message:

The commanders haven't asked for more men; they feel they have adequate strength to meet the situation now, and as far into the future as they project. I don't want to foreclose the possibility of requests in the future, but we have received none to date.

While I'm on that, let me simply say we're prepared to send more men if more are required. We've sent three carriers into the Korean waters, plus substantial reinforcements to our air power there, all out of our active forces, without in any way reducing the forces in Western Europe or Southeast Asia. We can send additional aircraft or additional ground forces from our active forces, should that prove necessary.[5]

Three days after announcing an 11,000-man emergency reinforcement for Vietnam (the 27th Marine Regiment, and the 3rd Brigade, 82nd Airborne Division), and with the battle of Hue still going on, the President was questioned again on February 16:

Q.: Mr. President, are you giving any thought to increasing the level of our forces in Vietnam?

Johnson: Yes, we give thought to that every day. We never know what forces will be required there. We have, tentatively, a goal. We would like to reach that goal as soon as we can. In light of the circumstances that existed when we set that goal, we hoped to reach it sometime this year.

In light of the developments and the subsequent substantial increases in the enemy force, General Westmoreland asked that he receive approximately half of the remaining numbers under that goal during February or early March.

Did you mean enemy forces or our forces?

Q.: Our forces.

Johnson: I said in light of substantial increases in the enemy force. You understood that, didn't you?

Q.: Yes.

Johnson: So General Westmoreland told us that.

We carefully reviewed his request in light of the information that had come in. We made certain adjustments and arrangements to comply with his request forthwith. That will be done.

When we reach our goal, we will be constantly reviewing the matter many times every day, at many levels. We will do whatever we think needs to be done to insure that our men have adequate forces to carry out their mission.[6]

In Saigon, after the onset of Tet, Westmoreland made no public statement about increased troop needs until his AP interview published on February 25. The date coincided with the departure of visiting Gen. Earle Wheeler, who, as will be noted, had his own ideas about increased manpower needs. Westmoreland said only that, pending the "development" of the ARVN, "additional United States forces may be required." He did not specify numbers of reinforcements or their mission.

Finally, in his March 31 speech announcing a partial pause in the bombing of North Vietnam and his own decision not to seek re-election, President Johnson finally let it be known what additional troops Westmoreland was to get: The old figure of 525,000 was to be boosted by only 13,500 support troops and the 11,000 emergency reinforcements already sent. It was a figure far lower than those mentioned earlier in news stories:

On many occasions I have told the American people that we would send to Vietnam those forces that are required to accomplish our mission there. So, with that as our guide, we have previously authorized a force level of approximately 525,000.

Some weeks ago—to help meet the enemy's new offensive—we sent to Vietnam about 11,000 additional Marine and airborne troops. They were deployed by air in 48 hours, on an emergency basis. But the artillery, tank, aircraft, medical, and other units that were needed to work with and to support these infantry troops in combat could not then accompany them by air on that short notice.

In order that these forces may reach maximum combat effectiveness, the Joint Chiefs of Staff have recommended to me that we should prepare to send—during the next five months—support troops totaling approximately 13,500 men.

A portion of these men will be made available from our active forces. The balance will come from reserve component units which will be called up for service.[7]

In the light of subsequent press accounts of the "Great Turna-round" of March 1968 in Vietnam War policy, it is important to note what President Johnson did *not* say on March 31. He set no ceiling on future U.S. manpower commitments, nor did he describe the new troop reinforcements as the last that would be sent to Vietnam, even as he lay heavy stress on new war efforts by the South Vietnamese.

The man who, in effect, nailed down subsequent policy was the new (since March 1) Defense Secretary, Clark Clifford, who had come to believe that a limit on U.S. involvement and a de-escalation of the war were in order. Clifford was a secondary figure during the pre-March 31 decision-making period. But he later moved in skill-fully to exploit the President's ambiguity. He spoke out repeatedly to insure that the press (and public) saw the President's speech as sig-naling a turn in American policy. By his own account, Clifford sought to create an irrevocable impression that the latest deployment did, in fact, represent an upper limit on U.S. involvement and that a decision had been made to turn over the major share of the war effort to the Saigon regime. With increasing success, he put this "troop limitation" message across—in his first press conference on April 11 and in sub-sequent statements on April 22, June 20, and August 15. He used the figure of 549,500—the achieved authorization level—on occasion as an *implicit* top figure. Not until September 5, however, did the De-fense Secretary firmly fix the figure of 549,500, attributing it to the President. "The so-called 'bottomless pit' has been capped," Clifford told the National Press Club. By the time the President left office in 1969, as Herbert Schandler emphasizes, "the tentative decision he had made in March to send only a few thousand troops to Vietnam at that time had been transformed [by Clifford's deliberate moves to ad-vance, in public, policy positions not yet reached by the President] into a positive limitation on the American troop commitment."[8]

But during February and March 1968, there was very little "official" public word from the Johnson Administration concerning what it planned to do militarily in response to the Tet offensive. The President made numerous exhortatory "we will hold the line" speeches. But he gave little inkling of what were, in reality, major in-tra-Administration debates taking place over what course to pursue. The troop reinforcement question at first was central to the discus-sion.

The *Times:* "Numbers" and "Sources" in Washington

Together with much of Washington officialdom, newsmen like "numbers," which give a semblance of precision and clarity, even significance, to otherwise complicated policies or events. Predicting the number of troops to be sent to Vietnam was a perennial game in Washington journalism. Often as not, what the numbers meant—in terms of combat strength, or choice of strategy, or mobilization policy—was ignored as a "technicality," or misunderstood by editors and commentators alike. As in federal budgets or draft calls, the numbers alone seemed impressive enough.

In February–March 1968, this penchant for numbers was especially true of the New York *Times* editors. As the Johnson Administration reexamined its Vietnam policy in a variety of ways, the *Times* devoted far more attention to the prospects of troop reinforcement than did other news organizations. Indeed, in the face of public Administration silence or evasion, the *Times* was almost alone in February in Washington in producing "inside" information on the reinforcement issue; no one else in our study produced more than one or two stories that went beyond the official statements. Hence, this chapter deals primarily with the work of the *Times,* and of its "psychological" competitor in Washington, the *Post.*[9]

The *Times* had a tradition of unearthing foreign-policy-in-the-making, dating back to James Reston's revelations at the 1944 Dumbarton Oaks Conference on international finance. The paper had uncovered the plans for the 1961 Bay of Pigs invasion, although—to some editors' subsequent regret—it did not publish them in full. Now, in February–March 1968, the onset of Tet convinced many at the *Times* that the White House would react militarily to what some of its editors perceived as a major military setback.[10]

The *Times*'s Washington bureau, then headed by Tom Wicker (who also wrote a column) was larger, with some 30 reporters, than the *Post*'s contingent devoted to national news. The bureau men were no lightweights. Wicker's deputy, as news editor, was Robert Phelps, a widely respected professional. Its Pentagon staff was led by William Beecher, a former *Wall Street Journal* reporter, who had traveled to Vietnam and specialized in broad policy stories. Keeping tabs on Vietnam affairs in particular was veteran Vietnam reporter Neil Sheehan. At the State Department was Hedrick Smith, another *Times* veteran of Vietnam (1964). And operating out of the New York office, aided by his own large specialized library and sizable files, and with the help of an experienced research assistant, was Hanson Baldwin, an Annapolis graduate, the *Times*'s military affairs editor. His access to the Joint Chiefs of Staff (among others) and his breadth of knowledge had long made him a formidable asset to the paper.

Baldwin was among the last of a breed of *Times* newsmen brought to prominence in the '40s and '50s: the painstaking, semischolarly specialist who was recognized as an authority and permitted by editors to write "long and dull," if necessary, on important matters. In the turbulent late 1960s, however, Baldwin was out of fashion at the *Times;* the changing management, reacting to critics' accusations that the paper was stodgy and "hard to read," strove for more "lively writing" about "people" and "issues" rather than "systems" and "institutions." Moreover, Baldwin was also out of fashion politically: He was, privately, a hawk and a conservative, while his fellow members of the *Times* editorial board, led by John Oakes, were mostly Democratic doves. Bitterness over what he considered offhand treatment of his news copy, and dismay over what he saw as a tilt away from balance in *Times* news columns, speeded Baldwin's retirement in 1968.

Baldwin had his professional biases: against McNamara's yardsticks of "cost-effectiveness" as applied to real war; against "technology" as a substitute for devoted leadership and well-trained men; against "civilians," as opposed to military professionals, as "operators" of military policy. This writer—and the *Times* Saigon bureau—felt that Baldwin's 1967 year-end series on Vietnam suffered from his "listening only to generals" who took too narrow a view of the war. Nevertheless, in early 1968, Baldwin was recognized by his colleagues as unsurpassed in one key area, among others: his ability to comprehend and translate for the lay reader what his high-level sources told him under skillful interrogation.

Baldwin had long been aware of the recurrent civilian-military debate within the Johnson Administration over escalation of the war. Indeed, prior to the U.S. buildup in Vietnam, Baldwin accurately conveyed the Joint Chiefs' private view: To "win" the war *quickly* would take much more money and manpower (and a more forceful strategy) than either Johnson or McNamara was willing to permit—or than the Joint Chiefs were willing to press for, to the point of resigning in protest. Like the dovish civilian doubters-in-office, the hawkish

Joint Chiefs did not resign; hoping always to get "more," they ac-
quiesced in the President's "limited war" policy of piecemeal bombing and troop commitment, a policy then known as "keeping your
options open." It was a pattern which persisted through Tet 1968.
Baldwin did not rebuke the Chiefs for this. But in *The New York
Times Magazine* of February 21, 1965, only two weeks before the
first Marines landed at Da Nang, he warned that "partial mobilization," and as many as "10 to 12 divisions," "perhaps 200,000 to
1,000,000 Americans" (counting Air Force, Navy, and logistics
manpower), would be needed in Southeast Asia in a "major war" to
save South Vietnam from a takeover by Hanoi, as he (and the Joint
Chiefs) saw it. At the time, it seemed a highly inflated proposition.

In early 1968, as in the past, Baldwin could pick up the telephone
and call any of the Joint Chiefs—and have his call returned in person.
He did so as the 1968 Tet tempest broke, and reported the Chiefs'
views on February 3 in the *Times:*

The widespread enemy attacks in South Vietnam and the consequent
dispersion of United States forces there have again focused attention in
Washington on the size and strength of United States units in Vietnam.
Gen. William C. Westmoreland . . . has about half a million men
from all four armed services and the Coast Guard in South Vietnam. He
has been authorized a total of 525,000. No plans were approved, before
the current crisis, for reinforcements beyond this figure. . . .
The buildup of United States troops in South Vietnam has not met either the schedules or totals asked by the military.
There has long been general agreement in the armed services that the
attempt to maintain half a million men in Vietnam, without mobilization
and on the basis of a one-year rotation plan and a two-year draft, meant
that elsewhere than in Southeast Asia the Army, Navy, and Air Force
have been spread thin and their experience level, inventories, and combat
effectiveness have declined.
The Korean diversion highlighted this and led to what the *services
regard as only a first step*, the mobilization of about 14,800 Air reservists.
The Navy has assigned two aircraft carriers, the *Enterprise* and the
Ranger, plus an antisubmarine-warfare carrier to the Sea of Japan, and
this has added an immense strain to the Navy's burden.

Baldwin correctly reflected the Joint Chiefs' position at this point:
no more troops for Vietnam without mobilization and a big reserve
call-up to strengthen the "worldwide military posture." The latter
was perhaps their prime concern. This view was overruled by the
President when he ordered 11,000 more troops (Marines and Army

Airborne) flown to Vietnam on February 12 as emergency reinforcements, after Westmoreland was urged to ask for them by General Wheeler under prodding by Johnson himself.[11]

Baldwin's story continued:

Senior officers in the Army and Marines believed in the early stage of the war that 600,000 to 750,000 men would be required.

However, in the last year, military men have been heartened by what they considered the improved combat effectiveness of the South Vietnamese armed forces—and have been saying that the 526,000 would probably be enough if the South Vietnamese continued to improve.[12]

Now, the strong enemy thrusts into nearly all the major cities of South Vietnam this week and what is believed to be an impending large-scale battle around Khe Sanh at the western end of the Demilitarized Zone appear to cast some doubt on this assumption.[13]

Shortly after, the *Times*'s Max Frankel, then the White House correspondent, wrote an unsigned piece in the "News of the Week in Review" section analyzing the President's problems in Asia after Tet; the piece strongly indicated another, different view in Washington of what Tet "proved":

Now, through a concentration of their manpower and with more sophisticated planning and weaponry than ever before, they have proved that city-dwellers and even some American installations are not immune to attack. No more than one or two such major assaults a year could well create the impression of the stalemate that the Administration has so vigorously denied.

If that should ever become the analysis of the American electorate, President Johnson would indeed be vulnerable to the charges of both doves and hawks that he can neither end the war nor win it. No one who knows him expects the President ever to reduce his objectives in Vietnam merely for political profit, but the combined pressures of the war itself and its political consequences at home are *thought to have raised once again the temptation of further military escalation.*[14]

Frankel raised some straw men. The North Vietnamese, repeatedly in the past, had shown that cities and "even some American installations" were not "immune" from attack. Even the most optimistic Administration statements before Tet claimed no "immunity" from such attacks. The scale and intensity of the Tet attacks, as MACV's Brig. Gen. John Chaisson noted on February 3, were what surprised the military—and Saigon newsmen.

Although Frankel, like others in Washington, thought Tet would tempt the President to escalate, it was rather clear on the record by 1968 that Johnson had found escalation—in the hawks' sense—as unappealing as the withdrawal urged by extreme doves. He had only slowly increased the troop commitment to Vietnam, always finally drawing the line at mobilization or calling up the reserves.[15] For a time in early February, he may have been sufficiently worried, notably by Khe Sanh, to open the door to suggestions that he send major reinforcements to Westmoreland, and this was the impression conveyed by Wheeler to Saigon. But it was hardly a *tempting* prospect for Johnson.

During and after Wheeler's important February 23–25 visit to Saigon, the *Times* began to print some "numbers" stories on more troops for Vietnam. For example, it published a vague "50,000 to 100,000" figure by UPI out of Saigon, along with a Pentagon "no comment."[16] UPI, we know now, was not totally wrong. But the story is complex: The visit of Wheeler to Saigon, at his own request, was ordered by Johnson. For the President, Wheeler was to determine Westmoreland's needs. On behalf of the worried Joint Chiefs, Wheeler would also examine these needs in terms of a new military strategy in Vietnam, and *equally important,* in the light of U.S. worldwide troop needs—in Korea and Europe, and for the strategic reaction forces in the United States.

As *Times* reporter William Beecher was to note in print, the Joint Chiefs had been repeatedly turned down when they asked the Johnson Administration to mobilize the reserves, as President Truman had mobilized them during the Korean War. McNamara had opposed any such move and, in 1967, had opposed sending more major forces to Vietnam. Now—with Tet provoking an Administration "new look" at Vietnam, and with McNamara replaced by a reputedly more hawkish Clark Clifford—an opportunity arose to press the Joint Chiefs' old arguments once more.

In Saigon, Wheeler and Westmoreland agreed that it was also a good time to urge a bolder Vietnam strategy, with more troops to gain quicker results: i.e., forays into Laos, Cambodia, and possibly that part of North Vietnam just above the DMZ. Westmoreland was concerned about the enemy threat to Khe Sanh and northern I Corps in late February, but neither he (nor any newsman in Saigon) saw the overall military situation as precarious. The "requirement" for 206,000 troops was linked in Westmoreland's thinking to adoption by the White House of the Laos-Cambodia-DMZ strategy, and the number was approximately what Westmoreland had sought in vain in 1967.[17]

Moreover—and here Wheeler's "worldwide" concerns came into play—Westmoreland agreed to Wheeler's verbal caveat: Even if the 206,000 "package" were accepted by the White House, only half of it—or about 100,000 men—would be definitely committed in increments to Vietnam. Deployment of the rest would be conditioned by future developments both in Southeast Asia and elsewhere. In any event, Wheeler said, Westmoreland could not expect sizable reinforcements until late in the year. Westmoreland could accept that; he wanted more troops to pursue a new strategy and exploit enemy Tet losses, not to "save" the current situation, which he saw as improving markedly.

Wheeler, however, went home to make a different argument: The "worst possibilities" (an ARVN collapse, a major future escalation by Hanoi) now justified a 206,000-man increase, ostensibly all for Vietnam. Readying a force of 206,000 men—only half of it really committed to Vietnam—would require a wider buildup and, Wheeler reasoned, a decision to mobilize reservists. As the Joint Chiefs desired, the "worldwide posture" would thereby gain. In his gloomy report to the President on February 27, Wheeler did not mention the new strategy. Once he got the troops, he would argue strategy.

Wheeler's translation of Westmoreland's troop request, couched in terms of offsetting future and present perils, caused a furor. It seemed to confirm the doves' worst fears. Johnson ordered Clifford to set up a secret task force to present recommendations. They did so on March 4.

As General Wheeler finished his Saigon visit, Beecher wrote an unsigned piece, in the "News of the Week in Review" section, suggesting, as had Frankel, that escalation—notably a reserve call-up—was probable:

> On at least four other occasions prior to last week during the Vietnamese War, the Joint Chiefs of Staff have recommended a mobilization of reserves: twice in 1965, and once each in 1966 and 1967. Each time the recommendation has been rejected by the Secretary of Defense and the President. Now the Chiefs are urging a reserve call-up once again. And this time, though nothing is certain in war or politics, the *expectation is that President Johnson will go along*.[18]
>
> The decision is believed to hinge on whether Gen. William C. Westmoreland can make a convincing case for requiring substantial rein-

forcements fairly quickly to help stem the new enemy offensive in Vietnam. . . .

At week's end, the Texas White House reported that the whole matter was under continuing review. A decision, it was generally felt, would probably not be made until General Wheeler returned to Washington at midweek.[19]

Again, Beecher assumed, as did most other newsmen at the time (including this one), that Wheeler was merely presenting Westmoreland's "case," not acting as Chairman of the Joint Chiefs, who had other interests and uses for troops besides the war in Vietnam. On February 29, Beecher had a remarkably accurate if incomplete page-one exclusive after General Wheeler returned and visited the White House. Beecher's story attributed the "indicated" troop request ("100,000 to 200,000") solely to Westmoreland, but it implied (correctly) that the numbers had been under discussion in the Pentagon prior to Wheeler's visit to Vietnam. More interestingly, well before his *Times* colleagues' March 10 exclusive, Beecher noted the strategy dispute then going on between Pentagon civilians and the Joint Chiefs over the "what next" question. But unlike his colleagues, Beecher did not identify the factions involved. There were, he said, advocates of "pull back" and advocates of "no change." There were other advocates, he reported, of "mobilization," who said "100,000" more men would enable Westmoreland to "regain the initiative" (a Wheeler phrase later erroneously attributed to Westmoreland by the *Times* in its March 10 story) and reconstitute his own mobile reserve. The story did not explain what "regain the initiative" meant in terms of new strategy, i.e., hitting Laos and Cambodia. After citing the 200,000 figure in his lead, Beecher did not mention it again.[20]

Beecher's story began:

High government officials said today that the Johnson Administration was making a reappraisal of American military strategy in Vietnam. The reports came amid indications that Gen. William C. Westmoreland was seeking 100,000 to 200,000 more troops for the war effort.

Central to the review, the reports say, will be discussions between government officials and Gen. Earle G. Wheeler . . . who returned from an inspection of the combat theater this morning. He went promptly to the White House for a two-hour breakfast, meeting with many leading government planners on Vietnam.

Officials stressed that any proposal by General Wheeler for reinforcements would be tentative and *would not constitute a formal request for a specific number of men.* . . .

As in the past, they said, a formal request will not be made until Washington is able to give Saigon a clear indication of what forces may be made available over the next year or so. That cannot be done until the strategy review has been completed.[21]

A few days later, while the behind-the-scenes troops debate went on in Washington, James Reston visited the fifth wheel of the Vietnam cart—the U.S. Pacific Command in Hawaii. He accurately reported Adm. U. S. Grant Sharp's call to Washington for escalation, particularly in terms of bombing, to "regain the initiative":

HONOLULU—The pressure is obviously rising here at U.S. Pacific Command *for more men and more bombing targets in Vietnam.* Adm. U. S. Grant Sharp now has over a million men under his command in the entire Pacific area, but the estimates here call for a substantial increase to regain the initiative in Southeast Asia. . . .

Officers here seem confident that the trend of policy in Washington is going their way. There were no tears in this command when Secretary of Defense McNamara left the Pentagon. "He was never really for the bombing of the North," one officer observed. More important, President Johnson is now regarded here as coming over to a military solution of the war, playing down the talk of negotiation, and beginning to deal with what is called here "the realities of the military situation."[22]

The same Sunday Beecher reprised his February 29 story, and again predicted that Johnson would "opt" for mobilization of the reserves:

WASHINGTON—At the Pentagon everyone was waiting last week to hear what Gen. Earle G. Wheeler had to say. The Chairman of the Joint Chiefs of Staff had just returned from Vietnam, where he was *reported to have* heard a request from Gen. William C. Westmoreland for 100,000 to 200,000 more fighting men.

"He wants closer to 200,000 than 100,000 more," one knowledgeable source disclosed. . . .

The attacks demonstrated a spectrum of vulnerabilities, the defense of which is at the heart of the strategic review in Washington.[23]

In essence, the military options most seriously considered were these: Mobilize for a substantial infusion of new manpower. . . .

Pull back American troops from more or less static defense positions near Vietnam's borders, as at Khe Sanh, into the populated regions along the coastal plain. Present troop levels, it is argued, could more effectively

protect the cities while Saigon attempts to improve its military and political hold on the people. Long-range patrols would be pressed in the va-
cated territories in an attempt to find the enemy for air strikes and occasional attacks. . . .[24]

A more-of-the-same approach, patching up the present strategy by adding a few tens of thousands of troops and hoping that air attacks, when
the weather clears, will punish the enemy sufficiently to make him lose
heart and seek an accommodation.

Betting in the nation's capital is that, hard as the choice may be, President Johnson will opt for a mobilization of the reserves in a massive
effort to prevail in Vietnam.[25]

Beecher in effect was reporting what *his* prime sources—on the National Security Council and among the aides of the Joint Chiefs—were
hoping and predicting. He and they did not suggest that the manpower "infusion" was tied to a revived proposal for the long-range
Laos-Cambodia strategy, rather than the immediate situation. During
the following week, fueled by such stories, the debate in Congress
over the war was spurred by what Senator William Fulbright called
"reports or rumors" of a 200,000-man troop increase for Vietnam.[26]

The Administration, as we have noted, was still officially silent or
noncommittal on any new strategy or troop increase for Vietnam—
even as the President continued to make "hold that line" speeches
around the country. Thus, Washington's rumor mills, rivaling any in
Saigon, continued to work overtime. The possibility of a reserve call-
up and troop increases grew as a subject of speculation among newsmen. And, a few days after Wheeler's return from Vietnam, the
Times reporters began to pick up echoes of the intra-Administration
debate outside the Pentagon.

Just as Beecher's best contacts in the Pentagon (like Baldwin's)
were the hawkish, if not monolithic, high-ranking uniformed military,
so his colleague Neil Sheehan enjoyed most rapport with the more
dovish, disenchanted "McNamara civilians" (led by former Washington lawyer Paul Warnke, the Assistant Secretary of Defense for International Security Affairs) and their friends on Capitol Hill. Sheehan
had little access to the Joint Chiefs. He was one of those whose "pessimism" while in Vietnam had incurred the wrath of the U.S. Mission
in the last days of Ngo Dinh Diem. Some senior Army veterans of
that period retained no love for either Sheehan or *Times* reporter
David Halberstam. "We would have been all right in Vietnam," Maj.
Gen. Hal D. McGown later observed, combining the two young vil-

lains in his mind, "if it hadn't been for people like Neil Halberstam."[27] Sheehan, it is fair to say, mustered little sympathy for Westmoreland or that commander's military superiors in the Pentagon. He viewed their public optimism in 1967 as a case of self-delusion as old as the U.S. involvement in Vietnam. During the Tet period, he reported several instances of apparent Pentagon duplicity and of Westmoreland's alleged optimism in pre-Tet reports to Washington—the result of "leaks" to Sheehan on the Hill or downtown.[28] Long after Tet, Sheehan was to expose fraudulent atrocity tales in investigating a war-crimes anthology compiled after the My Lai massacre by Mark Lane. In 1971, he was Daniel Ellsberg's conduit for the secret Pentagon Papers, and chief writer and organizer of the subsequent *Times* series (which began June 13, 1971).

Another *Times* Washington man heavily involved in the Tet story was Hedrick Smith, a UPI alumnus, who had served the New York *Times* in Cairo before his assignment to Vietnam. Essentially, he was no more enchanted with Administration Vietnam policy than was Sheehan. Since Smith covered the State Department, he daily sought out its middle- and upper-middle-echelon officials. These officials, by education and bureaucratic bias, tended to find little congenial in the propositions put forward by the Joint Chiefs during the periodic debates over Vietnam policy. Just as the Joint Chiefs or their aides "talked" to a few newsmen like Beecher and Baldwin,[29] so the civilians at ISA and State "talked" to Sheehan, Smith, and others (such as Chalmers Roberts and Murrey Marder of the *Post*) whom *they* found congenial. And the civilians "talked" far more.

In public testimony on Capitol Hill during 1967–68, McNamara drew the spotlight, often with a bemedaled Wheeler sitting impassively behind him. The individual branches of the armed forces were not mute, however. They had their hawkish friends in Congress who occasionally rebroadcast their frustrations (notably during the 1967 Senate Preparedness Subcommittee hearings on McNamara's curbs on the bombing of North Vietnam). There was a strong defense industry lobby. But Wheeler and his peers had few social or "business lunch" contacts with newsmen or their superiors; the two worlds—of military "doers" and civilian "kibitzers"—were too far apart for them to meet with comfort or even convenience. On the other hand, to Washington newsmen, the military's bureaucratic antagonists (at State, CIA, DOD), their academic critics, and their Congressional foes were PLUs ("people like us"), as the West Point graduates were not. Like the newsmen, the civilians were kibitzers—articulate, politically sensitive, often semi-"intellectual." Especially under a Democratic regime, the civilians were accessible; they were good company at the Federal City Club or at dinners in Georgetown. Their shock over Tet, shared by newsmen, was readily transmitted—without attribution—into public print as anonymous but expert testimony.

Even before Tet, journalistic contact with the military remained confined largely to the remote exiles in the green-painted Pentagon newsroom. Reporters often had difficulty arousing the interest of their deskmen in "dull" but important defense issues. By and large, the senior military view of the world was not only different from their own, but also couched in either technical jargon or brutal-sounding clichés. Thus, the Washington editors' reaction to military issues was all the more to lean toward the familiar, accessible, "civilian" view, especially if it was critical of military policy. Moreover, the military were not "winning the war," and newsmen disdain "losers." As the generals' image eroded (no one is more susceptible to "images" than busy editors), newsmen who tried to cover the vast military bureaucracy also lost status, and their advice to deskmen was often suspect as axe-grinding for the military. As some of the Pentagon "regulars" complained to me in 1969, the "market" changed. Their role as "explainers" of complex military issues had to cede almost wholly to their other role as exposers of specific military follies, important or not. Otherwise, they often were regarded by their offices as "captives" of the military, particularly during the post-1966 Vietnam era.

Oddly enough, few Washington reporters other than those assigned to the military felt this "in-house" pressure in 1967–69. No one, for example, then or later, accused newsmen on Capitol Hill of being overly kind to congressmen or the legislative process—even if few Congressional warts were described in print. Notably absent from the media in 1968 was any suggestion that senators were apt to substitute rhetoric on Vietnam for hard facts and hard questions, a flaw often apparent in Foreign Relations Committee hearings despite generally excellent work by the committee staff. Instead, then as later, prominent senators (hawks and doves alike) were treated not only as advocates but as *informed* sources on the war in South Vietnam and on the psychology of the South Vietnamese.

The Making of the *Times* "Exclusive"

The sum total of the Baldwin-Beecher-Smith-Sheehan access to information and to the contending Administration factions was impressive. But this reportorial potential was not realized, for the *Times* effort was not made by a team; each specialist mined his own vein of information, without collaborating with his fellows. This dispersion of effort is common in the press (Max Frankel, when he became Washington bureau chief in 1969, made a special effort to overcome the gaps). But at Tet there were also other factors involved. Both Wicker and James Reston, his predecessor as chief and the *Times*'s Washington-based columnist and "senior statesman," were preoccupied with internal matters, namely, a dispute with the senior editors in New York, who wanted to establish greater control over the Washington bureau.[30] With a feud in process, the senior New York editors were adamant about how various "angles" of Washington stories should be handled by Wicker's bureau. Wicker and Robert Phelps were "under the gun"—in a poor position either to argue with New York or even to think through day-to-day news operations.

In any event, in early March 1968, when the *Times* bureau's Smith and Sheehan unearthed part of a major policy-in-the-making story (essentially a follow-on to Beecher's and Baldwin's February reporting), the *Times* did not use all its assets to investigate all sources. The story as developed seemed devastatingly simple: Westmoreland had requested, through Wheeler, a 206,000-man troop increase to contain and roll back enemy gains at Tet, thereby setting off a still-lively debate inside the Administration over whether to meet the request and thus vastly increase the war's cost.

In March 1968, Johnson, Rusk, and newcomer Clifford were "inaccessible" to newsmen, even to the White House man, Frankel. But the *Times,* potentially at least, had access, through Beecher and, above all, Baldwin, to a second obvious set of "actors" in the President's 1968 decision-making process—the Joint Chiefs. These two reporters were not invited to join the search. Yet, besides their special "access," they were the two *Times* staffers at home most sensitive to the bureaucratic history of troop requests, the repeated Westmoreland request for a new strategy (Laos-Cambodia), and the historic linkage between the two.

Moreover, Beecher and Baldwin were conscious—as their February reports indicate—of the Joint Chiefs' concern over troop needs *outside* Vietnam. That Wheeler used the "worst possible" contingencies in Vietnam as an initial rationale for his troop request, made in Westmoreland's name but aimed primarily at strengthening the United States worldwide, might have been too complex a bureaucratic gambit for Baldwin and Beecher to uncover in four days. But it seems at least highly likely that these two reporters, especially Baldwin, would have discovered the two crucial points:

1. The 206,000-man request for Vietnam, or any such major reinforcement, was no longer seen as a live issue by the Joint Chiefs by the time the Smith-Sheehan story appeared on March 10.

2. The "request," in any case, was not Westmoreland's response to the post-Tet situation in Vietnam, but a *repeat* request tied to a long-sought change in strategy.

Indeed, Beecher, at one point during that first week of March, ventured to warn his bureau colleagues not to take the troop request too literally. His advice was ignored. And the Saigon bureau was not asked for its advice.

There was pressure from the New York office to produce—and preserve—an "exclusive." Sheehan and Smith were willing to believe that their sources were sufficiently knowledgeable, and to believe with those sources that the post-Tet military outlook was sufficiently bleak to justify a plea for help from Westmoreland. Their sources' worst fear was of major escalation by Johnson to salvage a deteriorated battlefield situation, and this seemed reinforced by Johnson's publicly hawkish stance and by much media reporting from Vietnam.

On Friday, March 1, Edwin L. Dale, the *Times*'s Washington economic reporter, and Townsend Hoopes, Undersecretary of the Air Force who had sat in on the Pentagon discussion of Wheeler's troop request earlier in the week, attended a party at the home of Representative William Moorhead, a Pennsylvania Democrat. All three had been at Yale together in the 1940s, and all three had been members of Skull and Bones, the Yale senior society.

As they talked, Hoopes, without mentioning numbers, told Dale that he and other Pentagon civilians were opposed to any major troop reinforcements and favored a new look at the whole war policy. Dale passed the word to Robert Phelps on Monday, March 4. What aroused Phelps's interest, and that of others at the *Times*, was Hoopes's allusion to high-echelon dissent over the much-rumored troop request (cited by Beecher the previous week). The fact that disagreement had occurred before, notably over Westmoreland's rejected 1967 troop proposal, was not then generally recalled outside the Pentagon, despite accurate 1967 press accounts. The widespread assumption among newsmen not in the Pentagon was that, so far, Westmoreland had gotten almost everything he asked for, and still could not win a "military victory." That McNamara had come to question publicly the bombing of North Vietnam in 1967 was generally remembered; that privately he had successfully opposed further troop reinforcements was not. Reporters—and their editors—as author-journalist Frances Fitzgerald later remarked to this writer, "have the memories of rabbits."

Phelps persuaded the New York editors that the story was worth pursuing, and assigned Smith and Sheehan to the job. In addition to their "downtown" sources, both reporters had good friends on the staffs of the Senate Foreign Relations Committee and among the aides of individual senators.

On Tuesday, March 5, after one day's work, Smith got the 206,000 figure from a committee staffman on Capitol Hill—and got confirmation that the internal debate cited by Hoopes was underway in the Pentagon. Comparing notes, Smith and Sheehan then pursued the story with everyone they could find, bluff, or cajole into yielding details of the intra-Administration debate. Both were professionals; they knew Washington; they cited the 206,000 figure to officials they could reach and watched for reaction; they got confirmation of the number from three separate sources and began writing Friday morning, March 8. By this time, of course, the White House had the March 4 Clifford task force report, recommending only a 22,000-man reinforcement for Westmoreland.

When queried by this author later (1970), both Sheehan and Smith invoked the reporter's privilege of not disclosing his sources. As their story partly indicates, their range of information was necessarily limited. But Schandler, after interviewing a wide range of 1968 actors and observers for his analysis of the troop decision, concludes that the Times's major sources were not "disaffected bureaucrats" but certain senators and their aides on Capitol Hill. These men, Schandler writes, "had long since decided ، . . to do what they could to change the direction of the war." One of the sources was William Miller, assistant to Senator John Sherman Cooper. Miller told Schandler: "It was not clear that Lyndon Johnson did not propose to continue the buildup in Vietnam as recommended by his military advisors, and to them [the Senate doves and their aides] this had become an intolerable policy." There was an "interlocking network" between the disaffected bureaucrats and sympathetic, less inhibited senators "which kept Congress fully informed," Miller added.[31]

This was particularly true on the Senate Foreign Relations Committee, headed by Senator William Fulbright, who repeatedly warned against escalation. One former member of that committee's staff, who asked anonymity, said that the diligent *Times* reporters, in early March 1968 and later, found the Fulbright committee staffers a good source of Vietnam "leaks." However, he added, the Congressional staff people tended to get their information on Vietnam policy from the like-minded "downtown," who also tended to talk to one another and to the *Times*. Thus, one may speculate that, in checking separate sources, Smith and Sheehan may simply have been tapping different points on the same narrow circuit of impressions and information. There were also delays and intervening interpretations in this informal syndication of inside "facts." These factors may explain some of the omissions and misplaced emphasis in the March 10 story.

As it turned out, the *Times* uncovered only one level of the story—the arguments within the middle-echelon Clifford task force—and conveyed the impressions of only this one set of actors. These actors were the civilians of the ISA ("McNamara's State Department") and their allies elsewhere in Defense, State, the CIA, and, above all, on Capitol Hill. Subsequent historical accounts seem to confirm that the two reporters accurately reported what their sources told them. But these actors played a secondary role in the President's February–March 1968 decision-making on troop reinforcements for Vietnam. And they were not privy to three more important dialogues involving: (1) the President and Secretary Rusk; (2) the President, Rusk, Clifford, Wheeler, and other senior officials; and (3) Wheeler, Westmoreland, and the Joint Chiefs.

The revealing backchannel messages between Wheeler and Westmoreland were not available to the *Times* reporters as they pressed for details during the first week of March; nor were these messages distributed on Capitol Hill or to Pentagon civilians. (They were later made available by the Army to civilian historians.) The messages make clear the concern of Wheeler and the Joint Chiefs with military commitments other than Vietnam, the White House's reluctance to mobilize and reinforce, and, *prior* to publication of the New York *Times* story, Wheeler's realization that the troop issue was dead.

On March 5, General Wheeler informed Westmoreland of the March 4 recommendations made by the Clifford task force. He noted that emphasis had been placed in the task force report on "the fact that [the] CONUS (Continental United States) strategic reserve is badly depleted" to the point where "we can provide only a fraction of a portion of the first [100,000-man] increment" of the 206,000-man package agreed to by Westmoreland during Wheeler's February visit. "Highest authority" (the President), Wheeler told Westmoreland, had "instructed me to inform you of the committee recommendations," which included a 22,000-man deployment to Vietnam, and a reserve call-up not for Vietnam but to "increase and improve our strategic reserve in the United States."

In a second message to Westmoreland on March 5, after the White House Tuesday luncheon meeting (Johnson, Rusk, Clifford, Wheeler), Wheeler noted the President's relief at receiving Westmoreland's optimistic March 3 cable concerning imminent offensive operations by allied forces following the recapture of Hue (February 24). This cable, Wheeler said, "has raised a lot of interest." Westmoreland's optimism—reflected in his public statements and briefings on February 25 and March 6 in Saigon—reassured the President. It meant that the General was going on the offensive *without* additional troops.

As we have noted, Johnson had dispatched 11,000 men to Vietnam in mid-February as emergency reinforcements (almost pressed on Westmoreland by Wheeler), without the reserve call-up sought by the Joint Chiefs. Worried in February, he had briefly opened the door to a massive troop request by asking Westmoreland to state his needs, and by dispatching General Wheeler to evaluate them. But now he was closing the door—noiselessly—and reverting to his pre-Tet reluctance to meet repeated Joint Chiefs' demands for "more." President Johnson let the Pentagon debate go on, even as he began to think about other Vietnam matters, notably Dean Rusk's private suggestion on March 5 that the United States, to buy time and appease the doves, try a partial bombing pause.[32]

But Wheeler was not deceived. His gambit had failed. On March 8, he informed Westmoreland that there was "strong resistance in all quarters to putting more ground-force units in South Vietnam." A 30,000-man package—up from the 22,000 men first proposed by Clifford—was probable, but a "decision has not yet been taken" to deploy that number. A reserve call-up, he also noted, would raise "unshirted hell" in Congress. While mobilization of the reserves, still a matter of discussion by Clifford, would improve the ready forces in the United States, Wheeler told Westmoreland, "You should not count on an affirmative decision for additional forces. With this cheerless counsel, I will sign off."

In short, by March 8, both Wheeler and Westmoreland knew escalation was dead, at least in terms of the major reinforcements that a new strategy would require. So did a number of military men on the ISA staff. Still unresolved was the question of the reserve call-up, but this was a separate issue, and it died somewhat later.

On that same date, across the Potomac from the Pentagon, Smith was writing with Sheehan the story they had researched. "Our feeling," Smith said later, "was that the big story was not the 206,000 figure, but the fact *that a major policy fight* (at least in DOD) was going on in the government over Vietnam policy."

Accordingly, Smith wrote the first lead paragraph to deal with the policy fight, not the number. But the editors in New York, responding to a chronic journalistic thirst, insisted to Phelps that the lead paragraph be rewritten to include the number. As Don Oberdorfer was later to observe: "The fact that this was not a rounded number—not 200,000 or even 205,000, but precisely 206,000—added greatly to its authenticity and impact."[33] For added effect, the *Times*'s New York editors held the story for Sunday's paper, and gave it the lead position under a three-column headline. This delay meant, as seen in retrospect, that the headline was even more misleading and more outdated.

In this story, Smith and Sheehan accurately portrayed the "groggy," pessimistic sub-Cabinet officials, but not the Senate aides who were also prime sources; the debate (over "enclave" strategy, "broadening the base," negotiation) going on at the sub-Cabinet level;[34] Westmoreland's desire to expand the war into Laos and Cambodia; the hawks' unhappiness on Capitol Hill; and, *well down in the story*, the rejection of the 206,000-troop request as "unrealistic" by "some senior officials." But the opening paragraphs of the story, as revised on New York's orders, made the troop request a Westmoreland "plea" for strength to "regain the initiative" from the enemy—a "plea" implicitly tied to recovery from the Tet offensive, not linked to a new, expanded Laos-Cambodia strategy. The military argument cited further down in the story by the writers was in fact advanced by General Wheeler in his report to the President, not by

Westmoreland: "Only a massive infusion of troops will restore the allied initiative."[35] Furthermore, the story made it appear that the 206,000-troop request was still a live issue—as Sheehan and Smith were led to believe it was. In fact, as we have seen, Wheeler had warned Westmoreland on March 8 it was all but dead.

The use by Wheeler of the "worst possible" contingencies in Vietnam as his opening argument for more worldwide U.S. military strength was only slowly discerned by Clifford. The purpose of the argument also went unrecognized by some of those at sub-Cabinet level.[36] They initially accepted Wheeler's presentation as Westmoreland's formal request for troops to recover from the Tet blows in Vietnam, and they relayed this impression to their friends on Capitol Hill and, presumably, in some cases, to the inquiring *Times* reporters.[37] This was the result:

WASHINGTON, Mar. 9—Gen. William C. Westmoreland has asked for 206,000 more American troops for Vietnam, but the request has touched off a divisive internal debate within high levels of the Johnson Administration.

A number of sub-Cabinet civilian officials in the Defense Department, supported by some senior officials in the State Department, have argued against General Westmoreland's plea for a 40 percent increase in his forces "to regain the initiative" from the enemy.

There are now about 510,000 American troops in Vietnam, and the President has authorized a level of 525,000 by next fall. Many of the civilian officials are arguing that there should be no increase beyond the movement of troops now under way.

Fear Matching Rise

The contention of these high-ranking officials is that an American increase will bring a matching increase by North Vietnam, thereby raising the level of violence without giving the allies the upper hand.

Senior Pentagon civilians have put forward a written counter-proposal to President Johnson, calling for a shift in American strategy to a concept of close-in defense of populated areas with more limited offensive thrusts than at present. Much of the military hierarchy is reported to oppose this approach.

General Westmoreland, the American commander in Vietnam, has been seeking to persuade the President to approve bolder strategy. Officials report that he has been proposing ground actions into Laos and Cambodia to disrupt the enemy's base areas and infiltration routes.[38]

Compromise Suggested

But the enemy's winter offensive has had such stunning impact on some high civilian officials here that they question privately whether the government should not lower its war objectives. Some have suggested that the ground be prepared for a political compromise with the Vietcong. But this is a position that President Johnson and his inner circle of advisors firmly reject at this point.

The President has not yet decided on the question of substantial increases in American forces in Vietnam.

"He is keeping an open mind," said one senior advisor.

For the time being Mr. Johnson is reported to be holding to current strategy and urging General Westmoreland to wring the utmost combat capacity out of the 510,000 American troops already in Vietnam. The White House maintains officially that the question of more troops is "not a matter of decision at this point."[39]

Offensive Causes Doubts

Nonetheless, the scope and depth of the internal debate within the government reflect the wrenching uncertainty and doubt in this capital about every facet of the war left by the enemy's dramatic wave of attacks at Tet, the Lunar New Year holiday, six weeks ago. More than ever, this has left a sense of weariness and irritation over the war.

Officials themselves comment in private about widespread and deep changes in attitudes, a sense that a watershed has been reached and that its meaning is just now beginning to be understood.

One high official commented that the enemy's Tet offensive was "a body blow." Another remarked that Washington was "still groggy." Said a third: "There's no disguising it—we got a real punch in the nose." Others speak bitterly of Vietnam as a "bottomless pit." Even more pervasive is the comment, "We don't really know where we stand yet. Our information is poor."[40]

Another official intimately acquainted with the Vietnam situation recalled the government's optimistic estimates of progress last fall. "We know now that we constantly underestimated the enemy's capacity and his will to fight, and overestimated our progress," he said. "We know now that all we thought we had constructed was built on sand."[41]

The President and his inner circle of advisors, especially Secretary of State Dean Rusk and Walt W. Rostow, a special assistant to the President for national security affairs, project an air of confidence that the situation can somehow be righted and the balance restored.[42]

The 206,000 figure received wide attention. UPI came out next day with a "curtain raiser" on Secretary Rusk's coming appearance before the Senate Foreign Relations Committee, correctly tying the cited troop increase to strategy proposed by Westmoreland: "Some officers felt this might require as many as 206,000 additional troops by this time next year." Administration officials, UPI accurately said, "discounted any idea that the escalation this year would be more than 30,000 to 40,000 men."[43]

Thomas B. Ross of the Chicago *Sun-Times* (March 14) shrewdly sounded a note of warning, saying that the "political and military realities appear to be dictating great caution in [Johnson's] handling of the war" despite the President's hawkish public stance.

Orr Kelly of the Washington *Evening Star* said (March 12): "The tendency to try to solve the problems [of Tet] with another quick infusion of American troops apparently seemed most attractive about three weeks ago. Since then, it has reportedly appeared less and less certain to be the obvious thing to do."

The Philadelphia *Inquirer* cast doubt on the likelihood of the increase. The Baltimore *Sun* talked of a "reported request for 200,000 more troops." Max Lerner of the New York *Post* (March 12) said the Tet offensive had "forced" Westmoreland to ask for 200,000 men.

On March 13, the *Times's* William Beecher provided the latest correct number—30,000—but applied it to an "initial" reserve call-up being urged by "high Pentagon officers" to help Westmoreland "regain the initiative" (which the General had already told Saigon newsmen and the President he was regaining). The story was buried on page fifteen. But Beecher's report was timely and accurate in that it also cited discussion of a 100,000-man reserve call-up (sought by Wheeler) and an increased role for the South Vietnamese Army, whose Tet performance had encouraged Westmoreland, Rusk, and Johnson. The 206,000 figure was briefly mentioned by Beecher, but as the extreme end of "a spectrum of options."[44] In fact, of course, it was no longer a serious option.

On March 17, a week after the 206,000-man story, the *Times,* still getting leaks, held to the probability of a reserve call-up and said 35,000 to 50,000 more troops for Vietnam was the likely figure. The story landed on page one:

WASHINGTON, Mar. 16—The Johnson Administration has decided to send more troops to Vietnam. Reliable sources said today that the number would be moderate, compared with the 206,000 men requested by Gen. William C. Westmoreland.

The President was reported to have made no decision on the exact number. But military observers speculated that the pattern of past increases indicated that he might approve the dispatch of one more division with supporting units, about 35,000 men over the next several months.[45]

The following Sunday, March 24, James Reston reported on the intra-Administration situation, after Johnson's announcement of Westmoreland's promotion to Army Chief of Staff:

WASHINGTON, Mar. 23—Dean Rusk says the Vietnam policy is being reassessed from A to Z, and President Johnson talks as if the reappraisal were going merely from A to B, but obviously something is afoot here.

Several things we know. President Johnson brought General Westmoreland prominently into the politics of the war, and in the process promised the General publicly he would get all the troops he needed. General Westmoreland asked for 206,000 more troops, which he isn't going to get, and now he's coming home to be Army Chief of Staff. Maybe there's no connection between these things, but they're intriguing.[46]

As his "curtain raiser" for President Johnson's speech on March 31, Max Frankel kept the reserve call-up question alive in his lead, and noted the President's pre-speech dismissal of speculation on a massive troop increase:

WASHINGTON, Mar. 30—President Johnson will address the nation at 9 p.m. tomorrow to deal "rather fully" with the situation in Vietnam, including further troop buildups, the possibility of reserve call-ups, and the additional costs thereof.

The President announced his speech, by radio and television from his office, at a news conference in the White House Rose Garden this noon. He said it would also cover "other questions of some importance," including the government's "entire fiscal policy."

Mr. Johnson said that new troop deployments and reserve needs would not be "anything like" the hundreds of thousands mentioned in speculation. He put the new defense spending at "a few billion dollars," but not so much as the $10 billion to $20 billion mentioned in some quarters. . . .

The President said the Administration's review of policies in Vietnam, prompted by the enemy offensive, would in a sense never end until peace had been found. But his speech should supply "generally the government's position and the course that we intend to take," he said.

He would not comment on speculation that he might order another halt in the bombing of North Vietnam. He said his offer to halt the bombing if Hanoi pledged not to take advantage of the halt still stood. But he had seen no indication of Hanoi's interest, he added.[47]

It had been a busy, productive month for the *Times*'s Washington bureau. The irony was, of course, that its "biggest" story was the most incomplete. One can argue that, as in the case of so many Washington "bureaucratic" conflicts, the reality behind the March 10 story was so complex, and so inaccessible in its vital details, that even the best reporters could not describe it without serious distortion. Other reasons have already been cited: haste, lack of memory, management interference, too narrow a range of sources, and, perhaps, a willingness on the part of some *Times* editors and reporters to believe—despite contrary evidence—only the worst.

As historian John Henry was to note later, the March 10 headline had "enormous impact." Congress renewed its Vietnam debate. The readers, Henry wrote, "still recovering from the shock of the Tet offensive, automatically jumped to the conclusion—just as Clifford [and others] had two weeks earlier—that the military situation in Vietnam was falling apart. Lacking any knowledge of past bureaucratic battles over troop strength, the American public panicked upon learning of the military's recommendations . . . presented out of context. They did not fully understand that President Johnson had not authorized previous recommendations and that the military had been attempting to [exploit the Tet shock] to get the forces they had wanted . . . for some time."

The *Post:* A More Restrained Story

As noted, the *Post,* in terms of numbers, had no resources in Washington comparable to those of the *Times* for penetrating official secrecy on possible troop increases. In late February, the *Post*'s Pentagon man, George Wilson, a former *Aviation Week* writer, was preparing to leave for Vietnam as a badly needed reinforcement.[48] The *Post*'s senior editors, including Managing Editor Benjamin Bradlee and National Editor Laurence Stern, enjoyed no special advantage over their *Times* counterparts in knowledge of military-diplomatic matters. Moreover, they devoted far less page-one space to such matters than did the *Times.* The *Post*'s one managerial-level specialist in this area was Philip Geyelin, editor of the editorial page, who had been in Vietnam for the *Wall Street Journal* and written extensively on Johnson's foreign policy. But Geyelin was not engaged in the day-to-day news operation. As its national news deskmen were well aware, the *Post*'s prime interest and expertise in 1968 was in politics, political issues, and "political personalities"—not the complexities of Administration war policy.

The burden of keeping track of the latter fell on two men—Murrey Marder, a veteran State Department reporter known for his skepticism and careful reporting, and Chalmers Roberts, the *Post*'s chief diplomatic correspondent. Roberts' contacts covered few generals but a wide range of politicians and civilian officials in State, Defense, and the White House.[49] During Tet, both Marder and Roberts, in the *Post* tradition, wrote an abundance of Vietnam analyses, focusing often on Washington evaluations of U.S. and enemy "strategy," and usually achieving no better results than did their colleagues in Saigon or Hong Kong. But as reporters, both men were professionals of long experience: They did not succumb to the "numbers game." Marder, in particular, sensed accurately that Vietnam issues broader than troop increases occupied the Administration.

The contacts of both men were primarily with CIA and State. The *Post*'s Pentagon coverage during this period was thin; by all accounts, there was no managerial thrust for a breakthrough in terms of uncovering issues in the on-going confused Administration debate until after the *Times*'s March 10 exclusive. Nor was there any systematic effort by the *Post*—or by the *Times*—to tie in Saigon and Washington reporting on what Wheeler's obviously important trip produced, or what increased numbers of troops would accomplish in Vietnam. The *Post*'s efforts were erratic; other matters, such as enemy strategy, Administration "mood," and Tonkin Gulf hearings had more appeal on any given day for the paper's editors. The *Post* did report that a "reexamination" was underway, but without attempting to disclose the issues—possibly an impossible job—except in terms of hawk-versus-dove talk on Capitol Hill. Unlike the *Times,* the paper did not involve itself in the "numbers" and "debate" stories. In a sense, by its omissions, the *Post* probably caused less confusion, since the *Times*'s March 10 exclusive proved to be distorted and incomplete.

The *Post* had front-paged UPI's (50,000–100,000) troop request story and Westmoreland's AP interview on the need for more troops.[50] It had printed its own Saigon bureau's reports of U.S. troops being spread thin in I Corps. On February 29, the headline of its page-one story following Wheeler's visit to the White House to discuss Westmoreland's troop requirements mentioned no figures: "LBJ Sees Top Aides on War; No Decision Reported on Troop Increase." On March 1, the day after Beecher's "100,000 to 200,000 more troops" story appeared in the *Times,* Roberts wrote a brief, vague story. He did not mention any troop requests, but instead concentrated on pending mobilization "decisions"—notably on reserve call-ups—and quoted "Administration officials" as saying that: "President Johnson is considering more troops to Vietnam on a long-haul rather than a quickie basis. Officials pointed out that the present Presidentially approved ceiling is 525,000 men and that of this number the last 14,500 have yet to be committed . . . the question of the call-up of reserves would be reviewed in the 'next two weeks.'" Roberts found slim pickings, but stayed clear of numbers. His story ran well inside the paper.[51]

On March 3, in a quasi-editorial in the Sunday "Outlook" section, Roberts asked, "Is There a Choice on More Troops?" He gloomily assessed Hanoi's skill and the unworthiness of the South Vietnamese, and said, "Even if Mr. Johnson wanted to send enough men to defeat Giap's strategy, there are simply not enough troops [available] . . . to do so quickly." Then he urged that no more troops be sent, so that Saigon would be prompted to "galvanize" its followers into "fighting for themselves." Roberts suggested that it was "far easier to decide to send more men," a sentiment, we now know, not shared by President Johnson, then or earlier.

In the same day's issue, in a shirttail following a page-one story on a Presidential speaking tour, there was a short "assessment of Vietnam policy developments in Washington." It said little more than that "a major reassessment is underway inside the Administration on the heavy military, political, and economic damage inflicted on U.S. plans [*sic*] by the continuing communist offensive," calling it "the most comprehensive reexamination ever made of U.S. policy in Vietnam," and noting "grim conferences going on behind the scenes."

Next day, John Maffre, the second Pentagon man, was as vague as Roberts in a page-one story about the shortage of ready forces available to send to Vietnam: "Gen. William C. Westmoreland's newest troop request is going to be a tough military nut to crack, even in the highly unlikely prospect that he'd settle for a few battalions." However, Maffre did report—with imprecision—what Westmoreland needed or wanted: "Some Pentagon officers say Westmoreland doesn't need just individual battalions. . . . They feel he will want units the size of brigades or the somewhat larger Marine regimental landing teams, at least. Probably divisions."⁵²

On March 6, Carroll Kilpatrick reported that the President "is continuing a thorough review of the Vietnamese situation, but had made no decisions regarding an increase in the number of troops to be sent there, the White House said." Kilpatrick cited "speculation" about a one-division reinforcement, and added: "Wheeler had made no formal recommendation to the President as yet (according to George Christian, White House spokesman)."⁵³

The *Times* exclusive came off the presses in mid-evening on Saturday, March 9. AP routinely photographed page one of the paper's first edition and transmitted it by wirephoto to other newspapers throughout the country. The *Post* night news editors—as was their custom—carefully scanned the wirephoto.⁵⁴ What they saw made them rush the wirephoto to Benjamin Bradlee, who was attending the annual Gridiron Club dinner at the Statler-Hilton Hotel, across L Street from the *Post*. Bradlee called Chalmers Roberts, and the two men began questioning the tuxedoed luminaries in the ballroom, who included Vice President Humphrey, Cabinet officials, and the Joint Chiefs of Staff. "The evasive and noncommittal answers indicated to Bradlee and Roberts that the story was right."⁵⁵

Back in the *Post*'s fifth-floor news room, Murrey Marder was summoned to write a hasty, catch-up story, which duly appeared in late editions of the *Post*, with a new figure (196,000) and a less than candid denial by George Christian, the White House press secretary:

Intense debate is going on inside the Administration over military requests to regain the initiative in Vietnam by sending *up to 200,000 or more* additional U.S. troops into the battle.

Informed sources said last night that figures as high as 196,000 and 206,000 troops, in addition to 525,000 American men now earmarked for the war, are being proposed. Also under study are drastic revisions of American strategy to counter the major communist offensive that has been unfolding since January 30.⁵⁶

The highest Administration officials, however, said that all the reported force levels or strategy changes represent speculation at this stage.

White House press secretary George Christian issued the following statement last night in the midst of the Gridiron Club dinner which he was attending at the Statler-Hilton Hotel:

"There are a lot of figures kicking around, including this one (206,000 additional troops). The President has received no specific request from General Wheeler or General Westmoreland. No specific recommendation has been made by the Joint Chiefs." . . .

Gen. Earle G. Wheeler, Chairman of the Joint Chiefs, conferred in Saigon last month with Gen. William C. Westmoreland . . . to assess the damage inflicted by the first stage of the communist offensive.[57]

It was not a glorious moment for the *Post;* but its editors might have felt better had they known that, in fact, the 206,000 figure was already dead.

Next day, Chalmers Roberts discussed the "internal debate" aspects of the *Times* story in a page-one piece: "War Is Undergoing Searching Scrutiny." In the same issue, inside the paper, the *Post* also ran two more troop stories—"GI Buildup in Vietnam Is Opposed by Bundy" and "Troop Call Seen Helping McCarthy"—as well as a column by Alsop: "Why Senator Clark's Non-Facts Don't Lessen Viet Troop Need."

On March 11–12, Secretary Rusk was on the Foreign Relations Committee stand, and the troop issue again got page-one prominence in the *Post:* "Critics Press Rusk at Six-Hour Hearing, Troop Issue Skirted" (March 12) and "Rusk Shuns Pledge on Troops" (March 13).

By the following Saturday, the "troop issue" had faded from the *Post.* Further, on Sunday, March 17, the paper had a page-one story on Johnson which incorporated an Administration put-down of the *Times* story that the editors a week earlier had rushed to "match:"

President Johnson said yesterday the United States will fight on to a battlefield victory in Vietnam if necessary. He called for home-front austerity, including federal budget cuts, to support the war effort.

"We must tighten our belts," he said. "We must adopt an austere program. We must adopt a program of fiscal soundness."

At the same time, an authoritative source confirmed that more than the previously planned number of U.S. troops will be sent to Vietnam.

The exact number has not been agreed upon, the source said. But he asserted that the increase—an addition to the 525,000 planned by this summer—will be "moderate" as compared with the 206,000 reportedly suggested by military leaders in Vietnam.

The source declined to say how many more would be sent but he described as "a dove scare" figure the report that Westmoreland wanted 206,000 more men. Another source said that a guess of even 100,000 additional troops would be far out of line.

There now are at least 506,000 U.S. troops in Vietnam and the previously established limit was 525,000, scheduled to be reached by mid-year.[58]

The same issue carried a page-eight analysis of Robert Kennedy's entrance into the race for the Presidential nomination, with Murrey Marder repeating the Administration's denial of the 206,000 figure: "The Administration chose to make it known within an hour of the Kennedy announcement that the increases it contemplates in the size of U.S. forces in Vietnam will be 'quite moderate' in contrast to the 206,000 figure now being circulated. The 206,000 was described, scoffingly, as 'a dove scare figure.' "

Finally, on March 31, in a "curtain raiser" to the President's speech, Marder reported the bombing halt speculation and ventured some troop numbers:

> On the military front, it is widely expected that the President will authorize new reinforcements of up to 30,000 to 40,000 *or more* U.S. troops, and a new mix of tactics to diminish "search-and-destroy" strategy and gain more manpower to hold the countryside in Vietnam.[59] Recent pledges of up to 135,000 more South Vietnamese troops are expected to mesh with the revised American deployments.
>
> On the diplomatic front, the President is expected to try to outmaneuver his rivals for the Democratic Presidential nomination with a new offer on suspending the bombing of North Vietnam.
>
> There is wide speculation that the President will flatly announce a halt in the bombing to test Hanoi's readiness to negotiate. Others suspect the President will stop short of that and produce a more flexible variation of the September 29 San Antonio offer to halt the bombing if Hanoi is prepared to guarantee prompt talks.[60]

The President's March 31 speech was to quash the "numbers game." The game, however, was resumed in 1969, as President Nixon began to withdraw U.S. troops—in varying increments—from Vietnam.

12

The Debate at Home: How Did It Affect Johnson War Policy?

As we have seen, there were considerable differences between perceptions of the Tet attacks by senior American officials in Saigon on the one hand, and those in Washington on the other. Similar differences also became evident, as time went on, between news managers and reporters on opposite sides of the Pacific. Such gaps between the "field" and headquarters are common in both government and journalism; they often become particularly acute in times of crisis, and especially in an election year. As a general rule, strikingly illustrated by the Tet experience, it may be said that the further one is removed from a crisis, the more alarming it seems.[1]

American newsmen and officials on both sides of the Pacific, however, immediately shared one reaction: The Tet offensive would stir an uproar in the United States, which was getting ready for a Presidential election. Journalists in Saigon were ill-equipped to gauge South Vietnamese psychological reactions. But they knew their own fellow-countrymen well enough to realize that the Tet shock would be considerable at home. Their colleagues in New York and Washington had a keener awareness that the shock would be expressed (or exploited) by Administration foes. That was part of the political game in America.

A vigorous outcry in Washington would have ensued, this writer believes, even without the credibility gap over Vietnam policy that the White House and Defense Secretary McNamara had been helping to widen since 1962. What Johnson Administration post-mortems do not emphasize is that: (1) the Tet attacks came without any prior White House warning of heavy fighting ahead—although Westmoreland and Wheeler had publicly issued such warnings; (2) the attacks followed by less than 10 weeks the end of an Administration "progress" propaganda campaign designed to show that the enemy was "losing"; (3) the attacks came on the heels of another apparent setback to U.S. prestige, the January 23 capture by the North Koreans of the U.S.S. *Pueblo;* (4) the President's own party was split, with Senator Eugene McCarthy seeking the 1968 Democratic nomination as the candidate of much of the campus-based peace movement, and Senator Robert Kennedy contemplating similar rebellion, with Vietnam as his major issue; and (5) within the Administration in Washington, Tet struck dissatisfied hawks and nonhawks alike as an opportunity for *change,* with each side arguing (in part via the press) for or against a new look at proposals (e.g., a reserve call-up, a total bombing halt) which the White House had previously rejected. For these and other reasons, the conditions for consensus were not present in America in early 1968.

Debate and controversy were inevitable. Unpleasant foreign-policy surprises, even in nonelection years, have seldom been greeted with equanimity in the United States, whose politicians and plain citizens are accustomed to thinking of themselves as the inhabitants of the most powerful nation in the world.[2] Yet, to any reasonably alert, well-read citizen (or editor or commentator), the attacks on the cities of Vietnam produced few new "facts" about the U.S. commitment. By January 30, 1968, the costs—human and financial—of the war were already a matter of public debate. The strain on the U.S. worldwide military and financial position was clear, as was the impact of the war's costs on domestic outlays. The frustrations of "limited war" (no invasion of North Vietnam, no massive reserve call-up at home, no ground attacks on key enemy supply lines in Laos and Cambodia) had been voiced by Congressional hawks. The limited military benefits of step-by-step bombing of North Vietnam, especially the heavily defended Hanoi-Haiphong area, had been aired in public, partly by McNamara himself. The allied battlefield advantages of mobility and firepower had been noted, as were the foe's stout qualities as rural guerrilla and infantryman. The weaknesses—real and imagined—of the South Vietnamese regime and its army had been abundantly decried (only their virtues were unknown). Conventional military victory had been ruled out by the Administration. The goal, variously ornamented, was to weaken the foe sufficiently by attrition to permit the survival of a noncommunist South Vietnam and block communist expansion in Southeast Asia. It was not an inspiring vision. No *quick* end was in sight or even promised in 1967, and "progress," despite all the public rhetoric, was accurately portrayed by the media as slow and uneven. General Westmoreland himself had publicly foreseen no U.S. troop withdrawals before late 1969.

Thus, for all their destruction and drama, the Tet attacks and their aftermath did not suddenly bring to light any basic new weaknesses or virtues in Administration Vietnam policy. What the attacks did do, specifically, was forcefully to direct attention to the war, at least for a few weeks, to highlight the lack of a White House strategy for ending it, and to underline the President's chronic prior refusals to tell the public what he knew about the war's bleaker side and its probable further costs. In the case of Tet, he had failed to warn the people personally that heavy fighting probably lay ahead, and that the foe, far from being at the end of his resources, was preparing "kamikaze attacks."[3]

This Presidential failure received considerable press comment right after the attacks, as we have noted earlier. Moreover, Tet was linked to this failure, particularly in terms of commentary and photographic and television coverage, as a "disaster." Nor did the media stop there. As time went on, the ruins of Hue, the refugees of Saigon, the wounded Marines at Khe Sanh were not only made to represent destruction and human suffering, but they were presented as symbolic evidence of a stunning "defeat" (variously implied or defined) for allied forces, and hence *proof* of failure of the Administration's conduct of the war in Vietnam. The enemy was omnipresent, the South Vietnamese lacked the will to fight, American firepower was obliterating Vietnam, the allies had ceded the "initiative" to the "wily Giap"—these vivid themes shaped the scenario for television and radio, for the picture editors, and for *Newsweek* into late March. These themes provided a context for Congressional rhetoric and Administration reaction. In this sense, the media shaped the "climate" of public debate.

My interviews with colleagues who were in Washington during Tet suggest that a good many newsmen there were preoccupied, as always, with Administration *words*. They simply concluded that, since Tet had exposed the fragility of the White House's 1967 "progress" rhetoric, it had also exposed the fragility of the 1968 allied military-political position in Vietnam. The public post-Tet analyses by McNamara, Wheeler, and others—usually expressed in chastened tones—were largely dismissed as more of the same. Few realized that the Johnson Administration, shocked into relative candor, had more or less stopped gilding the lily. Many Washington newsmen and their superiors were willing to give credence to almost any criticism or interpretation that now seemed to show the Administration's Vietnam policy in the worst light—a common form of journalistic retribution for past official sins. This sentiment helped shape coverage of the "debate" that followed Tet, and thus, to some degree, shaped the debate itself.

The Presidential Reaction: Setting the Tone

In any major crisis, the President's response helps to set the tone in Washington, especially for newsmen and the politicians on Capitol Hill. His words, his decisions, even his facial expressions contribute to creating a mood. In retrospect, Lyndon Johnson, in February–March 1968, seems to have conveyed a sense of frustration, even of indecision. In contrast to John F. Kennedy during the 1962 Cuban missile crisis, or to Franklin D. Roosevelt after Pearl Harbor, he started by setting a hesitant tone—which did not go unnoticed in the media.

Initially, the President sought to repeat his 1967 public-relations strategy, dominating the media with reassuring statements about Vietnam by subordinates. On January 31, for example, at the height of the Tet fighting, General Westmoreland received this message from Wheeler:

The President desires that you make a brief personal comment to the press at least once each day during the current period of mounting VC/NVA activity. The purpose of such statements should be to convey to the American public your confidence in our capability to blunt these enemy moves, and to reassure the public here that you have the situation under control.

These instructions were repeated to both Westmoreland and Ambassador Bunker later that same day by George Christian, press secretary to the President:

We are facing, in these next few days, a critical phase in the American public's understanding and confidence toward our effort in Vietnam. . . .

To be specific, nothing can more dramatically counter scenes of VC destructiveness than the confident professionalism of the Commanding General. Similarly, the dire prognostications of the commentators can best be put into perspective by the shared experience and wisdom of our Ambassador. . . . Appearances by you, in the immediate situation, will make a greater impact here at home than much of what we can say.

Westmoreland and Bunker agreed that it would be both unnecessary and foolish for them to hold a press conference daily, as this might give newsmen the impression that they were panicking.[4] Instead, as we noted earlier, for several days, subordinates (including Weyand and Chaisson) briefed the Saigon press on particular aspects of the situation.

Bunker, in view of the scarcity of solid information, limited himself to a background briefing on February 3 in which he could not be quoted directly.[5] His briefing, as we have seen, received little attention. General Westmoreland dutifully briefed the press on February 1. His analysis did not meet White House desires for "reassurance"; the General emphasized the next phase in the enemy campaign, which he saw as the largest phase, including attacks in the Quang Tri/Thua Thien area. (These attacks, aside from lunges at Khe Sanh, did not materialize.)

On February 2, at his first post-Tet press conference, President Johnson opened by reading a statement which stressed the failure of the enemy's "general uprising," but warned that "at this very moment" the foe might launch another phase up north—a worried reflection of Westmoreland's more confident appraisal. He closed by saying, "As all of you know, the situation is a fluid one. We will keep the American people informed as these matters develop." In the question-and-answer period which followed, reporters sought, for the most part, an overall assessment of the war. Johnson's answers were couched in tentative terms; he gave the impression of being on uncertain ground. The questions presented to him were not "loaded." Newsmen were shaken by the Tet attacks, but there also seemed to be implicit in their questions the hope that the President would admit that the allies had been surprised, and promise that they would now rally to roll back the Vietcong. Instead came a claim, repeated thrice over, that the allies had not been caught off guard, and a rather ambivalent response as to what the final outcome would be.[6]

Thereafter, for two weeks, President Johnson went back to his earlier tactic: assigning his subordinates to push the public Administration view and to reassure the public. But the fact of the matter was that the President and much of his Administration had been shaken not only by the Tet attacks but by communist initiatives elsewhere: the seizure of the *Pueblo;* the breakup of an assassination plot by the North Koreans against South Korea's President Park Chung Hee; intelligence reports of possible East German or Soviet designs around Berlin. With General Westmoreland predicting a "third round" in South Vietnam, the outlook was not reassuring to the men in Washington.

Moreover, vivid portrayals of disaster in Vietnam by the press and television were strongly felt within the Administration, as among its foes and among commentators in Washington. Harry McPherson, a Presidential speech-writer and special counsel, recalled his reactions later:

I felt we were being put to it as hard as we ever had and I was extremely disturbed. I would go in two or three mornings a week and study the cable book and talk to Rostow and ask him what had happened the day before, and would get from him what almost seemed hallucinatory from the point of view of what I had seen on network television the night before. . . . Well, I must say that I mistrusted what he said, although I don't say with any confidence that I was right to mistrust him, because, like millions of other people who had been looking at television the night before, I had the feeling that the country had just about had it, that they would simply not take any more. . . . I suppose, from a social-scientist point of view, it is particularly interesting that people like me—people who had some responsibility for expressing the Presidential point of view —could be so affected by the media as everyone else was, while downstairs, within 50 yards of my desk, was that enormous panoply of intelligence-gathering devices—tickers, radios, messages coming in from the field. I assume the reason this is so . . . was that like everyone else who had been deeply involved in explaining the policies of the war and trying to understand them and render some judgment, I was fed up with the "light at the end of the tunnel" stuff. I was fed up with the optimism that seemed to flow without stopping from Saigon.

William P. Bundy, Assistant Secretary of State for Far Eastern Affairs, also felt pessimistic, as did some old Vietnam hands in Washington:

I quickly came to the view that the attacks had been damaging to the North, but they had also been shattering to the South, especially in the area of pacification. The net balance, therefore, depended on whether the country could pull itself together. My view of the situation was formed by reports from people in the field out in Vietnam. I remember in particular one view that impressed me. Leroy Wehrle, who was with the AID office in Washington, was a staunch fellow with wide experience in Vietnam. He wrote a memo on February 5 which said that the South Vietnamese were through, that they had too many defects in their society to survive this blow. It was a poignant memo which said in effect, "They've had it." That memo reflected my view for a period.[7]

As the press soon reported, the strain affected even the usually imperturbable Secretary of State, Dean Rusk. At a background session at the State Department on February 9, Rusk blew up at persistent questions concerning the failure of United States intelligence in Vietnam. "There gets to be a point when the question is, 'Whose side are you on?'" the Secretary told startled newsmen. "I don't know why . . . people have to be probing for the things that one can bitch about. . . ."

What was striking—and important—about the public White House posture in February and March 1968 was how defensive it was. In retrospect, it seems that President Johnson was to some degree "psychologically defeated" by the threat to Khe Sanh and the onslaught on the cities of Vietnam. If he did not appear in public to be as depressed as those subordinates whom he later chided for their gloom, he did not strike a decisive public stance. In a sense, the inherent contradictions of his limited-war policy came home to roost. Between escalation (politically and economically very costly) and a "phasing down," Johnson did not choose. Essentially, he sought to buy time for "more of the same." This approach led to two months of Presidential inaction in the face of a perceived "disaster," at least in public. The only public war decision by the President prior to March 31 was the dispatching of 11,000 emergency reinforcements to Vietnam in mid-February. For the rest, he sought to rally public opinion with exhortation. He emphasized the need to stand firm, but he did not spell out what this meant, or how the battlefield situation was changing, as he saw it, in Vietnam. He left a big void, which others hastened to fill.[8]

The Congressional Reaction: A Cacophony

In Congress, the Tet attacks provoked some initial off-the-cuff comment, as newsmen routinely sought "reaction." Then, the Wash-

ington atmosphere was enlivened for a week by Senator Eugene
McCarthy's offhand remarks on February 8 in a Boston television in-
terview, concerning "some demands" for the emergency use of tactical nuclear weapons in Vietnam. At the end of February, the Senate
Foreign Relations Committee, presided over by Senator J. William
Fulbright as Chairman, held hearings, with Defense Secretary McNamara among the badgered witnesses, on long-obscure aspects of the
North Vietnamese PT boat attacks on U.S. destroyers in the Gulf of
Tonkin in August 1964; the much-publicized proceedings threw more
doubt on White House credibility at a time of crisis. Stirred by the reports of "more troops for Vietnam," the Fulbright committee heard a
noncommittal Dean Rusk testify for two days on March 11–12. Neither he nor Senator Fulbright appeared to budge from earlier positions. Thereafter, the Kennedy-McCarthy Presidential campaigns
preoccupied the political writers and politicians, with Vietnam as a
major but ill-defined issue.

All during this period, there were frequent rhetorical emanations
from Capitol Hill, with the more controversial bits drawing the most
attention from the media. Some hawks, such as Representative L.
Mendel Rivers of South Carolina, Chairman of the House Armed
Services Committee, urged escalation; others, including Senator Richard Russell of Georgia, suggested that Administration policy was not
working, and another way out of the Vietnam situation should be
sought. Senator Everett Dirksen, the Republican minority leader, was
one of the few senators who continued to back the Administration's
limited war policy, even as he asked for more troops.

As always, the Congressional "debate" was less a debate than an
intermittent cacophony of expressions of varying degree of dismay,
optimism, or disillusionment, coupled with vague proposals for
"more bombing," a "coalition government" in Saigon, or a negotiated peace after a bombing halt. On the G.O.P. side, Richard Nixon
and Governor George Romney of Michigan were equally critical, but
in even vaguer terms. The chief themes of the media's portrayal of
the Tet offensive repeatedly cropped up as the context and underpin-
ning for the discussion. Senator Harry Byrd, Democrat of Virginia,
quoted a *Times* article by Hanson Baldwin, "the sum and substance
[of which was] that the Vietcong's aim, it is believed, is to spur allied
war-weariness." Senator Joseph Clark, Democrat of Pennsylvania,
cited newspaper articles that hit at previous "false predictions" of security, the failure of the GVN to protect the people, and the allegedly

THE DEBATE AT HOME

faulty strategy of stripping southern areas to reinforce I Corps. Senator Stephen Young, Ohio Democrat, described the weakness and corruption of the Saigon government that he had found during a recent trip to Vietnam. Senator Ernest Gruening, the Alaska Democrat, quoted at length from a speech titled "Corruption in South Vietnam—Must Our Boys Die to Defend It?" by Senator Edward Kennedy, who had just returned from Vietnam. Kennedy related the Tet attacks to the "deadly apathy" of the South Vietnamese. Another recent visitor to Vietnam, Senator Charles Percy, Illinois Republican, charged that the Administration had "deliberately" misled the public about Vietcong capabilities. He joined Senator Mike Mansfield, the Senate majority leader, in calling on the President to reassess the U.S. commitment to Vietnam.[9] Senator Jacob Javits, Republican of New York, challenged past Administration appraisals, particularly noting Westmoreland's November 1967 statements to the effect that the enemy's "guerrilla force was declining at a steady rate." The Senator said that the Tet attacks "do not represent a significant threat to our basic military position," but he felt that the political and psychological impact was significant. He attacked the Thieu-Ky regime and said that the Secretary of State had brushed off the real importance of the shock by describing U.S. opinion as "grumpy." Javits took the position that the war was stalemated.

On February 11, Mansfield said that the Tet attacks had proven that no part of South Vietnam was secure and that there was "not the beginning of a stable political situation." In a speech at the University of Idaho, Senator Albert Gore, Tennessee Democrat, said that he was now convinced that Americans were destroying the nation they "profess to be saving," and he called for negotiations to get out of Vietnam "on condition that Vietnam be neutralized." Senator Fulbright subsequently called for a "full-scale reexamination of the purposes and objectives of our policy in Vietnam," while Senator Mansfield, supported by Senators John Sherman Cooper, Robert Kennedy, and Eugene McCarthy, suggested a trial suspension of bombing of North Vietnam. Senator Gruening went further and suggested that the President unilaterally end the war with a phased military withdrawal. Radio Hanoi followed by complimenting Mansfield, Cooper, Kennedy, and McCarthy for having "seen the right way" by calling for bombing halts.[10]

Many in the Senate still held views opposite to these. However, as time went on, Congressional hawks and/or supporters of LBJ's Viet-

nam war policy seemed to object less and less to the statements of
the doves; most hawks remained silent. Inevitably, the press play
went to the more talkative doves. Few Congressmen, their speechwriters, or the reporters who selected and "rebroadcast" excerpts
from the speeches, had any broad knowledge of Vietnam; all relied
on hasty reading of contemporary press accounts and on their own
diverse professional instincts.

John Finney of the New York *Times*'s Washington bureau early
caught the mood of the Senate during February:

WASHINGTON, Feb. 11—Like a delayed time fuse, the current communist offensive in Vietnam seems to be setting off within the Senate a
critical political reaction against the *validity* as well as the *credibility* of
the Administration's policy. . . .

Of all the recent military events, perhaps the most disillusioning to
many senators was the failure of South Vietnamese forces to come to the
defense of the American Embassy or to protect provincial capitals. In the
Senate cloak rooms, there is considerable grumbling that the South Vietnamese forces failed to heed American warnings of an impending communist offensive and instead "took off" for the Tet holidays. . . .

Senator Henry M. Jackson, Democrat of Washington, an Administration supporter, said that recent events "demonstrate the need to take a
good hard look at the attitude of the South Vietnamese government in the
military effort and the pacification program." . . .

The recent turn of military events, in contrast to the optimistic appraisals offered by the Administration last fall, also seems to have resulted in widespread skepticism about the Administration's analysis of the
war.

For the moment, the skepticism is directed most personally at Deputy
Ambassador Robert W. Komer and his computerized [*sic*] approach to
analyzing the progress of the pacification program in South Vietnam.

Reflecting the skepticism, [Republican] Senator [Thruston] Morton
said in an interview that within the Senate "there has been an immediate
and measurable reaction, decidedly negative, to the continued bland and
probably inaccurate statements of confidence from Westmoreland,
Komer, and the White House."

As seen by Senator Morton, the critical reaction against Administration
policy is developing from several angles—the "massive slaughter" of civilians, the credibility of the Administration, corruption in the South Vietnamese government. . . .

The potential political reaction building up against the Administration
was illustrated in a private "bull session" among members of the Senate
Foreign Relations Committee last week.

The discussion was a gloomy one, with the members generally concurring in the appraisal of one senator that "the nation is caught in the worst crisis since the Civil War."[11]

The few firm expressions of Administration optimism uttered after the first week of February were treated on Capitol Hill as absurd. During the President's trip to military bases in late February, Walt Rostow told newsmen that the Tet attacks "may have left the ARVN and the government stronger institutions than before." Senator Fulbright was prompted to respond: "A fantastic analysis of what is happening."[12]

At about the same time, George Wilson, the *Post*'s Pentagon correspondent, recorded some of the Congressional discordance:

Three separate discussions in Congress yesterday dramatized the way the Vietnam War is bringing demands for a reshuffling of national priorities.

Senator Frank Church (Democrat-Idaho) took the floor of the Senate to declare that the United States is trying to do far too much militarily, and should retrench.

As he spoke, Gen. John P. McConnell, Air Force Chief of Staff, was telling the Senate Armed Services Committee that the United States is not doing enough. He sounded grave warnings about the Soviet threat and requested money for a host of new weapons.

And late in the day, a House Armed Services subcommittee declared that the priorities must be shifted within the Vietnam War itself. The subcommittee said the military leaders must be given a freer hand so they can "win."

Neither the hawks nor the doves, these statements showed, like the way things are going for the United States. But the unity of opinion stops there. . . .

. . . .

The American involvement in Vietnam, [Church] said, is so massive that the South Vietnamese government we sought to bolster had been *"reduced to puppetry in the eyes of its own people.* The banner of nationalism has passed to the Vietcong."[13]

The Congressional "Nuke" Uproar

One special feature of the Vietnam debate in Congress after Tet was the prolonged flurry of speculation over the possible use of tactical atomic weapons ("tactical nukes") in Vietnam, specifically to save the Marines at Khe Sanh. "Congress, in a snappish, irritable mood, and ready to believe the worst, fell prey to rumors that the government might consider using tactical weapons as a last resort to defend the Marine positions at Khe Sanh," wrote an anonymous *Times* Washington bureau man in mid-February.[14]

The same might be said of the media. The episode began, in terms of public utterances, with the already noted remarks of Senator Eugene McCarthy, the peace candidate, during a WBZ-TV television interview in Boston. The interchange was as follows:

. . . "Are you at all concerned that if there is a repetition of the events in Vietnam of the last week that there will be a demand for use of tactical nuclear weapons?"

"Well, I expected that there would be a demand for the use of tactical nuclear weapons by someone. As a matter of fact, there have been some demands for their use already. I hesitate to say that these demands—I hope that it would not be seriously entertained by the Administration," McCarthy replied.[15]

Senator Fulbright, archcritic of Administration Vietnam policy, let it be known that he was querying Secretary of State Dean Rusk. That was sufficient to launch the controversy in earnest. As AP reported, the fever mounted. The White House issued a denial. McCarthy, also, began to deny his Boston statement:

WASHINGTON (AP)—Senator J. W. Fulbright . . . has written Secretary of State Dean Rusk asking for a report on rumors that the United States is prepared to use tactical nuclear weapons if American forces meet military reverses in Vietnam.

Fulbright . . . said in a telephone interview he is "deeply concerned about this, as I am sure many people are."

The question was raised Friday as to whether such weapons would be used if American troops are dealt a setback in the expected major battle at Khe Sanh, site of a massive communist buildup.

White House press secretary George Christian branded as false a statement attributed to Senator Eugene J. McCarthy . . . that the U.S. command in Vietnam had asked for authority from President Johnson to use tactical nuclear weapons in an emergency. McCarthy denied making the statement.

Senate Democratic leader Mike Mansfield said in an interview there had been only rumors of such action discussed within the Foreign Relations Committee, of which he is a member.

Another member, Senator Bourke B. Hickenlooper, Republican-Iowa, said he is satisfied tactical nuclear weapons will be quickly available to

U.S. forces in South Korea if there's a North Korean attack. But he said he knew nothing about the situation regarding Vietnam.

State Department press officer Robert J. McCloskey declined comment on a story from Washington published in the St. Louis *Post-Dispatch* that rumors persist "the United States has stockpiled tactical nuclear weapons in South Vietnam for use if the communists threaten to overrun the allied force at Khe Sanh."

McCloskey added he knew nothing about the newspaper's report that some senators had heard four nuclear scientists had been flown to Vietnam.

Later, the Defense Department said four scientists are in Vietnam to appraise new weapons "which have no relationship whatsoever to nuclear systems of any kind." The Pentagon said no other scientists have been sent to Vietnam in connection with nuclear matters "and there is no intention" to do so.

Christian was asked if President Johnson had received a request for the use of tactical nuclear weapons in Vietnam if this becomes necessary. He replied the President had "considered no decision of this nature."

A newsman told the press secretary that McCarthy, campaigning against Johnson for the Democratic Presidential nomination on an antiwar theme, had said in Boston that a request for tactical nuclear weapons for use in Vietnam had been made. McCarthy was quoted as saying that he expected a renewed demand for them and hoped it would be rejected.

"Senator McCarthy's statement is false and it is also unfair to the armed forces," Christian said.

In Miami, Florida, McCarthy denied making the statements. He said he was asked by a reporter in Boston about rumors that permission to use nuclear weapons had been asked of the President.

McCarthy, another member of the Foreign Relations Committee, said he told the newsman: "It wouldn't surprise me if some generals had been asking for nuclear weapons." He added he didn't say anyone had asked for them.[16]

As James Reston once noted, "If reporters tend to play up spectacular charges or statements of extremists on Capitol Hill and to play down or ignore the careful analytical speeches of the more moderate and responsible members—as unfortunately they do most of the time—this inevitably has its influence on many other members [of Congress]."[17]

The *Times* ran the initial stories on page thirteen on February 10: "White House Disputes McCarthy on Atom Arms" (AP), and "Query by Fulbright" (UPI). The *Post* ran the story on page one, covering roughly the same ground as AP, but adding a "hard" translation of what General Wheeler allegedly told "several senators" in secret session, namely that "the [Joint] Chiefs would recommend the use of nuclear or any other type weapons to hold Khe Sanh. But Wheeler said he did not think this would be necessary." Then the *Post* noted:

> . . . Even if President Johnson should receive a request to use nuclear weapons in the Khe Sanh battle, Pentagon weapons experts contend the technical problems are almost as large as the political ones.
> Small nuclear weapons are "dirty," since they split the atomic ingredients for their power, spewing the landscape with radioactivity. The close quarters fighting of Khe Sanh would seem to rule out their use on these grounds. The weapons could be made "clean," but this, too, carries penalties.[18]

McCarthy raised the matter again at reporters' urgings on "Meet the Press" on February 11, as the AP reported:

> WASHINGTON, Feb. 11 (AP)—Senator Eugene J. McCarthy . . . target of White House fire in an atomic tangle, said today he would be very surprised if the Pentagon has not considered use of nuclear weapons in the war in Vietnam.
> McCarthy, citing Washington rumors, said, "There have been suggestions around the edges that nuclear weapons—tactical weapons—have been recommended, have been considered."
> He started to add, "I'm sure they've been in some way"—but stopped and went on. "If they haven't been considered by the Pentagon in some kind of program planning, I would be very much surprised."
> The Senator said the Administration's public response that it does not plan to use such weapons "tends to relieve me somewhat." . . .
> McCarthy said he had gone no further in his original remarks than to confirm that rumors were circulating in Washington.[19]

It was the kind of Washington story that tends to titillate newsmen. It was simple: "nukes" to save Khe Sanh? And it involved a pet Washington media theme: the confrontation of the Administration—Fulbright versus Rusk, McCarthy versus the White House. Reporters asked politicians what they thought of the "issue." Richard Nixon said nukes were neither necessary nor desirable. Senator Hugh Scott, Republican of Pennsylvania and Senate minority whip, and Senator Joseph Clark duly expressed opposition to the notion, with Clark adding a note of foreboding. CBS interviewers on "Face the Nation" got visiting British Prime Minister Harold Wilson to condemn the use of tactical atomic weapons in Vietnam as "sheer lunacy," and it was reported in the *Times*.[20] On February 13, Senator Mike Mansfield observed that an anonymous telephone call (to the Senate Foreign Relations Committee) had started the whole thing, and expressed concern that such unsubstantiated speculation could "get such widespread circulation."[21]

Next day, after giving closed-door testimony on Capitol Hill, General Wheeler was pressed by newsmen on the "nuke issue." Wheeler, as Chairman of the Joint Chiefs, was not ready to rule out any weapon; it was something no military man could be expected to say. Moreover, the President, not Wheeler, decided such matters. Wheeler's interview on February 14 was brief and very military:

Q.: There is a lot of speculation up here on the Hill that ultimately we may have to use nuclear weapons. What can you say on that subject?
Wheeler: I do not think that nuclear weapons will be required to defend Khe Sanh.
Q.: Not under any circumstances, General?
Wheeler: I refuse to speculate any further on that question. I merely said that I do not think nuclear weapons will have to be used.[22]

Fulbright next day argued that the General's answer "leaves the impression that, if needed to defend Khe Sanh, they would be used."[23]

Meanwhile, Fulbright had involved himself in another dispute with Secretary of State Dean Rusk, who had implied that Fulbright's public raising of the atomic weapons issue was a "disservice." Fulbright suggested that, rather than introducing the nuclear issue, he was merely exposing the disastrous decision to hold Khe Sanh:

. . . "I reject the implication that the discussion of the subject of the use of nuclear weapons in Vietnam is a disservice to the nation," Fulbright declared in a statement serving as the latest chapter in a strong controversy that began with an anonymous phone call some days ago suggesting he look into the matter.

"I believe," the committee Chairman went on, "it would be a grave disservice to our country, in truth a disaster, if our leadership should so expose our troops in Vietnam as to require nuclear weapons to prevent their destruction."[24]

On February 15 Defense Secretary McNamara, on Capitol Hill, also attacked the "nuke" speculation:

Q.: Mr. Secretary, yesterday General Wheeler touched on the subject of nuclear weapons. Can you say if their possible use in Vietnam, particularly Khe Sanh, has been discussed by the Administration?

McNamara: It has not been discussed.
Q.: It's never been raised in any discussion?
McNamara: It has not been raised in any discussion, and it has not been discussed.[25]

The story finally began to die after the President himself called a press conference on February 16 to lay it to rest. Said Johnson:

The President must make the decision to deploy nuclear weapons. It is one of the most awesome and grave decisions any President could be called upon to make.

It is reasonably apparent and known to all that it is very much against the national interest to carry on discussions about deployment of nuclear weapons. . . .

I have been in the executive branch of the government for seven years. I think I have been aware of the recommendations made by the Joint Chiefs of Staff, by the Secretary of State, and the Secretary of Defense during that period.

So far as I am aware, they have at no time ever considered or made a recommendation in any respect to the employment of nuclear weapons. They are on our planes on training missions from time to time.

We do have problems. There are plans with our allies concerning what they do.

There is always a person available to me who has full information in connection with their deployment, as you newspapermen know. I think if any serious consideration were ever given, and God forbid there ever will be, I don't think you would get it by some anonymous caller to some committee of the Congress. I think most of you know that, or ought to know that.

No recommendation has been made to me. Beyond that, I think we ought to put an end to that discussion.

Such stories as the nuclear uproar during Tet-1968 seem to have a life of their own. As we have noted, the New York *Times* started with the story on page thirteen, on February 10. Thereafter, however, the paper put it on page one four times.[26] The Washington *Post* put the story on page one on February 10 and on two days thereafter.[27] The *Times* also incorporated the "nuke" talk in its Sunday "News of the Week in Review," discussing the Washington mood after the President's press conference:

. . . The White House branded the rumors false and irresponsible. Gen. Earle G. Wheeler, Chairman of the Joint Chiefs of Staff, said nuclear weapons would not be needed at Khe Sanh. Mr. Johnson said none of his military commanders had recommended using them. But no one in authority would categorically rule out such a move.

And with diplomatic hopes all but dead at the moment and the military initiative in the enemy's hands, Washington's uneasiness over the trend of events in Vietnam remained, to say the least, undiminished.[28]

The "issue" finally culminated in a demonstration in New York against atomic weapons:

About 2,000 persons marched in United Nations Plaza yesterday to protest escalation of the Vietnam War and possible use of nuclear weapons. Some of the signs carried by the marchers said "No Nuclear Weapons in Vietnam" and "No More Hiroshimas." . . .
The demonstration and rally were arranged by the Fifth Avenue Vietnam Peace Parade Committee, a coalition of 150 peace groups. The committee said that it was concerned by the "frightening rumor that tactical nuclear weapons might be used in Vietnam."[29]

The "nuke" story also snowballed on the networks. CBS started out by recording White House and Pentagon denials, but its anchorman, Harry Reasoner, added, confusingly, that "the denials still did not wipe out the *basis* for concern."[30]

On February 11, both Reasoner and Bob Pierpoint commented:

Reasoner: Reporters spending a quiet Sunday at the White House have been probing again the question of Khe Sanh and the rumor that some of the military would like to be ready to use tactical nuclear weapons there in some eventuality. . . .
Pierpoint: Khe Sanh has now become the key to more war or possibly to peace in Vietnam. This is the view of top Administration officials who don't particularly like the comparison with Dienbienphu, but concede that Khe Sanh can be a similar turning point.
. . . President Johnson has not considered using tactical nuclear weapons to aid in their [Khe Sanh's] defense because his military advisors do not think this will be necessary. *Still, nuclear weapons are not ruled out,* and that's the decision the President hopes he won't have to make.[31]

All told, the television networks kept the story alive, mentioning it fairly often on weekday evenings throughout the period from February 9 through February 16, the date of the President's press conference: CBS, four times; NBC, two times;[32] ABC, three times.

The news magazines also found the story irresistible. *Newsweek* persisted in it, running this in its "Periscope" section:

In secret testimony before the Senate Armed Services Committee last week, Gen. Earle G. Wheeler, Chairman of the Joint Chiefs of Staff, was asked a hypothetical question about the use of nuclear weapons at Khe Sanh. Reportedly, he replied that a military man would recommend using any weapon including nuclear if the objective was important enough—such as holding Khe Sanh. He added, however, that he and the Joint Chiefs felt the United States could defend Khe Sanh with the conventional weapons and forces available. Of what use would such nuclear weapons be? They could annihilate enemy troop concentrations or remove entire hilltops.

Senators Fulbright and McCarthy have raised the question of whether the United States is shipping tactical nuclear weapons to Vietnam, and the Defense Department categorically denies it. The Pentagon recently did send four scientists to Vietnam, but they are studying the construction of the electronic barrier system across the 17th parallel. The Pentagon clincher: The artillery and aircraft that use nuclear weapons are now in Vietnam, and if President Johnson decided the weapons were needed, they could be shipped in quickly from 7th Fleet aircraft carriers in the area or from U.S. bases in Okinawa.[33]

The following week, *Newsweek* took note of the President's February 16 press conference:

. . . he sought to put down a squabble between Secretary of State Dean Rusk and Senator J. William Fulbright as to whether the United States is contemplating the use of tactical nuclear weapons in Vietnam, saying: "The President must make the decision to deploy nuclear weapons. It is one of the most awesome . . . (he) could ever be called upon to make. . . . God forbid that (he ever does)."[34]

Time waited until mid-February, saying:

. . . The President himself was finally confronted with the rumors at a White House press conference at week's end. "As far as I am aware," said Johnson, "they (the Joint Chiefs) have at no time ever considered or made a recommendation in any respect to the employment of nuclear weapons." By implying that he might not be "aware" of such considerations, Lyndon Johnson left a gaping loophole of doubt.

There was, in fact, logic to the Administration's public ambiguity. By refusing to rule out flatly the use of nuclear weapons in Vietnam (or Korea), the Administration sought to keep the communists guessing. Unfortunately, it also kept some Americans worrying about whether Vietnam's one-time guerrilla war was now in danger of escalating into World War III. That fear seemed ill-founded. Tactical weapons have only a limited blast area, and as far as Khe Sanh is concerned, a high officer in the field pointed out that the hilly terrain would minimize their range and thus their usefulness.[35]

In retrospect, there is considerable irony in this blurred sequence of events so typical of Washington: (1) the anonymous telephone call to the Fulbright committee; (2) the repetition (and partial retraction) by a Presidential candidate and antiwar senator of the report; (3) the embroidery and exploitation of the report/rumor by dovish senators and the press; (4) the carefully worded denial by General Wheeler; (5) the flat denial by Secretary McNamara; and (6) the seemingly final flat denial by the President himself.

The fact of the matter, we now know, is that President Johnson was sufficiently worried about Khe Sanh to ask Westmoreland, via Wheeler (not McNamara), if he (Johnson) would be confronted with an unwelcome decision to use nuclear weapons. Westmoreland replied in early February that the "use of tactical nuclear weapons should not be required in the present situation" (essentially Wheeler's reply to the press). However, in case of a major NVA offensive across the whole DMZ, Westmoreland said, "I visualize that either tactical nuclear weapons or chemical agents would be active candidates for employment." Because the foe had uncommitted divisions in North Vietnam, Westmoreland later told Schandler, "I was sensitive to the possibility of a massive attack across the DMZ. This would have been the worst possible case."[36]

In short, although no reporter or senator ever proved it, there was some fire amid all that billowing smoke in February 1968. Westmoreland and the Joint Chiefs were not demanding nuclear weapons to save Khe Sanh; but when a worried President raised the issue, Westmoreland was not inclined to rule out a request for any weapon should the "worst case" occur. In historical terms, the incident was more revealing of the President's anxiety than of the military's preoccupations. Oddly enough, few Saigon correspondents, except Time's men, were asked for advice by their home offices. It was a Washington controversy.

In late February, the matter finally died. The "nuke" episode illuminated the Administration's continuing lack of credibility and the willingness of its political adversaries to stir public apprehensions. It demonstrated the newsman's taste for Washington "confrontation," and the power of an anonymous telephone call, in time of crisis, to a Senate committee hostile to the incumbent Administration's policy.

Judging by the rhetoric, and the "play" given the story, the affair also strikingly illustrated the impact of media reporting from Vietnam concerning the plight of Khe Sanh—and of "leaks" about the President's own worries about another Dienbienphu—on editors and Congress alike.

Kennedy and the Media Themes

Perhaps no public figure used (selectively) media versions of the Tet situation in Vietnam to demonstrate the inadequacies of the Administration's war policy as faithfully as did Robert F. Kennedy, the senator from New York. He announced his candidacy for the 1968 Democratic nomination on March 16. Kennedy—and his speechwriters—relied heavily on the media for source material about current battle conditions, U.S. tactics in Vietnam, Westmoreland's "plea" for more troops and, above all, accounts of destruction, damage, and South Vietnamese failures. Indeed, as time went on, it sometimes seemed that Kennedy was campaigning not against Lyndon Johnson, but against Nguyen Van Thieu.

Moreover, Kennedy began echoing the media just after Tet. As the situation on the ground became clearer, and some newspapers, notably the *Times* and *Post,* began to report (on back pages) allied recovery from Tet's effects and a muddling-through by ARVN forces, Kennedy persisted in the earlier "disaster" themes, as did television and radio. In the context of media commentary and of much reporting, his simplifications and exaggerations did not seem out of line. His "facts" about the current situation in Vietnam were not then challenged in the media,[37] as were those of the Administration; they were "rebroadcast."

On February 8, Kennedy delivered his first major post-Tet speech at the Chicago Book and Author luncheon. He began by criticizing the Administration's pre-Tet optimism and then cast doubt on the veracity of official figures for enemy losses. These losses, he implied, were probably terrible, but irrelevant: "The central battle in this war cannot be measured by body counts or by bomb damage, but by the extent to which the people of South Vietnam act on a sense of common purpose and hope with those who govern them."[38] He said Tet showed that "none of the population is secure and no area is under sure control" and "there are no protected enclaves." The prime reason for the enemy's success at Tet, he went on, was not lack of bravery or effectiveness on the part of "our men," but because "we have sought to solve by military might a conflict whose issue depends on the will and conviction of the South Vietnamese people. It is like sending a lion to halt an epidemic of jungle rot." He declared that corruption caused the South Vietnamese people to "close their eyes and shut their doors in the face of their government—even as they did last week [at Tet]." Kennedy's conclusion: "More than any election, more than any proud boast, that single fact reveals the truth. We have an ally in name only. We support a government without supporters. Without the efforts of American arms, that government would not last a day."

In the same speech, Kennedy's second major theme was the destruction resulting from the urban battles and the use of U.S. bombs in the "tiny land," caused by U.S. preoccupation with "military victory." He said: "Imagine the impact in our own country if an equivalent number—over 25 million Americans—were wandering homeless or interned in refugee camps, and millions more refugees were being created, as New York and Chicago, Washington and Boston, were being destroyed by war raging in their streets." He suggested, oddly enough, that the execution by General Loan of a Vietcong prisoner was an American crime:

. . . Nor does it serve the interests of America to fight this war as if moral standards could be subordinated to immediate necessities. Last week, a Vietcong suspect was turned over to the chief of the Vietnamese security services, who executed him on the spot—a flat violation of the Geneva Convention on the Rules of War.

The photograph of the execution was on front pages all around the world—leading our best and oldest friends to ask, more in sorrow than in anger, what has happened to America?

In essence, Kennedy not only chided the Administration for its 1967 progress campaign and the credibility gap, but blamed Tet on the old sins of the South Vietnamese government. He did not mention the South Vietnamese battle losses or South Vietnamese combat performance, only the refugees and destruction.[39]

Kennedy was to repeat these themes often during the next few months. His views and his description of the situation on the ground in Vietnam were to be widely publicized.[40]

Typical were the comments of Eric Sevareid, who greeted the Senator's February 8 speech with sober approval:

Senator Robert Kennedy's speech today is his strongest attack yet on the President's Vietnam policies, and it comes when those policies appear to have reached their weakest stage.

· ·

Kennedy does not ask for withdrawal, but he does contend that a complete military victory is impossible, not necessary to our vital interests, and that the effort for one is harming our interests worldwide. The logic of this line of talk would seem to be, then, the regrouping to a defensive strategy and acceptance of the idea of a compromise peace. . . .

· ·

"We must show as much willingness to risk some of our prestige for peace," said Kennedy today, "as to risk the lives of our young men."[41]

On March 18, two days after he announced his candidacy for the Democratic nomination, Kennedy spoke at Kansas State University. His speech followed the recapture of Hue, the announced resumption of allied offensive operations in the hinterland around Saigon, and the appearance of a few *Times* and *Post* articles suggesting that all was not lost and that Thieu was even beginning to mobilize his countrymen. It also followed *Newsweek*'s famed "Agony of Khe Sanh" cover story, the pessimistic Walter Cronkite and Frank McGee explanations of Tet, and the New York *Times*'s revelation of Westmoreland's "plea" for 206,000 more troops to "regain the initiative."

Kennedy repeated most of the media themes that he had echoed in his February 8 speech in Chicago, and added a few:

. . . The *reversals of the last several months* have led our military to ask for 206,000 more troops. This weekend, it was announced that some of them—a "moderate" increase, it was said—would soon be sent. But isn't this exactly what we have always done in the past? If we examine the history of this conflict, we find the dismal story repeated time after time. Every time—at every crisis—we have denied that anything was wrong; sent more troops; and issued more confident communiqués. Every time, we have been assured that this one last step would bring victory. [Emphasis added.]

He shared the assessment of Walter Cronkite on that newsman's February 27 TV "special" that U.S. troops would have to garrison the countryside.

. . . what are the true facts? What is our present situation?

First, our control over the rural population—so long described as the key to our efforts—has evaporated. The Vice President tells us that the pacification program has "stopped."

. . . It is this effort that has been most gravely set back in the last month. We cannot change the minds of people in villages controlled by the enemy. The fact is, as all recognize, that we cannot reassert control over those villages now in enemy hands without repeating the whole process of bloody destruction which has ravaged the countryside of South Vietnam throughout the last three years. Nor could we thus keep control without the presence of millions of American troops. . . .

. . . already the destruction has defeated most of our own purposes. . . . As a consequence, the political war—so long described as the only war that counts—has gone with the pacification program that was to win it. In a real sense, it may now be lost beyond recall.

He repeated his condemnation of the Saigon government:

. . . The second evident fact of the last two months is that the Saigon government is no more or better an ally than it was before; that it may even be less; and that the war inexorably is growing more, not less, an American effort. American officials continue to talk about a government newly energized, moving with "great competence," taking hold "remarkably well," doing "a very, very good piece of work of recovery." I was in the executive branch of the government from 1961 to 1964. In all those years, we heard the same glowing promises about the South Vietnamese government. . . .

. . . The facts are that 18-year-old South Vietnamese are still not being drafted; though now, as many times in the past, we are assured that this will happen soon. The facts are that thousands of young South Vietnamese buy their deferments from military service while American Marines die at Khe Sanh.

Kennedy, then as later, ignored Saigon's mobilization effort and the presence of the South Vietnamese 37th Ranger Battalion at Khe Sanh—as did much of the media, particularly television. He stressed heavily, again like much of the media, the plight of Hue and AP's anonymous quote of the major at Ben Tre:

. . . it is becoming more evident every passing day that the victories we achieve will only come at the cost of destruction for the nation we once hoped for. Even before this winter, Vietnam and its people were disintegrating under the blows of war. Now hardly a city in Vietnam has been spared from the new ravages of the past two months. Saigon officials say that nearly three-quarters of a million new refugees have been created, to add to the existing refugee population of two million or more. No one really knows the number of civilian casualties. The city of Hue, with most of the country's cultural and artistic heritage, lies in ruins: Of

488 BIG STORY

its population of 145,000, fully 113,000 are said to be homeless. There is not enough food, not enough shelter, not enough medical care. There is only death and misery and destruction.

An American commander said of the town of Ben Tre, "It became necessary to destroy the town in order to save it." It is difficult to quarrel with the decision of American commanders to use air power and artillery to save the lives of their men; if American troops are to fight for Vietnamese cities, they deserve protection. What I cannot understand is why the responsibility for the recapture and attendant destruction of Hue, and Ben Tre and the others, should fall to American troops in the first place.

He gave credit to "some of the South Vietnamese Army," but then suggested that most were unwilling to fight:

. . . If communist insurgents or invaders held New York or Washington or San Francisco, we would not leave it to foreigners to take them back, and destroy them and their people in the process. . . . There is no question that some of the South Vietnamese Army fought with great bravery. The Vietnamese—as these units, and the Vietcong have both shown us—are a courageous people . . . it is also true that in the height of the battle for Hue, as trucks brought American dead and wounded from the front lines, millions of Americans could see, on their television screens, South Vietnamese soldiers occupied in looting the city those Americans were fighting to recapture.

If the government's troops will not or cannot carry the fight for their cities, we cannot ourselves destroy them. . . . If it becomes "necessary" to destroy all of South Vietnam in order to "save" it, will we do that too?

In discussing military tactics as tied to negotiation, Kennedy shared a predilection for an "enclave" policy endorsed by many Washington analysts: "We can—as we are refusing to do today—begin to de-escalate the war, concentrate on protecting populated areas, and thus save American lives and slow down the destruction of the countryside."

Tet, if it demonstrated anything, showed how much *less* destructive it was to fight the enemy in the peripheral jungles than it was to fight big-unit battles in and around "populated areas." But Kennedy and others made "defense of populated areas" sound painless and tactically feasible.

In sum, Kennedy's first two speeches show how gaps, misplaced emphasis, and hasty assumptions in Vietnam coverage and Washington punditry could add up to a faulty context at home for public debate. Kennedy attacked not only prior Administration statements and the Vietnam commitment—which was fair enough—but sought to explain the U.S. problem in Vietnam in terms of events that allegedly occurred on the ground at Tet, notably with respect to South Vietnamese performance. To repeat, Kennedy's speeches were widely and uncritically reported in the media. Only Joseph Alsop took issue with *some* (not all) of Kennedy's "facts" about the Tet situation in Vietnam.

Daily Print and Network Coverage of the "Debate"

The Administration statements and "leaks," and Congressional "debate," of course, were not the only discussions of Vietnam policy that Tet provoked. The wire services offered editors and TV newsshow producers a plethora of nonofficial comment, polemic, and protest from all sides.

AP, for example, reported former Lt. Gen. James Gavin urging adoption of his "enclave" strategy; Alf Landon, the 1936 G.O.P. Presidential candidate, declaring that the use of nuclear weapons would be lunacy; 4,500 law school teachers and students signing petitions opposing Administration policy; antiwar demonstrations in Europe; a Tass report that the eminent pediatrician Dr. Benjamin Spock had thanked Soviet scientists for supporting the antiwar effort in the United States; an American Legion demand that all "restrictions be lifted from the military" in Vietnam; Theodore Sorensen saying he was "bleakly pessimistic" about the war; Harrison Salisbury, assistant managing editor of the New York *Times,* attacking Vietnam policy in a debate in Oxford, Ohio; Smith College students starting a protest fast; Dr. Martin Luther King saying he was opposed to the war because "injustice anywhere is a threat to justice everywhere"; South Vietnam's Ambassador Bui Diem predicting a "second wave" attack on Saigon on March 15 (it didn't happen); the "capture" of a U.S. Army exhibit at a Chicago museum by antiwar protesters; retired Marine Corps commandant David Shoup saying military victory was impossible; the organization of Business Executives Move for Vietnam Peace; the *Foreign Service Journal* refusing to accept an antiwar advertisement by a State Department employee group; former President Eisenhower accusing war dissenters of giving "aid and comfort to the enemy."

For the most part, unless there was a direct confrontation, or, for example, an Administration spokesman made a statement in the same place on the same day as a dove senator did, the wires simply reported the statements, pro or con, separately. The President, his Cabinet officers, and troubled supporters such as Senators Richard Russell and John Stennis had no trouble getting on the wire; nor did antiwar Senators Fulbright, Frank Church, and Joseph Clark, or the "name" dove professors, John Kenneth Galbraith, Chairman of Americans for Democratic Action, and Arthur Schlesinger, Jr., former speech-writer for Presidents Kennedy and Johnson. The wires also covered antiwar groups on the campuses, but often gave their statements lower priority.

The United States was short on "Vietnam experts": Almost anyone who had worked somewhere in Asia (e.g., Edwin O. Reischauer, former Ambassador to Japan) would do. The resulting plethora of opinions may not have clarified the issue, but, while it is possible to indict the wire services for oversimplifying a given "pro" or "anti" statement, one is hard put to accuse UPI or AP of slighting either side, or, if you will, the various sides. Given the limitations of wire-service manpower, knowledge (a shortage shared with academia), and space, not to mention the quality of the rhetoric reported, one cannot fault the wires for not producing articles on the great Vietnam debate worthy of *Foreign Affairs*.

As for the networks, the three major Sunday "talk shows" were evenly divided between pro- and anti-Administration figures:

CBS: "Face the Nation": February 4, Undersecretary Nicholas Katzenbach; February 18, Ambassador Ellsworth Bunker; February 25, President Nguyen Van Thieu; March 3, Mayor John V. Lindsay; March 10, Governor George W. Romney; March 17, Senator Eugene McCarthy; March 24, Representative Melvin Laird; March 31, George W. Ball.

ABC: "Issues and Answers": February 4, Senator Everett M. Dirksen; February 25, Senator J. William Fulbright; March 24, Senator Mark Hatfield; March 31, Presidential Assistant Walt W. Rostow.

NBC: "Meet the Press": February 4, Secretary Robert S. McNamara and Secretary Dean Rusk; February 11, Senator Eugene McCarthy; February 25, Assistant Secretary of State William P. Bundy; March 17, Senator Robert Kennedy; March 24, Senator Thruston B. Morton and Senator Jacob K. Javits; March 31, Gen. Maxwell D. Taylor.

Television networks broadcast several "specials" on Vietnam, with a strong "message" echoing dominant TV themes. No less important, there was participation in the debate by anchormen and reporters themselves, both on radio "analysis" shows and on television. For example, NBC's Elie Abel on radio: "Not all the bombs that we have dumped on North Vietnam or the supply routes in Laos, not all the valor of our GIs and Marines in battle, [have] *so far made a proud and enduring nation of South Vietnam.* . . . While it is clear that the communists cannot hope to defeat the United States in Vietnam, victory for our side is remote and, some would say, unobtainable."[42] CBS's Walter Cronkite, on radio, commented:

The bitter news from South Vietnam in the past week, once again, points up the misleading picture of those optimistic stories we've heard about the progress of the war and the pacification program. Reliable reports are hard to come by, and this must sharply increase the dilemma in which President Johnson finds himself. . . .

But where do we go from here? Can President Johnson continue to cry out "Help me, help me," and his plea for suggestions about a way out of the war? Or is the President, as some persons suspect, now a prisoner of his own policy and a captive of his advisors?

. . . Can we, as a nation, face up to the prospect of an overwhelmingly costly and bitter Asian war? To some observers, this seems more and more likely if we continue our present policy. President Johnson will have to come to grips with this if he has not already done so.[43]

Eric Sevareid, on CBS-TV, said:

The first wave of bitter argument over the turn of events in Vietnam has receded in this capital. . . .

The overall reaction . . . seems to break down this way. On the one hand, a sharp rise in popular support for the President and the war . . . because Americans instinctively rally to their leadership when things get rough.

On the other hand, a sharp rise in criticism and in doubts about our policies here in the capital among those who react *intellectually more than emotionally,* including congressmen and the press.

. . . .

A month ago and before, the *highest military authorities here were saying the military war was won,* the enemy beaten, that he could put on a show only near his sanctuaries, the Cambodian border and the Demilitarized Zone in the north, that he had nothing left elsewhere with which to stage an offensive. . . .[44]

. . . who in command is listening to whose advice?[45]

David Brinkley, on NBC-TV, injected his opinion:

Even among those in Congress who oppose the war, there has been little or no criticism of Gen. William Westmoreland himself.

But Representative [Margaret] Heckler of Massachusetts accused him of misleading the American people and deluding the members of Congress. She referred to the various highly optimistic reports Washington was hearing from Westmoreland and others about six weeks ago.

But other members rose to his defense and said it was the President, the Secretary of State, and others who had been deluding Congress, not the General.[46]

Another dove, Edward P. Morgan, put it this way:

. . . There is an ugly atmosphere of frustration and concern festering like a boil on the bleak winter face of Washington. . . . Remembering the Spanish artist's savage series of etchings protesting the disasters of war a century and a half ago, it is not hard to imagine what Goya would be producing from Khe Sanh or My Tho or Saigon today. . . .

. . . .

One important official described U.S. policy as mule-headed, stubbornly following a line that has repeatedly failed to produce promised results, an escalation, you might say, with questionable justification. . . .

One wonders if such disgust and frustration don't explain, in part, society's sudden hunger for books about our ancestors, the apes. Maybe a hopeful caricature could be made out of that.[47]

– On the more or less pro-Administration side was Chet Huntley, who also expressed his sentiments on radio:

Historians might one day, when this Vietnam War has ended, discover that it broke all known records in throwing off platitudes. They have floated out of the Vietnam confusion like clouds of little bubbles. For example, the Vietcong are frequently defined as patriotic nationalists. The war is frequently called a civil war. Ho Chi Minh's purposes are sometimes described as only a desire to unite his country.

We have had "seek and destroy," the "redoubt or garrison tactic," "stop the bombing," and, finally, there is the one which reads, "There can be no military decision in Vietnam."

If [captured documents] *can be given any credence* whatsoever, it becomes *clear that military results* are going to determine when and under what circumstances the enemy will come to the negotiating table.[48]

ABC's Howard K. Smith was the one big-name hawk on the three major networks:

There exists only one real alternative, but no one suggested it because it's considered one of those thoughts that is unthinkable, that is, to escalate, but this time on an overwhelming scale. At home, declare a state of national emergency and stop pretending that this is not a major war. Use the urgency thus created to raise taxes, not 10 percent as the President requested, but 20 percent to pay for the war. Mobilize not a few more thousand men, but three or four hundred thousand men, enough to turn future Khe Sanhs into Stalingrads that destroy the besiegers. Begin treating the communists the way they treat the South Vietnamese: Bomb their irrigation dikes and deprive them of food, as they are now depriving Saigon of food. Give civilians 48 hours to get out, then level the harbor of Haiphong so not a bullet more can be unloaded there.[49]

The big shift on the war on network television (as opposed to radio commentary) by a "star" anchorman came with Cronkite's return from his flying visit to Vietnam and his gloomy conclusions voiced on his February 27 "special":[50] "But it is increasingly clear . . . that the only rational way out . . . will be to negotiate, not as victors, but as an honorable people who lived up to their pledge to defend democracy, and did the best they could."[51]

On March 10, NBC followed with its Frank McGee "special" on Vietnam, in which McGee said what many network reporters had been inferring or saying flatly on radio, that "the war is being lost by the Administration's definition." In yet another tribute to AP's anonymous major at Ben Tre, McGee added that the United States must decide whether "it's futile to destroy Vietnam in the effort to save it."

The New York *Times*'s television critic, Jack Gould, was worried less by the sentiment than by its precedent-setting expression on a TV news show. Under a neatly incongruous headline ("U.S. Is Losing the War in Vietnam, NBC Declares") Gould wrote that "the posture of both NBC and CBS is not that they are engaging in editorializing, but rather that they are using the *reportorial candor* that current events dictate." Gould suggested that this form of commentary by hitherto "objective" anchormen, addressing an audience of 60 million, "could be a new and unpredictable factor in influencing critical decisions."[52]

McGee's show received raves from *Variety,* the national show business weekly, which reviews news shows along with entertainment:

Television's big speak-out—the turn since the Tet offensive to telling it like it is on the war in Vietnam—hit a high mark Sunday in a special edition of NBC-TV's "Frank McGee report."

Not that the show's hard line on U.S. setbacks and barely screened scorn for the Administration's hawking was out of the current trend by the gen-

eral press. The *Wall Street Journal,* the New York *Times,* and now even
Newsweek and others have recently been outspoken dissenters. . . .

. . . This was difficult journalism executed with a special excellence
that made a great deal of the electronic medium's very special impact.

With methodical precision, anchorman McGee and correspondents
Dean Brelis, Howard Tuckner, and Paul Cunningham *set up Administration leaders, then bowled them over like so many tenpins. Opening
clips featured* President Johnson, the then Defense Secretary McNamara,
and General Westmoreland expressing their specific optimism of recent
months. Then with fire footage, maps, and interviews, the [Adminis-
tration] leaders' assurances were shrapneled.

. . . .

Viewers were spared nothing in the program's assemblage of all the
shocking footage that has come out of Vietnam in the changed war—
from the ruins of Hue—"the loveliest city in Vietnam"—and the looting
there, to the cold-blooded murder of a suspected Vietcong officer by
Saigon's police chief [General Loan].

Just how far this show was willing to go was pointed up in the execution footage. When the sequence first appeared on the Huntley-Brinkley
nightly news strip, producer Shad Northshield ordered an upcut between
the first and second feeds of the half-hour because the victim's head in
the early take (just off the satellite) was seen to bleed slightly as it hit
the pavement. On the McGee hour, viewers saw the entire take with an
enormous pool of blood forming as the officer lay dying in the street. To
close the segment, Tuckner noted that the executioner was still chief of
police.

McGee's closing words impressed after an hour to challenge a viewer's
immunity to two years of cameo fire footage: "Now there are finite limits
to the destruction Vietnam can absorb. There are only so many buildings
and so many people and too many of the buildings lie in rubble and far
too many of the people lie dead.

"Laying aside all other arguments, and there are a great many more,
the time is at hand when we must decide whether it's futile to destroy Vietnam in the effort to save it."

Laying aside any argument on the show's subjectivity, it must be
assessed as *responsible, fair,* and *authoritative.*[53]

In terms of page-one coverage of the debate at home, the New
York *Times* gave the President, Administration spokesmen, and Congressional supporters better "play" and bigger headlines than domestic foes: 26 stories to 24. The same was true of the Washington *Post:*
32 to 15. Inside the two newspapers during February–March 1968,
the ratios were far different. The *Times* published a total of 64 stories

inside on antiwar politicians or groups, versus 28 on the President, hawks, and other Administration spokesmen. For the *Post,* the corresponding inside totals were 29 to 20.

If one adds up all the February–March domestic page-one stories in these two newspapers showing, on the one hand, that the Administration was popular or performing adequately vis-à-vis Vietnam, or, on the other, that it was under fire (from left or right), or unpopular (including polls), or that its policies were not working, or that it was possibly contemplating nuclear weapons, the result is: *Times:* 27 "pro-Administration" to 36 "anti-Administration," and *Post:* 36 "pro-Administration" to 31 "anti-Administration." (In this count, stories from abroad—that is, other than Saigon—are excluded, as are independent *Times* stories disclosing possible troop increases.)

The problem of "balance," or reporting "both sides"—a traditional newspaper and wire-service goal—was not always successfully resolved in the *Times* and *Post* as the Vietnam debate at home grew increasingly loud during the Tet offensive. In most *Times* page-one stories about Administration spokesmen and statements, some indication was given that the points made were questioned by doves, or that disagreement with or within the Administration existed. However, in most *Post* or *Times* page-one stories about antiwar critics or statements, no such "balancer" was added. There were exceptions: for one, Edward B. Fiske's *Times* story, written in New York, about the anthology of alleged allied atrocities, *In the Name of America;* the *Times* included the State Department's point of view.[54] The *Post,* in its own story on the book, omitted a similar "balancer."[55]

Both newspapers also participated in the domestic debate through editorials and commentary and through the publication of articles written by nonstaffers. As may be clear in the earlier chapters, the *Times* reader found little but dismay, despair, or disapproval in the paper's analyses and commentaries. During February and March 1968, the Sunday *New York Times Magazine* published three pieces on the war by "outsiders," none of whom had been to South Vietnam: Edwin O. Reischauer, who suggested that the much-reported Tet destruction made a Saigon government unviable; Richard Barnet, co-director of the Washington-based Institute for Policy Studies, who hailed the prospect of victory by the National Liberation Front; and Sol Stern, who suggested that mayhem would ensue when black combat veterans came home from Vietnam. The magazine also carried an analysis of the impact of the war on domestic policies and the coming election by former special counsel to the President, Theodore Sorensen.[56]

The *Times*'s own columnists, during February and March, were shocked by Tet but less inclined to pessimistic predictions than the editorial page (29 editorials concerning Vietnam appeared during the period). Appalled by press accounts of urban destruction, James Reston, for example, nevertheless did not suggest, as did John Oakes's editorial writers, that the allies were in a "perilous" position militarily. Both Reston and Tom Wicker, however, excoriated the Administration for past optimism and cast doubt on the "official" version of current events. Both argued for a change in policy. C.L. Sulzberger, no dove, suggested from Paris that: (1) militarily, Giap had Westmoreland in trouble; and (2) the U.S. military might revolt if Vietnam were abandoned, a far-fetched analogy to France's experience during the Algerian War in 1958–62.[57]

Overall, the *Times,* then as later, did not offer its readers a wide spectrum of opinion on the Vietnam War.

As usual, the *Post,* thanks to its array of syndicated columnists, provided a wide range of commentary (much of it flawed by factual error), from various breeds of hawks (Joseph Alsop, William S. White, Roscoe Drummond), to middle-of-the-roaders (Rowland Evans and Robert Novak), to doves (Joseph Kraft); and its Sunday "Outlook" section published the analysis of Vietcong failure in the cities by Douglas Pike. Its editorials on the war were few: 19, and moderately critical. The *Post,* unlike the *Times,* had taken a pro-Administration stand in 1965; its evolution toward a more dovish stance came as its long-time editor, J. Russell Wiggins, began to transfer more responsibility to his designated successor, Philip Geyelin, who opposed the Administration's Vietnam commitment.

On March 22, the *Post*'s "Letters to the Editor" column carried a letter which was picked up by AP. It was from Professor Arthur Schlesinger, Jr., sometime member of the White House staff and noted historian, who since Tet had been calling for Westmoreland's ouster and a new strategy. Describing what he had been seeing about the siege of Khe Sanh on television, Schlesinger urged that the garrison be evacuated promptly by air:

The saddest time in America today is the moment every night on the news when the television screen shows American Marines at Khe Sanh—

brave young men, trapped in a war they never made, waiting for the inevitable attack. . . .

How can people in their senses suppose that bombing will now "save" Khe Sanh in case of attack? Do they not understand that, the closer the enemy gets to our men, the less we can bomb, because we will be killing our own troops as well as the enemy? Do they not understand that, already at some points, the enemy is only a few hundred yards away?

. . . Yes, air power is one vital difference between Khe Sanh and Dienbienphu. For, if air power cannot save Khe Sanh, it may still save the men in Khe Sanh. The Air Force surely has contingency plans for the evacuation of the Marines. Let us put these plans into immediate effect, before enemy antiaircraft batteries interdict our flights, before enemy mortars destroy our landing strip, before enemy shock troops overrun the base. Let us not sacrifice our brave men to the folly of generals and the obstinacy of Presidents.[58]

If nothing else, Schlesinger's letter demonstrated the power of television, and also the attraction for academics (as for many others) of long-distance analysis of the Vietnam battlefield. As newsmen in Vietnam were well aware, there was no feasible method of evacuating the more than 5,000 U.S. and South Vietnamese troops from Khe Sanh and its outposts by air while the base was under fire (an overland U.S. ground attack was even then being planned). Moreover, as UPI had reported on March 20, and as Westmoreland had hinted on March 6, there were signs even then that enemy pressure at Khe Sanh was slackening. (We now know what was then not general knowledge—Marine intelligence had discovered that the foe was beginning to pull back by mid-March.)

News Magazine Coverage

As the uproar began in February, *Time* took a "balanced" approach in a lead story on the war:

Inevitably, a new wave of criticism washed over the Capital—and for the first time a good deal of it spilled onto Gen. William C. Westmoreland, the handsome U.S. commander in Vietnam for nearly four years. Some of the criticism was aimed at his consistently *sanguine estimates* of a struggle that has grown increasingly sanguinary. But more was directed at the overall strategy and conduct of the war.

Robert F. Kennedy mounted the harshest of the attacks. "It is time for the truth," said Kennedy. "It is time to face the reality that a military victory is not in sight and that it probably never will come." Agreed Bobby's senior colleague, Jacob Javits, in a Senate speech: "We do not yet have a winning strategy in Vietnam. The situation there is basically stalemated." Senate majority leader Mike Mansfield likewise called for a major reassessment of the U.S. commitment.

And in an emotional indictment of American conduct in the war, which admittedly ignored communist atrocities, 29 Protestant, Catholic, and Jewish clergymen published a 420-page catalogue of "U.S. War Crimes," called *In the Name of America.*

Washington and Westmoreland were by no means the only targets. The South Vietnamese government was blasted for *apathy, corruption, and incompetence*—though U.S. officials claimed that President Nguyen Van Thieu's Administration acted creditably during the communist attacks. . . .[59]

Edward Kennedy, *fresh* from a visit to Saigon, warned that if the Vietnamese "are unwilling to accept their responsibilities, then the American people, with great justification, may well consider their responsibilities fulfilled."[60]

Bobby Kennedy told a Chicago audience: "Enormous corruption pervades every level of South Vietnamese official life." Washington's Democratic Senator Henry Jackson, a staunch Johnson supporter, demanded that "the Saigon government get off its duff and get moving."

Nothing, naturally, would please the Johnson Administration more. The fact is, however, that *unless the U.S. wants to undertake a full-fledged colonial venture in South Vietnam,* its leverage in dealing with an independent and touchy Saigon government is severely limited. Militarily, too, U.S. options are notably restricted.[61]

In its cover story on John Kenneth Galbraith in the same issue, *Time* was even-tempered:

. . . Galbraith was counseling against the dispatch of even a few American combat troops to South Vietnam. "A few," he advised Kennedy in 1962, "will mean more and more and more." His forecast proved flawless. From 773 advisors at the start of the decade, the U.S. force grew to more than 16,000 under Kennedy and half a million under Lyndon Johnson today. The war that they are fighting, cries Galbraith, is "perhaps the worst miscalculation in our history," and he sees the Vietcong's bloody rampage through the cities of South Vietnam as complete vindication of his position. "We were winning," he argues, "only in the speeches of our generals and ambassadors. . . ."

Galbraith has spent a good half of his time in recent months focusing on the single issue of Vietnam. He has promoted his plan for de-escalation on TV, held forth from college platforms across the country, argued his case in publications as diverse as the *Wall Street Journal* and *Playboy.*

His *How to Get Out of Vietnam*, a 47-page, thirty-five-cent broadside, has gone through a printing of 250,000. As national chairman of the liberal, 50,000-member Americans for Democratic Action, he has helped push the group to the brink of a possibly irreparable split by promoting the Presidential candidacy of Vietnam critic Eugene McCarthy on the ground that no domestic gains can be achieved until the war is halted. . . .

Galbraith allows for the possibility that he might be wrong—a concession rarely made by the more dogmatic critics of the war. "Should our continued presence be necessary," he says, "the course I propose will accord us a foothold for a time and thus allow us a second look." In any event, he says in a tart aside, past policy "has been wrong so long and so alarmingly that even a modestly right one will seem superb."

Whether Galbraith's program can be considered superb—or even modestly right—is questioned by defenders of U.S. policy. It is hard to believe, for example, that abandoning most of the countryside to the communists—the very core of Galbraith's plan—would not embolden and stiffen them rather than give them greater reason to come to the conference table. Secure in the countryside and immune from interdiction by air, they could husband their forces and then assault the allied-held cities with far greater strength than they showed in the past two weeks. Nor is it true that the Vietcong alone guard the grail of Vietnamese nationalism. They are simply better organized than the hopelessly fragmented moderates, who also qualify as genuine nationalists; and the VC are far more adept at the use of terror and brutality to gain their ends. Still, despite more than a few drawbacks, Galbraith's proposals do offer at least a foundation for a responsible opposition policy.[62]

The following week, *Time* noted increasing problems for Johnson:

Once again the United States had to separate fond hope from grim fact. On successive days, the Johnson Administration announced that reinforcements would be sent immediately to South Vietnam[63] and that the latest rumors about peace feelers from Hanoi had added up to nothing. As if to underscore the news, communist forces over the weekend launched a savage new offensive across South Vietnam. . . .

The Senate, particularly, continues to scorch the Administration with criticism. Kentucky Republican Thruston Morton last week accused the Administration of "bland and probably inaccurate statements" about the war. By Morton's count, the number of antiwar senators has grown from 10 to 25 in the past year.[64] One of that number is Illinois Republican Charles Percy, who is now asking a phased withdrawal of U.S. forces from Vietnam, leaving the South Vietnamese government to survive or expire on its own. Ohio Democrat Stephen Young demanded that Westmoreland be replaced by "a more competent general" because he has been "outwitted and outgeneraled."

On the House side, Wisconsin Republicans Glenn Davis and Vernon Thomson predicted that Westmoreland would be fired by Easter. The General, after four grueling years in Vietnam, is due for relief, and Johnson does not rule out his return. Nevertheless, the President insisted: "I have no intention of seeing him leave. I have no plan for him to leave." . . .

If recent developments in Vietnam have failed to rally Congress, the public at large seems to be reacting differently. Opinion polls show that approval of Johnson's handling of the war remains low. Support of the war itself, however, seems to have risen since the communists' Tet offensive. The Gallup survey periodically asks people to classify themselves as hawks or doves. Since January, the self-described hawks have increased from 56 percent to 61 percent, and the doves have decreased from 28 percent to 23 percent. The latest Louis Harris survey found that those expressing general support for the war have increased from 61 percent in December, to 74 percent. Yet even Johnson, the indefatigable poll watcher, insisted last week that "you can't run a war by polls."[65]

Nor can a war be run—or at least well run—as long as the other side can repeatedly determine when and where the action is to be. Johnson responded to Westmoreland's latest request for help with determination, giving the marching orders just 48 hours after the General's message arrived. Yet once again the United States was on the defensive, reacting to the enemy's initiative.[66]

By the third weekend after the Tet attacks, *Time* began to reflect worry. In its lead "Nation" story, it scored Administration optimism and called allied prospects "grim."[67] Further down in the article, however, Lyndon Johnson got his say:

. . . Addressing American sailors on the deck of the 60,000-ton aircraft carrier *Constellation* last week during a tour of military facilities, he put his feelings into forceful words. "Men may debate and men may dissent, men may disagree," said Johnson, "and God forbid that a time should come when men of this land may not—but there does come a time when men must stand. And for Americans, that time has now come."

This was followed by an excerpt from the *Wall Street Journal's* much quoted February 23 editorial on a looming defeat, and a useful if anonymous warning about the dangers of excess:

. . . Warned the *Wall Street Journal*, a *firm supporter* of the Administration's war policies:[68] "We think the American people should be getting ready to accept, if they haven't already, the prospect that the whole Vietnam effort may be doomed; it may be *falling apart beneath our feet*. The actual military situation may be making academic the philosophical arguments for the intervention in the first place."

On the other hand, one of the oldest axioms about Vietnam, as a U.S. official reflected last week, is that "things are never as good as they seem when they are good, or as bad as they seem when they are bad."

Time rallied a bit the following week, but, amid rumors of the President's plans for escalation, noted a Hearst editorial: "Said the Hearst newspapers, firm supporters of Johnson on the war . . . 'This war has gone on too long, it is causing too much disaffection in the country, it is killing and maiming too many Americans. It must be brought to an end—with new ideas, new tactics and new methods.' "[69]

The next issue reflected "a groundswell of pessimism" and cited at length the doves' objections to the war on various grounds: moral, domestic, strategic. *Time* could offer no solace:

. . . If the U.S. were doing better in Vietnam, and if an end were somewhere in sight, most grounds for objection to the war—save perhaps the moral ones—would probably melt away rapidly. But no end is in sight, and at this juncture the United States cannot be said to be doing very well. . . .

In this situation, there is more and more talk of the need to find a formula to end the war.[70]

Stepped-up Congressional unhappiness and Kennedy's antiwar speeches also got attention in this piece, which noted that "only two senators countered the critics."

By the second week in March (*Time*'s March 22 issue), things had changed: Vietnam had given way to the "Vietnam issue" and McCarthy had been successful in the March 12 New Hampshire primary (McCarthy was on *Time*'s cover). McCarthy's Vietnam views were not explored in detail, however; the accent was on the politics and color.

On the weekend that Johnson gave his abdication speech, *Time* explained why he did it: "His popularity hit an all-time low in a Gallup poll released this week. Only 36 percent of those questioned approved of his conduct of the Presidency (versus 48 percent in January); only 26 percent approved of his conduct of the war (versus 39 percent). *Obviously, the Tet offensive had much to do with Johnson's slide.*"[71]

Newsweek handled the debate theme far differently. As we have seen, *Newsweek*'s New York editors in 1966–67 were divided on the war—as were those of most major publications. The magazine's solution prior to Tet seemed to be to take an even-handed stance—to run Walter Lippmann, who was anti-Johnson on Vietnam, Ken Crawford, who supported the President, and various staffers pro and con. There was no consistent "line" until after January 30. By early mid-March, *Newsweek* had clearly become "gloomy dovish," as Merton Perry put it. It was a deliberate decision by Osborn Elliott; it was in harmony with prevailing sentiment in the New York office, and, it was thought, among *Newsweek* readers.

From the start, it can be fairly said, *Newsweek*'s editors—relying on roughly the same mixture of "in-house," wire-service, and New York *Times* information as *Time,* but with shorter files from a smaller staff—took a more alarmist view of the Tet offensive than did *Time.* And, as becomes evident in the reading, *Newsweek*'s rather breathless writing style added to the net effect. In its first Tet issue, the magazine said:

. . . On Capitol Hill, hawks and doves alike lamented the "humiliation" inflicted on the allied cause and complained that they had been misled about the communists' capability.

Shock Value: No one could read the implications of the audacious attacks with any degree of certainty. . . .

But for sheer shock value, the assaults could not have come at a worse time. Red guerrilla successes in Laos, and North Korea's brazen seizure of the U.S. intelligence ship *Pueblo,* had freshly underscored the vulnerability of American power spread thin in Asia.[72]

Later, *Newsweek* wrote of the President that "a weary Lyndon Johnson reflected the temper of the times. 'I don't know how to do anything better than we are doing it,' the President told some visiting students who faced him with questions about Vietnam. 'If I did, I would do it. I would take the better way. We have considered everything.' "[73] And the same piece went on to say: "But there was little anywhere in last week's news to give them hope that the enemy's strength has finally begun to wane, that Vicksburg, if not Appomattox, is just around the corner."

In its next issue, *Newsweek*'s cover photograph was of actress Faye Dunaway, followed up by a quick discussion inside of "The New American Beauties." The lead article in the national news section, however, was devoted to the war, and was as relentlessly gloomy as it claimed Administration spokesmen were "relentlessly optimistic":

> Lyndon Johnson's Administration seemed as besieged last week as the lonely U.S. Marine outpost at Khe Sanh. With the military situation in Vietnam looking more precarious by the day,[74] the pressures intensified on every Presidential flank. From Capitol Hill to the judicious editorial page of the *Wall Street Journal*, a fresh clamor rose for a reexamination of America's prospects in Vietnam. But the Administration gave the *unmistakable impression* that all the big questions had been resolved long ago—and the answer was to *plunge on*.[75]

Newsweek then went on to cite at some length the *Wall Street Journal* editorial of February 23, but without the modifying comment of *Time*. The President was depicted as a fugitive from worldly cares: "Beset by troubles on all sides, a haggard Lyndon Johnson retreated to his Texas ranch."[76]

Finally, on March 18, following the lead of CBS's Walter Cronkite and NBC's Frank McGee, *Newsweek* published as its lead article an editorial denouncing present policy and suggesting a new one. The Vietnam coverage heavily supported the editorial, and the cover was the already discussed "Agony of Khe Sanh" one, with Merton Perry's cover story inside (see Chapter 8).

In its condemnatory editorial, *Newsweek* said:

> After three years of gradual escalation, President Johnson's war strategy for Vietnam has run into a dead end. Only the chronic optimist can now see "the light at the end of the tunnel" that used to illuminate the rhetoric of the military briefing officers. Only the deluded can console themselves with the comforting feeling that suddenly the war will turn a corner and the enemy will wither away.[77] The Tet offensive—those three brutal weeks that may have been only the first part of the communists' winter-spring campaign—*has exposed the utter inadequacy* of the Administration's war policy.
>
> . . . Those who supported the war—for whatever reasons—have had to reexamine their assumptions. They have had to ask whether the political imperatives which seemed to justify the war are worth the savagery and terror, the wholesale destruction which mark the struggle.[78] Those who opposed the war can now find new reasons to justify their criticism. . . .
>
> Though the Johnson Administration may not have misled the nation, it certainly has miscalculated.

Newsweek justified its pessimism as follows:

> This is the dismal balance sheet at the moment. It can be argued that it is too pessimistic an accounting; but the reports of the Administration have always been too optimistic—a habit that still persists.[79]

In its March 25 issue, *Newsweek*, like *Time* and the newspaper analysts, deserted the war for politics: the McCarthy-Kennedy challenge to Johnson. (It did, however, briefly note the start of the allied "Resolve to Win" offensive.) Like *Time*, *Newsweek* warned that the March 12 New Hampshire primary was not a true test of the Vietnam issue. It devoted a lot of space to Congressional "misgivings" about Vietnam:

> In the aftermath, it was immediately apparent that the upsurge in Congressional dissent over Vietnam was not confined to the basically dovish Foreign Relations Committee. Many congressmen noted that ever since the communists' Tet offensive, their mail has shown mounting dissatisfaction with the conduct of the war. *Newsweek*'s chief Congressional correspondent, Samuel Shaffer, summed up the mood on Capitol Hill this way: "The report[80] that the President has been asked by our military commanders in Vietnam to increase our troop commitment to 200,000 men has brought Congress as close to mutiny as I have ever seen it. Hawks are being converted overnight to doves and House members in particular are falling over each other to get resolutions to the hopper demanding that no more troops be sent."[81]

In the last week of March (April 8 issue), *Newsweek* rested on its oars:

> . . . President Johnson summoned reporters to the Rose Garden and announced that he would go on national television late Sunday night— just 36 hours before the polls open in Wisconsin—to give a review of the war in Vietnam.
>
> The President indicated he would propose a *moderate* increase in U.S. troop strength in Vietnam, and repeat his earlier request for a tax increase—*probably of some $9 billion.* He refused to comment on the possibility that he might announce a bombing pause, but did add that he would discuss "what our plans are—and I will talk about other questions of some importance."
>
> At the weekend, the President's staff was still working on his speech, and the word at the White House was that the President had a *bombing pause proposal going beyond* the San Antonio formula—first step in an elaborately orchestrated peace offensive that would almost certainly lead to a suspension of the bombing by sometime this summer—unless, of

course, the enemy should launch another major attack in the meantime.[82] Presidential staffers said that a moderate troop call-up would be announced to remove any suggestion that might permit the peace offensive to be interpreted as a retreat.[83]

Did the Media Shape the Results?

What impact did the post-Tet Washington uproar—so heavily shaped by the media—have on the course of the war? Nobody knows, exactly.

The conventional wisdom as late as 1976 was to assume that the Tet outcry "turned the war around," causing the President, for the first time, to reject a military request for escalation. As we have seen, the Pentagon Papers, John Henry, and Schandler showed this not to be so; the President was merely faithful to his earlier caveat of 1967: "We cannot call up the reserves." The historians also tell us that the "partial bombing pause" was not expected by Rusk to lead to negotiations; it was a device to soothe antiwar Democrats without incurring much military risk (the flying weather was bad over Hanoi in April). To the extent that it persuaded the President to venture a *temporary* partial bombing pause again, and to offer again to talk with Hanoi (if only to show domestic doves his willingness to seek "peace"), the outcry affected Johnson *policy*. To the Americans' surprise, Hanoi agreed to talk. Thereafter, the limits on U.S. military commitments and strategy gradually became fixed (largely by Clifford) in concrete; and the bombing of all North Vietnam ended on November 1, just before the election.

There is no evidence of a direct relationship between the dominant media themes in early 1968 and changes in American mass public opinion vis-à-vis the Vietnam War itself.[84] Indeed, public support for the war effort remained remarkably steady in February–March 1968, even as LBJ's popularity hit a new low, as measured by the pollsters. But we can observe unmistakable reflections of strong media themes (notably concerning Khe Sanh and the South Vietnamese) in the Congressional rhetoric and in the discussion by the politically active and media-sensitive elites outside Washington. Less obviously, we see the tendency of politicians and bureaucratic pressure groups to use media themes as new clothes for old arguments. The Tet experience suggests that the dominant media "image" of a major foreign-policy crisis, given the proper circumstances, may contribute hugely to a set of perceptions *in Washington* that variously alters, hastens, or delays decisions by both the President and his chief political opponents, especially under the pressures of an election year.

Amid the Tet uproar, the surprisingly strong showing against the President made by Senator Eugene McCarthy (42.2 percent of the Democratic vote) in the New Hampshire primary on March 12 was widely interpreted by media and politicians as an antiwar vote, despite some warnings to the contrary. Later studies have suggested that it was a generalized anti-Johnson vote, not a "peace vote." Among the pro-McCarthy voters, those who were dissatisfied with Johnson for not pushing a harder line in Vietnam outnumbered those who wanted a withdrawal by a margin of nearly three to two. Of those who favored McCarthy before the Democratic convention, but who switched to some other candidate by November 1968, a plurality switched to George Wallace, the ultra-hawkish American Independence Party candidate.[85]

It is plausible to argue that the media's "disaster" image of events in Vietnam further aggravated dissatisfactions with the Johnson war policy on the part of both hawks and doves, adding to the McCarthy vote in New Hampshire. Interpreted as a dove show of strength, the primary results then helped push Johnson and his political advisors to make moves designed to placate the doves. But the media did not "drive Johnson from office." At Tet, as earlier in the war, the President was his own worst enemy. As it happened, Lyndon Johnson temporarily calmed, but did not end, his own party's political crisis by withdrawing from the 1968 election. Some writers argue that Johnson might have been forced to "abdicate" in 1968 even without Tet; he had neglected his own party organization and lost the support, for diverse reasons, of major groups preoccupied with domestic issues.[86] Indeed, Johnson in his own memoirs suggests that he felt well before Tet that he had spent much of his political capital.[87] Tet hit LBJ when he was *already* in trouble.

A media portrayal of Tet closer to the historical realities would not have averted a new Washington debate over the war; the surprise alone would have forced a New Look. But one can speculate that had the events of February–March 1968 been portrayed with more cold light and less black fog, neither hawks nor doves would have had a "disaster" to exploit. Robert Kennedy might have deferred his candidacy. And Lyndon Johnson might have waited for a diplomatic initiative from Hanoi before launching his own, under pressure to "buy time." One suspects that in the wake of their Tet military set-backs, Hanoi's leaders were eager to buy a little time themselves.[88] Within South Vietnam the war did not end. The North launched a bloody "second wave" against Saigon in May–June; the allied commanders finally developed an urban defense plan. On the ground, the U.S. policy was "more of the same, but better" through 1968–69, with one important exception: Under pressure from Washington, Westmoreland and his successor, Gen. Creighton Abrams, began slowly to press Saigon to bring more South Vietnamese troops into the "big war." Pacification, abetted by general mobilization and the arming of the people, accelerated. So did U.S. efforts to "dig out" the foe. U.S. casualties were slightly *higher* in 1969 than in 1967, the year before Tet, but the troops' efforts got far less media notice. In mid-1969, as Westmoreland had prophesied in his 1967 National Press Club speech, the first U.S. troop withdrawals began, under the Nixon Administration, as negotiations at Paris dragged on. The last U.S. forces did not pull out until after Mr. Nixon's "Peace with Honor" in January 1973, almost five years after Tet '68. Hanoi finally conquered the South in 1975.

13

An Extreme Case

In overall terms, the performance by the major American television and print news organizations during February and March 1968 constitutes an extreme case.

Rarely has contemporary crisis-journalism turned out, in retrospect, to have veered so widely from reality. Essentially, the dominant themes of the words and film from Vietnam (rebroadcast in commentary, editorials, and much political rhetoric at home) added up to a portrait of defeat for the allies. Historians, on the contrary, have concluded that the Tet offensive resulted in a severe military-political setback for Hanoi in the South. To have portrayed such a setback for one side as a defeat for the other—in a major crisis abroad—cannot be counted as a triumph for American journalism.

Why did the media perform so unsatisfactorily? I have come to this general conclusion: The special circumstances of Tet impacted to a rare degree on modern American journalism's special susceptibilities and limitations. This peculiar conjuncture overwhelmed reporters, commentators, and their superiors alike. And it could happen again.

In most American foreign policy crises since World War II, there have been objective factors that assuaged journalistic needs and curbed journalistic excess. One thinks in particular of the 1962 Cuban missile crisis and Hanoi's 1972 offensive, the latter a far stronger military effort than Tet. In both cases, 1962 and 1972, there were perceived forewarnings of trouble, a well-defined geographical arena, a widely shared sense of the relative strengths and capabilities of the opposing sides, a conventional confrontation remote from journalistic havens, and a coherent Presidential response. None of these reassuring elements was fully present at Tet-1968.

In Vietnam, the sudden penetration of downtown Saigon by Vietcong sapper teams impacted personally on correspondents' lives. The geographical dispersion of the concurrent communist attacks elsewhere in the country led to uncertainty among newsmen about the enemy's intent, strength, and degree of success in the countryside. Journalists' unfamiliarity both with the South Vietnamese and with the relative military capabilities of each side increased this uncertainty.

Inevitably, then, the overall pattern of events in Vietnam in February 1968 was for a time obscure. But commentators and many reporters did not wait. By the time the fog of war began to lift later that month, the collective emanations of the major media were producing a kind of continuous black fog of their own, a vague conventional "disaster" image, which few newsmen attempted to reexamine and which few news managers at home sought to question. Indeed, in the case of *Newsweek*, NBC, and CBS, and of photo displays by others, the disaster theme seemed to be exploited for its own sake. The journalistic fog had thinned to a patchy haze by the time of President Johnson's March 31 speech, but it had not been penetrated by a cold, retrospective light. The record was not set straight. The hasty assumptions and judgments of February and early March were simply allowed to stand.

Indeed, Charles Mohr of the New York *Times* recalled, in a 1971 letter to the author, that when he wrote a piece later in 1968 analyzing the outcome of the Tet attacks as a setback to Hanoi, he received letters from *Times* readers expressing surprise and disbelief.

In late 1968, according to Edward J. Epstein, an NBC field producer named Jack Fern suggested to Robert J. Northshield a three-part series showing that Tet had indeed been a military victory for America and that the media had exaggerated greatly the view that it was a defeat for South Vietnam. The idea was rejected because, Northshield (an NBC News producer) said later, Tet was already established "in the public's mind as a defeat, and therefore it was an American defeat."[1]

Was this thematic persistence due to a sudden seizure of "antiwar" feeling among newsmen, an ideological media conspiracy against Johnson Administration war policy?

One must rely for the answer on contemporary impressions and in-

terviews obtained 18 months to two years after the fact—when time
and a new set of perceptions had clouded memories. What seems
fairly clear is that, in January 1968, there was little optimism among
newsmen, as among congressmen, with regard to the Vietnam venture. Many, as we have indicated, were simply skeptical of any success; a few were hostile to the military and sympathetic to the academicians and senators active in the peace movement; others hoped for
a negotiated settlement. Hawks were few, except on *Time*. Outspoken
doves were rare, except on the *Times*. At CBS and NBC, it appears,
there was both impatience with the war's length and revulsion at its
horrors. In Vietnam, there was little conversation about war policy;
instead, newsmen exchanged anecdotes about the war's various aspects. Overall, there seems to have been no ideological consensus
prior to Tet that could serve as an explanation for media treatment of the crisis.

It is true that, after the attacks broke, *Newsweek* became explicit
in its political stance, citing the "utter inadequacy" of Administration
war policy and calling for a negotiated settlement. (We have seen
that that magazine's Vietnam news coverage was more negative than
that of the other print media.) However, *Newsweek*'s editors may
have been equally concerned about keeping up with political fashion,
with the much more vocal antiwar opinion, with the pessimism of
Walter Cronkite and the New York *Times*'s editorial page.*

Thus, out of his own experience, and interviews with his colleagues, this writer is convinced that ideology, per se, played a relatively minor role in the media treatment of the Tet crisis. The big
problems lay elsewhere, and persist to this day.

Yet, downgrading the ideological factor in Tet media coverage—a
factor so heavily stressed by Nixon Administration spokesmen in
1969–72 in their attacks on the "Eastern establishment press"—
should not be taken to mean that newsmen, especially those in Washington and New York, were neutral with respect to the Johnson Administration. They were suspicious and resentful, on personal-profes-
sional grounds. As was noted at the beginning of this study, the
credibility among newsmen of President Johnson, Secretary McNa-

---

* At an editorial meeting around March 1, Oberdorfer noted, "one of the
editors expressed the fear that *Newsweek* would be the last to speak instead
of being the pacesetter it aspired to be." (*Tet!*, p. 274.) *Newsweek* was quick
off the mark during Hanoi's Easter offensive in 1972, prematurely invoking
"the specter of defeat" in early May.

mara, and senior officialdom by 1968 was low. Johnson, starting with his first public budget discussions in 1964, had gained a reputation in Washington for manipulation and half-truths. The public utterances of generals and civilian officials alike concerning the war had seldom been distinguished by brutal candor. And Tet, as we have noted, came after an Administration propaganda campaign intended to shore up support for a long-term limited-war policy that embraced neither a decisive military strategy nor a plausible diplomatic ending. The policy satisfied neither hawks nor doves. Yet, this 1967 "progress" campaign had, in effect, made implicit promises that no unpleasant surprises were in store.

Although they voiced misgivings, newsmen in Vietnam (or Washington) could not *prove* in 1967 that the Administration's professed optimism was overblown. They had to report what the Administration said. But there was an underlying journalistic resentment, especially in Washington, at being thus used, and, when the crisis came, Johnson was not given the benefit of the doubt, as Presidents usually are. As several Washington reporters later noted, the primary reaction of many newsmen in the capital after Tet was to indulge in retribution for prior manipulation by the Administration.[2] Thus, while formal ideology did not heavily flavor media treatment of Tet, to a rare degree the initial coverage reflected subjective reactions by newsmen—not only to the sights and circumstances of Tet itself, but also to the Administration's past conduct.

This coverage was also shaped by habit and convention. The press, and, most strikingly, television news since the early 1960s, have sought "themes" and "story lines" to routinize major developments and to make events intelligible. "Keep it simple," is the deskman's warning to reporters, as much for his own sake as for the reader's. Election campaigns are portrayed as horse races (with front runners and dark horses); votes on major issues in Congress are often defined as "defeats" or "victories" for the President; and, for a long time in the 1950s and 1960s, local struggles in Africa and Latin America were simplified as contests between "procommunists" and "anticommunists." These ingrained professional habits left newsmen ill-equipped to cope with the unusual ambiguities and uncertainties surrounding Tet. In Washington, the assault on the U.S. Embassy in Saigon came as a crisis piled on top of another (apparent) crisis—the dramatic seizure of the *Pueblo* by the North Koreans—which had preoccupied news managers for a week. Moreover, as we have noted,

President Johnson *did not seize the initiative* in terms of information or decision-making; and although Washington newsmen do not like to admit it, their dependence on the White House for a "news agenda" and a "frame of reference," especially in crisis, is considerable. When the President is vague, or delegates the discussion of bad news to subordinates (as Johnson largely did at Tet), without demonstrably responding to the crisis himself, the government seems incoherent, the future filled with uncertainty.

We have seen that in Vietnam, too, the circumstances for newsmen were at first ambiguous and uncertain. There was the personally threatening combat in Saigon, the looming drama of Khe Sanh, the destructive urban battle in Hue. There were the fragmentary reports of action in other towns and cities. And there was Westmoreland himself predicting a second wave. To newsmen accustomed to the relatively brief, localized rural battles that characterized the war until Tet, the very persistence of communist effort in Saigon, Hue, and Khe Sanh and along the highways was unsettling. The fate of the initially inaccessible countryside, the state of the long-neglected ARVN (suddenly a key actor), the intentions and capabilities of the foe were all question marks throughout much of February.

Could the official information machinery in Saigon have dispelled the ambiguities?

Certainly the daily "Five O'Clock Follies" and the fragmentary communiqués were inadequate for providing an overview of the countrywide trends or of ARVN performance (not included by MACOI). Indeed, the communiqués tended to mask both some enemy initiatives (in early February) and the allies' regaining of the tactical initiative (thereafter). Responding to a late 1968 survey, a number of journalistic veterans of the Tet period gave MACV a mixed report card. The Da Nang press center was faulted for "authoritarian handling" of reporters. MACV in Saigon was sharply (and appropriately) rebuked for its early "optimism" about the Hue battle and the state of security in Saigon. The two-week-long effort by MACV to show enemy defeat through detailed (and inflated) "body counts" and "kill ratios" was (again) cited as a blow to U.S. Mission "credibility." However, the New York *Times*'s Tom Buckley, who wrote many of his paper's Saigon war wrap-ups, was complimentary about the general MACV performance:

> MACV organization for press during the Tet offensive remained at extremely high level with respect to frequency of briefings, availability of

senior officers, logistics, and overall cooperation. Credibility was quite good, with exception of inflated casualty figures. It was an outstanding performance. JUSPAO less effective on all counts. . . . General Sidle was so good as to be miraculous. No other information officer approached him in competence, candor, and knowledgeability. For the rest, they did as well as they could in enormously difficult circumstances, but many seemed unequipped.[3]

For their part, Don Sider and Bob Wildau saw the need for: "A full-time private briefing room run by MACV in Saigon, and perhaps one at each corps headquarters, with the straight, current word on what is up, for major bureau chiefs or their representatives. . . . It would keep us honest, keep us up to date on how to disperse our people, and prevent us from filing stories that turn out to be wrong."[4]

The problem for MACV and JUSPAO in making such arrangements was the size and heterogeneity of the Saigon press corps, as Sidle and Zorthian frequently observed. On January 1, 1968, there were 181 Americans accredited as newsmen (plus 111 Vietnamese and 162 "Third Country" nationals); on February 2, there were 196 Americans (plus 116 Vietnamese and 174 others); on February 29, there were 248 Americans (119 Vietnamese and 260 others); by March 31, 1968, as the prospects of a climactic drama waned, the numbers had declined to 232 Americans, 123 Vietnamese, and 235 others.[5] It was difficult for MACV to include all—or even half—the Americans and still speak with candor about the current tactical situation, given the diverse professional and personal standards represented in the U.S. press corps. It was equally difficult to invite only "major bureau chiefs" to a regular briefing without strong protests from those excluded. In 1965–67, "major bureau chiefs" individually got to see Westmoreland and senior officials in Saigon by advance appointment, two to four times a year. At Tet, access was less easy, but, as Buckley noted, not prohibited. As we have observed earlier, those dozen backgrounders which CORDS, MACV, and the Marines did give to larger press groups at Tet received relatively little play at home, except when the journalistic focus was on future enemy threats.

In theory, one might have wished for a weekly summary of perceived regional military trends. Perhaps the strong local contrasts in tempo, persistence, and relative strength of enemy activity might have been underscored, and the gradual recovery of tactical initiative by U.S. forces in most areas made clear, along with the special character of the drawn-out Khe Sanh and Hue engagements. Yet, without censorship, one wonders how much detail MACV could have provided on the record. And, security aside, one wonders how well the MACV public information system, inevitably flawed, and geared to conventional official and journalistic needs for "particulars," would have been able in February to depict a fluid, dispersed combat pattern never before experienced in Vietnam. Most of all, one speculates that, given the suspicions and preoccupations of newsmen in Saigon and their bosses at home, a weekly MACV overview would have been greeted with indifference or extreme skepticism as a self-serving "handout."

In retrospect, after all is said and done, the problem for the major bureaus in Vietnam was not lack of *opportunity* to piece together the overall picture and dispel some confusion as time went on. It lay in their initial reactions to the Tet crisis, and in the subsequent preoccupation of most reporters and their managers with more compelling matters, such as Khe Sanh and upcoming enemy moves.

Faced with ambiguities and uncertainty, the major bureaus in Saigon, for the most part, reacted in two ways. The first generalized tendency was to follow standard Vietnam operating procedure, which in turn was conditioned by standard perceptions of "news." For newspapers and AP and UPI, this meant mining and processing the most dramatic elements out of the daily communiqués and briefings in Saigon. For everyone, it meant deploying reporters to the most dramatic action elsewhere. This approach throughout an episodic war had yielded both "hard news" and vivid human-interest "features" for print, and a steady flow of filmed vignettes, oftentimes film clichés, for televison. The tendency to head for "the action" (which noticeably faded among newsmen in Saigon in later years) was by no means universal in 1965–68. But it was common to the reporters most respected by their peers. Going to "the action" served the obvious professional requirements of seeing and experiencing the war one had been sent to cover; and it sustained a proud tradition in U.S. journalism. In the case of television, it also satisfied superiors' demands for GI combat stories. On another level, it legitimized (or seemed to legitimize) a newsman's claim to speak with authority on the war; it gave him a certain status. And the risks of brief exposure to danger justified his relative comfort amid so much courage and suffering.

Most newsmen in Vietnam, in their late twenties and thirties, sought the opportunity to witness a prolonged life-and-death drama of major importance to America. But their time horizons were short. Their focus was narrow. By temperament or training they were not "experts," systematic researchers, writers skilled in synthesis; they were adventurers and, to some extent, voyeurs; at their best they were also shrewd observers and interrogators, and perceptive tellers of tales. To them and their superiors, the inherent drama—and importance—of Saigon, Hue, and Khe Sanh were compelling, and obviously "news." And the concentration of journalistic manpower on these dramatic but isolated stories insured that they were treated at home as the significant "news." What else was worthy of sustained firsthand attention was less obvious; and the media in Vietnam committed major sins of omission as time went on.

The second generalized reaction by the major news bureaus in Saigon was in keeping with the more ambitious, more "intellectual" journalism of the late 1950s and 1960s. It was to "explain" or "interpret" what had happened and, implicitly or explicitly, to forecast the future, especially as the fighting at Hue and Khe Sanh dragged on.

The wire services were relatively constrained in this regard; in passing, to enliven their war wrap-ups, they dwelled on the possibilities of renewed anti-cities attacks or the prospect of a second Dienbienphu at Khe Sanh. Far less constrained were Time, and especially Newsweek, where "projecting the story" was a standard technique. And on television, similar projection was used to lend added "significance" to reporters' comments (e.g., "The war is no closer to an end tonight than it was this morning").

On the Times and, more markedly, the Post, some license had been given since the early 1950s to ordinary reporters (as opposed to columnists, whose independence was generally accepted) to "explain" events within the confines of conventional hard-news stories. Here, selected opinions and interpretations were often vaguely attributed to anonymous "officials," "insiders," "observers," or "senior officers," as in Time or Newsweek. Greater freedom was allowed to reporters when they wrote under the rubric of "news analysis" or "commentary." Foreign correspondents, faced with the task of explaining far-off events to American readers, were allowed the most leeway. They often went beyond observable events, attributed information, and quoted opinion to interpret developments on their own authority.

Such interpretative reporting had long been characteristic of the *Post*'s Washington coverage, occasionally to the point, in the early 1960s, where the analysis got more space and "play" than the hard news being analyzed. "News analysis" came to the *Times* in the 1950s, with James Reston among the first practitioners. The form caused early misgivings on the paper despite Reston's reputation for finding the facts, taking no sides, and eschewing the temptation to supply all the answers. But such fears eased. By Tet-1968, news analysis by *Times* reporters, especially in the Sunday "News of the Week in Review" section, was commonplace.

In the careful hands of Reston, Hanson Baldwin, Edwin Dale (the *Times* economist), and a few other specialists, the technique added considerably to reader understanding of complex matters. But no comparable competence existed among newsmen with regard to Vietnam. Indeed, as we have noted, both the war's circumstances and the media's own various organizational incentives worked against the acquisition of such competence in Vietnam (and Washington). Moreover, the problem in February 1968 for all would-be news analysts was that the Tet battlefields provided an insufficient "data base" from which to draw broad independent conclusions or to "project the story" in many areas. "Herd journalism" and the news focus on enemy threats and localized fighting in Saigon, Hue, and Khe Sanh—however important those battles might be—left many other crucial matters unexplored firsthand. Yet, the very existence of great uncertainty, added to the subjective responses noted earlier, appears to have impelled editors to publish, and reporters (and pundits) to compose, "analyses" of the crisis that would fill the vacuum. It proved a serious lapse of self-discipline. As we have seen, most analyses were the hasty reactions of the half-informed. Fewer than 15 percent of the *Times* and *Post* items about Vietnam were in explicit "commentary" categories, yet this segment of the coverage, often prominently displayed and "rebroadcast," accounted for a disproportionate share of both papers' sins of commission. And the "projection-analysis" technique, used so heavily on television and in *Newsweek,* produced more pervasive distortions.

These two immediate professional responses by major Vietnam news bureaus and their superiors back home—a focus of firsthand reporting on a few dramatic events, plus undisciplined "analysis" and "projection"—underlay the overall failure of the press and TV to cope with the formidable circumstances of February–March 1968. As often happens, these initial journalistic reactions set the tone and supplied the themes assigned to the crisis over the entire period.

The chronically short attention span of the media—four to six weeks in 1968—insured a feast-and-famine flow of information, aggravated by space and time limitations. As is usually the case in crisis, most space and "play" went to the Tet story early, when the least solid information was available. There was no institutional system within the media for keeping track of what the public had been told, no internal priority on updating initial impressions. As usual, the few catch-up or corrective stories later on were buried on back pages. This practice in turn gave Saigon correspondents little incentive to produce such stories. The *Post* was the most obvious example: On eight days in March, no story from Vietnam made page one. The networks cut their "Vietnam-related" weekday evening film reports: ABC went from 42 in the January 30–February 29 period to 24 in March; CBS, 38 to 17; NBC, 38 to 28 (according to Lichty's rough count based here, as elsewhere, on Defense Department television archives). For film reports out of Vietnam only, the networks dropped from 79 to 39. *Time* went from a weekly February average of 99.85 column inches of text on Vietnam at home and abroad to 71.87 in March; *Newsweek,* from 126.10 to 107.50.

The result was that the media tended to leave the shock and confusion of early February, *as then perceived,* "fixed" as the final impression of Tet, and thus as a framework for news judgment and public debate at home. At Tet, the press shouted that the patient was dying, then weeks later began to whisper that he somehow seemed to be recovering—whispers apparently not heard amid the clamorous domestic reaction to the initial shouts.

There is little disagreement among historians or even journalists that the dramatic Tet surprises of late January were indeed shocking —to official Washington and the public at home, and to the U.S. Embassy and the Presidential Palace in Saigon, to say nothing of urban South Vietnamese and U.S. newsmen caught in the fighting. But drama or shock does not automatically mean a decisive turn of events, in this case "defeat" or "demoralization" on the ground. At Tet, the media managers hastily assumed it did, and led their readers to do the same. A mind-set—most obvious in the selection of page-one stories, TV film, and newspaper photographs—quickly developed: Tet was a *disaster,* not only for the highly visible 10 percent of the South Vietnamese population caught up in the urban fighting, but, actually or imminently, for the allied armies, the pacification effort, the Thieu government. Tet, belying the Johnson Administration's "progress" campaign, *thereby* showed that the war was being "lost." Tet proved that the North Vietnamese were the "winners" and their foes the "losers." Tet was a triumph for the wily Giap—in South Vietnam.

Was anything other than allied "defeat" discernible to newsmen in February–March 1968 on the ground? The answer is: Yes, starting in late February. Earlier, the newsmen in Saigon called into question MACV's hasty cumulative totals of enemy losses, and noted contradictions between the first optimistic communiqués and the realities at Hue and on Saigon's outskirts. They were skeptical of Ambassador Bunker's early (but ultimately accurate) accounting of enemy failures (no procommunist uprisings, few ARVN defections). But they neglected to echo General Weyand's sensible warning in early February that it was premature to add up the final Tet score, good or bad; and, with the "disaster" mind-set, they pressed officials for predictions of future enemy initiatives—forgetting to keep posted on what was already happening as February ended.

Yet, after the recapture of Hue on February 24, the manpower was available, at least in the larger bureaus (AP, UPI, *Time,* the networks, the *Times*), to travel about for a systematic "second look." Moreover, the reporters were enormously helped by freedom from censorship—a freedom not enjoyed by their counterparts in both World Wars and Korea, or in coverage of the Arab-Israeli wars. Thanks to official cooperation and U.S. air mobility, they had unprecedented access to the battlefield. And they had facilities for relatively rapid transmission of film and prose. By March 1, it would have been possible to observe and to report that: (1) enemy military pressure had slackened, except at Khe Sanh; (2) the fighting was shifting back to the countryside; (3) ARVN, despite its 50 percent strength level and some extraordinarily incompetent senior leadership, had held together and fought back; (4) pacification, although hit hard, was not "dead"; and (5), amid many problems and much human suffering, urban recovery was beginning here and there. In short, it was a mixed picture, but clearly neither a military nor a psychological "disaster."

Time made a good effort to catch up. The other big organizations did not. Most of the scattered *Post* and *Times* catch-up stories— dealing with localized recovery—missed page one and landed inside the paper. In mid-March, *Newsweek,* CBS, and NBC were still portraying North Vietnamese troops as holding the "initiative," if only because of a fixation with Khe Sanh. Drama was perpetuated at the expense of information.

Competition did not make for more sophisticated journalism. The fierce rivalry between UPI and AP (with the outcomes judged on the basis of clients' choices of competing agency stories) and among networks (judged on the basis of news program audience "ratings") did not lead to breadth of coverage, and hence to a comprehensive countrywide portrait of a countrywide war. It led, as often happens, to clustering of rival newsmen at the same places, so that each agency "matched" the other on the same story. The wire services put out Saigon war wrap-ups competing for "impact" back home. Competition between NBC and CBS seemed at times a contest over who could shout the same words more loudly.

But in other media, where short-range competitive success was harder to quantify—and where *Time* and the *Times* clearly outgunned their putative rivals in Vietnam—the pressures were less severe, and duplication less frequent. Indeed, in terms of *staff*-written reports from Vietnam outside Saigon, the *Times* and *Post* overlapped relatively little after the first three weeks of February.

Traditional American journalistic skills—notably in reporting what can be seen or heard—served the print media well at Da Nang, Hue, in the Delta, and in some of the Saigon street fighting. AP's John Wheeler and others reported accurately from Khe Sanh, especially during the early stages of the siege of that base. But the newsmen, by and large, did not *see* very much of the countrywide Tet offensive or its aftermath. There were many gaps in their information (as in that initially available to officialdom). Yet, most news managers at home were apparently willing, even eager, to supply their audiences with quick, imaginative descriptions of the strategy of the "wily Giap," the psychological impact of Tet on South Vietnamese morale, the future of the Thieu regime, the "death throes" of pacification, the enemy's "awesome" weaponry—all mostly based on guesswork and secondhand sources in Saigon or Washington.

Most important, throughout Tet, the great bulk of the wire-service output actually used by U.S. newspapers (and its refined versions in network scripts) and of the newspapers' page-one Vietnam material did not come from eyewitness reports. It was secondhand or thirdhand information—reprocessed, as we have seen, several times over.

To produce its war wrap-ups, the UPI, in particular, added color and spice—"words that pop out at you"—to the bare fragments. The Saigon rewrite man sought a specific—a bombing raid, a downed aircraft, a montage of enemy mortar attacks, a "Dienbienphu angle"—to give his lead paragraphs competitive eye appeal for jaded stateside deskmen.† All this was conventional journalistic technique, but the accent on such specifics first exaggerated and then belittled the tempo of the war during February and March, since no context was provided. It was "news," but not information. It did not tell us how the war, overall, was going.

Even if one excludes the first week of Tet fighting (which heavily involved Saigon), the preponderance of Saigon stories is striking: 80 percent of all wire-service output (war wrap-ups, official statements, etc.), 80 percent of all *Times* and *Post* staff-written stories—but only 20 percent of TV film reports. (The network anchorman's nightly script, on the other hand, was largely based on wire-service Saigon war wrap-ups, and this script supplied two-thirds of all TV "reports" about Vietnam.) In the print media, news managers did indeed like eyewitness action stories, but unless it was Khe Sanh or Hue, the Saigon "headquarters" dateline got the page-one play.

Reporting: Superior and Otherwise

During the February–March 1968 period, there were individual instances of superior journalistic performance, in terms of supplying information as opposed to simple "drama." Many reporters for the major media produced *some* able journalism, whatever their sins on other occasions. And none, notably including this writer, was without sin. The "pluses" inform us as much as the "minuses."

† "One very fast gatekeeper [editor] took an average of four seconds to handle [read, and then decide on and indicate the changes he wanted made] a story of 225 words. Shorter items used would take two seconds, longer ones ten seconds at a maximum. The average for [such] observed gatekeepers was about six seconds per story selected for use.

"This is a virtuoso performance of decision-making. Judgment is exercised almost instantly without time for reflection or references. Whatever values the gatekeeper brings to these decisions he brings by reflex." (Ben H. Bagdikian, *The Information Machines: Their Impact on Men and the Media* [New York: Harper & Row, 1971], p. 103.)

Perhaps the consistently best reporting from Vietnam came from Charles Mohr of the New York *Times*. Mohr's prior experience in Vietnam (dating back to 1963) was, no doubt, a major asset; he was skeptical of rumor and of instant claims of "victory" or "disaster." But what best served Mohr and his readers were his professional self-discipline, clear prose, and willingness to see for himself. His "spot" coverage of the January 31 U.S. Embassy fight, the ARVN action in the Saigon suburbs, and the recapture of the Hue Citadel stand out as calm, comprehensive reporting under severe stress.

Rarer still at Tet was Mohr's instinct for the second look to clear up first impressions; for example, he explicitly set the *Times* record straight on the Vietcong's failure to get into the embassy chancery, took a helicopter ride over Saigon to assess the damage to the city, and reported the confused beginning of recovery in pacification. He wrote accurately about military matters, notably Westmoreland's tactics and strategy. He rarely indulged in speculation about the future. Mohr was not without error: He, too, had a bout (in Saigon) of "Dienbienphu fever" over Khe Sanh. But, during Tet, as before, his reporting stood out as superior. Much of it never made Page One.

(The one Pulitzer Prize for work done during the Tet offensive went to Eddie Adams, the AP photographer who produced the dramatic photographs of General Loan shooting a Vietcong suspect on a Saigon street. A Pulitzer Prize *related* to Tet events went to Seymour Hersh of Dispatch News Service in 1970 for his publicizing of the March 1968 My Lai massacre; interrogating ex-GIs and using Army sources in the United States, Hersh never set foot in South Vietnam.)

There were able "information" performances—within the confines of each medium—by others as manifested in some but not all of their stories on local developments at Tet. To recall some examples:

The Saigon coverage: AP's Peter Arnett; the *Times*'s Joseph Treaster; NBC's cameramen at the U.S. Embassy; *Newsweek*'s Francois Sully; UPI's Eugene Risher.

The early Da Nang fighting: CBS's George Syvertsen; NBC's Ron Nessen.

The Hue battle: AP's John Lengel and George McArthur; the *Times*'s Gene Roberts and Tom Johnson; the *Post*'s Lee Lescaze; CBS's Don Webster; ABC's Bill Brannigan; *Time*'s David Greenway and Karsten Prager.

The Khe Sanh siege: AP's John Wheeler; Merton Perry of *Newsweek;* Don Sider of *Time.*

The Delta post-mortems: the *Post*'s Lee Lescaze and George Wilson.

Pacification and recovery: the *Times*'s Bernard Weinraub and Joseph Treaster; the *Post*'s Stanley Karnow; *Time*'s Wallace Terry; UPI's Dan Southerland.

[For the record, others should be mentioned: William Tuohy of the Los Angeles *Times* (Delta); Don Oberdorfer of Knight newspapers (Hue); John Carroll of the Baltimore *Sun* (Khe Sanh); and Peter Kann of the *Wall Street Journal* (U.S. Embassy fight).]

Yet, it must be emphasized, even the best reportorial efforts of individuals had, in the main, a very narrow focus. Outside Saigon, newsmen usually produced "vignettes" of a small part of a larger, localized battle or its aftermath. These vignettes generally were drawn from, at most, a day or two of necessarily limited observation and interviews; there was seldom a deliberate longer-term effort to gain broader knowledge. And much good work got little "play" at home.

In retrospect, the most coordinated performance by a news bureau in Vietnam was turned in by *Time*'s reinforced eight-man reporting team. Bureau Chief William Rademaekers did not leave the capital during Tet, violating *Time* tradition. But as he later noted, "I had very good people, and I deployed them." His reporters were at all the major stories, and went out after the not-so-obvious as well. *Time* coverage, as we have noted, was hardly flawless. But no other big news bureau matched that magazine's effort to pin down—in late February and March—the military and civilian situation in the hinterland. After intensive condensation and "processing," the published version of this story ("After 'Tet': Measuring and Repairing the Damage," March 15, 1968) did not fully reflect the detailed reporting in all four regions of Vietnam by Rademaekers' people. There were minor errors of fact. But it was the most comprehensive such report to appear in print during Tet. *Time,* to be sure, had the advantage of weekly, not daily, deadlines. Its bureau long outnumbered rival *Newsweek*'s by two to one, and enjoyed vastly superior communications with the home office. *Time* did not throw away these advantages. And its editors at home, involved in debate, tended to cancel out extreme judgments most of the time; they relied more heavily than usual on the reporting from Vietnam.[6]

In contrast to the tightly coordinated *Time* effort, the New York

Times bureau, biggest of the newspaper bureaus, functioned more or less as an assemblage of lone operatives. Mohr, sent in to supervise new Bureau Chief Gene Roberts' break-in period, was a superb reporter but, as is often the case with newsmen, no manager. The six *Times* reporters covered Saigon, Hue, and Da Nang through February, but in March there was little effort to keep an eye on the country as a whole. Mohr, Roberts, Weinraub, Treaster, Tom Buckley, and Tom Johnson produced some excellent work, but 80 percent of the staff-written stories during March were filed out of Saigon. Much catch-up field reporting was not done. And there was little coordination with Washington.

The *Post,* with two men (briefly reinforced in February by Stanley Karnow, and then helped out in March by George Wilson), was simply too undermanned to handle the rush of events in February. The war wrap-ups had to be left largely to the wire services; and the *Times* inevitably produced much more staff coverage of Hue and Saigon than did the *Post.* But the tired *Post* men made efforts in late February and March to check out the hinterland and the ARVN performance. No comprehensive overview resulted, but some of the post-mortems challenged the conventional wisdom. The *Times* beat the *Post,* but not as severely as it could have.

The wire services were perhaps the most disciplined of the major media in terms of generalized "projection" and explicit commentary. They put their manpower into often superb coverage of the initial Saigon fighting and the Hue battle, and, in the case of AP, made a big effort at Khe Sanh. AP, in particular, gave officialdom its say, covering the U.S. Mission press conferences and the March announcements of the Thieu government. But the wires made relatively little effort to cover the nondramatic and, as a result, showed a very narrow range: official statements, "human interest" features, and the "action story" (with photograph). The Saigon war wrap-ups—the main offering to wire clients—were the principal "big picture" stories, and their built-in inadequacies have been demonstrated. In effect, the wire services' gravest sins, like those of the newspapers, in Vietnam were those of *omission.*

The three network television bureaus shared the wire services' penchant for the dramatic. CBS put more stress on Khe Sanh than its rivals, but NBC broadcast more Vietnam film.[7] The fleeting bits and pieces presented on the TV screen—the anonymous faces, voices, and sights of the war—buttressed by a reporter's hasty "analysis" or a lame interview, did not lend themselves to information but to vignettes or "short stories" which were often represented as "microcosms" of the whole war. Television's show-business tradition put little premium on breadth of coverage, fact-finding, or context. Brave as he often was, the television journalist in Vietnam was preoccupied with film and logistics, with little incentive to seek out sources or investigate nonfilmable aspects of events. Yet, like the anchorman back home, he had to pose on camera as an authority, dominating what he described. His commentary was thematic, and often highly speculative. The TV correspondent tended to tell viewers more than he knew or could know. Overall, then as now, television producers seemed preoccupied with impact, and to an even greater degree than their counterparts in the print media. As Michael Arlen wrote:

> Propaganda appears to be the vocabulary that people [in TV] have simply come to feel is best suited to the times—as if in considering an actual situation today (for example, Negro rioting in Newark or the burning of a village in Vietnam) one had made some sort of explicit decision that, although the actuality of the situation was real and important, what was more real and more important was what the [audience] could be brought to feel about it.[8]

In Washington, a city afloat with "leaks" and speculation, the *Times*'s Neil Sheehan unearthed one key military rationale for defending Khe Sanh (as a potential jump-off point for an invasion of Laos); and Max Frankel, John Finney, Hedrick Smith, and Tom Wicker wrote comprehensive pieces on Congressional and Administration reaction to Tet events. AP's Fred Hoffman and the *Times*'s William Beecher and Hanson Baldwin did solid work on Pentagon reactions and policy issues. The *Post*'s Murrey Marder was alone in noting the shift from triumph to caution in Radio Hanoi's emphasis. *Newsweek*'s Pentagon reporters vainly warned the home office against overreaction; while the *Time* bureau, led by John Steele, conveyed the inner White House gloom and concern. But most of the voluminous Washington reporting-cum-analysis, as usual, was not up to that from Vietnam in terms of *information* about Vietnam. Of the pundits, and the network anchormen, little should be said here, except that Joseph Alsop early reported the threat to Khe Sanh (which he later visited), and James Reston accurately sensed the late-March Washington policy atmosphere.

However, the relatively unimpressive performance of most Washington bureaus and of the *Post* national staff during the Tet period stemmed in part from a preoccupation with the politics of the Vietnam issue in an election year. Reporters accurately perceived the "siege atmosphere" in the White House and the tension on Capitol Hill; only the *Times* published much "policy" reporting. To editors, commentators, and producers, the chronic gap between Washington-New York perceptions (journalistic or official) on the one hand, and the realities of the battleground in Vietnam on the other, should have been clear by 1968. Nevertheless, we have seen that the *Times* and *Post,* in particular, published considerable "analysis" and secondhand reportage, much of it clouded by error and hypothesis, on the military-political situation in Vietnam, written far from the scene. Moreover, in the absence of detailed knowledge of the situation on the ground—and genuine specialists on Vietnamese affairs were rare—instant "experts" were created by the media at home. These press-anointed experts or advocates, hawk or dove, had two major advantages over the White House: (1) their statements were quoted and then forgotten without prejudice to their "expert" standing; and (2) they did not get challenged on their "facts." In their rush to judgment, the instant experts enjoyed rare immunity from journalistic skepticism.

The prevailing accent on the negative, or on disagreement—however partisan, irrelevant, or uninformed—with the government, varied among news organizations. Television provided perhaps the least balance, victimized by its thematic imperatives and the limitations of time. The news magazines had the most opportunity to provide balance and context: *Time,* for reasons already discussed, often did so, while *Newsweek,* edging to an outright editorial stand, more often did not. Newsmen and their critics may argue endlessly about what constitutes "balance" or even "negative" and "positive."

What we sought to discover, with the benefit of hindsight, was how the crude negative and positive trends, regardless of specific factual errors, varied over time, and with each medium. By the first week of March, in terms of the *knowable* improvement in the situation on the ground, something close to a balance of negative and positive statements concerning *that* situation (as opposed to the domestic political repercussions) should have begun to appear in each of the media. But in fact, that mix was not even approached in reporting from Vietnam in the wires and newspapers until mid-March, and on TV until late March. This lag may in turn have contributed to the more persistent negative trend in the newspapers' domestic reporting and commentary about Vietnam, which did not moderate. By the time the reporting from Vietnam became more positive (and less abundant), much of the commentary and space at home was being devoted to Vietnam as an *issue* within the Democratic Party. *Newsweek,* as we have noted, remained *more* negative; *Time* more or less followed the gradual March upturn of the newspaper and wire-service reporting from Vietnam. The negative accent remained strong in pictorial treatment. Of the television networks, CBS, with its steady emphasis on Khe Sanh, was most negative; ABC the most positive; NBC mixed.

To varying degrees, the persistent accent in March on the negative stemmed from important failures to "catch-up," from mind-set, from poor self-discipline by commentators in Washington and newsmen in Vietnam, from short attention span, from the traditional search for "drama."[9]

The Role of the Managers

Vietnam policy issues aside, the Tet experience makes clear the requirements for maximum candor on the part of the President and his spokesmen *before* crisis and for Presidential coherence *during* crisis: Congress and the public cannot rely only on the specialized reactions of the press and TV to threatening events. The Johnson Administration failed to meet these requirements.

But, ultimately, the remedies for most of the weaknesses evident in the 1968 performance of the major news organizations lie with the media managers. Reporters and sub-editors, the myths of the craft notwithstanding, are highly responsive to firm managerial direction, either implicit or explicit. To be sure, reporters may fasten on some events and neglect others; department heads engage in bureaucratic bargaining; habits and conventions of deskmen ("gatekeepers") are strong. Budgets and owner predilection may limit managerial initiatives. Sensitivity to competitive audience ratings (in TV) and to the pattern of client response (in the wire services) may influence news selection. But, particularly in newspapers and news magazines, "operational" policies are what the top editor and his senior editors say they are.

The February–March 1968 experience reflected in good measure a number of management policy failures persisting into the troubled 1970s. There were—and are—no universally accepted "objective standards" in the news business. However, already at Tet, there was a notable lack of management insistence on the "balance," professional discipline, and respect for the "naked facts" so often invoked as journalistic virtues. There was also a curious lack of imagination and common sense.

What did the media manager at home know when the first AP bulletins came off the ticker on January 31? Whether or not he was an "expert" on the war, he knew, or should have known from harsh experience, that in the first days of any battle, any crisis, no one (including his staffers in Saigon in this instance) has a clear picture; that most reactions will be partisan and off-the-cuff; that political Washington, like Wall Street, tends to overreact to big news, especially big bad news. Especially in crisis, even the most authoritative sources speaking in all objectivity may be victims of the fog of war or of sheer distance from the action—a gap in perception and communication which always separates headquarters from field. The manager should have reacted with wariness to first reports—especially in terms of initial "play" and receptivity to "instant analysis"—expecting the situation to clarify, and pressing his correspondents in Vietnam for such clarification, as time went on.[10]

Yet, we found few examples of such calls for clarification to newsmen in Saigon or Washington. By all accounts, queries on substance were rare (except in the *Time* and *Newsweek* system) and largely reflected the conventional instant wisdom at home: Wasn't the Administration covering up something? Wasn't Khe Sanh the important story, a potential Dienbienphu? Most managers did not exercise the traditional newspaper city editor's function of questioning a reporter's more sweeping assertions (a function painstakingly revived, for example, by prudent *Post* senior editors during much of the dogged 1972–73 Watergate reporting by Carl Bernstein and Bob Woodward). Instead, it would appear, some managers joined in the overreaction to Tet, and even exploited it, perhaps because they no longer felt that the Administration could supply them with a clear context or agenda for Vietnam "news," and they had no coherent framework of their own. Amid the uncertainty and clamor at home, consciously or unconsciously, many managers simply adopted the "disaster" scenario, and thus encouraged subordinates to do the same.

For lack of coherent managerial concepts, issues open and close swiftly in the media, like bad plays on Broadway. Only compelling dramas like Watergate and Presidential election campaigns enjoy a sustained run. It would seem that even the managers of serious newspapers and magazines have come to see television, with its emotive appeal and its fads, as a threatening rival worthy of closer emulation. At Tet, the short managerial attention span brought down the curtain while the play was still going on.

Increasingly painful limitations of time, space, and money, and the competitive quest for audiences seem to preclude easy recipes for better performance. As critics often forget, the major media do not constitute an organized, unified information conglomerate, but an array of relatively small, disparate, rival commercial organizations engaged in hurriedly assembling, variously processing, and distributing "news" which, as Walter Lippmann pointed out, is not—and cannot be—the same commodity as "truth." This frail "system" is easily overloaded in crisis, and tilted, and it was overloaded and tilted at Tet.

Yet, some compensatory remedies emerge from examination of the Tet experience. In crisis, the major media manager can remind his producers or deskmen—those harassed gatekeepers—of the need for skepticism, of the likelihood that the "facts" will change and need explicit correction. He can underline the difference between "drama" and "significance," and allocate space or time accordingly. He can discourage instant analysis and prediction. He can order his dispersed reporters to inform one another on the state of current knowledge and to remember the need for a future overview. He can insist on intense questioning of all actors in domestic debate. On television, he can see that a minimum of context is supplied to film reports ("no microcosms" is a good rule). He can order that a running summary be kept of his organization's pertinent news output, in order to detect gaps which need filling in or initial impressions which require fresh investigation.

In slack periods, the manager often must spur his subordinates on. But in times of crisis, the audience is hungry, and journalistic adrenalin flows freely; the leader's duty then is to challenge hasty judgments, while stressing dispassionate inquiry and persistent legwork. In short, he should reinforce the proclaimed journalistic virtues.

These remedies are modest, but they curb excess. They do not preclude vivid prose or "good film." They do not bar vigorous reporting. They should not inhibit sharp questioning of officialdom or efforts to unearth policy-in-the-making. They do not cost money or require a revolutionary upgrading of reportorial talent and training. But they require something more of managers than visceral reactions to events, "issues," and personalities. They require consistent leadership, imagination, some steady intellectual effort, and a strong awareness of the limited capacity of journalism to provide the public with broad knowledge on short notice.

Few models of such managerial leadership exist in the 1970s. Major newspapers and magazines, in particular, seem caught in identity crises; old, often constricting traditions have been eroded without being replaced by coherent new concepts. Since James Reston stepped down as Washington bureau chief and influential philosopher-king of the *Times* in 1964, there have been no towering figures of serious American journalism for other managers (and reporters) to emulate or dispute and few firm operational philosophies to debate or imitate.

In view of all these factors, unsatisfactory performance in another surprise crisis or near-crisis appears likely. The major media's various operating limitations and susceptibilities are seldom examined by managers, even inside their own organizations. Criticism, however mild, from outside groups (e.g., the National News Council) is too often greeted with resentment or disdain. The prospect is for a continuation of current volatile styles, always with the dark possibility in crisis that, if the managers do not themselves take action, then outsiders—the courts, the Federal Communications Commission, or Congress—will seek to apply remedies of their own. But a free society deserves better.

Notes

Chapter 1: The Press Corps in Vietnam

1. *The Making of a Quagmire* (New York: Random House, 1965), p. 319. For an evocative, detailed memoir of the "madness," "camaraderie," and "parasitic" qualities of the combat reporters in Vietnam in 1968, see Michael Herr's "The War Correspondent: A Reappraisal," *Esquire* (Apr. 1970), p. 95. Herr wrote, "We all had roughly the same position on the war; we were in it, and that was a position."

2. In *The Press and Foreign Policy* (Princeton: Princeton University Press, 1963), Bernard C. Cohen noted some survey results. One analysis of five newspapers circulating in April 1960 in Madison, Wisconsin, showed that "foreign news" took up 2.6 percent of the news "hole" in the local *Capital Times* (less than four columns a day), 6 percent in the highly regarded Milwaukee *Journal* (12 columns a day), and 10 percent in the New York *Times* (26 columns a day). AP alone produced some 22,000 words (roughly 27 columns) daily of foreign news in 1952–53, during U.S. involvement in the Korean War. But during the 1960s the average newspaper used the equivalent of about five columns daily of foreign news from all sources. In all but a handful of newspapers, Cohen found that "the presumption on the news desks runs against foreign stories and against complicated foreign policy issues."

3. MACV Weekly Report, Jan. 19, 1968.

4. MACV Accreditation List, Jan. 1968.

5. For a list of major media and their Saigon staffs, as of April 1, 1968, reflecting Tet reinforcements, see Appendix XXXVI, *Big Story*, 1977 Westview Press edition.

6. These audience figures are for the period October–November 1968 and come from Control Data's Advertising Research Bureau. The figures represent men and women over 18 years old who viewed the evening television news shows.

7. The conventional, tank-led 1972 Easter offensive launched by the North Vietnamese—after the effective departure of most U.S. ground forces—lent itself to far more clean-cut reporting and less distortion, since prolonged battlefield confrontations were the norm, not the "symbolic" exception.

8. The peak enemy bombardment at Con Thien was 1,065 rounds on July 2, 1967, according to USAF historians. See also Capt. Moyers S. Shore, USMC, *The Battle for Khe Sanh*, prepared for the Historical Branch, G-3 Division, U.S. Marine Corps (Washington, D.C.: Government Printing Office, 1969).

9. In 1967, ARVN reported 12,176 battle deaths, as against 9,378 for U.S. forces. (Source: Department of Defense.)

10. Based on U.S. advisors' ratings, as relayed privately by MACV officials, the 18th, 25th, and 5th ARVN Divisions around Saigon were cited as of poor quality; yet according to U.S. advisors, from October through December 1968, only eight U.S. newsmen out of 170 accredited visited any of them. In January 1969 I was the first American newsman to visit the 18th Division since the previous May.

11. Peter Kann of the *Wall Street Journal* and Lee Lescaze of the Washington *Post* were among the exceptions.

12. See F. M. Kail, *What Washington Said* (New York: Harper & Row, 1973) for a useful survey of public rhetoric on Vietnam by leading U.S. officials in 1949–69.

13. Professor Allan E. Goodman of Clark University observed that Vietnam received "little serious scholarship," despite the campus clamor. He reported that only 22 Ph.D. dissertations were written on Vietnam in 1954–68 out of a total of 7,615 written in the fields of modern history, international relations, and political science at U.S. universities. See Goodman's "Vietnam and the Limits of Scholarly Intervention," *Freedom at Issue*, no. 21 (Sept.–Oct. 1973), 19.

14. Joe McGinniss, "Going Back to Vietnam," *Bulletin of the American Society of Newspaper Editors*, no. 551 (May–June 1971), 4.

15. "Continuing Study: Report of the Foreign News Committee," APME *Red Book* (1968), pp. 118–24.

16. Elmer W. Lower, "Cost of Same Day Coverage: How They Get the Story Home," in the annual magazine of the Overseas Press Club of America, *Dateline: Moving the News*, 9, no. 1 (1967), 45. Emphasis added.

17. Kurt Volkert, "Combat Cameraman Vietnam," *Dateline: 1918–1968*, 12, no. 1 (1968), 97–98. Emphasis added.

18. Cited by William Small in *To Kill A Messenger* (New York: Hastings House, 1970), p. 99. Emphasis added.

19. *Newsweek*, Sept. 8, 1967. Offensive to South Vietnamese pride, the integration notion was also never appealing to Westmoreland because it

would add to his headquarters' burdens, make ARVN more dependent on the United States, and fuel communist charges that ARVN was a "puppet army."

20. On May 5, 1969, in a lecture at Memphis, Elliott discussed his magazine's "beneficial subjectivity" on the civil rights issue in 1967, and added that "no such consensus existed among us at that time, for example, on the subject of Vietnam." But at Tet, "common ground began to form among us [sic]. The result, in early March of 1968, was Newsweek's second excursion into advocacy . . . which we began with the headline 'More of the Same Won't Do' [and featuring on the cover, "The Agony of Khe Sanh"]. Within weeks, of course, President Johnson had announced the partial bombing halt and his own decision to stand down. I like to think that in the weeks that preceded that famous speech, Newsweek's voice was not ignored by the decisionmakers in Washington." Published in Howard K. Smith et al., The News Media—A Service and A Force, ed. Festus J. Viser (Memphis: Memphis State University Press, 1970), pp. 28–31.

21. The Times did, however, make a practice of alternating tours of duty between the New York desk and the Soviet Union for its "No. 2" men in Moscow. Correspondents going to Moscow also got time off for language training.

22. See Topping's highly readable memoir, Journey Between Two Chinas (New York: Harper & Row, 1972).

23. Shortly after Tet, with the wisdom of hindsight, several of us concluded, after long discussions, that the ideal minimum newspaper bureau for Vietnam during the 1964–69 period would be manned by five "Yankee" reporters—one in each of the three more remote corps areas, one "swing man," and one man in Saigon—plus a Vietnamese reporter, a night dictationist, an American secretary, and a messenger boy. This would make possible realistic wrap-ups and quick exploitation of news tips. This argument bore some fruit in 1972 during Hanoi's Easter offensive; then, through reinforcements of old Vietnam hands from Washington, the Post fielded five reporters in Vietnam, the New York Times, eight. For this and other reasons, coverage improved.

Chapter 2: Prelude

1. In a prescient article, Don Oberdorfer reported the vulnerability of the Administration's support to any adverse dramatic turns on the Vietnam battlefield. See "The Wobble on the War on Capitol Ilill," The New York Times Magazine, Dec. 17, 1967, p. 30. See also Oberdorfer's Tet!, (New York: Doubleday & Co., 1971), pp. 83–86.

2. This figure is exclusive of economic assistance. See "Impact of the Vietnam War," Committee on Foreign Relations, U.S. Senate, prepared by

Foreign Affairs Division, Congressional Research Service, Library of Congress, June 30, 1971.

3. Oberdorfer, *Tet!*, p. 158.

4. For a complete transcript, see "LBJ: 'Time Has Come for . . . New, Fresh Look at Dissent,' " the Washington *Post*, Nov. 18, 1967, p. A8; the New York *Times* also printed the full text.

5. Bunker's figure of 67 percent under "government control" got into the Washington *Post* ("Bunker Reports War Gain," Nov. 14, 1967, p. A1) and got into the New York *Times* ("Bunker Reports Gains," Nov. 15, 1967, p. 1).

6. Komer was less optimistic here than in other press appearances; he did not claim that "hearts and minds"—a phrase that made newsmen snicker —had been won; he said it was hard to "assess" progress; he stressed "hamlet protection," not the new wells and good roads and "revolutionary development" so heavily emphasized in 1965–66. But few of these nuances got into the stories about what Komer said. He, Bunker, and other officials cited the 67 percent figure, and that got the attention of the press, as the White House, no doubt, anticipated. American newsmen prefer statistics, even if they doubt their validity, to nuances "which just confuse the reader."

7. The "enclave" alternative to Westmoreland's strategy was repeatedly advanced by Lt. Gen. James Gavin (USA-Ret.) and, in various forms, by Professor John K. Galbraith and some middle-echelon Pentagon civilians even during Tet. It was not taken seriously by newsmen in Saigon.

8. Westmoreland did not, of course, disclose his repeated requests for far more men (200,000 more) than the White House felt it was politically feasible to mobilize and send, or his conviction that a broader strategy (e.g., operations into Laos and Cambodia) was required to shorten the war. See Mike Gravel, ed., The Senator Gravel Edition: *The Pentagon Papers*, 4 vols. (Boston: Beacon Press, 1971), 4:363–65.

9. "The New Vietnam War Plan," the Washington *Post*, Nov. 26, 1967, p. B6.

10. Emphasis added. This reference to the December 1944 German offensive through the weakest U.S. sector in the Ardennes was repeated *after* Tet by General Westmoreland in his February 25, 1968, AP interview and in a briefing with newsmen on March 6.

11. Source: Department of the Army.

12. Lyndon Baines Johnson, The Vantage Point: Perspectives of the Presidency 1963–1969 (New York: Holt, Rinehart and Winston, 1971), p. 379.

13. See R. W. Apple's story from Saigon, "U.S. Said to Press Sharply for Good Vietnam Reports," the New York *Times*, Jan. 1, 1968, p. 1.

14. Letter to the author, Apr. 24, 1970.

15. Komer, a better manager, pre-Tet, than prognosticator, told this reporter, and Bernard Kalb of CBS, in September 1967 that he expected the sheer weight of allied materiel and manpower to begin to tilt the balance in pacification by the beginning of 1968.

16. The stories were: "Re-examining the Conduct of the War," *Life*, Jan. 5, 1968, pp. 4–5; "How Goes the War?" *Newsweek*, Jan. 1, 1968, pp. 17–29; and "The War: Frontier Offensive," *Time*, Dec. 22, 1967, pp. 15–16.

17. "Captured Documents Indicate a Major Red Strategy Shift," the Washington *Post*, Dec. 15, 1967.

18. "Hanoi Seen Aiming for Talks on Red Terms, after Attack," the Washington *Post*, Jan. 8, 1968.

19. "Foe Seeks to Sway U.S. Public," the New York *Times*, Dec. 27, 1967, p. 1.

20. *Time*, Jan. 5, 1968, p. 31.

21. Statement before the Senate Armed Services Committee on the FY 1969–73 Defense Program and 1969 Defense Budget, Jan. 22, 1968.

22. Letter to the author, Apr. 24, 1970.

23. "Footnotes on the Vietnam Dispatches," *The New York Times Magazine*, Oct. 20, 1968, p. 34.

24. On December 30, 1967, Foreign Minister Nguyen Duy Trinh announced in a speech in Hanoi that the North Vietnamese government "will" sit down to talks with the United States if "bombing and all other acts of war against North Vietnam stop unconditionally." Much was made over the phrasing—"will" instead of "could" as in an earlier offer of Trinh on January 28, 1967.

·25. Reported by William Tuohy in the Los Angeles *Times*, in a story filed from Saigon, January 9. Ambassador Komer was to make the last such pre-Tet analysis; he predicted steady progress in pacification in a press conference on January 24.

26. There were, of course, no allied defensive "lines" in South Vietnam.

27. It was one of the few times when *Newsweek's* favorite word, "ominously," turned out to be totally justified. Emphasis added.

28. The Miami *Herald*, Jan. 12, 1968, p. 1.

29. According to Westmoreland's aides, COMUSMACV (Commander, U.S. Military Assistance Command, Vietnam) met with Weyand on January 11, 1968, to discuss the enemy's pressure. On the 13th, planned operations along the Cambodian border were put off. On the 15th, warnings were sent to local U.S. forces that attacks on Hue might be expected. A countrywide alert was sounded on January 22 for U.S. troops, and on January 24 Defense Secretary McNamara canceled a Tet total bombing halt over the North, allowing U.S. bombers to hit as far north as Vinh in the Panhandle.

On January 8, 1968, according to Westmoreland's aides, the first of two significant meetings was held with Vietnamese officials to discuss the Tet holiday cease-fire. Westmoreland asked for no cease-fire at all. Gen. Cao Van Vien, chief of the Joint General Staff, said he would try to limit the truce to 24 hours.

On January 15, President Thieu, in meetings with U.S. officials, including Westmoreland, made clear through Vien that he was reluctant to cancel the 48-hour Tet cease-fire: it would produce a poor reaction among his troops and play into the hands of the communists. However, he agreed to a 36-hour truce. And, presumably, made plans to visit his in-laws in My Tho in the Delta at Tet.

30. *The Viet Cong Tet Offensive, 1968* (Saigon, 1969), pp. 24–30, 74.
31. Robert L. Pisor, "Saigon's Fighting MPs," *Army* (Apr. 1968), p. 41.
32. Westmoreland later wrote: "Owing to an apparent mixup in coordination, the enemy attack was launched in I and II Corps 24 hours ahead of the attack in the remainder of the country. This gave us additional warning, but still did not reveal the nature of his plans in the Saigon area." (Adm. U. S. Grant Sharp and Gen. William C. Westmoreland, *Report on the War in Vietnam* [Washington, D.C.: Government Printing Office, 1969], p. 158.)
33. Letter to the author, Oct. 22, 1970.
34. Yet, as it developed, the Vietcong attacked areas in II Corps unaffected by the troop shift. A similar failure to keep up with details of friendly order of battle led this writer to report from Da Nang four days earlier that 3rd Marine Division headquarters had been moved from Dong Ha, within artillery range of the DMZ, south to Quang Tri. This was not true. Only the division "rear" and helicopters had gone to Quang Tri, where Westmoreland had (foresightedly) built a new airstrip for C-130 transports and helicopters.

Chapter 3: First Reports

1. Letter to the author, June 22, 1970.
2. The numbers following the dispatches indicate the time—e.g., as here, 2:20 p.m.,—that each message went on the AP wire.
3. Arnett wrote: "Jacobson, who spent most of his years in Vietnam with the U.S. military and now is a civilian, said at 4:30 a.m. in a telephone interview that one U.S. Marine had been wounded in the action.

"'There is a lot of sporadic small-arms fire around here,' Jacobson commented. 'Three rounds of heavy stuff landed a few minutes ago, but I couldn't tell whether it was mortar or rockets.' [He] . . . said the first enemy rounds fell around 2:45 a.m. 'The Vietcong sent in a few sapper units to celebrate Tet in their own inimitable way,' Jacobson said. 'They are calculating a big splash all over the world with their activities.'"
4. Pisor, "Saigon's Fighting MPs," p. 38.

5. Letter to the author, Mar. 11, 1971.

6. Emphasis here, and in the following stories, added.

7. Letter to the author, Mar. 11, 1971.

8. Letter to the author, Sept. 7, 1971.

9. It is worth repeating that, at home, the foreign editor's dependence on the wire services for fast-breaking stories from Vietnam was heightened by the fact that AP and UPI (like *Time*) had direct, expensive communications of their own via Tokyo or Manila. The dailies did not, and their stories had to wait in line at Reuters. The New York *Times* received its Saigon copy in London and relayed it on its own wire at once; the system of the Washington *Post* and Los Angeles *Times* was slower, and their stories took far longer to get from Saigon to the home office. This also meant that when Tet came, the *Post's* second edition (as well as its first 8:30 p.m. edition) was a wire-service wrap-up, and contained the wire-service errors. In 1968, neither the *Post's* nor the *Times's* home-office people (unlike those of the wires and *Time*) could instantly query their men in Saigon on apparent conflicts of fact. In 1972, when Hanoi launched its Easter offensive, and in the 1975 crisis, communications were vastly improved; *Post* and *Times* reporters could talk to their home offices by telephone.

10. Nineteen was the number.

11. Not so. They wore civilian clothes.

12. The paratroopers, as noted, arrived after the battle was all but over.

13. The helicopters did not operate against these "raiders" who, moreover, did not make it onto the Independence Palace grounds. They were repelled.

14. Thieu was in My Tho, visiting his in-laws. Ky was in Saigon.

15. Buckley promptly equipped himself with a flak vest and carbine.

16. This was perhaps the most serious battle of the day in Saigon, but we did not know it at the time.

17. The *Times*, unlike the wires, warned readers that all was not known.

18. Outgunned, no. Outmaneuvered, yes.

19. This was in error. I saw U.S. armored personnel carriers (APCs) racing down Cong Ly Boulevard into town just after daybreak, as noted earlier.

20. Or traffic jams?

21. Was the *Times* already calling the score? What "informed sources" are meant—other newsmen?

22. Letter to the author, June 22, 1971.

23. This was quite different from saying there was a floor-to-floor fight, as did UPI.

24. This was also described by Westmoreland as a hole made by an anti-tank rocket.

25. A second *Times* warning to the reader. Actually, newsmen were in the embassy yard only during the last act.

26. Said by whom? By the MPs, actually.

27. To evacuate a wounded Marine.

28. The attribution to "American officials" is not in UPI or AP files. We lack Reuters' records. Apparently there was a determination to fault the "attack-proof" embassy.

29. This is a stronger rewrite of the AP's post-Westmoreland hang-on.

30. Again, this was a common assumption, shared with AP and UPI.

31. The reference is to the battles that began January 29–30, the night before the Saigon attacks. For lack of clear information on what was happening in the Delta, the rest of III Corps, and the rest of Saigon, this is what seemed most certain at the time of writing.

32. All this came from the MACV morning communiqué.

33. A bit misleading. As Mohr noted in his story, there was not much debris (except for dead Vietcong).

34. Two VC were captured.

35. This implies that VC were on lower floors.

36. Indeed, as noted in the foreign desk's own newsletter issued a week later, "the only word Braestrup and Lescaze have received from Washington has come in a couple of faint phone calls. The nightly play messages [informing the Saigon bureau how its stories fared and what other Vietnam stories from other sources were used] are stacked up in Manila waiting for a clear circuit."

The New York *Times*'s Mohr bypassed the Reuters mess after early January 31 by moving into *Time*'s bureau next door, and using the magazine's direct Telex line to send his bureau's dispatches to *Time*'s Rockefeller Center headquarters, there to be picked up by *Times* messenger. The arrangement was a boon to the New York *Times*, whose editors nevertheless sent no word of thanks to *Time*. After five days, Richard Clurman, the magazine's chief of correspondents, a bit miffed, cut off the arrangement. By that time, Reuters was OK again.

37. See Oberdorfer, *Tet!*, Chapter 1.

38. "Johnson Receives Flow of Reports," the New York *Times*, Jan. 31, 1968, p. 1. We know now that LBJ and Rusk were not thinking in terms of a "possible pattern for compromise."

39. In fact, the design was not so bad: the B-40 rockets failed to penetrate the facade; the embassy interior was intact except for the first-floor lobby—penetrated through windows by grenades and rockets. Artistic considerations had apparently dominated the exterior: no corner watchtowers were built until late 1968; the doors were made of wood, not steel. Needless to say, there were only lame explanations later about why only five guards were on duty despite the Tet alert. A 30-man MP platoon later was deployed.

40. "Washington: The Law of Compensation in Korea and Vietnam," the New York *Times,* Jan. 31, 1968, p. 40. Reston might have added that "surrender" was not the allies' stated goal, at least not in any formal sense.

41. "Reds Boast New Capability—Claim Forces Can Now Wage Large Battles," the Washington *Post,* Jan. 31, 1968, p. A9.

42. "VC Seen Resorting to Multiple-Shock Offensive Strategy," the Washington *Post,* Jan. 31, 1968, p. A11.

43. The *Post's* afternoon (Washington) rivals, the *Star* and the *News,* did get in their indignant licks, based on the early wire-service accounts. The Washington *Daily News* ("Where Were We? Where *Are* We?" Jan. 31, 1968, p. 1) wrote:

> The bold, massive communist attacks yesterday on Saigon, eight provincial capitals, and 30 or 40 lesser towns were a shocker.
>
> American military police having to land on the roof of the U.S. Embassy in Saigon under fire to recapture the supposedly "guerrilla-proof" building from communists who held it six hours! That scene alone is enough to force the Johnson Administration to stamp invalid its optimistic assessment the war is showing "continual and steady progress." . . .
>
> If this kind of Vietcong attack had occurred as the war's opener—a sort of Pearl Harbor—it would be easier to understand, and more forgivable. But the war has now been raging five years, and the United States has been on the scene in strength for nearly three years. Is this the sort of defeat we should be suffering when we have a half-million men on the ground and our top officials, flown back from Saigon to report just two months ago, tell us things are going well?

The Washington *Evening Star* ("Explosion in Vietnam," Jan. 31, 1968, p. 14) commented:

> Once again, United States military strategists have demonstrated their capacity at underestimating the strength, the purpose, and the determination of an enemy. . . .
>
> The explosion of Vietcong terrorism that has rocked all of South Vietnam came, we are told, as no surprise. If that is true, then the degree of success achieved by the enemy in 10 provincial capitals, in 40 towns and villages, in U.S. military installations, and in Saigon itself is difficult to explain. A "Pearl Harbor" in Vietnam might be understood if, lulled by the promise of a Tet truce, there had been some lowering of the guard. . . .
>
> The "assault-proof" American Embassy in Saigon was attacked, blasted open, entered and—according to most reports—held in part for six hours by enemy suicide squads. . . .
>
> We have been assured that the Marines and the South Vietnamese

forces are ready; that Khe Sanh can never be another Dienbienphu. Let us hope that—this time—the military strategists have read their intelligence reports accurately, and not through the rose-tinted spectacles of self-deception, complacency, and tragic underestimation of the strength and the ability of a dedicated foe.

44. "Khe Sanh: Holding the End of the Line," the Washington *Post*, Jan. 31, 1968, p. A20. U.S. losses here were roughly 200 dead.

45. TV folk, like newspaper picture editors and magazine layout men, love pictures of fires—any fire.

46. CBS-TV, "CBS Evening News," Jan. 30, 1968.

47. See wire-service stories on those "suicide commandos" on the embassy first floor.

48. See UPI reports.

49. "Wrecked the gates," but were driven off.

50. CBS had the figure at $25 million. To laymen, dollar figures sound impressive, which is perhaps why writers for TV news shows and wire services like to use them. In military terms, the bombardment of Da Nang was small potatoes, of course: only three fighter aircraft were destroyed and the field was not knocked out.

51. NBC-TV, "Huntley-Brinkley Evening News," Jan. 30, 1968.

52. *Who* was "denying"?

53. Frank Reynolds was employing the "double-conditional," a favorite tool in television commentary. ABC-TV, "ABC News," Jan. 30, 1968.

Chapter 4: Military Victory or Defeat?

1. Sharp and Westmoreland, *Report on the War*, pp. 183–84.

2. Gravel, *Pentagon Papers*, 4:547. The North Vietnamese, after the Vietcong's Tet losses, assumed the chief battlefield burden. They launched progressively weaker attacks: a costly "second wave" against Saigon in May 1968, a "third wave" against border towns in August–September, a "fourth wave" in early 1969. Thereafter, until their 1972 Easter offensive, supported by Soviet-supplied tanks and artillery, the North Vietnamese generally stayed close to their base areas in Laos and Cambodia.

3. The COSVN documents and others are cited in Oberdorfer, *Tet!*, pp. 253–57.

4. Ibid., p. 34.

5. Ibid.

6. "Special Report from Vietnam," *Army* (May 1968), pp. 18–19. As AP reported, the sudden disruption of Saigon "normalcy" at Tet had its unsettling effects on journalistic routine. A 7 p.m. curfew required that *Post* and *Times* reporters, for example, summon a U.S. Military Police jeep to ride a few blocks to the Reuters office to file their night's copy; wives of some correspondents were flown out to Hong Kong and Sin-

gapore; JUSPAO distributed Army C-rations for possible emergency use; restaurants closed early; movement in the suburbs was curtailed; to get to Tan Son Nhut Airfield from downtown Saigon during the first few days, newsmen took Army helicopters from the U.S. Embassy roof.

7. "The allies are winning the battles," wrote the Los Angeles *Times*'s William Tuohy at the turn of the year, "but are we winning the war?" ("Despite Gains, Viet Peace Keeps Fading," Los Angeles *Times*, Jan. 14, 1968, p. 1G).

8. Lt. Gen. Frank T. Mildren, USA, "From Mekong to DMZ: A Fighting Year for the U.S. Army's Best," *Army* (Oct. 1968), p. 87.

9. "Offensive Is Running 'Out of Steam,' Says Westmoreland," the New York *Times*, Feb. 2, 1968, p. 1.

10. "Offensive Is Said to Pinpoint Enemy's Strengths," the New York *Times*, Feb. 2, 1968, p. 12.

11. "Allied Figures on Casualties Are Thrown into Question," the Washington *Post*, Feb. 3, 1968, p. A13.

12. "Needed: The Courage to Face the Truth and to Accept the Possible Consequences of a Realistic Compromise," *Newsweek*, Mar. 18, 1968, p. 39.

13. "The War: Picking Up the Pieces," *Time*, Feb. 16, 1968, p. 32.

14. See Bernard Fall, *Hell in a Very Small Place* (Philadelphia: J.B. Lippincott Co., 1966); and idem, *Street without Joy* (5th rev. ed.; Harrisburg, Pa.: Stackpole Books, 1966).

15. AP, B95—Thieu Text, Jan. 31, 1968.

16. They were, although this reporter allowed himself to mock the notion in print (the Washington *Post*, Feb. 2, 1968, p. A1).

17. Letter to the author, June 20, 1970.

18. "Vietcong Holding Position on Edge of Saigon Airport," the New York *Times*, Feb. 4, 1968, p. 1. Emphasis added.

19. "Siege Ebbs; New Raids Are Seen; Enemy Is Able to Hit Anew, U.S. Aides Say," the Washington *Post*, Feb. 4, 1968, p. A1.

20. The President had already been worried about Khe Sanh, whose siege began January 21. See Johnson, *The Vantage Point*, p. 381.

21. A half-truth, aimed at rebutting reports that the United States was taken by surprise at Tet. As we have seen, Westmoreland, Wheeler, and Weyand had warned of impending enemy activity prior to Tet. But General Chaisson's discussion on February 3 of "surprise" came far closer to the truth.

22. AP, A113 WX, US—Asia, Feb. 2, 1968. Emphasis added.

23. "North Vietnam's Strategy of Terror," the New York *Times*, Feb. 2, 1968, p. 34.

24. The previous summer, however, Westmoreland had said as much to newsmen in background briefings (Aug. 17 and 18, 1967).

25. Wheeler did not yet know about the attack on Hue; like West-moreland, he expected the major push to come farther north.

26. Feb. 1, 1968.

27. Feb. 2, 1968.

28. From an interview following his appearance before the Subcommittee on Department of Defense House Appropriations. Emphasis added.

29. AP, A395—War Spotlights, Feb. 21, 1968. This was not literally true. Both ARVN and U.S. firepower saved the day, and, as at Quang Tri, Kontum, Pleiku, and Ban Me Thuot, ARVN did counterattack. Most reporting did not reflect this "mixed" picture.

30. NBC-TV, "Vietcong Terror: A Guerrilla Offensive," Feb. 1, 1968. Emphasis added. By contrast, the wire services—which will not be discussed separately in this chapter—for the most part stuck to reporting the "action" in Vietnam and the conflicting statements of U.S. officials and of critics of the war policy, without attempting any explicit score-keeping as to Hanoi's victory or failure.

31. ABC-TV, "ABC Evening News," Feb. 1, 1968.

32. CBS-TV, "CBS Evening News," Feb. 2, 1968.

33. CBS-TV, "Report from Vietnam: Who, What, When, Where, Why," Feb. 27, 1968.

34. See Oberdorfer, *Tet!*, pp. 246–49.

35. "Vietcong Press Guerrilla Raids," the New York *Times*, Feb. 1, 1968, p. 1.

36. "U.S. Voices Confidence Raids Were Expected," the Washington *Post*, Feb. 1, 1968, p. 1.

37. "Khe Sanh Situation Now Shows Viet Foe Makes Strategy Work," the Washington *Post*, Feb. 1, 1968, p. A21.

38. "Red Raids on Cities Are Sign of Weakness, Not Strength," the Washington *Post*, Feb. 2, 1968, p. A19. For the full text see Appendix XII, *Big Story*, Westview Press edition.

39. "Red Glare of Battle Illuminates Lessons of Vietnam Nightmare," the Washington *Post*, Feb. 6, 1968, p. A15.

40. "Viet Reds' Drive Was a Giap 'Masterstroke,' " the Washington *Post*, Feb. 11, 1968, p. A8.

41. "Clashes Persist in Viet Cities, General Warns of DMZ Push," the Washington *Post*, Feb. 2, 1968, p. A1.

42. "Giap's Round on Points," the New York *Times*, Mar. 8, 1968, p. 39. Emphasis added.

43. This was, essentially, the U.S. official view.

44. Who "avowed" they were *suicidal?* Happily for the Thieu regime, and the United States, the VC sapper squads were not bent on suicide, but on successful hit-and-run attacks. Terrorism in the cities was surprisingly infrequent, given the opportunities.

45. This was reported by U.S. officials in Saigon. How typical these POW

reports were was not then known. "The War: The General's Gamble," *Time*, Feb. 9, 1968, pp. 22–23. Emphasis added.

46. General Weyand, among others, had seen "psychological" returns for Hanoi. See page 124.

47. "Devastatingly effective" in what sense—surprising the allies? Forcing allied bombardment of cities? Scaring U.S. newsmen? "Hanoi Attacks and Scores a Major Psychological Blow," *Newsweek*, Feb. 12, 1968, pp. 23–24. Emphasis added.

48. "Man on the Spot," *Newsweek*, Feb. 19, 1968, p. 33.

49. "The Tet Offensive: How They Did It," *Newsweek*, Mar. 11, 1968, pp. 65–66.

Chapter 5: North Vietnamese Performance

1. Walter G. Hermes, *United States Army in the Korean War: Truce Tent and Fighting Front*, prepared for the Office of the Chief of Military History, Defense Department, Army (Washington, D.C.: Government Printing Office, 1966), p. 148.

2. "Hanoi Says Aim of Raids Is to Oust Saigon Regime," Feb. 2, 1968; "Hanoi Indicates It Is Still Ready to Discuss Peace," Feb. 9, 1968.

3. "Hanoi's Leader Charges Allies Broke Tet Truce," Feb. 1, 1968.

4. This idealization of the Vietcong and North Vietnamese, whom the French-educated Prince Souvanna Phouma of Laos described to me and others as "the Germans of Southeast Asia," flowered again in the obituaries of Ho Chi Minh in 1969.

5. For a "Source Breadth" breakdown of New York *Times*, Washington *Post*, AP, and network television Vietnam coverage during Tet, see Tables in Westview Press edition of *Big Story*.

6. "Khe Sanh Waits and Probes Strategy," the Washington *Post*, Feb. 19, 1968, p. A19.

7. "Street Fighting in Some Cities Obscures a Success at Da Nang," the Washington *Post*, Feb. 13, 1968, p. A1.

8. "The Tet Offensive: How They Did It," *Newsweek*, Mar. 11, 1968, pp. 65–66.

9. Including the 7th and 8th Battalions of the 29th Regiment sent from Khe Sanh. See Sharp and Westmoreland, *Report on the War*, p. 160; and Maj. Miles D. Waldron and Sp. 5 Richard W. Beavers, *Operation Hue City*, Historical Study 2-68, 31st Military History Detachment, Headquarters Provisional Corps Vietnam, Aug. 1968.

10. Remarks at the American Management Association, New York, Mar. 5, 1968.

11. "Reds in Saigon Area Believed Hurt," the Washington *Post*, Mar. 11, 1968, p. A10.

12. "National Liberation Front" was seldom used by American newsmen in Saigon as a synonym for the popular term "Vietcong" (Vietnamese

communist) in referring to the native South Vietnamese communist organization. The formal NLF designation found greater favor with European journalists, State Department analysts, and, increasingly, American opponents of the war. The formation of the NLF was announced by Hanoi in 1960; it was described by Hanoi as an autonomous South Vietnamese coalition of communists and noncommunists. By U.S. accounts, the NLF was simply Hanoi's South Vietnamese branch; its military leaders were North Vietnamese or Northern-trained, even as its visible spokesmen and its rank and file were Southerners. At Tet, Southern units bore the brunt of the attacks in the Delta and Saigon; by then, however, infiltrated Northern regulars already accounted for about half of the 197 communist main force battalions in the South. See Sharp and Westmoreland, *Report on the War*, p. 176. By 1975, the Vietcong were no longer a significant factor in combat.

13. AP, A106–Hanoi-Vietnam Lead, Feb. 2, 1968.
14. AP, A031, Mar. 30, 1968.
15. AP, A050WX.
16. AP, Feb. 3, 1968.
17. Letter to the author, Mar. 11, 1971.
18. Arnett forgot Westmoreland's three-phase analysis, as well as subsequent briefings by the General's subordinates on the enemy's political objectives.
19. AP, A015–Vietnam News Analysis. Emphasis added.
20. AP, A396.
21. AP, A058–Evaluation.
22. "VC Drive Held Aid to Allies, LBJ Tells Ike Saigon May Be Stronger Now," the Washington *Post*, Feb. 19, 1968, p. A1.
23. AP, A041 and A042–Vietnam Outlook, Feb. 28, 1968.
24. AP, A069–Giap Strategy, Feb. 29, 1968.
25. AP, A072, Mar. 29, 1968. Emphasis added.
26. Entitled "Circular from Central Office of South Vietnam, Current Affairs Committee and Military Affairs Committee of South Vietnam Liberation Army (SVNLA) Headquarters, Concerning a Preliminary Assessment of the Situation," it was reprinted and analyzed by Patrick J. McGarvey, an old Vietnam hand, in *Visions of Victory–Selected Vietnamese Communist Military Writings, 1964–68* (Stanford, Calif.: Hoover Institution on War, Revolution, and Peace, 1969).
27. "Bunker Asks Role for General Palmer, Key Post Believed Sought in Revamping of Forces," by Bernard Weinraub.
28. "VC Document Gives Failures of Tet Drive," Mar. 30, 1968, p. A14.
29. What puzzled many Americans in Vietnam was the apparent failure of North Vietnamese intelligence and operations officers to capitalize on the detailed press reporting of allied troop movements, down to company

size (as at Hue), fortifications, losses, and morale. It was suggested by some U.S. Army officers that perhaps, in Hanoi, the U.S. media lacked credibility.

30. AP, A007—Citadel, Feb. 19, 1968. Oberdorfer also cites the request of the NVA commanders at Hue to withdraw (*Tet!* p. 221).

31. "Three Dead Enemy Soldiers Reported Chained to Gun, Allied Officers in Hue Assert; the Bodies Were Discovered When School Was Taken," the New York *Times*, Feb. 17, 1968.

32. CBS-TV, "CBS Evening News," Feb. 13, 1968.

33. ABC-TV, "ABC Evening News," Feb. 13, 1968.

34. ARVN, *Viet Cong Tet Offensive.*

35. NBC-TV, "Huntley-Brinkley Report," Mar. 5, 1968.

36. CBS-TV, "CBS Evening News," Feb. 2, 1968.

37. CBS-TV, "CBS Reports, 'Vietcong,'" Feb. 20, 1968.

38. In fact, as most newsmen in Saigon knew, there was nothing for U.S. officials to "insist" upon: Cu Chi was a garrisoned district capital in Hau Nghia province less than two miles from the U.S. 25th Division base camp, which was established there in 1966.

39. Not at all. Mines need fuses to be dangerous.

40. NBC-TV, "Huntley-Brinkley Report," Feb. 16, 1968. Emphasis added.

41. CBS-TV, "CBS Evening News," Feb. 16, 1968.

42. NBC-TV, "Huntley-Brinkley Report," Feb. 14, 1968. Emphasis added.

43. CBS-TV, "CBS Evening News," Mar. 4, 1968. Emphasis added.

44. CBS-TV, "CBS Morning News," Mar. 20, 1968.

45. CBS-TV, "CBS Evening News," Feb. 22, 1968. Emphasis added.

46. "Hanoi Says Aim of Raids Is to Oust Saigon Regime," Feb. 2, 1968; and "Hanoi Indicates It Is Still Ready to Discuss Peace; U.S. Interest Is Stirred by Official's Rephrasing of Conditions of Talks," Feb. 9, 1968. The *Times* was traditionally excited by "diplomacy" and "peace feeler" stories; the net effect, on reviewing the play given to them by the paper, is to make Hanoi seem accommodating and the United States very stubborn —an impression emphasized by *Times* editorials (e.g., "Vietnam Peace Talks," Feb. 11, 1968, p. 12E).

47. "Warning Is Given, President Terms U.S. Ready for a Push by Enemy at Khe Sanh," Feb. 3, 1968; and "Latest Soviet Tanks Used by Enemy near Khe Sanh," Feb. 8, 1968.

48. "North Vietnam's Strategy of Terror," the New York *Times*, Feb. 2, 1968, p. 34. Emphasis added.

49. Straw-man journalism: Komer claimed a lot for the Hamlet Evaluation Survey, but he did not claim *immunity* for pacified hamlets. See Appendix V, press conference, Jan. 24, 1968, *Big Story*, Westview Press edition.

50. "Offensive Is Said to Pinpoint Enemy Strengths; Despite U.S. Stress on Toll, VC Gains Are Seen in Morale and Prestige," the New York *Times*, Feb. 2, 1968, p. 12.

51. "Guerrilla Motivation Stressed: 'The VC Are Not Afraid to Die,'" the New York *Times*, Feb. 3, 1968, p. 9.

52. New enemy weapons sightings were announced by MACV spokesmen as they occurred during Tet. Westmoreland later noted the new weapons without assigning them much importance. See Sharp and Westmoreland, *Report on the War*, p. 185.

53. By official count, U.S. fixed-wing airplane losses in Indo-China during February and March were 132; helicopter losses were 216, without counting extensive damage to others. The United States had over 3,000 helicopters in Vietnam.

54. "Enemy's Use of New Soviet and Chinese Weapons Changes the Pattern of War in Vietnam," the New York *Times*, Mar. 2, 1968, p. 3.

55. Sharp and Westmoreland, *Report on the War*, p. 141.

56. Shore, *Khe Sanh*, pp. 106-7.

57. "Enemy Armory Goes Modern," the New York *Times*, Mar. 3, 1968, p. E4.

58. "Vietnam Issues: A Grim Military Chess Game," the New York *Times*, Mar. 3, 1968, p. E3.

59. For example, "Allies Disagree on Enemy's Aims: U.S. Girding at Khe Sanh, Saigon Looks to Highlands," Feb. 24, p. 5; "Saigon General Says Foe Has Replaced His Losses," Mar. 10, p. 1; and "U.S. Terms Enemy Weaker," Mar. 15, p. 2.

60. For example, "Foes of Regime Warned by Hanoi; Penalties, Including Death, Decreed for Subversion," Mar. 22, 1968, p. 3.

61. Nevertheless, Ho Chi Minh, hailing victory, got on page one on February 1, and subsequent statements by Hanoi got into the paper on inside pages. Some of these *Post* "Hanoi" stories, for example, were: "Hanoi's Leader Charges Allies Broke Tet Truce," Feb. 1, p. A1; "Reds Claim to Have 'Councils' in Cities," Feb. 2, p. A4; "Hanoi Says Foundation Is Laid for More Victories," Feb. 4, p. A9; "Vietcong Bars Coalition with Regime in Saigon," Feb. 7, p. A11; "North Vietnam Claims Complete Tet Victory," Feb. 20, p. A15; "General Giap Foresees Fierce Phase of War," Feb. 24, p. A8.

62. The attention given by *Post* editors to enemy performance (as to everything else *in* Vietnam) did not last. It waned rapidly as the Washington debate over what to expect next began, and as the domestic political season blossomed just prior to the New Hampshire primary on March 12—a time when the situation in Vietnam was beginning to become clearer here and there.

63. "Vietcong Seen Resorting to Multiple-Shock Offensive Strategy," by Murrey Marder, Jan. 31, 1968, p. A11.

64. "Reds Said to Marshal Power, Held Capable of Fighting Large Battles," Jan. 31, p. A9; "What Are the VC Trying to Prove?" Feb. 2, p. A18; "Vietcong Mount Political Offensive," Feb. 4, p. A8; "Vietcong Aim Seen to Boost Its Role in Settlement," Feb. 7, p. A16.

65. "What Are the Vietcong Trying to Prove?" by Stanley Karnow, the Washington *Post*, Feb. 2, 1968, p. A18. Emphasis added.

66. "U.S. Warily Eyes Hanoi Strategy," the Washington *Post*, Feb. 16, 1968, p. A14. Emphasis added.

67. As we now can see, this change, then unremarked by the New York *Times*, provided a tip-off to Hanoi's decision to cut its losses for the time being. It got more emphasis from the relatively hawkish Washington *Evening Star*, whose editorial writer, drawing on a dispatch from Saigon, said the same day:

> . . . Donald Kirk, our Asia correspondent, reports a major shift in the propaganda line from Hanoi. Just before the attacks on the cities, enemy troops were being told by their commanders that this was it—that the war would be over in a few months. Then came the fantastically extravagant victory claims—that Saigon was in ruins, that the Americans were devastated, that the South Vietnamese government was tottering on the verge of collapse. According to our correspondent, however, a new note is being sounded now by the Hanoi propagandists. Instead of instant victory, this, they say once again, as they were saying at the outset, is going to be a "long war" against the American "imperialists" and their puppet regime in South Vietnam.

68. This radio broadcast was also reported in the New York *Times*'s "News of the Week in Review," Feb. 25, 1968. It was wryly noted by newsmen in Saigon after listening to MACV spokesmen discussing a wide variety of possible enemy targets. As it turned out, the enemy was unable to land a "real blow" against any of the targets he named and the "feints," if that is what they were, were unrewarding.

69. "A Vietcong Pincer Strategy Is Unfolding," the Washington *Post*, Feb. 29, 1968, p. A23. Nine days later, Marder suggested that the enemy's claim was correct, and that the allies had been forced into an "enclave" strategy ("Cruel Irony of the Enclave Theory," Mar. 8, p. A20). In fact, by then this was no longer even a half-truth.

70. For this Alsop column, see Appendix XII. For other columnists, see Story Index, Washington *Post*, both in *Big Story*, Westview Press edition.

71. "The Red Glare of Battle Illuminates Lessons of Vietnam," the Washington *Post*, Feb. 6, 1968, p. A15.

72. Among these discussions in the *Post* were: "Brooding on Viet Setback Ignores Fearful Cost to Enemy," Feb. 7, p. A21; "Hanoi Places Heavy Stakes on Two Throws of the Dice," Feb. 9, p. A21; "Major Failure in the City Battles Was Enemy's Not Allies'," Feb. 19, p. A21;

"Pike's VC Attack Post-mortem Refutes Senate Doves' Views," Feb. 26, p. A13; "Kennedy's Viet Defeatism Contradicts Facts of War," Mar. 27, p. A23.

73. "The President Should Approve More GIs and Call Reserves," the Washington *Post*, Feb. 28, 1968, p. A15. This was answered in the paper next day by Kraft: "New Strategy, Redeployment Seen U.S. Need, Not More Men," Feb. 29, 1968, p. A25.

74. Bernard Fall in *Hell in a Very Small Place* (p. 45) makes clear that the French high command unwisely dispersed its own mobile reserves elsewhere in Indo-China prior to the Dienbienphu siege on its own initiative, notably in Operation Atlante, not because of any sudden diversionary urban efforts by Giap. Giap never tried anything remotely similar to Tet against the French. Khe Sanh bore certain resemblances to Giap's past experience; but the anti-cities attacks at Tet represented relatively untried techniques for him and his troops.

75. "A Vietcong Sees Fight to the End," by Mark Franklin, the Washington *Post*, Feb. 21, 1968, p. F7.

76. Some of these *Post* stories, for example, were: "Marines Dig In at Khe Sanh," Feb. 5, p. A1; "Question in Assessing Casualties Is Effect on Enemy Capability," Feb. 29, p. A20; and "A Somber View of the Foe," Feb. 23, p. A1.

77. I fumbled my Hue compass directions, mentioning the northwest *corner* of the Citadel instead of the *north*, and the *southwest* side of Hue instead of the *southeast*.

78. "Allies Assess Strengths and Failings," the Washington *Post*, Feb. 8, 1968, p. A1.

79. "VCs Uncertain of Objectives, First Data on POWs Suggest," the Washington *Post*, Feb. 13, 1968, p. A1.

80. "Viet Army Morale Seen Aim of Offensive," the Washington *Post*, Feb. 13, 1968, p. A10.

81. "Street Fighting in Some Cities Obscures a Success at Da Nang," the Washington *Post*, Feb. 13, p. A1.

82. "South Viets Prove Fighters in Hue," Mar. 2, p. A11; "Quang Tri Pushes Ahead Again," Mar. 4, p. A9; "Busy Spotter Pilot Helps Clear Road to Khe Sanh," Mar. 24, p. A1.

83. "The War: The General's Gamble," *Time*, Feb. 9, 1968, p. 22.

84. "The Enemy's New Weapons," *Time*, Mar. 15, 1968, p. 21.

85. "The Tet Offensive: How They Did It," *Newsweek*, Mar. 11, 1968, pp. 65–66.

86. The following week, however, *Newsweek*'s editors were to declare Administration policy a failure and suggest that Westmoreland should switch to a more defensive strategy ("More of the Same Won't Do," Mar. 18, 1968, p. 25).

87. A point made by Abrams in his briefing on February 8.

88. Partly straw-man journalism. Although surprised by Tet, Westmoreland and Wheeler—prior to Tet—as we have noted, had promised more hard fighting and enemy initiatives. See Chapter 2.

89. "New Rules in Vietnam," *Newsweek*, Mar. 11, 1968, p. 88.

Chapter 6: Civilian Deaths and Destruction

1. "Saigon Arrival: A Royal Welcome," the Washington *Post*, Feb. 6, 1968, p. A14.

2. One exception was a photograph in *Time*, Mar. 8, 1968, p. 28, with the caption: "Flares and Artillery Flashes on Saigon's Outskirts."

3. Early during the Tet offensive, the wires gave considerable attention to the U.S. missionaries' plight. Said AP (A032—Missionary Rescue, by Barry Kramer, Feb. 4, 1968): "Thirty-four missionaries were rescued from their hilltop mission in the resort town of Da Lat by U.S. forces a short time before it was overrun by the Vietcong, U.S. official said Sunday. . . . The attack on the mission, which is operated by the Christian Missionary Alliance and Overseas Crusade group, coincided with another guerrilla attack on the alliance's mission in Ban Me Thuot . . . in which six missionaries were killed, one was wounded, and two abducted."

The New York *Times* described the mission attacks in "Six U.S. Missionaries Killed by Vietcong," Feb. 3, p. 1; and "Thirty-Four Rescued by GIs at Mission in Da Lat" (AP), Feb. 5, p. 1. Accounts of Vietnamese war victims went inside the paper—"Saigon Appeals for Refugee Aid" (Reuters), Feb. 5, p. 16; "20,000 Refugees in Saigon" (AP), Feb. 5, p. 16; "Civilian Toll High in Mekong Delta" (AP), Feb. 6, p. 14; "Civilian Wounded Jam Hospital, Boy Scouts Carrying Stretchers," by Thomas Johnson, Feb. 7, p. 16.

The Washington *Post*, however, played down the missionary story; UPI's report went on p. A6, Feb. 3. For the most part, the *Post* incorporated the periodic official refugee statistics in its war wrap-ups, but like the *Times* published some firsthand accounts inside the paper concerning civilians caught in the Saigon-area battles ("U.S. Attack Traps Civilians; Death in the Saigon Suburbs," Feb. 4, p. A5; "Violence Lashes Out at Cholon Residents," by Lee Lescaze, Feb. 7, p. A11).

4. Bill Brannigan, "Brannigan's Stew in Vietnam," *Dateline: Who's Watching Who? The Press vs. the Politician* (1970), pp. 56–59. In the last sentence, Brannigan might more accurately have substituted "media" for "public."

5. The *official* pre-Tet refugee count as of December 31, 1967, was 800,000. On February 24, Ambassador Komer told newsmen that the number of "post-Tet evacuees," including those who had not lost their homes but took refuge from the fighting, was estimated at 473,000; that 63,700 houses were destroyed, 4,300 civilians killed, and 17,800 wounded. These figures were later revised upward. Oberdorfer cites these

figures: 821,000 Tet refugees, in addition to 904,000 refugees prior to Tet. (*Tet!* p. 179.) Pike cites Vietnamese government figures as: 7,424 civilians killed and 15,434 wounded. (Douglas Pike, *The Viet-Cong Strategy of Terror* [Saigon: United States Mission, Vietnam, 1970], p. 83.)

6. Saigon was depicted, often, as a Western-style city with big buildings flattened into "tons of rubble" by World War II style bombardment. Actually, Cholon and Gia Dinh, mostly composed of two-story dwellings and shanties, suffered from *fire* at Tet.

7. AP, 40—Civilians, Feb. 4, 1968.

8. AP, A0832—Vietnam Civilians, Feb. 10, 1968.

9. Few newsmen recalled that the United States had not compiled much of a record in helping refugees displaced by its military operations prior to Tet, as Senator Edward Kennedy had noted. Indeed, the New York *Times* reported (Jan. 18, 1968) that construction in South Vietnam of three U.S. hospitals for wounded civilians had been halted for lack of funds.

10. AP, A016—Refugees, Feb. 24, 1968.

11. AP, A022—Realities of War, by Peter Arnett, Feb. 5, 1968.

12. AP, A020—Northern Vietnam, Feb. 3, 1968.

13. "Vietnam Reds Resist Attacks in Hue Again," the Washington *Post*, Feb. 4, 1968, p. A1.

14. "Saigon: Scattered Fighting, but Battle Ebbs," the Washington *Post*, Feb. 2, 1968, p. A1.

15. "Allied Figures on Casualties Are Thrown into Question," the Washington *Post*, Feb. 3, 1968, p. A13.

16. "Enemy Is Able to Hit Anew," the Washington *Post*, Feb. 4, 1968, p. A1.

17. "Guerrilla Motivation Stressed; 'The VC Are Not Afraid to Die,'" the New York *Times*, Feb. 3, 1968, p. 9.

18. "War Crisscrosses Suburb of Saigon," the New York *Times*, Feb. 4, 1968, p. 5.

19. "U.S. Attack Traps Civilians; Death in the Saigon Suburbs," the Washington *Post*, Feb. 4, 1968, p. A5.

20. "Streets of Saigon Shelled in Drive to Rout Vietcong," the New York *Times*, Feb. 6, 1968, p. 1.

21. "Refugees Jam Saigon Camps; Rice on Hand but Milk Is Scarce," the New York *Times*, Feb. 24, 1968, p. 3.

22. "The War: The General's Gamble," *Time*, Feb. 9, 1968, pp. 23, 25.

23. "Man on the Spot," *Newsweek*, Feb. 19, 1968, p. 33.

24. ABC-TV, "ABC Evening News," Feb. 2, 1968. Emphasis added.

25. AP, A008, Feb. 2, 1968.

26. The street was in suburban Gia Dinh.

27. Exactly the reverse was true. Allied forces in Saigon and the Delta

towns lacked powerful "direct-fire" weapons, unlike the Marines who used the 106 mm. recoilless cannon to good effect on Hue's south side; elsewhere, for lack of alternatives, air strikes and helicopter gunships were used.

28. CBS-TV, "CBS Evening News," Feb. 2, 1968.

29. ABC-TV, "ABC Evening News," Feb. 6, 1968. In fact, Saigon was not short on food; prices doubled, then fell; that ABC's expenses at the Caravelle Hotel were affected seemed to bulk overly large in Young's account.

30. NBC-TV, "Huntley-Brinkley Report," Feb. 7, 1968.

31. NBC-TV, Frank McGee Report, "A New Year, A New War," Mar. 10, 1968.

32. AP, 75—Saigon Air View, by John Nance, Feb. 10, 1968. Emphasis added.

33. "Damage in Saigon Is Limited So Far," the New York Times, Feb. 11, 1968, p. 3. Emphasis added.

34. No doubt, but how many peasants did AP interview? In one day?

35. AP, A003, Feb. 5, 1968.

36. AP reported half of My Tho was destroyed, but gave a lower casualty total.

37. "A Third of My Tho Destroyed in Delta Battle," the Washington Post, Feb. 6, 1968, p. 1.

38. The New York Times used the Kramer story: "Civilian Toll High in Mekong Delta," Feb. 6, 1968, p. 14.

39. Letter to the author, Mar. 11, 1971.

40. AP, A110–111—Destroyed, Feb. 7, 1968.

41. Six weeks later, on March 22, the Washington Post's Saigon bureau received this query from the home office about a follow-up story from Ben Tre by William Tuohy of the Los Angeles Times knocking down the Arnett piece:

> ANY PLANS TO VISIT BEN TRE QUERY HAVE IN HAND TUOHY PIECE CASTING DOUBT OF OFFICIALS ON MAJOR'S FAMOUS QUOTE AND STATING THAT DAMAGE TO CITY MUCH LESS THAN AT FIRST RE-PORTED. APPRECIATE YOUR COMMENTS. REGARDS.

Lescaze replied:

> PRODESK TUOHY PIECE SOUNDS PUZZLING AND EYE VOTE AGAINST RUNNING IT. EYE SAW KIEN HOA AND DAMAGE IS ENORMOUS. WHETHER IT IS LESS ENORMOUS THAN FIRST THOUGHT SEEMS A QUIBBLE. ALSO MANY PEOPLE AROUND VIETNAM TALK AS THAT MAJOR DID ALTHOUGH THEIR PHRASES ARE NOT AS PITHY. . . .

Wrote Tuohy on March 24 in a story entitled by his paper "Ravaged Viet City Faces Uphill Battle to Rebuild":

> Ben Tre, hardest hit of the Mekong Delta's province capitals, is

trying to pull itself together again with the help of the 15 U.S. civilian advisors and 130 military men.
  . . . Their work is cut out for them. But they believe that it hasn't
been made easier by the widely circulated quote from an anonymous
major to the effect that "we had to destroy the town in order to save
it."
  Only 25 percent of the city—rather than the reported 80 percent
—was actually destroyed by the Vietcong attack and the Vietnamese
artillery and U.S. air strikes that followed. And the U.S. advisory
group doubts that the statement was actually made in that form.
  "It sounds too pithy and clever to have been made on the spot,"
says one U.S. civilian advisor. "It just rings wrong."
42. Letter to the author, Mar. 11, 1971.
43. UPI, 533B—Ben Tre, Feb. 7, 1968.
44. "Survivors Hunt Dead of Ben Tre, Turned to Rubble in Allied
Raids," the New York Times, Feb. 8, 1968, p. 14. For the full text, see
Appendix XVI, Big Story, Westview Press edition.
45. "The Flies That Capture the Flypaper," the New York Times, Feb.
7, 1968, p. 40. The column showed the impact on Reston of the Tet
"image." It was a reaction to Tet coverage, shared by others before and
after the Ben Tre quote.
46. "The War: Picking Up the Pieces," Time, Feb. 16, 1968, p. 34.
47. CBS-Radio, "Capitol Cloakroom," Feb. 11, 1968.
48. ABC-TV, "ABC Evening News," Feb. 12, 1968.
49. WTOP-Radio, Feb. 10, 1968.
50. "The Slaughter Goes On," The New Republic, Feb. 24, 1968, p. 13.
51. "Debate in a Vacuum," Time, Mar. 15, 1968, p. 13.
52. "Notes and Comment," The New Yorker, Mar. 20, 1971, p. 31. Emphasis added.
53. Our UPI files are incomplete.
54. Two of these were by AP.
55. UPI, 009A, Mar. 3, 1968.
56. "Allies Trying to Seize Offensive in the Delta," the Washington Post,
Mar. 10, 1968, p. A27.
57. "Ruined Viet Hamlet Rebuilds in Fear," the Washington Post, Mar.
17, 1968, p. A18.
58. Technically correct, but see Charles Mohr's New York Times story,
Feb. 11, 1968.
59. "The War: Picking Up the Pieces," Time, Feb. 16, 1968, p. 32. Emphasis added.
60. "Man on the Spot," Newsweek, Feb. 19, 1968, p. 39.
61. CBS-TV, "CBS Evening News," Feb. 5, 1968.
62. NBC-TV, "Huntley-Brinkley Report," Feb. 6, 1968.
63. "Hue, capital of the kingdom of Annam, site of the French High

Resident [governor], is situated 12 km. from the sea on the Hong-giang, 'The River of Perfumes.' . . . The Citadel, fortified à la Vauban, includes, in imitation of the Chinese capitals, three concentric areas separated by walls. The 'Kinh-Thanh,' or capital city, encloses the royal city (Hoang-Thanh) and the 'Tu-Cam-thanh,' Forbidden City (reserved for the royal family). . . . The plan [by a Frenchman, Olivier de Puymanel] of Hue has been laid out since the start of the Emperor Gia Long period (1802)." (Guide Madrolle, *Indochine du Nord* [Paris: Librarie Hachette, 1932], p. 253.) Explaining the complex plan in wire or newspaper terms, even when the facts were known, led to confusion. Nobody got it *all* right.

64. AP, A106–Hue Descriptive, Feb. 2, 1968.

65. The ancient imperial capital was Hanoi, not Hue, according to Pike, *Viet-Cong Strategy of Terror*, p. 23.

66. *Time*, Mar. 1, 1968, p. 20.

67. According to Oberdorfer, "It was officially estimated immediately after the battle that 80 percent of the houses and buildings in Hue were destroyed or damaged in the battle. This estimate was probably high but it did justice to the visual impression of the devastated city." (*Tet!*, p. 234.)

68. "War-Stricken City of Hue Digs Out to Face Host of Problems," the Washington *Post*, Feb. 28, 1968, p. A6.

69. Vietnam Press, No. 4440 (Evening), Mar. 11, 1968, pp. 12–13.

70. ARVN, *Viet Cong Tet Offensive*, p. 284.

71. Ibid.

72. ARVN, *Viet Cong Tet Offensive*, p. 281.

73. AP, A044, Feb. 2, 1968.

74. It was not a no man's land but an NVA stronghold.

75. At this point, the "Hue massacre" by the Vietcong was still unknown to newsmen.

76. AP, A010–Hue Descriptive, by John Lengel, Feb. 10, 1968. Emphasis added.

77. "Weather and Thin Ranks Slow Marines' Tough Fight in Hue," the Washington *Post*, Feb. 12, 1968, p. A1.

78. UPI, 7, Feb. 21, 1968.

79. "Vietnam Reds Resist Attacks in Hue Again," the Washington *Post*, Feb. 4, 1968, p. A1.

80. AP, A010–Firepower, Feb. 18, 1968. This was included in the Washington *Post* war wrap-up the following day.

81. "South Vietnamese Seize Hue Palace; Enemy Retreats," the New York *Times*, Feb. 25, 1968, p. 1.

82. AP, A079, Feb. 24, 1968. Emphasis added. Devastation, of course, was not "almost total" elsewhere in the Citadel, as Mohr's story and subsequent *Post* reports indicated. Hue was no Stalingrad.

83. AP, A015, Feb. 26, 1968. The "advisor" was Robert Kelly, the chief U.S. official in Hue. This writer was with Lengel to see Kelly ("War-Stricken City of Hue Digs Out to Face Host of Problems," the Washington *Post*, Feb. 28, 1968, p. A6):

> HUE, South Vietnam, Feb. 27—"Hue will never be the same," said Robert Kelly, senior U.S. relief coordinator here, "but the city could be back to relatively normal life in 90 days."
>
> As he spoke, this scarred, river city of 140,000 was still convalescing from the longest, hardest battle of the Vietnam War—25 days of bitter street fighting, allied bombardment, and Vietcong terrorism.
>
> Some parts of the city, where little fighting occurred, were troubled only by looters. But, said Kelly, "looting by the troops is no longer a problem, because there isn't much left to loot."
>
> Around Hue's broken bridges, in the vicinity of the U.S. advisors' compound and in the environs of the Citadel's 20-foot-high walls, the damage was particularly severe. There the scene is one of shattered stucco houses, splintered tamarind trees, crumpled garden walls, and burned-out shops. . . .
>
> . . . Some 19,000 people have been inoculated against cholera. There have been only two verified cases of the disease so far. No one still knows how many persons were killed and wounded here during the fighting.

84. AP, A080, Feb. 27, 1968.
85. UPI, 203A, Mar. 9, 1968.
86. CBS-TV, "CBS Morning News," Feb. 12, 1968.
87. CBS-Radio, "Dimension," Feb. 19, 1968.
88. NBC-TV, "The Today Show," Feb. 28, 1968.
89. "The War: The General's Gamble," *Time*, Feb. 9, 1968. *Time* was a bit premature; bombing of the Citadel, as noted, did not begin until three days later.
90. "Battle of Hue," *Time*, Feb. 16, 1968, p. 37.
91. "The VC's Week of Terror," *Newsweek*, Feb. 12, 1968, p. 29.
92. "The Death of Hue," *Newsweek*, Mar. 11, 1968, pp. 58–60.
93. In Vietnam in 1968, province chiefs and mayors of large cities were almost all Army officers.
94. "Sad, Sad Hue," *Newsweek*, Apr. 8, 1968, pp. 20–21.
95. AP, A093—Hue Communists, Feb. 8, 1968.
96. The McArthur story did not get into the *Times*, but was used in the Washington *Post*, Feb. 9, 1968, p. A10.
97. AP, A009—Viet Executions, by George McArthur, Feb. 11, 1968.
98. "Reds Said to Execute 300 in Hue," the Washington *Post*, Feb. 12, 1968, p. A11; "Hue's Mayor Says Foe Executed 300," the New York *Times*, Feb. 12, 1968, p. 1.

99. UPI, 280A–Viet, Feb. 28, 1968. The story, matched by AP, was used in the *Times,* Feb. 29, p. 4, but not in the *Post.*
100. UPI, 211A–Massacre, Mar. 3, 1968. The story was not used in the *Times* or *Post.*
101. "Death Holds Hue in a Quiet Agony," the New York *Times,* Mar. 1, 1968, p. 1.
102. AP, A035–Hue Aftermath, Mar. 6, 1968. Neither the *Times* nor the *Post* used the story.
103. "400 Hue Slayings Laid to Enemy," the Washington *Post,* Mar. 10, 1968, p. A18.
104. "Hue Lives in Fear of a New Attack," by Gene Roberts, the New York *Times,* Mar. 23, 1968, p. 13.
105. "War-Weary Hue's Animosities Grow," the Washington *Post,* Mar. 19, 1968, p. A11. The other *Post* aftermath story dealt with the dereliction of South Vietnamese doctors (also cited by Weinraub in the *Times*) at Hue provincial hospital: "Doctors Leave Hue Despite Direct Order," Mar. 21, p. A22.
106. "An Efficient Slaughter," *Time,* Apr. 5, 1968, p. 36. The New York *Times* published this account under the headline "In Hue, Graves Disclose Executions by the Enemy," Mar. 28, 1968, p. 4.
107. See also Oberdorfer, *Tet!,* Chapter 6.
108. Pike, *Viet-Cong Strategy of Terror,* pp. 25–31. The Hue massacre, although never investigated extensively in the media, became a minor point of political contention during the Nixon and Ford Administrations, when official spokesmen harked back to the massacre to justify their argument that a "blood bath" would follow a communist takeover in Vietnam.

Chapter 7: Performance of U.S. Troops

1. The Saigon fighting, as NBC's bureau chief, Ron Steinman, was later to note, was far more accessible to the heavily burdened TV camera crews than had been past Vietnam battles. Perhaps the most "convenient" continuing battle in Saigon was the two-day siege by Brig. Gen. Nguyen Ngoc Loan, director of the national police, and his police forces of a Vietcong sapper group holed up in a semicompleted hotel just across Nguyen Du Street from Independence Palace. The sappers had tried, and failed, to enter the grounds of the Independence Palace early on January 31, as their comrades hit the U.S. Embassy a few blocks away. The surviving Vietcong retreated to the hotel. The siege was promptly christened by UPI "the Battle of the Penthouse." Firing was sporadic. From their nearby offices, American newsmen strolled over to watch, sheltered behind the sidewalk acacia trees, like spectators at a big city fire. Loan, high on a balcony of the unfinished hotel, directed his men amid considerable confusion. The Vietcong were obviously doomed; Loan did not heedlessly

risk his troops. But for two days, until the surviving sappers, haggard and bleeding, surrendered, the scene provided TV film and newspaper features.

Television crews, in particular, ventured bravely through unfamiliar streets to provide vignettes of combat and destruction elsewhere in Saigon and Cholon, but the battles there were harder to assess. No newsmen could get to the Delta until the big battles in that area were over. The Highlands got initial coverage from men on the scene, but little more. The big out-of-town stories, rather, were up north—at Hue and Khe Sanh.

2. Ward Just, *To What End: Report from Vietnam* (Boston: Houghton Mifflin Co., 1968), pp. 126–27.

3. Oberdorfer, *Tet!*, pp. 231–32.

4. See Waldron and Beavers, *Operation Hue City*.

5. "Progress," of course, was not "good" at Hue on February 2. The allies were virtually stalled, and it was the allies who were in the "pockets" —the foe controlled most of the city, as AP's John Lengel was to point out.

6. At this point, American planes were *not* bombing Hue; the South Vietnamese were.

7. UPI, 439B—Hue, Feb. 1, 1968.

8. The optimism was apparently based on reports other than those of Brigadier General Truong, the 1st ARVN Division commander, whose troops were hard pressed on the north side of the river. General Truong, Chaisson recalled in a 1970 conversation with this writer, later chided the COC director for his optimism, and Chaisson replied sheepishly that he was merely relaying to the press the information he had at the time from General Lam.

9. Letter to the author, Mar. 26, 1971.

10. AP, A044, Feb. 2, 1968.

11. Letter to the author, Mar. 26, 1971.

12. Here again is the confused geography: It was the southeast wall.

13. There was nothing "sacred" about the Citadel walls or "bastions."

14. UPI, 224A—Citadel NL, Feb. 17, 1968. Neither AP nor UPI had any reporters with the ARVN, although some photographers were with them.

15. UPI, 079A—Viet, by Eugene V. Risher, 3rd LD, Feb. 22, 1968. Emphasis added. For the Marines, Hue was not an ordeal without parallel. During the 1967 Khe Sanh hill fighting, April 24–May 12, for example, the Marines lost 155 killed and 425 wounded, as against, at Hue, 142 killed and 857 wounded. The South Vietnamese, as noted, had far greater losses at Hue. The Army, pressing down from the north, suffered less severely.

16. The Marines did not "virtually seal off" the NVA "suicidal band"—
they took one corner of the Citadel, the east corner.

17. UPI, 079A–Viet, by Eugene Risher, 4th LD, Feb. 22, 1968. Emphasis added.

18. Weekday evening news shows: ABC–4, CBS–9, NBC–5.

19. The province headquarters had *tactical* significance; it had to be
taken to clear the south bank of the Perfume River. The VC flag was
merely an extra goad to the Marines.

20. The Marines' Regimental S-2 (intelligence officer), Maj. Joseph
Gratto, would not have agreed.

21. Both Marine battalion commanders involved, Lt. Col. Ernest
Cheatham and Lt. Col. Mark Gravel, told newsmen at the time that it
took the Marines a few days to get used to street fighting; they had been
used to rice paddies.

22. CBS-TV, "CBS Evening News," Feb. 7, 1968. Emphasis added.

23. In fact, as other newsmen learned at the time, the Marines were not
trying to blow up the Le Loi Street bridge to "trap" the enemy, but to
make it more difficult for the NVA to counterattack what had become
the Marines' flank. The NVA, of course, did not need bridges to "escape."

24. CBS-TV, "CBS Evening News," Feb. 10, 1968. CBS, like the other
networks, generally included film clips of the wounded being treated or
carried away, grimacing, on stretchers. This added an easy touch of
pseudo-realism to the two- or three-minute film reports, establishing the
"human drama" in combat.

25. Huntley's writers had their geography confused (as did most newsmen and MACV briefers on occasion): (1) the Marines executed no
"wide flanking movement," but simply boated across the Perfume River
and went to the east corner, site of 1st ARVN Division headquarters;
(2) Hue's square Citadel walls did not run north to south or east to
west. They linked corners which pointed in the four principal compass directions. Thus the "southeast corner" was in reality the south corner; but
the map of Hue was usually tilted, for easier reading, and confusion
resulted.

26. NBC-TV, "Huntley-Brinkley Report," Feb. 12, 1968. Emphasis
added.

27. CBS-TV, "CBS Evening News," Feb. 15, 1968. Emphasis added.

28. This story of planned "summary executions," irrelevant to the "critical" battle situation in any case, was later knocked down (AP, Feb.
21), and Colonel Khoa was sacked for incompetence and panic. The
wires were keen on execution stories.

29. NBC-TV, "Huntley-Brinkley Report," Feb. 20, 1968. Emphasis
added. This "Pyrrhic victory" theme cropped up repeatedly in TV and in
Newsweek, a bit of extrapolation. The palace was not destroyed.

30. CBS-TV, "CBS Evening News," Feb. 21, 1968. Emphasis added.

31. "Attacks on Hue Fail to Rout Foe," the New York Times, Feb. 5, 1968, p. 1.

32. "Hue to Da Nang: A Perilous Boat Ride," the New York Times, Feb. 11, 1968, p. 1.

33. For example, the New York Times stories: "Marines Gain in Hue," Feb. 14, 1968, p. 3; "U.S. Marines Gain 200 Yards in Day at Hue's Citadel," Feb. 16, 1968, p. 1.

34. "The U.S. Negro in Vietnam," the New York Times, Apr. 29, 1968.

35. Joseph Treaster of the Times was also received by Tolson, to the latter's regret. Treaster nearly lost his accreditation for telling all: In "Airmobile Division Short of Copters and Supplies; Force, Believed to Be Reserve for Khe Sanh, Is Fighting at Hue and Quang Tri" (Feb. 22, 1968, p. 10), he quoted Tolson as saying: "I hope for the time being we don't have to go to Khe Sanh." MACV subsequently imposed a tighter code for newsmen.

36. AP, B51–Hue Press, Feb. 17, 1968.

37. "Weather and Thin Ranks Slow Marines' Tough Fight in Hue," the Washington Post, Feb. 12, 1968, p. A1.

38. "Hue: Fires Pinpoint the Foe," the Washington Post, Feb. 16, 1968, p. A1.

39. Michael Herr, "Illumination Rounds," New American Review: Number 7 (New York: New American Library, 1969), p. 81.

40. There were two Washington Post stories: "Shortage of Men, Air Support Slow Marine Drive in Hue," Feb. 19, p. A1; "Hue Marines: Bitter As They Are Brave," Feb. 20, p. A1.

41. "Marine Leader Sees Weeks of Hue Battle," the Washington Post, Feb. 21, 1968, p. A1.

42. "U.S. Relieves Unit Hard Hit at Hue," the Washington Post, Feb. 22, 1968, p. A1.

43. "Marine Leader Sees Weeks of Hue Battle," the Washington Post, Feb. 21, 1968, p. A1.

44. Herr, "Illumination Rounds," pp. 82–83.

45. See "Weather and Thin Ranks Slow Marines' Tough Fight in Hue," the Washington Post, Feb. 12, 1968, p. A1.

46. This assertion was widely made. However, historians do not confirm it: The NVA came from the outside, joining Vietcong cadres inside. See Waldron and Beavers, Operation Hue City.

47. "Battle of Hue," Time, Feb. 16, 1968, p. 34.

48. Compare, to cite only two, UPI's "foot by bloodsoaked foot" (Feb. 22) and CBS's "bloody inch by inch" (Feb. 7).

49. "Grappling for Normalcy," Time, Feb. 23, 1968, p. 31. There was no mystery. This information was not filed by Time's men in Vietnam.

Which allied officers declared south Hue "sealed off"? This remains a *Time* exclusive.

50. *Time*'s weekly column, "A Letter from the Publisher" (Mar. 1, 1968, p. 7), gave Greenway, wounded, a pat on the back:

Also in Hue early in the week was correspondent David Greenway. Moving with a Marine company at the Citadel, Greenway decided to go forward with a squad that was assigned to knock out a North Vietnamese Army machine-gun post. As the squad reached a wall still standing amid the rubble, a Marine stood up to look through what had been a window, and an enemy soldier shot him through the neck. Greenway and a medical corpsman dragged the victim to the company command post and, once out of the line of fire, laid him down on a road behind a burned-out bus.

There, three other newsmen joined to help carry the man back to the rear. Just as the newsmen picked up the dying Marine, an enemy mortar round landed a few yards from them, blowing them into a ditch. Shrapnel hit Greenway in the left leg. He was taken out of Hue in a helicopter and treated at the U.S. military hospital at Phu Bai.

At week's end, walking with a crutch, Greenway was back at work, but from his home in Hong Kong.

51. The accompanying pictures, mostly by wire services, covered the fight of 1st Battalion, 5th Marines, the only Marine battalion committed to the north side of the river. There was plenty of rubble to be seen there. But the whole Citadel was not like that. It was battered, but not "the ruins of Monte Cassino."

52. There was no later evidence that napalm had been used against the Imperial Palace. Normally helicopters cannot "spray" napalm. This remains still another *Time* exclusive.

53. *Time*, like the other media, was confused about the position of the walls.

54. The correct designation: 5th Regiment's 1st Battalion. This is the kind of military error that *Time*, then staffed by World War II and Korean War veterans, did not make in the 1950s.

55. What was the "imperial city": the palace, the Citadel, or all of Hue? *Time*, like so many other publications, never made the geography clear. "Fight for a Citadel," *Time*, Mar. 1, 1968, p. 20. Emphasis added.

56. One new battalion (the 1st, 5th Marines) was thrown into the Citadel fight. The others were deployed to the southwest.

57. It was something less than an "all-out attack," as those newsmen who covered the Citadel fighting observed, since bad weather curbed air strikes and a 500-foot ceiling curbed helicopter gunships.

58. The chief "architectural treasures," of course, were both outside Hue (the royal tombs) and inside the palace. In neither place were they

"crumbling into debris," it turned out. The Citadel was often confused in reports with the Imperial Palace.

59. This implied that Hue's population was starving to death or dropping dead of illness, which was not so.

60. Battered or damaged, but not "flattened." Very little of Hue was "flattened," i.e., razed.

61. This was one standard Vietnam cliché. "Death of a Monument," *Newsweek,* Feb. 26, 1968, p. 34. Emphasis added.

62. As noted, only one tired, understrength three-company Marine battalion was involved in the Citadel assault. Six to eight understrength ARVN battalions were also involved, but never cited by *Newsweek.* Hue accounted for a minor share of U.S. troops killed in action in February.

63. "Waiting for the Second Wave," *Newsweek,* Mar. 4, 1968, p. 28.

64. AP, A032, Mar. 16, 1968.

65. UPI, 212A–Viet, by Thomas Cheatham, NX Night Lead, Mar. 16, 1968.

66. UPI, 281A–Viet, 2nd Add 1st Night Lead, Mar. 16, 1968. Emphasis added.

67. See Seymour Hersh, *My Lai 4: A Report on the Massacre and Its Aftermath* (New York: Random House, 1970).

68. Not so quiet, as subsequent court-martial testimony on the My Lai massacre was to reveal. But neither MACV information officers nor Saigon newsmen knew otherwise in 1968.

69. The operation was hardly an "offensive"; it was a small, standard search-and-destroy effort; and the enemy was not "threatening" Quang Ngai city, but recuperating from the Tet attacks.

70. "GIs in Pincer Move, Kill 128 in a Day-Long Battle," the New York *Times,* Mar. 17, 1968, p. 1.

71. "U.S. Infantrymen Kill 128 in Attack near Coast," the Washington *Post,* Mar. 17, 1968, p. A18.

72. One not atypical example was CBS's Jeff Gralnick interviewing a Marine at Hue on February 19. Asked Gralnick: "What d'you think of at a time like this?" The reply: "Um. Keepin' down."

Chapter 8: Khe Sanh

1. Even by Dienbienphu or Korean War standards—and in terms of the large (half a square mile) target—this average was less than "devastating," a favorite media adjective. A total of 103,000 rounds fell on Dienbienphu, averaging over 2,000 rounds daily. (Fall, *Hell in a Very Small Place,* p. 451.) In Korea, in four days the Chinese fired more than 45,000 rounds on one small area during the March 26–29, 1953, battle for the "Nevada complex" outposts. (Hermes, *United States Army in the Korean War,* p. 397.)

2. Shore, *Khe Sanh,* p. 130. No figures are available for ARVN losses,

which were considerably smaller; nor does this total apparently include those Marines lost aboard aircraft downed outside the Khe Sanh perimeter, according to Headquarters Marine Corps.

3. Fall, *Hell in a Very Small Place*, p. 455.

4. In contrast to far heavier losses of helicopters on the ground elsewhere at Tet, and to the loss of 30 helicopters reportedly downed in one day by NVA ground fire, April 19, during the allies' Operation Delaware raid on the A Shau Valley. (Brig. Gen. Edwin H. Simmons, USMC, "Marine Corps Operations in Vietnam, 1968," *United States Naval Institute Proceedings*, Naval Review Issue, 96, no. 5/807 [May 1970], 304.)

5. Shore, *Khe Sanh*, p. 131.

6. The interview got newspaper and network attention. The New York *Times* ran only two paragraphs from AP as a follo (a brief story following a major dispatch): "U.S. Force Kills 80 in Vietnam Clash . . . Westmoreland Expects Action," Jan. 18, 1968, p. 3. The Washington *Post* ran it the same day under the head: "U.S. General Sees Heavy Viet Fighting," p. 1.

7. The *Times* ran the story (p. 2) following "U.S. Pessimistic on Hanoi's Stand . . . Westmoreland Warns on Raids," Jan. 23, 1968, p. 1. *Post* coverage (p. 8) was also a follo, to "Allies Quitting Khe Sanh . . . Westmoreland Says Halt Would Aid Foes," Jan. 23, 1968, p. 1.

8. See Sharp and Westmoreland, *Report on the War*, p. 163; Simmons, "Marine Corps Operations," pp. 295–96; Shore, *Khe Sanh*, pp. 47–48.

9. Briefing by Maj. Gen. Philip B. Davidson, Feb. 4, 1968.

10. El Toro Marine Corps Air Station, California, Feb. 17, 1968.

11. Oberdorfer, *Tet!*, p. 110. Rostow saw "marked similarities" (terrain, weather, local ground firepower), but also "key differences" between Dienbienphu and Khe Sanh, and so told President Johnson. (Walt W. Rostow, *The Diffusion of Power* [New York: Macmillan, 1972], p. 465.)

In his well documented account of Washington policy-making ("Making a Decision: Tet 1968," Ph.D. thesis, Harvard University, 1974), Col. Herbert Yale Schandler, a Pentagon Papers contributor, emphasizes the chronic gap in perceptions between senior Washington policy-makers and General Westmoreland after the Tet attacks. President Johnson and his advisors did not share Westmoreland's confidence that Khe Sanh was not a Dienbienphu, nor the General's feeling that he need not put any great emphasis on Khe Sanh per se. "The thought of an American Dienbienphu following on the heels of the Tet offensive was enough to shake Washington to its roots," Schandler writes.

A written endorsement by the Joint Chiefs of Westmoreland's views, presented to Johnson by General Wheeler on January 29, did not end the worries. Rostow and Gen. Maxwell D. Taylor, former Ambassador to South Vietnam and a special consultant to the President, were also concerned. Westmoreland was pressed for reassurances that he could reinforce Khe Sanh; he gave them. The President, Taylor, and Rostow, far from the scene, remained worried; their state of mind, if not Westmoreland's, was communicated to subordinates and, via leaks, to the press in Washington.

12. Michael Herr, "Khe Sanh," *Esquire* (Sept. 1971), p. 122.

13. "Vietnam Outpost Awaiting Attack," the New York *Times,* Oct. 2, 1966.

14. Fall puts French Union losses at 8,221, including 1,293 known dead from November 21, 1953, to May 5, 1954, three days before the fall of Dienbienphu, or about 50 percent of the total French manpower committed. Marine casualties for the entire Operation Scotland (November 1, 1967–March 31, 1968) were 205 killed and 852 seriously wounded, or roughly 18 percent of the garrison at peak strength.

15. Giap, it has fairly well been established, did not "personally supervise" the Khe Sanh siege, as rumors enthusiastically cited by the wires frequently had it; indeed, a "senior U.S. military source" threw cold water on this theory at a briefing at Phu Bai on March 5 (AP). Giap was defense minister of North Vietnam, with much else to occupy him.

16. "U.S. Girding at Khe Sanh to Avoid a Dienbienphu," Hedrick Smith, Feb. 10, 1968; "Khe Sanh Disturbs Many in Marines," Hanson Baldwin, Mar. 14, 1968.

17. "The Military Dilemma," *Newsweek,* Mar. 18, 1968, p. 26.

18. "Viet Reds' Drive Was a Giap 'Masterstroke,' " the Washington *Post,* Feb. 11, 1968, p. A8.

19. "And the Debate over VN Deepens," the New York *Times,* Feb. 4, 1968, p. 1E.

20. Sharp and Westmoreland, *Report on the War,* p. 176.

21. Simmons, "Marine Corps Operations," p. 297; Oberdorfer, *Tet!,* p. 209.

22. Oberdorfer suggests that a lucky bomb hit on NVA headquarters in Laos may have thrown enemy commanders off stride. The NVA command radio went off the air for a fortnight. (*Tet!,* pp. 110–11.)

23. The Paterson (New Jersey) *Call.*

24. Bernard Kalb, "I Remember Da Nang," *Saturday Review,* LI, no. 48 (Nov. 30, 1968), 27.

25. Michael Herr, "Conclusion at Khe Sanh," *Esquire* (Oct. 1969), p. 123.

26. UPI, 017A–Cushman NX, by Robert C. Miller, Mar. 11, 1968. Emphasis added. Cushman was not spontaneously offering Dienbienphu analogies, but was responding to newsmen's queries and citations.

27. Shore, *Khe Sanh,* p. 49.

28. See Appendix XX for William Tuohy's description, *Big Story,* Westview Press edition.

29. "At Khe Sanh: Life on the Bull's-eye," the New York *Times*, Feb. 13, 1968, p. 1. Wheeler's story was widely used, but not in the Washington *Post*.
30. AP—Khe Sanh Hills, Mar. 1, 1968. This story did not get into either the New York *Times* or the Washington *Post*.
31. AP—Khe Sanh, by Lewis Simons, Feb. 24, 1968.
32. Especially after Tet, MACV tended to discuss "elements" of as many as four divisions in Khe Sanh and adjoining Laos and North Vietnam, stretching Khe Sanh "area" widely, possibly as further public justification for the U.S. effort at the base. Marine intelligence at the base during the siege put NVA strength nearby at two divisions (20,000 men at full strength), with another (the 320th) 20 kilometers away at the closest. This third NVA unit could conceivably have been committed to an attack on Khe Sanh; it was not.
33. Actually four.
34. Twenty rounds was hardly a "barrage"; it was harassing fire.
35. Despite the "barrages," the C-130s continued to land until February 12. The smaller two-engine C-123s came and went throughout the siege.
36. The AP and UPI war wrap-ups both had a sports-page statistics flavor, especially when dealing with air operations.
37. In military terms, these casualties are extremely light for a 5,000-man force.
38. "Reds Bombed at Khe Sanh, Foe Still Shells Marine Base Despite Record Air Assault," the Washington *Evening Star*, Jan. 25, 1968, p. 1. Emphasis added.
39. Herr, "Conclusion at Khe Sanh," pp. 121–22. Thanks to modern communications, Lownds was subject to considerable official kibitzing. Once, just before Tet, as he came out of his command post, he shook his head in wonder at this writer. The Colonel had just received a call from the President of the United States, who wanted to know if everything was coming along all right.
40. This, again, is exaggeration. Needless to say, the enemy mortars were relatively ineffective, considering the target. The daily death toll, including losses inflicted in infantry combat, from *all* enemy action averaged three men. Emphasis added.
41. "Khe Sanh," *Life*, Feb. 23, 1968, p. 28B.
42. Khe Sanh was not burrowed into a thickly jungled valley, but sat on a plateau, with hill outposts. Hanoi's "shortest" invasion route was, of course, not an end run via Khe Sanh, but across the DMZ.
43. AP, A004—Khe Sanh, by George McArthur. Emphasis added.
44. There is no record of Giap using tanks at Dienbienphu. AP, A012, Feb. 8, 1968. Emphasis added.
45. AP, A023—Khe Sanh-Dienbienphu, 480, Feb. 9, 1968. The Washington *Post* used the story on Feb. 10, 1968, p. A6.

46. AP, A103—Dienbienphu Special Report 430, advance for Wed. PMs, Mar. 13, 1968.

47. AP—Vietnam, A004 114 pes, Mar. 22, 1968. Emphasis added. A later night lead (AP, A109, Mar. 22) described the guns as a "new peril" to U.S. planes.

48. "Mobile Guns Imperil Khe Sanh," the New York Times, Mar. 23, 1968, p. 13; "B-52s Strike Enemy Bases near Saigon," the Washington Post, Mar. 23, 1968, p. A1.

49. UPI, 6—Viet, Feb. 7, 1968. Emphasis added.

50. UPI, 122—Viet, Feb. 7, 1968. Emphasis added.

51. The tanks were old PT-76 models.

52. UPI, 126—Viet, Feb. 8, 1968. Emphasis added.

53. The geographical similarities were minor. The enemy was not "crushed"; they backed off.

54. It was a "tiny" fort two days earlier.

55. UPI, 110—Viet, Feb. 9, 1968. Emphasis added.

56. UPI, 096A—Flight, by Robert Ibrahim, NX, Feb. 29, 1968.

57. C-130s had stopped landing on February 12. UPI, 094A—Viet, NX, 1st Add 2nd LD Viet Saigon 093A, Feb. 28, 1968. Emphasis added.

58. The story of the written guarantee had been reported by Time, and continued to be echoed, as here, in print. (See below, note 112.) The ground attack was the first one against the main perimeter, after three efforts against hill outposts (Hills 861, 861 Alpha, 64).

59. UPI, 212A—Viet, by Jack Walsh, NX, Night LD, Mar. 1, 1968. Emphasis added.

60. UPI, 208A—Viet, by Jack Walsh, NX, Bulletin, 1st Night LD, Mar. 2, 1968.

61. It was the 304th Division (10,000 men), not a battalion (400), but it got Dienbienphu into the picture again. UPI—Saigon, by Jack Walsh, Night LD, Mar. 2, 1968.

62. UPI, 203A, RS1240 pes, by Robert Ibrahim, Night LD, Mar. 2, 1968.

63. UPI, 206A—Viet, by Jack Walsh, NX, Night LD, Mar. 11, 1968. Emphasis added.

64. UPI, 234A—Battle, by Richard V. Oliver, Mar. 12, 1968.

65. UPI, 027A—Viet, by Eugene Risher, Mar. 12, 1968.

66. UPI, 208A—Viet, by Jack Walsh, NX, Night LD, Mar. 13, 1968.

67. UPI, 028A—Viet, by Jack Walsh, Mar. 18, 1968.

68. UPI, 76—Khe Sanh, Mar. 20, 1968.

69. UPI, 217A—Viet, Mar. 20, 1968.

70. Shore, Khe Sanh, pp. 126–27.

71. News conference, Apr. 11, 1968.

72. AP, A091—Khe Sanh, Mar. 21, 1968.

73. On April 3, after asking guidance on a second but "unpublished"

withdrawal report, and getting another MACV denial on March 29, the *Post* foreign desk sent this semi-reproachful cable to Saigon: "INFORMATIVELY SHEEHAN [Neil Sheehan] HAD UNNAMED DOD OFFICIALS SAYING NORTH VIETNAMESE HAD SUBSTANTIALLY REDUCED FORCES AT KHE SANH OVER PAST MONTH. OFFICIALS SAY NOW *SOME* DOUBT PREDICTED ATTACK WILL TAKE PLACE . . . THAT DIVISION [withdrawn from Khe Sanh] IDENTIFIED AS THREE-TWO-FIVE CCC." Sheehan had scored again.

74. UPI—Cushman, by Richard Oliver, NX, Mar. 26, 1968.

75. UPI, 231A—Viet, by Thomas Cheatham, Night LD, Mar. 30, 1968. Emphasis added.

76. NBC-TV, "Huntley-Brinkley Report," Jan. 29, 1968. Emphasis added.

77. It should be remembered, as noted, that, unbeknownst to newsmen, the Tet attacks, against Hue in particular, caught Cushman in the middle of a reshuffle of Marine units in northern I Corps, and in the middle of a shift (which was publicized) of Army units to the area as well. Tet, in effect, caught the U.S. troops in coastal northern I Corps with one foot in the air.

78. CBS-TV, "CBS Morning News," Jan. 29, 1968.

79. As the Khe Sanh siege went on, the traditional thirst of television producers for combat footage began to excite less and less enthusiasm among TV newsmen in Vietnam. Reported *Time*'s television section, Mar. 15, 1968, p. 58:

> . . . Last week two ABC men, Bill Brannigan and Jim Deckard, were injured in the bombardment of Khe Sanh. As a result, many members of TV's standard three-man teams (correspondent, cameraman, and sound man) have begged off from hazardous assignments, and the networks are having trouble reporting all the battles. CBS Tokyo Bureau Chief Igor Oganesoff, who was frequently shuttled into Vietnam for fill-in duty, has refused further combat assignments; ABC's Don North, a veteran of 18 months there, asked to be transferred. ABC's Hong Kong Bureau Chief, Sam Jaffe, also decided after three recent weeks in Vietnam that "I won't cover Khe Sanh, and I refuse to go back to Hue." Summed up Jaffe, 38, who saw action as a merchant seaman in World War II and with the Marines in Korea: "The longer you stay here, the more inevitable it is that you're going to be hurt, maimed, or killed."

80. According to a tabulation for this book by Professor Lawrence Lichty.

81. David Douglas Duncan, "Khe Sanh," *Life*, Feb. 23, 1968; and idem, *I Protest!* (New York: New American Library, 1968).

82. A week earlier CBS had shown a film report by Jeff Gralnick

("CBS Evening News," Jan. 31, 1968) about what a "bad week" it had been at Khe Sanh; but this was filmed prior to Tet.

83. This was reading Hanoi's mind again.

84. ABC-TV, "ABC Evening News," Feb. 6, 1968.

85. CBS-TV, "CBS Evening News," Feb. 14, 1968. Emphasis added. Fromson voiced the common impression among newsmen.

86. CBS-TV, "CBS Evening News," Feb. 15, 1968. Emphasis added. Of course, Khe Sanh turned out to be a "trap" for neither side.

87. U.S. B-52s were trying to knock out enemy artillery and infantry.

88. Assaults against Lang Vei, Hill 861, and Hill 64 had taken place.

89. ABC-TV, "ABC Evening News," Feb. 19, 1968. Emphasis added.

90. ABC-TV, "ABC Evening News," Feb. 23, 1968. Emphasis added.

91. *Newsweek* also said that the U.S. position at Khe Sanh "simply reflects in microcosm the entire U.S. military position in Vietnam." ("The Military Dilemma," *Newsweek*, Mar. 18, 1968, p. 27.)

92. "Roadblock"? Khe Sanh blocked Highway Nine, if nothing else.

93. Khe Sanh was isolated and tied down, but 20,000 "reserves" were not. They were operating vigorously on the "coastal plain."

94. As noted elsewhere, MACV officials were prudently repeating the old military cliché: Any fortified position can be taken if the enemy wants to pay the price and has the necessary men and firepower. I heard this phrase about Khe Sanh, as about Con Thien, before Tet at MACV and at the III MAF press camp. Few old Vietnam hands were surprised by the caveat that Cronkite found disheartening.

95. "Certitude" but not "conviction"?

96. CBS-TV, "CBS Evening News," Feb. 29, 1968. Emphasis added.

97. CBS-TV, "CBS Evening News," Mar. 1, 1968.

98. It was the same C-130 transport cited by Duncan.

99. CBS-TV, "CBS Evening News," Mar. 6, 1968. Emphasis added.

100. CBS-TV, "CBS Evening News," Mar. 14, 1968. Emphasis added.

101. ABC-TV, "ABC Evening News," Mar. 15, 1968. The report was UPI's.

102. NBC-TV, "Huntley-Brinkley Report," Mar. 15, 1968.

103. CBS-TV, "CBS Evening News," Mar. 18, 1968. Four-engine C-130s were dropping supplies by parachute, and the twin-engine C-123s were regularly landing and taking off, carrying such items as artillery pieces and other heavy gear.

104. ABC-TV, "ABC Evening News," Mar. 19, 1968.

105. CBS-TV, "CBS Evening News," Mar. 22, 1968. Emphasis added.

106. CBS-TV, "CBS Evening News," Mar. 28, 1968. Emphasis added.

107. Again, there was no mention of total U.S. losses, and no context for the film.

108. CBS-TV, "CBS Evening News," Mar. 29, 1968. Emphasis added. Ironically, casualties were light that month.

109. CBS-TV, "CBS Morning News," Mar. 26, 1968.
110. ARVN morale, as AP's John Wheeler later pointed out, was to drop somewhat, partly because they were told they would be relieved by another battalion in mid-March, and were not. (AP, Mar. 17, 1968.)
111. CBS-TV, "CBS Evening News," Mar. 9, 1968.
112. "In a rainbow display of his kaleidoscopic personality, Johnson was by turns wryly humorous, cautious, defensive, patriotic, and pugnacious. 'I don't want any damned Dienbienphu,' he warned the Joint Chiefs of Staff during a White House discussion of Khe Sanh, cross-examining them at great length about the wisdom of defending the isolated outpost. In an extraordinary gesture, apparently designed to alert everyone to the gravity of the situation, Johnson then made each Chief sign a paper stating that he believed Khe Sanh could be defended." ("The Presidency: A Long Way from Spring," Time, Feb. 9, 1968, p. 16.) Joseph Alsop had cited "two questions which were long ago put to [Westmoreland] from a high level in Washington." They were: Could Khe Sanh be held or should the garrison withdraw east to the Rock Pile area? Westmoreland answered appropriately. (The Washington Post, Jan. 29, 1968.)
113. On June 24, long after Tet, in a speech to the New York Society of Newspaper Editors, Wheeler dated the Joint Chiefs' response to the President as coming just before Tet, on January 29.
114. ABC-TV, "ABC Evening News," Feb. 5, 1968.
115. NBC-Radio, "Emphasis: Plain Talk," Feb. 6, 1968. Huntley did not explain how captured documents hinted that Khe Sanh could be a Dienbienphu for the foe.
116. CBS-Radio, "First-Line Report," Feb. 7, 1968.
117. CBS-Radio, "Dimension," Feb. 7, 1968.
118. CBS-Radio, "The World This Week," Feb. 10, 1968.
119. NBC-Radio, "Weekend Report," Feb. 11, 1968. Emphasis added.
120. NBC-TV, "The Today Show," Mar. 4, 1968.
121. NBC-TV, Mar. 9, 1968. This was a non-parallel; tunnels were not used to blow up the command bunkers at Dienbienphu.
122. NBC-TV, "The Today Show," Mar. 11, 1968.
123. CBS-TV, "CBS Evening News," Mar. 12, 1968.
124. CBS-Radio, "The World Tonight," Mar. 13, 1968. The "new communist road" has already been noted: It was UPI's highly touted but irrelevant "jungle road" (Route 547) through the A Shau Valley, 35 miles from Khe Sanh. General Cushman had not read UPI.
125. According to a survey made by Professors Lawrence Lichty and Thomas Hoffer, covering the January 29–March 22 period.
126. CBS-TV, "CBS Evening News," Feb. 29, 1968, and Mar. 12, 1968.
127. Alsop's reports in the Washington Post were: "Curious Facts Lie Behind Flurry of Vietnam Negotiations Talk," Dec. 13, 1967; "Captured

Documents Indicate a Major Red Strategy Shift," Dec. 15, 1967; "Hanoi Plans 'Coalition Ploy' as Easy Way Out of its Bind," Dec. 18, 1967.
128. A question asked by another reporter.
129. "Marines Are Digging In at Khe Sanh," by Peter Braestrup, the Washington *Post,* Feb. 5, 1968, p. A10.
130. "Security Is a Bunker for Khe Sanh Platoon," the Washington *Post,* Feb. 17, 1968, p. A10.
131. "Khe Sanh Waits and Probes Strategy," by Peter Braestrup, the Washington *Post,* Feb. 19, 1968, p. A19.
132. "Marines at Khe Sanh Clean Rifles and Dig Deeper, Find They 'Gotta Keep Busy' to Counteract the Tension and Tedium of Waiting," the New York *Times,* Feb. 14, 1968, p. 2.
133. "Marines at Khe Sanh Find Flaws in Their Defenses," the New York *Times,* Feb. 22, 1968, p. 1. The *Times* editors accompanied the story with the usual inaccurate Khe Sanh map and inserted a cross-reference to a second yarn by Joseph Treaster (p. 10): "The Army's 1st Cavalry Division (Airmobile), widely viewed as a possible reinforcing unit for Khe Sanh, has faced a shortage of manpower supplies and helicopters." (Treaster's story included the previously noted quote of Maj. Gen. John Tolson—see the preceding chapter, note 35.)
134. Shore, *Khe Sanh,* pp. 55–56.
135. "Plight of Khe Sanh Called Not So Dire," the Washington *Post,* Mar. 3, 1968, p. A20.
136. AP, 47—Vietnam—Censor, Mar. 5, 1968.
137. "The Analogy of Dienbienphu," the Washington *Post,* Feb. 10, 1968, p. A6. Emphasis added.
138. "Khe Sanh and Dienbienphu: A Comparison," the New York *Times,* Mar. 8, 1968.
139. "Now It's a New and Much Meaner War," the New York *Times,* Mar. 10, 1968, p. 3E. Trenches, not the widely reported suspected "tunnels," were plentiful around Khe Sanh's perimeter, as post-siege inspection was to show. See Shore, *Khe Sanh,* pp. 120–21. Roberts, like the *Post* reporters and most other "analysts" in March, suffered from a lack of firsthand, current information on Khe Sanh. This shows up repeatedly in failures to examine, or even mention, the abortive attack against the South Vietnamese Rangers, which, historians now believe, was the last gasp before the March 12 withdrawals began. Even AP's Peter Arnett, who was there March 1, did not stay long enough to do a post-mortem of what Lownds first saw as a "probe."
140. "North Vietnam's Comments Stress New Attacks near Khe Sanh," the New York *Times,* Mar. 17, 1968, p. 7. The "move," we now know, was withdrawal.
141. "Copters Run Constant Risks to Supply Khe Sanh Outposts," by Peter Braestrup, the Washington *Post,* Mar. 5, 1968, p. A10.

142. "Busy Spotter Pilot Helps Clear Road to Khe Sanh," by Peter Braestrup, the Washington *Post*, Mar. 24, 1968, p. 1. Security considerations, however, forbade explaining the overall system set up for air support of Khe Sanh. The writer blacked out three times during the roller-coaster flying, which also blurred his perceptions during a subsequent interview with spotter pilots in Da Nang.

143. "U.S. Officers Say Air Power Makes Khe Sanh a Disaster for Foe," the New York *Times*, Mar. 28, 1968.

144. In fact, trench construction had largely ceased. We did not know that the foe had begun to withdraw. The Marines raided the enemy trenches for the first time March 30, the day before Roberts' story was printed, an event announced by MACV and AP.

145. "U.S. Builds Up Forces in Two Northern Provinces As Enemy Threatens Bases," the New York *Times*, Mar. 31, 1968, p. 3. After a major buildup in the Calu Valley area 12 miles east of Khe Sanh, the Marines and Army launched Operation Pegasus on April 1, the day after the *Times* published this story, and after abundant hints in the *Post* and AP that a move was coming.

146. For example, "5,000 Men Massed at Khe Sanh by U.S.," by Charles Mohr, the New York *Times*, Jan. 24, 1968.

147. AP, A031–534 a.m.–Red Bombers, Feb. 10, 1968.

148. UPI, 61–Viet, 2:15 p.m., Feb. 10, 1968.

149. As already noted, the cavalrymen were hard at work—at Quang Tri, and, against heavy resistance, north of Hue. "Jet Bombers Seen at Base in North During U.S. Raids," the New York *Times*, Feb. 11, 1968, p. 1. Emphasis added.

150. "North Viet Bombers Sighted, Three Russian Jets Seen on Field North of Hanoi," the Washington *Post*, Feb. 11, 1968, p. A1.

151. Despite the low U.S. plane losses at Khe Sanh, individual fixed-wing aircraft and even helicopters shot down or destroyed on the ground by communist gunners accounted for two Khe Sanh war leads for the *Times*, three for AP, and one for the *Post*, not to mention plentiful TV commentary and film during February and March 1968. Rarely, despite the American penchant for air war scorekeeping, were low cumulative plane losses at Khe Sanh cited.

152. "The Little Marine and His New Boots," the Washington *Post*, Mar. 24, 1968, p. B1.

153. The weather remained about the same—bad. The U.S. position was unchanged, except that the Marines had made progress in digging in, and the North Vietnamese had begun digging approach trenches.

154. "Khe Sanh Is Quite Takeable," the Washington *Post*, Feb. 25, 1968, p. D1.

155. Feb. 23, 1968, p. A10.

156. "Force at Khe Sanh Is Foe's Largest," Jan. 26, 1968.

157. "Battle for Khe Sanh May Be Major Turning Point of War," Jan. 29, 1968, p. A15.
158. "Red Raids on Cities Are Sign of Weakness, Not Strength," Feb. 2, 1968, p. A19; "Hanoi Places Heavy Stakes on Two Throws of the Dice," Feb. 9, 1968, p. A21; "Major Failure in City Battles Was Enemy's, Not the Allies'," Feb. 19, 1968, p. A21.
159. "Khe Sanh: Holding the End of the Line," the Washington *Post*, Jan. 31, 1968, p. A20.
160. "Policy-Makers and Generals Worry over Massive Buildup at Khe Sanh," the Washington *Post*, Jan. 31, 1968, p. A21. Emphasis added. Westmoreland did not, publicly at least, "predict" that sort of "victory," only a serious enemy effort.
161. "Khe Sanh Situation Now Shows Viet Foe Makes Strategy Work," the Washington *Post*, Feb. 1, 1968, p. A21.
162. "Washington Stunned by One-Two Blow," Feb. 4, 1968, p. 2E; "Latest Soviet Tanks Used by Enemy near Khe Sanh," by William Beecher, Feb. 8, 1968, p. 1; "U.S. Girding at Khe Sanh to Avoid a Dienbienphu, Washington Mood Tense," by Hedrick Smith, Feb. 10, 1968, p. 1; "Johnson Holds Reins," by Max Frankel, Feb. 10, 1968, p. 1; "Khe Sanh: Why U.S. Is Making a Stand," by Neil Sheehan, Feb. 23, 1968, p. 1; "Khe Sanh Disturbs Many in Marines, Some Voice Objections to a Static Defense but Doubt a Dienbienphu Parallel," by Hanson Baldwin, Mar. 14, 1968, p. 1.
163. Feb. 4, 1968, p. 1E.
164. "Latest Soviet Tanks Used by Enemy at Khe Sanh."
165. "U.S. Girding at Khe Sanh to Avoid a Dienbienphu, Washington Mood Tense."
166. "Khe Sanh: Why U.S. Is Making a Stand." This last point, though not stressed by Sheehan, was the prime revelation in his well-written story. As noted, Westmoreland in July 1967 had proposed to visiting Defense Secretary McNamara that such thrusts be made, based on Khe Sanh, the only possible staging area in mountainous northwestern South Vietnam. Westmoreland had moved in the Marines in October 1966 (not in February 1967, as Sheehan reported) and begun to improve the Khe Sanh airstrip.
167. "Khe Sanh Disturbs Many in Marines."
168. "Hanoi Places Heavy Stakes on Two Throws of the Dice," Feb. 9, 1968, p. A21.
169. "U.S. Had to Scrap 1968 War Plan Even Before Assault on Viet Cities," Feb. 16, 1968, p. A21.
170. "Disturbing Parallels Noted in Saigon," Mar. 15, 1968, p. B15.
171. "Vets of Dienbienphu Appraise Khe Sanh," Feb. 14, 1968, p. A18.
172. "Plight of Khe Sanh Called Not So Dire," Mar. 3, 1968, p. A20.
173. "U.S. Warily Eyes Hanoi Strategy," the Washington *Post*, Feb. 16,

1968, p. A14. Such "growing doubt" did not get into the New York *Times*.

174. There was only one day in March when the *Times* did not have a page-one story from Vietnam.

175. Like his AP counterpart, the *Times*'s war wrap-up writer in Saigon, partly in response to the accent on Khe Sanh, highlighted and interpreted Khe Sanh items out of the Five O'Clock Follies, but without firsthand information.

176. For picture captions, see Picture Indexes, the New York *Times* and the Washington *Post*.

177. This was a persistent rumor, but U.S. officials, even long after the battle, said it was unconfirmed.

178. The communists had to go uphill to take the Marine hill outposts on the west; the terrain on Khe Sanh's eastern and southern sides was rolling. The terrain was no problem except on the north or ravine side.

179. No "barrier" existed or was attempted west of Con Thien, a few miles from the sea. Khe Sanh blocked only one of many easy access routes into South Vietnam; it had primarily regional significance as a hindrance to an enemy end run into Quang Tri province's coastal flats. It did not prevent attacks on Hue, Quang Tri city, or Phu Loc.

180. *Who* was *hoping* Giap would strike?

181. "The War: The General's Gamble," *Time*, Feb. 9, 1968, p. 22. The last sentence was a foray into mind-reading.

182. *Newsweek* upped the enemy strength from 20,000 (two divisions) to 40,000, all of them "tough." The Marines were just Marines.

183. And, more importantly, they probably wanted to leave a free-fire zone for artillery, air, and B-52 strikes. "Hanoi Attacks and Scores a Major Psychological Blow," *Newsweek*, Feb. 12, 1968, p. 23.

184. This was one of many examples of the erroneous rewriting of history during the Khe Sanh-Tet period. It was the French, not the Vietminh, who launched attacks far from the Dienbienphu area. There was nothing comparable to Tet in 1954. Westmoreland suggested, then quickly abandoned, the idea that the Tet offensive was a "diversion."

185. "The War: The General's Biggest Battle," *Time*, Feb. 16, 1968, p. 19. Emphasis added.

186. The concrete bunker was simply the command post for the Green Berets, and not indicative of the earthwork defenses of the outpost as a whole, which were, by all accounts, as vulnerable to assault as any other Special Forces outpost in Vietnam, as well as being vulnerable (and hardly "immune") to artillery fire. Some of the material for this story was supplied by Don Sider, from Khe Sanh; some came from the Saigon bureau.

187. "Fall of Lang Vei," *Time*, Feb. 16, 1968, p. 36. Emphasis added. Actually, aside from Lang Vei, the ground attacks that week were against

Hills 861 Alpha (near Hill 558) and Hill 64, a small platoon outpost 500 meters west of the Khe Sanh perimeter. No newsmen were able to get to these outposts by this time; and Lownds's aides were not preoccupied with press relations. Information on anything occurring on the hill outposts bearing the brunt of the siege was secondhand and sketchy; they tended to go unmentioned by the media, although their role was vital. Hill 64, in fact, was abandoned, after the NVA won and lost it.

188. "Khe Sanh: Ready to Fight," *Time*, Feb. 16, 1968, p. 38. Marine historians place the "incoming" record for one day at 1,307 rounds, received February 23. (Shore, *Khe Sanh*, p. 183.) But Sider's total, based on contemporary Marine reports, was widely echoed.

189. The story is error-ridden. Only two such NVA assaults were made the previous week and repulsed; nine tanks were employed; and the Ilyushin jets, as we have seen, did not reappear.

190. There was little other choice: Khe Sanh was encircled on the ground.

191. This remains a *Newsweek* exclusive.

192. *Newsweek* was hedging. No attack can be beaten down "instantly."

193. "Man on the Spot," *Newsweek*, Feb. 19, 1968, p. 33. Emphasis added.

194. Correct. Compare with *Time*'s description of sure-fire defenses at Lang Vei.

195. The PT-76 tank, which mounted a 76 mm. gun, was not "modern." As noted, the New York *Times* erroneously made it "modern" on February 9.

196. This was a point *Newsweek* might have made at the start.

197. "How the U.S. Lost Lang Vei," *Newsweek*, Feb. 19, 1968, p. 42. Emphasis added.

198. For a 6,000-man force these were extremely light casualties—well below the casualty rate of Marine forces engaged at Hue or south of Da Nang. But that was not the impression given by the media.

199. The "dawning realization" was not, as implied, among U.S. military commanders. The possibility was repeatedly mentioned by Cushman and by MACV officials that the enemy might be able to take Khe Sanh if "he wants to pay the price." The realization had dawned on—indeed preoccupied—the press corps and their superiors back home; since January 21, apocalyptic visions of Dienbienphu swam in everybody's head.

200. "Waiting for the Thrust," *Time*, Feb. 23, 1968, p. 32. Emphasis added. The insight about Giap's musings on the use of warplanes in the south is a *Time* exclusive. See UPI, and also "Jet Bombers Seen at Base in North," the New York *Times*, Feb. 11, 1968, p. 1.

201. "The War: More Men, More Doubts," *Newsweek*, Mar. 4, 1968, p.

19. Emphasis added. Was the last comment prompted by the New York *Times*'s "flaws" story of February 23?

202. In eight hours on February 23, the Khe Sanh combat base took 1,307 rounds, many of them from the 130 mm. and 152 mm. guns in Laos. But casualties were relatively light: 10 killed, 21 medevacked. (Shore, *Khe Sanh*, pp. 121–22.) The enemy artillery and mortar fire— by comparison with enemy fire as reported at Dienbienphu or in Korea— seemed curiously erratic and ill-aimed, especially when enemy artillery observers overlooked the base and, theoretically, could fire rounds on any one of a number of obvious targets. This failure on the enemy's part to exploit his low-cost opportunities was later attributed by some of the media to heavy air strikes which upset his ammunition-supply system. But during the siege, as elsewhere in Vietnam, the focus was on the damage suffered by the allies, not on the enemy's failures to inflict more. This focus was natural to civilians under fire. There were occasional exceptions in *Time* and the Washington *Post*.

203. "Dark Clouds," *Newsweek*, Mar. 4, 1968, pp. 29–30. Emphasis added.

204. "The War: On the Defensive," *Time*, Mar. 1, 1968, p. 18.

205. "Living on Air: How Khe Sanh Is Sustained," *Time*, Mar. 1, 1968, p. 19.

206. Evacuation was, of course, impossible, as most newsmen, and presumably Thieu, were well aware.

207. "The Administration: Clifford Takes Over," *Time*, Mar. 8, 1968, p. 17. Emphasis added.

208. First mention of the ARVN at Khe Sanh.

209. "Waiting: Khe Sanh and Saigon," *Newsweek*, Mar. 11, 1968, p. 58. Emphasis added. *Newsweek*'s account is based on AP, Mar. 1. In retrospect, it proved a turning point, not a "probe," according to Marine historians. As no one thought to report, at the onset of March the weather was getting better. Twelve days later, the foe began to withdraw.

210. This is still another *Time* exclusive. But *Time* was on to something. USMC historians record that the 304th Division stayed at Khe Sanh, while the 325C NVA Division started moving *into Laos* in early March. (Shore, *Khe Sanh*, p. 126.)

211. "The War: Period of Adjustment," *Time*, Mar. 15, 1968, p. 21.

212. "The Dusty Agony of Khe Sanh," *Newsweek*, Mar. 18, 1968, p. 28.

213. However, Francois Sully was touched by the "Dienbienphu syndrome," as noted earlier.

214. "The Military Dilemma: The New Math of Escalation Adds Up to One-to-One," *Newsweek*, Mar. 18, 1968, p. 26. This is an exclusive. Comparisons for March 13 were as follows: 190 NVA/VC battalions versus 296 allied battalions (including 107 U.S.; 26 Thai, Korean, Australian; 155 South Vietnamese). (Sharp and Westmoreland, *Report*

on the War, p. 178.) It should be noted that U.S. battalions in the field (600 to 800 men) ran larger by 50–100 percent than the NVA/VC units; there was nothing near a "one-to-one" ratio in combat manpower. 215. "A Day at Dong Ha," *Newsweek,* Mar. 25, 1968, p. 40. During the Tet period, *Newsweek* ran 29 Khe Sanh photographs (including the cover of March 18)—more than one-third of all its Tet Vietnam photos. Almost half (13) showed American or ARVN troops dead or wounded. None showed U.S. troops firing back. Four showed damage inflicted by the foe—e.g., wrecked planes. *Time* ran only four pictures of Khe Sanh, out of 62 Tet-period photographs.

Chapter 9: South Vietnamese Performance

1. In 1972, *Newsweek* had the wisdom to employ, as a stringer, perhaps the war's only American journalist specializing in monitoring ARVN performance. He was Alexander Shimkin, a lanky young Indiana University graduate who spoke Vietnamese, kept tabs on individual ARVN units and their leaders, and based his scholarly reporting on systematic firsthand observation in combat. He generously shared his information with Saigon colleagues. During Hanoi's 1972 Easter offensive, Shimkin told this writer that he covered both excellent South Vietnamese units (e.g., the airborne) and battalions that fell apart. "The magazine didn't use the favorable reports," he said. "But I guess I shouldn't complain. They pay me." Shimkin was reported missing near Quang Tri city while covering the ARVN in late 1972.

2. Sharp and Westmoreland, *Report on the War,* p. 154. The RVNAF strength figures are from a memorandum from Gen. Earle Wheeler to President Johnson, Feb. 27, 1968, published in "Key Texts from Pentagon's Vietnam Study," the New York *Times,* July 4, 1971, p. 15. Comparable figures are cited by McNamara in his statement to the Senate Armed Services Committee, Jan. 22, 1968, which also mentions the 70,000-man national police, badly hit at Tet.

3. Reflecting the confusion of the time, minor disparities exist in various official reports on the number of localities that were actually *assaulted* by Vietcong or NVA troops at Tet. We use throughout this book the data from Sharp and Westmoreland, *Report on the War* (p. 158), which also states that the enemy "penetrated in strength" into Saigon, Hue, and 10 other cities (p. 159). By official count, probably understated, RVNAF lost 4,954 killed, 15,097 wounded, and 926 missing in action during February and March 1968. (ARVN, *Viet Cong Tet Offensive,* p. 55.) Losses were particularly heavy in the elite units—Marines and airborne—used as reaction forces. Total U.S. casualties from January 29 to March 31, 1968, included 3,895 deaths; communist dead totaled 58,373; and 14,300 South Vietnamese civilians died, according to official allied figures. (Oberdorfer, *Tet!,* p. v.)

4. UPI, 201A–Viet, by Jack Walsh, Feb. 25, 1968. In this book, for such enumerations, "leads" have been defined as the first *two* paragraphs of a war wrap-up or omnibus Vietnam story.

5. They were: "S. Viets Got Tet Leave Despite Raid Warning," Feb. 10, p. A6; "Capture of Hue Citadel Was a Must for S. Viet Unit," Feb. 29, p. A22; "South Viets Prove Fighters in Hue," Mar. 2, p. A11; "Saigon Army Missing 10 Percent Since Tet," Mar. 2, p. A10; "Ky Praises His Troops' Valor," Mar. 10, p. A26; "Militia Unit Presses VC Hard," Mar. 20, p. A23.

6. One was a brief AP file: "Half Saigon Army on Leave for Tet," Feb. 9, p. 17; another, also by AP, was about the execution of a VC prisoner by a South Vietnamese Marine, with two photos illustrating the act: "The Execution of a Vietcong Suspect Marks a Day of Violence in Saigon," Feb. 19, p. 14. The only staff-written reports were by Charles Mohr: "War Crisscrosses Suburb of Saigon," Feb. 4, p. 5; and "Saigon Tries to Recover from the Blows," Mar. 10, p. 3E.

7. Speech before the annual convention of the Colorado Construction Association, Denver, Colorado, Jan. 19, 1968; in "Selected Statements on Vietnam by Department of Defense and Other Administration Officials, January 1–June 30, 1968," prepared and xeroxed by the Research and Analysis Division, Office of the Administrative Assistant to the Secretary of the Air Force (SAFAA), p. 189.

8. Speech before the Indianapolis Junior Chamber of Commerce, Jan. 26, 1968; ibid., p. 191. Americans were also deeply involved in the Vietnamese side of the war. A parallel U.S. (advisory) structure matched the ARVN's. The military advisors had their own communications net, reporting system, and supply sources. Every 450-man ARVN battalion was accompanied by a three-to-five man U.S. advisory team (with its own radio). As many as 300 Americans were assigned, as liaison-advisory-logistics specialists, to an ARVN infantry division, as at Hue. Moreover, U.S. advisory teams (primarily used to prod ARVN counterparts and to obtain and coordinate U.S. supplies and helicopter and fire support) were present at every level of ARVN territorial command, including "sector" (province) and "sub-sector" (district). These advisors, perhaps 12,000 in all, were usually hospitable to the few American newsmen who came to visit. But relatively little press attention was given the senior advisors' crucial roles at Tet, or, indeed, after Tet through 1972, notably as brokers between jealous ARVN commanders and as sources of moral, as well as material, support for the South Vietnamese military.

9. Speech before the National Association of Secondary School Principals, Atlantic City, New Jersey, Feb. 10, 1968; SAFAA, "Selected Statements on Vietnam," p. 213.

10. Interview following appearance before House Subcommittee on Department of Defense Appropriations, Feb. 14, 1968; ibid., p. 214.

11. Speech at testimonial dinner for Representative Jack Brooks, Beaumont, Texas, Mar. 1, 1968; ibid., p. 193.

12. AP, A093—Viet Comment, Feb. 3, 1968; and "Vietcong Holding Position on Edge of Saigon Airport," the New York *Times*, Feb. 4, p. 1.

13. "Offensive Is Said to Pinpoint Enemy's Strengths," the New York *Times*, Feb. 2, 1968, p. 12. The *Times* also carried the later AP story.

14. The degree to which ARVN battalions actually shielded or "supported" the exposed 51-man Revolutionary Development teams or the militia against enemy attack even prior to Tet remained a matter of dispute. Like American units, if U.S. advisors' complaints were valid, the ARVN tended to "button up" in their own perimeters at night, delaying any relief expeditions until dawn, and even then proceeding with great caution.

15. AP, A003—Westmoreland, Feb. 25, 1968.

16. It got little play: "Ky Praises His Troops' Valor," the Washington *Post*, Mar. 10, 1968, p. A26.

17. AP, A029—Vigilantes, Feb. 1, 1968. Emphasis added.

18. AP, A021-022—Battletown, Feb. 1, 1968. A week later, in his discussion of the action at Ban Me Thuot, General Abrams quoted Simons' host, the 23rd Division advisor, Col. Henry A. Barber of Waco, Texas, as saying that the ARVN commander did a superior job; the foe came into town four times and was driven out four times.

19. AP, A018—Battle, Feb. 2, 1968.

20. AP, A016—Golf Course, Feb. 3, 1968.

21. AP, A063—Vietnam Execution Wirephoto, Feb. 1, 1968.

22. Said the *News* next day ("Grim and Ghastly Picture," Feb. 3, 1968):

> The picture reproduced herewith ran on the front page of yesterday's *News*.
>
> It shows South Vietnam's national police chief, Brig. Gen. Nguyen Ngoc Loan, at the instant after firing a bullet into the brain of a Vietcong (communist) officer caught disguised and armed during Thursday's fighting in Saigon.
>
> It is a grim and ghastly picture, showing just how glorious war is not.
>
> There are a couple of facts we should bear in mind, however, about the picture: (a) the executed Vietcong was out to kill as many people on our side of this war as he could; (b) so are all his surviving pals.
>
> This gives you an idea of how perilously idiotic are the demands of our doves for a one-sided allied pause in bombing Red North Vietnam.

23. "Raids on Cities Caught Vietnamese Off Guard," the Washington *Evening Star*, Feb. 6, 1968, p. 1.

24. "Saigon Troops Lolling in Sun as Reds Attacked," the Philadelphia *Inquirer*, Feb. 6, 1968, p. 1.

25. NBC-TV, "Huntley-Brinkley Report," Feb. 2, 1968.

26. ABC-TV, "ABC Evening News," Feb. 2, 1968.

27. NBC-TV, "Huntley-Brinkley Report," Feb. 12, 1968.

28. CBS-TV, "CBS Evening News," Feb. 12, 1968. Emphasis added.

29. NBC-TV, "Weekend Special Report," Feb. 3, 1968. Emphasis added.

30. NBC-TV, "Weekend Special Report," Feb. 3, 1968. Emphasis added.

31. NBC-Radio, "Emphasis: Newsbeat," Feb. 6, 1968.

32. CBS-TV, "CBS Evening News," Feb. 14, 1968.

33. CBS-Radio, Feb. 17, 1968. Emphasis added.

34. ABC-TV, "ABC Evening News," Feb. 29, 1968. See also Oberdorfer, *Tet!*

35. ABC-TV, "ABC Evening News," Feb. 21, 1968. Emphasis added.

36. ABC-TV, "ABC Evening News," Feb. 27, 1968.

37. CBS-TV, "CBS Morning News," Feb. 28, 1968. This report was not used on the Cronkite show.

38. NBC-TV, "The Today Show," Feb. 28, 1968.

39. CBS-TV, "CBS Evening News," Mar. 26, 1968.

40. This was the first time this point was made on television about "our Vietnamese."

41. ABC-TV, "ABC Evening News," Mar. 6, 1968. As Brannigan indicated, his last statements were guesswork. It was rumored that some Popular Forces in Tay Ninh province had gone over to the enemy, given that choice or death, but no one had any hard information then or later on defections, except that none were reported up the U.S. advisory chain.

42. NBC-TV, "Huntley-Brinkley Report," Mar. 19, 1968.

43. "By Bus, By Truck, on Foot, Foe Built Forces in Saigon," the New York *Times*, Feb. 4, 1968, p. 1.

44. The *Times* editors forgot they had reported it (see above, note 13), and when the AP caught up with the story (Feb. 8), the *Times* ran the dispatch: "Half Saigon Army on Leave for Tet," Feb. 9, 1968, p. 17.

45. "The VC Launch Their Revolution," the New York *Times*, Feb. 4, 1968, p. 1E.

46. "A Kennedy on Saigon Corruption," the New York *Times*, Feb. 4, 1968, p. 2E.

47. "War Crisscrosses Suburb of Saigon," the New York *Times*, Feb. 4, 1968, p. 5.

48. "South Vietnamese Seize Hue Palace, Enemy Retreats," the New York *Times*, Feb. 25, 1968, p. 1.

49. "Saigon General Says Foe Has Replaced His Losses," the New York *Times*, Mar. 10, 1968, p. 1. Thang turned out to be a bit overly pessi-

mistic, for no major Vietcong ground attacks were launched thereafter in the Delta.

50. "Saigon Tries to Recover from the Blows," the New York Times, Mar. 10, 1968, p. 3E.

51. "Kennedy Challenges 'Illusions' on War," the New York Times, Mar. 17, 1968, p. 59.

52. "Saigon's Inertia Disappoints U.S.," the New York Times, Mar. 17, 1968, p. 3.

53. "New Test for Military," the New York Times, Mar. 17, 1968, p. 2E.

54. "General Sees Foe Set for New Attacks," the Washington Post, Feb. 5, 1968, p. A5.

55. Inside the paper that day, the Post also ran this writer's lengthy, week-old description of Khe Sanh. It included three paragraphs on the ARVN 37th Ranger Battalion's "cocky" presence, and these were reduced to a single brief one in the published version: "Marines Are Digging In at Khe Sanh," the Washington Post, Feb. 5, 1968, p. A10.

56. "S. Viets Got Tet Leave Despite Raid Warning," the Washington Post, Feb. 10, 1968, p. A6.

57. "U.S. and Vietnam: Test in Battle of Saigon," the Washington Post, Feb. 11, 1968, p. A1.

58. "War-Stricken City of Hue Digs Out to Face Host of Problems," the Washington Post, Feb. 28, 1968, p. A6.

59. "Capture of Hue Citadel Was a Must for S. Viet Unit," the Washington Post, Feb. 29, 1968, p. A22, covered the Hoc Bao Company; "South Viets Prove Fighters in Hue," the Washington Post, Mar. 2, 1968, p. A11, covered the 3rd Regiment.

60. "A Delta City's Puzzle: Can the Pieces Be Put Together?" the Washington Post, Mar. 16, 1968, p. A10. See also in the Post: "Allies Trying to Seize Offensive in the Delta," Mar. 10, 1968, p. A27, and "Island Begins New Life Under VC Rule," Mar. 15, 1968, p. A9.

61. "Saigon Army Missing 10 Percent Since Tet," the Washington Post, Mar. 2, 1968, p. A10.

62. "Is There a Choice on More Troops?" the Washington Post, Mar. 3, 1968, p. B6. Emphasis added.

63. "Ky Praises His Troops' Valor," the Washington Post, Mar. 10, 1968, p. A26.

64. "Allies Trying to Seize Offensive in the Delta," the Washington Post, Mar. 10, 1968, p. A27.

65. March 13, 17, 20, 25, 26, 28, 29, and 30.

66. "The War: Picking Up the Pieces," Time, Feb. 16, 1968, pp. 32–34.

67. "By Book and Bullet," Time, Feb. 23, 1968, p. 32.

68. "The War: On the Defensive," Time, Mar. 1, 1968, p. 18. Emphasis added.

578 NOTES TO PAGES 369-74

69. "The War: On the Offensive," *Time,* Mar. 22, 1968, p. 25.
70. "The War: End of the Tour," *Time,* Mar. 29, 1968, p. 21. This statement, of course, assumes that an American could "build" the army —one not under his command—of an independent foreign nation.
71. "A Reformer Rejected," *Newsweek,* Feb. 12, 1968, p. 33.
72. "The War Around the Corner," *Newsweek,* Feb. 12, 1968, p. 66. Actually, according to AP's John Lengel, Schneider went into Hue with the U.S. Marines.
73. "Man on the Spot," *Newsweek,* Feb. 19, 1968, pp. 33-34.
74. Fifty percent of the ARVN—or more—by U.S. estimate were on leave at Tet. *Newsweek* was unique in speculating that many of those on leave "would wait to see" who was winning before coming back.
75. "Man on the Spot," *Newsweek,* Feb. 19, 1968, p. 39. Emphasis added.
76. The Thieu-Ky regime, which excited little admiration in Vietnam, somehow was still in being four years later.
77. "More of the Same Won't Do," *Newsweek,* Mar. 18, 1968, p. 25. This argument was a standard one: The Administration is too optimistic, hence we are justified in being too pessimistic. But it was not helpful to the reader.
78. "The Political Morass," *Newsweek,* Mar. 18, 1968, p. 38. If *Newsweek's* reporters and the other U.S. newsmen, including this writer, had spent more time at Tet with ARVN, facts would have been available to back up such analyses.
79. "Allied Offense: Morale Victory?" *Newsweek,* Apr. 1, 1968, p. 13. The problem, as General Westmoreland and other U.S. commanders told newsmen, was not "sagging morale," but the caution of ARVN commanders, whom Westmoreland urged to get out of the urban areas and into the field again.
80. "McNamara Says VC Suffered Big Losses, Warns of New Raids," the Washington *Post,* Feb. 2, 1968, p. A12. Emphasis added.
81. "Vietcong Mount Political Offensive," the Washington *Post,* Feb. 4, 1968, p. A8.
82. "McCarthy Derides Johnson on War," the New York *Times,* Feb. 4, 1968, p. 11.
83. "As the Enemy Changes Tactics, Concern Grows About Two Critical Zones," the New York *Times,* Feb. 25, 1968, p. 1E.
84. "Man on the Spot," *Newsweek,* Feb. 19, 1968, p. 33. Emphasis added. This comment, like so many others, says less than it seems to at first glance. How much is "much of the population"? How does one lend "passive support"?
85. "The Political Morass," *Newsweek,* Mar. 18, 1968, p. 38.
86. CBS-TV, "Face the Nation," Feb. 16, 1968.
87. Oberdorfer, *Tet!,* pp. 132–34.

88. Visiting U.S. antiwar politicians had little trouble, either. Periodically, that old ghost from Graham Green's *The Quiet American*—a "Third Force," neither "military" nor "communist"—would be exhumed on the visitor's return home as a political solution for Vietnam's woes. It was not taken seriously by Saigon newsmen. "Broadening the political base" was another recipe often stressed by U.S. Embassy analysts. It meant, essentially, representation in the Thieu Cabinet of such diverse groups as the Cao Dai and Hoa Hao sects, the old VNQDD and Tan Dai Viet parties, the labor groups, and the main Buddhist and Catholic factions. Thieu never embraced the principle.

89. "Test of Thieu's Regime Now Is Its Capacity to Restore Order," the Washington *Post*, Feb. 8, 1968, p. A5; "Vietcong Program Held Better, House Report Censures AID and Saigon on Land Reform," the Washington *Post*, Mar. 4, 1968, p. A1; "Saigon Inertia Disappoints U.S.," the New York *Times*, Mar. 17, 1968, p. 3.

90. Statement before the Senate Armed Services Committee on the FY 1969–73 Defense Program and 1969 Defense Budget, Jan. 22, 1968.

91. CBS-TV, "Face the Nation," Feb. 4, 1968.

92. Address before the National Association of Secondary School Principals, Atlantic City, New Jersey, Feb. 10, 1968.

93. AP, A053—Vietnam, NL, Feb. 2, 1968.

94. AP, A081—Viet Prisoners, Feb. 4, 1968. After the March 1965 entry of U.S. battalions into Vietnam, the wire services and major newspapers conveyed a vivid, if fragmentary, picture of the random cruelties inflicted, wittingly and unwittingly, by allied troops and firepower on hamlets, Vietcong prisoners, and individual rural South Vietnamese caught up in the war. Indeed, just before Tet, a 421-page compilation of press accounts to support its charges of U.S. "war crimes" in Vietnam was published by the antiwar group, Clergy and Laymen Concerned About Vietnam, and titled *In the Name of America* (New York: 1968). The book was described at length in the news columns of the Washington *Post* and New York *Times* on January 30, 1968. No comparable anthology was published by any other antiwar group, or by any other private body, of the excesses of the other side.

95. AP, A078—Thieu, Feb. 9, 1968.

96. AP, A040WX—Vietnam-AID, Feb. 10, 1968.

97. AP—Hue Officials, Feb. 27, 1968.

98. AP, A047, Mar. 2, 1968.

99. AP, A602 and A604, Mar. 26, 1968.

100. NBC-Radio, "Emphasis," Feb. 2, 1968.

101. CBS-TV, "CBS Evening News," Feb. 14, 1968. Emphasis added.

102. CBS-TV, "CBS Evening News," Feb. 28, 1968.

103. NBC-TV, "Huntley-Brinkley Report," Feb. 19, 1968.

104. NBC-TV, "Huntley-Brinkley Report," Feb. 22, 1968. Emphasis added.
105. ABC-TV, "ABC Evening News," Mar. 7, 1968.
106. AP reported one form or another of this story several times during Tet. The New York *Times* published a worried-sounding reaction story by Hedrick Smith, "Saigon Cautioned on Invasion Talk," Mar. 15, 1968, p. 2.
107. ABC-TV, "ABC Evening News," Mar. 21, 1968. Emphasis added.
108. Oberdorfer, *Tet!*, p. 179.
109. "A Kennedy on Saigon Corruption," the New York *Times*, Feb. 4, 1968, p. 2E.
110. "Saigon's Authority Believed to Be in Critical Stage," the New York *Times*, Feb. 11, 1968, p. 3.
111. "U.S. Admits Blow to Pacification," the New York *Times*, Feb. 25, 1968, p. 1.
112. "U.S. Pressed Shift of Vietnam General," the New York *Times*, Feb. 25, 1968, p. 25. The story was cut for the final editions and these final paragraphs appeared only in the early version of the story.
113. "South Vietnam Is Reported Giving Arms to Civilians," the New York *Times*, Feb. 25, 1968, p. 21.
114. "Citizens in 10 Areas of Saigon Organize Groups for Defense," the New York *Times*, Mar. 3, 1968, p. 1. The post-Tet self-defense effort, observed by Treaster in Saigon and by this reporter in Quang Tri city, finally became organized in mid-1968 and grew steadily through mid-1970. But in 1969–70, it was ignored by the media, even as its beginnings were ignored, except by the *Times* and the *Post*, in March 1968.
115. "Pacification Teams Returning to Hamlets Abandoned After Vietcong Drive," the New York *Times*, Mar. 3, 1968, p. 7.
116. "One Reform Is Achieved," the New York *Times*, Mar. 17, 1968, p. 3.
117. "Kennedy Challenges 'Illusions' on War," the New York *Times*, Mar. 17, 1968, p. 59. The drafting of 19-year-olds had already begun, and the drafting of 18-year-olds began in June.
118. "Saigon's Inertia Disappoints U.S.," the New York *Times*, Mar. 17, 1968, p. 3.
119. "Thieu Expected to Dismiss at Least Six More Provincial Chiefs," the New York *Times*, Mar. 24, 1968, p. 7.
120. "Washington: Vietnam Reappraisal—A to Z or A to B?" the New York *Times*, Mar. 24, 1968, p. 16E. It turned out to be a perceptive title. The reappraisal was A to B, with a partial bombing pause to placate the doves and "Vietnamization" as a substitute for U.S. reinforcements.
121. "Enemy Is Able to Hit Anew," the Washington *Post*, Feb. 4, 1968, p. A1.

122. "Thieu Lost Prestige in VC Thrusts," the Washington *Post*, Feb. 18, 1968, p. A1.

123. "Khe Sanh: A U.S. Obsession?" the Washington *Post*, Mar. 3, 1968, p. A1.

124. The story was edited by this writer as bureau chief. "Thieu seems determined" might have been more accurately put as "Thieu has said he is determined."

125. "Thieu's Rule Unshaken by Tet," the Washington *Post*, Mar. 17, 1968, p. A16.

126. "The War: The General's Biggest Battle," *Time*, Feb. 16, 1968, p. 19. Emphasis added.

127. "The War: Picking Up the Pieces," *Time*, Feb. 16, 1968, p. 34.

128. "The War: Critical Season," *Time*, Mar. 1, 1968, p. 11. Emphasis added.

129. "South Vietnam: A Time of Doubt," *Time*, Mar. 1, 1968, p. 22. Emphasis added. There was no firm figure on arrests. The "Salvation Front" soon faded, as JUSPAO's Zorthian glumly predicted it would.

130. "A Sense of Urgency," *Time*, Mar. 8, 1968, pp. 29–30. *Time* was a bit generous to the Thieu regime. Compare, below, *Newsweek*'s handling of this development.

131. "The Road Ahead: How Vietnamese Leaders See It," *Time*, Mar. 8, 1968, p. 29.

132. "First Step Toward Reform," *Time*, Mar. 22, 1968, pp. 25–26.

133. This measure by autumn had indeed beefed up the ARVN and, most markedly, the militia, despite desertions and casualties.

134. "State of the Union," *Time*, Mar. 29, 1968, pp. 34–36. There were still more than a million "permanent" refugees on USAID rolls. This total was not to decline noticeably until heavy fighting eased in the fall of 1968.

135. *Newsweek* was well ahead in the three-legged "jumping-to-conclusions" race. Others were to catch up.

136. "The VC's Week of Terror," *Newsweek*, Feb. 12, 1968, p. 30. Emphasis added.

137. "The Devastating Effect on the People," *Newsweek*, Feb. 12, 1968, p. 32. Emphasis added.

138. When did McNamara publicly set target dates in Vietnam after U.S. intervention in 1965? We find no such dates in his 1965–67 reports.

139. "Swan Song," *Newsweek*, Feb. 12, 1968, p. 40.

140. Who is "not everyone"?

141. GVN communication always "took days."

142. "Politicians" or "administrators"?

143. "Supreme Test," *Newsweek*, Feb. 26, 1968, pp. 34–36. Emphasis added.

144. "Odd Men Out," *Newsweek*, Mar. 4, 1968, pp. 30–31.

145. This remains one of *Newsweek*'s many political exclusives.

146. It was thwarted because GVN officials were traditionally reluctant to arm anybody, fearing the weapons would go to the Vietcong, and because no organization then existed to provide the weapons and training. By year's end the self-defense program was well under way. The "deep-rooted antipathy" between northerners and southerners had little to do with the delay.

147. "Semi-coup"? Political arrests in Vietnam had occurred before, notably in 1966, during the Buddhist movement's last surge, and in 1967, and no one spoke of "semi-coups."

148. This hardly sounds "something like a return to military rule."

149. The example seems minor, and quite in accord with Third World administrative procedures, which foreigners and citizens alike commonly found irritating. How it resulted from "internecine bickering" is not clear.

150. Vietnamese industrialists, whose small plants in Cholon and the suburbs were badly damaged at Tet, constituted an insignificant political-economic factor in Vietnam in 1968. That there was confusion over government disaster aid five weeks after the Tet onslaughts seems about par, again, for the Third World, and a delay not entirely foreign to Western bureaucracies. *Newsweek,* like the rest of the press, might better have checked out how fast food and shelter were being provided to the refugees.

151. "The Political Morass," *Newsweek,* Mar. 18, 1968, pp. 37–38. Emphasis added.

Chapter 10: Pacification

1. Robert S. McNamara, Statement before the Senate Armed Services Committee on the FY 1969–73 Defense Program and 1969 Defense Budget, Jan. 22, 1968.

2. Komer press briefing and "fact sheet," Jan. 24, 1968.

3. The Baltimore *Sun,* Feb. 11, 1968.

4. The *Post*'s Lee Lescaze pointed this up in a story on a tour by Senator Joseph S. Clark of I Corps provinces, where a province advisor told Clark about problems whose existence was denied by his superior, the senior State Department advisor at Da Nang. ("Senator Finds That I Corps Has Its Own Credibility Gap," the Washington *Post,* Jan. 21, 1968, p. A29.) A notable contrast: John Vann, the retired Army colonel who ran pacification in III Corps and was quick to debunk Washington optimism.

5. "Vietnam: Signs of Stalemate," the New York *Times,* Aug. 8, 1967, p 1.

6. Brannigan, "Brannigan's Stew in Vietnam," p. 58. According to Professor Lawrence Lichty, out of a total of 187 Vietnam film reports from September 1, 1967, through January 31, 1968, there were nine on

pacification and eight on "refugees" and "relocation." The breakdown was: ABC—two on pacification, one on refugees; CBS—four on pacification, six on refugees; NBC—three on pacification, one on refugees.
7. CBS-TV, "CBS Evening News," Feb. 5, 1968.
8. AP, A006—Recovery, Feb. 8, 1968. Emphasis added.
9. CBS-TV, "CBS Evening News," Feb. 14, 1968.
10. Emphasis added. This is full of straw-man journalism. For example, it is unknown by whom the specified area was cited as a "prime example" of pacification success. Moreover, few villagers could be expected to do otherwise than leave the fighting to the soldiers. There were plenty of warnings of impending attack, but the GVN refused to heed them. The militia which fought the Vietcong was made up of "villagers."
11. CBS-TV, "CBS Evening News," Feb. 20, 1968.
12. "Vietnam Reds Resist Attacks in Hue Again," the Washington *Post,* Feb. 4, 1968, p. A1.
13. "Guerrillas Wreck Pacification Plan," the Washington *Post,* Feb. 4, 1968, p. B1.
14. "Viet Reds' Drive Was a Giap 'Masterstroke,' " the Washington *Post,* Feb. 11, 1968, p. A8.
15. "U.S. and Vietnam: Test in Battle," the Washington *Post,* Feb. 11, 1968, p. A1.
16. "Asian Pressures: Cruel Dilemma for Johnson," the New York *Times,* Feb. 11, 1968, p. 1E.
17. "Illusions and Deceptions," the New York *Times,* Feb. 11, 1968, p. 13E.
18. "Offensive Is Said to Pinpoint Enemy's Strengths," the New York *Times,* Feb. 2, 1968, p. 12.
19. "Saigon's Authority Believed to Be in Critical Stage," the New York *Times,* Feb. 11, 1968, p. 3.
20. "Heavy Setback for Saigon and More Trouble Ahead," the New York *Times,* Feb. 11, 1968, p. 1E.
21. "Pacification Program Is Almost at Standstill in South Vietnam," the New York *Times,* Feb. 14, 1968, p. 4.
22. "Officials Seek to 'Reprime the Pump' of Pacification," the New York *Times,* Feb. 16, 1968, p. 2.
23. Mohr, Roberts, Weinraub, Buckley, Johnson, Treaster, and White.
24. "A Pacification Drive Setback in Key Area," the New York *Times,* Feb. 21, 1968, p. 1.
25. "Pacification Future in Doubt," the Washington *Post,* Feb. 16, 1968, p. A15.
26. "Pacifying Did Stop, Says HHH," the Washington *Post,* Feb. 20, 1968, p. A1.
27. "The War: The General's Gamble," *Time,* Feb. 9, 1968, p. 22. Emphasis added.

28. "The War: Picking Up the Pieces," *Time*, Feb. 16, 1968, p. 32.
29. "The War: Critical Season," *Time*, Mar. 1, 1968, p. 11. Emphasis added.
30. "The War: On the Defensive," *Time*, Mar. 1, 1968, p. 18. Emphasis added. What are the "largest population centers"? All 16 province capitals and some 70 district towns were in allied hands. Most main Delta roads were safe by daylight for military convoys. The enemy used no "artillery" in the Delta, and few "piles" of mortar and rocket ammunition were stacked in the open. The enemy, south of Saigon, never required "massive" supplies.
31. "The VC's Week of Terror," *Newsweek*, Feb. 12, 1968, p. 30.
32. "The Devastating Effect on the People," *Newsweek*, Feb. 12, 1968, p. 32.
33. "Man on the Spot," *Newsweek*, Feb. 19, 1968, p. 33.
34. Ibid., p. 39. Emphasis added.
35. "The Supreme Test," *Newsweek*, Feb. 26, 1968, p. 36. Emphasis added. *Newsweek*, apparently, had forgotten the "vacuum" described by its writer only the previous week.
36. "U.S. Admits Blow to Pacification; High Official in Saigon Says Foe's Attacks Resulted in a Rural 'Vacuum,'" the New York *Times*, Feb. 25, 1968, p. 1.
37. "U.S. Pressed Shift of Vietnam General," the New York *Times*, Feb. 25, 1968, p. 25. The story did not explain what the situation was in 1963, but it implied that Komer had lost five years' work overnight.
38. "Vacuum Remains in South Vietnam's Rural Areas," the Washington *Post*, Feb. 25, 1968, p. A10.
39. "Westmoreland Said to Want 50,000 GIs," and "Allies Clear Enemy from Hue's Palace."
40. "Reds' Offensive Leaves U.S. with Maze of Uncertainties," the Washington *Post*, Feb. 26, 1968, p. A1. The treatment of pacification was misleading; no one in Saigon claimed to know, even prior to Tet, what "the farmers *thought*."
41. This portion of the interview was noted in the next day's Washington *Post* ("Fulbright Asks Policy Review," Feb. 26, 1968, p. A1) but ignored by the New York *Times*.
42. Again, Rusk's remarks were cited in the Washington *Post* at length ("Rusk at Hearing: . . . Not Just a Problem of South Vietnam," Mar. 12, 1968, p. A10), but excluded from the *Times*'s excerpts of the hearing transcript.
43. NBC-TV, "Huntley-Brinkley Report," Feb. 27, 1968.
44. His talk about the "vacuum," he said later, was intended not only to inform newsmen, but also to prod Thieu into pushing ARVN back out into the countryside. Westmoreland was similarly preoccupied with prodding ARVN, and convinced that the Vietcong had temporarily "shot their

wad," at least in the southern three-fourths of South Vietnam. He said as much to Wes Gallagher (AP interview, Feb. 25).

45. CBS-TV, "Report from Vietnam: Who, What, When, Where, Why," Feb. 27, 1968.

46. "The Other War in Vietnam: Can Pacification Succeed?" by Daniel Southerland, Feb. 25, 1968.

47. CBS-TV, "CBS Evening News," Feb. 28, 1968.

48. CBS-Radio, "Dimension," Feb. 28, 1968. Emphasis added.

49. CBS-Radio, "First-Line Report," Feb. 28, 1968.

50. NBC-TV, "Huntley-Brinkley Report," Mar. 5, 1968.

51. NBC-Radio, "David Brinkley Report," Mar. 5, 1968. Indeed, the CIA *in Washington,* if not in Vietnam, was saying that "the vacuum was being filled by the Vietcong." Disheartened junior CORDS officials in Vietnam were talking about an 18-month delay; Komer ventured no prediction.

52. CBS-Radio, "The World Tonight," Mar. 5, 1968.

53. NBC-TV, Frank McGee Report, "A New Year, A New War," Mar. 10, 1968.

54. AP, 001–112A–Delta.

55. Figures on Hue refugees varied—60,000 and 70,000 were used by the wire services.

56. These figures expressed also as a percentage of total population would have been more informative.

57. "After 'Tet': Measuring and Repairing the Damage," *Time,* Mar. 15, 1968, pp. 22–23.

58. "U.S. Aide in Saigon Quits in Protest; He Charges U.S. Programs in Vietnam Are Failing," the New York *Times,* Mar. 26, 1968, p. 1; the paper carried Komer's rebuttal the following day: "Critical Ex-Official Disputed by Komer," p. 3. The Washington *Post* ran both stories on its inside pages.

59. "Pacification Teams Returning to Hamlets Abandoned After Vietcong Drive," the New York *Times,* Mar. 3, 1968, p. 7.

60. "Mekong Delta Still Paralyzed Five Weeks After Foe's Offensive," the New York *Times,* Mar. 8, 1968, p. 4.

61. "Saigon General Says Foe Has Replaced His Losses," the New York *Times,* Mar. 10, 1968, p. 1.

62. There had been a report by Tom Johnson on a critique of pre-Tet pacification efforts: "U.S. Study Assails Pacification Plan," the New York *Times,* Mar. 11, 1968, p. 13.

63. "Fear in Hamlets Is Still Hampering Pacification; Officials Term Psychological Blows a Greater Setback Than Physical Damage," the New York *Times,* Mar. 29, 1968, p. 14.

64. Some examples of these Washington *Post* stories in March 1968 were: "Quang Tri Pushes Ahead Again," Mar. 4, p. A9; "Reds in Saigon

Area Believed Hurt," Mar. 11, p. A10; "Island Begins New Life Under VC Rule," Mar. 15, p. A9; "Ruined Viet Hamlet Rebuilds in Fear," Mar. 17, p. A18; "Hamlet Safety Is Post-Tet Problem," Mar. 18, p. A12; "Militia Unit Presses VC Hard," Mar. 20, p. A23; "Bien Hoa Is 'Running Scared,'" Mar. 29, p. A14.

65. The pacification story would have been an ideal one on which to pool newspaper manpower—as was done during the 1967 elections in Vietnam —to provide a collective, independent overview of the countryside during the last week of February and in early March. It was not done and, as far as I know, the suggestion never came up.

66. In a cable to Saigon on March 17, for example, the foreign desk noted that several pacification and urban recovery stories were still awaiting publication, adding: "ASK PATIENCE, AS HARD TO ACCOMMODATE FOUR-MAN [sic] BUREAU WITH SPACE SHORT IN DOMESTIC AND FINANCIAL NEWS EXPLOSION."

Chapter 11: Reinforcement and Escalation

1. Ever intrigued by the possibilities (real or imagined) of diplomacy, the New York *Times* published no less than six page-one stories on the Vietnam-related "diplomatic" activity of the Tet period. Few of the events reported, or statements quoted, we now know, had any relevance to the Administration's eventual decision to try a partial bombing pause on March 31.

2. Infantry and armored battalions, varying in strength from 600 to 1,000 men.

3. Statement before the Senate Armed Services Committee on the FY 1969–73 Defense Program and 1969 Defense Budget, Jan. 22, 1968.

4. News conference, Feb. 2, 1968.

5. NBC-TV, "Meet the Press," Feb. 4, 1968.

6. News conference, Feb. 16, 1968.

7. Radio and TV address to the nation, Mar. 31, 1968.

8. Schandler, "Making a Decision," p. 248.

9. For "more troops" stories in the other media, see Story Indexes, the Westview Press edition of *Big Story*.

10. Much—good and bad—has been writen about the Washington decision-making of the February–March 1968 period. By far the best overall accounts available are John B. Henry, "March 1968: Continuity or Change?" (Honors thesis, Harvard University, 1971) and Schandler, "Making a Decision." Henry was the first historian to interview Rusk and Wheeler, among others; Colonel Schandler, the anonymous author of the relatively skimpy section of the Pentagon Papers (Gravel, *Pentagon Papers*, 4:538–604) dealing with the 1967 and February–March 1968 periods, expanded greatly on his earlier efforts, benefiting from Henry's work and additional interviews and documents. Schandler's study was published as *The Unmaking of a President* (Princeton: 1977). Also

helpful to this writer were Maj. Paul Miles, a Rhodes scholar and aide to General Westmoreland, and other Army historians who supplied copies of key backchannel messages between Wheeler and Westmoreland during the period.

11. Gravel, *Pentagon Papers,* 4:541–42.

12. This report is corroborated by the Pentagon Papers. Westmoreland (and the Joint Chiefs) asked for 556,000 men in 1966, cut to 470,000, and for 670,000 in April 1967, cut to 525,000. The Vietnam commander prepared to live with the compromise. He envisioned an effort to "Vietnamize" the war, as he noted in his public speech of November 21, 1967, before the National Press Club. See also Henry, "March 1968," p. 34, and Schandler, "Making a Decision," pp. 15–17.

13. "U.S. Manpower Needs for War, Foe's Drives Focus Attention on Troop Ceiling at 525,000," the New York *Times,* Feb. 3, 1968, p. 10. Emphasis added.

14. "Asian Pressures: Cruel Dilemma for Johnson," the New York *Times,* Feb. 11, 1968, p. 1E. Emphasis added.

15. Schandler, "Making a Decision," p. 15, and Gravel, *Pentagon Papers,* 4:527–28.

16. "Westmoreland Bid for Troops Related," the New York *Times,* Feb. 25, 1968, p. 21.

17. See Henry, "March 1968," pp. 42–43, 84.

18. This was largely correct, but the "expectation" should have been attributed to the Joint Chiefs.

19. "Troops, More Men for a Tougher War," the New York *Times,* Feb. 25, 1968, p. 2E. Emphasis added.

20. This was possibly because his sources—among the aides to the Joint Chiefs—thought in terms of the first 100,000 "to be deployed" directly to Vietnam, and the second 100,000 to build up the depleted strategic reserve in the United States "prepared" to go to Vietnam if necessary. This was Wheeler's thinking.

21. "U.S. Reappraising Its Use of Troops in Vietnam War; Westmoreland Said to Seek 100,000 to 200,000 More," the New York *Times,* Feb. 29, 1968, p. 1. Emphasis added.

22. "Honolulu: A View from Pearl Harbor," the New York *Times,* Mar. 3, 1968, p. E12. Emphasis added.

23. The "strategic review" was being conducted, of course, in several places—by Johnson-Rusk-Wheeler, by the lower-level Clifford task force, and, no doubt, by the Joint Chiefs.

24. This was the position of the International Security Affairs (ISA) civilians in the Defense Department.

25. "The Manpower Cupboard Is Nearly Bare," the New York *Times,* Mar. 3, 1968, p. 3E. Emphasis added.

26. "Criticism of War Widens in Senate on Buildup Issue," the New York *Times,* Mar. 8, 1968, p. 1.

27. In a 1967 conversation with this reporter in Bangkok, where McGown was chief of the U.S. Military Assistance Command, Thailand.

28. Westmoreland's 1967 annual report on the war was sent to Washington on January 26, 1968; the General was optimistic on U.S. military prospects, but less sanguine than before about the GVN, pacification, and Vietcong strength. The report concluded: "Clearly our work is cut out for us in 1968." This point did not get into the *Times.* (Maj. Paul Miles, USA, interview with this author, Mar. 17, 1971; see also Schandler, "Making a Decision," p. 17.) Westmoreland, as we noted earlier, also warned Washington about impending enemy large-scale offensives in December 1967 and January 1968, even as he did not predict the pattern of enemy urban targets.

29. And to a few sympathetic publications like *U.S. News and World Report.*

30. See Talese, *The Kingdom and the Power.*

31. Schandler, "Making a Decision," pp. 141–42.

32. Henry, "March 1968," pp. 59–60, 120–22.

33. Oberdorfer, *Tet!,* p. 269.

34. The debate was reflected in later accounts by sub-Cabinet alumni. See Hoopes, *The Limits of Intervention* and Goulding, *Confirm or Deny.*

35. As the *Times* had earlier reported, Westmoreland had already contended he was taking the offensive, without having received anything but minor reinforcements. See his AP interview published on February 25 and his briefing to newsmen on March 6. In private, both Bunker and Westmoreland, on March 3, had assured Johnson by cable that U.S. troops were taking the offensive. See Johnson, *The Vantage Point,* p. 396, and Henry, "March 1968," p. 99.

36. Henry, "March 1968," p. 83.

37. According to Paul Miles, Westmoreland in 1969 explained to Townsend Hoopes what the 206,000-troop request really signified. Hoopes did not include this revelation in his book. The anonymous authors of the Pentagon Papers, dependent on the sketchy ISA files for the February–March 1968 period, did not fully understand the matter either. The New York *Times* summary of their analysis does not probe much further, although it cites the gaps. See Gravel, *Pentagon Papers,* 4:594–95.

38. This was a repeated Westmoreland proposal, starting in late 1966, and the reason *Westmoreland* wanted the troops.

39. To repeat, at Johnson's suggestion, Wheeler on March 5 had told Westmoreland to expect 22,000 more men, and that strong opposition had developed to sending any more. On March 8, Wheeler told Westmoreland to expect no more than 30,000 more men, at most. See John-

son, *The Vantage Point*, p. 399. This information was also given by Maj. Paul Miles, in an interview with the author (Mar. 23, 1972).

40. This accurate reflection of the political mood in Washington illustrated again the vast difference between the states of mind there and in Saigon. By March 10, it may be fairly said, newsmen and officials in Saigon had largely recovered from their Tet shock, and a few were so reporting. One interesting aspect cited by Schandler and Henry was that the earlier vivid media accounts from Vietnam had considerable impact on Washington officialdom in February, including Wheeler and Clifford. The *Times* and *Post* were easier to read than the cautiously worded official cables; and, after Tet, civilians, in particular, were ready to believe the worst.

41. The accuracy of these unattributed remarks is not questioned, even implicitly, by the *Times* reporters. Judging by Goulding and Hoopes, it now seems that such comments constituted largely a civilian-official reaction to press accounts.

42. Implicitly the writers are skeptical here: The Administration was claiming that "somehow" the situation could be "righted" and "the balance restored." They did not know that Rusk had counseled Johnson not to send more troops, because, Rusk felt, more troops were not needed. See Henry, "March 1968," pp. 108–09.

43. "Rusk Will Shun Troop Issue at Fulbright Quiz," the Philadelphia *Inquirer*, Mar. 11, 1968, p. 2.

44. "High Pentagon Aides Urge Call-up of 30,000 Men," the New York *Times*, Mar. 13, 1968, p. 15.

45. "U.S. to Put More Men in Vietnam; Call-up Moderate; 35,000–50,000 Men May Go—Reservists Face Active Duty," the New York *Times*, Mar. 17, 1968, p. 1. The story was by Robert Phelps, who was pretty up to date on numbers, if not on units; Pentagon plans changed almost daily. See Gravel, *Pentagon Papers*, 4:591.

46. "Washington: Vietnam Reappraisal—A to Z or A to B?" the New York *Times*, Mar. 24, 1968, p. 16E.

47. "Johnson to Talk to Nation Tonight on Vietnam War; Speech to Deal 'Rather Fully' with Buildup of Forces and Additional Costs," the New York *Times*, Mar. 31, 1968, p. 1.

48. There, in contrast to many another visiting Pentagon reporter, Wilson promptly went into the field with the infantry battalions to learn what war was about. John Maffre, Wilson's sidekick, was shortly to leave the *Post*.

49. The *Post*, of course, also offered its readers syndicated columnists who discussed escalation during and after Wheeler's February Vietnam trip: the dovish Joseph Kraft ("New Strategy, Redeployment Seen U.S. Need, Not More Men," Feb. 29); the hawkish Joseph Alsop ("The President Should Approve More GIs and Call Reserves," Feb. 28, and

"General Wheeler's War Report Asks Painful and Crucial Action," Mar. 6); and middle-of-the-roaders Evans and Novak ("Johnson's Decision on Men, Money Could Add Third to Viet War Budget," Feb. 29).

50. "Westmoreland Said to Want 50,000 GIs," Feb. 25, 1968, p. A1; and "Troop Increase 'Probably' Needed, Westmoreland Says," Feb. 26, 1968, p. A1.

51. "Johnson Reported Studying Long-Haul, Not Quickie, Troop Increase," the Washington *Post*, Mar. 1, 1968, p. A13.

52. "Large Units Scarce for Vietnam Buildup," the Washington *Post*, Mar. 4, 1968, p. A1.

53. "Johnson Presses War Study," the Washington *Post*, Mar. 6, 1968, p. A7. The White House, not for the first time, was less than candid, for we know that Wheeler had presented the request for 206,000 men on February 28, and that the Clifford task force recommendation for a 22,000-man increment had been approved, with strong opposition to sending any more than that. Rusk was dead set against any more troops, as being unnecessary. By then, the debate was on broader matters: a reserve call-up, and a partial bombing halt as urged by Rusk on March 5 to appease public opinion. See Henry, "March 1968," p. 105.

54. The *Post* night editor checks off with a red grease pencil *Times* stories "matched" by the *Post*, and tries to recoup, for a later edition, important *Times* stories not so "matched." The *Times* in New York follows roughly the same procedure with the first edition of the *Post*—neither paper likes to be left trailing on Washington news. The result is not always thorough coverage.

55. Oberdorfer, *Tet!*, p. 270.

56. The "major communist offensive" stopped "unfolding," of course, in mid-February.

57. "206,000 Draft Call Hinted," the Washington *Post*, Mar. 10, 1968, p. A1. Emphasis added.

58. "LBJ Seeks Austerity, Victory; Troops Will Be Boosted," the Washington *Post*, Mar. 17, 1968, p. A1.

59. "Widely expected" among some newsmen with a fixation on the term "search-and-destroy operations."

60. "Stage Set for New Viet Move," the Washington *Post*, Mar. 31, 1968, p. A1. Emphasis added.

Chapter 12: The Debate at Home

1. Conversely, in times of no crisis, the "home office" tends to be a good deal more complacent, even inattentive, with respect to warnings from abroad that trouble may be brewing. This trait manifested itself journalistically in the modest "play" given to Westmoreland's and Wheeler's pre-Tet warnings.

2. Far more serious than Tet was the surprise entry of the Chinese Com-

munists into the Korean War in 1950, after the defeat of the North Koreans by the United Nations forces. China's entry signified a "new war." It resulted in a costly U.S. retreat down the Korean peninsula, alarms at home over the possible resort to atomic weapons (as at Tet), and right-wing Republican demands that the Truman Administration broaden its limited-war policy and bomb China. Later, the Chinese were stopped, and the war remained limited. But the Korean "conflict" became increasingly unpopular, as did President Truman, who decided not to run for re-election. "Korea, communism, and corruption" became the 1952 G.O.P. campaign themes against the Democrats, who lost.

3. He privately mentioned such attacks, in advance, to the Australian Cabinet in December 1967. (Johnson, *The Vantage Point*, pp. 378–79.)

4. See Schandler, "Making a Decision," pp. 30–31.

5. For a discussion of this and other official statements following the initial Tet attacks, including President Johnson's February 2 press conference, see Chapter 4.

6. This point was made (pp. 179–80) in a useful, unpublished study paper by Chandler Goodnow, Louis G. Michael, Edward A. Partain, and Sidney R. Steele, "News Coverage of the Tet Offensive" (U.S. Army War College, Carlisle Barracks, Pennsylvania, March 25, 1969). The authors, all infantry lieutenant colonels, analyzed a broad random spectrum of media output before and during Tet. They compared this coverage to that of the 1944 Battle of the Bulge.

7. The recollections of McPherson and Bundy are cited in Schandler, "Making a Decision," p. 29.

8. Johnson's tone is suggested by these New York *Times* headlines: "President Honors Lincoln and Likens Their War Ordeals," Feb. 13; "President Urges Firmness on War in First Visit to Dallas Since Assassination; He Sees a Turning Point in Vietnam," Feb. 28; "President Asks for Austerity to Win the War; Tells Farm Union Delegates in Minnesota It's Time for Total National Effort," Mar. 19; "Johnson Defiant on Vietnam View, Tells Foes Course Is Set and America Will Prevail," Mar. 20; "Johnson Warns of 'Phony Peace,'" Mar. 21; "Johnson Affirms Vietnam Resolve, Declares Will of U.S. Won't Break Under Frustration," Mar. 22. See also Doris Kearns's important *Lyndon Johnson and the American Dream* (Harper & Row; 1976), especially pp. 280–85 and 334–52, for insights into LBJ's reactions.

9. See *Congressional Record*, 90th Cong., 2nd sess., 1968, 114, pt. 2: S761; S795–97; S799; S863–68; CBS-TV, "Face the Nation," Feb. 11, 1968.

10. "Mansfield Warns on War Realities," the New York *Times*, Feb. 12, 1968, p. 8; "Gore Urges U.S. Quit War Morass," the New York *Times*, Feb. 18, 1968, p. 8; "Sen. Fulbright Derides Rostow," the Washington *Post*, Feb. 20, 1968, p. A6; "Mansfield Urges Peace Emphasis," the New

York *Times*, Feb. 27, 1968, p. 1; "Hanoi Lauds Four Senators for Asking Halt in Bombing," the Washington *Post*, Mar. 2, 1968, p. A10.

11. "War Doubts in Senate; Misgivings over Administration Policy Said to Spread As Offensive Continues," the New York *Times*, Feb. 12, 1968, p. 6. Emphasis added.

12. "Rostow's Rosy Views on War Are Challenged by Fulbright," by Peter Lisagor, the Philadelphia *Inquirer*, Feb. 23, 1968. Rostow turned out to be right. But in mid-February, as we have noted, it was too early to say whether the ARVN or the Saigon government would be "stronger" —or weaker. One knew only that the South Vietnamese, caught on a holiday, had not caved in under the Tet shock, and that a recovery effort was (barely) starting. The Pentagon Papers and Johnson's own statements in *The Vantage Point* suggest that there was great uncertainty in the Administration, at this point in February, about Saigon's future performance.

13. "War Stirs Conflict on Priorities," the Washington *Post*, Feb. 22, 1968, p. A10. Emphasis added.

14. The New York *Times*, Feb. 18, 1968, p. 1E.

15. AP, A050WX—Nuclear Weapons, Feb. 9, 1968.

16. AP, A003WX—North Vietnam Nuclear, by Jack Bell, Feb. 10, 1968.

17. James Reston, *The Artillery of the Press* (New York: Harper & Row, 1967), p. 73.

18. "No A-Arms Requested for Vietnam, U.S. Says," the Washington *Post*, Feb. 10, 1968, p. A1.

19. "Possible Viet A-Bomb Use Studied, McCarthy Suspects," the Baltimore *Sun*, Feb. 12, 1968, p. 2.

20. "Wilson Cautions on A-Arms in War," the New York *Times*, Feb. 12, 1968, p. 4.

21. CBS-TV, "CBS Evening News," Feb. 13, 1968.

22. Interview following appearance before House Subcommittee on Department of Defense Appropriations, Feb. 14, 1968.

23. "Fulbright Denounces Rusk in Nuclear Arms Use Row," the Baltimore *Sun*, Feb. 16, 1968, p. 1.

24. Ibid.

25. Interview following appearance before House Subcommittee on Department of Defense Appropriations, Feb. 15, 1968.

26. "Anonymous Call Set Off Rumors of Nuclear Arms for Vietnam," Feb. 13; "Wheeler Doubts Khe Sanh Will Need Atom Weapons," Feb. 15; "Fulbright Query Attacked by Rusk, but Senator Rejects Charge That Atomic Arms Debate Is Disservice to Nation," by John Finney, Feb. 16; "Johnson Denies Atom Use in Vietnam Is Considered," Feb. 17.

27. "A-Arm Use Called Lunacy by Wilson," Feb. 12; and "Fulbright and Rusk Clash on Atom Talk," Feb. 16.

28. "U.S. Pessimistic on Talks," the New York *Times*, Feb. 18, 1968, p. 1E.

29. "2,000 March Here to Protest War; Also Ask Ban of Any Use of Nuclear Arms in Vietnam," the New York *Times*, Feb. 25, 1968, p. 21.

30. CBS-TV, "CBS Evening News," Feb. 9, 1968.

31. CBS-TV, "CBS Sunday News," Feb. 11, 1968. Emphasis added.

32. Our NBC files are incomplete.

33. "Nuclear Weapons for Khe Sanh," *Newsweek*, Feb. 19, 1968, p. 17.

34. "Watching and Waiting," *Newsweek*, Feb. 26, 1968, p. 22.

35. "The Nuclear Rumble," *Time*, Feb. 23, 1968, p. 17.

36. Schandler, "Making a Decision," p. 35. In his own researches in 1969–70, John Henry told this writer in 1975, he found none of the leading civilian Pentagon officials aware of this Johnson-Wheeler-Westmoreland interchange. The possible use of nuclear weapons in Vietnam, at any rate, does not seem to have arisen as a subject for extensive planning or discussion within the Pentagon in early 1968.

37. Hawkish columnist Joseph Alsop was an exception. He wrote, in the Washington *Post:* "RFK Is Unwise in Accepting Peace at Any Price Counsel," Feb. 12, 1968, p. A15; "Pike's VC Attack Post-mortem Refutes Senate Doves' Views," Feb. 26, 1968, p. A13; and "Kennedy's Viet Defeatism Contradicts Facts of War," Mar. 27, 1968, p. A23.

38. CBS-TV, "CBS Evening News," Feb. 8, 1968.

39. He also demolished one straw man—the Administration goal of "military victory, whatever its cost"—and suggested that a "political compromise" between Hanoi and Saigon was not only possible, "but the best [easiest] path to peace." This was a notion widely shared in the United States; it found less credence among newsmen in Vietnam, if only because no compromise seemed tolerable to either side. Kennedy, like many Americans, underestimated the tenacity of both South and North Vietnam.

40. For example: "Criticism of War Widens in Senate on Buildup Issue . . . Kennedy Scores Policy," the New York *Times*, Mar. 8, 1968, p. 1; "Kennedy Challenges 'Illusions' on War," the New York *Times*, Mar. 17, 1968, p. 59; "RFK Says Johnson Divides the Nation," the Washington *Post*, Mar. 22, 1968, p. A1. Kennedy's statements were reported on all three networks.

41. CBS-TV, "CBS Evening News," Feb. 8, 1968.

42. NBC-Radio, "The World in Washington," Feb. 4, 1968. Emphasis added.

43. CBS-Radio, "Dimension," Feb. 6, 1968.

44. This was still another case of lazy, straw-man journalism. Sevareid (1) ignored Wheeler's December 17 warning speech and Westmoreland's January 17 warning of "resurgence," and (2) attributes the statement that the "military war was won" to the highest military "au-

thorities." One finds no such statements in the record from the "highest military authorities," e.g., McNamara, Wheeler, Westmoreland.

45. CBS-TV, "CBS Evening News," Feb. 12, 1968. Emphasis added.

46. NBC-TV, "Huntley-Brinkley Report," Feb. 12, 1968.

47. WETA-TV, "Public Broadcast Laboratory," Feb. 25, 1968.

48. NBC-Radio, "Emphasis," Feb. 28, 1968. Emphasis added.

49. ABC-TV, "ABC Evening News," Mar. 13, 1968.

50. In "The Presentation of the Vietnam War on the CBS Evening News with Walter Cronkite, and Effects of This . . . on Public Opinion" (May 1969), an unpublished analysis of CBS Vietnam coverage, Johannes A. Binnendijk, a graduate student at Fletcher School of Law and Diplomacy, Tufts University, observed, as we did, that CBS's view on the war was sour *prior* to Tet:

> Tracing the CBS attitude toward the war in Vietnam, it is found that in 1966 the news broadcast seemed quite pro-Administration, in some cases (March 7, 1966, and September 5, 1966) more so than public opinion. In December 1966 and March 1967 it was found that the Cronkite show seemed critical of the Administration, as was the population. In September of 1967 the Cronkite show seemed more optimistic than public opinion. In December of 1967 both seemed to support the Administration to a certain extent. But in January of 1968 the Cronkite show began to present the war in a very bad light. In February, while public opinion seemed to favor the war, CBS News was calling for a negotiated peace. This situation continued into early March, the only change being a move by public opinion in the same direction. After Johnson had taken the initial steps toward negotiation, the Cronkite reports of July and October 1968 were not as critical.

51. CBS-TV, "Report from Vietnam: Who, What, When, Where, Why," Feb. 27, 1968.

52. The New York *Times*, Mar. 12, 1968, p. 50. Emphasis added.

53. "NBC-TV Busts Out with Downbeat on Vietnam via Frank McGee & Co.," by Bill Greeley, *Variety*, Mar. 13, 1968, p. 44. Emphasis added.

54. "Clerics Accuse U.S. of War Crimes," the New York *Times*, Feb. 4, 1968, p. 1.

55. "Religious Leaders Publish Study Accusing U.S. of War Crimes in Vietnam," the Washington *Post*, Feb. 4, 1968, p. A22.

56. Richard J. Barnet, "The Last Act in Vietnam," Feb. 4, 1968, p. 26; Edwin O. Reischauer, "We Have Failed in Vietnam . . . What Now?" Mar. 10, 1968, p. 23; Theodore C. Sorensen, "Sorensen Says, Of Course the War Will Be a Campaign Issue," Mar. 17, 1968, p. 30; and Sol Stern, "When the Black GI Comes Back from Vietnam," Mar. 24, 1968, p. 26.

57. "The Strategy of Error," Mar. 1, 1968, p. 36; and "Giap's Round on Points," Mar. 8, 1968, p. 39.

58. "Khe Sanh Can Still Be Averted," the Washington *Post,* Mar. 22, 1968.

59. See "Man on the Spot," *Newsweek,* Feb. 19, 1968, which did not mention U.S. claims—more correct than incorrect in this case—that Thieu's regime acted "creditably" at Tet.

60. Kennedy returned from Saigon *prior* to Tet.

61. "The War: The General's Biggest Battle," *Time,* Feb. 16, 1968, p. 19. Emphasis added.

62. "The Great Mogul," *Time,* Feb. 16, 1968, p. 24.

63. These were the 11,000 "emergency" reinforcements of Marines and paratroopers sent to I Corps.

64. "War Doubts in Senate; Misgivings over Administration Policy Said to Spread As Offensive Continues," the New York *Times,* Feb. 12, 1968, p. 6.

65. Unlike *Newsweek, Time* did not point out that, in the Gallup polls, a sizable percentage of self-classified hawks were portrayed as being as dissatisfied with the President's conduct of the war as the self-described doves.

66. "The War: Thin Green Line," *Time,* Feb. 23, 1968, pp. 15–16.

67. "The War: Critical Season," *Time,* Mar. 1, 1968, p. 11; see above, Chapter 9. Indeed, the U.S. newsmen in Vietnam were also feeling a bit low, for the Tet crisis was going on too long (three weeks). If the fighting at Hue had ended, it was still going on around Saigon, where curfew was still in effect. It was still hard to file stories, and, up in I Corps, the weather was bad and the Khe Sanh story—involving scary descents by air into the main base—was still dragging on. Westmoreland was still getting U.S. troops sorted out. There were nothing but gloomy reports from the countryside, which, aside from brief circumscribed tours the week after Tet, remained closed to newsmen. In short, there was no apparent movement. This seemed even truer to newsmen in Washington and New York. In fact, however, as we know now, the worst was over.

68. Actually, the *Wall Street Journal* had been uneasy, if not apocalyptic, about Vietnam before. Emphasis added.

69. "The Administration," *Time,* Mar. 8, 1968, p. 17.

70. "The War: Debate in a Vacuum," *Time,* Mar. 15, 1968, p. 14.

71. "The Presidency: The Bombing Pause," *Time,* Apr. 5, 1968, p. 19. Emphasis added.

72. "Hanoi Attacks and Scores a Major Psychological Blow," *Newsweek,* Feb. 12, 1968, p. 23.

73. "Watching and Waiting: A Grimly Determined Capital Listens for the Other Shoe," *Newsweek,* Feb. 26, 1968, p. 21.

74. In fact, Khe Sanh aside, the military situation had begun to ease, with Hue about to be retaken.

75. "The War: More Men, More Doubts," *Newsweek*, Mar. 4, 1968, p. 19. Emphasis added.

76. Ibid., p. 20.

77. This straw-man journalism was an overreaction to Administration optimism. Neither Westmoreland nor Johnson promised that the foe would *suddenly* wither away.

78. An echo of the AP Ben Tre quote?

79. "More of the Same Won't Do," *Newsweek*, Mar. 18, 1968, p. 25. Emphasis added. This last paragraph was a standard journalistic argument: The Administration is too optimistic, hence we are justified in being too pessimistic. What about the reader?

80. The New York *Times* exclusive, Mar. 10, 1968.

81. "Foreign Policy: Growing Dissent," *Newsweek*, Mar. 25, 1968, p. 39.

82. *Newsweek* was hedging.

83. "Foreign Policy: Peace Offensive," *Newsweek*, Apr. 8, 1968, p. 35. Emphasis added. There was no troop call-up; and no "peace offensive."

84. As Schandler notes in "Making a Decision," public opinion studies have shown how little was the change in popular support for the war (as opposed to fluctuating approval of Lyndon Johnson as President) between the fall of 1967 and the spring of 1968, *prior* to Johnson's March 31 speech. Indeed, the crisis of Tet caused an initial upward surge in public support for (or acquiescence in) the Administration war effort (Schandler, p. 135). See also Hazel Erskine, "The Polls: Is War a Mistake?" *Public Opinion Quarterly*, Spring 1970, pp. 135, 142–53. For Burns Roper's extended analysis of the 1967–68 public opinion polls, see the Westview Press edition of *Big Story*, Chapter 14.

85. See Schandler, "Making a Decision," pp. 157–58, and Oberdorfer, *Tet!*, pp. 275–76; see also Philip E. Converse, Warren E. Miller, Jerrold G. Rusk, and Arthur C. Wolfe, "Continuity and Change in American Politics: Parties and Issues in the 1968 Election," *American Political Science Review*, LXIII (Dec. 1969), 1083–1105.

86. See David Broder, *The Party's Over: The Failure of Politics in America* (New York: Harper & Row, 1972).

87. Johnson, *The Vantage Point*, p. 432.

88. Oberdorfer so indicates. And, on March 20, 1968, he notes, the North Vietnamese invited CBS's Walter Cronkite to come to Hanoi. Charles Collingwood went instead, assured that CBS would be granted "important interviews." At the same time, Harry C. Ashmore, executive vice president of the Center for the Study of Democratic Institutions, and William Baggs, a Center board member and Miami *News* editor, got permission to make their second quasi-diplomatic trip to North Vietnam. All three Americans arrived in Hanoi on March 29. Collingwood was upbraided by his hosts for his delay; he was told to await an "important in-

terview" with Foreign Minister Nguyen Duy Trinh on April 2. The North Vietnamese, Collingwood felt, expected the interview to make news around the world. After Johnson's speech on March 31, the interview was postponed for three days and Trinh merely repeated his government's acceptance of Johnson's proposal to talk. It is interesting to ponder what would have happened had Trinh spoken first. See Oberdorfer, *Tet!*, pp. 303, 323.

Chapter 13: An Extreme Case

1. See Epstein's *Between Fact and Fiction* (Vintage: 1975), p. 225.
2. In the spring of 1970, a similar overreaction occurred after the U.S.-South Vietnamese "incursions" into Cambodia. The limited ground operations against communist base areas were preceded by high-level State Department assurances that no such actions were contemplated. They were accompanied by a television speech by President Nixon who exaggerated their real scope and objectives and thereby contributed further to media alarmism and public alarm. Washington *Post* ombudsman Richard Harwood, in a January 26, 1971, memo to the editors, noted that "following the events of last spring a couple of our summer interns examined our Cambodia coverage—foreign and domestic. They concluded that it was one-sided and unfair [to the Nixon Administration]." He followed with a plea for the *Post* to "use the naked facts if at all possible and to use them with precision" in future coverage of Cambodian fighting. See Laura Langley Babb, ed., *Of the Press, by the Press, for the Press (and Others, Too)* (Washington, D.C.: Washington *Post* Co., 1974).
3. Goodnow et al., "News Coverage of the Tet Offensive," p. 84. Responding to the survey, besides Buckley, were Don Oberdorfer, then of the Knight newspapers; Robert Schakne and Jeff Gralnick of CBS News; Bob Kaylor of UPI; Bob Wildau and Don Sider of *Time;* and Ron Nessen, Jack Fern, and Garrick Utley of NBC.
4. Ibid., p. 88.
5. Source: Department of Defense. There were only 117 Americans accredited in 1972.
6. The *Time* staff included Karsten Prager, Peter Vanderwicken, Glenn Troelstrup, Don Sider, John Cantwell, Wallace Terry, H.D.S. Greenway, and Dan Coggin. *Newsweek* was belatedly reinforced by Joel Blocker, Kevin Buckley, and Maynard Parker.
Newsweek had no such healthy debate among its editors as did *Time.* Although Sully and Perry filed a major review of the initial communist performance ("The Tet Offensive: How They Did It," Mar. 11, 1968), the published version was marred by hasty judgments and "projection" into the future.
7. Professor Lawrence Lichty of the University of Wisconsin, analyzing for this book Vietnam film reports on the weekday evening TV news

shows for January 30–March 29, 1968, found in a preliminary study the cumulative total of such film to be: ABC, 98.6 minutes; CBS, 135.8 minutes; NBC, 162.1 minutes. Of this total, on each network, just under half was devoted to various categories of "battle" footage. Some of this was "nonviolent" (i.e., troops moving into battle but not shooting), or "semiviolent" (troops shooting but no apparent enemy fire). CBS led with "violent" battle film (33.7 minutes), NBC with "semiviolent" (34.6 minutes). Besides "battle" footage, CBS ran twice as much field "situationer" film (38.3 minutes) as NBC, due in part to its preoccupation with analysis of Khe Sanh. Pacification got no film on CBS, 6.5 minutes on NBC, and two minutes on ABC. CBS broadcast the only film on South Vietnamese government activity (2.7 minutes); NBC ran a total of 8.6 minutes on the "enemy." Length of film reports averaged 1.5 minutes on ABC, 2.3 minutes on NBC and CBS.

8. *The Living Room War* (New York: Viking, 1969), p. 143.

9. Analyzing the more heterogeneous 1968 output contained in the daily Defense Department selection of press clippings and radio-TV transcripts, through March 10, Goodnow et al. found roughly similar negative persistence even as coverage began to decline in March. See "News Coverage of the Tet Offensive," p. 116 ff.

10. In 1972, returning to Vietnam for the *Post*, this writer was told by Foreign Editor Philip Foisie to "collect string" for a major portrait of overall ARVN and NVA performance as soon as Hanoi's Easter offensive had ebbed and the dust settled a bit. After 10 weeks of field reporting and Saigon interviews, a three-part series was produced in July with new data and (properly) tentative conclusions. No follow-up examination, however, was undertaken by the *Post* when the front stabilized that fall, or, indeed, prior to the 1975 collapse. This failing was widespread.

ADDITIONS AND CORRECTIONS

Page 20   Second paragraph: What was not widely perceived by newsmen then or later was the fact that the U.S. advisors to the South Vietnamese army were not only useful in coordinating U.S. air and logistic support for ARVN but also constituted a crucial parallel command structure that compensated for the lack of cohesion and coordination between ARVN commanders, particularly at Tet 1968 and during Hanoi's 1972 Easter offensive. For all their frustrations and shortcomings, these Americans were the "glue" that kept the South Vietnamese forces together. The withdrawal of the advisors in 1973, as few newsmen noted, was no less damaging to the South Vietnamese cause than the withdrawal of U.S. airpower and logistic support—a fact which became recognized only after the final collapse in 1975.

Page 38   Second paragraph should read: "According to the Lichty-Hoffer analysis for this book, home-based TV newsmen, mostly anchormen, supplied 339 of 461 oral 'key statements' about pacification, combat in various areas, victory or defeat, etc., on the weekday TV network evening news shows from January 29 to March 29, 1968. Of 187 Vietnam-related film reports, 118 came from correspondents in Vietnam. Lichty found the cumulative two-month total per network of such film from Vietnam to average a little over 2 hours. (See p. 597, note 7.)"

Page 116   To correct an important omission, the third paragraph should read: "Walter Cronkite of CBS opened the show with a 'tell' story. Like his ABC and NBC rivals, he relayed a studio writer's rehash of early AP and UPI wire service reports, including the erroneous report that a 'communist suicide squad held part of the first floor' of the U.S. embassy in Saigon, before focusing on the earlier upcountry attacks." His report is reprinted here:

Good evening. The biggest Communist offensive of the Vietnam War has begun. In an unprecedented display of military strength, the Vietcong have attacked eight major South Vietnamese cities, scores of towns and villages, and five American airfields, and early Wednesday, Vietnam time, the Communists struck at the heart of Saigon, and seized part of the new American embassy. At dawn, American military police tried to storm into the embassy, but were driven back by the Vietcong force, estimated at 20 men. The Communist suicide squad held part of the first floor. Other guerrillas attacked the Presidential Palace, the government radio station, three American officers' billets, and Tan Son Nhut airbase. Enemy rockets and mortars set off a series of fires in Saigon, causing substantial damage. There was no immediate word on casualties.

The intensity of the enemy assault up and down the country, and the coordination that went into it, indicate the big battles are yet to come. Far to the north, along the demilitarized zone, an estimated 40,000 North Vietnamese troops have massed for an invasion that American commanders believe is imminent. It seemed probable that today's coordinated attacks were intended to tie down Allied forces to prevent reinforcement of the marines when the northern offensive kicks off.

Late reports said fighting still is raging tonight around Da Nang, and in several of the provincial capitals invaded by the Vietcong as the lunar New Year began today. Those cities are the equivalent of American state capitals. . . . Casualty reports are fragmentary, but the Vietcong, taking advantage of the Allied-proclaimed cease-fire, caught some government units off guard and inflicted heavy casualties. Saigon immediately cancelled the remainder of the 36-hour truce. In a moment, we'll have film reports on the attack at Da Nang.

Page 117   In justice to NBC, it should be noted that later in the show, in a "live" narrative from Tokyo over film hastily relayed via satellite of the final Embassy mop-up, Jack Perkins said: "They [the Vietcong] did not, as far as we know, get into the building itself."

Page 238   A postscript: On June 13, 1980, by order of General Robert H. Barrow, the Marine Corps commandant, at a special parade at Marine Barracks, Washington, D.C., Mohr, Webb, and Greenway received Bronze Star medals (with V for Valor) in recognition of their February 19, 1968 rescue effort. Among the guests: 100 Washington newsmen and Steve Bernston, a former Marine sergeant, who had also been wounded during the rescue effort and had been awarded a Bronze Star.

Page 291   In an internal CBS memorandum (February 21, 1978), producer Les Midgely analyzed the 1977 edition of *Big Story*, saying "I don't understand why it was written." The book, he noted, said the media distorted the realities of the Tet attacks. "I don't agree," Midgeley wrote. But even if historians agreed that Tet was a setback for Hanoi, he said, "I still think our people did a marvelous job of reporting it at the time; they did their job." As for Khe Sanh, "Well, it was a terrific story . . . we had more men in and out of Khesanh than anyone [else] and they did the finest job."

Pages 438–59   At my request, Neil Sheehan (February 14, 1982) and Hedrick Smith (February 5, 1982) commented by letter on my account of their March 10, 1968, New York *Times* story on the Westmoreland-Wheeler request for 206,000 more troops.
     Smith properly chides me for not stressing earlier in the chapter the two reporters' feeling that the "major revelation was not the number but the high-level disaffection within the Administration caused by the shock effect of so large a request." Secondly, Smith writes, "I believe there was significance in reporting the 206,000 number even though President Johnson was moving more modestly (which we did not know that day). . . . Think of it this way: Without that story, we'd have missed out on some vital information and insight into the Johnson Administration's policy debates and considerations at a crucial moment."
     Both Sheehan and Smith correct the description of their sources on pp. 446–47. Smith's daily contacts outside the State Department were National Security Council staff, Congressional foreign policy and military specialists, and some Pentagon officials. Sheehan's best sources as Pentagon reporter were not "McNamara civilians" or the Senate Foreign Relations Committee staff, but hawkish anti-McNamara Congressional staffers and *their* military friends in the Pentagon, including Sheehan's old contacts from Vietnam, colonels and majors, who worked for senior officers and "read the cables." He did have some dovish sources, "but they came late in the game. . . . I still retained my hawk sources because I think they saw I was honest in my reporting."
     Sheehan, referring to the bureaucratic stratagems employed by Wheeler in conveying the troop request and by LBJ in dealing with it, observed wryly that "Penetrating beyond a memorandum to the President from the Chairman, JCS (Wheeler) is pretty difficult."
     When the two *Times*men started writing on March 8, their sources thought the argument was still alive (even though Wheeler had cabled Westmoreland that the troop issue was all but dead). Their sources included people on the JCS Joint Staff, in State "just below Rusk," Congressional staffers. They did not include Paul Warnke or Townsend Hoopes, says Sheehan.

The *Times* editors did not hold up the Smith-Sheehan story (p. 454) for Sunday. "We finished writing at 5 a.m. Saturday, March 9. The story was then run as soon as it could be printed." Nor, Sheehan says rightly, should the "numbers game," not played by the *Post* (p. 460), be pooh-poohed: U.S. troop numbers, proposed or actual, wére important throughout the war; they represented levels of U.S. commitment.

The March 10 story, Sheehan observes, "had errors in it but it was not alarmist. Westmoreland and Wheeler should have thought through the repercussions of asking for 206,000 more troops."

Overall, Smith and Sheehan correct several inaccuracies; overall, they confirm, I think, the notion that even the best reporters in Washington must necessarily rely on the available sources. And on this complex story, the prime sources, including LBJ, Rusk, and Wheeler, were simply not talking to reporters—or to many others—about the true state of play.

SOURCES AND METHOD

Footnotes cite the chief written sources. Citations or texts of New York *Times* and Washington *Post* newspaper stories come from late editions in library microfilm archives, except where noted. AP and UPI stories are identified by code "slugs" and time-date groupings where noted; most are from the main "A" wire; some are from the services' respective Washington wires, which carry shorter dispatches. Television transcripts were taken from the author's own audio tracks of news programs available in the Pentagon archives, from Department of Defense transcripts of radio and television programs, or, in the case of CBS, from transcripts in the CBS library. *Time* and *Newsweek* stories are from the U.S. editions of those publications.

I did not subject the entire mass of available material to the kind of sentence-by-sentence "content" analysis that has been employed by other researchers. I was primarily interested in numbers, prominence, and origin of stories on given subjects, and then in the themes these stories tended to convey.

In the end, I found that a determination of how much a given topic is covered and how much "play" it gets reveals as much about press performance as does a (more subjective) analysis of how "objectively" it is covered.

For a bibliographic essay on the Vietnam literature, too long to be included here, see my "Vietnam as History," *The Wilson Quarterly*, Vol. II, No. 2, Spring 1978, and a follow-up survey-letter by Douglas Pike, *The Wilson Quarterly*, Vol. II, No. 3, Summer 1978.

ACKNOWLEDGMENTS

A number of persons worked long and hard in the search for material for this book. In 1970, Martha Damm and Ruth Silverman processed and reproduced the wire service reports in New York, thanks to help from the Associated Press library and the United Press International management. Later, in Washington, Kathy Lee, Judy Sorenson, Peter Rodaikis, and Karen Nicola typed copies of news clippings, wire service material, television transcripts, and drafts of the manuscript. Crucial research was done in Washington by John Doyle, Jo Ann Acosta, Therese Gibbons, Anne-Marie Gibbons, and Virginia Hamill. Indexes to wire service stories were compiled by Josette Selim. Archives and documents were acquired in Saigon by Joyce Bolo of the Washington *Post* and Daniel Southerland of the *Christian Science Monitor*, who also supplied his recollections.

Over the years, virtually every newsman and news organization mentioned in this book was helpful, either in offering critical comments or in supplying information. I wish to pay particular tribute to the following colleagues: the late Merton Perry of *Newsweek*; Lee Lescaze and Don Oberdorfer of the Washington *Post*, the latter also author of his own fine *Tet!*; Wally Terry, Don Sider, and H. D. S. Greenway of *Time*; Eugene Roberts, Charles Mohr, Joseph Treaster, Hedrick Smith, Neil Sheehan, and Robert Phelps of the New York *Times*; Eugene Risher of UPI; John Lengel and Peter Arnett of AP; the late George Syvertsen of CBS; and Peter Kann of the *Wall Street Journal*. At home, others most helpful were A. M. Rosenthal of the New York *Times*, Lou Boccardi of AP, and Philip Foisie of the Washington *Post*.

Still others, given the sensitivities of their employers, must remain nameless.

On the nonjournalistic side, I am particularly indebted to the late Lt. Gen. John Chaisson, USMC, whose candor and humor were most helpful; to Gen. William C. Westmoreland, USA, and his aide-historian, Maj. Paul Miles; to Col. David Lownds, USMC, the commander at Khe Sanh, for his comments on the manuscript; to Charles MacDonald, director of the Army's own long-term Vietnam history effort, for his warnings on the pitfalls of writing history; to Robert Komer, former chief of the pacification effort, and to Brig. Gen. Robert Montague, USA, his deputy, for comments and insights; to Tom Scoville, for a young historian's view of the impact of Tet on pacification and pacifiers; to John Henry, whose own well-researched account of the February–March 1968 policy debate in Washington challenged many cherished Washington myths; to Col. Marcus Gravel and Lt. Col. Ernest C. Cheatham, the able commanders of the first two Marine battalions into Hue; to the late John Paul Vann, for his recollections; to Brig. Gen. E. H. Simmons, USMC, director of Marine Corps history; to Maj. Gen. Robert Ginsburgh, USAF, White House aide at Tet and later secretary to the Joint Chiefs; and to the late Gen. Creighton Abrams, USA, whose informal reflections in 1968–69 and again in 1972 were of great help.

The project received indispensable help from key personnel in charge of Pentagon film and print archives, notably Harry Zubkoff, chief media archivist; Norman T. Hatch, head of the Defense Department's audio-visual branch; and John L. Sullivan, archivist for the Defense Department's information branch. Comdr. Joseph Lorfano, USN, was most helpful, as were Maj. Gen. Gordon Hill, USA; Francis J. Falatko; Assistant Secretary of Defense Jerry W. Friedheim; and Maj. Gen. Winant Sidle, USA.

Barry Zorthian, former head of the Joint United States Public Affairs Office (JUSPAO), as well as U.S. Ambassador to South Vietnam Ellsworth Bunker, provided insights, as did several younger members of the U.S. Mission in Vietnam, notably Frank G. Wisner and Paul Hare. Samuel Lubell and Irving Kristol offered early advice and encouragement. Historian Herbert Y. Schandler was generous with drafts of his own work on Tet, published as *The Unmaking of a President* (Princeton, 1977). Lawrence Lichty was no less generous with his own work on TV, and a perceptive critic of *Big Story*'s imperfections.

Index

Peter Braestrup was born in New York City June 8, 1929, the son of Elsebet Kampmann Braestrup and the Danish-born physicist Carl Bjorn Braestrup. He grew up in Scarsdale, New York, attended Riverdale Country School, and secured his first newspaper job as a summer stringer for the New Haven (Connecticut) *Register*. At Yale (B.A. 1951), he worked on the Yale *Daily News*, went to the 1948 Presidential conventions as a *Life* messenger boy, and with three classmates ran a summer weekly, *The Connecticut Shore* (circ. 1200), in 1949.

In 1951–53, Mr. Braestrup served in the Marine Corps as a 2nd Lieutenant, went to Korea, was wounded in the defense of Outpost Reno (1952), and later was released to inactive duty. In 1953, *Time* hired him as a staff writer, then sent him to Chicago to cover labor, politics, and civil rights in the Midwest and South (1955–57). He joined the New York *Herald Tribune* in 1957 as an investigative reporter; he spent a month in Tunisia and Algeria with the Algerian FLN guerrillas.

Awarded a Nieman Fellowship at Harvard in 1959–60, Mr. Braestrup was recruited for the New York *Times* Washington bureau by James B. Reston; he covered the New Frontier as general assignment reporter. The *Times* sent him abroad, first to newly independent Algeria (1962–65), then to Paris (1965), then to Bangkok (1966–68), whence he began to cover the Indo-China war. In January 1968, just before Tet, he joined the Washington *Post* as Saigon bureau chief, returning to the home office in 1969 as a staff writer. In 1972, he returned to Vietnam to help cover Hanoi's Easter offensive.

In 1973, Mr. Braestrup became a Fellow at the Woodrow Wilson International Center for Scholars at the Smithsonian. In 1975, he joined the Center staff as the founding editor of the *Wilson Quarterly*. Completed at the Center, his *Big Story* won the 1978 Sigma Delta Chi Award.

He is married to the former Angelica Hollins. They have three children: Angelica, Elizabeth Kate, and Carl Peter.